PROTESTANT NONCONFORMIST TEXTS
VOLUME 2

This book is one of four substantial volumes designed to demonstrate the range of interests of the several Protestant Nonconformist traditions from the time of their Separatist harbingers to the end of the twentieth century.

In this volume we are concerned with the eighteenth century. It was a period in which Old Dissent – the Congregationalists, Baptists, Presbyterians and Quakers – had to face challenges from Enlightenment thought on the one hand and Evangelical Revival enthusiasm on the other. Largely in their own words, though with introductions contributed by the editors, we enter into the philosophical world of Isaac Watts, Richard Price, and others; we overhear doctrinal disputes over the doctrine of the Trinity; we meet such new arrivals on the religious scene as the Moravians, Sandemanians, Swedenborgians and Methodists (Calvinistic and Arminian). We consider the Nonconformists' views on the Church, the ministry and the sacraments; on Church, state and society; and on Christian nurture, piety and church life.

From philosophical tomes to hymns, from sacramental questions to prison reform, from the most strait-laced Presbyterian to the most enthusiastic Jumper: this volume will remind scholars of, and aquaint others with, the intellectual excitements, the practical witness and the worship of the eighteenth-century Nonconformists.

PROTESTANT NONCONFORMIST TEXTS

Series editor: Alan P. F. Sell

This series of four substantial volumes is designed to demonstrate the range of interests of the several Protestant Nonconformist traditions from the time of their Separatist harbingers in the sixteenth century to the end of the twentieth century. It represents a major project of the Association of Denominational Historical Societies and Cognate Libraries. Each volume comprises a General Introduction followed by texts illustrative of such topics as theology, philosophy, worship and socio-political concerns. This work has never before been drawn together for publication in this way. Prepared by a team of twelve editors, all of whom are expert in their areas and drawn from a number of the relevant traditions, it provides a much-needed comprehensive view of Nonconformity told largely in the words of those whose story it is. The works will prove to be an invaluable resource to scholars, students, academics and specialist and public libraries, as well as to a wider range of church, intellectual and general historians.

Other titles in the series:

Protestant Nonconformist Texts Volume 1
1550 to 1700
Edited by R. Tudur Jones
with Arthur Long and Rosemary Moore

Protestant Nonconformist Texts Volume 3
The Nineteenth Century
Edited by David Bebbington
with Kenneth Dix and Alan Ruston

Protestant Nonconformist Texts Volume 4
The Twentieth Century
David M. Thompson
with J. H. Y. Briggs and John Munsey Turner

Protestant Nonconformist Texts
Volume 2

The Eighteenth Century

Edited by
ALAN P. F. SELL

with
DAVID J. HALL
and
IAN SELLERS

ASHGATE

Published by
Ashgate Publishing Limited
Gower House
Croft Road
Aldershot
Hants GU11 3HR
England

Ashgate Publishing Company
Suite 420
101 Cherry Street
Burlington
VT 05401-4405
USA

Ashgate website: http://www.ashgate.com

British Library Cataloguing in Publication Data
Protestant nonconformist texts
    Vol. 2: The eighteenth century
    1.Dissenters, Religious – England – History – Sources 2.Dissenters, Religious – Wales –
    History – Sources 3.Protestant churches – England – History – Sources 4.Protestant
    churches – Wales – History – Sources 5.England – Church history – Sources 6.Wales –
    Church history – Sources
    I. Sell, Alan P. F. (Alan Philip Frederick)
    280.4'0942

Library of Congress Cataloging-in-Publication Data
Protestant nonconformist texts
        p. cm
    Includes bibliographical references.
    Contents: v. 1. 1550 to 1700 / edited by R. Tudur Jones – v. 2. The eighteenth century
    / edited by Alan P. F. Sell – v.3. The nineteenth century / edited by David Bebbington –
    v.4. The twentieth century / edited by David M. Thompson.
    ISBN 0-7546-3864-2 (v. 1 : alk. paper) – ISBN 0-7546-3853-7 (v. 2 : alk. paper) –
    ISBN 0-7546-3850-2 (v. 3 : alk. paper) – ISBN 0-7546-4013-2 (v. 4 : alk. paper)
    1. Dissenters, Religious. I. Jones, R. Tudur (Robert Tudur) II. Sell, Alan P. F. III.
    Bebbington, D. W. (David William) IV. Thompson, David M.

BR1609.5.P76 2003
280'4'0942–dc21

2003052257

ISBN-13: 978-0-7546-3853-7
ISBN-10: 0-7546-3853-7

Typeset by Manton Typesetters, Louth, Lincolnshire, UK
Printed and bound in Great Britain by CPI Antony Rowe Ltd, Chippenham

Contents

Part IV: Evangelism, Revival and Mission

Part V: Church, State and Society

Part VI: Nurture, Piety and Church Life

Series Editor's Preface

I had long felt the need of a series which would present texts from the history and thought of Protestant Nonconformity in England and Wales in such a way that the breadth of the Nonconformists' interests, the extent and variety of their activities, and the depth of their devotion from the days of the sixteenth-century Separatists onwards would become plain. When the Association of Denominational Historical Societies and Cognate Libraries was formally constituted on 23 October 1993, with the objective of sharing intelligence and facilitating co-operative scholarly activity across the several denominational boundaries, I formally proposed the preparation of a series of Protestant Nonconformist Texts to the membership.

There was unanimous agreement that a need existed which could, and should, be met. It was determined that the series should comprise four volumes covering the periods 1550–1700, the eighteenth century, the nineteenth century and the twentieth century; and that each volume should be in the hands of a co-ordinating editor assisted by two co-operating editors drawn from different church traditions. The secretaries of the member societies, with the guidance of their respective committees, nominated scholars who might be approached to serve as editors. I am pleased to say that within a month the twelve editors were mustered, and I am most appreciative of their enthusiasm for the task, and of the expeditious way in which they have carried it out. It is proper to make special and grateful mention of the late Reverend Professor R. Tudur Jones who, in addition to serving as the coordinating editor of the first volume – a task he completed within days of his sudden and much-lamented death on 23 July 1998 – also cordially agreed to act as consultant on Welsh matters to the editors of all four volumes. The sudden death of the Reverend Dr Ian Sellers, a contributing editor of Volume II has left a further significant gap in the ranks of scholars of English Nonconformity.

The editors were given a fairly free hand in the organisation of their volumes: indeed, the nature of the materials has been permitted to suggest the layout of the several volumes. It is claimed that the order of each volume is clear and justifiable, even if in format one may differ slightly from another.

It is hoped that the series will prove helpful to students and interested readers, and that scholars may find it useful to have a checklist of sources which, though necessarily limited by considerations of space, is intended as an appetiser and a stimulus to further quarrying.

Above all, it is hoped that worthy tribute is paid here to those who, often at great personal cost, and in face of socio-political obstacles of various kinds, declared their faith and bore their witness. Indeed (to advert to realities, not to utter a lament), in a time of general apologetic caution, widespread doctrinal ignorance and apathy, fitful ecumenism, queried national institutions and overall numerical decline among the Protestant Nonconformists of England and Wales, it may even be that forebears have something to teach those who inherit their mantle – and any others who may care to listen.

On behalf of my editorial colleagues I should like to thank Sarah Lloyd, Liz Pearce and all at Ashgate Publishing for their commitment to this project and for the care they have lavished upon it.

Alan P. F. Sell

Acknowledgements

I wish to record my thanks to David J. Hall and the late Ian Sellers, my co-operating editors, for the care and promptness they displayed in discharging their tasks. This volume has benefited greatly from the former's knowledge of eighteenth-century Quakerism, and from the latter's through acquaintance with Methodism. The delivery of his sections of this work must have been among the last tasks that Dr Sellers was able to perform before his sudden and untimely death on 10 December 1997. Students of Nonconformity everywhere will give thanks for the legacy of Dr Sellers's writings, which amply testify to his enthusiasm for, and industry within, the field.

Every effort has been made to ensure that copyright has not been violated. Thanks are due to the staff of the following libraries, for their assistance in locating and in some cases copying eighteenth-century texts: The British Library; Cambridge University Library; Dr Williams's Library, London; Friends' Library, London; Harris-Manchester College Library, Oxford; Hugh Owen Library, University of Wales, Aberystwyth; John Rylands University Library of Manchester; Luther King House Library, Manchester; The National Library of Wales; The United Theological College Library, Aberystwyth. Special mention must be made of The British Library, whose officers granted permission to reproduce extracts from A 891 and A 891a, concerning the musical contribution of Caleb Ashworth.

The publisher and I are most grateful to the Association of Denominational Historical Societies and Cognate Libraries for a grant towards the publication of this volume.

Alan P. F. Sell

Abbreviations

BCE   *The Blackwell Companion to the Enlightenment*, ed. J. Yolton, R. Porter, P. Rogers and B. M. Stafford, Oxford: Blackwell, 1991

DEB   *Dictionary of Evangelical Biography*, ed. D. M. Lewis, Oxford: Blackwell, 1995

DECBP   *The Dictionary of Eighteenth-Century British Philosophers*, ed. John W. Yolton, John Valdimir Price and John Stephens, Bristol: Thoemmes Press, 1999

DH   *John Julian, A Dictionary of Hymnology* (1892), London: John Murray, 1925

DNB   *The Dictionary of National Biography*, 1882– (now published as *The Oxford Dictionary of National Biography* (2004) by OUP)

DWB   *The Dictionary of Welsh Biography*, ed. J. E. Lloyd, R. T. Jenkins, W. L. Davies, M. B. Davies, London: Honourable Society of Cymmrodorion, 1959

ODCC   *The Oxford Dictionary of the Christian Church*, ed. E. A. Livingstone, 3rd edn, Oxford: OUP, 1997

Introduction

As compared with the period from 1550 to 1700, covered by the first volume in this series, with its Separatist martyrs, the saga of the Pilgrims and the sufferings under the Clarendon Code; and with the excitements of Christianity's outreach to many parts of the world through the modern missionary movement, the challenges of evolutionary thought and of industrialisation, and the growth of Nonconformity to numerical parity with the Church of England, with which the third volume will be concerned, the eighteenth century may seem – and has by some been deemed – dull to the point of boring: except, of course, for the Evangelical Revival and John Wesley, than whom no other eighteenth-century religious personage has been more enthusiastically promoted and skilfully merchandised. It is hoped that the closer inspection of the period invited by this collection of very varied texts will convince any who may require to be persuaded that the 'long' eighteenth century – that is, the period from the Toleration Act of 1689 to the early years of the nineteenth century – is more interesting than might at first sight appear. It is, in fact, the seed-bed of many of the religious departures and intellectual challenges which continue to stimulate, challenge or haunt the churches today.

As the following six parts will make plain, the eighteenth-century Nonconformists wrestled with such philosophical problems as personal identity, which was highly germane to Christian understandings of immortality, and the foundations of ethics. They discoursed upon – even squabbled over – doctrinal points which, however much they may appear to be nit-picking to some early twenty-first-century readers, were to them crucial to the understanding and presentation of the Gospel. They were for the most part concerned for the right ordering of the ministry, they took differences of opinion on the sacraments – especially baptism – with great seriousness, and they had to take the measure of such newcomers as the Moravians, the Sandemanians and the Swedenborgians. They pioneered evangelisation at home and abroad, sometimes against doctrinal opposition from their own kind, and frequently in face of Establishment hostility. They continued to press for fuller toleration for themselves and often for others, for although orthodox Protestants (only) were given a measure of religious freedom in 1689, their position remained precarious and their social position constrained throughout the eighteenth century – as witness the proposed Schism Act of 1714, the Church and King riots of the 1790s, and the continuing impact of the Test Acts. Despite inhibitions – legal and ecclesiastical – some of their number pioneered Sunday schools and prison reform, and embraced the anti-slavery cause. Through it all the faithful gathered for worship – their hymns being among their lasting monuments, and churchly life went on at the local level and in wider associations. Discipline was exercised, the young were educated in a variety of academies, personal piety was encouraged, and the faithful departed were commemorated and their lives 'improved' in funeral sermons of sometimes considerable length. Nor should we forget that the several Nonconforming traditions made their way in a land served by poor communications, with frequently impassable roads, the menace of highwaymen and inadequate health provision in many places – the Presbyterian Ebenezer Latham of Findern (c. 1688 – 1754) was not unique in combining the roles of pastor, academy tutor and physician within his person.

Since each of the following six parts will have its own brief introduction, it will suffice here to draw attention to certain general points which need to be borne in mind, and to say a little concerning the process of selecting and classifying the texts.

It must first clearly be understood that a collection of texts of this kind however varied, creates a relatively narrowly focused picture. With a wide-angle lens we should be able to see more of the socio-political environment in which the Nonconformists lived and, in particular, we should hear more of the Establishment opposition to them. We should also be able to witness the activities of such friendly Anglican evangelicals as William Grimshaw and Thomas Haweis; we should observe the beginnings of modern evangelical internationalism through contacts with the likes of Jonathan Edwards; and the American War of Independence and the French Revolution would loom larger than they can do here. This wider picture should not only be remembered when we study Protestant Nonconformist texts, but it should be evaluated accurately. This means above all that we must eschew accounts of the eighteenth century which would have us believe that the Established Church was rotten through and through, populated with dissolute, absentee, huntin'-shootin'-fishin' clerics, who dragged their flocks into the mire of godlessness, and that all was changed when John Wesley clip-clopped into view (Doddridge, Whitefield and the Welsh pioneers of Revival frequently being overlooked). In fact, many parsons were models of conscientiousness in the early eighteenth century, and a good number were simply overtaken by events as industrialisation with its attendant population shifts – especially in the north of England – began to flood their geographically extensive, increasingly unworkable, parishes.[1] For example, whereas George Leigh, vicar of Halifax, reported to Archbishop Herring that in his parish in 1743 there were just '300 Presbyterian families; scarce any Baptists or Independents; 60 Quaker families and very few Papists', by the end of the century Nonconformists outnumbered Anglicans in that unwieldy parish.[2]

Secondly, we must make due allowance for the degree of fluidity within Protestant Nonconformity itself. Although by the beginning of the eighteenth century it had become current to refer to 'the three denominations' (the Independent, Baptist and Presbyterian), these were not the clearly defined, highly centralised structures with which we are familiar today. There were indeed such co-operative ventures as the Common Fund for the support of students which was established by the Presbyterians and Independents in 1691, and which bifurcated in the Presbyterian and Congregational Funds on the breakdown of the 'Happy Union' between those parties in 1695 – a breakdown prompted by Daniel Williams's accusation that the Congregationalists were Antinomians, and their rejoinder that he was a Socinian![3] There were also Associations surviving from the seventeenth century, among them the Worcestershire (1652), the Cumberland and Westmorland (1656), the Exeter

(1691) and the Lancashire (1693). Some of these were composed of both Presbyterians and Independents, some included laymen, but that at Exeter was entirely ministerial and largely Presbyterian. Crucially, however, these Associations, while they could and did offer guidance, were voluntary bodies only, having no executive authority over local churches.[4]

Congregations were frequently composed of people with various church-polity sympathies (and, no doubt, of some who were there because that is where they and their family had always been); and it was not exceptional for ministers to serve now in a Presbyterian, now in an Independent church. Thus, for example, Philip Doddridge served among the Presbyterians, and was approached by both Presbyterians and Independents prior to accepting a call to the Independent church in Northampton, where he was ordained in 1730. As for the local churches, a number of them changed their label during the century, either because their theology (or that of a sufficient number of members, or a small number of influential members) changed – normally from trinitarianism to Arianism and thence to Unitarianism among the Presbyterians and General Baptists; or because it remained the same, as when the church at Carlton, Bedfordshire, moved from Independent to Baptist and subsequently to Strict Baptist, retaining its original Calvinism throughout. Such changes were facilitated by the fact that the majority of chapel and meeting-house trust deeds referred to the worshippers as 'Protestant Dissenters' rather than as followers of more specific traditions. Those who could not abide such changes frequently seceded and established new causes of their own, as we shall see.

Thirdly, we must bear in mind that the inspiration of Methodism, whether Calvinistic or Arminian, was evangelistic and religious, not ecclesiological. By contrast, Old Dissent, from its Separatist harbingers onwards, entailed a claim that the nature of the Church was other than that proposed by the Anglican Establishment. Organiser though he was, John Wesley had no such motive – indeed, by profession and in fact he remained an Anglican to his dying day (though his breaches of parochial discipline and the ordinations of Methodist preachers paved the way for the subsequent parting of the ways); indeed, within living memory local Methodist congregations were referred to as societies rather than as churches. Although during the nineteenth century the Arminian Methodists (by now of various stripes) aligned themselves ever more closely with Old Dissent, the implications of the different starting-points of the respective traditions have continuing ecumenical significance. As for the Calvinistic Methodists, it may, without disrespect, be said that they 'came by' Presbyterianism in the early nineteenth century, just as many influenced by the Revival in Scotland 'came by' Congregationalism. Certainly in neither case was the original motivation ecclesiological.

There are, fourthly, some basic questions which are easy to pose and not so easy to answer. How many Nonconformists were there in the eighteenth century? M. R. Watts has estimated that in the early eighteenth century there were some 338,120 Dissenters, comprising 6.21 per cent of the total population of England. Of these, Presbyterians accounted for 179,350, Independents for 59,940, Particular Baptists for 40,520, General Baptists for 18,800, and Quakers for 39,510.[5] His estimates for Wales, where the 17,770 Dissenters comprised 5.74 per cent of the total population are: Presbyterians 6,080, Independents 7,640, and Particular Baptists 4,050.[6] As the century progressed the number of Presbyterians and Quakers declined – J. S. Rowntree estimated that there were 19,800 Quaker members and some 8,000 adherents in England and Wales in 1800,[7] while the Independents and Baptists, influenced as many of them were by the Revival, began to increase dramatically in the last quarter of the century. The Census of 1851 revealed that Nonconformists now numbered 17 per cent of the English and 45 per cent of the Welsh populations. Slightly more than half of the increase consisted of Arminian Methodists in England (of whom there were already 80,000 by 1791, the year of Wesley's death) and Calvinist Methodists (Presbyterian Church of Wales) in Wales.[8]

Of what sort were the Nonconformists? Again, this is a complicated question which can here be answered in only the most general terms. Excluded from civic life, Dissenters frequently devoted themselves to trade, and some became prosperous. In the early decades of the eighteenth century Dissenting congregations had a sizeable proportion of merchants, traders and rural freeholders among their members, though there were significant variations within the 'denominations'. For example, John Evans's List of 1718-29 shows that at Whitehaven Presbyterian Church there was one merchant worth more than £20,000, and four worth more than £4,000 each, while at Salkeld there was but one gentleman, the remainder being 'the meaner sort of yeomen and poor farmer'.[9] With industrialization and the influx of new converts under the Revival, while some Quaker meetings, a number of Presbyterian congregations and a few Independent churches remained prosperous, the majority of Nonconformists were drawn from the new, poor, skilled and semi-skilled workers and their families.[10]

Where did the Nonconformists worship? In the twenty years following the Toleration Act of 1689 licences, which had to be issued by bishops, archdeacons or magistrates from that date until 1852, were granted to some 3,000 premises. Many of these were dwelling houses; others, as at Maesyronnen, Powys (1696), were converted barns; some were new buildings. Many of the latter, like the Presbyterian chapel at Knutsford (1689) and the Presbyterian-turned-Independent chapel at Chinley, Derbyshire (1711), were in the traditional meeting-house style consistent with the vernacular architecture of the period; but some, like Old Meeting Norwich (1693), with its brick pilasters with Corinthian capitals, and the Presbyterian cause at St Saviourgate, York (1693), designed in the form of a Greek cross, made more original architectural statements. In the middle of the century the influential Presbyterian congregation of John Taylor of Norwich had an octagonal chapel erected (1754–56), and among a number of Methodist octagons are those at Yarm (1763) and Heptonstall (1764). The latter two were by no means as grandly appointed as the former, of which John Wesley, never slow to exercise his facility in making theological points, turned architecture to polemical use and, following his visit on 23 December 1757, declared,

> I was shewn Dr. Taylor's new meeting-house, perhaps the most elegant one in all Europe. It is eight square, built of the finest brick, with sixteen sash-windows below, as many above, and eight sky-lights in the dome, which are indeed purely ornamental. The inside

4

is furnished in the highest taste, and is as clean as any nobleman's saloon. The communion-table is fine mahogany; the very latches of the pew-doors are polished brass. How can it be thought that the old coarse gospel should find admission here?[11]

In Long Sutton, Somerset, the Friends' Meeting House (1717), with its Georgian, Wren-like features, is relatively grand, while its exact contemporary at Pales, Powys, in the Radnor Forest, the oldest Quaker property in Wales, is small, thatched and secluded. Square Independent Chapel, Halifax (1772) was one of a number of chapels built by the increasingly important industrial barons of northern England, while Ebenezer Baptist Chapel, Llangefni (1781), Angelsey, exemplifies chapels with adjoining houses. So much for the merest glimpse of eighteenth-century's Nonconformist 'texts in stone', the renewed interest in which in recent years is most gratifying if somewhat belated.[12]

It remains to offer some remarks upon the selection and classification of the material presented in this volume. The process of selection has been painful. So much of what one's friends wrote has had to be excluded, so many local excitements – doctrinal, evangelistic and socio-political – have been passed by. Difficult decisions have been taken, prompted by the number of pages allowed, the onset of deadlines and the need to clear the floors of two rooms in the co-ordinating editor's home of heaps of candidate texts.

The selection made, the attempt to classify the favoured items has also been fraught with difficulty, and there is something inevitably arbitrary about the arrangement of the resulting six parts of this work. Thus, for example, most of the English and Welsh eighteenth-century philosophers were also divines; the laicising of philosophy, on which Gilbert Ryle once remarked, had yet to take place.[13] No hard-and-fast distinctions can be drawn between what we should nowadays regard as philosophical questions on the one hand and theological questions on the other (though Henry Grove pioneered the curriculum distinction between dogmatics and ethics). The attempt to make two parts out of 'Philosophy' and 'Christian Doctrine' is thus done for convenience and with latter-day hindsight. Again, many of the texts gathered under 'Church, Ministry and Sacraments' and 'Church. State and Society' are intensely doctrinal in tone and might have appeared under 'Doctrine'. But, once more, the topical classification seems convenient. But where to place local church covenants, so important in the Baptist and Independent traditions? Many of these are doctrinal in tone, and some are concerned to make theological points against those from whom the drafters have recently seceded; and they all have to do with the way in which the nature of the Church is understood. On balance, however, in view of their local origin it seemed most fitting to place them under 'Nuture, Piety and Church Life'. Yet again, Sunday schools, prison reform and the anti-slavery movement have sometimes been regarded as products of the Evangelical Revival, and so the brief references to them here might have been allocated to Part Four, 'Evangelism, Revival and Mission'. But the circulating schools in Wales which pre-date the major Welsh and English itinerant evangelists, and the fact that the first designated Sunday school in England was founded in 1764 by Theophilus Lindsey who, though not yet an avowed Unitarian was certainly a latitudinarian Anglican, gave one pause, and so they appear under 'Church, State and Society'. Ordinations were no doubt red letter days in the life of local churches and might therefore have appeared in Part Six. But our interest in them here is primarily ecclesiological, and hence they are considered in Part Three. Similarly, while Doddridge's thoughts on the ministry might well have appeared under 'Church, Ministry and Sacraments', they were stimulated by the urgent need for revival, and so are included in Part Four.

However inadequate the principles of classification, it is hoped that the overriding intention of the collection is clear: to present as comprehensive a view as possible of the philosophical, doctrinal, ecclesiological, socio-political, evangelistic and missionary concerns of the eighteenth-century Nonconformists, and to afford a glimpse into their devotional life – private and public, their churchly activities, and their heaven-orientated motivations and aspirations.

> The Lamb shall lead his heav'nly flock
>> Where living fountains rise,
> And love divine shall wipe away
>> The sorrow of their eyes.[14]

Notes

1. See, for example, the careful work of John Walsh and others in John Walsh, Colin Haydon and Stephen Taylor, eds, *The Church of England c. 1689–c. 1833: From Toleration to Tractarianism*, Cambridge: CUP, 1993. In the light of such work the assertion of Henry Bett, typical of popularisers of earlier times, requires serious qualification: 'In the first years of the eighteenth century in this country religion had lost all its passionate reality. It amounted to little more than a moral life and decent observance of the rites of the Church'. See his *What Methodists Believe and Preach*, 4th printing, London: Epworth Press, 1952, p. 5
2. So John Hargreaves in *Thunderclaps from Heaven: Calderdale's Heritage of Nonconformity*, Halifax: Metropolitan Borough of Calderdale, 1984, p. 11
3. See Walter D. Jeremy, *The Presbyterian Fund and Dr. Daniel Williams's Trust: With Biographical Notes of the Trustees, and Some Account of their Academies, Scholarships and Schools*, London: Williams and Norgate 1885; John H. Taylor, *The Congregational Fund Board 1695 – 1995*, a supplement to *The Congregational History Circle Magazine*, III, suppl. 1, 1995, *The Journal of the United Reformed Church History Society*, V, suppl. 1, 1995, and *Y Cofiadur, Cylchgrawn Cymdeithas Hanes Annibynwyr Cymru*, 59 A, 1995
4. See Geoffrey F. Nuttall, 'Assembly and Association in Dissent, 1689–1831', in G. J. Cuming and Derek Baker, eds, *Councils and Assemblies* (Studies in Church History, VII), Cambridge: CUP, 1971, pp. 289–309.
5. The figure for the Quakers is in broad agreement with that deduced by William C. Braithwaite who, however, reminds us that records are imperfect. See *The Second Period of Quakerism*, 2nd edn, Cambridge: CUP, 1961, p. 459. For Wales, see the pioneering but still valuable work of Thomas Rees, *History of Protestant Nonconformity in Wales*, London: John Snow, 1883, 259–66.

6. M. R.Watts, *The Dissenters,* vol. 1: *From the Reformation to the French Revolution,* Oxford: Clarendon Press, 1978, p. 270; and see the important appendix.

7. J. S. Rowntree, *Quakerism, Past and Present; being an Inquiry into the Causes of its Decline in Great Britain and Ireland,* 1859. For Quaker record-keeping, see R. T. Vann and D. Eversley, *Friends in Life and Death,* Cambridge: CUP, 1992, ch. 1.

8. See M. R. Watts, *The Dissenters,* vol. 2: *The Expansion of Evangelical Nonconformity,* Oxford: Clarendon Press, 1995, pp. 23, 28, 29. Original sources for such statistical analysis include John Evans's *List,* compiled 1715–18, and Josiah Thompson's MS (1772–3), both of which are at Dr Williams's Library, London.

9. Evans's *List,* Dr Williams's Library, London, MS. 38.4.

10. See further, James Bradley, *Religion, Revolution and English Radicalism,* Cambridge: CUP, 1990, pp. 63–9; R. T. Vann, *The Social Development of English Quakerism,* Cambridge, MA: Harvard University Press, 1969; M. R. Watts, *The Dissenters,* I, pp. 346–57.

11. J. Wesley, *Works,* 1872, II, p. 431. See further, John and Edward Taylor, *History of Octagon Chapel, Norwich,* 1848.

12. See further, for example, Frederick J. Jobson, *Chapel and School Architecture* (1850), reprinted Peterborough: Methodist Publishing House, 1991; Ronald P. Jones, *Nonconformist Church Architecture,* London: Lindsey Press, 1914; George W. Dolbey, *The Architectural Expression of Methodism,* London: Epworth Press, 1964; Kenneth Lindley, *Chapels and Meeting Houses,* London: John Baker, 1969; Kenneth H. Southall, *Our Quaker Heritage: Early Meeting Houses,* London: Quaker Home Service, 1974; David A. Barton, *Discovering Chapels and Meeting Houses,* Princes Risborough: Shire Publications, 1975; David M. Butler, *Quaker Meeting Houses of the Lake Counties,* London: Friends Historical Society, 1978; idem, *The Quaker Meeting Houses of Britain,* 2 vols, London: Friends Historical Society, 1999. Ken Powell, *The Fall of Zion: Northern Chapel Architecture and its Future,* London: SAVE Britain's Heritage, 1980; Benjamin G. Cox, *Chapels and Meeting Houses in the Vale of Evesham,* Gloucester: Alan Sutton for the Vale of Evesham Historical Society, 1982; Anthony Jones, *Welsh Chapels,* Cardiff: National Museum of Wales, 1984; H. Godwin Arnold et al., *Hallelujah! Recording Chapels and Meeting Houses,* London: Council for British Archaeology, 1985; Graham Hague, *The Unitarian Heritage: An Architectural Survey,* Sheffield: Unitarian Heritage, 1986; and Christopher Stell's exemplary volumes on *Nonconformist Chapels and Meeting Houses* in *Central England* (1986), *South-West England* (1991), and *Northern England* (1994), London: HMSO, and *Eastern England,* Swindon: English Heritage, 2002. These last are notable for the detail of the architectural descriptions, the quality of the photographs and the range of the bibliographies.

13. Gilbert Ryle, *The Revolution in Philosophy,* London: Macmillan, 1960, p. 2.

14. Isaac Watts, *The Psalms and Hymns of the Rev. Isaac Watts, D.D.,* London, [1718], p. 350, hymn 41 verse 6.

PART I

PHILOSOPHY

Introduction

The eighteenth-century Protestant Nonconformists displayed attitudes to philosophy ranging from lively interest to dark suspicion. By far the majority of those who viewed philosophy askance counted themselves evangelical – Arminian or Calvinist. Thus, when John Fletcher of Madeley, President of the Countess of Huntingdon's college at Trevecka (1768), visited the students, his concern for their souls would outweigh the dictates of the syllabus: 'His full heart would not suffer him to be silent'. As for the students, 'they were readier to hearken to this servant and minister of Jesus Christ than to attend to Sallust, Virgil, Cicero, or any Latin or Greek historian, poet, or philosopher they had been engaged in reading'. Before long 'they were all in tears and every heart caught fire from the flame that burned in [Fletcher's] soul'.[1] Again, John Newton who, although an evangelical Anglican, was the motivating force behind the Nonconformist evangelical academy at Newport Pagnell (1783) recommended the use of Isaac Watts's *Logic and the Improvement of the Mind* – a standard text of fifty years previously, but declared, 'I have no great opinion of metaphysical studies', and despised the study of the evidences for Christianity, a staple of the curriculum of older Dissenting academies.[2]

For the most part, therefore, the practice and teaching of philosophy rested in the hands of Dissenters who lived and worked prior to, or untouched by, the Evangelical Revival. In some academies of the previous century scholastic philosophy was still taught. For example, of Matthew Warren of Taunton academy it was said that 'though bred himself in the old logic and philosophy and little acquainted with the improvements of the new, yet he encouraged his pupils in a freedom of inquiry and in reading those books which would better gratify a love of truth and knowledge, even when they differed widely from those writers on which he had formed his own sentiments … [Thus] Locke, Le Clerc and Cumberland were guides to the students in their closets'.[3]

The crucial name here is that of Locke, viewed with suspicion by many Erastians. His *Essay concerning Human Understanding* (1690) was proscribed at Oxford University in 1703 (though read surreptitiously by some). It was Locke with whom most philosophers – whether Dissenters of not – felt they had to reckon, especially though by no means exclusively in the four decades following the Toleration Act of 1689. The *Essay* was on the syllabus of moderate and liberal Dissenting academies. The Dissenters valued Locke's writings on toleration, though some, Priestley among them, would have gone further than Locke (who opposed toleration for Roman Catholics because they owed allegiance to a foreign power, and atheists because they were untrustworthy), and would have extended toleration to all.[4] Concerning other aspects of Locke's thought Dissenters were selective. While some welcomed his attack upon innate ideas, Watts was not entirely persuaded by it; some were highly suspicious of Locke's suggestion that, had he so chosen, God might have endowed matter with the power of thought; and although many appreciated Locke's encouragement to those who would read biblical books whole, a number, among them Philip Doddridge, challenged him on particular points of interpretation. With Newtonian science behind him, Locke further stimulated many in what might be called the century of the cosmological argument for God's existence to ground their theism in (and, as we shall see in Part Three, to frame their ordination confessions in accordance with) that argument.[5]

The extracts which follow suggest (they do no more than that) the concerns of eighteenth-century Dissenting philosopher-divines with metaphysics, ethics and political theory. Among a number of recurring themes as the century progresses are those concerning the right of private judgement and the foundation of ethics. In the latter case the debate between the good friends Richard Price and Joseph Priestley over the latter's materialism and the former's deontological approach (over against Hutcheson's moral sense theory) in ethics are of particular importance.

It remains only to add that one of the most influential philosophers of the eighteenth century was trained at Samuel Jones's academy but, on conforming to the Church of England he slipped the Dissenting net and eventually became *Bishop* Joseph Butler.[6]

Notes

1. [A.C.H. Seymour], *The Life and Times of Selina, Countess of Huntingdon*, 1860, II, p. 102. For Fletcher (1729–85) see DEB, DNB, ODCC; L. Tyerman, *Wesley's Designated Successor*, 1882; G. Lawton, *Shropshire Saint: A Study in the Ministry and Spirituality of Fletcher of Madeley*, 1960; Patrick Streiff, *Reluctant Saint? A Theological Biography of Fletcher of Madeley*, Peterborough: Epworth Press, 2001. Biographical references to significant individuals are given in the notes to the Introduction to each part of this work only when those concerned are not the authors of texts to be introduced subsequently. For the position of philosophy in eighteenth-century academies see Alan P.F. Sell, *Philosophy, Dissent and Nonconformity 1689–1920*, Cambridge: James Clarke, 2004.
2. Newton to William Bull, December 1786, in *Memorials of the Rev. William Bull*, 1864, p. 162. For William Bull (1738–1814), and ardent Calvinist in whose charge the Newport Pagnell academy was placed, see DNB. For Newton (1725–1807) see DEB, DH, ODCC and a number of *Lives*.
3. J. Toulmin, *An Historical Account of the State of the Protestant Dissenters*, 1714, pp.230–2. For Warren (c. 1642–1706) see DNB.
4. J. Priestley, *The Theological and Miscellaneous Works of Joseph Priestley*, ed. J.T. Rutt, 1817–31, XXII, p. 63 n.
5. See further Alan P.F. Sell, *John Locke and the Eighteenth-Century Divines*, Cardiff: University of Wales Press, 1997, reprinted Eugene, OR: Wipf & Stock, 2006.
6. For Samuel Jones (1680?–1716), see DNB, DWB.

Document I.1

Samuel Clark's Advice to Philip Doddridge

Samuel Clark (1684–1750) was minister at Dagnal Street, St Albans, where he be-friended the orphaned Philip Doddridge (1702–51), and received him as a communicant church member in 1719. Supported by Clark, Doddridge attended Kibworth academy under John Jennings, succeeding to the Kibworth pastorate on Jennings's death in 1723. In 1729 the academy was reopened in Northampton, where Doddridge settled as min-ister of the Independent Church and academy tutor. An open-minded Calvinist, Doddridge was an early proponent of mission, and a hymn-writer of note. Among his students was Samuel Clark's son, also Samuel (1727–69), who became assistant to Doddridge and, following the latter's death, tutor at Daventry (1752–6) and teacher of Joseph Priestley, removing thence to Old Meeting, Birmingham, where he remained until his death. In the following letter of 3 October 1721, Dr Clark recommends the student Doddridge to read Locke's *Essay*, and cautions him to develop both mind and soul.

For Clark of St Albans see William Urwick, *Nonconformity in Herts.*, London: Hazell, Watson and Viney, 1884, pp. 191–297; Doddridge's funeral sermon for Clark in *The Works of the Rev. P Doddridge, D.D.*, 10 vols, Leeds: Edward Baines, 1803, III. For Doddridge see DEB, DECBP, DH, DNB, ODCC; Job Orton's Memoir in Doddridge's *Works*; Geoffrey F. Nuttall, ed., *Philip Doddridge 1702-51: His Contribution to English Religion*, London: Independent Press, 1951; M Deacon, *Philip Doddridge of Northampton 1702–51*, Northampton: Northamptonshire Libraries, 1980. For Jennings (d. 1723) see DNB. For Samuel Clark the Younger see George Eyre Evans, *Midland Churches*, Dudley, 1899 (though beware of confused dates). The following extract is taken from J.D. Humphreys, *Correspondence and Diary of Philip Doddridge*, 5 vols, London, 1829–31, I, p. 39.

I am sensible of the difficulties pneumatology has attending it. The only method of extricating oneself out of them is to see that we have clear ideas of all the terms we use, whether single, or connected with propositions, and that we take nothing for granted without sufficient evidence; and, which flows from the other two, that we do not pretend to reason upon things about which we have no ideas: that is, that we do not pretend to impossibilities. Mr. Locke's Essay is so useful to direct the mind in its researches, that methinks it should have been read before you entered upon pneumatics ... As to your contemplations upon the being and attributes of God, take heed of suffering your mind to rest in barren speculations. Whatever clear and en-larged ideas you attain to of the divine excellencies, see that they have proportionable effect upon the soul, in producing reverence, affection, and submission.

Document I.2

Isaac Watts's Philosophical Stance

Remembered especially for his hymns, Isaac Watts (1674–1748) was honoured by
many in his own day for his philosophical acumen. He studied under Thomas Rowe in
the Dissenting academy at Newington Green, London, and then served as assistant at
Mark Lane Independent Church, London, from 1699, and as pastor there from 1702.
Owing to ill health he resigned in 1712, and spent the rest of his life at Stoke
Newington.

   For Watts see BCE, DECBP, DH, DNB, ODCC; B. L. Manning, *The Hymns of
Wesley and Watts*, London: Independent Press, 1942; Arthur Paul Davis, *Isaac Watts:
His Life and Works*, London: Independent Press, 1948; J. Hoyles, *The Waning of the
Renaissance 1640–1740: Studies In the Thought and Poetry of John Norris and Isaac
Watts*, The Hague: Marinus Nijhof, 1971; I. Rivers, *Reason, Grace and Sentiment: A
Study of the Language of Religion in England, 1660–1780*, Cambridge: CUP, 1991.
For Rowe (1657–1705) see DNB. The following concise statement of Watts's episte-
mological position is taken from his *Works*, Leeds: Edward Baines, 1880, VI, p. 529,
where he counters Locke's view that the soul is not thinking at all times.

Now though I never was, nor could persuade myself to be a disciple of *Des Cartes*
in his doctrine of the nature of matter, or *vacuum*, or of *plenum*, &c. and I have many
years ago given up his opinions as to the chief phaenomena of the corporeal world,
yet I have never seen sufficient ground to abandon all his scheme of sentiments of
the *nature of mind* or *spirit*, because I could not find a better in the room of it, that
should be free from objections and difficulties.

Document I.3

Isaac Watts on the Resurrection of the Same Body

The following passage, in which Watts again adjusts himself to Locke's position, is
taken from his *Works*, Leeds: Edward Baines, 1800, VI, pp. 554–9.

There has been a warm dispute among men of learning and particularly between Mr.
Locke and Bishop Stillingfleet, whether the same individual body which is buried
shall be raised at the resurrection of the dead? Or, whether it may not be another
new-made body, composed of any other atoms, and united to the same soul. Those
who with Bishop Stillingfleet affirm the resurrection of the same body, may give
such reasons as these for it.

   1.   It is fit and proper, that the same body which has been a companion and instrument of the soul in duties of holiness should arise and share with the soul in the
reward of heaven; and that the same body, which has been a temptation or instrument
of the soul in sin, should also rise to share the torment. I must confess, I do not think
this argument has very great weight in it; because the body alone is mere insensible

matter, and can neither share in pleasure or pain. It is the soul only that has sense of pain and pleasure, and whatsoever body it is vitally united to, is still its own body, and may be the medium of pleasure or pain to it.

2.   Since body and soul united constitute the man, if it be not the same body that died which is raised, then one essential part of man is lost. If it be another body, it is another man that is raised from the earth, and not the same man that died. Besides, the soul never dies; and if the same animal body that died be not raised to life, there is nothing at all to be raised to life: There may be another inanimate body which has life given to it indeed, but nothing is revived. Perhaps this sort of argumentation many have some weight in it.

3.   Christ himself saith; John v. 28, *They that are in the graves shall come forth*: This must refer to the same body that died; for it is not the soul, nor is it any other body that was properly put into the grave, but the animal body of man which is now inanimate dead.

4.   It seems to be the design of the apostle, to shew that it is the same body which died in some respects, though not in all respects, which shall be raised again to life: 1 Cor. xv.42. *So is the resurrection of the dead.* It, i.e. the body, *is sown in corruption, it is raised in incorruption, &c.* It, i.e. the body, *is sown a natural boy, it is raised a spiritual body.* It is the same human body still, but with different qualities. So *ver.* 52, 53. 'The dead shall be raised incorruptible, and we shall be changed. This corruptible shall put on incorruption, this mortal shall put on immortality;' which seems to be spoken both with regard to those who shall be raised from the dead, as well as those who shall be changed at the coming of Christ. It is this *mortal and this corruptible*, that is, this very animal body, which was mortal and corruptible, must be raised immortal.

To this I might add, that the apostle; Rom. viii. 11. speaks of these very mortal bodies which we now have, and affirms they shall be quickened, &c. and *Phil.* iii. *ult.* 'this body of our vileness or humiliation is to be changed, and made like to the glorious body of Christ.' Surely such expressions denote the same body. But the substance and strength of all the arguments derived from Scripture to prove the resurrection of the same body, may be found well put together in Dr. Whitby's Preface to the First Epistle to the Corinthians. Those who with Mr. Locke make the resurrection of the same individual body needless, may alledge such reason as these.

1.   It attains no valuable purpose to confine the resurrection to the same atoms of matter; for if the same soul be united to any mass of the same sort of substance, *i.e.* to any matter, there is a sufficient provision for every thing that regards the happiness or misery of the rising dead: Since the body itself, or mere matter, has no sensation and the soul will have the same sort of sensations, (whether pleasant to reward it, or painful to punish it) whatsoever other particles of matter it may be united to, as if it were united to the same particles it had in this world, and in which it obeyed or sinned.

Besides it is worthy of our observation what Mr. Locke says on this subject. 'If it should be demanded what greater congruity the soul hath to any particles of matter which were once vitally united to it, but are no so no longer, than it hath no particles of matter to which it was never united, this would be hard to determine'.

15

2.   The apostle shews it shall be different matter from that which was laid in the grave, by the very manner of his arguing: For when he uses the simile of a 'grain of wheat dying in the ground,' he says, *ver.*37,38. 'Thou sowest not that body that shall be, but thou sowest a bare grain; and God giveth it a body (*i.e.* another body) as pleaseth him. And then he goes on to shew what different sorts of bodies there are, and how different the bodies in the resurrection shall be from what were buried.

3.   It is hardly possible that all the very same bodies should rise; that is, all the same atoms or particles that were buried: For when bodies turn to dust, this dust or earth grows up in vegetation, and becomes the body of grass or plants; sheep and oxen eat these plants, and other men eat the sheep and oxen; and thus the particles of one man's body may frequently become the parts of another man's body. And this is more conspicuous in the country of *cannibals*, where they kill and eat their slaves. How then is is possible that each human body should have its own particles?

4.   There is sufficient ground to say, the same person rises again from the dead though there be not one atom of the same matter that was buried, which goes to make up the body in the resurrection; for *Methuselah*, when a child, and when one, two, three, four or five hundred years old, and when he had lived nine hundred and sixty years before his death, had actually by perspiration, and attrition &c. changed the atoms that composed his body perhaps thirty or forty times over, and yet it is the same compound substance of soul and body, the same conscious being or person still, it is *Methuselah* both at his birth, at five hundred years old, and at his death. Besides, if all the same atoms that ever belonged to *Methuselah* must be raised, what a bulky man would that be? And further, what need is there that the last dying withering particles should be raised to make *Methuselah* again, when any other atoms that ever belonged to him, and in which he practised virtue or vice, are as much the same *Methuselah*? And yet all of these cannot be crouded into his body, without making a giant of him. So that we see there is no need of the same atoms or particles to make the same person, if there be but the same thinking mind conscious of his actions in this life, united to a proper portion of matter. It is consciousness makes the person.

This is the force of the arguments of those who deny the necessity of having the same body raised. And I think the arguments on both sides have some real strength in them. Now I would humbly enquire, whether all the differences of these disputants, which I have endeavoured briefly to set in their strongest light, may not be compromised in this manner.

I.   It is granted that it cannot be the very same body in all the particles or atoms of it which were united to the soul in this world, that shall be raised and united to it in the resurrection:

(1.)   Because all the atoms that ever belonged to the animal body of *Methuselah* in nine hundred and sixty nine years would make a most bulky and disproportionate figure at the resurrection: And for the same reason all the antediluvians, who lived so many hundred years, would be raised as giants in comparison of us in later days. And on the same account also, every man at the resurrection would be so much larger than his contemporaries and neighbours, as he lived longer on earth; which is a vain and groundless conceit.

(2.) All the same particles, even of the body when it died and was buried, can hardly be raised again and united to the soul of any man, because several of the particles that made one man's body at the time of his death are very probably turned to grass or plants, and so become food for cattle, or other men, and are become part of the bodies of other men several times over. And thus there might be great confusion, because the self-same particles would belong to the bodies of several men. Besides, here's one pious man perhaps died of a dropsy, or excessive fat and unwieldy, must he be raised in that unwieldy bulk and those extravagant dimensions? Another was worn out to a mere skeleton by a consumption; must his raised body be of this slender and withered shape or size? Others it may be from their very birth were in some part defective, or redundant; and in these cases must not some particles be left out or added in the resurrection to form a proper body for the glorified soul? All these considerations prove that all the precise number of atoms that ever made up a man's body here on earth, or even those that belonged to it at the hour of death, are not necessary to be summoned together to form the same man at the resurrection.

II. It is also granted, that it must be in some sense the same body raised which was buried, in order to answer several expressions both of Jesus Christ and of the apostle Paul in the discourse of the resurrection. And we may allow without any difficulty, that so many of the same particles of any man's body which were buried may go to constitute the new raised body, as justly to denominate it the same body, and which being united to the same soul, do render the new-raised man the same man and the same person who died: For it is evident that a very few of the same atoms or particles which were laid in the grave are sufficient for this purpose, if we consider these two things:

I. It is very probable that a new-born infant in its muscles and nerves (and especially in its bowels and bones) has some original, essential, and constituent tubes, fibres or staminal particles (if I may so call them) which remain the same and unchanged through all the stages and changes of life in following years, how much soever the external and fleshy parts may be changed. And some philosophers maintain that the growth of the animal body is nothing but the dilation, stretching or spreading of these essential and staminal parts, these fibres, tubes or membranes, by the interposition of new additional particles; which additional and accidental particles are the only things which are in perpetual flux, and always changing. And it may be added also, that perhaps these essential staminal particles are of such a nature as not to join and unite with other animal or human bodies, and become an essential constituent of them: And therefore if mankind were all *cannibals*, and eat one another as well as the flesh of bests, yet the same staminal or constituent particles cannot belong to the bodies of two or more human persons. It has been said by some philosophers that the mere membranaceous parts of an animal body, though eaten by other animals, will not easily if at all digest; and then they cannot be sanguified or turned into blood, nor become nutritive juices, nor form the constituent and essential parts of other animals; Now a great many of the original constituent parts of human bodies are membranaceous; for some suppose almost the whole body to be made of tubes and juices, with little interspersed fibres which are added by nutrition. And how far the bones, *i.e.* original mere osseous substances may be indigestible also, who can tell?

Upon the whole, it seems that these essential, constituent or staminal particles, whatsoever they may be, whether osseous, or membranaceous, or of any other quality, and how many or how few soever they be, always abide the same, even when the body is greatly enlarged by the perpetual new interposition of additional nutritive particles, which are in continual flux. I say also, that it seems that these unchanging parts, whether few or many, in union with the same soul, are abundantly sufficient to denominate *Methuselah the infant, and Methuselah the aged*, the same person; and then also these few essential constituent particles preserved by divine providence, and raised in the formation of the new body, and united to the same soul, are sufficient to denominate *Methuselah dying* and *Methuselah rising* the same person still, both soul and body.

Here it may be *objected* indeed, that there is no need of running to such *essential constituent particles* of the body of a man in order to denominate him the *same* man at sixteen or sixty, or six hundred years of age; for these philosophical ideas of *constituent particles* come not within the notice of the bulk of mankind, and yet all mankind agree to call *Methuselah* the *same man*, and his body the *same body*, though it be maintained by the continual succession of new particles of matter, since they are united to the same soul. This seems to be sufficient for this purpose.

This *objection* may be *answered* two ways, (1.) that as these constituent and unchangeable particles of the body do not come within the notice of the bulk of mankind, so neither does the continual change and succession of new particles by perspiration and nutrition come within their notice; and therefore the bulk of manking call it the *same body* because it appears in the gross to be the same: But if you prove *it is not the same* by insensible alterations, I may prove *it is the same* by these insensible unchanging parts. In one case the alteration is insensible; and the constituent particles abide unchanged without sensible notice in the other case; and if one disputant borrows his objection from *philosophical ideas*, the other may borrow his solution from *philosophical ideas* too.

It may be answered (2.) that the language of scripture and the reasons for the resurrection of the body, in some respects *the same* with that which was buried, are so strong, that I think they cannot well be answered without supposing so many particles of the same body which was buried to be raised again, as may be sufficient upon some just principles to give it the name of the *same body*, and there can be no more required.

2. The similitude which the apostle uses in that discourse concerning *a grain of wheat, v.* 37, 38. plainly teaches us, that though there should be but a very few of the same individual particles raised from the dust, and mixed with a multitude of other new particles, yet these few are sufficient to denominate it the *same body*, so far as the apostle's argument requires it. For it is evident that when a grain of wheat is sown into the ground, far the greatest part of the grain quickly dies and rots in the eartb; and there are but a very few small particles of the same grain which compose the *germen* or bud of the new plant, and which do really grow up into, and help to form and compose the new stalk and the ear of corn, together

with the addition of a multitude of other new atoms borrowed from the earth and water.

In the same manner the apostle leads us to suppose there may be a few of the same original and essential parts of the body of a man which are buried in the grave, which are the original, the spring and foundation of the new-raised body, though there may be thousands of other new atoms mixt with them. Now it is easy to suppose, that the power and providence of God may according to this supposition, preserve and raise the same body at the resurrection. For if the new-raised body has but as many essential atoms of the dead body in it, as the new stalk and ear of wheat has of the grain that was sowed, it is enough: And the union of the same conscious mind or spirit, makes it the same man.

I would ask leave to conclude this Essay with this short and plain remark. There are some of those who follow Mr. Locke and his way of thinking in many of these matters, who also go a step further, and supposed the spirit or conscious principle in man to lose all consciousness when the body dies, and that at the resurrection God shall give consciousness to the person again, or make a conscious principle to exist in the new-raised body. Now if this is the case, then it is neither the same body nor the same spirit that is raised from the dead, but a new spirit and a new body, which I think must necessarily be called *another person*, as well as Mr. Locke would call it *another man*: and I am sure such a new-made creature consisting of another mass of matter, and another conscious principle, can never be justly rewarded or punished for *personal* virtues and vices, good or evil actions done in the former life by a different body and spirit, *i.e. by another person*.[1]

Note

1. I have not observed any distinction here between the *same man* and the *same person* though Mr. Locke makes a great difference.

Document I.4

Abraham Taylor on Locke

Abraham Taylor (*fl.* 1727–40), Independent minister at Little Moorfields, London, was tutor at the Clerkenwell-Deptford Dissenting academy from its inception in 1730. This academy was constituted by the Independents of the King's Head Society, which body was formed in the same year to combat the growth of Arianism. Not surprisingly, then, Taylor was an ardent – even a belligerent – Calvinist. His general position is made plain in the following extract, which concludes with a characteristically English put-down.

For Taylor see DNB. The following extract is from his *An Introduction to Logick, with a few Lectures on Perception, the first part of that Science*, 1739, pp. 43–4, MS 69.24 at Dr Williams's Library, London.

The Popish writers have run into great confusion in endeavouring to make free thinking consistent with implicit faith in the dictates of their church; and Mr. Locke, who let his admirers say what they will of him, was no better than a Socinian in principle, and but a mean Divine for that sort, and no great friend of revelation, has interlarded his work with a great many subtleties, which tend to bring persons to have a mean and low view of what is properly mysterious. These men were certainly persons of deep thought, and penetrating genius, but their learning was very inconsiderable, and their reading was not large. This, in a particular manner, was true of Mr. Locke. Those that knew him personally were satisfied, that, as to ancient literature he was but very superficial.

Document I.5

Henry Grove on Locke

Henry Grove (1683/4–1738), Presbyterian divine, was the ablest student in philosophy to emanate from the Taunton Dissenting academy conducted by Matthew Warren. He completed his studies under Thomas Rowe, his cousin, at Moorfields academy, London. After a brief pastorate at Ilchester (1705) he succeeded Warren at Taunton. Of an eirenic disposition, his open-mindedness as a tutor prompted some to suspect his doctrinal soundness, and he remained aloof from the Salters' Hall conference of 1719. That religion is reasonable is a theme which runs through his writings. Against Locke, Grove defends the immateriality of the soul, denying that matter can think, and proves to his own satisfaction that Mr Locke was not infallible.

For Grove see DECBP, DNB; James Strong's sermon at Grove's funeral: *The suddenness of Christ's coming consider'd and improv'd*, 1738; Thomas Amory's 'Account' of Grove's life prefixed to the latter's *Works*, 1747; Alan P. F.Sell, *Dissenting Thought and the Life of the Churches*, Lewiston, NY: Edwin Mellen Press, 1990, ch. 6; Alan P. F. Sell, *Testimony and Tradition: Studies in Reformed and Dissenting Thought*, Aldershot: Ashgate, 2004 ch. 5; Brian Kirk, *The Taunton Dissenting Academy*, Taunton: Somerset Archaeological and Natural History Society, 2005. For Warren (1642–1706) see DNB. The following extract is from Grove's *Works*, 4 vols, 1747 (reprinted Bristol: Thoemmes Press, 2000), III, pp. 203, 230–1.

Matter cannot *think; and if so*, unquestionably the soul is immaterial … [He states Locke's contrary view, and continues] Is this reasoning worthy of so great a Philosopher? Excepting the instances of sense and spontaneous motion in animals … in which Mr. *Locke* begs the question, all the other properties which Mr. *Locke* saith are superadded to *matter*, really conclude no more that that *matter* may be figured and moved by almighty power in ten thousand ways, than which nothing more true; and therefore because the qualities of *matter* may be acted upon and new modified, *matter* may receive a new quality of a kind perfectly differing from all the qualities it was possessed of before; than which, in my opinion, nothing can be more false.

Document I.6

Henry Grove on our Obligation to Love God

Grove's favourite field of study was ethics, and he was among the first to differentiate ethics from dogmatics in the theological curriculum. Grove looks back to Locke (not uncritically, as we have seen), and forward to Price. The following passage is from the sermon he preached at Taunton at the ordination of Thomas Amory and William Cornish on 7 October 1730, *Works*, 1747, I, reprinted 2000, pp. 470–1.

The nature of man being considered, together with the relations he stands in to God, and his fellow-creatures, love is the first duty he owes both of them, and to himself; a love of desire, delight, and gratitude, mingled with an awful veneration to his Maker; a love of benevolence to other intelligent Beings; and a love enlightened by wisdom, not flowing from blind instinct, to himself. To this love, and by consequence, to all the actions that are the necessary effects, and genuine expressions of it, there must be an obligation antecedent in nature to any laws and precepts concerning it, whether human or divine. We are obliged to love God, not merely because he hath commanded us to love him, but because he hath made us capable of loving him, and both by his perfections and his benefits challenges our love. Did not these oblige us to love him as soon as we were in a condition to make an reflection on them, no subsequent command could oblige us to it. Why else are these things (viz, the perfections of the divine nature, and the kindness and love of God to us) mentioned as reasons of love which no ingenuous mind can resist? For if they are good reasons why we should love God, now that he commands it, they must be equally reasons for love antecedent to the consideration of any command whatsoever.

Document I.7

Henry Grove on Religion as the Foundation of Morality

If Grove will not have reason constricted by dogma, he will not have ethics divorced from religion either, as the following passage shows. It is from his *A System of Moral Philosophy*, edited and with eight concluding chapters by Thomas Amory, 2 vols, London, 1749 reprinted 2000, I, pp. 56–7.

As all Morality has its foundation in Religion, or the belief of a Supreme Being, and the hopes and fears of mankind relating to him, if there be no other life of man but what is animal and dying, Religion vanishes of course, and with that Morality, as far as it flows from conscience, regulates the habit and temper of the mind, and is supported by the awe or love of a Divine Being ...

Document I.8

Thomas Amory on the Doctrines of Natural Religion

Thomas Amory (1701–74) studied under his uncle, Henry Grove, at Taunton, and then proceeded to Moorfields academy under John Eames, where he studied experimental physics. In 1725 he became assistant minister at Bishops Hull, and assistant in the Taunton academy. He was ordained in 1730 and became assistant to Edmund Batson at Paul's Meeting, Taunton. Theological differences coupled with Batson's reluctance to divide the stipend prompted Amory's friends to build a new meeting house in Tancred Street, over which he presided until 1738, when Grove died and Amory took charge of the academy. In 1759 he removed to London and became afternoon preacher and, from 1766, co-pastor at the Old Jewry. A number of other lectureships and preaching appointments came his way. In 1772 he was among those Dissenters who pressed for the relaxations of the law requiring subscription to the Anglican articles on the part of schoolmasters and others. In the text to follow Amory is typical of the more liberal Dissenting divines of his day in underlining the importance of the doctrines of natural religion, and of the appeal to reason, whilst giving due place to divine revelation.

For Amory see DECBP, DNB; Brian Kirk, *The Taunton Dissenting Academy*, 2005. He argues as follows in *Ministers not Lords over the Faith of Christians, but Helpers of their Joy. A Sermon Preached at Lewin's-Mead, Bristol, at the Ordination of the Reverend Mr. William Richards, May the 22d. 1751*, London, [1751], pp. 12-14.

As to the great Doctrines therefore of *Natural Religion*, which the *Gospel*[1] takes for granted, and which are the foundations of our Faith in any Divine Revelation, because these can only be proved by reasonings on the nature of things, the frame of the world, and the like; we must, by arguments of this sort, addressed to the Reason of Men, endeavour to establish in them the belief of the Being, Perfections, and moral Providence of God; of the moral and essential differences of characters and actions, and of a future state of recompences. *He that cometh to God*,[2] says the Apostle, *must believe that he is, and that he is a rewarder of them who diligently seek him.* As all men therefore are obliged to receive these Truths, and are *capable*[3] of discerning the evidences of them; all they, whom we would confirm in the faith of these, have a right to demand from us *rational* grounds for their faith. To require that they should believe, without good reasons, what we affirm on these heads, is to exalt ourselves into *Lords of Faith*, and degrade them to a level with *brutes*.

As to the Articles and Duties of *Revelation*, which we would have them receive and practise, we must, by an appeal to the Scriptures, explained according to the rules of fair interpretation, prove to them, that the Doctrines, which we assert to be contained in such passages of Scripture, are really taught therein by Christ, and the Precepts really enjoined by him. For any Man, or Body of Men, either alone, or assembled in *Councils* or *Synods*, to require of others to submit to his or their determinations, as Rules of Faith or Practice, without first making it plain to their Understandings, that they have determined according to the mind of Christ, is really to make themselves *Lords of Faith*, and to exercise the *Dominion* which St. *Paul* renounces. If the *Council* of *Nice* or of *Trent*; if a *Convocation* at *London*, or the *Synod* at *Westminster*, have determined Articles of Faith, and proved them by the Scriptures, they are to be received by all who *discern the proof*. Not for any Authority in these Ecclesiastical Bodies, but on account of the Evidence they bring with them. And where this Evidence does not appear, their *Decrees* are to be rejected as warrantably, as if they were merely the determinations of a single undignified Person.

Nor ought we, after having nobly cast off the Authority of *others* as *Lords* over our *Faith*, to assume *Dominion* to *ourselves*, by exacting Faith or Obedience merely on the pretence of our own Authority. To Reason, *to the Law and to the Testimony*,[4] all are authorised to appeal; and by these our Doctrines are as subject to be tried as the Doctrines of any others. If Persons do not immediately yield to our Arguments, we must not pronounce them dishonest or stupid, but carefully examine, whether we ourselves are not mistaken. And if after a review we see good reason to conclude, that we have Truth of our side, we should try whether placing our Arguments in other Lights, or offering new, taken from Reason and Scripture; whether continued kindness and candor, joined with a good Example, may not prevail over their Prejudices. *For the servant of the Lord must not strive, but be gentle unto all men, apt to teach, patient; in meekness instructing those who oppose themselves, because God may thus give them repentance to the acknowledgement of the Truth.*[5]

Where we cannot by good Arguments convince others, to pronounce them Enemies to Truth and Goodness, is to exalt ourselves into *Lords* indeed. 'Tis claiming not only *infallibility* as to Doctrine, but such a *knowledge of the heart* as qualifies us certainly to determine, that it is a want of honesty and of love to the Truth, not a want of ability to discern the evidence, which occasions persons to differ from us.

Notes

1. John vi. 44, 45. Matt. vi. 26.
2. Heb. xi. 6.
3. Rom. i. 20. ii. 14. Acts xiv. 15. xvii. 24.
4. Isa. viii. 20.
5. Tim. ii. 24.

Document I.9

Richard Price on Moral Obligation

Wales's most prominent philosopher, Richard Price (1723–91), recoiling from his father's staunch Calvinism, became an Arian Presbyterian divine of wide interests. His education included periods under Samuel Jones at Pen-twyn, Vavasor Griffiths at Talgarth and John Eames at Moorfields. From 1758 he served at Newington Green and also for a period as tutor at the liberal Hackney College. A noted actuary, Price was also an ardent supporter of the American War of Independence and the French Revolution. In some respects anticipating Kant, Price maintained that actions are intrinsically right or wrong; and that while these concepts are not susceptible of further analysis, we see immediately by rational intuition that it is so.

For Price see BCE, DECBP, DNB, DWB, ODCC; W. Morgans's Memoir, London, 1815; C. B. Cone. *Torchbearer of Freedom: The Influence of Richard Price on Eighteenth-Century Thought*, Lexington, KY: University of Kentucky Press, 1952; D. O. Thomas, *The Honest Mind: The Thought and Work of Richard Price*, Oxford: Clarendon Press, 1977; W. D. Hudson, *Reason and Right: A Critical Examination of Richard Price's Moral Philosophy*, London: Macmillan, 1970; W. B. Peach and D. O. Thomas, eds, *The Correspondence of Richard Price*, Cardiff: University of Wales Press and Durham, NC: Duke University Press, 3 vols, 1983–94; D. O. Thomas, ed., *Political Writings, Richard Price*, Cambridge: CUP, 1991; D. O. Thomas, J. Stephens and P. A. L. Jones, *A Bibliography of the Works of Richard Price*, Aldershot: Scolar, 1993. For Samuel Jones (*fl.* 1715–64), see DWB; for Vasavor Griffiths (d. 1741) see DWB. The following passage is from Price's major ethical work, *A Review of the Principle Questions in Morals*, (1758), 3rd edn, 1787, ch. 6.

Obligation to action, and *rightness* of action, are plainly coincident and identical; so far so, that we cannot form a notion of the one, without taking in the other. This may appear to any one upon considering, whether he can point out any difference between what is *right*, *meet* or *fit* to be done, and what ought to be done.[1] It is not indeed plainer, that figure implies something figured, solidity resistance, or an effect a cause, that it is that *rightness* implies *oughtness* (if I may be allowed this word) or *obligatoriness*. And as easily can we conceive of figure without extension, or motion without a change of place, as that it can be *fit* for us to do an action, and yet that it may not be what we *should* do, what it is our *duty* to do, or what we are under an *obligation* to do. – *Right, fit, ought, should, duty, obligation*, convey, then, ideas necessarily including one another. From hence it follows,

First, That virtue, *as such*, has a real obligatory power antecedently to all positive laws, and independently of all will; for obligation, we see, is involved in the very nature of it. To affirm, that the performance of that, which, to omit, would be wrong, is not obligatory, unless conducive to private good or enjoined by a superior power, is a manifest contradiction. It is to say, that it is not true, that a thing is what it is: or that we are *obliged* to do what we *ought* to do; unless it be the object of a command, or, in some manner, privately useful. – If there are any actions fit to be done by an agent, besides such as tend to his own happiness, those actions, by the terms, are *obligatory*, independently of their influence on his happiness. – Whatever it is *wrong* to do, that it is our *duty* not to do, whether enjoined or not by any positive law.[2] – I cannot conceive of any thing much more evident than this. – It appears, therefore, that those who maintain that all obligation is to be deduced from positive laws, the Divine will, or self-love, assert what (if they mean any thing contrary to what is here said) implies, that the words *right* and *just* stand for no real and distinct characters of actions; but signify merely what is *willed* and *commanded*, or conducive to private advantage, whatever that be; so that any thing may be both right and wrong, morally good and evil, at the same time and in any circumstances, as it may be commanded or forbidden by different laws and wills; and any the most pernicious effects will become just, and fit to be produced by any being, if but the smallest degree of clear advantage or pleasure may result to him from them.

Those who say, nothing can oblige but the will of God, generally resolve the power of this to oblige to the annexed rewards and punishments. And thus, in reality, they subvert entirely the independent natures of moral good and evil; and are forced to maintain, that nothing can *oblige*, but the prospect of pleasure to be obtained, or pain to be avoided. If this be true, it follows that *vice* is, properly, no more than *imprudence*; that nothing is right or wrong, just or unjust, any farther than it affects self-interest; and that a being, independently and completely happy, cannot have any moral perceptions. The justness of these inferences cannot be denied by one, who will attend to the coincidence here insisted on between obligation and virtue.

But to pursue this point farther; let me ask, would a person who either believes there is no God, or that he does not concern himself with human affairs, feel no *moral obligations*, and therefore not be at all *accountable*? Would one, who should happen not to be convinced, that virtue tends to his happiness here or hereafter, be released from every *bond* of duty and morality? Or, would he, if he believed no future state, and that, in any instance, virtue was against his *present* interest, be truly *obliged*, in these instances, to be wicked? – These consequences must follow, if obligation depends entirely on the knowledge of the will of a superior, or on the connexion between actions and private interest. – But, indeed, the very expression, *virtue tends to our happiness*, and the supposition that, in certain cases, it may be inconsistent with it, imply that it may exist independently of any connexion with private interest; and would have no sense, if it signified only the relation of actions to private interest. For then, to suppose virtue to be inconsistent with our happiness, would be the same with supposing, that what is *advantageous* to us, may be *disadvantageous* to us.

It is strange to find those who plead for self-interest, as the only ground of moral obligation, asserting that, when virtue clashes with present enjoyments, all motives to it cease, supposing no future state. For, upon their principles, the truth is not, that all motives to practise virtue, would, in these circumstances, cease, but that virtue itself would cease; nay, would be changed into vice; and what would otherwise have been fit and just, become unlawful and wrong: For, being under an obligation in these circumstances not to do what appeared to us fit, it could not in reality *be* fit; we could not do it without violating our duty, and therefore certainly, not without doing wrong. Thus, all who find not their *present* account in virtue, would, upon these principles (setting aside another world) be under an obligation to be wicked. Or, to speak more properly, the subject-matter of virtue and vice (that is, the relation of particular actions to private good) would be altered; what was before *wickedness* would become *virtue*, and what was before *virtue* would become *wickedness*. – It should be carefully minded that, as far as another world creates *obligation*, it creates *virtue*; for it is an absurdity too gross to be maintained, that we may act contrary to our obligations and yet act virtuously.

Another observation worthy our notice in this place, is, that rewards and punishments suppose, in the very idea of them, moral obligation, and are founded upon it. They do not *make* it, but *enforce* it. They are the *sanctions* of virtue, and not its *efficients.* A reward supposes something done to *deserve* it, or a conformity to *obligation subsisting previously to it*; and punishment is always inflicted on account of some breach of *obligation.* Were we under no obligations, antecedently to the proposal of rewards and punishments, it would be a contradiction to suppose us subjects capable of them. – A person without any light besides that of nature, and supposed ignorant of a future state of rewards and punishments and the will of the Deity, might discover these by reasoning from his natural notions of morality and duty. But were the latter dependent on the former, and not *vice versa*; this could not be said, nor should we have any principles left, from which to learn the will of the Deity, and the conditions of his favour to us.

Secondly, From the account given on *obligation,* it follows that *rectitude* is a *law* as well as a *rule* to us; that it not only *directs,* but *binds* all, as far as it is perceived. – With respect to its being a *rule,* we may observe, that a rule of action signifying some measure or standard to which we are to conform our actions, or some information we possess concerning what we ought to do, there can, in this sense, be no *other* rule of action; all besides, to which this name can be properly given, implying it, or signifying only helps to the discovery of it. To perceive or to be informed how it is *right* to act, is the very notion of a *direction* to act. And it must be added, that it is such a direction as implies *authority,* and which we cannot disregard or neglect without remorse and pain. Reason is the guide, the *natural* and *authoritative* guide of a rational being. Where he has no discernment of right and wrong, there, and there only, is he (morally speaking) *free.* But where he has this discernment, where *moral good* appears to him, and he cannot avoid pronouncing concerning an action, that it is fit to be done, and evil to omit it; here he is tied in the most strict and absolute manner, in bonds that no power in nature can dissolve, and from which he can at no time, or in any single instance, break loose, without offering the most unnatural violence to himself; without making an inroad into his own soul, and immediately pronouncing his own sentence.

That is properly a *law* to us, which we always and unavoidably feel and own ourselves *obliged* to obey; and which, as we obey or disobey it, is attended with the immediate sanctions of inward triumph and self-applause, or of inward shame and self-reproach, together with the secret apprehensions of the favour or displeasure of a superior righteous power, and the anticipations of *future* rewards, and punishments. – That has proper *authority* over us, to which, if we refuse submission, we transgress our duty, incur guilt, and expose ourselves to just vengeance. All this is certainly true of our moral judgment, and contained in the idea of it.

Rectitude then, or virtue, is a LAW.[3] And it is the *first* and *supreme* law, to which all other laws owe their force, on which they depend, and in virtue of which alone they oblige. It is an *universal* LAW. The whole creation is ruled by it: under it men and all rational beings subsist. It is the source and guide of all the actions of the Deity himself, and on it his throne and government are founded. It is an *unalterable and indispensible* LAW. The repeal, suspension or even *relaxation* of it, once for a moment, in any part of the universe, cannot be conceived without a contradiction. Other laws have had a date; a time when they were enacted, and became of force. They are confined to particular places, rest on precarious foundations, may lose their vigour, grow obsolete with time, and become useless and neglected. Nothing like this can be true of this law. It has no date. It never was made or enacted. It is prior to all things. It is self-valid and self-originated; and must for ever retain its usefulness and vigour, without the possibility of diminution or abatement. It is coeval with eternity; as unalterable as necessary, everlasting truth; as independent as the existence of God; and as sacred and awful as his nature and perfections. – The *authority* it possesses is native and essential to it, underived and absolute. It is superior to all other authority, and the basis and parent of all other authority. It is indeed self-evident, that properly speaking, there is not other authority; nothing else that can claim our obedience, or that *ought* to guide and rule heaven and earth. – It is, in short, the *one* authority in nature, the same in all times and in all places; or, in one word, the DIVINE authority.

Thirdly, From the account given of obligation, it appears how absurd it is to enquire, what *obliges* us to practise virtue? as if obligation was no part of the idea of virtue, but something adventitious and foreign to it; that is, as if what was *due*, might not be our *duty*, or what was *wrong*, *unlawful*; or as if it might not be true, that what it is *fit* to do, we *ought* to do, and that what we *ought* to do, we are *obliged* to do. – To ask, why are we *obliged* to practise virtue, to abstain from what is wicked, or perform what is just, is the very same as to ask, why we are *obliged* to do what we are *obliged* to do? – It is not possible to avoid wondering at those, who have so unaccountably embarrassed themselves, on a subject that one would think was attended with no difficulty; and who, because they cannot find any thing in *virtue and duty themselves*, which can induce us to pay a regard to them in our practice, fly to self-love, and maintain that from hence alone are derived all inducement and obligation.

Fourthly, From what has been observed, it may appear, in what sense obligation is ascribed to God. It is no more that ascribing to him the perception of rectitude, or saying, that there are certain ends, and certain measures in the administration of the world, which he approves, and which are *better* to be pursued than others. – Great care, however, should be taken, what language we here use. *Obligation* is a word to which many persons have affixed several ideas, which should be no means be retained when we speak of God. Our language and our conceptions, whenever he is the subject of them are *always* extremely defective and inadequate, and *often* very erroneous. – There are many who think it absurd and shocking to attribute any thing of *obligation* or *law* to a being who is necessarily sufficient and independent, and to whom nothing can be prior or superior. How, I conceive, we are to frame our apprehensions on this subject, has already, in some measure, appeared. It should, methinks, be enough to satisfy such persons, that the obligations ascribed to the Deity arise entirely from and exist in his own nature; and that the eternal, unchangeable LAW, by which it has been said, he is directed in all his actions, is no other than HIMSELF; *his own infinite, eternal, all perfect understanding.*

Fifthly, What has been said also shews us, on what the obligations of religion and the Divine will are founded. They are plainly branches of universal rectitude. Our obligation to obey God's will means nothing, but that obedience is *due* to it, or that it is *right and fit* to comply with it. What an absurdity is it then, to make obligation *subsequent* to the Divine will, and the *creature* of it? For why, upon this supposition, does not *all* will oblige equally? If there be any thing which gives the preference to one will above another; that, by the terms, is *moral rectitude*. What would any laws or will of any being signify, what influence could they have on the determinations of a moral agent, was there no good reason for complying with them, no obligation to regard them, no *antecedent right* of command? – To affirm that we are *obliged* in any case, but not in virtue of *reason and right*, is to say, that in that case we are not obliged at all. – Besides, nothing could be ever commanded by the Deity, was there no prior reason for commanding it. To which add, that one ground of our obligation to obey His will is this, its being under the direction of reason, or always a wise, righteous, and good will. Thus, therefore, on all accounts, and in every view of things, do will and law presuppose reason and right. And it is upon the whole, un-questionable, that if we take away the latter, the former lose all support and efficacy; and that were there nothing in itself just and obligatory, nothing could be made so by law, will, commands, compacts, or any means whatever. ...

One cannot but observe on this occasion, how the ideas of right and wrong force themselves upon us, and in some form or other, always remain, even when we think we have annihilated them. Thus, after we have supposed all actions and ends to be in themselves indifferent, it is natural to conceive, that it is *right* to give ourselves up to the guidance of unrestrained inclination, and *wrong* to be careful of our actions, or to give ourselves any trouble in pursuing any ends. Or, if with *Hobbs* and the ora-tor in *Plato*'s *Gorgias*, we suppose that the strongest may oppress the weakest, and take to themselves whatever they can seize; or that unlimited power confers an un-limited right; this plainly still leaves us in possession of the idea of *right*, and only establishes *another species* of it. – In like manner, when we suppose all the obliga-tions of morality to be derived from laws and compacts, we at the same time find ourselves under a necessity of supposing something *before* them, not absolutely in-different in respect of choice; something good and evil, right and wrong, which gave rise to them and occasion for them; and which, after they are made, makes them regarded.

But to return to the subject under consideration. The necessary perfections of the Deity; the infinite excellencies of his nature as the fountain of reason and wisdom; the entire dependence of all beings upon him, and their deriving from his bounty existence and all its blessings and hopes – from hence, and not merely from his al-mighty power, arises his SOVEREIGN AUTHORITY. These are the reasons that render him the proper object of our supreme homage, constitute his right of government, vest him with universal and just dominion, and make it the first duty of the whole intelligent world to obey, to please, and honour him in all they think and do. – Those who will allow of no other motive to regard the Deity, no other meaning of the obli-gation to obey him, besides what is implied in his power to make us happy or miserable, maintain what it is wonderful how any human mind can seriously em-brace. They maintain, that were it possible to suppose that we had nothing to hope or fear from him, we should not have the least desire of his approbation, or the least concern about his expectations from us, or any reason for paying him any kind of regard; that setting aside the consideration of our own interest, it is entirely indiffer-ent what our dispositions and behaviour are with respect to him; that his nature, attributes and benefits, however glorious, are, in themselves, incapable of having any effect upon any rational nature; and that though (retaining power) we were ever so much to change or reverse his character, it would still be equally incumbent upon us to love, revere, and obey him, to resign our wills to his, and to endeavour to approve ourselves to him.

Notes

1. *Obligatory* answers to *oportet, decet, debitum,* in *Latin*; and to δεῖ, δέον ἐστί, θεμιτόν, καθῆκον, δίκαιον, in *Greek*.
2. It is obvious, that this is very different from saying (what it would be plainly absurd to say) that every action, the performance of which, in certain circumstances is wrong, will continue wrong, let the circumstances be ever so much altered, or by whatever authority it is commanded.
3. Τὸ μὲν ὀρθὸν νόμος ἐστὶ βασιλικός. Plat. Minos.

Document I.10

Richard Price contra Francis Hutcheson

In the following extended note from 'Of Degrees of Virtue and Vice', in his *A Review of the Principle Questions in Morals,* Price counters the moral sense view as propounded, in the wake of Shaftesbury, by Hutcheson.

For Hutcheson (1694–1746) see BCE, DNB; William Blackstone, *Francis Hutcheson and Contemporary Ethical Theory,* Athens, GA: University of Georgia Press, 1965.

The human mind would appear to have little order or consistency in it, were we to consider it as only a system of passions and affections, which are continually drawing us different ways, without any thing at the head of them to govern them, and the strongest of which for the time necessarily determines the conduct. But this is far from being its real state. It has a faculty essential to it, to which every power within it is subjected, the proper office of which is to reconcile the differences between all our particular affections, to point out to us when and how far every one of them shall or shall not be gratified, and to determine which, in all cases of competition, shall give way. This faculty is our *Moral faculty,* and it is therefore the reference of all within us to this faculty, that gives us the true idea of human nature. This supremacy of the moral faculty, I have observed, is implied in the idea of it; but we have also a demonstration of it from fact: For whereas the *least* violation of this faculty, in compliance with *all our other powers* in conjunction, would give us pain and shame; the *greatest* violation, on the contrary, of our other powers, in compliance with *this,* is approved by us; nay, the more we contradict our other powers in compliance with it, and the greater sacrifice we make of their enjoyments and gratifications to it, the more we are pleased with ourselves, and the higher inward satisfaction and triumph we feel. – See Dr. *Butler*'s Sermons on *Human Nature,* and the *Preface.* I find also Dr. *Hutcheson*, in his *System of Moral Philosophy*, asserting to the same purpose that our moral faculty, or, as he calls it, the *Moral sense*, is the 'directing principle within us, destined to command all our other powers; and that the desire of moral excellence is the supreme determination or affection of our minds, and *different from all our kind affections*.' See p. 61, 67, 68, 70, 77, &c. Vol. I.

Though I entirely approve these sentiments, I cannot help detaining the reader while I make a few remarks, in order to shew him how difficult it is to reconcile them with this writer's other sentiments of virtue. It is much to be wished that he had been more explicit on this subject, and explained himself more particularly. Had he done this, he would, I fancy, either not have writ in this manner, or given a different account of the nature of moral approbation, and of our moral faculty.

If *Moral approbation* be only a kind of *sublimer sensation*, or a *species of mental taste*, it can surely have no influence on our purposes and actions; much less can it have such influence, as to be the supreme and commanding principle within us. The *Moral sense* is properly the determination in our natures to be pleased or displeased with actions proceeding from certain motives. It therefore always supposes some distinct motives, and can never be itself a spring of action. Is it not then wonderful to find this very ingenious and able writer, contrary to what he had done in his *Illustrations on the Moral Sense*,[1] confounding *senses* with *instincts*; and, contrary to what the very idea of *the Moral sense*, as he seems to have explained it, admits of, representing it as a distinct spring of conduct in the mind, talking of its *force and efforts within us, its recommending, enjoining, controuling, and governing*,[2] nay, setting it up as the *sovereign director of our affections and actions, superior even to Benevolence?* This can be consistent and proper on no other supposition, than that our Moral faculty is the Understanding, and that moral approbation implies in it the perception of truth, or the discernment of a real character of actions.

Again; what is *Moral excellence*? On the principles I am considering, it must mean, either those affections and actions themselves to which we give the denomination of *excellent*, or that *grateful sensation*, of which, when observed, they are the occasions. – If it means the former, or, in other words, the having and exercising an extensive and ardent benevolence; how can the desire of it be different from benevolence? How can it be, as Dr. *Hutcheson* says it is,[3] in *another order of affections*? – If it means the latter, how can it be proper to speak of the desire and love of it? Can the desire of the *relish* we have for particular objects, as distinct from the desire of the objects themselves, mean any thing, besides the desire of enjoying the pleasures attending it; and can it therefore influence our actions any otherwise than by means of self-love? In short, it must appear, I should think, to every one, very absurd to speak of the desire of Moral excellence, to suppose a calm, immediate determination to *Moral good itself*, and to ascribe a commanding power to the faculty which perceives it, if *Moral good*, or *Moral excellence*, signifies nothing distinct from a *feeling of the heart*, or nothing absolute and immutable and independent of the mind. It is however some indication of the truth on this subject, that those, with whose sentiments it is inconsistent, find themselves led insensibly to write and think of our moral faculty, (or the sense of duty and moral excellence) as the ultimate and supreme guide of our actions. Nor can it be easy for any one who will examine this matter, not to feel that it is unavoidable to conceive this to be indeed the case, and that therefore every account of morality must be false that implies the contrary.

Once more. Our moral faculty, Dr. *Hutcheson*, we find, acknowledges to be the supreme commanding power within us. But can there be a higher power in a reasonable being than reason? and is this power a *sense*? How strange would this seem? – I do not find that *Plato*, and others of the antient moralists, had any notion that the τὸ ἡγεμονικόν in man, which they insist so much upon, was any thing else than *reason*. τὸ φύαει δεσποτικόν, τουτέστι τὸ λογιστικόν, says *Alcinous de Doctrina Platonis*, Chap. xxviii.

Let me add, that the very question which has been asked, and which naturally arises when we are settling a scheme of life and conduct; 'what *ought* to be the end of our deliberate pursuit, *private* or *public* happiness;' or, 'which *ought* to give way, (that is, which is it *right* should give way) in case of opposition, the calm selfish, or the calm benevolent affection?' See the *Preface* just quoted, page 45, &c. This question, I say, plainly implies, that the idea of *right* in actions is something different from and independent of the idea of their flowing from kind affections, or having a tendency to universal happiness; for certainly, the meaning of it cannot be, which will proceed from kind affection, or which has a tendency to promote universal happliness, following our desires of private or of universal happiness. – It also supposes, that the perception of *right* influences our choice; for otherwise such a question could never be asked with any view to the determination of our choice, nor could an answer to it have any effect this way. – It supposes finally, that the appeal in all cases is to our moral faculty, as the ultimate judge and determiner of our conduct; and, that the *regard* to *right*, to *duty*, or to *moral excellence*, is a superior affection within us to *benevolence*; for it comes in, in cases of interference between self-love and benevolence, to turn the scale in favour of benevolence, to recommend and order the generous part, or, as Dr. *Hutcheson* speaks,[4] to make the determination to public happiness the supreme one in the soul.

Thus then, here, as in other parts of this work, we find an object, 'Moral Good, of unrivalled worth; of supreme influence; eternal, divine, all-governing; perceived by reason; necessarily loved and desired as soon as perceived; and the affection to which (including benevolence, but not the same with it) is the chief affection in every good being, and the highest dignity and excellence of every mind.'

Notes

1. See Chap. I.
2. See his *Moral Philosophy* [1755].
3. Ibid. p. 70 – See also *the Preface* by the excellent Dr. *Leechman*, p. 44, &c.
4. Ibid. p. 77.

Document I.11

Joseph Priestley on the Materiality of the Soul

Joseph Priestley (1733–1804) was a Presbyterian divine who became a Socinian; a scientist, a writer on metaphysics, politics and education; and a supporter of the French Revolution – a fact which, together with his heterodoxy, placed him at the centre of the Birmingham riots of 1791. He removed to America in 1794, where he died. Already questioning the Calvinism of his parents, he refused to attend Zephaniah Marryatt's academy at Plasterers' Hall, London, because of the requirement of subscribing every six weeks to ten Calvinistic articles, and went instead to Daventry on its opening in 1751 under Caleb Ashworth. From Ashworth he received orthodox doctrine; from Samuel Clark the younger, 'heresy'. He passed through Arianism to Socinianism, and ended a Unitarian. In addition to pastoral appointments in Leeds and Birmingham, Priestley was tutor at Warrington academy from 1761 to 1764. In philosophy he was a materialist, a matter on which he and his friend Price could never agree.

For Priestley see BCE, DECBP, DNB, ODCC; *Memoirs of Dr. Joseph Priestley, to the Year 1795, written by himself, with a Continuation ... by his son*, London, 1806, reprinted Bath, 1790; Robert E. Schofield, *The Enlightenment of Joseph Priestley: A Study of his Life and Work from 1733 to 1773*, University Park, PA: Pennsylvania State University Press, 1998. For Marryatt (1684?–1754) see *A Sermon occasioned by the sudden death of the Reverend and learned Zephaniah Marryatt, D.D. preached in Southwark, September the 22ⁿᵈ. By Thomas Hall. To which is added, The Funeral Oration at his Interment, by Thomas Towle. Both published at the People's Request*, London, 1754; Walter Wilson, *History and Antiquities of Dissenting Churches and Meeting-Houses*, 1814, IV, pp. 199–203. For Ashworth (1722–75) see DNB. The following extract is from Priestley's *Disquisitions Relating to Matter and Spirit*, 1777, section IV, pp. 33–8.

In the preceding section I have represented how unphilosophical it is to conclude that all the powers of man do not belong to the same substance when they are observed to have a constant and necessary dependence upon one another, and when there is not, as far as we know, the least inconsistency or incompatibility between them. If there be any foundation for the established rules of philosophising, the argument ought to be conclusive with us and everything that can be added to it is really superfluous. However, for the greater satisfaction of some of my readers I shall, in this section, subjoin some additional arguments, or considerations, or rather, in some cases, distinct illustrations of the preceding argument.

1.　That the faculty of thinking necessarily depends for its exercise at least upon a stock of ideas about which it is always conversant, will hardly be questioned by any person. But there is not a single idea of which the mind is possessed but what may be proved to have come to it from the bodily senses, or to have be consequent upon the perceptions of sense. Could we, for instance, have had any idea of colour, as red, blue, etc. without the eyes, and optic nerves; of sound without the ears and auditory nerves; of smell, without the nostrils and the olfactory nerves, etc. etc.? It is even impossible to conceive how the mind could have become possessed of any of its present stock of ideas, without just such a body as we have; and consequently judging from present appearances (and we have no other means of forming any judgment at all) without a body of some kind or other we could have had no ideas at all, any more than a man without eyes could have any particular ideas belonging to colours. The notion, therefore, of the possibility of thinking in man without an organized body, is not only destitute of all evidence from actual appearances, but is directly contrary to them; and yet these appearances ought alone to guide the judgment of philosophers.

Dr. Clark seems to have imagined that he had fully answered the argument for the materiality of the human soul from its having received all its ideas from the bodily senses, by asking whether there might not possibly have been other inlets to ideas besides our present senses. 'If these,' says he, 'be arbitrary, then the want of these does by no means infer a total want of perception, but the same sould may, in another state, have different ways of perception.'

To this it is easy to reply that mere possibility is no foundation for any conclusion in this case. We see, in fact, that all our sensations come to us by the way of the corporeal senses; and though our observing this will authorize us to say that if the Divine Being had so pleased, we might have had more, or fewer, or quite different senses, and, of course, should have had very different sets of sensations and ideas, it will by no means authorize us to say that it was even possible for us to have had sensations and ideas without any corporeal senses at all. We have no example of any such thing, and therefore cannot say that it is even possible, much less that it is actually the case. Present appearances certainly lead us to think that our mental powers necessarily depend upon our corporeal ones; and till some very different appearances present themselves, it must be exceedingly unphilosophical to imagine that the connection is not necessary.

2.   The only reason why it has been so earnestly contended for that there is some principle in man that is not material, is that it might subsist and be capable of sensation and action when the body was dead. But if the mind was naturally so independent of the body, as to be capable of subsisting by itself and even of appearing to more advantage after the death of the body, it might be expected to discover some signs of its independence before death and especially when the organs of the body were obstructed so as to leave the soul more at liberty to exert itself, as in a state of sleep or swooning which most resemble the state of death in which it is pretended that the soul is most of all active, most active, and vigorous.

But, judging by appearances, the reverse of all this is the case. That a man does not think during sleep, except in that imperfect manner which we call dreaming, and which is nothing more than an approach to a state of vigilance, I shall not here dispute, but take for granted; referring my readers to Mr. Locke, and other writers upon that subject; and that all power of thinking is suspended during a swoon I conclude with certainty, because no appearance whatever can possibly lead us to suspect the contrary.

3.   If the mental principle was, in its own nature, immaterial and immortal, all its particular faculties would be so too; whereas we see that every faculty of the mind, without exception, is liable to be impaired and even to become wholly extinct before death. Since, therefore, all the faculties of the mind, separately taken, appear

to be mortal, the substance or principle in which they exist must be pronounced to be mortal too. Thus we might conclude that the body was mortal from observing that all the separate senses and limbs were liable to decay and perish.

4.   If the sentient principle in man be immaterial it can have no extension, it can neither have length, breadth, nor thickness, and consequently everything within it, or properly belonging to it, must be simple and indivisible. Besides, it is universally acknowledged that if the substance of the soul was not simple and indivisible, it would be liable to corruption and death, and therefore that no advantage would be gained by supposing the power of thinking to belong to any substance distinct from the body. Let us now consider how this notion agrees with the phenomena of sensation and ideas which are the proper subject of thought.

It will not be denied but that sensations or ideas properly exist *in the soul* because it could not otherwise retain them, so as to continue to perceive and think after its separation from the body. Now whatever ideas are in themselves, they are evidently produced by eternal objects, and must therefore correspond to them; and since many of the objects or archetypes of ideas are divisible, it necessarily follows that the ideas themselves are divisible also. The idea of a man, for instance, could in no sense correspond to a man which is the archetype of it, and therefore could not be the idea of a man if it did not consist of the ideas of his head, arms, trunk, legs etc. It therefore consists of parts and consequently is divisible. And how is it possible that a thing (be the nature of it what it may) that is divisible should be contained in a substance, be the nature of it likewise what it may, that is indivisible?

If the archetypes of ideas have extension, the ideas which are expressive of them and are actually produced by them according to certain mechanical laws, must have extension likewise; and therefore the mind in which they exist, whether it be material or immaterial, must have extension also. But how anything can have extension and yet be immaterial without coinciding with our idea of mere empty space, I know not. I am therefore obliged to conclude that the sentient principle in man, containing ideas which certainly have parts and are divisible and consequently must have extension, cannot be that simple, indivisible and immaterial substance that some have imagined it to be; but something that has real extension and therefore may have the other properties of matter.

Document I.12

Joseph Priestley contra Thomas Reid

Priestley contends that the view of the common sense of mankind as propounded by the Scottish divine and philosopher Thomas Reid is untenable, and facilitates dogmatism. He cannot see how we can proceed from sensation to external objects. Moreover, Reid's multiplication of instinctive principles lands us in a scepticism as deep as that with which Reid charges Hume.

For Reid (1710–96) see BCE, DNB; S.A. Grave, *The Scottish Philosophy of Common Sense*, Oxford: Clarendon Press, 1960; and for this debate, Alan P. F. Sell,

'Priestley's Polemic against Reid', in *idem, Dissenting Thought and the Life of the Churches*, Lewiston, NY: Edwin Mellen Press, 1990, ch. 15. The following extract is from Priestley's *Works*, ed. J. T. Rutt, 25 vols, London, 1817–31, III, pp. 11, 27.

Dr. Reid meets with a particular sentiment, or persuasion, and not being able to explain the origin of it, without more ado he ascribes it to a *particular original instinct*, provided for that very purpose. He finds another difficulty, which he also solves in the same concise and easy manner. And thus he goes on accounting for everything, by telling you, not only that he cannot explain it himself, but that it will be in vain for you, or any other person, to endeavour to investigate it farther than he has done. Thus avowed ignorance is to pass for real knowledge, and, as with the old Sceptics, that man is to be reckoned the greatest philosopher who asserts that he knows nothing himself, and can persuade others that they know no more than he does. There is this difference between the ancient and these modern sceptics, that the ancients professed neither to *understand* nor *believe* any thing, whereas the modern believe every thing, though they profess to understand nothing. And the former, I think, are the more consistent of the two ...

It is impossible to contemplate such a theory of the human mind as that of Dr. Reid with any satisfaction, and the farther study of the subject is thereby rendered exceedingly disgusting and unpromising. I flatter myself, therefore, that I may be doing some service to future enquirers, by endeavouring to shew that this new system has in it as little of truth, as it has of beauty, that we may safely take up the subject where Mr. Locke left it, and proceed to attend to what Dr. Hartley has done, by following his steps; when, if I have any foresight, we shall smile at Dr. Reid's hypothesis, or rather string of hypotheses, as a mere puzzle, and look back upon it as upon a dream.

Document I.13

Thomas Reid contra Joseph Priestley

Reid's rejoinder is in his *Works*, ed. William Hamilton, Edinburgh, 1846, p. 52. He teases Priestley for thinking that mental powers originate in the organical structure of the brain.

Dr. Priestley, in his last book, thinks that the power of perception, as well as all the other powers that are termed mental, is the result of such an organical structure as that of the brain. Consequently, says he, the whole man becomes extinct at death, and we have no hope of surviving the grave, but what is derived from the light of Revelation. I would be glad to know your Lordship's opinion, whether, when my brain has lost its original structure, and when, some hundred years after, the same materials are again fabricated so curiously as to become an intelligent being, whether, I say, that being will be *me*; or, if two or three such beings should be formed out of my brain, whether they will all be *me*, and consequently all be one and the same intelligent being.

This seems to me a great mystery, but Priestley denies all mysteries. He thinks, and rejoices in thinking so, that plants have some degree of sensation. As to the lower animals, they differ from us in degree only, and not in kind. Only they have no promise of a resurrection. If this be true, why should not the King's advocate be ordered to prosecute criminal *brutes*, and you criminal judges to try them? You are obliged to Dr Priestley for teaching you one-half of your duty, of which you knew nothing before. But I forgot that the fault lies in the legislature, which has not given you laws for this purpose. I hope, however, when any of them shall be brought to a trial, that he will be allowed a *jury of his peers*. ...

Document I.14

Joseph Priestley on Divine Foreknowledge

From *The Doctrine of Philosophical Necessity Illustrated*, 1777, pp. 19–24.

As it is not within the compass of power in the author of any system that an event should take place without a cause, or that it should be equally possible for two different events to follow the same circumstances, so neither, supposing this to be possible, would it be within the compass of knowledge to foresee such a contingent event. So that, upon the doctrine of philosophical liberty, the Divine Being could not possibly foresee what would happen in his own creation, and therefore could not provide for it, which takes away the whole foundation of divine providence, and moral government, as well as all the foundation of revealed religion in which prophecies are so much concerned.

That an even truly contingent, or not necessarily depending upon previous circumstances, should be the object of knowledge has, like other things of a similar nature in modern systems, been called a difficulty and a mystery; but in reality there cannot be a greater absurdity or contradiction. For as certainly as nothing can be known to exist but what does exist, so certainly can nothing be known to arise from what does exist, but what does arise from it or depend on it. But according to the definition of the terms a contingent event does not depend upon any previous known circumstances, since some other event might have arisen in the same circumstances.

All that is within the compass of knowledge in this case is to foresee all the different events that might take place in the same circumstances; but which of them will actually take place cannot possibly be known. In this case all degrees of knowledge or sagacity are equal. Did the case admit of approximation to certainty, in proportion to the degree of knowledge, it would be fully within the compass of infinite knowledge; but in this case there is no such approximation. To all minds the foretelling of a contingent event is equally a matter of conjecture; consequently infinite knowledge makes no difference in this case. For knowledge supposes an object which, in this case, does not exist and therefore cannot be known to exist. If man be possessed of

36

a power of proper self-determination, the Deity himself cannot control it (as far as he interferes it is no self-determination of the man), and if he does not control it he cannot foresee it. Nothing can be known at present except itself, or its necessary cause, exist at present. Yet the whole history of Revelation shows that every determination of the mind of man is certainly foreknown by the Divine Being, determinations that took place from natural and common causes, where the mind was under no supernatural influence whatever; because men are censured and condemned for actions that were so foreseen.

The death of our Saviour is a remarkable instance of this kind. This event was certainly foreseen and intended, for it most particularly entered into the plan of divine providence; and yet it appears from the history that it was brought about by causes perfectly natural and fully adequate to it. It was just such an event as might have been expected from the known malice and prejudice of the Jewish rulers, at the time of his appearance. They certainly needed no supernatural instigation to push them on to their bloody and wicked purpose; and Pilate, dispose and situated as he was, needed no extraordinary impulse to induce him to consent to it, notwithstanding his hesitation and his conviction of the malice and injustice of the proceedings; and both he and the Jews were righteously condemned and punished for it; which, I doubt not, will have the happiest effect in the system of the divine moral government.

This argument from the divine prescience is briefly but clearly stated by Mr. Hobbes. 'Denying necessity' says he, 'destroys both the decrees and prescience of Almighty God. For whatever God has purposed to bring to pass by man, as an instrument, or foresees shall come to pass, a man, if he has liberty might frustrate and make not come to pass; and God should either not foreknow it and not decree it, or he shall foreknow such things shall be as shall never be and decree what shall never come to pass.'

Indeed many of the most zealous advocates for the doctrine of philosophical liberty, aware of its inconsistency with the doctrine of divine prescience, have not scrupled to give up the latter altogether. With respect to such persons, I can only repeat what I have said upon this subject in my *Examination of the Writings of Dr. Beattie*, etc.

'Thus our author, in the blind rage of disputation, hesitates not to deprive the ever-blessed God of that very attribute by which, in the books of scripture, he expressly distinguishes himself from all false gods, and than which nothing can be more essentially necessary to the government of the universe, rather than relinquish his fond claim to the fancied privilege of self-determination; a claim which appears to me to be just as absurd as that of self-existence and which could not possibly do him any good if he had it.'

What is more extraordinary, this power he arrogates to himself without pretending to advance a single rational argument in favour of his claim; but expects it will be admitted on the authority of his instinctive common sense only. And yet if a man express the least indignation at such new and unheard-of arrogance, and in an argument of such high importance as this, what exclamation and abuse must he not expect?

Document I.15

Richard Price contra Joseph Priestley

Price refers to the Quaker physician John Whitehead (1740?–1804) and to Samuel Horsley (1733–1806), who became successively bishop of St Davids, Rochester and St Asaph. For both see DNB. The following text is from *A Free Discussion of the Doctrines of Materialism, and Philosophical Necessity, in a Correspondence between Dr Price and Dr Priestley*, London, 1778, pp. 321–5.

Newington-Green, Sept. 19,1778.

Dear Sir,

The desire you have expressed that I would give you my sentiments of the Controversy between us, *on a view of the whole of it as now printed*, has induced me once more to apply my thoughts to it. I have done this with care and attention; but am not sure that any thing which you will judge of great importance has occurred to me. I might, therefore, have been right to resolve to say no more; and indeed, I am so much afraid of perplexing by a multiplicity of words, and of giving disgust by too many repetitions, that this would have been my resolution, had I not thought, that the *Additional Observations* which you will receive with this letter, contain some *new* matter; and place several of the arguments already insisted on, in a light that my render them to some persons more intelligible and striking. I have now said the best I can; and I leave our readers to judge between us, hoping that whether they decide in your favour or mine, they will be candid, and believe that we are both of us governed alike by a sincere love of truth and virtue. I feel deeply that I am in constant danger of being led into error by partial views, and of mistaking the suggestions of prejudice for the decisions of reason; and this, while it disposes me to be candid to others, makes me ardently wish that others would be candid to me.

I am, in a particular manner, sensible of my own blindness with respect to the nature of matter and spirit, and the faculties of the human mind. As far as I have gone in this dispute I am pretty well satisfied; but I cannot go much further. You have asked me some questions (and many more may be asked me) which I am incapable of answering.

I cannot help taking this opportunity of repeating to you, what I dislike more than I can easily express, the malevolence expressed by most of the writers against you. I have myself, as you well know, been long an object of abuse for a publication which I reckon one of the best actions of my life, and which events have fully justified. The consciousness of not deserving abuse has made me perfectly callous to it; and I doubt not but the same cause will render you so.

It is certain that, in the end, the interest of truth will be promoted by a free and open discussion of speculative points. Whatever will not bear this must be superstition and imposture. Instead, therefore, of being inclined to censure those who, with honest views, contribute to bring about such a discussion, we ought to thank and honour them, however mistaken we may think them, and however sacred the points of discussion may be reckoned. I wish I could see more of this disposition among the defenders of religion. I am particularly sorry to find that even Mr Whitehead does not perfectly possess this temper. Had he avoided all uncandid insinuations, and treated you constantly with the same just respect that he does in general, his book in my opinion would have done him much honour.

Dr. Horsley is, I fancy, the only person who, in opposing your opinions, has discovered a just liberality. This is worthy of an able Philosopher; and you have, therefore, very properly distinguished him from your other antagonists, by addressing him, in your letter to him, with particular respect. His method of arguing agrees very much with mine. There is, likewise, an agreement between some of Mr Whitehead's arguments and those I have used. But this agreement has been accidental; for our correspondence was begun and finished long before I knew anything of either Dr Horsley's or Mr Whitehead's publications.

Wishing you every possible blessing, I am, with the most affectionate respect,

Yours,

Richard Price.

Document I.16

Joseph Priestley's Reply to Richard Price

From *A Free Discussion of the Doctrines of Materialism, and Philosophical Necessity, in a Correspondence between Dr Price and Dr Priestley*, London, 1778, pp. 407–15.

Calne, Oct. 2. 1778.

Dear Sir,

With this letter you will receive a few remarks on your *Additional Observations*, which I have read with that *attention* which every thing from you demands. That it has not been with *conviction*, your candour, I know, will not impute to any peculiar *obstinacy*, but to my unavoidably seeing the subjects of our discussion in a light different from that in which you see them. We have not the same idea of the nature of the human mind, or of the laws to which it is subject, but we are both sufficiently aware of the force of *prejudice*, and that this may equally throw a bias on the side of the *long established*, or of *novel* opinions. Also, equally respecting the Christian maxim of *doing to others as we would that others should do to us*, we are each of us ready to give to others that liberty which we claim ourselves; while we equally reprobate those rash sentiments which proceed from a decision without a previous discussion of the reasons for and against a question in debate.

I am not a little proud of your commendation of me for my 'fairness in the pursuit of truth, and following it in all its consequences, however frightful, without attempting to evade or palliate them' (p. 352). It is a conduct that I hope I shall always pursue, as the first of duties to that God who has given me whatever *faculties* I possess, and whatever *opportunity of inquiry* I have been favoured with; and I trust I shall continue to pursue this conduct at all risks. As he is properly no christian, who does not *confess Christ before men*, or who is *ashamed* of his religion in an unbelieving age, like the present; this maxim, which the author of our religion inculcates with respect to christianity in general, the reason of the thing requires that we extend to every thing that essentially affects christianity.

So long, therefore, as I conceive the doctrine of a *separate soul* to have been the true source of the grossest corruptions in the christian system, of that very *antichristian system* which sprung up in the times of the apostles, concerning which they entertained the strongest apprehensions, and delivered, and left upon record, the most solemn warnings, I must think myself a very lukewarm and disaffected christian if I do not bear my feeble testimony against it.

With respect to the private conduct of individuals, as affecting our happiness after death, I do not lay any stress upon this, or upon *any opinion whatever*, and there is no person of whose christian temper and conduct I think more highly than I do of yours, though you hold opinions the very reverse of mine, and defend them with so much zeal; a zeal which, while you maintain the opinion at all, is certainly commendable. But with respect to the *general plan of christianity*, the importance of the doctrines I contend for can hardly, in my opinion, be rated too high. What I contend for leaves nothing for the manifold corruptions and abuses of popery to fasten on. Other doctrinal reformations are partial things, while this goes to the very root of almost all the mischief we complain of; and, for my part, I shall not date the proper and complete downfall of what is called *antichrist*, but from the general prevalence of the doctrines of materialism.

This I cannot help saying appears to me to be that fundamental principle in true philosophy which is alone perfectly consonant to the doctrine of the scriptures; and being at the same time the only proper deduction from natural appearances, it must, in the progress of inquiry soon *appear to be so*; and then, should it be found that an unquestionably true philosophy teaches one thing, and revelation another, the latter could not stand its ground, but must inevitably be exploded, as contrary to *truth and fact*. I therefore deem it to be, of particular consequence, that philosophical unbelievers should be apprized in time, that there are christians, who consider the *doctrine of a soul* as a tenet that is so far from being *essential* to the christian scheme, that it is a thing quite *foreign* to it, derived originally from heathenism, discordant with the genuine principles of revealed religion, and ultimately subversive of them.

As to the doctrines of *necessity*, I cannot, after all our discussion, help considering it as *demonstrably true*, and the only possible foundation for the doctrines of a *providence*, and the *moral government of God*. Continuing to see things in this light, after the closest attention that I have been able to give to them, before, or in the course of our friendly debate (and you will pardon me, if I add, feeling this in a stronger light than ever) you will not be displeased with the *zeal* that I have occasionally shewn; as I, on my part, intirely approve of yours, who consider yourself as defending important and long received truth, against fundamental and most dangerous innovations.

We are neither of us so far blinded by prejudice as not to see, and acknowledge, the wisdom of constituting us in such a manner, as that every thing *new* respecting a subject of so much consequence as *religion*, should excite a great alarm, and meet with great difficulty in establishing itself. This furnishes an occasion of a thorough examination, and discussion of all new doctrines, in consequence of which they are either totally exploded, or more firmly established. The slow and gradual progress of christianity, and also that of the reformation, is a circumstance that bids fairer for their perpetuity, than if they had met with a much readier reception in the world. You will allow me to indulge the hope of a similar advantage from the opposition that I expect to this article of reformation in the christian system, and that the truth I contend for will be the more valued for being dearly bought, and slowly acquired.

As to the *odium* that I may bring upon myself by the malevolence of my opposers, of which, in your letter to me, you make such obliging mention, I hope the same consciousness of not having deserved it, will support me as it has done you, when much worse treated than I have yet been, on an occasion on which you deserved the warmest gratitude of your country, whose interests you studied and watched over, whose calamities you foresaw, and faithfully pointed out; and which might have derived, in various respects, the most solid and durable advantages from your labours. But we are no christians, if we have not so far imbibed the principles and spirit of our religion, as even to *rejoice that we are counted worthy of suffering* in any good cause.

Here it is that, supposing me to be a defender of *christian truth*, my object gives me an advantage that your excellent *political writings* cannot give you. All your observations may be just, and your advice most excellent, and yet your country, the safety and happiness of which you have at heart, being in the hands of infatuated men, may go to ruin; whereas christian truth is a cause *founded on a rock*, and though it may be overborne for a time, we are assured that the *gates of death shall not prevail against it*.

Having now, each of us, defended, in the best manner that we can, what we deem to be this important truth, we are I doubt not, equally satisfied with ourselves, and shall chearfully submit the result of our discussion to the judgment of our friends, and of the public; and to the final and infallible determination of the *God of all truth*.

I am, notwithstanding this, and every other possible difference in *mere opinion*, with the most perfect esteem,

Dear Sir,
Yours most affectionately
J. Priestley.

Document I.17

Richard Price on the Nature of Liberty in General

The following extract is section I of *Observations on the Nature of Civil Liberty, the Principles of Government, and the Justice and Polity of the War with America, 1776.*

In order to obtain a more distinct view of the nature of liberty as such it will be useful to consider it under the four following general divisions.

First, physical liberty; secondly, moral liberty; thirdly, religious liberty; and fourthly, civil liberty. These heads comprehend under them all the different kinds of liberty. And I have placed civil liberty last because I mean to apply to it all I shall say of the other kinds of liberty.

By physical liberty I mean that principle of spontaneity, or self-determination, which constitutes us agents, or which gives us a command over our actions, rendering them properly ours, and not effects of the operation of any foreign cause. Moral liberty is the power of following, in all circumstances, our sense of right and wrong, or of acting in conformity to our reflecting and moral principles, without being controuled by any contrary principles. Religious liberty signifies the power of exercising, without molestation, that mode of religion which we think best, or of making the decisions of our own consciences respecting religious truth, the rule of our conduct, and not any of the decisions of our fellow-men. In like manner civil liberty is the power of a civil society or state to govern itself by its own discretion or by laws of its own making, without being subject to the impositions of any power in appointing and directing which the collective body of the people have no concern and over which they have no controul.

It should be observed that, according to these definitions of the different kinds of liberty, there is one general idea that runs through them all; I mean the idea of self-direction, or self-government. Did our volitions originate not with ourselves, but with some cause over which we have no power; or were we under a necessity of always following some will different from our own, we should want physical liberty.

In like manner, he whose perceptions of moral obligation are controuled by his passions has lost his moral liberty, and the most common language applied to him is that he wants self-government.

He likewise who, in religion, cannot govern himself by his convictions of religious duty, but is obliged to receive formularies of faith, and to practise modes of worship imposed upon him by others, wants religious liberty. And the community also that is governed, not by itself, but by some will independent of it, wants civil liberty.

In all these cases there is a force which stands opposed to the agent's own will, and which, as far as it operates, produces servitude. In the first case, this force is incompatible with the very idea of voluntary motion; and the subject of it is a mere passive instrument which never acts, but is always acted upon. In the second case, this force is the influence of passion getting the better of reason, or the brute overpowering and conquering the will of the man. In the third case, it is human authority in religion requiring conformity to particular modes of faith and worship, and superseding private judgment. And in the last case, it is any will distinct from that of the majority of a community which claims a power in making laws for it and disposing of its property.

That it is, I think, that marks the limit between liberty and slavery. As far as, in any instance, the operation of any cause comes in to restrain the power of self-government, so far slavery is introduced. Nor do I think that a preciser idea than this of liberty and slavery can be formed.

I cannot help wishing I could here fix my reader's attention, and engage him to consider carefully the dignity of that blessing to which we give the name of liberty, according to the representation now made of it. There is no a word in the whole compass of language which expresses so much of what is important and excellent. It is, in every view of it, a blessing truly sacred an invaluable. Without physical liberty, man would be a machine acted upon by mechanical springs, having no principle of motion in himself, or command over events; and, therefore, incapable of all merit and demerit. Without moral liberty, he is a wicked and detestable being, subject to the tyranny of base lusts, and the sport of every vile appetite. And without religious and civil liberty, he is a poor and abject animal, without rights, without property, and without a conscience, bending his neck to the yoke, and crouching to the will of every silly creature who has the insolence to pretend to authority over him. Nothing, therefore, can be of much consequence to us as liberty. It is the foundation of all honour, and the chief privilege and glory of our natures.

In fixing our idea on the subject of liberty, it is of particular use to take such an enlarged view of it as I have now given. ...

PART II

CHRISTIAN DOCTRINE

Introduction

The standard exposition of Quaker theology available in the eighteenth century re-mained the earlier classic *An Apology for the True Christian Divinity As the same is held forth, and preached by the People, Called, in Scorn, Quakers*, by Robert Barclay. First available in English in 1678, relatively large quantities of later editions were printed after 1700. Professing himself no admirer of the schoolmen, and claim-ing to write from the heart rather than from the head, Barclay nevertheless set forth his views on revelation, the Scriptures, the Fall, universal redemption in Christ, the saving light which enlightens every person, justification, perfection, perseverance and the possibility of falling from grace, the ministry, worship, baptism, the com-munion of the body and blood of Christ, the civil magistrate, and salutations and recreations, with reference to authors ancient and modern, with a view to refuting alternative views.[1] Barclay's doctrinal positions were widely accepted and seldom queried until the rise of evangelicalism amongst Friends in the first half of the nine-teenth century.

If the doctrinal position of the Quakers remained more or less static during the eighteenth century, the same cannot be said of that of Old Dissent. At the beginning of our period the (Arminian) General Baptists were embroiled in a saga surrounding the Christological views of Matthew Caffyn which had rumbled on since 1672. Caffyn seems to have been indebted to Melchior Hoffman for the view that on the one hand Christ could not have received his flesh from his mother because the Word could not assume accursed flesh, and on the other hand, he could not be of the uncre-ated nature and substance of the Father.[2] In part the difficulties arose because Caffyn expressed his views cautiously – some said evasively; in part the imprecise wording (certainly as compared with that of the Particular Baptists' Second London Confession of 1677) of the General Baptist Standard Confession of 1660 did not assist heresy-hunters and aided Caffyn. The upshot was that the General Baptist Assembly of 1700 concluded that Caffyn's views were not inconsistent with the terms of the 1660 Confession. Among the consequences of this dispute was the for-mation in 1696 of the General Association of General Baptists. This body, though presenting itself as more orthodox than the Assembly, was not inclined to tolerate those who veered too far in the direction of Calvinism – hence it disciplined and dismissed Joseph Stennett, who joined the Particular Baptists, to which fold other General Baptists had already transferred.[3]

Churches as well as individuals were affected by doctrinal discord. For example, at Smarden, Kent, the General Baptists were excluded by the Particulars in 1706. In 1767 John Simmonds, pastor at Wivelsfield Particular Baptist Church, was dismissed for teaching Arian doctrine, while in 1793 nineteen members of Bond Street Particular Baptist Church, Brighton, who had embraced the universalism of Elhanan Winchester, were excommunicated and constituted themselves as a General Baptist

Church.[4] By the end of the century most of the rationalistic Arminian General Baptist Churches were set in the direction of Unitarianism (to which denomination their survivors now belong), while their more orthodox and evangelical members were embraced by Dan Taylor's New Connexion of General Baptist Churches (1770).

Differences over Christology and the Trinity became a running theme of the eighteenth century. The debate was fuelled in part by the publication of the Anglican Samuel Clarke's *The Scripture-Doctrine of the Trinity* (1712),[5] an Arian work, but it became prominent in Dissenting circles in the events leading up to the Salters' Hall conference of 1719. The Exeter Presbyterian minister James Peirce, though denying that he was an Arian, held that the God and Father of Jesus Christ is the one God, and that it is not the case that the Father, Son and Holy Spirit together constitute the one God.[6] At the conference the issue of subscription became interwoven with that of doctrinal orthodoxy, and most of those who did not *subscribe* to orthodox articles nevertheless professed belief in the Trinity (albeit the non-subscribers' pamphlet on this matter was unanimous only because of the omission from the list of signatories of such avowed Arians or Semi-Arians as Luke Langdon and Martin Tomkins). There can be no doubt, however, that many Presbyterian divines (as well as some General Baptist pastors) were tending in an Arian direction, but it is most important to recognise that this was not on rationalist but on scriptural grounds. The reiterated use of the phrase 'The Scripture-Doctrine of' in theological works of the period is significant. Thus John Taylor of Norwich, the Arian Presbyterian divine, whose book *The Scripture Doctrine of Original Sin* powerfully argued the moral case against humanity's being punished for the sins of Adam, based his views on the principle of the sufficiency of Scripture, on which subject he also wrote at length. It would seem that the long-lived Micaijah Towgood was the last of the Arians to favour the public worship of Christ. Richard Price's Arianism did not go that far, and the Socinianism of Joseph Priestley disinclined him to think of Jesus as anything other than the noblest human being – a view reinforced by the uncompromising Unitarianism of Thomas Belsham.

While six Independent congregations only (and a number of prominent Independent individuals including Nathanael Lardner) became Arian, many Presbyterian causes moved in that direction as the century proceeded. Frequently, as at Elder Yard, Chesterfield, in 1772 orthodox members withdrew to form an Independent Church; in other cases, as at Billericay, Essex, the Church dismissed a heterodox minister – in this case Richard Fry, who, together with his supporters, constituted the short-lived New Meeting. Similar secessions were suffered by the Independent churches at Castle Hill, Northampton and Dagnal Street, St Albans. There were a number of less common cases. For example, Duke's Alley Independent Church, Bolton, was founded in 1754 by John Bennet, one of Wesley's preachers who turned Calvinist, and its numbers were swollen by the accession of a group which had already seceded from the Presbyterian cause. In Kendal in 1763 thirty-one orthodox members seceded from the Presbyterian Church and, on appealing for preachers to the General Associate Presbytery in Scotland, received James McQuhae as their first minister. He turned Independent, and Lowther Street Independent Church was constituted. In Yorkshire twenty-three Presbyterian churches became

Independent, while three, unusually, became Anglican. Equally unusually, the heterdox congregation at Loscoe, Derbyshire, became Baptist, calling its first minister in 1784.

It would be quite wrong to suppose that the flames of doctrinal discord were universally fanned by partisan preachers. The ministers' doctrinal views were sometimes known, but in the pulpit they had other homiletic fish to fry, and many, like Micaijah Towgood, dropped their disputes 'at the shrine of piety'.[7] Of Doddridge's Arian/ Arminian pupil Benjamin Fawcett, who served the doctrinally diverse Church at Kidderminster, it was said that 'he managed so far to conceal his opinions as to be very popular with his hearers, and these were very numerous'.[8]

Why did the Presbyterians turn more readily to Arianism and thence to Unitarianism than the Congregationalists? To answer a vexed question unduly bluntly: the evidence suggests that whereas the Presbyterians had not been able to establish their polity across the land following the Great Ejectment of 1662 – and hence had become *de facto* independents, lacking presbyterial discipline and being variously at the mercy of, or in sympathy with, sometimes powerful (and sometimes absentee) trustees who appointed ministers without regard to the niceties of doctrine – the Independents, with their church meeting, their congregational discipline, their local covenants and their orthodox hymns had more checks upon possible doctrinal vagaries.[9]

To the end of the eighteenth century there was Presbyterian vitality in some quarters – notably in Exeter; and it would be a serious error to attribute numerical decline (which there undoubtedly was) to doctrinal change alone. Certainly some orthodox members were lost through secession on doctrinal grounds, but there are ways of proclaiming the Canons of Dort which are equally prone to kill congregations. Moreover demographic considerations became important as churches of all theological stripes closed as populations shifted with the growth of industrialisation. It seems quite clear that the Presbyterians were for the most part intellectually disinclined to the style and message of the revivalists, and this, while it does not explain their numerical decline, does suggest why (unlike the Baptists and Congregationalists) they did not experience overall growth.[10]

As if the disputes over Christology and the Trinity were not enough, such high Calvinists as the Baptist John Gill, evangelical Calvinists such as George Whitefield, and evangelical Arminians including the Wesleys found themselves in doctrinal squabbles from time to time. The issues between Gill and Wesley concerned Calvinistic views of election, predestination and perseverance, while Wesley's understanding of free grace pitted him against Whitefield. Prominent underlying themes included the nature of election, the freeness of grace, and the degree to which, if at all, human beings may co-operate with God in the matter of their salvation.[11]

Into the midst of all this home-grown discussion there came, from Scotland, Sandemanianism, with its insistence that faith is intellectual assent to an understood divine testimony; and from further afield, the evangelical piety of Moravianism and the mystical musings of Emanuel Swedenborg.

As for John Wesley's distinctive theological contribution: we cannot expect his ideas, many of them worked out literally on the hoof, to have the character of a rounded system. Like Paul and Augustine before him, he frequently wrote to meet pressing needs, practical and doctrinal. For all that, his theological contribution, not least his emphases upon the new birth, justification by faith, assurance, perfect love and the practicalities of Christian living, was by no means negligible. Its interest lies not least in Wesley's eclecticism. For just as Wesley the evangelist-organiser subsumed the 'rounds' of other itinerants into his own tightly knit structure, adding his own 'societies' along the way, so Wesley the theologian summoned patristic divines, German pietists, Spanish mystics and others, moulding their insights to his own ends.

Notes

1. For Barclay (1648–90) see DNB, ODCC; and for further bibliographical references, Alan P. F. Sell, 'Robert Barclay (1640–1690), the Fathers and the Inward Universal Saving Light: A Tercentenary Reappraisal', in *idem, Commemorations: Studies in Christian Thought and History*, Calgary:University of Calgary Press and Cardiff: University of Wales Press, 1993, reprinted Eugene, OR: Wipf & Stock, 1998, ch.6. Barclay's *Apology* was reprinted in English in 1701, 1703, 1736, 1765 and 1780 in London. Other editions appeared in Birmingham, Dublin and North America. It was translated into Dutch, German, French, Danish and Spanish.

2. For Hoffmann (c. 1500–c. 1543) see ODCC; K. Deppermann, *Melchior Hoffman: Social Unrest and Apocalyptic Visions in the Age of Reformation*, Engl. trans., Edinburgh: T. & T. Clark, 1987; G. H. Williams, *The Radical Reformation*, Philadelphia: Westminster Press, 1962.

3. For Stennett (1663–1713) see DH, DNB. See further Alan P. F. Sell *Testimony and Tradition: Studies in Reformed and Dissenting Thought*, Aldershot: Ashgate, 2004, ch. 4.

4. For Winchester (1751–97) see *Dictionary of American Biography* (1927), New York: Scribners, [1995]; Ernest Cassara, *Universalism in America*, Boston: Skinner House, 1984; Russell E. Miller, *The Larger Hope: History of the Universalist Church in America,* 2 vols, Boston: Unitarian Universalist Historical Society, 1979, 1985; Elmo Arnold Robinson, *American Universalism: Its Origins, Organization and Heritage*, Jericho: Exposition Press, 1970.

5. For Clarke (1675–1729) see BCE, DECBP, DNB, ODCC; J.P. Ferguson, *An Eighteenth Century Heretic*, Kineton: The Roundwood Press, 1976; T. C. Pfizenmaier, *The Trinitarian Theology of Dr. Samuel Clarke*, Leiden: Brill, 1997.

6. See his *Letter to a Dissenter in Exeter*, 1719, pp. 10, 11. For Peirce (1674?–1726) see DNB.

7. James Manning, 'A Sketch of the Life and Writings of the Rev. Micaijah Towgood', *The Protestant Dissenter's Magazine*, November 1794, p. 426.

8. G. Hunsworth, *Memorials of the Old meeting House, Kidderminster*, 1874, p. 41. For Fawcett (1715–80) see DNB.

9. Ironically, the post-Revival influx of converts to Congregationalism, with its associated emphasis upon the individual's experience, weakened the idea of the covenanted fellowship, to the extent that the polity began to suffer and, in some places, baptism was regarded as optional. This is not to deny that it is more important that people hear and receive the Gospel than that polity be preserved intact. But there can be no doubt that

the catholicity of Congregationalism accords ill with nineteenth-century individualism. If it be asked, Why did Unitarianism flow from Congregationalism rather than from Presbyterianism in America, the answer is probably to be sought in the increasingly liberal Congregational ministers issuing from Harvard on the one hand, and, on the other hand, in the fact that the Presbyterianism of the time, heavily Scottish and Irish, was a Presbyterianism whose institutions and discipline had not suffered under the Clarendon Code.

10. See further Alan P. F. Sell, 'Confessing the Faith in English Congregationalism' and 'Presbyterianism in Eighteenth-Century England: The Doctrinal Dimension', in *idem, Dissenting Thought and the Life of the Churches: Studies in an English Tradition*, Lewiston, NY: Edwin Mellen Press, 1990, chs. 1 and 5.

11. On this last point see, for the eighteenth century, Alan P. F. Sell, *The Great Debate: Calvinism, Arminianism and Salvation*, Worthing: H.E. Walter, 1982 and Grand Rapids: Baker Book House, 1983, reprinted Eugene, OR: Wipf & Stock, 1998, ch.3.

Quaker Belief and Practice

Concerning the Holy Scriptures

Benjamin Holme (1683–1749), a Quaker travelling minister, visited Friends all over Britain, as well as in Holland, America and the West Indies. Widely respected, his writings are practical, and much less demanding on the reader than Barclay's.

For Holme see DNB. The following extract is from his *A Serious Call in Christian Love To all People To turn to the Spirit of Christ in Themselves*, (1st edn, 1725), 1753. It was followed by at least another eighteen editions.

Altho' some have misrepresented us, as tho' we undervalued or disesteemed the Holy Scriptures of the Old and New Testament; yet we do bless the Lord, and have great Cause so to do, that the excellent Counsel therein contained, which proceeded from the Spirit of God, is preserved upon Record to this Day; and it is a great Favour that we live under a Government, where we have the Liberty to read them, this being a Privilege that many called *Christians* are deprived of, in some other Countries; and I wish that all would be frequent in reading of them: The Apostle *Paul* commended *Timothy, in that from a Child he had known the Holy Scriptures, which,* saith he, *are able to make thee wise unto Salvation, through Faith, which is in Christ Jesus. All Scripture given by Inspiration of God, is profitable for Doctrine, for Reproof, for Correction, for Instruction in Righteousness, that the Man of God may be perfect, throughly furnished unto all good Works.*[1] *Search the Scriptures,* saith Christ, *for in them ye think ye have eternal Life, and they are they which testify of me, and ye will not come to me that ye might have Life.*[2] They are greatly to be valued, in that they testify of Christ, in whom there is Power to give Men Victory over their Corruptions, and Passions, and enable them to do the Will of God; we read that Christ *came unto his own, and his own received him not; but as many as received him, to them gave he Power to become the Sons of God.*[3] They that receive Christ by his Spirit into their Hearts, they receive Power; for Christ's Spirit is a *Christian*'s Strength: *I can do all Things,* saith the Apostle, *through Christ, which strengthens me.*[4] We read, that *No Prophesy of the Scripture is of any private Interpretation; for the Prophecy came not in old Time by the Will of Man, but holy Men of God spake as they were moved by the Holy Ghost.*[5] Now we say, the most true Interpreter of the Holy Scriptures, is the Holy Ghost, or Spirit, from which they did proceed; we read, that *The natural Man receives not the Things of the Spirit of God, neither can he know them,* saith the Text, and there is a strong Reason laid down for it, *because they are spiritually discerned*; they are beyond his Reach and Comprehension; *For what Man knoweth the Things of a Man, save the Spirit of a Man which is in him: even so the Things of God knoweth no Man, but the Spirit of God.*[6] This is the Key which opens the Mysteries of the Kingdom of God to Men; I take this to be the great Reason why there are such great Mistakes about Religion, and why many put such gross Constructions upon many Parts of the Holy Scriptures, as they do, because they do not come to that divine Spirit which gives a right and true Understanding; as *Elihu* said, *There is a Spirit in Man, and the Inspiration of the Almighty giveth them Understanding.*[7] Till Men come to the Holy Spirit of God in themselves, they can neither know God nor the Things of God; for we read, that *No Man knoweth the Father save the Son, and he to whomsoever the Son will reveal him.*[8] Now if Revelation was ceased, as some do imagine it is, what a sad condition would Mankind be in? For we read, *the World by Wisdom knows not God*; there is no knowledge of God, but by the Revelation of his Son; and it is as Men come to have an inward Knowledge of God, that they come to have a right Understanding of the Holy Scriptures, which proceeded from the good Spirit of God, wherefore we highly value them; though it is to be feared, some called *Christians* do disbelieve many of the great Truths therein contained; for I believe, that a Man, through often rebelling against the Holy Spirit of God in himself, may arrive to such a Degree of Wickedness, that he may reject the Scriptures, and count them but Fables; and may be so far from owning of any Thing of God in Man, as to deny the Lord that bought him, and according to *Psalm* xiv.1, he may say in his Heart, *there is no God.* It is the Work of the Enemy of all Righteousness to persuade Men that there is no God, and that the Scriptures are but a Fiction, and that Men are not accountable for their Words or Actions, and that there are no future Rewards and Punishments; that they might walk at large, and take their full Swing in Wickedness. It is greatly to be desired, if there be any such now living, whose Day of Mercy is not wholly over, that have arrived to such a Degree of Hardness and Wickedness as this is, that they may be brought to a Sense of their Iniquity and Error, and be so truly humbled in Soul because thereof, that if possible, they might find Mercy at the Lord's Hand. The better *Christian* that any man is, the more true and real Value he has for the Holy Scriptures.

Notes

1. 2 Tim. iii. 15, 16, 17.
2. John v. 39–40.
3. John i. 11–12.
4. Phil. iv. 13.
5. 2 Pet. i. 20, 21.
6. 1 Cor. ii. 11.
7. Job xxxii. 8.
8. Mat. xi. 27.

Document II.2

Concerning Swearing

> Friends were markedly distinguished from those they called the world's people by a number of strongly held and internally enforced tenets generally known as testimonies. These included objecting to swearing and to taking oaths, and the refusal to pay tithes and church rates, to use pagan terminology in the calendar, and to observe traditional religious and non-religious festivals. They required plainness and simplicity in speech and dress, and opposed war and the support of it through militia service.
>
> The following extract is from Benjamin Holme's *A Serious Call in Christian Love To all People To turn to the Spirit of Christ In Themselves*, 1st edn, 1725; it was followed by at least another eighteen editions.

We do not only deny vain, rash and false Swearing, but we also conscientiously refuse to swear in any Case, or on any Account whatsoever, because we believe that our Saviour, *Mat.* v. 33, 34, 35, 36, 37, did positively forbid all Swearing, for he saith, *Again, ye have heard, that it hath been said by them of old Time, thou shalt not forswear thyself, but shalt perform unto the Lord thine Oaths. But I say unto you,* Swear not at all; *neither by Heaven, for it is God's Throne; nor by the Earth, for it is his Footstool; neither by* Jerusalem, *for it is the City of the great King: Neither shalt thou swear by thy Head, because thou canst not make one Hair white or black. But let your Communication be* Yea, Yea; Nay, Nay; *for whatsoever is more than these, cometh of evil.* From which it is very plain, that as they of old allowed true Swearing, but forbad Forswearing, or Perjury; so our Saviour here forbids both the *One* and the *Other*, declaring, without any Exception, that whatsoever is more than *Yea, Yea; Nay, Nay*, cometh of evil. As for profane, vain and rash Swearing, it was also forbidden under the Law; for the third Command saith, *Thou shalt not take the Name of the Lord thy God in vain, for he will not hold him guiltless that taketh his Name in vain.*[1] And as this our conscientious Refusal of an Oath, in all Cases, is grounded upon the express Command of Christ; we have great Cause to be thankful to the King and Government, for their Favour, by enacting, that our Word, or Affirmation, shall pass in Cases of Evidence, instead of an Oath. For many of our elder Friends underwent great and grievous Sufferings, by Fines, Confiscations, Banishments, and Imprisonments to Death, for this their *Christian* Testimony. Swearing is now become so common, that it may with Sorrow be observed, that vain and profane Swearing abounds; Multitudes in their common Conversation, being guilty of it, in open Defiance and Violation, both of the Laws of God and Man.

It is very much to be desired, that all who profess themselves to be Followers of Christ, may live in Subjection to the Spirit of Christ in themselves, which leads into all Truth, and consequently to speak Truth on all Occasions: Men and Women under this Influence, may be very safely trusted. And it is a Reproach to any under the Denomination of *Christians*, that they cannot be depended upon for the Truth of *what they say.* Religion, however, is not yet at so low an Ebb, but that there are many honest well-minded People of different Professions and Perswasions, who have gained so great Credit and Reputation amongst such as know them, that they are, and can be relied on for the Truth of what they write or speak. And were all to live up to the Doctrine of Christ, there would be no Occasion for Swearing to awe Men into Truth-speaking; for the Fear of God, which is a stronger and more forcible Tye than any Oath that ever can be made, would always oblige and engage them thereunto.

Note

1. Exod. xx. 7.

Document II.3

Pride and Plainness

Plainness is illustrated from the Yearly Meeting Epistle of 1715. Yearly Meeting Epistles were issued annually, and are an important source for both the official Quaker position and for observing the development of Quaker thought and practice.

See *Epistles from the Yearly Meeting of Friends held in London, to the Quarterly and Monthly meetings in Great Britain, Ireland and Elsewhere, from 1681 to 1857, inclusive: with an historical introduction* ... , 2 vols, 1858. For plainness see David J. Hall, 'Plainness of Speech, Behaviour and Apparel in Eighteenth-Century English Quakerism', in *Monks, Hermits and the Ascetic Tradition*, ed. W. J. Sheils (Studies in Church History, XXII), Oxford: Blackwell, 1985, pp. 307–18.

A tender concern being upon the spirits of many brethren, for the keeping up our ancient testimonies in the truth against pride, and the vain fashions and customs of the world; it is desired and advised, that Friends in all places (in the wisdom of God) endeavour to train up their children in the fear of the Lord, and be good examples to them, in keeping to the cross of Christ, both in plainness of habit and speech; and, that none do countenance or connive at them, in going from the ancient simplicity of the truth, in which we have appeared as a people called of God, to bear testimony to his name; nor make light of those testimonies, which, by our ancient Friends (who trod out the way before us) were borne through great perils and dangers, to the hazarding the lives and estates of many; the weight of whose exercises remains fresh upon the minds of a remnant, to the stirring up of a godly zeal in them, against all false liberty, and sinful ease in the flesh, which is too apt to grow among some professing the same truth with us, in this our day, for want of due watchfulness and obedience to the light of Christ, and keeping low and humble before the Lord; by reason whereof, many evils get in amongst us; viz. Pride of apparel; making of mixed marriages with persons of contrary judgment; bowing, and giving flattering titles to men; the saying of ye or you to a single person; and calling the days of the week, and the months, by heathen names, to the declining of truth's testimony, and giving occasion of stumbling to such as are seeking after the knowledge of the same, as it is in Jesus.

Document II.4

[Matthew Green] on Robert Barclay

It is not easy to find balanced views of eighteenth-century Quakerism from outside the Society. Thomas Clarkson's sympathies place him in a special category, though his observations in *A Portraiture of Quakerism* (3 vols, 1806) are of considerable value because of their detail. The poet Matthew Green appears also to have been sympathetic – if he was in fact the author of the following poem on Barclay's *Apology*. Green was not himself a Friend, and his approval of Quaker principles did not imply that he felt able to adopt them in practice.

For the anti-slavery agitator Clarkson (1760–1846) see DNB, ODCC. For the poet Matthew Green (1696–1737), who rebelled against a puritanical upbringing in favour of 'some free notions on religious subjects', see DNB. Green's poem was first printed in 1735. The text used here is from his *The Spleen and Other Poems*, London: T. Cadell, 1796, pp. 69–72.

These sheets primæval doctrines yield,
Where revelation is reveal'd;
Soul-phlegm from literal feeding bred,
Systems lethargic to the head
They purge, and yield a diet thin,
That turns to gospel-chyle within.
Truth sublimate may here be seen
Extracted from the parts terrene.
In these is shewn, how men obtain
What of Prometheus poets feign:
To scripture-plainness dress is brought,
And speech, apparel to the thought.
They hiss from instinct at red coats,
And war, whose work is cutting throats,
Forbid, and press the law of love.
Breathing the spirit of the dove.
Lucrative doctrines they detest,
As manufactur'd by the priest;
And throw down turnpikes, where we pay
For stuff, which never mends the way;
And tythes, a Jewish tax, reduce,
And frank the gospel for our use.
They fable standing armies break;

But the militia useful make:
Since all unhir'd may preach and pray,
Taught by these rules as well as they;
Rules, which, when truths themselves reveal,
Bid us to follow what we feel.

The world can't hear the small still voice,
Such is its bustle and its noise;
Reason the proclamation reads,
But not one riot passion heeds.
Wealth, honour, power the graces are,
Which here below our homage share:
They, if one votary they find
To mistress more divine inclin'd,
In truth's pursuit to cause delay
Throw golden apples in his way.

Place me, O heav'n, in some retreat,
There let the serious death-watch beat,
There let me self in silence shun,
To feel thy will, which should be done.

Then comes the Spirit to our hut,
When fast the senses' doors are shut;
For so divine and pure a guest
The emptiest rooms are furnish'd best.

O Contemplation! Air serene,
From damps of sense, and fogs of spleen!
Pure mount of thought! Thrice holy ground,
Where grace, when waited for, is found!

Here 'tis the soul feels sudden youth,
And meets exulting, virgin Truth;
Here, like a breeze of gentlest kind,
Impulses rustle through the mind;
Here shines that light with glowing face,
The fuse divine, that kindles grace;
Which, if we trim our lamps, will last,
'Till darkness be by dying past,
And then goes out at end of night,
Extinguish'd by superior light.

Ah me! the heats and colds of life,
Pleasure's and pain's eternal strife,

Breed stormy passions, which confin'd,
Shake, like th'Æolian cave, the mind,
And raise despair my lamp can last,
Plac'd where they drive the furious blast.

    False eloquence, big empty sound,
Like showers that rush upon the ground,
Little beneath the surface goes,
All streams along and muddy flows.
This sinks, and swells the buried grain,
And fructifies like southern rain.

    His art, well hid in mild discourse,
Exerts persuasion's winning force,
And nervates so the good design,
That King Agrippa's case is mine.

    Well-natur'd, happy shade, forgive!
Like you I think, but cannot live.
Thy scheme requires the world's contempt,
That, from dependence life exempt;
And constitution fram'd so strong,
This world's worst climate cannot wrong.
Not such my lot, not Fortune's brat,
I live by pulling off the hat;
Compell'd by station every hour
To bow to images of power;
And in life's busy scenes immers'd,
See better things, and do the worst.

    Eloquent Want, whose reasons sway,
And make ten thousand truths give way,
While I your scheme with pleasure trace,
Draws near, and stares me in the face.
Consider well your state, she cries,
Like others kneel, that you may rise;
Hold doctrines, by no scruples vex'd,
To which preferment is annex'd,
Nor madly prove, where all depends,
Idolatry upon your friends.
See, how you like my rueful face,
Such you must wear, if out of place. ·
Crack'd is your brain to turn recluse
Without one farthing out at use.
They, who have lands, and safe bank-stock,

With faith so founded on a rock,
May give a rich invention ease,
And construe scripture how they please.

The honour'd prophet, that of old
Us'd heav'n's high counsels to unfold,
Did, more than courier angels, greet
The crows, that brought him bread and meat.

Document II.5

Voltaire on the Quakers

Voltaire's view is of particular interest. While it cannot be argued that it is reliable, it represents the view of an acute observer standing outside English and Welsh Nonconformity. The first four of his *Letters Concerning the English Nation* (1733) concern the Quakers, and the first two are printed here from the 1760 London edition. They are readily accessible in a version translated and introduced by Leonard Tancock, *Letters on England*, Harmondsworth: Penguin Books, 1980. A Quaker rejoinder to Voltaire came from Josiah Martin, *A Letter from one of the People called Quakers, to Francis de Voltaire, occasioned by his Remarks on that People in his Letters concerning the English Nation*, 1741. Martin's objective was 'to give that Author an Opportunity of correcting in subsequent Editions the Errors of his first; that by such a Demonstration of his sincere Attachment to Truth, he might at once have done himself Honour and the Quakers Justice'. Voltaire did not oblige.

For Voltaire (Françoise-Marie Arouet, 1694–1778) see BCE, ODCC. For Martin (1683–1747) see DNB.

Letter I.
on the
Quakers.

I was of opinion, that the doctrine and history of so extraordinary a People, were worthy the attention of the curious. To acquaint myself with them, I made a visit to one of the most eminent Quakers in *England*, who after having traded thirty years, had the wisdom to prescribe limits to his fortune and to his desires, and was settled in a little solitude not far from *London*. Being come into it, I perceiv'd a small, but regularly built house, vastly neat, but without the least pomp of furniture. The Quaker who own'd it was a hale ruddy complexion'd old man, who had never been afflicted with sickness, because he had always been insensible to passions, and a perfect stranger to intemperance. I never in my life saw a more noble or a more engaging aspect than his. He was dress'd like those of his persuasion, in a plain coat, without plaits in the sides, or buttons on the pockets and sleeves; and had on a beaver, the brims of which were horizontal, like those of our clergy. He did not uncover himself when I appear'd, and advanc'd towards me without once stooping his body; but there appear'd more politeness in the open, humane air of his countenance, than in the custom of drawing one leg behind the other, and taking that from the head, which is made to cover it. Friend, says he to me, I perceive thou art a stranger, but if I can do any thing for thee, only tell me. Sir, says I to him, bending forwards, and advancing as is usual with us, one leg towards him, I flatter myself that my just curiosity will not give you the least offence, and that you'll do me the honour to inform me of the particulars of your religion. The people of thy country, replied the Quaker, are too full of their bows and compliments, but I never yet met with one of them who had so much curiosity as thyself. Come in and let us first dine together. I still continued to make some very unseasonable ceremonies, it not being easy to disengage one's self at once from habits we have been long us'd to; and after taking part of a frugal meal, which began and ended with a prayer to God, I began to question my courteous host. I open'd with that which good Catholicks have more than once made to Huguenots. My dear sir, says I, were you ever baptiz'd? I never was, replied the Quaker, nor any of my brethren. Zouns, says I to him, you are not Christians then. Friend, replies the old man in a soft tone of voice, swear not; we are Christians, and endeavour to be good Christians, but we are not of opinion, that the sprinkling water on a child's head makes him a Christian. Heavens! says I, shock'd at his impiety, you have then forgot that *Christ* was baptiz'd by St. *John.* Friend, replies the mild Quaker once again, swear not. *Christ* indeed was baptiz'd by *John,* but he himself never baptiz'd any one. We are the disciples of *Christ,* not of *John.* I pitied very much the sincerity of my worthy Quaker, and was absolutely for forcing him to get himself christened. Were that all, replied he, very gravely, we would submit chearfully to baptism, purely in compliance with thy weakness, for we do not condemn any person who uses it; but then we think that those who profess a religion of so holy, so spiritual a nature as that of *Christ,* ought to abstain to the utmost of their power from the *Jewish* ceremonies. O unaccountable! says I , what? baptism a *Jewish* ceremony? Yes, my friend, says he, so truly *Jewish,* that a great many *Jews* use the baptism of *John* to this day. Look into ancient authors, and thou wilt find that *John* only reviv'd this practice; and that it had been us'd by the *Hebrews,* long before his time, in like manner as the Mahometans imitated the *Ishmaelites* in their pilgrimages to *Mecca. Jesus* himself submitted to the baptism of *John,* as he had suffered himself to be circumcis'd; but circumcision and the washing with water ought to be abolish'd by the baptism of *Christ,* that baptism of the spirit, that ablution of the soul, which is the salvation of mankind, thus the forerunner said, *I indeed baptize you with water unto repentance; but he that cometh after me, is mightier than I, whose shoes I am not worthy to bear: he shall baptize you with the Holy Ghost and with fire.*[1] Likewise *Paul,* the great apostle of the Gentiles, writes as follows to the *Corinthians; Christ sent me not to baptize, but to preach the Gospel;*[2] and indeed *Paul* never baptiz'd but two persons with water, and that very much against his inclinations. He circumcis'd his disciple *Timothy,* and the other disciples likewise circumcis'd all who were willing to submit to that carnal ordinance. But art thou circumcis'd, added he? I have not the honour to be so, says I. Well, friend, continues the Quaker, thou are a Christian without being circumcis'd, and I am one without being baptiz'd. Thus did this pious man make a wrong, but very specious application, of four or five texts of scripture which seem'd to favour the tenets of his sect; but at the same time forgot very sincerely an hundred texts which made directly against them. I had more sense that to contest with him, since there is no possibility of convincing an enthusiast. A man shou'd never pretend to inform a lover of his mistress's faults, no more than one who is at law, of the badness of his cause; nor attempt to win over a fanatic by strength of reasoning. Accordingly I wav'd the subject.

WELL, says I to him, what sort of a communion have you? We have none like that thou hintest at among us, replied he. How! no communion, says I? Only that spiritual one, replied he, of hearts. He then began again to throw out his texts of scripture; and preach'd a most eloquent sermon against that ordinance. He harangued in a tone as tho' he had been inspir'd, to prove that the sacraments were merely of human invention, and that the word *sacrament* was not once mention'd in the gospel. Excuse, says he, my ignorance, for I have not employ'd an hundredth part of the arguments which might be brought, to prove the truth of our religion, but these thou thyself mayest peruse in the Exposition of our Faith written by *Robert Barclay*. 'Tis one of the best pieces that ever was penn'd by man; and as our adversaries confess it to be of dangerous tendency, the arguments in it must necessarily be very convincing. I promis'd to peruse this piece, and my Quaker imagin'd he had already made a convert of me. He afterwards gave me an account in few words, of some singularities which make this sect the contempt of others. Confess, says he, that it was very difficult for thee to refrain from laughter, when I answer'd all thy civilities without uncovering my head, and at the same time said *Thee* and *Thou* to thee. However, thou appearest to me too well read, not to know that in *Christ's* time no nation was so ridiculous as to put the plural number for the singular. *Augustus Cæsar* himself was spoke to in such phrases as these, *I love thee, I beseech thee, I thank thee*; but he did not allow any person to call him *Domine*, Sir. 'Twas not till many ages after, that men wou'd have the word *You*, as tho' they were double, instead of *Thou* employed in speaking to them; and usurped the flattering titles of lordship, of eminence, and of holiness, which mere worms bestow on other worms, by assuring them that they are with the most profound respect, and an infamous falshood, their most obedient, humble servants. 'Tis to secure our selves more strongly from such a shameless traffick of lies and flattery, that we *thee* and *thou* a king with the same freedom as we do a beggar, and salute no person; we owing nothing to mankind but charity, and to the laws respect and obedience.

Our apparel is also somewhat different from that of others, and this purely, that it may be a perpetual warning to us not to imitate them. Others wear the badges and marks of their several dignities, and we those of christian humility. We fly from all assemblies of pleasure, from diversions of every kind, and from places where gaming is practis'd; and indeed our case wou'd be very deplorable, should we fill with such levities, as those I have mention'd, the heart which ought to be the habitation of God. We never swear, not even in a court of justice, being of opinion that the most holy name of God ought not to be prostituted in the miserable contests betwixt man and man. When we are obliged to appear before a magistrate upon other people's account, (for law-suits are unknown among the friends) we give evidence to the truth by sealing it with our *yea* or *nay*; and the judges believe us on our bare affirmation, whilst so many other Christians forswear themselves on the holy Gospels. We never war or fight in any case; but it is not that we are afraid, for so far from shuddering at the thoughts of death, we, on the contrary, bless the moment which unites us with the Being of beings; but the reason of our not using the outward sword is, that we are neither wolves, tigers, nor mastiffs, but men and Christians. Our God who has commanded us to love our enemies, and to suffer without repining, would certainly not permit us to cross the seas, merely because murtherers cloathed in scarlet, and wearing caps two foot high enlist citizens by a noise made with two little sticks on an ass's skin extended. And when, after a victory is gain'd, the whole city of *London* is illuminated; when the sky is in a blaze with fireworks, and a noise is heard in the air of thanksgivings, of bells, of organs, and of the cannon, we groan in silence, and are deeply affected with sadness of spirit and brokenness of heart, for the sad havock which is the occasion of those public rejoicings.

Notes

1. St. Matth. iii. 11.
2. 1 Cor. i. 17

Letter II.
on the
Quakers.

Such was the substance of the conversation I had with this very singular person; but I was greatly surpriz'd to see him come the *Sunday* following, and take me with him to the Quakers meeting. There are several of these in *London*, but that which he carried me to stands near the famous pillar call'd the Monument. The brethren were already assembled at my entering it with my guide. There might be about four hundred men and three hundred women in the meeting. The women hid their faces behind their fans, and the men were cover'd with their broad-brim'd hats; all were seated, and the silence was universal. I past through them, but did not perceive so much as one lift up his eyes to look at me. This silence lasted a quarter of an hour, when at last one of them rose up, took off his Hat, and after making a variety of wry faces, and groaning in a most lamentable manner, he partly from his nose, and partly from his mouth, threw out a strange, confus'd jumble of words, (borrow'd as he imagin'd from the Gospel) which neither himself nor any of his hearers understood. When this distorter had ended his beautiful soliloquy, and that the stupid, but greatly edified, congregation were separated, I ask'd my friend how it was possible for the judicious part of their assembly to suffer such a babbling. We are oblig'd, says he, to suffer it, because no one knows when a man rises up to hold forth, whether he will be mov'd by the spirit or by folly. In this doubt and uncertainty we listen patiently to every one, we even allow our women to hold forth; two or three of these are often inspired at one and the same time, and 'tis then that a most charming noise is heard in the Lord's house. You have then no priests, says I to him. No, no, friend, replies the Quaker, to our great happiness. Then opening one of the friends books, as he call'd it, he read the following words in an emphatic tone: God forbid we should presume to ordain any one to receive the Holy Spirit on the Lord's day, to the prejudice of the rest of the brethren. Thanks to the Almighty, we are the only people upon the earth that have no priests. Wouldest thou deprive us of so happy a distinction? Why shou'd we abandon our babe to mercenary nurses, when we ourselves have milk enough for it? These mercenary creatures wou'd soon domineer in our houses, and destroy both the mother and the babe. God has said, freely you have receiv'd, freely give. Shall we after these words cheapen, as it were, the gospel; sell the Holy Ghost, and make of an assembly of Christians a mere shop of traders? We do not pay a set of men clothed in black, to assist our poor, to bury our dead, or to preach to the brethren; these offices are all of too tender a nature, for us ever to entrust them to others. But how is it possible for you, says I, with some warmth, to know whether your discourse is really inspir'd by the Almighty? Whoever, says he, shall implore *Christ* to enlighten him, and shall publish the Gospel truths, he may feel inwardly, such an one may be assur'd that he is inspir'd by the Lord. He then pour'd forth a numberless multitude of Scripture-texts, which prov'd, as he imagin'd, that there is no such thing as Christianity without an immediate revelation, and added these remarkable words: When thou move stone of thy limbs, is it mov'd by thy own power? Certainly not, for this limb is often sensible to involuntary motions; consequently he, who created thy body, gives motion to this earthly tabernacle. And are the several ideas of which thy soul receives the impression form'd by thyself? Much less are they, since these pour in upon thy mind whether thou wilt or no; consequently thou receivest thy ideas from him who created thy soul: But as he leaves thy affections at full liberty, he gives thy mind such ideas as thy affections may deserve; if thou livest in God, thou actest, thou thinkest in God. After this thou needest only but open thine eyes to that light which enlightens all mankind, and 'tis then thou wilt perceive the truth, and make others perceive it. Why this, says I, is *Malebranche*'s doctrine to a tittle. I am acquainted with thy *Malebranche*, says he; he had something of the *friend* in him, but was not enough so. These are the most considerable particulars I learnt concerning the doctrine of the Quakers; in my next letter I shall acquaint you with their history, which you will find more singular than their opinions.

Old Dissent and Orthodox Doctrine

Document II.6

Matthew Caffyn and the General Baptists

Matthew Caffyn's Christological difficulties with the General Baptists have been out-
lined in the introduction to this part. Four extracts will indicate the flow of the debate:
(a) the relevant, less than watertight, clause of the Standard Confession of 1660; (b) a
clause from the doctrinally tighter Orthodox Creed prepared by Thomas Monk and
fifty-four General Baptists from Buckinghamshire, Hertfordshire, Bedfordshire and
Oxford in 1679; (c) the affirmation of a group of messengers at the General Baptist
Assembly of May 1770, where Caffyn was tried; (d) the Assembly's judgement.

For Caffyn (1628–1714) see DNB; Alan P. F. Sell, *Testimony and Tradition*, Aldershot:
Ashgate, 2005, ch. 4. Extracts (a) and (b) are in William L. Lumpkin, *Baptist Confessions
of Faith*, Valley Forge, PA: Judson Press, 1969, pp. 225 and 229–300; extracts (c) and
(d) are in W.T. Whitley, *Minutes of the General Assembly of the General Baptist
Churches in England*, London: Baptist Historical Society, 1909, I, pp. 66 and 67.

(a)
We believe … III. That there is one Lord Jesus Christ, by whom are all things, who
is the only begotten Son of God, born of the Virgin *Mary*; yet as truly *Davids* Lord,
and *Davids* root, as *Davids* Son, and *Davids* Offspring, Luke 20.44. Revel. 22.26.
whom God freely *sent into the world* (because of his great love unto the World) who
as *freely gave himself a ransome for all, I Tim, 2.5,6. Tasting death for every man,
Heb.2.9. a propitiation for your sins; and not for ours only, but also for the sins of
the whole World*, I John 2.2.

(b)
We confess and believe that the Son of God, or the eternal word, is very and true
God, having his personal subsistence of the father alone, and yet for ever of himself
as God; and of the father as the son, the eternal son of an eternal father; not later in
the beginning. There was never any time when he was not, not other in substance
… not a metaphorical, or subordinate God; not a God by office, but a God by nature,
coequal, coessential, and coeternal, with the father and the holy ghost … [T]he second person in the sacred Trinity, took to himself a true, real, and fleshly body, and
reasonable soul, being conceived in the fulness of time by the holy ghost, and born
of the virgin Mary, and became very and true man.

(c)
[We believe] That Christ as he was the word is from the Beginning But in Time that
words tooke not on him the Nature of Angells but he took on him the Seed of

Abraham & as such is Emanuell God with us or God manifest in the flesh & as he is the word is one with the ffather & the Holy Ghost & as he was God manifest in the flesh so is he Jesus that Tasted Death for Every Man And further whereas that have been & yet are Debates about the most high God wee Conceive he is one Infirmative Unchangable and Eternall Spiritt & Incomnprehensable Godhead & doth Subsist in the father ye word & the Holy Ghost.

(d)
Agreed that the Defence Bror Matthew Caffin made in the Assembly and his Acknowledgment was in the satisfaccon of the Assembly.

Document II.7

Isaac Watts on John Locke

Like many others, Watts queried whether Locke was doctrinally sound on Christ's person and satisfaction. Unlike most, he turned to verse to express himself. The poem is from Watts's *Works*, Leeds: Edward Baines, 1800, VII, p. 261. For Watts see Document I.2.

On Mr. Locke's Annotations upon Several Parts of the New Testament, left behind him at his Death.

Thus reason learns by slow degrees,
    What faith reveals; but still complains
  Of intellectual pains;
And darkness from the too exuberant light.
  The blaze of those bright mysteries
  Pour'd all at once on nature's eyes
  Offend and cloud her feeble fight.

  Reason could scarce sustain to see
  Th' Almighty One, th' eternal Three,
  Or bear the infant deity;
  Scarce could her pride descend to own
  Her Maker stopping from his throne,
  And drest in glories so unknown.
  A ransom'd world, a bleeding God,
  And heav'n appeas'd with flowing blood,
Were themes too painful to be understood.

  Faith, thou bright cherub, speak, and say
  Did ever mind of mortal race
  Cost thee more toil, or larger grace,
  To melt and bend it to obey,
'Twas hard to make so rich a soul submit,

And lay her shining honours at thy sovereign feet.

> Sister of faith, fair charity,
> Shew me the wondrous man on high,
> Tell how he sees the godhead Three in One;
> The bright conviction fills his eye,
> His noblest powers in deep prostration lie
>   At the mysterious throne.
> 'Forgive, he cries, ye saints below,
> 'The wav'ring and the cold assent
> 'I gave to themes divinely true;
> 'Can you admit the blessed to repent?
>   'Eternal darkness veil the lines
>   'Of that unhappy book,
> 'Where glimmering reason with false lustre shines.
>   'Where the mere mortal pen mistook
>   'What the celestial meant![1]

Note

1. See Mr. Locke's Annotations on Rom. iii. 25 and Paraphrase on Rom. ix.5. which has inclined some readers to doubt whether he believed the deity and satisfaction of Christ. Therefore in the fourth stanza I invoke charity, that by her help I may find him out in heaven, since his Notes on 2 Cor. v. ult. and some other places, give me reason to believe he was no Socinian, though he has darkened the glory of the gospel, and debased christianity, in the book which he calls The Reasonableness of it, and in some of his other works.

Document II.8

The Subscribers at Salters' Hall

Documents II.8 and II.9 confirm the statement made earlier that both subscribers and most non-subscribers at the Salters' Hall conference of 1719 found ways of affirming their belief in the Trinity. It appears that 29 Presbyterians and 28 Independents subscribd, and that 47 Presbyterians were among the non-subscribers, of whom Benjamin Avery and Nathanael Lardner were decided Arians. Most subscribers were over forty years of age; most non-subscribers were under forty.

For the conference see A.Gordon, *Addresses Biographical and Historical*, London: Lindsey Press, 1922, pp. 124–53; F.J Powicke, 'The Salters' Hall Controversy', *Congregational Historical Society Transactions*, VII, no 2, 1916, pp. 110–24; R. Thomas in C. G. Bolam, J. Goring, H. L. Short and R. Thomas, *The English Presbyterians: From Elizabethan Puritanism to Modern Unitarianism*, London: Allen and Unwin, 1968; C. G. Bolam, 'The Non-Subscription Controversy amongst Dissenters in 1719: The Salters' Hall Debate', *Journal of Ecclesiastical History*, IV, 1953, pp. 162–86; Alan P. F. Sell, *Dissenting Thought and the Life of the Churches*, Lewiston,

NY: Edwin Mellen Press, 1990, *passim*. For Avery (d. 1764), who resigned from the Presbyterian ministry following the conference and practised as a physician, see DNB. For Lardner (1694–1768) see DECBP, DNB, ODCC. The following extract is from *A True Relation of some Proceedings at Salters-Hall By those Ministers who sign'd The First Article of the Church of England, and The Answers to the Fifth and Sixth Questions in the Assemblies Shorter Catechism, March 3. 1719*, London, [1719], pp. 11–17.

II.   Advices with the Letter accompanying.

Some of our Number having been apply'd to by several Worthy *Gentlemen* at *Exon* for *Advice* how to conduct themselves under their unhappy Circumstances: We are clearly of OPINION,

That there are ERRORS in DOCTRINE of such a Nature, as will not only *warrant*, but *oblige* the People to withdraw from those *Ministers* that maintain and teach them.

And that the *People* have a Right to judge what those Errors are, and when they are so maintain'd and taught, as will justify them in withdrawing from such a *Ministry*. But as the PURITY of the Faith, the PEACE of the CHURCHES, the *Reputation* and *Usefulness* of *Ministers*, are Matters of very great Weight and Consequence, the utmost *Care* and *Caution* ought to be had *on both Sides* in all Proceedings of such a Nature; and therefore we humbly advise:

1.   That when such *Differences* do arise, the *People* would consider, tho' they have the Power of judging what *Ministers* and *Doctrines* are fit for them to hear, yet they must by no Means suffer their Passions, Prejudices, or unreasonable Jealousies, to *byass* their Judgment; but must search the *Scriptures*, and be determined by them, both as to the *Merits* of the Cause and the *Manner* of *Proceeding*. All Rashness and intemperate Zeal must be suppress'd, and every thing managed *clearly, calmly*, in the *Fear* of GOD, with Meekness and tender Compassion towards *all* with whom they are concerned.

2.   If the *People* shall see fit (which in many Cases may be expedient) to call for the Advice of Neighbouring Ministers and others, that are most like to give them good Direction in the Matter before them; *those Ministers* and *Others*, whose Counsel is desired, should be *free, open* and *faithful* in the Advice they give, without being *in the least* influenced by the any personal *Respect* of *Disrespect* on either Hand.

3.   If any *Minister* is suspected by his *Hearers* to hold *dangerous Errors*, and the *People* in a *serious* and *respectful Manner* desire him to be *plain* with them, and let them know what his *real Belief* is, that they may not by Mistake either wrong *him* or their *own Souls*; we think it reasonable he should comply with their Desire, and *be ready to give an Account of the Hope that is in him with Meekness and Fear*, that the People may have no Ground to charge him with Pride or Prevarication, sacrificing his own Peace and theirs too, to a Stiffness of *Humour*, or Punctilio of *Honour*.

4.   That the *People* in this Case should be always ready to receive a *reasonable* Satisfaction; and if it does appear either that their Ministers *never held* those Errors

of which they were suspected, or have upon maturer Thoughts *relinquish'd* them and return'd to the Truth, the People should regard them with *all Respect* and *Kindness*, not suffering *any Jealousies* to lodge in their Breasts; but should *receive them in the* LORD, and attend upon their Ministry, and treat them with as much Affection, Freedom and Confidence, as if no such Suspicions had ever taken place among them.

5.   If *all Attempts* for mutual Satisfaction, Union and Agreement, between Ministers and People should prove ineffectual, and either *the Minister* should judge it *his Duty* to withdraw from the People, as those that will not endure that which he takes to be *sound Doctrine*, or *the People* shall judge it *their Duty* to withdraw from their Minister, as maintaining what they take to be *dangerous Error*, they should re-solve to part *without Wrath* and *Bitterness* according to the *Gospel Rule*; and *how much soever* they may judge that Error to be in its Nature of the most dangerous Tendency, yet that neither *they* nor *others* should interpret such their *Separation*, as if thereby they presum'd to *judge* and *condemn* each other as to *their eternal State*: Being perswaded, that tho' our LORD and SAVIOUR is justly and highly offended with the sinful Errors and Divisions of those that call upon his Name, yet he is that *merciful High-Priest* that knows how to have Compassion on the Ignorant and those that are out of the Way, and to *give them Repentance to the Acknowledgment of the Truth*.

As we have with very good Reason declared the Right of the People to judge what those Doctrines are that will justify them in withdrawing from their Minister, so we take the Freedom to declare it as our Judgment, That *the Denying of the true and proper Divinity of the* Son *of* GOD *and the* HOLY SPIRIT, viz. *that they are One* GOD *with the* Father, *is an Error contrary to the* HOLY SCRIPTURES *and common Faith of the* REFORMED CHURCHES.

We who have subscrib'd these *Advices*, have also subscrib'd the *First* Article of the Church of *England*, and the Answers to the *Fifth* and *Sixth* Questions of the *Assemblies Catechism*; as what we believe to be the DOCTRINE of the Blessed TRINITY revealed in the HOLY SCRIPTURES. ...

Document II.9

The Non-Subscribers at Salters' Hall

The following extract is from *An Authentick Account of Several Things Done and agreed upon by the Dissenting Ministers Lately assembled at Salters-Hall*, London, 1719, pp. 22–9.

III.   We did not think fit to subscribe because we thought *no sufficient Reasons* were offered, for our subscribing.

We were prest to it, that we might *clear ourselves* from the *Suspicions* of *Arianism*. But, as we knew no just Ground of Suspicion, much less of any Charge against us, we thought it would ill become us so far to indulge an *unreasonable jealousy*, as to take a Step of this Nature for removing it; especially since doing so would have been inconsistent with *one* of the *Advices* which we thought necessary to be given, and which was founded upon an *Apostolical Rule*. And we see no End of such Jealousies: For, if we may be suspected of *Arianism* without having taught any Thing like it, and tho' we have taken all proper Occasions to offer our Reasons against it, and that not only from the *Pulpit* but some of us from the *Press*; We say, if we must be suspected, merely because we would not subscribe what our Brethren would have us; why may we not be suspected of *Hypocrisy* after we have done it? And then pass in the World for *Arians*, and *Cheats* into the Bargain. We never yet thought *Jealousy* and Suspicion to be such good-natured Things as to be satisfied with a *few Good Words*.

It was also urged, That to subscribe as they would have us, would give the *greater Weight* to our *Advices*, in Case we should send them to *Exeter*. On the contrary we could not but think, that tho' they might be regarded by *One Party*, because they would interpret what we did so as to justifie their own Conduct; yet they could be taken by the *other* side in no other Sense, but making ourselves a Party *against them*, which we thought would no Way suit with Advices intended to make *Peace*, as well as to secure *Truth*. And we have Ground to hope that our Advices would be received by all *impartial Men* on Account of what was contain'd in them, as far as they carried Reason and Evidence along with them.

There was another Thing offered, That, if we subscribed it would prevent the *spreading of Erroneous Opinions* amongst Those whom our Names might be supposed to Influence; whereas if we refused, They might be in Danger from a *wrong Apprehension* of our Sentiments. But we could not think ourselves answerable for any Arguments drawn by others from groundless *Suspicions* concerning us; nor that those Suspicions were a just Reason for our coming into such a Subscription: We thought we had sufficiently guarded against them in the *Course of our Publick Ministrations*; And we are still fully persuaded that a Faith built upon our Authority is a vain Thing in *itself*. We think ourselves obliged often to inculcate this Principle upon our Hearers, That they ought not to form their judgment in Matters necessary to Salvation, by the private Sentiments of their *Ministers* and farther than they are supported by the *Word of God*.' And we shall assure ourselves that a tender and scrupulous Regard for *the Word of God alone*, will never be thought either dangerous, or inconvenient, to the *Body* of *Protestant Dissenters*.

IV.   We saw *no* Reason to think, That a *Declaration* in *other Words* than those of *Scripture*, would serve the Cause of *Peace* and *Truth*; but rather be the Occasion of *greater Confusions* and *Disorders* We have found it always so in *History*; And in *Reason*, the *Words* of *Men* appear to us more liable to *different* Interpretations, than the *Words* of *Scripture*; Since all may fairly think themselves *more at Liberty*, to put their own Sense upon *Humane Forms*, than upon the Words of the *Holy Ghost*. And in this Case, what Assurance could we have that all who subscribed meant precisely the *same Sense* any more than if they had made a Declaration in *express Words* of *Scripture*.

V.   The Subscription insisted on, Was *beyond even what the Legislature itself* requires of us. For the Legislature has thought fit to require only our *once subscribing*; and this being a necessary Condition of exercising our Ministry, we should be highly blameable to neglect that Work, by refusing to comply with what is required of us, when we can do it with a safe Conscience: But we have always thought that *such Humane Declarations of Faith*, were far from being eligible on their *own Account*; since they stood to *narrow* the Foundations of Christianity, and to restrain that *Latitude* of Expression in which our great *Legislator* has seen fit to deliver his Will to us.

VI.   We did not think fit, to pay such a new an unwarrantable Regard to the *Catechism of the Assembly of Divines*: It being what they themselves, have in Effect declared against; and we fear, many pious Christians will be less ready to make the proper Use of this *Compendium*, when they see such Colour given for its standing in the Place of the *Word of God*.

VII.   We take it to be an inverting the Grace Rule of *deciding Controversies among Protestants*: Making the Explications and Words of *Men* determine the Sense of *Scripture*, instead of making the *Scriptures* to determine how far the *Words of Men* are to be regarded. We therefore, could not give our Hands to do that, which in present Circumstances, would be like to mislead others to set up Humane Explications for the *Decisive Rule* of Faith. We then did, and do now judge it our Duty to remonstrate against such a *Priestdom*, as opening a Way to (what we dread) the most fatal *Breaches on Gospel Liberty*.

VIII.   Tho' we would not charge our Brethren that requir'd our Subscriptions with a Design which any of them do disclaim, yet to us it appeared, and does still appear to have the *Nature of Imposition*; which has been the great Engine of Division among Christians from the Beginning, and has done unspeakable Mischief to the *Christian Church*.

IX.   We thought it would be a Reproach upon us, to do any Thing that look'd like *giving up our Christian Liberty when others* with so great *Strength* of Argument are pleading for it.

X.   We foresaw the Subscription insisted on would occasion *Reflections*, and become a *Mark of Distinction* set on those who should not subscribe: And we knew that several, who had the *same* Faith and Opinions concerning the TRINITY, with *ourselves* and our *Brethren*, yet could not be satisy'd to come into any Humane Explications.

XI.   We could not but think it would highly reflect on *those among ourselves*, who hd been known often to declare against every Thing of this Nature.

XII.   We observed the *Enemies* of the *Protestant Dissenters* to be great Encouragers and Approvers of such kind of Proceedings; and we have seen how many Ways they are ready to take Advantage of our Brethrens Subscription since.

To add but one Thing more, We did not think it proper to subscribe because if this Humour was *once* complied with, we could not tell *where it would stop*.

Document II.10

Edmund Calamy's Veiled Charge of Hypocrisy

Edmund Calamy (1671–1732), a Dissenting divine educated at Dissenting academies in England and in Utrecht, was an astute observer of the religious scene, and the leading biographer of Nonconformity of his day. A biographer of Richard Baxter, the ninth chapter of his *Abridgment of Baxter's History* (1702), new edn, 2 vols, 1713), entitled 'A Particular Account of the Ministers, Lecturers, Fellows of Colleges, &c., who were silenced and ejected by the Act for Uniformity; with the characters and works of many of them', is of great value. See A.G. Matthews, *Calamy Revised: Being a Revision of Edmund Calamy's account of the Ministers and Others Ejected and Silenced*, Oxford: Clarendon Press (1934), 1988. Calamy's remark is a commentary upon the latitudinarianism of the Church of England, to which in his day a number of Presbyterians in particular – including Joseph Butler and Thomas Secker the future archbishop of Canterbury – were conforming. Some of these Presbyterians felt constricted by Dissent; some noticed that since Arians who were within the Established Church were not proceeded against, it was not necessary to remain outside the Church of England on doctrinal grounds (and, in any case, heterodox Dissenters could equally well be prosecuted under the Act of Toleration, but were not); and some continued to value the idea of an Established Church, even if its polity were not the one they would have preferred.

For Calamy see DNB, ODCC. The following comment is in his *Thirteen Sermons concerning the Doctrine of the Trinity, Preach's at the Merchant's-Lecture, at Salter's Hall*, London, 1722 (unpaginated) 12–13.

[I]t appears to me a very pardonable Thing, for Persons to be the less inclin'd to regard or value Subscriptions, when they observe how awkwardly they are manag'd by the Arian Subscribers to Trinitarian Articles, and the Arminian Subscribers to Calvinistical Articles, of both which Sorts I doubt there are great Numbers in the church of England.

Document II.11

Abraham Taylor contra Isaac Watts

His querying of Locke's Christology and soteriology notwithstanding (Document II.7 above), Watts himself was suspected by some of veering in the direction of Socinianism in his declining years. That this was the view of Abraham Taylor, whose doctrinal antennae were ever more sensitive than his tongue, is clear from this extract from his *The Scripture Doctrine of the Trinity Vindicated. In opposition to Mr. Watts's Scheme of One Divine Person and Two Divine Powers*, 2nd edn, London, 1728, pp. 114–17.

For Watts see Document I.2 above; for Taylor see Document I.4 above.

In case Mr. Watts should think his scheme is not overturned, by what has been objected to him, if he will fairly go to work, he should not only shew the insufficiency of the arguments, brought against him, but should give the positive proofs of his opinions from Scripture.

I.   It will lie upon him to prove, that it is any way possible for us, finite creatures, to gain adequate conceptions of an infinite Being, and consequently to acquire clear and bright ideas of the three divine persons.

II.   He ought to shew, how, and wherein, the scheme he advances, differs from the Sabellian scheme, or the Socinian, except in words, and his adding the fancy of Christ's having a super-angelic Spirit, to supply the place of a human soul.

III.   He should bring plain and positive proof from Scripture, that the one God is properly but one person.

IV.   It may be expected of him, to make it evident, that the Scripture represents the Son, and holy Spirit, as properties, faculties, or powers of the divine nature.

V.   It will be necessary for him to manifest that the Scripture has ever given us any caution, against taking the personal ascriptions, which it applies, without difference, to Father, Son, and Spirit, in the same sense, when applied to the Son and Spirit, as when applied to the Father.

VI.   It will be incumbent on him to shew, that there is the least countenance, directly or indirectly, given, in Scripture, to his fancy of a created Logos, or of a glorious super-angelic spirit being to Christ, instead of a human soul.

These are things which Mr. Watts ought, in justice to truth, (if he thinks what he has advanced to be truth) to make out clearly and fully, if he is able. But as I am satisfied, this is above his power, I cannot but think, he ought to beg pardon of the Church of Christ, for many mistakes he has run into.

1.   For pretending to give a scheme of the Trinity, which has clear and bright ideas annexed to it, and yet giving us a scheme full of thick darkness, and mere confusion, and for his numerous self-contradictions:

2.   For introducing great numbers of hard and unintelligible terms, which can only perplex and confound his readers:

3.   For obtruding upon us the Socinian scheme, in a new dress, and yet not knowing he does so:

4.   For making Christ to be, as to his Divinity, only a property of God, and for denying his true humanity, by making him to have a soul vastly above what is human:

5.   For representing Nestorianism as an innocent notion, and yet not proving it to be so:

6.   For hinting, that the human soul of Christ, a creature, might be employed in the works of creation and providence:

7.   For making the holy Spirit to be a power, or property, and yet not a mere attribute of God:

8.   For saying[1] the holy Spirit has not the pronoun I attributed to him, in the new Testament:

9.   For representing the doctrine of the eternal generation of the Son, and the procession of the Spirit, to be a popish and scholastic hypothesis:

10.   For making it a matter of indifference whether doxologies are to be addressed to the Spirit, or no:

Christian Doctrine

11. For giving a false and partial account of antiquity, in making the Spirit to be addressed to, by way of doxology, only two, or three times, in the primitive writings.

12. For abusing the Apostle John, as a poor Jewish fisherman, who could not know the Greek learning, when he had spoke Greek above sixty years.

These are things for which Mr. Watts ought openly to beg pardon; and were he to do so, it would make but small amends, for the grief and trouble he has occasion'd, to those who have at heart the welfare of Christianity.

It is high time now to draw towards a close. I would therefore earnestly desire Mr. Watts, to lay his hand upon his heart, and seriously to consider what he has been doing: he bears the character of a person of great devotion; have his devotions, all the past years of his life, been directed to wrong objects? Has he had communion with Father, Son and Spirit, without knowing, whether he held communion with persons, or properties? Can he think it becoming one, who has a long time dispensed the Gospel, to shift his notions of the prime doctrine of revelation, two or three times, in the compass of two or three years, without giving any reasons for his so frequently veering about? Can he, in his conscience, believe that the jargon of words he has made use of, can convey clear and bright ideas? Can he reckon it safe to give a scope to a working fancy, in things of such a high nature? Can he think he rightly employs his time, in only puzzling and confounding plain truths, and raising a dust before the eyes of weak readers? Can he think, with comfort, of appearing before Christ, when he makes him to be neither perfect God, nor intirely man? And can he expect the consolations of the holy Spirit, when he, in effect, reduces him to nothing? These things, I hope, he will seriously revolve in his mind, and will not think the product of a fertil invention, too dear a sacrifice to be offer'd up to the honour of the Gospel.

If I find my weak endeavours are made by God successful, for the establishment of Christians in their most holy religion, I shall have the end answer'd, which I proposed in drawing up this work. I think, I can truly say, my aim in it is right, however I may have failed in the management of it: I design'd it as a mark and token of my high value for the true Scripture and catholic doctrine of the Trinity, in the faith of which I hope to live and to die.

Now to the Father, the Son, and the holy Spirit, three persons, but one infinitely glorious God, be ascribed all honour and glory, might, majesty, power and dominion, henceforth, and for evermore. Amen.

Note

1. Mr. Watts has acknowledg'd, that as to this matter, he had forgot himself. (See his Sermons, Vol. iii, p. 426.) and this is the only mistake he has retracted, tho' he has again been on the subject.

Document II.12

Samuel Bourn on Fundamental Truths and the Trinity

Samuel Bourn the Younger (1689–1754), Presbyterian divine, was educated at the Manchester Dissenting academy conducted by James Coningham and John Chorlton. He ministered at Crook, near Kendal (1711–20), Tunley (1720–7), Chorley (1727–32), and Coseley and New Meeting, Birmingham (1732–54). A zealous pamphleteer who at times exemplified a knockabout style, he also published sermons and prayers.

For Bourn see DNB; Alan P. F. Sell, 'A Little Friendly Light: the Candour of Bourn, Taylor and Towgood', in *idem, Dissenting Thought and the Life of the Churches,* Lewiston, NY: Edwin Mellen Press, 1990, ch. 7. For Coningham (1670–1716) and Chorlton (1666–1705) see DNB. Text (a) is extracted from *The True Christian Way of Striving for the Faith of the Gospel (passim)*, reprinted 1771, a sermon preached at Dudley Yearly Meeting on 23 May 1735 against what Bourn regarded as one of the greatest evils among Protestant Dissenters in the Dudley area, namely, that of introducing unwarranted terms of fellowship. Text (b) is extracted from *A Dialogue between a Baptist and a Church-Man. By a Consistent Christian*, 1737, pp. 10–11.

(a)
It has been an antient Practise for Church Bigots, and Orthodox Zealots to make many Fundamentals in Religion, many Conditions of Salvation, which God never made so; and then to miscall, curse, excommunicate and damn those who do not believe and submit to them. We *wish* there would be no like instances in any Christian Church. However, we *hope* this Anti-Christian Spirit will not haunt the Christian Church much longer ...

[I]t is possible for good Men to believe, preach, and to impose upon Others, and *fundamental Truths*, very great Errors ... A great many ... very hurtful Errors ... may conflict with *Grace*. [Such errors are] That human inventions in *Creeds* are very lawful and necessary ... That private Christians and Ministers are not to have the free use of their *own Reason*, and of the *Holy Scriptures,* but are *obliged* to understand them as their Fathers did; tho' they are *not able* so to understand them ... That Candour and Justice are not due to an Erroneous Brother ...

[The doctrine of the Trinity is plain and not disputed]. But if we give up any Points relating to this Doctrine, it is only *Human Explications* of it; and we give them up only because, either wholly Incomprehensible to us, or utterly indefensible by us ...

You must use none of *Satan's Weapons* in defending the Truths and Cause of Christ ... This hating and hurting Men, under pretence of Religion, is the very *Spirit of Anti-Christ*.

[In a post-script to the printed version of his sermon Bourn declares that 'It is just Ground both Wonder and Lamentation' that his sermon which was designed to promote peace should have stirred up such a commotion. Since his motive was pacific, the cause of the unrest must lie elsewhere.]

(b)

[In answer to the Baptist's claim that Baptist preachers, however plain, preach true doctrine – for example, the Trinity]: If by the Doctrine of the Trinity you mean the Doctrine of the *Father, Son and Holy Spirit*; they might have stay'd at home; in regard as far as I know the Town, this Doctrine is firmly believ'd by every preacher in Town, and by all their Hearers … For my Part, I hold Jesus Christ to be God, or a God … But I can't bring my self to believe his *Supreme Deity*, because I believe in the same supreme Deity of God the Father; and it appears to me a plain contradiction to say that there are two Persons or Beings who are both of 'em *Supreme* or *Most High God*, and I never yet had Faith eno' to believe two contradictory Propositions.

Document II.13

John Taylor on Original Sin

John Taylor (1694–1761), Presbyterian divine, was educated under Thomas Dixon at the Dissenting academy at Whitehaven, and then under Thomas Hill at Findern academy. He ministered at the extra-parochial chapel at Kirkstead, Lincolnshire (1716–33) and Norwich (1733–57). In 1757 he became the first tutor in divinity and moral philosophy at Warrington academy, where he remained until his death. Taylor published biblical works, a Hebrew concordance, books on prayer, the atonement and moral philosophy, and a collection of psalmody tunes with an introduction on the art of singing. In *An Examination of the Scheme of Morality advanced by Dr. Hutcheson* (1759) he follows the deontological line of Price (see Documents I.9 and I.10 above.)

For Taylor see BCE, DECBP, DNB, ODCC; Alan P. F. Sell, *Dissenting Thought and the Life of the Churches*, Lewiston, NY: Edwin Mellen Press, 1990, ch. 7; G. T. Eddy, *Dr Taylor of Norwich: Wesley's Arch-heretic*, Peterborough: Epworth Press, 2003. The following extract is from *The Scripture-Doctrine of Original Sin Proposed to Free and Candid Examination*, London, 1740, pp. 2–6, 63–4, 249–60. This work was widely influential, not least in America. Nearer home it prompted the warning of an Irish Calvinistic minister to his flock: 'I desire that none of you will read it; for it is a bad book, and a dangerous book, and a heretical book; and what is worse than all, the book is unanswerable.'

All TRUTH necessary to Salvation is revealed in the Holy SCRIPTURES; and the SCRIPTURES, not the Opinions of *Men*, not of *learned Men*, no, not of *good Men*, no, not of many *learned* and *good Men*, are the Rule of our Faith. Men of Knowledge and Integrity may indeed be useful to us, as Instructors, to open the Sense of God's Word: But it is the Word and Revelation of God alone upon which my Faith is to be founded. And as for human Wisdom and Knowledge, I ought to value it, in religious Matters, just so much, and so far only, as it serves to unfold the Mind and Meaning of God in the Scriptures; in the interpreting of which, we ought not to admit any thing contradictory to the common Sense and Understanding of Mankind. For the Scriptures can be no Rule to us, if the Understanding God hath given us is not a Rule in judging of their Sense, and Meaning. Nothing ought to pass for Divine Revelation which is inconsistent with any of the known Perfections of the Divine Nature. Difficult Places are to be explained by those that are easy to be understood. We must not allow ourselves to *feign* any thing; but must attend to the true, strict and proper Sense of every Place, without daring to add or diminish by our own Imaginations: and whatever we find is plainly added, or diminished, by human Interpretations or Schemes, we ought peremptorily to reject as dangerous Innovation. Lastly, we should not content ourselves with Scraps, and single Sentences, which in Sound may seem to mean one Thing, but really have, taken with what goes before, and what follows after, a quite different Signification. This is a very fallacious Way of proving Things from Scripture; and, for my own Part, I cannot satisfy my self in grounding Articles of Faith upon it ...

You want to be satisfied about *Original Sin*: that is, you would know, How far we, the Posterity of *Adam*, are involved in the Consequences of his first Transgression.

Come then, my dear Friend, let me lead you by the Hand into the most fruitful and pleasant Garden of God, his Holy Word. I have laid out a good deal of Study upon it, and, with some Care, have observed the several Plants which grow therein; and, with a particular Eye to the Point before us, the *Consequences of the first Transgression*: Which I find are spoken of *certainly* and *plainly* but five times in the whole Bible; namely, twice in the Old and thrice in the New Testament. Many other Places indeed are quoted by Divines, as relating to this Affair, but they are apparently doubtful; no Mention being made in them of *Adam*, or any Effects that his Sin hath upon us. However, the right way of proceeding is, to consider and examine first those Places where the Consequences and Effects of *Adam*'s Sin are *plainly* and *certainly* spoken of; and then we shall be better able to judge of the *doubtful* and *uncertain* Places, to which we shall next turn our Thoughts.

I find no more than five Places in all the Bible where the Consequences of the first Sin are *certainly* spoken of: The first is, *Gen.* ii. 17. The second is, *Gen.* iii. from the 7th verse to the end of the Chapter. The third Place is, in *Rom.* v. 12, to the 20th verse. The fourth Place is, in 1 *Cor.* xv. 21,22. The fifth and last Place is, 1 *Tim.* ii. 14.

The Bible is open to every body, and if any Man can produce more than these five Places where the Consequences of the first Transgression are *plainly* and *certainly* spoken of, it will be easy for every body to see, and I shall be very ready to own, I am mistaken. Of the Consequences of the first Transgression, there is not one *certain* Word spoken from the third Chapter of *Genesis* to the last of *Malachi* in the Old Testament. *David*, *Solomon*, and the *Prophets* say nothing *certain* about them. Our Saviour saith not ONE WORD of them in any of his Doctrines and Instructions, nor any of the Apostles and Writers of the New Testament in their Sermons and Epistles, except the Apostle *Paul*, and he but thrice ...

The Sum of all that we have found is this: *That upon the Sin of* Adam *God subjected him and his Posterity to Sorrow, Labour and Death; from which Death we are delivered, and are restored to Life at the Resurrection, by the Grace of God having Respect to the Righteousness and Obedience of* Christ. *And further more, That God in Christ hath bestowed upon us Mercy and Gifts, Privileges and Advantages, both in this and a future world, abundantly beyond the reversing of any Evils we are subject to in Consequence of* Adam'*s Sin.*

It appeareth therefore, for any thing I can see, that the true Answer to this Question, *How far we are involved in the Consequences of* Adam*'s Sin?* is this: *We are thereby, or thereupon, subjected to temporal Sorrow, Labour and Death.* All which (Thanks be to God for his unspeakable Gift!) are in the Redeemer turned into Great Advantages, as to our present spiritual Improvements; and at length we shall, if obedient to the Son of God, and sanctified by the Methods of Salvation established in him, not only be delivered from them all, but we shall also reign for ever with him in Glory.

But besides these five Places there are many others quoted by Divines as relating to this Affair, tho' in them no mention is made of *Adam*, or of any Effects that his Sin hath upon us. But having been long, and by many, taken in that Sense, they demand our Consideration, and you shall have my Thoughts upon them as Leisure admits. ...

For a Conclusion, give me leave to suggest a few Things worthy of serious Consideration.

Is it not highly injurious to the God of our Nature, whose Hands have fashioned and formed us, to believe our Nature is originally corrupted, and in the worst Sense of Corruption too? And are not such Doctrines, (which represent the Divine Dispensations as unjust, cruel and tyrannical) the Source of those gloomy and blasphemous Thoughts that infest and distract many good and honest Souls? For I am apt to think common Experience will make it good, that the more any study, and persuade themselves of the Truth of such Points, the more they are liable to dreadful, terrifying Apprehensions of the Deity, and the most ugly Thoughts and Injections. ...

Doth not the Doctrine of *Original Sin* teach you to transfer your Wickedness and Sin to a wrong Cause? Whereas in Truth you ought to blame or condemn *yourself alone* for any wicked Lusts, which prevail in your Heart, any evil Habits you have contracted, any sinful Actions you commit, you lay the whole upon *Adam.* ...

What can be more destructive of Virtue than to have a Notion that you must, in some Degree or other, be necessarily vicious? And hath not the common Doctrine of *Original Sin* a manifest Tendency to propagate such a Notion? And is it not to be feared so many Children of good Parents have degenerated, because in the Forms of religious Instruction they have imbibed ill Principles, and such are really are contrary to Holiness? For to represent Sin as *natural*, as altogether *unavoidable*, is to embolden in Sin, and to give not only and Excuse, but a Reason for sinning.

If we believe we are in Nature worse than the BRUTES, and this Doctrine represents us as such, what Wonder if we act worse than BRUTES? The Generality of Christians have embraced this Persuasion. And what Wonder if the Generality of Christians have been the most wicked, lewd, bloody, and treacherous of all Mankind? Certainly nothing generous, great, good, pure can spring from Principles, to say the least, so low and grovelling. ...

Is not this Doctrine hurtful to the Power of Godliness, not only as it filleth Mens Heads with frightful Chimeras, and loads their Consciences with the heaviest Fetters of Error, but also as it diverts their Thoughts from the heavenly and substantial Truths of Religion? As it throws the Method and Means of our Salvation into Perplexity and Confusion, and renders all religious Principles uncertain? We are made Sinners we know not how, and therefore must be sorry for, and repent of, we know not what. We are made Sinners in an arbitrary Way, and we are made Saints in an arbitary Way. But what is arbitrary can be brought under no Rules.

Which Notions are most likely to operate best upon Parents Minds, and most proper to be instilled into a Child? That it is born a Child of Wrath, that it cometh into the World under God's Curse, that its Being, as soon as given, is in the worst and most deplorable State of Corruption? Or, that it is born under the Smiles of Heaven, endowed with noble Capacities, and formed in Love, for the Glory of God and its own Happiness, if his Goodness is not despised and neglected. ...

Lastly, consider seriously, are those that look into the Scriptures, and compare the Doctrines of Men with the pure Word of God, to be blamed or commended? Is it not our Duty to search the Scriptures? It was the Sin of the *Pharisees* and *Jewish Doctors,* that they made the Commandment of God of none Effect by their Traditions; and shall we incur the like Guilt by making the Love and Goodness of God of none Effect by our traditionary Doctrines? What other Way is there of contending for the Faith once delivered to the Saints, but by seeking for it in the Word of God? Do we not blame the *Papists* for their implicit Faith, for believing as the Church believeth? And how are we better than they, if we take up our religious Principles upon Trust, and do not carefully adjust them by the Standard of Divine Revelation? ...

Thus I have, as well as I am able, gone through this useful and important Inquiry. May the Father of Lights illuminate our Understandings! I do not know that I have put a wrong Gloss upon any one Scripture (I am sure I never designed to do so:) nor am I in any Doubt or Uncertainty, at present, in my own Thoughts, about any thing I have advanced. But that is no Proof I am every where right. I make no Pretensions to Infallibility.

THE WORD OF GOD is infallible; and that, not any thing I say or judge, is the common Rule of Faith. And observe, while we love the Truth, and honestly endeavour, as we are able, all our Days to understand what God hath revealed, whether the Knowledge we gain be more or less, we discharge the Duty of good Christians; nor can we be defective in that Faith which is necessary to a righteous and holy Life, and the Acceptance of God. The Word of God is the Rule of Faith: and if I have pointed out the Light shining therein, it is well; you ought to turn your Eyes to THAT LIGHT. But as for me, I am a weak and imperfect Man, and may have said several weak and imperfect Things; and therefore declare, If upon further Examination, or the kind Information of any Person of more Skill and Knowledge, I find myself in any Mistake, I shall be very glad to see, and ready to own it. And if any one undertaketh to give you a better Account of Things, hear him willingly; but give him no Dominion over your Understanding or Conscience. Judge for yourself; weigh coolly and impartially what he advances. And if he convinceth you by Scripture Evidence, that I have taken any thing wrong, you are bound in Conscience and Duty to receive the Truth he discovers, and to reject my Error; but in the Spirit of Christian Love and Peace. And in so doing you will approve yourself to God, and please every honest Man; and among the rest,

Your Friend and Servant,

NORWICH,
Feb. 5. 1735/6

JOHN TAYLOR

* * *

READER,

If in perusing this Book you have discovered any Truth you did not before understand, 'tis my earnest Request, you would rather lay it up in your Heart for your own use, than make it the Subject of Contention and Strife, the Fewel of party Zeal, or the Occasion of despising or censuring those who do not yet see it. And if you should enter into Discourse about it, let it be with Moderation and Coolness on your Part; in the Spirit of Peace and mutual Forbearance. And therefore never converse upon this or any other Point with an *angry* Man; Passion and Heat blind the Judgment: nor with a *Bigot*, who is determined for a Scheme, and resolved to open his Eyes to no further Evidence. And whenever Anger and Bigotry appear in a Conversation already begun, break it off: For you cannot proceed to any good Purpose, and will be in Danger of catching a Spirit which is quite contrary to the Gospel. HOLD THE TRUTH IN LOVE. Fear God, and keep his Commandments; despise earthly Things; restrain and regulate your Passions; be constant in reading the Scriptures, fervent in Prayer to God, kind and compassionate to all Men, punctual and cheerful in ever Duty, humble in all your Deportment, upright and honest in all your Dealings, temperate and sober in all your Enjoyments, patient under all Afflictions, watchful against every Temptation, and zealous in every good Work: And then with Joy look for the coming of our Lord JESUS CHRIST, for he will assuredly appear to your everlasting Salvation.

Document II.14

John Taylor on Scripture Sufficiency

Taylor sketches the way in which Popery constricted the intellectual freedom of Christians, and deeply regrets that a Protestant 'Popery' has sprung up which is intent upon doing precisely the same thing. Against this he appeals to the principle of the sole sufficiency of Scripture (which, it must be granted, has in his hand a distinctly Arian cast). The extract is from the 1829 edition of *A Defence of the Common Rights of Christians*, 1737, pp. 12–16, a work which appeared in the context of the Castle Gate case, the subject of Document II.15 below.

This is ROMISH POPERY: whereby, as Revelation foretold, the Gospel, which is the power of God to promote goodness, love, humility, and benevolence amongst men, is unnaturally turned into an engine of usurpation, pride, tyranny, hatred, malice, and all manner of mischief.

To this sort of Popery our first Reformers, about two hundred years ago, gave a violent shock, by separating from the Church of Rome, casting off the Pope's supremacy and infallibility, translating the Scriptures into the vulgar tongues, and asserting them alone to be the only rule of faith and doctrine. But having been born and educated in the error and superstition of Popery, we cannot suppose, at their first emerging out of that profound darkness, their minds were at once completely illuminated. Many gross errors they rejected, some they retained. But the grand mistake was, after they had drawn schemes of faith from the Scriptures, honestly no doubt, and to the best of their abilities, either they or their followers, as if they had delivered the whole of Scripture truth, without any mixture of error, erected those schemes, though differing very much from one another, into rules to be universally received. The Scriptures were permitted to be read, but only in the sense of those schemes. Any that disputed them were loaded with odious party names, and Christian professors were again led to disparage and hate, to cast out and separate from one another, on account of difference in sentiments; in which yet they could not but differ, seeing that a free and peaceable study of God's Word was not allowed them. In Protestant schools, they that were educated for the ministry were taught the doctrine they were to preach, not from the Holy Scriptures, but from systems of divinity after the model of the Popish school-men, and taken chiefly from them. Their abstract metaphysical notions, terms of art, divisions and distinctions were retained, and still applied to Christian principles. Among Protestants their several creeds and Churches were established by the secular power, and the magistrate required his people to believe after the particular confession or articles he espoused. Subscription to human schemes was demanded; *Convocations* and *Committees for preserving the purity of faith* were erected; men were constituted judges of Scripture doctrine for whole nations and communities, and conscience was again made responsible to earthly tribunals. Worldly emoluments were annexed to a supposed right belief, and heavy penalties inflicted upon recusants.

This is PROTESTANT POPERY; which, though in some respects better than the ROMISH, is yet more inconsistent, because it renounceth infallibility, and yet imposeth and persecuteth as if infallible; rejected human authority, and yet in many cases pleadeth and resteth upon it; lastly, permitteth the Scriptures to be read, but not understood; or, which is all one, to be understood only in the sense of schemes formed and established by men.

... Within the last twenty years, since the confirmation of LIBERTY by the accession of the present Royal Family, greater freedom of inquiry hath been used, and many among us have generously declared for it; while others, tenacious of the received opinions, as stiffly opposed it. Hereupon some few congregations have divided; some ministers that could not fall in with common schemes, have been cast out as unfit to officiate in the sacred office, though otherwise men of the first accomplishments and characters.

This is DISSENTING POPERY; – for Popery is not mere error, seeing the best of Protestants may be in error more or less; but Popery is *human infallibility and persecution*, wherever they are found, whether among Papists, Protestants, or Dissenters. *Human infallibility* is making the judgement or writings of any man, or body of men, since the Apostles' days, the rule of Christian faith, not to be doubted, questioned, or departed from. *Persecution* is any degree of hatred, or any kind of injury done to those who differ from us in religious sentiments. And if *human infallibility* and *persecution* are found among Protestants in general, and Dissenters in particular, it is true, they so far retain a species of Popery, as they ground their faith upon human schemes, and hate or injure those that reject them. An instance of both these antichristian principles you have in the case of Mr. Rawson; wherein you find a Dissenting minister openly avowing and acting upon them.

Document II.15

The Castle Gate Case

The Congregationalists of Castle Gate church, Nottingham, were among those in the eighteenth century who fended off a heterodox challenge from within. This well-documented case furnishes us with an example of Independent church discipline at work. James Sloss arrived as minister of Castle Gate in 1733, and at once discovered that the Arian trends at work within the neighbouring High Pavement Church were affecting some of his own members also, hence extract (a) concerning Sloss's orthodox lectures. Joseph Rawson fell under suspicion of Arianism and was questioned about his views on a number of occasions: extracts (b) and (c). Sloss accused him of associating with heretics, and challenged him with test questions. At last Sloss pronounced the sentence of excommunication upon Rawson: extract (d). These extracts come respectively from the Castle Gate Church Book, February 1734, 25 May 1736, and two for 9 July 1736. John Taylor of Norwich rose in defence of Rawson with his *A Narrative of Mr. Joseph Rawson's Case*, 1742, from the Prefatory Discourse of which extract (e) is taken. Extract (f) is from Sloss's reply, *True Narrative of the Case of Joseph Rawson*, 1738, p. 2 (which in turn prompted Taylor's *A Further Defence of the Common Rights of Christians*, 1738); and extract (g), a Church Book entry for 28 December 1739, records the church's action in relation to High Pavement Church.

For Sloss (1698–1772) see *Derby Mercury*, 17 May 1772; A. R. Henderson, *History of Castle Gate Congregational Church*, London: James Clarke, 1905, pp. 140–50; Benjamin Carpenter, *Some Account of the Original Introduction of Presbyterianism in Nottingham and the Neighbourhood; With a Brief History of the Society of Protestant Dissenters assembling of the High Pavement in that Town*. [1852].

(a)
[S]ubscriptions were collected for a lecture on Sabbath evenings once a fortnight, to be continued for one year, to vindicate the doctrine of the Trinity and the proper Divinity of our Lord Jesus Christ and the Holy Ghost, and to promote serious godliness in the youth of this day ...

(b)

Some time was spent in prayer and humiliation, to ask direction of God how to proceed about Mr. Joseph Rawson, a member with us, who was suspected of having imbibed the Arian notion, and denying the Supreme Deity of Jesus Christ.

(c)

This congregations being informed that Joseph Rawson, one of their number, departing from the faith, was generally reputed to have drank in the Arian heresy, and some of our members, having conversed with him privately, and not being satisfied with the way he delivered himself upon the subject of the Trinity, and considering how much that dangerous error prevails in this place, to the great dishonour of Christianity in generally, and the Dissenting interest in particular, and how fatal it might prove to this congregation if it should get any footing amongst us, therefore we judge ourselves bound in conscience for the glory of God the Redeemer, and the preservation of the purity of this Church, to put a timely stop to that infection. And for that purpose did appoint some of our number to converse with the said Joseph Rawson concerning the Divinity of our Lord Jesus Christ; who reported that they did not receive that satisfaction that they could have wishes. Whereupon they appointed others to inquire into his sentiments; who also conversed with him again and again on the same subject, and put several questions to him. But in his answers he increased their suspicions more and more; which being reported to the Church, they found themselves obliged to call him before themselves. And upon his appearing before them, he treated the Church in a most insolent manner, altogether unbecoming the spirit of Christianity, and denied their authority to inquire into his sentiments.

(d)

I do in the name of our Lord Jesus Christ debar you, Joseph Rawson, from all sealing ordinances with us, and excommunicate you from all Christian communion with our Church and fellowship, and deliver you over to Satan for the destruction of the flesh that you may learn not to blaspheme, and that your spirit may be saved in the Day of the Lord Jesus.

(e)

Infallibility and *Persecution* are widely remote from the Principles of Dissenters as such; and this Narrative is published, not to expose Mr. *S.* or his Congregation, much less to disparage the Dissenting Cause, but to vindicated and guard it, by holding up this Case before their Eyes, that they may see how much such Practices are a Contradiction to their Profession and avowed Principles, how odious in themselves, and how injurious to true Religion; that unwary Minds may not be deceived into the worst of Crimes, and that this Spirit may not spread among us to our Ruin. ... To what Purpose is our boasted Liberty, if we dare not use it? To what Purpose do we enjoy the Light, if we may not open our Eyes to it? To what Purpose the Word of God, if we must not seek for its real and genuine Sense; but must be tied to the Dictates and Sentiments of any Divines that have been or now are? How can we, without the grossest Inconsistency, pray in our publick Assemblies, *that the*

Reformation may be carried on to still greater Degrees of Perfection; if in our Practice we defeat the very Blessing we desire? What Advantage hath the Dissenter, if not to reform, without the Formalities and Delays of human Laws and Edicts, whatever shall be discovered to be at any Time, or in any Respect, wrong in his Scheme? Why doth he reject human Impositions in one Way, if he tamely submits to them in another? Our Forefathers rejected what they thought was of human Invention; and what we find to be so that escaped them, we, upon their Principles are to reject; otherwise we only exchange one kind of Bondage for another, and while we refuse Establishments by Law, we shall come under the no less grievous Establishments of Custom.

And if this Spirit is let loose among us, what Ravages will it make in Congregations? What Fires will it kindle? What Animosities, Contentions and Divisions will it create? How will it lay waste Peace and Love, and Brotherly-kindness, the grand virtues of the Gospel; go on to spread Deism and make Christianity, through the false Principles, and inhuman Practices of Christians, the Scorn and Detestation of the World? Thus the very Men, who profess great Zeal for reviving the Power of Religion, will be found the greatest Obstructers of it.

How different from this, how amiable, happy and honourable is the Spirit of the Gospel, Peace, Love, Meekness, Gentleness, Goodness, mutual Forbearance, candid Allowance for Infirmity and Mistake, an honest Endeavour to promote Knowledge, impartial Study and Search of the Scriptures, free Communication and ready Admittance of what is found in them? These are the Virtues which make us truly Christian; thus we shall grow up into Christ in all Things; thus our Hearts, and in time our Heads too, will be united, as far as the present State of Things will admit; thus Religion will flourish and shine with a charming Lustre in the Eyes of the World.

If the Dissenters stand firm in Liberty and Love; if they lift themselves under no other Head and Leader but Christ alone; if they refuse all Party-Schemes, and stand upon the single Basis of universal Christianity; if they allow the free Study of the Bible, and encourage the Labours of their honest and learned men; if they are stedfastly determined to establish their Faith, Practice, and Worship, upon the Word of God alone, as it shall from time to time be made known unto them; and upon this Bottom, and no other, have true Affection to one another, and to all Men; then they will act up to their own true Principles; And tho' they may not be able at once to bring the whole Body of Truth out of Revelation, yet the Day will shine still brighter upon them; and their Cause, thus set upon its proper Basis, will stand, nor shall the Gates of Hell prevail against it. But if ever they abandon *Liberty* and *Love*; if they stiffly adhere to Party-Names and Schemes; if they set Bounds to Scripture-Knowledge, and presumptuously say, *Hither shalt thou go, and no further*; if they discourage the Honest and Learned, that would throw in more Light and Truth among them, they will become weak, and waste, and dwindle into nothing.

(f)
It is well known that there are, in the congregation that meet in Castle Gate, Presbyterians, Independents, Baptists, and others who sit down together in Christian fellowship with a becoming Christian love and charity, notwithstanding any differenc

there may be in their judgment about smaller matters; and it is a fixed principle with our society, as we think it ought to be with all Christians, to receive those whom, in the judgment of a true Christian charity, we have reason to believe Christ has received, though they may differ from us in some things that do not affect the essentials of Christianity. But where there is a going off the foundation, as we reckon there is when Emmanuel, the true Supreme God in our nature, is not believed in, then we openly profess before the world that, in that case, we believe there is no foundation for a Christian communion, because the communion of Christians is founded on the union with one Head; and therefore when *one* professes faith in, and union with Emmanuel, the true Christ, and *another* in a super-angelic being, united to a body of human shape, such, differing so widely in the Person who is the object of their faith, in the nature of the thing, cannot have communion together; because the foundation thereof is cut off, to wit, union with the true Christ as a common Head, the only bond and living spring of union among Christians.

(g)
Resolved that no person be received from the High Pavement congregation as a member of this congregation without giving in their experience, unless they have been received members of that Church before the Rev. Mr. Hewes left that congregation.

Document II.16

Joseph Priestley on the Importance of Free Enquiry in Religion

This extract is from *The Importance and Extent of Free Inquiry in Matters of Religion: A Sermon, Preached before the Congregations of the Old and New Meeting of Protestant Dissenters, at Birmingham, November 5, 1785*, 1785; in Priestley's *Works*, ed. J. T. Rutt, 25 vols, London, 1817–31, XV, pp. 73–5.
    For Priestley see Document II.11 above.

As new errors and mistakes are continually arising, it is of importance that these be corrected, even to keep the ground that we have already got; and it may well be presumed that the great corruption in doctrine, discipline and worship which began in the very age of the apostles, and which kept advancing for the space of near fourteen hundred years afterwards, may furnish matter for the laborious and spirited inquiries of a later period than ours. We have seen, indeed, the *dawn* of a reformation, but much remains to the light of *perfect day*; and there is nothing that we can now allege as a plea for discontinuing our researches, that might not have been said with equal plausibility at the time by *Wickliffe*, by *Luther*, or by later reformers, who stopped far short of the progress which you who now hear me have made. We think that they all left the Reformation very imperfect, and why may not our posterity think the same concerning us? What peculiar right have we to say to the spirit of reformation, *So far shalt thou go and no farther*.

Luther and *Calvin* reformed many abuses, especially in the discipline of the church, and also some gross corruptions in doctrine; but they left other things, of far greater moment, just as they found them. They disclaimed the worship of Jesus Christ, which led the way to it, which had the same origin, and which is an equal infringement of the honour due to the supreme God, who has declared that he will not give his glory to another. Nay, the authority of the names of those reformers who did not see this and other great errors, now serves to strengthen and confirm them; for those doctrines of original sin, predestination, atonement, and the divinity of Christ, which deserve to be numbered among the grossest of all errors, are even often distinguished by the appellation of *the doctrines of the Reformation*, merely because they were not reformed by those who have got the name of *the reformers*; as if no others could have a right to it but themselves; whereas, excepting the doctrine of *atonement*, (which, in its full extent, was an error that originated with the reformers themselves, who were led into it by an immoderate opposition to the popish doctrine of merit,) they are, in fact, the doctrines of the Church of *Rome*, which *Luther* and *Calvin* left just as they found.

It was great merit in them to go so far as they did, and it is not *they*, but *we* who are to blame, if their authority induce us to go no farther. We should rather imitate them in the boldness and spirit with which they called in question, and rectified, so many long-established errors; and, availing ourselves of their labours, make farther progress than they were able to do. Little reason have we to allege their name, authority, and example, when they did a great deal, and we do nothing at all. In this, we are not imitating *them*, but those who opposed and counteracted them, willing to keep things as they were, among whom were many excellent characters, who apprehensions at that day were the very same with those of many very good and quiet persons at present, viz. the fear of *moving foundations*, and overturning Christianity itself. Their fears, we are now all sensible, were groundless, and why may not those of the present age be so too?

Dissenters, who have no creeds dictated to them by any civil governors, have, nevertheless, at this day, no less need of such admonitions as these than members of established churches, because they may have acquired as blind an attachment to the systems in which they were educated as the members of any establishment whatever, and may be as averse to any farther improvement. Indeed a similar temper is necessarily produced in similar circumstances, which human nature is the same in us all; and, therefore, a person educated a Dissenter may be as much *a bigot* as any person educated a Churchman, or a Papist; and if he now be what he was brought up to, the probability certainly is, that had he been educated differently, his prejudices would have been no less strong, though entirely different; so that the rigid Dissenter would have been as rigid a Papist or a Churchman.

No person whose opinions are not the result of his own serious inquiry can have a right to say that he is a Dissenter, or any thing else, *on principle*; and no man can be absolutely sure of this whose present opinions are the same with those he was taught, though he may think, and be right in thinking, that he sees sufficient reason for them, and retains them on conviction. This, however, is all that can be expected of any man; for it would be most absurd for a man to adopt new opinions, opinions entertained by no person besides himself, merely for the sake of proving that he has actually thought for himself. But still, thinking as others have thought, and for reasons which others have given, is no *proof* of a man having thought for himself, and therefore will not authorize his censuring of others. Such a person *may* have the true spirit of inquiry, he may have exerted it, and have found the truth; but he is incapable of giving that satisfactory *evidence* of it which can be given by one whose present sentiments are different from those in which he was educated, and which he could not have learned but from his own researches.

How few, then, of those of you who were educated Dissenters can have a right to say that you would have been Dissenters if you had *not* been so educated! It is more than I would presume to say concerning myself. If those persons who now dislike the spirit of innovation were to go back in history, and place themselves in every age of reformation, still censuring that spirit which always gave offence in its day, (being always the rebellion of *a few* against the authority of *the many*,) they could not stop till they came to the Heathenism of our barbarous ancestors; for it was the bold spirit of inquiry that made them Christians.

Let all those who acquiesce in any system in which they were educated, or which they have learned from others, consider that, in censuring more modern innovators, they are censuring the *spirit* and *example* of the very persons whose opinions they have adopted, and of whose name they make their boast; and that if it had not been for that very spirit which they now censure, only exerted a century or two ago, their own opinions would have been very different from what they now are. They ought, therefore, to respect the *principle*, even though it should lead some into error. If the spirit of inquiry that carries some to *Socinianism* be wrong, that which carries others to *Arianism* is no less so; and if *Arminius* is to be condemned for abandoning the doctrine of Calvin, *Calvin* himself must be condemned for abandoning the doctrines of Popery.

Document II.17

Joseph Priestley's Doctrinal Stance

This extract is from Priestley's *Letter to the Inhabitants of Northumberland*, of 1 November 1799, reprinted in his *Works*, ed. J. T. Rutt, 25 vols, London, 1817–31, XXV, pp. 143–6.

For Priestley see Document I.11 above.

MY FRIENDS AND NEIGHBOURS,

Mr. COBBETT calls me sometimes an *Unitarian*, sometimes a *Deist*, sometimes an *Atheist*, and always a *hypocrite*. And a great hypocrite I must, indeed, be, if, in reality, I do not believe in the being of a God, or in the truth of Christianity, when I have written more in defence of those articles of faith than any other man now living, or almost that ever did live, and have officiated as a Christian minister more than forty years.

I must also have a greater want of common sense than he ascribes to me, to maintain opinions so inconsistent with one another as those above-mentioned. An Atheist acknowledges no God, and no future state; Deists acknowledge the former, but few of them the latter, and they believe in no revelation; whereas Unitarians deny, indeed, a trinity in God, but they believe in one God, the Father, and in the divine mission of Christ. They believe that he worked miracles by the power of God, that God raised him from the dead, and that he will come again to raise all the dead, and judge all the world. The same man cannot, therefore, be at the same time an *Atheist*, a *Deist*, and an *Unitarian*. If I be a *hypocrite*, in pretending only to be no Atheist or Deist, while, in reality, I am either the one or the other, what have I got by my hypocrisy? When, though I have been a preacher, as I have observed, more than forty years, my profession has never yielded me half a maintenance; and here I get nothing at all by it. Men are not at the trouble of acting the hypocrite, and especially for so long a time, for nothing.

It is true that I do not join in the public worship of this place; but it is because I cannot join in your devotions, which are altogether Trinitarian, as they ought to be while you are Trinitarians. For it would be absurd to acknowledge Christ to be God, and not to render him the honours of divinity by praying to him as an omnipresent and omnipotent Being, the maker and constant preserver of all things. But though I do not worship with you, I have divine service every Lord's-day in my own house, which is then open to every body, and where several of you occasionally attend. Now did any of you ever hear me preach anything like Atheism or Deism, or indeed any thing contrary to your own opinions? And when you have heard me pray, could not you join me in every word I said? If you be Christians at all, I am confident you always might. It never was my custom to preach on the controverted subjects of religion, or only on particular occasions. These I discuss in my publications, in which you may see what my opinions on those subjects are, and the arguments I have to advance in support of them.

Had I been permitted to officiate in either of your meeting-houses (which I should have done *gratis*, thankful for such an opportunity of being useful among you), you would never have heard from me any thing but the principles of our common Christianity. And this will furnish topics of discourse in great abundance, and such as are of far greater importance than all the things about which we differ. The substantial duties of the Christian life, to inculcate which is, or ought to be, the great end of all our preaching, are the same on all our principles; and do I in my preaching (and I hope I may add in my practice) contradict any of these?

We all agree in acknowledging the same books of scripture and we profess to derive our faith from them, though we interpret them differently. This, surely, is not Atheism or Deism. If I do not believe the Divinity of Christ, it is because I do not believe it to be the doctrine of the Scriptures, and because I cannot help thinking, that if Christ, and also the Holy Spirit, be possessed of all the attributes of divinity, equally with God the Father, there must be three Gods, and not one only, which the Scriptures assert, and on which they lay the greatest stress. In this you will not agree with me; being of opinion that, in some sense or other, three may be one, and one three. But you will not say that, because I am not a Trinitarian, I am an Atheist or a Deist.

You do not call the Jews Atheists or Deists, because they do not believe the divinity of Moses, or of the Messiah whom they expect. They believe that Moses delivered to them the laws and commands of God; and therefore they respect them as much as if they had all come from the mouth of God himself. I do the same with respect to all that Christ, speaking in the name of God, has delivered to us. He has repeatedly said, (*John* vii. 16, xiv. 24,) that the words which he spake were not his own, but the Father's who sent him; that the Father who was in him, or with him, worked the miracles which proved his divine mission, (*John* xiv. 10,) for that of himself he could 'do nothing'. (*John* v. 30.) The Apostle Peter calls Christ 'a man approved of God by signs and wonders which God did by him'. (*Acts* ii. 22.) And the Apostle Paul says, (1 *Cor.* viii. 6, 1 *Tim* ii. 5,) 'To us there is one God, one Father; and one Mediator beween God and men, the man Christ Jesus'.

But though I think the clear sense of scripture, such as is intelligible to the meanest capacity, is on my side, I can easily suppose that you see things in a very different light, and that you are as conscientious in differing from me as I am in differing from you. I, no doubt, wish that you could come to think as I do, on these subjects, as you do with respect to me. This is unavoidable in us both, if we lay any stress on our opinions, and have any good-will for one another. But I do not obtrude my opinions upon you, or offend you with disputation. Few of you have ever heard me mention the subject of our differences with respect to religion, and then the occasion has never been sought by me. I do not condemn those who act otherwise, but my habits are different; and though I have no less zeal, I take a different method of propagating my principles. I have seldom seen any good produced by disputing, in conversation. It too often tends to irritate; and though men are often silenced in this way, they are seldom convinced. But because I am not always talking about religion, do you suppose, Mr. Cobbett, that I have none?

Mr. Adams, your President, is unquestionably a religious man, and on this account, as well as on many others, I greatly respect him. He knows me well; and do you think he would have attended me constantly, as he did, when I delivered my first set of Discourses in Philadelphia, and have consented that I should dedicate them to him, if he had known or suspected me to be an Atheist or Deist, and consequently a hypocrite? He entertains no doubt of my being a sincere Christian, though our opinions may not be exactly the same.

I wish we had all more religion than we have. We should then think more of another world, and make less account of this, and of all things in it, than we do now. It would give us an habitual regard to God, and his providence, respecting both individuals and societies of mankind, and especially the great and interesting events which are now taking place in the old world. Firmly believing that a wise and good Providence superintends all events, and will bring good out of all evil, so that the final issue of the most calamitous events will be glorious and happy, we shall view them as they pass before us, not without interest, but with more tranquillity, and without ill-will towards any part of the human race, even our personal or national enemies.

Whatever you may think in the prime of life, while your spirits are high and your prospects good, the value of religion at my time of life is beyond all estimation.

Without such prospects as religion sets before us, the evening of life would be cheerless and gloomy, but with them it is most serene and happy; far more so than any preceding period. I am far, I assure you, from wishing to be young again, though I enjoyed that part of life as much as any of you can do.

On this account I regard unbelievers at the close of life with much compassion. And late converts, and nominal Christians, who give little attention to the subject, are not much better. It requires time before the principles of Christianity can be of much use in this respect. An habitual attention must be given to them, so that in every intermission of necessary business they shall, even without any effort, be uppermost in a man's thoughts, affording relief under all his troubles and cares. This state of mind cannot, in the natural course of things, be acquired in a short time. In this respect faith is a different thing from mere conviction, and admits of degrees, giving consolation and joy in proportion to its strength.

Atheist or Deist as I may be considered, and attached as I am to philosophical pursuits, my chief satisfactions are derived from the daily study of the Scriptures, and reflections on the momentous subjects that are there proposed to us. Religion is the only effectual support under all the troubles of life, (and in saying this you know that I may speak from experience,) as well as in the hour of death. It also tends to make men less ambitious, and to allay the heat of party spirit, which is too often the bane of a good neighbourhood, and separates those who would otherwise be happy in a pleasing and beneficial intercourse. If nations, or their governors, were really Christians, all mankind would live in peace and friendship with one another.

Call this a sermon if you please, and let Mr. Cobbett call it cant and hypocrisy. Only believe me to be, notwithstanding every difference of opinion, religious or political,

My Friends and Neighbours,
Your sincere well-wisher,
JOSEPH PRIESTLEY.

Northumberland, Nov. 1, 1799.

Document II.18

The Dismissal of an Anti-Trinitarian

Some members having already left the Independent Church at Billericay, Essex, the minister, Richard Fry, was invited to make a statement of his beliefs before the whole congregation. This he did on 5 September 1798. At the ensuing meeting 26 members and 25 subscribing non-members voted against Fry, 2 members and 19 subscribing non-members voted for him. John Mabbs, the senior deacon, then wrote the following letter to Fry on 28 September 1798, and a breach ensued.

The letter is quoted by William Taylor, *Calling the Generations: A History of the Independent Protestant Dissenters of Billericay (1672 – 1972)*, n.d., p. 27.

We are convinced it is our indispensable duty and we are come to a determination to be looking for another pastor, and hope that our particular situation will be thought a sufficient excuse for our fixing so short a time as Sunday the 7th October 1798 for the last time of your preaching in our pulpit. But encouraged by your declaration of submitting to our decisions and desirous of testifying our esteem for you and concern for the inconvenience you may experience, we shall request your acceptance of six months' salary from us.

Document II.19

Reluctance to Own the Name 'Unitarian'

It was not until 21 July 1813 that 'An Act to relieve persons who impugn the doctrine of the Trinity from certain penalties' found its way to the statute books (53 George III, c.160). Previously, profession of Unitarianism in England and Wales was punishable by loss of citizenship and imprisonment. However, not all liberal Dissenters favoured the new name. Older Arians did not, and neither did those who wished their views to permeate a number of denominations rather than become the 'creed' of one. In the following extract Henry Solly (1813–1903), who was raised in Marsh Street Congregational Church, Walthamstow (but became a General Baptist/Unitarian minister) looks back to his childhood, when heterodox opinions were being proclaimed in the chapel.

The extract is taken from H. Solly, *These Eighty Year's, or, The Story of an Unfinished Life*, London: Simpkin, Marshall, 2 vols, 1893, I, pp. 54–5. See also DNB *Missing Persons*.

My father and mother were in the habit of attending public worship regularly every Sunday, twice a day, morning and afternoon, at the New Gravel Pit Chapel (where Dr. Priestly officiated for a time) while they were living at Homerton and Clapton; and subsequently at the 'Old Meeting', Marsh Street, Walthamstow, after they came to live at Leyton. As children, we were all brought up to attend 'Meeting' with our parents, my little sister and I for years trotting backwards and forwards up Capworth Street (pronounced Capper) and along Hoe Street, both of which were then, for the most part, pretty green lanes, and sometimes over Mark-House Common, a pleasing variety in the route. At that 'Old Meeting' House the Rev. Benjamin Fawcett preached splendid sermons in the morning to about fifty people, which he repeated in the evening at the English Presbyterian Chapel in the Old Jewry, to about 500. The Rev. Eleazer Cogan, the schoolmaster of Higham Hill (whom my father had brought from Cheshunt, and established in those two-fold offices), conducted Divine Service there for many years. He was followed, on resigning his ministerial duties, by the late Dr. Hutton, afterwards of Leeds, and of Carter Lane, London. At one time, so great were the number of carriages bringing the surrounding gentry to worship in that humble four-square edifice, that two new stepping stones were erected in the court-yard, at which the occupants of those vehicles could alight instead of having to wait till there was room for them at the front door. These were shown to me, as a boy, moss-grown with age, as a proof of the former glories of the 'Old Meeting'. For about the year 1780 a great secession took place in consequence of theological differences, the minority swarming off into a new hive lower lower down the street, called the 'New Meeting', the congregation of which gradually increased in numbers as, during the succeeding half-century it declined in our own. One circumstance connected with this 'Old Meeting' – which struck me as a child, with some amount of wonder – took place whenever our carriage was required to convey us to 'Meeting'. For at the conclusion of the hymn following the sermon, the coachman and footman, who sat in the gallery, always got up and went out (missing the last prayer and benediction), to get the horses and carriage ready that the master and mistress might not have to wait. Some audacious questionings, I believe, which however I scarcely dared to propound openly, arose in my mind as to the relative importance of religion to the coachman and footman compared with their 'betters'. During the half century just referred to, heterodox doctrines, more or less of the Unitarian description, were held by the ministers who occupied this Walthamstow pulpit, although controversial or even doctrinal preaching was seldom or never heard within its walls, which, indeed, was a characteristic of almost all the old English Presbyterian congregations in the Southern portion of the kingdom. The sermons, in fact, were chiefly, as far as I can judge from various printed volumes, expositions of practical morality of a very superior character, often eloquent, and of inestimable value, especially to young people; but certainly not deeply imbued with that evangelical Christian spirit which marks the writings of the later Unitarians, such as Dr. Channing, Henry Ware, Dr. Martineau, the Rev. Hamilton Thom, Dr. Sadler, and the Rev. Charles Wickstead. My grandfather and grandmother Solly had an extreme dislike, as I have heard my father say, to the name 'Unitarian'; and though my father and mother were somewhat reconciled to it, by their friendship and esteem for Dr. Priestly, they would not have tolerated for a moment the 'Old Meeting' in Marsh Street being called a Unitarian Chapel.

Document II.20

The Uncompromising Unitarianism of Thomas Belsham

Thomas Belsham (1750–1829) was educated under John Aikin at Kibworth Academy, then at Wellingborough and Ware, and finally at Daventry under Caleb Ashworth, where in 1768 he became a member of the Independent Church. He continued at Daventry as a tutor until he was called to Angel Street Church, Worcester, in 1778. IN 1781 he returned to the academy in Daventry, resigning in 1789 consequent upon his adopting Unitarian views. He proceeded in the following year to the new liberal academy at Hackney, where Priestley was lecturing, and in 1794, when Priestley left for America, he assumed the charge of Gravel Pit Chapel. In 1796 the college closed, and he continued to take private pupils. In 1805 he accepted the pastorate of Essex Street Chapel. In the following passage he distinguishes between the older Arians and the new Unitarians.

For Belsham see DNB; Alexander Gordon, *Addresses Biographical and Historical,* London: The Lindsey Press, 1922. Like Belsham, Carpenter (1752–1816) was educated at Daventry under Caleb Ashworth. The following extract is from *Letters upon Arianism, and other Topics in Metaphysics and Theology, in Reply to the Lectures of the Rev. Benjamin Carpenter,* 1803, pp. 25–8.

My friend designates the body of christians who assert the proper humanity of Jesus Christ by the name of Socinians, at the same time professing, (p. 42) that 'he does not use the word as a term of reproach'. We, however, do not answer to that name, nor do we approve of being distinguished by it. In the first place, because the doctrine we hold is not borrowed from Socinus, but is known and universally allowed to have been coeval with the apostles. And, further, we differ very materially from the opinions of that very great and good man, and his immediate followers, who strangely imagined that Christ, though a human being, was advanced by God to the government of the whole created universe, and was the proper object of religious worship. It is the part of candour to give to every party and denomination of Christians the appellation which they themselves prefer: though not perhaps in every respect strictly appropriate. We call ourselves Unitarians, or, to distinguish ourselves from other classes of christians who assume that name, proper, or original Unitarians; and we regard ourselves as entitled to this distinction from prescription, from the reason of the thing, and now from the custom of the language. *Quem penes arbitrium est, et jus, et norma loquendi.*

My worthy friend and our Arian brethren in general, dispute our exclusive claim to this distinction, and I have often been disposed to smile when I have seen how dexterously they elude the arguments of their opponents against the Arian doctrine, by raising a cloud of dust about a verbal question which has no connection with the main point in dispute. In the present stage of the controversy it is incumbent upon the learned Arians to shew that the doctrine of a created Logos occupying the place of a human soul in the body of Christ had any existence before the fourth century: or to explain how the universal church for three complete centuries could remain in total ignorance of the person of its founder. Instead of which, till my friend's book appeared, we have heard nothing from the Arians for the last twenty years but lugubrious complaints against the Unitarians for appropriating to themselves that honourable name. Indeed, I have myself been pretty much schooled upon the subject, as if I had invented and propagated an invidious distinction, though I have done nothing more than taken up the word as I found it, and used it uniformly in the sense which appeared to me the most proper, leaving to others the option of using it in whatever sense they think fit. I admire the policy of our Arian brethren, and to do them justice, I must own that they have in some measure succeeded amongst persons who attend more to sound than sense, in bringing a degree of odium upon a cause which they could not easily refute. I rejoice however that Unitarianism is become an honourable distinction, and I sincerely wish that our Arian brethren might become Unitarians, not in name and in word only, but in deed and in truth. In the mean time I will take leave to state the grounds upon which I think that the assertors of the proper humanity of Jesus Christ are exclusively entitled to the destinction of Unitarians.

New Religious Movements

Document II.21

The Moravians

Under the impact of the revival of 1727, the Moravians were reorganised by Count Nikolaus Ludwig Graf von Zinzendorf (1700–60) on his German estates. Persecuted in the Roman Catholic territories of south Germany, they became a world-wide diaspora. Some came to England and Wales, where a number of them became involved in the Evangelical Revival.

For Zinzendorf see BCE, DEB, DH, ODCC; A. J. Lewis, *Zinzendorf the Ecumenical Pioneer*, London: SCM Press, 1962; A. G. Spangenberg, *The Life of Nicholas Lewis Count Zinzendorf*, Engl. trans., 1838; J. R. Weinlick, *Count Zinzendorf*, Nashville, TN: Abingdon Press, 1956.

Extract (a) comes from the preface to John Cennick's *Sacred Hymns for the Children of God*, 1741, part 1. For Cennick (1718–55), a Moravian missionary in the West Country, see DEB, DH, DNB; J.E. Hutton, *John Cennick: A Sketch*, London: Moravian Publication Office, 1906; V.W. Couillard, *The Theology of John Cennick*, Nazareth, PA, 1957.

In his letter to Philip Doddridge of 29 December 1746 (extract (b); Bedfordshire Record Office, MO/561), Andrew Parminter, a young man with his heart strangely warmed, does not hesitate to query the Christian standing of one of the most distinguished divines of the day.

Extract (c) is a letter of Johannes Loretz to Benjamin La Trobe of 27 November 1785; (d) is La Trobe's reply of 6 January 1786 (Herrnhut MSS R 13, A 43, both reproduced in W. G. Addison, *The Renewed Church of the United Brethren*, London: SPCK, 1932, pp. 198–200). The letters clearly indicate the dilemma facing the Moravians. On the one hand their Germanic discipline (in a Moravian community like Fulneck the compulsory habits were so designed as to make it impossible to distinguish a brother from a sister), their long liturgical services – possibly a reflection of German court ritual – and their memories of persecution set them apart from those around them; on the other hand the easy-going British government in 1749 allowed them to settle here as 'an ancient Episcopal church'. How should they respond? How should they define themselves in relation to the Church of England and the Methodists? The latter seemed to the Moravians most irregular, and it is interesting to see the conformist Charles Wesley being played off against his wayward brother John. Such issues had been debated in their Synods of 1754, the upshot of which was that the Moravians' evangelistic thrust was blunted.

For Benjamin La Trobe (1728–86), General Superintendent of the English Moravians, see DEB. Johannes Loretz was a Moravian missionary who had travelled all over the world. See J. Taylor Hamilton and Kenneth G. Hamilton, *History of the Moravian Church*, 2nd edn, Bethlehem, PA: Interprovincial Board of Christian Education, Moravian Church of America, 1983; Colin Podmore, *The Moravian Church in England,*

1728–1760, Oxford: Clarendon Press, 1998; J. C. S. Mason, *The Moravian Church and the Missionary Awakening in England 1760–1800*, Woodbridge: The Boydell Press, 2001.

The bibliography of John Wesley (1703–91), founder of Arminian Methodism, is vast. See BCE, DEB, DECBP, DH, DNB, ODCC; and among modern studies, Richard P. Heitzenrater, *The Elusive Mr. Wesley*, 2 vols, Nashville, TN: Abingdon Press, 1984; Henry D. Rack, *Reasonable Enthusiast*, London: Epworth Press, 3rd edn. 2002. For Charles Wesley (1707–88) see DEB, DH, DNB, ODCC; F. Baker, *Charles Wesley as Revealed by His Letters*, London: Epworth, 1948, S. T. Kimbrough, Jr., ed., *Charles Wesley, Poet and Theologian*, Nashville: Abingdon/Kingswood, 1992.

John Wesley's letter to Benjamin Ingham of 8 September 1746 (extract (e); John Telford, ed., *The Letters of Rev. John Wesley, A.M.*, London: Epworth Press, 1931, II, p. 80f.) reminds us that in the early days Methodists and Moravians had been very close. But at a crucial period the latter were affected by an exaggerated, pietistic, Quaker-like doctrine of 'stillness', a total passivity which prompted Wesley to reject them.

For Benjamin Ingham (1712–72) see DEB, DNB; D.F. Clarke, 'Benjamin Ingham (1712–1772), with Special Reference to His Relations with the Churches … ', unpublished M. Phil. dissertation, University of Leeds, 1971; R.P. Heitzenrater, *Diary of an Oxford Methodist*, Durham, NC: Duke University Press, 1985; H.M. Pickles, *Benjamin Ingham: Preacher amongst the Dales of Yorkshire, the Forests of Lancashire, and the Fells of Cumbria*, published by the author, 1995; R.W. Thompson, *Benjamin Ingham and the Inghamites*, Kendal, 1958.

(a)

I here (in Bristol) spent my time till Thursday, as far as I had power, in waiting upon God; when I was asked by some to go to Kingswood, to hear a young man read a sermon to the colliers. I readily consented, having been desirous of seeing the people of that place a long time.

When we were come to the place (which was under a sycamore tree near the intended school) we waited some time amongst the colliers, who were seriously attending round the tree, in number about four or five hundred, till the young man should come. But while he delayed beyond the appointed time, a gentlewoman of St Philip's-plain, and a young man who came with us, desired me either to read a sermon or expound a chapter. I had no power to refuse or gainsay; and though I was naturally fearful of speaking before company, having never done such a thing, yet so much was I pressed in spirit to testify the salvation of Jesus to the people, that I fell on my knees, and besought the Lord to be with me in the work, and prevent me if His Majesty were offended.

Scarcely had we ended prayer, when the young man came who was to read; and though he was urged to begin by many friends, yet he would not consent, but intreated, if I were inclined, to expound. Yet after all this I was afraid, lest the Lord should not teach me what to say. Again I prayed, and finding great freedom, I then tarried no longer, but rose up and went to the congregation, the Lord bearing witness with my word, insomuch that many believed in that hour.

On Friday I again expounded a part of St James's Epistle at White Hill, about a mile distant from the school, where many behaved in the most devout way I had ever seen. Tears fell from many eyes; and when we had joined in singing a hymn we parted, and were brought on our way home by several of the colliers.

(b)

I wish Dear Sir your heart was inclined to give up yourself as a poor sinner among mankind, to the light and Salvation of Christ alone, and that you would become a fool for his sake, and that you might be convinced of the real Redemption and happiness that there is in his wounds. You would then find that our Saviour could teach more to a simple believing sinner's Heart in a few days or hours than all the reasoning and studies of the wisest Heads could ever penetrate.

(c)

The beginning of the present awakening was in the Established Church, the few orthodox dissenting congregations were at that time sunk into mere systematic laodicean religion and were the greatest opposers of the simple truth as it is in Jesus and of the practical profession of it. The Wesleys and their adherents and other clergy of the Established Church at Oxford were awakened and Brother Boehler when he went there found a preparation for the Gospel.

[The sojourn of the two Wesley brothers in Georgia strengthened the bond, and]

Georgia was also a means of the connexion with Mr Ingham who was minister of the established Church in which the awakening began in Yorkshire. Societies established under the direction or patronage of the Bishop of London held in the Vestries of several churches were also a preparation for the Gospel. To these, Hutton, West, Edmonds, &c belonged. During the connexion with Messrs. Wesley the late Ordinary began his connexion with the Archbishop of Canterbury and he then declared by Charles Wesley who was sent to Archbishop Potter with a message from him that the Brethren would not draw the good souls from the Church, but labour to keep them in it and preserve a good seed in it.

After the Wesleys separated from the Brethren and it was found well to form a congregation the general plan was not immediately altered nor have we ever theoretically and synodically altered our plan, but we have altered it practically. The first Congregation settled in England was a Pilgrim Congregation: it was that of Yorkshire (I pass over the German and Sea Congregations). This congregation was settled in London and the members removed to Yorkshire from whence the Yorkshire congregation sprung, the members of the Society going until that time to the Communion in the Church of England. The London Congregation was soon after settled and that upon a pilgrim footing and indeed the greatest part of the first members became pilgrims and labourers.

[Thereupon many applied for membership.]

But, a rule was made, That no person should be proposed for reception into the congregation who had been within two years at the Holy Communion in the Established Church. This arose from a supposition that no one who could with a good conscience go in the established church would stay from the Communion two years, in hopes of being received in that time into the Congregation and therefore it would be a means of keeping the awakened people in it and this was the ground of the Societies being formed. The reason here assigned for the above rule of two years abstaining from the holy Communion I have learned repeated from the late Ordinary and other Brethren who were then active. It is confirmed by the *Form of a Testimonial &c* laid before Parliament, to be found in *Acta Fratum Un, in Anglia*, No. LXXIV in the Appendix of Vouchers. This must have been before my time discontinued as I never saw or knew anything of the kind. Here it appears that not only the person received were to have a time of trial of two years that their call to the Congregation might be clear, but that after reception, if it was found that their consciences would allow them to communicate in their former church, they should be sent back to it, though they had been received ... I know these were the principles of the late Ordinary to the end of his days, as I have heard him declare his sentiments upon this head very frequently, roundly and warmly ... the National Church being in extreme distress in spiritual matters and in expectation of losing more of her true foundation cannot but be glad that there is another Episcopal Church besides in the world entrusted with ye Treasury of a Church and the Christian faith itself, and the hearts and good wishes of all good clergy cannot but be with us ... and this makes the *vox populi christiani* here in England to be always with us, tho' they will not venture always to say so publickly, yet they cannot help being so minded and occasionally showing it and promoting it *sotto mane*. The extravagant course of these two or three years will perhaps have its bad effects for a time but in two or three years all will be forgotten and our good fame be re-established by experience and the life and real nature of the thing as it is now related will thrill again in the veins of the old Christians in England, we will be restored again to be the object of the good wishes and hearty rememberance of all who expect consolation in Israel. The spiritual race of them will never forget or neglect us, will always wish well to us, and respect us; be it a Peer, or a Bishop, a Dean or a Lawyer, or Curate, he will do so.

(d)
Wesley's pretensions to ordain cannot be maintained according to Canon Law (Ecclesiastical Right) and therefore the Methodist ordinations and ministerial acts cannot be valid. For although church constitutions do not touch the inner essence of Christianity – which is a religion of Spirit and Truth – nevertheless the lack of true qualifications will lead to trouble in the Methodist church because all right thinking men hold good order as healthy and necessary. As Charles Wesley said to you, there are many people who are friendly to the Brethren and seek their help. We must therefore consider whether it is now the time to become busy and adopt plans for God's work among this favourable party, or remain quiet for them to make their way to us. Our inclination and circumstances recommend the first but we must wait to see what is God's will – perhaps the way of private visits and conversations with individuals, not propaganda in Methodist chapels, by those who have experienced salvation and who understand our plan and are hungry for souls. Men must seek communion with God and with the Brethren and thence human fellowship will spring. Charles Wesley is right in saying that if the Brethren, according to their original plan, will help the awakened in the Church and nourish them, and not allow

members of the Church to join our church, then the clergy will not have reason to be jealous of the Brethren.

No one can reproach us with making schisms and sects or with proselytizing. That is not a matter of indifference, but the chief thing is that we do all we can to make the work of the Lord to increase.

(e)
To Benjamin Ingham

September 8, 1746.

MY DEAR BROTHER, – On Tuesday last I light upon a letter of yours in Devonshire, which I understand has been a great traveller. I think it is the part of brotherly love to mention to you some points therein wherein I doubt whether you are not a little mistaken; if I mistake, you will set me right. You say, –

1. 'First, as to *stillness*: The thing meant hereby is that man cannot attain to salvation by his own wisdom, strength, righteousness, goodness, merits or works; that therefore, when he applies to God for it, he is to cast away all dependence upon everything of his own, and, trusting only to the mercy of God through the merits of Christ, in true poverty of spirit to resign himself up to the will of God, and thus quietly wait for His salvation.' I conceive this to be the first mistake. I have nothing to object to this *stillness*. I never did oppose *this* in word or deed. But this is not 'the thing meant thereby,' either by Molther, or the Moravians, or the English Brethren, at the time that *I* (and *you* at Mr. Bowers's) opposed them.

2. 'That the Brethren teach that people who are seeking after salvation are all the while to sit still and do nothing – that they are not to read, hear or pray – is altogether false.' This I apprehend to be a second mistake. Whatever *the Brethren* do now, they did teach thus, and that explicitly, in the years 1739 and 1740. In particular, Mr. Brown, Mr. Bowers, Mr. Bell, Mr. Bray, and Mr. Simpson, then with the Moravians. Many of their words I heard with my own ears; many more I received from those who did so. And Mr. Molther himself, on December 31, 1739, said to me, in many and plain words, that the way to attain faith is '*to be still* – that is:

'Not to use (what we term) the means of grace;
'Not to go to church;
'Not to communicate;
'Not to fast;
'Not to use *so much* private prayer;
'Not to read the Scriptures;
'Not to do temporal good; and
'Not to attempt to do spiritual good.'

These things I myself heard him speak, as I am ready to give upon oath whenever required. You ought not, therefore to say, 'This is altogether false,' on the bare denial of Mr. Molther or any other …

8. The account you give of the Moravians in general is the very same I had given before – viz. that next to those of our own Church, 'who have the faith and love which is among them, without those errors either of judgement or practice, *the body* of the Moravian Church, however mistaken *some of them are*, are *in the main*, all of

whom I have seen, the best Christians in the world.' In the same tract I sum up my latest judgement concerning them in these terms: 'I believe they love the Lord Jesus in sincerity and have a measure of the mind that was in Him. And I am in great earnest when I declare once more, that I have a deep, abiding conviction by how many degrees the good which is among them overbalances the evil, and that I cannot speak of them but with tender affection, were it only for the benefits I have received from them; and that at this hour I desire union with them (were those stumbling-blocks once put away which have hitherto made that desire ineffectual) above all things under heaven.'

9.   In what respects the Brethren are Antinomians, in what sense they lean to Quietism, I have spoken at large. If they can refute the charge, I shall rejoice more than if I had gained great spoils.

Document II.22

The Sandemanians

From Scotland there emanated what to the evangelicals was 'a cold blast from the north'. This was Sandemanianism, a development by Robert Sandeman (1718–71) of the views of his father-in-law John Glas (1695–1773). A restorationist movement which sought to restore such New Testament practices as the love feast, the kiss of charity and the community of goods, the Sandemanians were at the rationalist edge of Calvinism, maintaining that intellectual assent to the apostolic testimony concerning the work of Christ suffices for salvation, and that considerations respecting the believer's will, emotions and obedience are beside the point lest faith be mistaken for a work. For the devastating impact of Sandemanianism upon some of the Inghamite causes in the North of England see Alan P. F. Sell, *Church Planting: A Study of Westmorland Nonconformity*, Worthing: H. E. Walter, 1986, pp. 50, 52, 75 reprinted Eugene, OR: Wipf & Stock, 1998; for an example of a minister's defection from Independency to Sandemanianism see *idem*, 'John Chater: From Independent Minister to Sandemanian Author', in *Dissenting Thought and the Life of the Churches*, Lewiston, NY: Edwin Mellen Press, 1990, ch. 14. Contemporary critiques of Sandemanianism include that of the evangelical Calvinist Baptist Andrew Fuller, *Strictures on Sandemanianism*, London, 1820. For Sandeman and Sandemanianism see DEB, DNB; G. Cantor *Michael Faraday, Scientist and Sandemanian: A Study of Science and Religion in the Nineteenth Century*, London: Macmillan, 1991; L. A. McMillan, *Restoration Roots*, Dallas, TX, 1983. For the Anglican evangelical Calvinist divine William Romaine (1714–95) see DEB, DNB, ODCC.

Extract (a) is from a 'Memoir of the Late Rev. B. Ingham', by 'Adolescens', *Evangelical Magazine*, 1814, p. 308; (b) from R. Sandeman, *Letters on Theron and Aspasio*, 1757, Letter 1 – these letters were addressed to the Anglican clergyman James Hervey (1714–58) in reply to his defence of Calvinism in *Theron and Aspasio*, 1755. For Hervey see DEB, DNB.

In his *History and Antiquities of Dissenting Churches and Meeting-houses in London, Westminster and Southwark*, 1810, III, p. 264, Walter Wilson describes Sandemanian church practice (extract c)), extract (d) is from John Evans's account of Sandemanianism, in which he refers to Sandeman's reply to Hervey and describes the practices of the sect. It is taken from his *A Sketch of the Denominations of the Christian World* ... (1795), 12th edn, 1811, pp. 207–9. For the Baptist minister Evans (1767–1827) see DNB, DWB.

In extract (e) Christmas Evans, the Welsh Baptist minister who became one of the most notable preachers of Wales, records his deliverance from Sandemanianism.

For Evans (1766–1838) see DEB, DNB, DWB. The extract is taken from B.A. Ramsbottom, *Christmas Evans*, Luton: The Bunyan Press, pp. 52–4.

(a)

The writer of this note was in company with the late venerable Mr Romaine, about the year 1780, at the house of the late D. Parker, Esq. in the King's Mews, when the conversation turned upon the congregations in Yorkshire and Lancashire, raised by the labours of Mr Ingham and his associates; and among the scattered remnants of whom the writer occasionally preached while he resided at Lancaster. Mr Romaine took up the subject with warmth; and referring to the period in which the gospel gloriously prevailed in Mr Ingham's connexion (which was also the period in which Mr Romaine was greatly opposed and almost excluded from the (National) Church) he said, 'If ever there was a church of Christ upon earth, that was one. I paid them a visit, and had a great mind to join them. There was a blessed work of God among that people, till that horrid blast from the North came upon them, and destroyed all.'

(b)

Every doctrine which teaches us to do, or endeavour, anything toward our acceptance with God, stands opposed to the doctrine of the Apostles; which instead of directing us what to do, sets before us all that the most disquieted conscience may require, in order to acceptance with God, as already done and finished by Jesus Christ. What Christ has done is that which pleases God; what he hath done is that which acquits the guilty conscience of man as soon as he knows it; so that, whenever he hears of it, he has no occasion of any other question but this, Is it true or not? If he finds it true, he is happy; if not, he can reap no comfort by it. If then we slight the comfort arising from the bare possession of this, it must be owing, at bottom, to our slighting this bare truth, to our slighting the bare work of Christ, and our considering it as too narrow a foundation whereon to rest the whole weight of our acceptance with God.

(c)

their weekly administration of the Lord's Supper; their love feasts of which every member is not only allowed but required to partake, and which consists in dining either in the vestry of the meeting house or at each other's houses in the interval between the morning and afternoon services; their kiss of charity ... their weekly collection before the Lord's Supper for the support of the poor ... mutual exhortation; abstinence from blood and things strangled; washing each other's feet ... community of goods ... the unlawfulness of laying up treasures on earth ... they do not allow of putting out money to interest ... they maintain a plurality of elders, pastors or bishops in each church ... no one married for the second time can hold such an office ... in their discipline the Sandemanians are strict and severe ... in their church proceedings they are not governed by majorities but esteem unanimity to be absolutely essential ... female members are allowed to vote equally with the male.

(d)

Mr. Robert Sandeman, an elder in one of these churches in Scotland, published a series of Letters addressed to Mr. Hervey, occasioned by his Theron and Aspasio, in which he endeavours to show, that *his* notion of faith is contradictory to the Scripture account of it, and could only serve to lead men, professedly holding the doctrines called Calvinistic, to establish their own righteousness upon their frames, feelings, and acts of faith. In these letters Mr. Sandeman attempts to prove, that faith is neither more nor less than a simple assent to the divine testimony concerning Jesus Christ, delivered for the offences of men, and raised again for their justification, as recorded in the New Testament. He also maintains that the word faith or belief, is constantly used by the apostles to signify what is denoted by it in common discourse, viz. a persuasion of the truth of any proposition, and that there is no difference between believing any common testimony and believing the apostolic testimony, except that which results from the testimony itself, and the divine authority on which it rests. This led the way to a controversy among those who are called Calvinists, concerning the nature of justifying faith, and those who adopted Mr. Sandeman's notion of it; and they who are denominated Sandemanians, formed themselves into church order, in strict fellowship with the churches of Scotland, but holding no kind of communion with other churches. Mr. Sandeman died in 1772, in America.

The chief opinion and practices in which this sect differs from other Christians, are their weekly administration of the Lord's Supper; their love-feasts, of which every member is not only allowed, but required to partake, and which consist of their dining together at each other's houses in the interval between the morning and evening service; their KISS of charity used on this occasion, at the admission of a new member, and at other times when they deem it necessary and proper; their weekly collection before the Lord's Supper, for the support of the poor and defraying other expences; mutual exhortation; abstinence from blood and things strangled; washing each other's feet, when, as a deed of mercy, it might be an expression of love; the precept concerning which, as well as other precepts, they understand literally – community of goods, so far as that every one is to consider all he has in his possession and power liable to the calls of the poor and the church; and the unlawfulness of laying up treasures on earth, by setting them apart for any distant, future, or uncertain use. They allow of public and private diversions so far as they are not connected with circumstances really sinful; but apprehending a lot to be sacred, disapprove of lotteries, playing at cards, dice, &c.

They maintain a plurality of elders, pastors, or bishops, in each church, and the necessity of the presence of two elders in every act of discipline, and at the administration of the Lord's Supper.

In the choice of the elders, want of learning and engagement in trade are no sufficient objections, if qualified according to the instructions given to Timothy and Titus;

but second marriages disqualify for the office; and they are ordained by prayer and fasting, imposition of hands, and giving the right hand of fellowship.

In their discipline they are strict and severe, and think themselves obliged to separate from the communion and worship of all such religious societies, as appear to them not to profess the simple truth for their only ground of hope, and who do not walk in obedience to it. We shall only add, that in every transaction they esteem unanimity to be absolutely necessary.

(e)

I was weary ... of a cold heart towards Christ, and His sacrifice, and the work of His Spirit – of a cold heart in the pulpit, in secret prayer, and in the study. For fifteen years previously, I had felt my heart burning within, as if going to Emmaus with Jesus. On a day ever to be remembered by me, as I was going from Dolgellau to Machynlleth, and climbing up towards Cader Idris, I considered it to be incumbent upon me to pray, however hard I felt in my heart, and however worldly the frame of my spirit was.

Having begun in the name of Jesus, I soon felt, as it were, the fetters loosening, and the old hardness of heart softening, and, as I thought, mountains of frost and snow dissolving and melting within me. This engendered confidence in my soul in the promise of the Holy Ghost. I felt my whole mind relieved from some great bondage; tears flowed copiously, and I was constrained to cry out for the gracious visits of God, by restoring to my soul the joys of His salvation; and that He would visit the churches in Anglesey that were under my care. I embraced in my supplications all the churches of the saints, and nearly all the ministers in the principality by their names.

This struggle lasted for three hours; it rose again and again like one wave after another, or a high flowing tide driven by a strong wind, until my nature became faint by weeping and crying. Thus I resigned myself to Christ, body and soul, gifts and labours – all my life – every day and every hour that remained to me; and all my cares I committed to Christ. The road was mountainous and lonely, and I was wholly alone, and suffered no interruption in my wrestlings with God.

From this time, I was made to expect the goodness of God to the churches and to myself. Thus the Lord delivered me and the people of Anglesey from being carried away by the flood of Sandemanianism.

In the first religious meetings after this, I felt as if I had been removed from the cold and sterile regions of spiritual frost into the verdant fields of divine promises. The former striving with God in prayer, and the longing anxiety for the conversion of sinners, which I had experienced at Llŷn, were now restored. I had a hold of the promises of God. The result was, when I returned home, the first thing that arrested my attention was that the Spirit was working also in the brethren in Anglesey, inducing in them a spirit of prayer, especially in two of the deacons, who were particularly importunate that God would visit us in mercy, and render the Word of His grace effectual amongst us for the conversion of sinners.

Document II.23

The Swedenborgians

The followers of the Swedish scientist and mystic Emanuel Swedenborg (1688–1772) came on to the English religious scene in the 1770s, and began to organise themselves as the New Church in the last decade of the century. The extracts which follow indicate their high doctrine of humanity and their understanding of the Trinity; the nature of Jesus Christ as Jehovah-God (though the atonement is downplayed); the levels of truth in Scripture (a neo-Platonic influence here – Swedenborg was indebted to Henry More); the importance of good works, or 'uses'; angels; the Second Advent, which Swedenborgians identify with the publication of Swedenborg's writings (or, more properly, The Writings) in 1757, the year of the Descent to earth of the new Jerusalem; and the New Church. An intriguing combination of the mystical with the rational/scientific, Swedenborgianism is sometimes regarded as abstruse; nevertheless, it had a considerable appeal to working people, not least in Lancashire. William Blake, alternately an enthusiast, a critic and then a cautious believer, powerfully portrayed the Swedenborgian mind-set in his 'Jerusalem'.

For Swedenborg see BCE, ODCC; E. J. Brock et al., *Swedenborg and His Influence*, Bryn Athyn, PA: Academy of the New Church, 1988; C. O. Sigstedt, *The Swedenborg Epic: The Life and Works of Emanuel Swedenborg*, New York: Bookman Associates, 1952. The extracts are from *The True Christian Religion* (1771) London: The Swedenborg Society, [1933], pp. 8, 75, 86, 117, 237, 241, 682, 272, 284, 83, 288, 392–3, 804, 810 and 816–17.

(a)   God
There is a universal influx from God into the souls of men to the effect that there is a God, and that He is one ...

I.   Omnipotence, omniscience, and omnipresence are attributes of the divine wisdom from the divine love. II. The omnipotence, omniscience, and omnipresence of God cannot be understood unless it is know what order is; God is order, and at the creation He imposed order upon the universe and all its parts. III. The omnipotence of God, in the universe and all its parts, proceeds and operates according to the laws of His order. IV. God is omniscient, that is, He perceives, sees and knows everything, even to the minutest details, that is done according to order, and thereby whatever is done contrary to order. V. God is omnipresent in all things from first to last of His order. VI. Man was created a form of divine order. VII. So far as he lives according to divine order, man has power against evil and falsity from the divine omnipotence, wisdom concerning good and truth from the divine omniscience, and is in God from the divine omnipresence.

(b)   Man
Man was created a form of divine order, because he was created an image and likeness of God; and, since God is order itself, man was created an image and likeness of order. Order originated from and is perpetuated by divine love and wisdom, and

man was created their receptacle; wherefore he was created according to the order whereby these two act in the universe, and especially in the angelic heaven.

(c)   The Redeemer

It is believed at this day in the Christian churches, that God, the creator of the universe, begat a Son from eternity, and that this Son descended and assumed human nature, in order to redeem and save mankind; but this is an error, and falls to the ground when it is considered that God is one, and that it is utterly opposed to reason to say that the one God begat a Son from eternity, and that God the Father, together with the Son and the Holy Spirit, each of whom is separately God, is one God. This absurd notion is dissipated like a meteor, when it is demonstrated from the Word that Jehovah God Himself descended and became Man and the Redeemer.

(d)   The Trinity

There is a divine Trinity, which consists of the Father, Son, and Holy Spirit ...

Before the creation of the world this Trinity did not exist; but after the creation of the world, when God became incarnate, it was provided and came into existence, and was then in the Lord God, the Redeemer and Saviour, Jesus Christ.

   In the Christian church, at the present day, a divine trinity is acknowledged as existing before the creation of the world. It is believed that Jehovah God begat a Son from eternity, and the Holy Spirit then proceeded from both; each of these three being God separately or by Himself, since each one is a self-subsistent personality. But this belief, being incomprehensible, is called a mystery, which can be made clear only by regarding these three, as possessing one divine essence, by which is meant eternity, immensity, and omnipotence, and consequently equal divinity, glory, and majesty. This trinity, however, is a trinity of three gods, and therefore in no sense a divine trinity, as will be proved below. But that a trinity of Father, Son, and Holy Spirit, which was provided and came into existence after God was incarnated, consequently after the creation of the world, is the divine trinity, because it pertains to one God, is evident from all that was said above. This divine trinity is in the Lord God, the Redeemer and Saviour, Jesus Christ, because the three essentials of one God, which constitute one essence, are in Him ...

The faith and imputation of the new church differ totally from the faith and imputation of the former church. For the faith of the former church teaches that three divine persons have existed as so many creators from eternity, each of whom singly, or by Himself, is God. But the faith of the new church is that there is only one divine Person from eternity, consequently only one God, and that there is no other God beside Him.

(e)   Scripture

The spiritual sense of the Word is not that which shines from the literal sense when the Word is studied to prove some dogma of the church. This may be called the literal and ecclesiastical sense of the Word; but the spiritual sense is not apparent in the sense of the letter; it is within it as the soul is in the body, or intelligence in the eyes, or affection in the countenance. It is this sense especially that makes the Word spiritual, not only for men but also for angels; and the Word thereby communicates with the heavens. Since the Word is inwardly spiritual, it is written by pure correspondences; and this produces in the ultimate sense a style like that of the prophets, the evangelists, and the Revelation; although it seems commonplace, it yet conceals within it divine and angelic wisdom ...

The science of correspondences, which is the key to the spiritual sense of the Word, is to-day revealed, because the divine truths of the church are now being brought to light. These are the truths of which the spiritual sense consists; and when there are in a man's mind, the literal sense of the Word cannot be perverted. For the literal sense can be used in two ways; if it is diverted to prove what is false, its internal and external holiness both perish; but if it is used to prove what is true, its holiness remains ...

(f)   Heaven and hell

The angels of heaven can see whatever is done in hell, and also the monsters therein; but the spirits of hell can no more see the angels nor anything that is done in heaven, than if they were blind or looking into empty air ...

There are three heavens, the highest, the middle, and the lowest; the highest heaven is the Lord's celestial kingdom, the middle heaven His spiritual kingdom, and the lowest heaven His natural kingdom. And just as there are three heavens, so there are three senses in the Word – the celestial, the spiritual, and the natural; and this agrees with what was said above ... , that the primary is in the middle, and thereby in the ultimate, just as the end is in the cause, and thereby in the effect. This shows the true nature of the Word. The literal sense which is natural contains an interior sense which is spiritual, and this again contains an inmost sense which is celestial; thus the ultimate natural or literal sense is the containant, basis and support of the two interior senses.

(g)   Faith and charity

It is now necessary to explain what faith and charity are in their essence, and this shall be done in the following sequence of articles: I. A saving faith is faith in the Lord God the Saviour, Jesus Christ. II. The sum and substance of faith is that he who lives well, and believes aright, is saved by the Lord. III. A man acquires faith by approaching the Lord, learning truths from the Word, and living according to them. IV. Faith is exalted and perfected by truths systematically arranged. V. Faith without charity is not faith, and charity without faith is not charity, and neither has any life except from the Lord. VI. The Lord, charity, and faith make one, like life, will, and understanding in man; and if they are divided, each perishes like a pearl reduced to powder. VII. The Lord is charity and faith in man, and man is charity and faith in the Lord. VIII. Charity and faith exist together in good works. IX. There is a true faith, a spurious faith, and a hypocritical faith. X. The wicked have no faith.

(h)   The Second Advent

The second coming of the Lord is taking place in order that the evil may be separated from the good, and that those who believe in Him may be saved and may form a new angelic heaven and a new church on earth; otherwise no flesh could be saved (Matt. xxiv 22).

772. This second coming of the Lord does not involve the destruction of the visible heaven and the habitable earth. He has come not to destroy but to build, consequently not to condemn but to save those who, since His first coming, have believed in Him, as is plain from these word: *God sent not his Son into the world to judge the world, but that the world through him might be saved. He that believeth in him is not judged; but he that believeth not is judged already, because he hath not believed in the name of the only-begotten Son of God.* (John iii 17,18).

(i)   Swedenborg's Testimony

The Lord has disclosed to me the spiritual sense of His Word, in which divine truth is in its light; and in this light He has been continually present with me. For the Lord's presence is in the spiritual sense of the Word, through whose light it passes into the shade of the literal sense; just as the light of the sun passes into the shadow of the clouds. It has been shown above that the literal sense of the Word is like a cloud, while the spiritual sense is the glory; and that the Lord Himself is the Sun from which the light proceeds, and is therefore the Word.

(j)   The New Church

As shown above, there have existed on this earth four churches – one before the flood, another after it, a third called the Israelitish church, and a fourth the Christian. All churches depend on the knowledge and acknowledgement of one God, with whom the members of the church can enter into communion. But, since the four churches had not that knowledge, it follows that a church is to succeed which shall possess it …

This new church is the crown of all the former churches, because it will worship one visible God, in whom is the invisible God as the soul is in the body.

Wesley, Whitefield and the Dissenters

The Teaching of John Wesley

We have already suggested that John Wesley did not leave a rounded theological system behind him; and what he did leave has been variously interpreted. Some have charged that experience looms large at the expense of other Christian doctrines; others have detected continuity throughout his writings, still others a progression from justification *via* assurance to perfection. Do we have an early Wesley (to 1735), a middle one (to 1765) and a later one (to 1791)? Again, are the Standards of Methodist Belief (the 'Wesley Canon'), namely, the forty-six Sermons (or should it be fifty-three?), the Large Minutes (1789 edition) and the Notes of the New Testament an altogether reliable introduction to the original emphases? Where do the controversial writings, the Journal, Diaries, Letters, the Library of Christian Classics, the scientific and medical treatises fit in to the overall picture? What of the regulative Hymn Book of 1780, almost wholly the work of Charles, yet edited and arranged by John?

Should we look beneath the surface – perhaps following J. Scott Lidgett's suggestion that Wesley transformed the Puritan monarchical conception of God into the gentle Father, with a corresponding emphasis upon the incarnation as well as the atonement? Is the Wesleyan emphasis upon regeneration a perhaps unconscious attempt to play down the substitutionary idea of the atonement, as the Victorian W. B. Pope surmised? And what of the Wesleyan idea of the Church and the Anglican factor? Whatever the practice (with which Wesley constantly outran and sometimes subverted the theory), 'the Church of England is that part, those members, of the Universal Church who are inhabitants of England'.

For Wesley see Document II.21 above. For his evangelical Arminianism see Herbert Boyd McGonigle, *Sufficient Saving Grace*, Carlisle: Paternoster, 2001. The extracts (those from the Sermons being in Wesley's *Works*, 1872, V, VI) are as follows.

From Sermons 39 on 'The new birth' and 5 on 'Justification by faith' are selected passages (extract (a)) on those doctrines which Wesley believed to be the foundation doctrines of the Christian faith.

Extract (b) from Sermon 10 on 'The witness of the Spirit' shows Wesley attempting to distinguish between true and counterfeit assurance. In this connection we may observe that later in the nineteenth century Wesleyans spoke of the Wesleyan Quadrilateral, suggesting that the founder's teachings were that all needed salvation, all could be saved, all could know that they were saved (assurance), and all could be saved to the uttermost (holiness, perfect love). The first is unexceptionable; the second, on Arminian principles, is understandable; the third, sometimes known as the witness of the Spirit, is more singular: it is an angry rejection of Calvinism turned inward and/or legalistic, whereby believers would look within, or to their 'godly walk' for signs of their election, but could never be sure of it.

Perfect love is even more singular, as extract (c) from *A Plain Account of Christian Perfection* (1776) shows (in *Works*, 1872, XI, p. 394 f.). Wherever this teaching came from – and the Spanish mystics are the most likely candidates – this characteristic Wesleyan teaching, an embarrassment to some and an inspiration to others, seemed to work consolingly for a generation faced with unparalleled economic, political, social and international instability – a reminder that expressions of doctrine derive some of their colour from the context in which they are articulated.

Wesley's thought was never far from the practice of the Christian life. In extract (d) from *The Character of a Methodist*, 1742 (*Works*, 1872, p. 339 f.), he emphasises proper behaviour over against correctness of doctrine.

In extract (e) from Sermon 39 on 'The Catholic spirit' Wesley applies his ethic to the world at large.

In Sermon 44 on 'The use of money' (extract (f)), Wesley's injunction to gain, save and give all you can reveals him as the homespun Lincolnshire countryman which, for all his sophistication, he ever seemed to be. This simple creed, so effective within the highly disciplined world of the Wesleyans, proved readily adaptable to the needs of an industrial society.

(a)

Ye must be born again. – John iii. 7.

If any doctrines within the whole compass of Christianity may be properly termed 'fundamental', they are doubtless these two, – the doctrine of justification, and that of the new birth: the former relating to that great work which God does *for us*, in forgiving our sins; the latter, to the great work which God does *in us*, in renewing our fallen nature. In order of *time*, neither of these is before the other; in the moment we are justified by the grace of God, through the redemption that is in Jesus, we are also 'born of the Spirit'; but in order of *thinking*, as it is termed, justification precedes the new birth. We first conceive His wrath to be turned away , and then His Spirit to work in our hearts ...

I.   1.   And, first, Why must we be born again? What is the foundation of this doctrine? The foundation of it lies near as deep as the creation of the world; in the scriptural account whereof we read, 'And God,' the three-one God, 'said, Let us make man in our image, after our likeness. So God created man in His own image, in the image of God created He him' (Gen. i. 26, 27): – not barely in his *natural image*, a picture of His own immortality; a spiritual being, endued with understanding, freedom of will, and various affections; nor merely in his *political image*, the governor of this lower world, having 'dominion over the fishes of the sea, and over all the earth': but chiefly in his *moral image*; which, according to the Apostle, is 'righteousness and true holiness' (Eph. iv. 24). In this image of God was man made. 'God is love'; accordingly, man at his creation was full of love; which was the sole principle of all his tempers, thoughts, words, and actions. God is full of justice, mercy, and truth; so was man as he came from the hands of his Creator. God is spotless purity; and so man was in the beginning pure from every sinful blot; otherwise God could not have pronounced him, as well as all the other works of His hands, 'very good' (Gen. i. 31). This he could not have been, had he not been pure from sin, and filled with righteousness and true holiness. For there is no medium: if we suppose an intelligent creature not to love God, not to be righteous and holy, we necessarily suppose him not to be good at all; much less to be 'very good'.

2. But, although man was made in the image of God, yet he was not made immutable. This would have been inconsistent with that state of trial in which God was pleased to place him. He was therefore created able to stand, and yet liable to fall. And this God Himself apprised him of, and gave him a solemn warning against it. Nevertheless, man did not abide in honour: he fell from his high estate. He 'ate of the tree whereof the Lord had commanded him, Thou shalt not eat thereof.' By this wilful act of disobedience to his Creator, this flat rebellion against his Sovereign, he openly declared that he would no longer have God to rule over him; that he would be governed by his own will, and not the will of Him that created him; and that he would not seek his happiness in God, but in the world, in the works of his hands. Now, God had told him before, 'In the day that thou eatest' of that fruit, 'thou shalt surely die.' ...

4. And in Adam all died, all human kind, all the children of men who were then in Adams' loins. The natural consequence of this is, that every one descended from him comes into the world spiritually dead, dead to God, wholly dead in sin; entirely void of the life of God; void of the image of God, of all that righteousness and holiness wherein Adam was created. Instead of this, every man born into the world now bears the image of the devil, in pride and self-will; the image of the beast, in sensual appetites and desires. This, then, is the foundation of the new birth, – the entire corruption of our nature. Hence it is, that being born in sin, we must be 'born again.' Hence every one that is born of a woman must be born of the Spirit of God.

II. 1. But how must a man be born again? What is the nature of the new birth? This is the second question. And a question it is of the highest moment that can be conceived. We ought not, therefore, in so weighty a concern, to be content with a slight inquiry: but to examine it with all possible care, and to ponder it in our hearts, till we fully understand this important point, and clearly see how we are to be born again ... .

4. Before a child is born into the world he has eyes, but sees not; he has ears, but does not hear. He has a very imperfect use of any other sense. He has no knowledge of any of the things of the world, or any natural understanding. To that manner of existence which he then has, we do not even give the name of life. It is then only when a man is born, that we say he begins to live. For as soon as he is born, he begins to see the light, and the various objects with which he is encompassed. His ears are then opened, and he hears the sounds which successively strike upon them. At the same time, all the organs of sense begin to be exercised upon their proper objects. He likewise breathes, and lives in a manner wholly different from what he did before. How exactly doth the parallel hold in all these instances! While a man is in a mere natural state, before he is born of God, he has, in a spiritual sense, eyes and sees not; a thick impenetrable veil lies upon them: he has ears, but hears not; he is utterly deaf to what he is most of all concerned to hear. His other spiritual senses are all locked up: he is in the same condition as if he had them not. Hence he has no knowledge of God; no intercourse with Him; he is not at all acquainted with Him. He has no true knowledge of the things of God, either of spiritual of eternal things; therefore,

though he is a living man, he is a dead Christian. Butt as soon as he is born of God, there is a total change in all these particulars. The 'eyes of his understanding are opened' (such is the language of the great Apostle); and, He who of old 'commanded light to shine out of darkness shining on his heart, he ses the light of the glory of God,' His glorious love, 'in the face of Jesus Christ.' ...

III. 1. It is not difficult for any who has considered these things, to see the necessity of the new birth, and to answer the third question, Wherefore, to what end, is it necessary that we should be born again? It is very easily discerned, that this is necessary, first, in order to holiness ... Now, this holiness can have no existence till we are renewed in the image of our mind. It cannot commence in the soul till that change be wrought; till, by the power of the Highest overshadowing us, we are 'brought from darkness to light, from the power of Satan unto God'; that is, till we are born again; which, therefore, is absolutely necessary in order to holiness.

2. But 'without holiness no man shall see the Lord,' shall see the face of God in glory. Of consequence, the new birth is absolutely necessary in order to eternal salvation ...

3. For the same reason, except he be born again, none can be happy even in this world. For it is not possible, in the nature of things, that a man should be happy who is not holy ...

I fear you have had a thousand opportunities of doing good which you have suffered to pass by unimproved, and for which therefore you are accountable to God. But if you had improved them all, if you really had done all the good you possibly could to all men, yet this does not at all alter the case; still 'you must be born again.' Without this nothing will do any good to your poor, sinful, polluted soul. 'Nay, but I constantly attend all the ordinances of God: I keep to my church and my sacrament.' It is well you do: but all this will not keep you from hell, except you be born again. Go to church twice a day; go to the Lord's table every week; say ever so many prayers in private; hear ever so many good sermons; read ever so many good books; still 'you must be born again': none of these things will stand in the place of the new birth; no, nor anything under heaven. Let this, therefore, if you have not already experienced this inward work of God, be your continual prayer: 'Lord, add this to all Thy blessings, – let me be born again! Deny whatever Thou pleasest, but deny not this; let me be "born from above"! Take away whatsoever seemeth Thee good – reputation, fortune, friends, health – only give me this, to be born of the Spirit, to be received among the children of God! Let me be born, "not of corruptible seed, but incorruptible, by the word of God, which liveth and abideth for ever"; and then let me daily "grow in grace, and in the knowledge of our Lord and Saviour Jesus Christ"!'

To him that worketh not, but believeth on Him that justifieth the ungodly, his faith
is counted for righteousness. – Rom. iv. 5.

How a sinner may be justified before God, the Lord and Judge of all, is a question of no common importance to every child of man. It contains the foundation of all our hope, inasmuch as while we are at enmity with God there can be no true peace, no solid joy, either in time or in eternity. What peace can there be, while our own heart condemns us; and much more, He that is 'greater than our heart, and knoweth all things'? What solid joy either in this world or that to come, while 'the wrath of God abideth on us'?

2.　And yet how little hath this important question been understood? What confused notions have many had concerning it! Indeed, not only confused, but often utterly false; contrary to the truth, as light to darkness; notions absolutely inconsistent with the oracles of God, and with the whole analogy of faith. And hence, erring concerning the very foundation, they could not possibly build thereon; at least, not 'gold, silver, or precious stones,' which would endure when tried as by fire; but only 'hay and stubble,' neither acceptable to God, nor profitable to man.

3.　In order to do justice, as far as in me lies, to the vast importance of the subject, to save those that seek the truth in sincerity from 'vain jangling and strife of words,' to clear the confusedness of thought into which so many have already been led thereby, and to give them true and just conceptions of this great mystery of godliness, I shall endeavour to show, –

I.　WHAT IS THE GENERAL GROUND OF THIS WHOLE DOCTRINE OF JUSTIFICATION;

II.　WHAT JUSTIFICATION IS;

III.　WHO THEY ARE THAT ARE JUSTIFIED; AND,

IV.　ON WHAT TERMS THEY ARE JUSTIFIED.

I.　I am first to show, what is the general ground of this whole doctrine of justification …

9.　This, therefore, is the general ground of the whole doctrine of justification. By the sin of the first Adam, who was not only the father, but likewise the representative, of us all, we all fell short of the favour of God; we all became children of wrath; or, as the Apostle expresses it, 'judgement came upon all men to condemnation.' Even so, by the sacrifice for sin made by the second Adam, as the Representative of us all, God is so far reconciled to all the world, that He hath given them a new covenant; the plain condition whereof being once fulfilled, 'there is no more condemnation' for us, but 'we are justified freely by His grace, through the redemption that is in Jesus Christ.'

II.　1.　But what is it to be *justified*? What is *justification*? This was the second thing which I proposed to show. And it is evident, from what has been already observed, that it is not the being made actually just and righteous. This is *sanctification*; which is, indeed, in some degree, the immediate fruit of justification, but, nevertheless, is a distinct gift of God, and of a totally different nature. The one implies, what God does for us through His Son; the other, what He works in us by His Spirit. So that, although some rare instances may be found, wherein the term *justified* or *justification* is used in so wide a sense as to include *sanctification* also; yet, in general use, they are sufficiently distinguished from each other, both by St. Paul and the other inspired writers …

III.　1.　But this is the third thing which was to be considered, namely, Who are they that are justified? And the Apostle tells us expressly, the ungodly: 'He' (that is,

God) 'justifieth the ungodly' the ungodly of every kind and degree; and none but the ungodly. As 'they that are righteous need no repentance,' so they need no forgiveness. It is only sinners that have any occasion for pardon: it is sin alone which admits of being forgiven. Forgiveness, therefore, has an immediate reference to sin, and, in this respect, to nothing else. It is our *unrighteousness* to which the pardoning God is *merciful*: it is our *iniquity* which He 'remembereth no more.' ...

IV. 1. But on what terms, then, is he justified, who is altogether *ungodly*: and till that time *worketh not*? On one alone, which is faith: he 'believeth in Him that justifieth the ungodly.' And 'he that believeth is not condemned'; yea, he is 'passed from death unto life.' 'For the righteousness' (or mercy), 'of God is by faith of Jesus Christ unto all and upon all them that believe: whom God hath set forth for a propitiation, through faith in His blood; that He might be just, and' (consistently with His justice) 'the justifier of him which believeth in Jesus'; 'therefore we conclude, that a man is justified by faith, without the deeds of the law'; without previous obedience to the moral law, which, indeed, he could not, till now, perform. That it is the moral law, and that alone, which is here intended, appears evidently from the words that follow: 'Do we then make void the law through faith? God forbid! Yea, we establish the law.' What law do we establish by faith? Not the ritual law: not the ceremonial law of Moses. In no wise; but the great, unchangeable law of love, the holy love of God and of our neighbour. ...

9. Thou ungodly one, who hearest or readest these words! thou vile, helpless, miserable sinner! I charge thee before God the Judge of all, go straight unto Him, with all thy ungodliness. Take heed thou destroy not thy own soul by pleading thy righteousness, more or less. Go as altogether ungodly, guilty, lost, destroyed, deserving and dropping into hell; and thou shalt then find favour in His sight, and know that He justifieth the ungodly. As such thou shalt be brought unto the *blood of sprinkling*: as an undone, helpless, damned sinner. Thus *look unto Jesus*! There is *the Lamb of God*: who *taketh away* thy *sins*! Plead thou no works, no righteousness of thine own! no humility, contrition, sincerity! In no wise. That were, in very deed, to deny the Lord that brought thee. No: plead thou singly the blood of the covenant, the ransom paid for thy proud, stubborn, sinful soul. Who are thou, that now seest and feelest both thine inward and outward ungodliness? Thou are the man! I want thee for my Lord! I challenge *thee* for a child of God by faith! The Lord hath need of thee. Thou who feelest thou art just fit for hell, art just fit to advance His glory; the glory of His free grace, justifying the ungodly and him that worketh not. O come quickly! Believe in the Lord Jesus, and thou, even thou, art reconciled to God.

(b)
9. 'But how may one who has the real witness in himself distinguish it from presumption?' How, I pray, do you distinguish day from night? How do you distinguish light from darkness; or the light of a star, or a glimmering taper, from the light of the noonday sun? Is there not an inherent, obvious, essential difference between the one and the other? And do you not immediately and directly perceive that difference, provided your senses are rightly disposed? In like manner, there is an inherent, essential difference between spiritual light and spiritual darkness; and between the

light wherewith the Sun of righteousness shines upon our heart, and that glimmering light which arises only from 'sparks of our own kindling': and this difference also is immediately and directly perceived, if our spiritual senses are rightly disposed.

10. To require a more minute and philosophical account of the manner whereby we distinguish these, and of the *criteria*, or intrinsic marks, whereby we know the voice of God, is to make a demand which can never be answered; no, not by one who has the deepest knowledge of God. Suppose, when Paul answered before Agrippa, the wise Roman had said, 'Thou talkest of hearing the voice of the Son of God. How dost thou know it was His voice? By what *criteria*, what intrinsic marks, dost thou know the voice of God? Explain to me the *manner* of distinguishing this from a human or angelic voice.' Can you belive, the Apostle himself would have once attempted to answer so idle a demand? And yet, doubtless, the moment he heard that voice, he knew it was the voice of God. But *how* he knew this, who is able to explain? Perhaps neither man nor angel.

11. To come yet closer: suppose God were now to speak to any soul, 'Thy sins are forgiven thee,' He must be willing that soul should know His voice; otherwise He would speak in vain. And he is able to effect this; for, whenever he wills, to do is present with Him. And He does effect it: that soul is absolutely assured, 'This voice is the voice of God.' But yet he who hath that witness in himself cannot explain it to one who hath it not: nor indeed is it to be expected that he should. Were there any natural medium to prove, or natural method to explain, the things of God to un-experienced men, then the natural man might discern and know the things of the Spirit of God. But this is utterly contrary to the assertion of the Apostle, that 'he cannot know them, because they are spiritually discerned'; even by spiritual senses, which the natural man hath not.

12. 'But how shall I know that my spiritual senses are rightly disposed?' This also is a question of vast importance; for if a man mistake in this, he may run on in endless error and delusion. 'And how am I assure that this is not my case; and that I do not mistake the voice of the Spirit?' Even by the testimony of your own spirit: by 'the answer of a good conscience toward God.' By the fruits which He hath wrought in your spirit, you shall know the testimony of the Spirit of God. Hereby you shall know that you are in no delusion, that you have not deceived your own soul. The immediate fruits of the Spirit, ruling in the heart, are 'love, joy, peace, bowels of mercies, humbleness of mind, meekness, gentleness, long-suffering.' And the outward fruits are, the doing good to all men; the doing no evil to any; and the walking in the light- a zealous, uniform obedience to all the commandments of God.

13. By the same fruits shall you distinguish this voice of God from any delusion of the devil. That proud spirit cannot humble thee before God. He neither can nor would soften thy heart, and melt it first into earnest mourning after God, and then into filial love. It is not the adversary of God and man that enables thee to love thy neighbour; or to put on meekness, gentleness, patience, temperance, and the whole armour of God. He is not divided against himself, or a destroyer of sin, his own work. No; it is none but the Son of God who cometh 'to destroy the works of the devil.' As surely therefore as holiness is of God, and as sin is the work of the devil, so surely the witness thou hast in thyself is not of Satan, but of God.

112

14.   Well then mayest thou say, 'Thanks be unto God for His unspeakable gift!' Thanks be unto God, who giveth me to 'know in whom I have believed'; who hath 'sent forth the Spirit of His Son into my heart, crying, Abba, Father, and even now, 'bearing witness with my spirit that I am a child of God'! And see, that not only thy lips, but thy life life show forth His praise. He hath sealed thee for His own; glorify Him then in thy body and thy spirit, which are His. Beloved, if thou hast this hope in thyself, purify thyself, as He is pure. While thou beholdest what manner of love the Father hath given thee, that thou shouldest be called a child of God, cleanse thyself 'from all filthiness of flesh and spirit, perfecting holiness in the fear of God'; and let all thy thoughts, words, and works be a spiritual sacrifice, holy, acceptable to God through Christ Jesus!

(c)

The following tract is by no means designed to gratify the curiosity of any man. It is not intended to prove the doctrine at large, in opposition to those who explode and ridicule it; no, nor to answer the numerous objections against it, which may be raised even by serious men. All I intend here is, simply to declare what are my sentiments on this head; what Christian perfection does, according to my apprehensions, include, and what it does not; and to add a few practical observations and directions ...

As these thoughts were at first thrown together by way of question and answer, I let them continue in the same form. They are just the same that I have entertained for above twenty years.

QUESTION.   What is Christian perfection?

ANSWER.   The loving God with all our heart, mind, soul and strength. This implies, that no wrong temper, none contrary to love, remains in the soul; and that all the thoughts, words, and actions, are governed by pure love.

Q.   Do you affirm, that this perfection excludes all infirmities, ignorance, and mistake?

A.   I continually affirm quite the contrary, and always have done so.

Q.   But how can every thought, word, and work, be governed by pure love, an the man be subject at the same time to ignorance and mistake?

A.   I see no contradiction here: 'A man may be filled with pure love, and still be liable to mistake.' Indeed I do not expect to be freed from actual mistakes, till this mortal puts on immortality. I believe this to be a natural consequence of the soul's dwelling in flesh and blood. For we cannot think at all, but by the mediation of those bodily organs which have suffered equally with the rest of our frame. And hence we cannot avoid sometimes thinking wrong, till this corruptible shall have put on incorruption.

But we may carry this thought farther yet. A mistake in judgement may possibly occasion a mistake in practice. For instance: Mr. De Renty's mistake touching the nature of mortification, arising from prejudice of education, occasioned that practical mistake, his wearing an iron girdle. And a thousand such instances there may be, even in those who are in the highest state of grace. Yet, where every word and action springs from love, such a mistake is not properly a sin. However, it cannot bear the rigours of God's justice, but needs the atoning blood.

Q. What was the judgment of all our brethren who met at Bristol in August, 1758, on this head?

A. It was expressed in these words: (1) Every one may mistake as long as he lives. (2) A mistake in opinion may occasion a mistake in practice. (3) Every such mistake is a transgression of the perfect law. Therefore, (4) Every such mistake, were it not for the blood of atonement, would expose to eternal damnation. (5) It follows, that the most perfect have continual need of the merits of Christ, even for their actual transgressions, and may say for themselves, as well as for their brethren, 'Forgive us our trespasses.'

This easily accounts for what might otherwise seem to be utterly unaccountable; namely, that those who are not offended when we speak of the highest degree of love, yet will not hear of living without sin. The reason is, they know all men are liable to mistake, and that in practice as well as in judgment. But they do not know, or do not observe, that this is not sin, if love is the sole principle of action.

Q. But still, if they live without sin, does not this exclude the necessity of a Mediator? At least, is it not plain that they stand no longer in need of Christ in his priestly office?

A. Far from it. None feel their need of Christ like these; none so entirely depend upon him. For Christ does not give life to the soul separate from, but in and with, himself. Hence his words are equally true of all men, in whatsoever state of grace they are: 'As the branch cannot bear fruit of itself, except it abide in the vine; no more can ye, except ye abide in me: Without' (or separate from) 'me ye can do nothing.'

In every state we need Christ in the following respects: (1) Whatever grace we receive, it is a free gift from him. (2) We receive it as his purchase, merely in consideration of the price he paid. (3) We have this grace, not only from Christ, but in him. For our perfection is not like that of a tree, which flourishes by the sap derived from its own root, but, as was said before, like that of a branch which, united to the vine, bears fruit; but, severed from it, is dried up and withered. (4) All our blessings, temporal, spiritual, and eternal, depend on his intercession for us, which is one branch of his priestly office, whereof therefore we have always equal need. (5) The best of men still need Christ in his priestly office, to atone for their omissions, their short-comings, (as some not improperly speak,) their mistakes in judgment and practice, and their defects of various kinds. For these are all deviations from the perfect law, and consequently need an atonement. Yet that they are not properly sins, we apprehend may appear from the words of St. Paul, 'He that loveth, hath fulfilled the law; for love is the fulfilling of the law.' (Rom. xiii.10). Now, mistakes, and whatever infirmities necessarily flow from the corruptible state of the body, are noway contrary to love; nor therefore, in the Scripture sense, sin.

To explain myself a little farther on this head: (1) Not only sin, properly so called, (that is, a voluntary transgression of a known law,) but sin, improperly so called, (that is, an involuntary transgression of a divine law, known or unknown,) needs the atoning blood. (2) I believe there is no such perfection in this life as excludes these involuntary transgressions which I apprehend to be naturally consequent on the ignorance and mistakes inseparable from mortality. (3) Therefore *sinless perfection* is a phrase I never use, lest I should seem to contradict myself. (4) I believe, a person filled with the love of God is still liable to these involuntary transgressions. (5) Such transgressions you may call sins if you please: I do not, for the reasons above-mentioned. ...

Q. How shall we avoid setting perfection too high or too low?

A. By keeping to the Bible, and setting it just as high as the Scripture does. It is nothing higher and nothing lower than this, – the pure love of God and man; the loving God with all our heart and soul, and our neighbour as ourselves. It is love governing the heart and life, running through all our tempers, words, and actions.

Q. Suppose one had attained to this, would you advise him to speak of it?

A. At first perhaps he would scarce be able to refrain, the fire would be so hot within him; his desire to declare the loving-kindness of the Lord carrying him away like a torrent. But afterwards he might; and then it would be advisable, not to speak of it to them that know not God (it is most likely, it would only provoke them to contradict and blaspheme); nor to others, without some particular reason, without some good in view. And then he should have especial care to avoid all appearance of boasting; to speak with the deepest humility and reverence, giving all the glory to God. ...

Q. When may a person judge himself to have attained this?

A. When, after having been fully convinced of inbred sin, by a far deeper and clearer conviction than that he experienced before justification, and after having experienced a gradual mortification of it, he experiences a total death to sin, and an entire renewal in the love and image of God, so as to rejoice evermore, to pray without ceasing, and in everything to give thanks. Not that 'to feel all love and no sin' is a sufficient proof. Several have experienced this for a time, before their souls were fully renewed. None therefore ought to believe that the work is done, till there is added the testimony of the Spirit, witnessing his entire sanctification, as clearly as his justification.

Q. But whence is it, that some imagine they are thus sanctified, when in reality they are no?

A. It is hence: they do not judge by all the preceding marks, but either by part of them, or by others that are ambiguous. But I know no instance of a person attending to them all, and yet deceived in this matter. I believe, there can be none in the world. If a man be deeply and fully convinced, after justification, of inbred sin; if he then experience a gradual mortification of sin, and afterwards an entire renewal in the image of God; if to this change, immensely greater than that wrought when he was justified, be added a clear, direct witness of the renewal; I judge it as impossible this man should be deceived herein, as that God should lie. And if one whom I know to be a man of veracity testify these things to me, I ought not, without some sufficient reason, to reject his testimony.

Q. Is this death to sin, and renewal in love, gradual or instantaneous?

A. A man may be dying for some time; yet he does not, properly speaking, dies, till the instant the soul is separated from the body; and in that instant he lives the life of eternity. In like manner, he may be dying to sin for some time; yet he is not dead to sin, till sin is separated from his soul; and in that instant he lives the full life of love. And as the change undergone, when the body dies, is of a different kind, and infinitely greater than any we had known before, yea, such as till then it is impossible to conceive; so the change wrought, when the soul dies to sin, is of a different kind, and infinitely greater than any before, and than any can conceive till he experiences it. Yet he still grows in grace, in the knowledge of Christ, in the love and image of God; and will do so, not only till death, but to all eternity.

Q.   How are we to wait for this change?

A.   Not in careless indifference, or indolent inactivity; but in vigorous, universal obedience, in a zealous keeping of all the commandments, in watchfulness and painfulness, in denying ourselves, and taking up our cross daily; as well as in earnest prayer and fasting, and a close attendance on all the ordinances of God. And if any man dream of attaining it any other way (yea, or of keeping it when it is attained, when he has received it even in the largest measure), he deceiveth his own soul. It is true, we receive it by simple faith: But God does not, will not, give that faith, unless we seek it with all diligence, in the way which he hath ordained. ...

Q.   But may we not continue in peace and joy till we are perfected in love?

A.   Certainly we may; for the kingdom of God is not divided against itself; therefore, let not believers be discouraged from 'rejoicing in the Lord always.' And yet we may be sensibly pained at the sinful nature that still remains in us. It is good for us to have a piercing sense of this, and a vehement desire to be delivered from it. But this should only incite us the more zealously to fly every moment to our strong Helper, the more earnestly to 'press forward to the mark, the prize of our high calling in Christ Jesus.' And when the sense of our sin most abounds, the sense of his love should much more abound.

Q.   How should we treat those who think they have attained?

A.   Examine them candidly, and exhort them to pray fervently, that God would show them all that is in their hearts. The most earnest exhortations to abound in every grace, and the strongest cautions to avoid all evil, are given throughout the New Testament, to those who are in the highest state of grace. But this should be done with the utmost tenderness; and without any harshness, sternness, or sourness. We should carefully avoid the very appearance of anger, unkindness, or contempt. Leave it to Satan thus to tempt, and to his children to cry out, 'Let us examine him with despitefulness and torture, that we may know his meekness and prove his patience.' If they are faithful to the grace given, they are in no danger of perishing thereby; no, not if they remain in that mistake till their spirit is returning to God ...

Q.   But what does it signify, whether any have attained it or no, seeing so many scriptures witness for it?

A.   If I were convinced that none in England had attained what has been so clearly and strongly preached by such a number of Preachers, in so many places, and for so long a time, I should be clearly convinced that we had all mistaken the meaning of those scriptures; and therefore, for the time to come, I too must teach that 'sin will remain till death.'

(d)

The Character of a Methodist

1. The distinguishing marks of a Methodist are not his opinions of any sort. His assenting to this or that scheme of religion, his embracing any particular set of notions, his espousing the judgment of one man or of another, are all quite wide of the point. Whosoever, therefore, imagines that a Methodist is a man of such or such an opinion, is grossly ignorant of the whole affair; he mistakes the truth totally. We believe, indeed, that 'all Scripture is given by the inspiration of God'; and herein we are distinguished from Jews, Turks, and Infidels. We believe the written word of God to be the only and sufficient rule both of Christian faith and practice; and herein we are fundamentally distinguished from those of the Romish Church. We believe Christ to be the eternal, supreme God; and herein we are distinguished from the Socinians and Arians. But as to all opinions which do not strike at the root of Christianity, we think and let think. So that whatsoever they are, whether right or wrong, they are no distinguishing marks of a Methodist.

2. Neither are words or phrases of any sort. We do not place our religion, or any part of it, in being attached to any peculiar mode of speaking, any quaint of uncommon set of expressions. The most obvious, easy, common words, wherein our meaning can be conveyed, we prefer before others, both on ordinary occasions, and when we speak of the things of God. We never, therefore, willingly or designedly, deviate from the most usual way of speaking; unless when we express scripture truths in scripture words, which, we presume, no Christian will condemn. Neither do we affect to use any particular expressions of Scripture more frequently than others, unless they are such as are more frequently used by the inspired writers themselves. So that it is as gross an error, to place the marks of a Methodist in his words, as in opinions of any sort.

3. Nor do we desire to be distinguished by actions, customs, or usages, of an indifferent nature. Our religion does not lie in doing what God has not enjoined, or abstaining from what he hath not forbidden. It does not lie in the form of our apparel, in the posture of our body, or the covering of our heads; nor yet in abstaining from marriage, or from meats and drinks, which are all good if received with thanksgiving. Therefore, neither will any man, who knows whereof he affirms, fix the mark of a Methodist here, – in any actions or customs purely indifferent, undetermined by the word of God.

4. Nor, lastly, is he distinguished by laying the whole stress of religion on any single part of it. If you say, 'Yes, he is; for he thinks " we are saved by faith alone",' I answer, You do not understand the terms. By salvation he means holiness of heart and life. And this he affirms to spring from true faith alone. Can even a nominal Christian deny it? Is this placing a part of religion for the whole? 'Do we then make void the law through faith? God forbid! Yea, we establish the law.' We do not place the whole of religion (as many do, God knoweth) either in doing no harm, or in doing good, or in using the ordinances of God. No, not in all of them together; wherein we know by experience a man may labour many years, and at the end have no religion at all, no more than he had at the beginning. Much less in any one of these; or, it may be, in a scrap of one of them: Like her who fancies herself a virtuous woman,

only because she is not a prostitute; or him who dreams he is an honest man, merely because he does not rob or steal. May the Lord God of my fathers preserve me from such a poor, starved religion as this! Were this the mark of a Methodist, I would sooner choose to be a sincere Jew, Turk, or Pagan.

5.　'What then is the mark? Who is a Methodist, according to your own account?' I answer: A Methodist is one who has 'the love of God shed abroad in his heart by the Holy Ghost given unto him'; one who 'loves the Lord his God with all his heart, and with all his soul, and with all his mind, and with all his strength.' God is the joy of his heart, and the desire of his soul; which is constantly crying out, 'Whom have I in heaven but thee? And there is none upon earth that I desire beside thee! My God and my all! Thou art the strength of my heart, and my portion for ever!"

6.　He is therefore happy in God, yea, always happy, as having in him 'a well of water springing up into everlasting life', and overflowing his soul with peace and joy. 'Perfect love' having now 'cast out fear', he 'rejoices evermore'. He 'rejoices in the Lord always', even 'in God his Saviour'; and in the Father, 'through our Lord Jesus Christ, by whom he hath now received the atonement'. 'Having' found 're-demption through his blood, the forgiveness of his sins'; he cannot but rejoice, whenever he looks back on the horrible pit out of which he is delivered; when he sees 'all his transgressions blotted out as a cloud, and his iniquities as a thick cloud'. He cannot but rejoice, whenever he looks on the state wherein he now is; 'being justified freely, and having peace with God through our Lord Jesus Christ' ...

7.　And he who hath this hope, thus 'full of immortality, in everything giveth thanks'; as knowing that this (whatsoever it is) 'is the will of God in Christ Jesus concerning him.' From him, therefore, he cheerfully receives all, saying, 'Good is the will of the Lord;' and whether the Lord giveth or taketh away, equally 'blessing the name of the Lord'. ...

16.　Lastly. As he has time, he 'does good unto all men'; unto neighbours and strangers, friends and enemies: And that in every possible kind; not only to their bodies, by 'feeding the hungry, clothing the naked, visiting those that are sick or in prison'; but much more does he labour to do good to their souls, as of the ability which God giveth; to awaken those that sleep in death; to bring those who are awak-ened to the atoning blood, that, 'being justified by faith, they may have peace with God'; and to provoke those who have peace with God to abound more in love and in good works. And he is willing to 'spend and be spent herein', even 'to be offered up on the sacrifice and service of their faith', so they may 'all come unto the measure of the stature of the fullness of Christ.'

17.　These are the principles and practices of our sect; these are the marks of a true Methodist. By these alone do those who are in derision so called, desire to be distinguished from other men. If any man say, 'Why, these are only the common fundamental principles of Christianity!' thou hast said; so I mean; this is the very truth; I know they are no other; and I would to God both thou and all men knew, that I, and all who follow my judgment, do vehemently refuse to be distinguished from other men, by any but the common principles of Christianity, – the plain, old Christianity that I teach, renouncing and detesting all other marks of distinction. And whosoever is what I preach (let him be called what he will, for names change not the nature of things), he is a Christian, not in name only, but in heart and in life. He is inwardly and outwardly conformed to the will of God, as revealed in the written word. He thinks, speaks, and lives, according to the method laid down in the revelation of Jesus Christ. His soul is renewed after the image of God, in righteousness and in all true holiness. And having the mind that was in Christ, he so walks as Christ also walked.

18. By these marks, by these fruits of a living faith, do we labour to distinguish ourselves from the unbelieving world, from all those whose minds or lives are not according to the Gospel of Christ. But from real Christians, of whatsoever denomination they be, we earnestly desire not to be distinguished at all, not from any who sincerely follow after what they know they have not yet attained. No: 'Whosoever doeth the will of my Father which is in heaven, the same is my brother, and sister, and mother.' And I beseech you, brethren, by the mercies of God, that we be in no wise divided among ourselves, Is thy heart right, as my heart with thine? I ask no farther question. If it be, give me thy hand. For opinions, or terms, let us not destroy the work of God. Dost thou love and serve God? It is enough. I give thee the right hand of fellowship. If there be any consolation in Christ, if any comfort of love, if any fellowship of the Spirit, if any bowels and mercies; let us strive together for the faith of the Gospel; walking worthy of the vocation wherewith we are called; with all lowliness and meekness, with long-suffering, forbearing one another in love, endeavouring to keep the unity of the Spirit in the bond of peace; remembering, there is one body, and one Spirit, even as we are called with one hope of our calling; 'one Lord, one faith, one baptism; one God and Father of all, who is above all, and through all, and in you all'.

(e)
For, from hence we may learn, First, that a catholic spirit is not *speculative* latitudinarianism. It is not an indifference to all opinions: This is the spawn of hell, not the offspring of heaven. This unsettledness of thought, this being 'driven to and fro, and tossed about with every wind of doctrine,' is a great curse, not a blessing; and irreconcilable enemy, not a friend, to true Catholicism. A man of a truly catholic spirit, has not now his religion to seek. He is fixed as the sun in his judgment concerning the main branches of Christian doctrine. It is true, he is always ready to hear and weigh whatsoever can be offered against his principles; but as this does not show any wavering in his own mind, so neither does it occasion any. He does not halt between two opinions, nor vainly endeavour to blend them into one. Observe this, you who know not what spirit ye are of; who call yourselves men of a catholic spirit, only because you are of a muddy understanding; because your mind is all in a mist; because you have no settled, consistent principles, but are for jumbling all opinions together. Be convinced, that you have quite missed your way; you know not where you are. You think you are got into the very Spirit of Christ; when, in truth, you are nearer the spirit of Antichrist. Go, first, and learn the first elements of the gospel of Christ, and then shall you learn to be of a truly catholic spirit.

2. From what has been said, we may learn. Secondly, that a catholic spirit is not any kind of *practical* latitudinarianism. It is not indifference as to public worship,

or as to the outward manner of performing it. This, likewise, would not be a blessing, but a curse. Far from being an help thereto, it would, so long as it remained, be an unspeakable hinderance to the worshipping of God in spirit and in truth. But the man of a truly catholic spirit, having weighed all things in the balance of the sanctuary, has no doubt, no scruple at all, concerning that particular mode of worship wherein he joins. He is clearly convinced, that *this* manner of worshipping God is both scriptural and rational. He knows none in the world which is more scriptural, none which is more rational. Therefore, without rambling hither and thither, he cleaves close thereto, and praises God for the opportunity of so doing.

3. Hence we may, Thirdly, learn, that a catholic spirit is not indifference to all congregations. This is another sort of latitudinarianism, no less absurd and unscriptural than the former. But it is far from a man of a truly catholic spirit. He is fixed in his congregation as well as his principles. He is united to one, not only in spirit, but by all the outward ties of Christian fellowship. There he partakes of all the ordinances of God. There he receives the supper of the Lord. There he pours out his soul in public prayer, and joins in public praise and thanksgiving. There he rejoices to hear the word of reconciliation, the gospel of the grace of God. With these his nearest, his best-beloved brethren, on solemn occasions, he seeks God by fasting. These particularly he watches over in love, as they do over his soul; admonishing, exhorting, comforting, reproving, and every way building up each other in the faith. These he regards as his own household; and therefore, according to the ability God has given him, naturally cares for them, and provides that they may have all the things that are needful for life and godliness.

4. But while he is steadily fixed in his religious principles, in what he belives to be the truth as it is in Jesus; while he firmly adheres to that worship of God which he judges to be most acceptable in his sight; and while he is united by the tenderest and closest ties to one particular congregation, – his heart is enlarged toward all mankind, those he knows and those he does not; he embraces with strong and cordial affection, neighbours and strangers, friends and enemies. This is catholic or universal love. And he that has this is of a catholic spirit. For love alone gives the title to this character: Catholic love is a catholic spirit.

5. If, then, we take this word in the strictest sense, a man of a catholic spirit is one who, in the manner above-mentioned, gives his hand to all whose hearts are right with his heart: One who knows how to value, and praise God for, all the advantages he enjoys, with regard to the knowledge of the things of God, the true scriptural manner of worshipping him, and, above all, his union with a congregation fearing God and working righteousness: One who, retaining these blessings with the strictest care, keeping them as the apple of his eye, at the same time loves, – as friends, as brethren in the Lord, as members of Christ and children of God, as joint-partakers now of the present kingdom of God, and fellow-heirs of his eternal kingdom, – all, of whatever opinion, or worship, or congregation, who believe in the Lord Jesus Christ; who love God and man; who rejoicing to please and fearing to offend God, are careful to abstain from evil, and zealous of good works. He is the man of a truly catholic spirit, who bears all these continually upon his heart: who, having an unspeakable tenderness for their persons, and longing for their welfare,

does not cease to commend them to God in prayer, as well as to plead their cause before men; who speaks comfortably to them, and labours, by all his words, to strengthen their hands in God. He assists them to the uttermost of his power in all things, spiritual and temporal. He is ready 'to spend and be spent for them;' yea, to lay down his life for their sake.

6.   Thou, O man of God, think on these things! If thou art already in this way, go on. If thou hast heretofore mistook the path, bless God who hath brought thee back! And now run the race which is set before thee, in the royal way of universal love. Take heed, lest thou be either wavering in thy judgment, or straitened in thy bowels: But keep an even pace, rooted in the faith once delivered to the saints, and grounded in love, in true catholic love, till thou art swallowed up in love for ever and ever!

(f)

I.   1.   The first of these [rules] is (he that heareth, let him understand!) 'Gain all you can.' Here we may speak like the children of the world: we meet them on their own ground. And it is our bounden duty to do this: we ought to gain all we can gain, without buying gold too dear, without paying more for it than it is worth. But this it is certain we ought not to do; we ought not to gain money at the expense of life, nor (which is in effect the same thing) at the expense of our health. Therefore, no gain whatsoever should induce us to enter into, or to continue in, any employ, which is of such a kind, or is attended to with so hard or so long labour, as to impair our constitution. Neither should we begin or continue in any business which necessarily deprives us of proper seasons for food and sleep, in such a proportion as our nature requires. Indeed, there is a great difference here. Some employments are absolutely and totally unhealthy; as those which imply the dealing much with arsenic, or other equally hurtful minerals, or the breathing an air tainted with streams of melting lead, which must at length destroy the firmest constitution. Others may not be absolutely unhealthy, but only to persons of a weak constitution. Such are those which require many hours to be spent in writing; especially if a person write sitting, and lean upon his stomach, or remain long in an uneasy posture. ...

2.   We are, secondly, to gain all we can without hurting our mind, any more than our body. For neither may we hurt this: we must preserve, at all events, the spirit of an healthful mind. ...

II. 1.   Having gained all you can, by honest wisdom, and unwearied diligence, the second rule of Christian prudence is, 'Save all you can.' Do not throw the precious talent into the sea, leave that folly to heathen philosophers. Do not throw it away in idle expenses, which is just the same as throwing it into the sea. Expend no part of it merely to gratify the desire of the flesh, the desire of the eye, or the pride of life. ...

III. 1.   But let not any man imagine that he has done anything, barely by going thus far, by 'gaining and saving all he can,' if he were to stop here. All this is nothing, if a man go not forward, if he does not point all this at a farther end. Nor, indeed, can a man properly be said to save anything, if he only lays it up. You may as well throw your money into the sea, as bury it in the earth. And you may as well bury it in the earth, as in your chest, or in the Bank of England. Not to use, is effectually to throw it away. ... Give all you can ... give all you have to God. ...

7.   Brethren, can we be either wise or faithful stewards unless we thus manage our Lord's goods? We cannot, as not only the oracles of God, but our own conscience, beareth witness. Then why should we delay? Why should we confer any longer with flesh and blood, or men of the world? Our kingdom, our wisdom, is not of this world: heathen custom is nothing to us. We follow no men any farther than they are followers of Christ. Hear ye him: yea, to-day, while it is called to-day, hear and obey his voice! At this hour, and from this hour, do his will: fulfil his word, in this and in all things! I entreat you, in the name of the Lord Jesus, act up to the dignity of your calling! No more sloth! Whatsoever your hand findeth to do, do it with your might! No more waste! Cut off every expense which fashion caprice, or flesh and blood demand! No more covetousness! But employ whatever God has entrusted you with, in doing good, all possible good, in every possible kind and degree, to the household of faith, to all men! This is no small part of 'the wisdom of the just.' Give all ye have, as well as all ye are, a spiritual sacrifice to Him who withheld not from you his Son, His only Son: so 'laying up in store for yourselves a good foundation against the time to come, that ye may attain eternal life!'

Document II.25

John Wesley and George Whitefield on Grace

During George Whitefield's absence in America John Wesley, against Whitefield's wishes, published his sermon on 'Free Grace' (though he did have the grace to omit it from his Standard Sermons on account of its manner). Here is the great negation in Wesley's thought: his utter rejection on moral grounds of predestinarian doctrine. Like Arminius before him (though in an evangelical rather than a rationalistic Arminian way) he interpreted the New Testament passages referring to election as indicative of the foreknowledge of God, not as implying divine decrees established from eternity. This, he said, was the 'hair's-breadth' which separated him from Calvinism – though many in his own day and since have perceived an unbridgeable chasm between the two. The Welsh Calvinistic evangelical Howel Harris sought to mediate between the Englishmen, but following Whitefield's letter to Wesley a breach occurred between the two men which lasted until 1742 – though their personal reconciliation did not imply doctrinal accord.

For Wesley see Document II.21. For Whitefield (1714–70) see DEB, DECBP, DNB, ODCC; A. Dallimore, *George Whitefield*, London: The Banner of Truth Trust, 1970, (vol. I) and 1980 (vol. II), H. S. Stout, *The Divine Dramatist: George Whitefield and the Rise of Modern Evangelicalism*, Grand Rapids: Eerdmans, 1991. For Harris see DEB, DNB, DWB, ODCC; Geoffrey F. Nuttall, *Howel Harris 1714–1773: The Last Enthusiast*, Cardiff: University of Wales Press, 1965; Eifion Evans, *Howel Harris, Evangelist*, Cardiff: University of Wales Press, 1974; Geraint Tudur, 'A Critical Study, Based on His Own Diaries, of the Life and Work of Howell Harris and His Contribution to the Methodist Revival in Wales between 1735 and 1752', unpublished doctoral dissertation, University of Oxford, 1989; idem, *Howell Harris: From Conversion to Separation, 1735–1750*, Cardiff: University of Wales Press, 2000.

Extract (a) is from Wesley's Sermon 128 on 'Free grace', in *Works*, 1829, VII, pp. 382–4.

In a letter of 27 October 1740 (extract (b)) Howel Harris informs John Cennick that he has been attempting to mediate between Wesley and Whitefield (reprinted in *The Journal of the Historical Society of the Presbyterian Church of Wales*, LX, no. 2, October 1975, p. 48).

Whitefield's reply to Wesley, the last part of which is reproduced here in extract (c), was written from Georgia on 24 December 1740 and makes plain his distress at Wesley's content and manner. It is from Whitefield's *Works*, London, 1771, pp. 72–3.

Extracts from Wesley's *Journal* (*Works*, 1829, I, p. 305; and III, p. 421) are printed in text (d).

Given the tone of Wesley's published sermon on 'Free grace', extract (e), from his *History of Methodism* (*Works*, 1872, VIII, p. 349), may be thought to display a rather smugly 'pious' tone.

(a)

24.   This premised, let it be observed, that this doctrine represents our blessed Lord, 'Jesus Christ the righteous,' 'the only begotten Son of the Father, full of grace and truth,' as an hypocrite, a deceiver of the people, a man void of common sincerity. For it cannot be denied, that he everywhere speaks as if he was willing that all men should be saved. Therefore, to say he was not willing that all men should be saved, is to represent him as a mere hypocrite and dissembler. It cannot be denied that the gracious words which came out of his mouth are full of invitations to all sinners. To say, then, he did not intend to save all sinners, is to represent him as a gross deceiver of the people. You cannot deny that he says, 'Come unto me, all ye that are weary and heavy laden.' If, then, you say he calls those that cannot come; those whom he knows to be unable to come; those whom he can make able to come, but will not; how is it possible to describe greater insincerity? You represent him as mocking his helpless creatures, by offering what he never intends to give. You describe him as saying one thing, and meaning another; as pretending the love which he had not. Him, in 'whose mouth was no guile,' you make full of deceit, void of common sincerity; – then especially, when, drawing nigh the city, He wept over it and said, 'O Jerusalem, Jerusalem, thou that killest the prophets, and stonest them that are sent unto thee; how often *would I* have gathered thy children together, – and *ye would not;* ηθελησα – και ουκ ηθελησατε. Now, if you say, *they would*, but *he, would not*, you represent him (which who could hear?) as weeping crocodiles' tears; weeping over the prey which himself had doomed to destruction!

25.   Such blasphemy this, as one would think might make the ears of a Christian to tingle! But there is yet more behind; for just as it honours the Son, so doth this doctrine honour the Father. It destroys all his attributes at once: It overturns both his justice, mercy, and truth; yea, it represents the most holy God as worse than the devil, as both more false, more cruel, and more unjust. More *false;* because the devil, liar as he is, hath never said, 'He willeth all men to be saved:' More *unjust;* because the

devil cannot, if he would, be guilty of such injustice as you ascribe to God, when you say that God condemned millions of souls to everlasting fire, prepared for the devil and his angels, for continuing in sin, which, for want of that grace *he will not* give them, they cannot avoid: And more *cruel*; because that unhappy spirit 'seeketh rest and findeth none;' so that his own restless misery is a kind of temptation to him to tempt others. But God resteth in his high and holy place; so that to suppose him, of his own mere motion, of his pure will and pleasure, happy as he is, to doom his creatures, whether they will or no, to endless misery, is to impute such cruelty to him as we cannot impute even to the great enemy of God and man. It is to represent the most high God (he that hath ears to hear let him hear!) as more cruel, false, and unjust than the devil!

26.   This is the blasphemy clearly contained in *the horrible decree* of predestination! And here I fix my foot. On this I join issue with every assertor of it. You represent God as worse than the devil; more false, more cruel, more unjust. But you say you will prove it by Scripture. Hold! What will you prove by Scripture? That God is worse than the devil? It cannot be. Whatever that Scripture proves, it never can prove this; whatever its true meaning be, this cannot be its true meaning. Do you ask, 'What is its true meaning then?' If I say, 'I know not,' you have gained nothing; for there are many scriptures the true sense whereof neither you nor I shall know till death is swallowed up in victory. But this I know, better it were to say it had no sense at all, than to say it had such a sense as this. It cannot mean, whatever it mean besides, that the God of truth is a liar. Let it mean what it will, it cannot mean that the Judge of all the world is unjust. No scripture can mean that God is not love, or that his mercy is not over all his works; that is, whatever it prove beside, no scripture can prove predestination.

27.   This is the blasphemy for which (however I love the persons who assert it) I abhor the doctrine of predestination, a doctrine, upon the supposition of which, if one could possibly suppose it for a moment, (call it election, reprobation, or what you please, for all comes to the same thing,) one might say to our adversary, the devil, 'Thou fool, why dost thou roar about any longer? Thy lying in wait for souls is as needless and useless as our preaching. Hearest thou not, that God hath taken thy work out of thy hands; and that He doeth it much more effectually? Thou, with all thy principalities and powers, canst only so assault that we may resist thee; but He can irresistibly destroy both body and soul in hell! Thou canst only entice; but His unchangeable decree, to leave thousands of souls in death, compels them to continue in sin, till they drop into everlasting burnings. Thou temptest; He forceth us to be damned; for we cannot resist his will. Thou fool, why goest thou about any longer, seeking whom thou mayest devour? Hearest thou not that God is the devouring lion, the destroyer of souls, the murderer of men? Moloch caused only children to pass through the fire; and that fire was soon quenched; or, the corruptible body being consumed, its torment was at an end; but God, thou art told, by his eternal decree, fixed before they had done good or evil, causes, not only children of a span long, but the parents also, to pass through the fire of hell, the " fire which never shall be quenched;" and the body which is cast thereinto, being now incorruptible and immortal, will be ever consuming and never consumed, but " the

smoke of their torment," because it is God's good pleasure, "ascendeth up for ever and ever.'"

(b)

I have been long waiting to see if Brother *John* and *Charles* should receive farther Light, or be silent, and not *oppose Election* and *Perseverance*; but finding no Hope thereof, I begin to be stagger'd about them what to do. I plainly see that we preach two Gospels, one sets *all on God*, the other *on Man*; the one on *God's Will*, the other on *Man's Will*; the one on *God's chusing*, the other on *Man's chusing*; the one on *God's Distinguishing Love, making one to differ from another*, the other on *Man's being better than another, and taking more pains, and being a better husband of his Grace than another, more* passive *under the Hand of the Spirit than the other*; and if both shou'd come to Heaven they cou'd not harmonize in Praises. The one must say, 'Lord, had it not been for thy Special Distinguishing Grace making me to differ, giving me the Will and the Power, and loving me with an Unchangeable, Free, Sovereign, and Everlasting *Love*, I shou'd have been in *Hell* for ever.' The other must say, I praise thee for offering Salvation to me as well as to all others, but I must thank *myself* for being passive under thy Hand, which others were not, or they might have believed too as well as me. I thank *myself* for receiving thee, and I must thank *myself* for being constant, faithful, and persevering, and improving it well.'

One Reason staggers me much about all *Universalists*, when there is an Appeal made to their Experiences, if then they will not come to see *Electing Love*. For whoever has *Distinguishing Love*, has Light with that, to see that he has a *particular Favour*, and so is under a *particular Obligation* to glorify God, and willingly takes away all Occasion of glorying or boasting but that. For it is a wide Difference to be saved or to be lost, to be for ever with God, and forever with the Devil. And it is a Matter of the highest Moment, that *whoever* or *whatever* makes the Difference should have the Glory of it; it being the Hinge on which turns our Salvation. The one is no more than the Covenant of Works, or the keeping of Man in himself, *viz. Do this, be passive*, and live: Not telling them that *they are dead*, and *cannot make themselves alive*, &c. setting him to look for a Power in himself which must be derived from Christ, and freely given by Christ, I mean the *Power of receiving Power*, the renewed submissive Will, the Power of believing, resting, and confiding in Christ. Christ saith, *No Man can come to me except the Father who hath sent me to draw him.* Man says, All can come; 'tis not in God's drawing but in Man's willing or chusing that the Difference lies. Christ saith, *All that the Father hath given to me shall come to me, and because I change not, none shall pluck them out of my Hands, for they must be confident of this one Thing, that he that hath begun the good Work, will carry it on 'till it is finished.* But Man says, *God* draweth all alike, but some resist him. But did not we all resist him 'till he drew us irresistibly, so that we could not be unwilling. The Father gave us all to Christ (say they) though all do not come. And so the one or the other must be false. The one puts the poor Soul's Comfort on *God's* Unchangeableness, and the other on Man's Faithfulness. How can that poor Soul have Assurance, who believes that to Day he may be justified, and so be a Child of God, and to morrow be a Child of the Devil and be damned. My dear Brother, deal faithfully with Brother *John* and *Charles*; if you will you may read this Letter to them. I must own the Difference did not appear to be so great as it doth now. But as the *Glory of God's Grace* is concern'd in it, I must declare to all the World who made us and all the Children of God to differ from the rest; as well as call all to Christ, *and let him that hath Ears to hear hear*. And as you must answer to your Father for every Thing he has taught you, to see that in this you are faithful to declare the *whole Counsel of God*, and teach others as *God* has taught you: And beware of the Sophistry of human Reasoning. While the Doctrine of final Perseverance is not fully and clearly set forth to the Children of the *Covenant*, they are *robbed of the Food* that their Father has prepared for them, and are kept under the Bondage of a slavish Fear of Hell: And *if thou lovest me, feed my Lambs* (saith Christ) and this is their Food, to tell them, that *that God who once loved them loveth them to the End*. And as it was God that gave them the Will, he will give them the Power also. ...

(c)

I purposely omit making any further particular remarks on the several last pages of your sermon. Indeed had not your name, dear Sir, been prefixed to the sermon, I could not have been so uncharitable as to think you were the author of such sophistry. You beg the question, in saying, 'That God has declared, (notwithstanding you own, I suppose, some will be damned) that he will save all,' *i.e.* every individual person. You take it for granted (for solid proof you have none) that God is unjust, if he passed by any, and then you exclaim against the horrible decree: and yet, as I before hinted, in holding the doctrine of original sin, you profess to believe that he might justly have passed by all.

Dear, dear Sir, O be not offended! For Christ's sake be not rash! Give yourself to reading. Study the covenant of grace. Down with your carnal reasoning. Be a little child; and then, instead of pawning your salvation, as you have done in a late hymn book, if the doctrine of *universal redemption* be not true; instead of talking of *sinless perfection*, as you have done in the preface to that hymn book, and making man's salvation to depend on his own *free-will*, as you have in this sermon; you will compose a hymn in praise of sovereign distinguishing love. You will caution believers against striving to work a perfection out of their own hearts, and print another sermon the reverse of this, and entitle it free-grace *indeed*. Free, because not free to all; but free, because God may withhold or give it to whom and when he pleases.

Till you do this, I must doubt whether or not you know yourself. In the mean while, I cannot but blame you for censuring the clergy of your church for not keeping to their articles, when you yourself by your principles, positively deny the 9th, 10th and 17th. Dear Sir, these things ought not so to be. God knows my heart, as I told you before, so I declare again, nothing but a single regard to the honour of Christ has forced this letter from me. I love and honour you for his sake; and when I come to judgment, will thank you before men and angels, for what you have, under God, done for my soul.

There, I am persuaded, I shall see dear Mr. *Wesley* convinced of election and everlasting love. And it often fills me with pleasure, to think how I shall behold you casting your crown down at the feet of the Lamb, and as it were filled with a holy blushing for opposing the divine sovereignty in the manner you have done.

But I hope the Lord with shew you this before you go hence. O how do I long for that day! If the Lord should be pleased to make use of this letter for that purpose, it would abundantly rejoice the heart of, dear and honoured Sir,

> Your affectionate, though unworthy brother
> and servant in Christ,
> GEORGE WHITEFIELD.

(d)

Sat. 28. – Having heard much of Mr. Whitefield's unkind behaviour, since his return from Georgia, I went to him to hear him speak for himself, that I might know how to judge. I must approved of his plainness of speech. He told me, he and I preached two different gospels, and therefore he not only would not join with, or give me the right hand of fellowship, but was resolved publicly to preach against me and my brother, wheresoever he preached at all. Mr. Hall (who went with me) put him in mind of the promise he had made but a few days before, that, whatever his private opinion was, he would never publicly preach against us. He said, that promise was only an effect of human weakness, and he was now of another mind. ...

Sat. 10. – I returned to London, and had the melancholy news of Mr. Whitefield's death confirmed by his executors, who desired me to preach his funeral sermon on Sunday, the 18th. In order to write this, I retired to Lewisham on *Monday*; and on *Sunday* following, went to the chapel in Tottenham Court Road. An immense multitude was gathered together from all corners of the town. I was at first afraid that a great part of the congregation would not be able to hear; but it pleased God so as to strengthen my voice, that even those at the door heard distinctly. It was an awful season: All were still as night: Most appeared to be deeply affected; and an impression was made on many, which one would hope will not speedily be effaced.

The time appointed for my beginning at the Tabernacle was half-hour after five: But it was quite filled at three; so I began at four. At first the noise was exceeding great; but it ceased when I began to speak; and my voice was again so strengthened that all who were within could hear, unless an accidental noise hindered here or there for a few moments. O that all may hear the voice of Him with whom are the issues of life and death; and who so loudly, by this unexpected stroke, calls all his children to love one another!

(e)

11. In March, 1741, Mr. Whitefield, being returned to England, entirely separated from Mr. Wesley and his friends, because he did not hold the decrees. Here was the first breach, which warm men persuaded Mr. Whitefield to make merely for a difference of opinion. Those, indeed, who believed universal redemption had no desire at all to separate; but those who held particular redemption would not hear of any

accommodation, being determined to have no fellowship with men that 'were in so dangerous errors.' So there were now two sorts of Methodists, so called; those for particular, and those for general, redemption.

Document II.26

John Wesley contra John Gill on Predestination

John Wesley returned to the theme of predestination, publishing his *Predestination Calmly Considered* in 1752. This was a critique of the position of John Gill (1679–1771), the leading Particular Baptist Theologian of his day. Towards the end of his tract Wesley makes it plain that his complaint is not merely doctrinal, but practical: he fears that those who hold to predestination will, because they consider themselves elect, lapse into Antinomianism and loose living. Extract (a) is from pp. 78–9. For Gill see DEB, DNB; the bibliography in Alan P. F. Sell, *The Great Debate: Calvinism, Arminianism and Salvation*, Worthing: H. E. Walter, 1982 and Grand Rapids: Baker Book House, 1983; repr. Eugene, OR: Wipf and Stock, 1998, p. 127, to which may now be added, Timothy George, 'John Gill', in T. George and David S. Dockery, eds, *Baptist Theologians*, Nashville, TN: Broadman Press, 1990, pp. 77–101; George M. Ella, *John Gill and the Cause of God and Truth*, Eggleston, Co. Durham: Go Publications, 1995; Michael A. G. Haykin, ed., *The Life and Thought of John Gill (1697–1771). A Tercentennial Appreciation*, Leiden: Brill, 1997.

Wesley's tract drew a prompt reply from Gill, who published *The Doctrine of Predestination Stated and set in the Scripture-Light; in Opposition to Mr. Wesley's Predestination Calmly Consider'd*, London, 1752. Extract (b) is from the second edition, 1752, pp. 5–6, 8, 10, 12, 18–19.

(a)

LXXXIV. The Truth is, neither this Opinion nor that, but the Love of God humbles Man, and that only. Let but this be shed abroad in his Heart, and he abhors himself in Dust and Ashes. As soon as this enters into his Soul, lowly Shame covers his Face. That Thought, What is God? What hath he done for *me*? is immediately followed by, What am I? And then he knoweth not what to do, or where to hide, or how to abase himself enough, before the great God of Love, of whom he now knoweth, that as his Majesty is, so is his Mercy. Let him who has *felt* this, (whatever be his Opinion) say, whether he could ascribe to himself any Part of his Salvation, or the Glory of any good Word or Thought? Lean then, who will, on that broken Reed for Humility: but let the Love of God humble my Soul!

LXXXV. 'Why this is the very Thing which recommends it. This Doctrine makes Men love God.' I answer as before: Accidentally it may; because God can draw Good out of Evil. But you will not say, all who hold it, love God; so it is no *certain* Means to that End. Nor will you say, that none love him who hold it not. Neither therefore is it a *necessary* Means. But indeed when you talk at all of its 'making Men love God,' you know not what you do. You lead Men into more Danger that you are aware of. You almost unavoidably lead them into *resting* on that Opinion. You cut them off from a true Dependence on the Fountain of living Waters, and strengthen then in hewing to themselves broken Cisterns, which can hold no Water.

LXXXVI. This is my grand Objection to the Doctrine of Reprobation, or (which is the same) unconditional Election. That it is an Error I know; because if this were true, the whole Scripture must be false. But it is not only for this, because it is an Error, that I so earnestly oppose it, but because it is an Error of so pernicious Consequences to the Souls of Men; because it directly and naturally tends, to hinder the inward Work of God in every Stage of it.

(b)

I.   In *general*, as respecting all things that have been, are, or shall be, or done in the world; every thing comes under the determination and appointment of God; 'he did, as the *assembly* of divines say in their confession, from all eternity, unchangeably ordain whatsoever comes to pass;' or, as they express it in their catechism, 'God's decrees are the wise, free and holy acts of the counsel of his will; whereby from all eternity, he hath, for his own glory, unchangeably fore-ordained whatsoever comes to pass in time:' and this predestination and foreappointment of all things, may be concluded from the fore-knowledge of God ...

To deny this, is to deny the providence of God, and his government of the world, which none but *Deists* and *Atheists* will do; at least it is to think and speak unworthily of God, as not being that all-knowing and all-wise, and sovereign ruler of the world, he is ...

II.   Predestination may be considered as *special*, and as relating to particular persons, and to things spiritual and eternal; whereas predestination in general respects all creatures and things, even things temporal and civil. ...

Predestination which the scriptures chiefly treat of, is what respects men, and consists of two parts, *election* and *reprobation*; the one is a predestination unto life, the other unto death.

Election, which is a predestination unto life, is an act of the free grace of God, of his sovereign and immutable will, by which from all eternity he has chosen in Christ, out of the common mass of mankind, some men, or a certain number of them, to partake of spiritual blessings here, and happiness hereafter, for the glory of his grace.

The objects of election are *some* men, not all, which a choice supposes to take all would be no choice; called therefore a *remnant according to the election of grace*, Rom. xi. 5. ...

This act of election is irrespective of faith, holiness and gook [good] works, as causes or conditions of it; faith flows from it, is a fruit and effect of it, is secured by it, and is had in consequence of it ...

The act of election was made in Christ, as the head, in whom all the elect were chosen, and into whose hands, by this act of grace, were put their persons, grace and glory; and this is an eternal act of God in him ...

First, Preterition is God's act of passing by, or leaving some men when he chose others, according to his sovereign will and pleasure; of which act of God there is clear evidence in the sacred Scripture; as well as it is necessarily implied in God's act of election, which has such clear and incontestable proof. ...

Secondly, Pre-damnation is God's decree to condemn men for sin, or to punish them with everlasting damnation for it: and this is the sense of the Scriptures; and this is the view which they give us of this doctrine, *Prov.* xvi.4. *The Lord hath made all things for himself, yea, even the wicked for the day of evil*: Not that God made man to damn him; the scripture says no such thing, nor do we; nor is the sense of the doctrine we plead for; nor is it to be inferred from it. God made man neither to damn him, nor save him, but for his own glory; that is his ultimate end in making him, which is answered whether he is saved or lost: but the meaning is, that God has appointed all things for his glory and particularly he has appointed the wicked man to the day of ruin and destruction for his wickedness. *Jude* ver. 4. ...

Thirdly, This decree, we say, is according to the sovereign will of God; for nothing can be the cause of his decree but his own will ...

Document II.27

John Wesley contra John Gill on the Final Perseverance of the Saints

In the same year, 1752, Wesley and Gill clashed over the final perseverance of the saints, with Gill maintaining that the elect cannot finally fall from grace, Wesley that they may.

Extract (a) is from Wesley's *Serious Thoughts upon the Perseverance of the Saints* (*Works*, 1872, X, pp. 285, 297–8).

Gill's first response to Wesley is entitled *The Doctrine of the Saint's Final Perseverance, Asserted and Vindicated*: *In Answer to a late Pamphlet, called, Serious Thoughts on that Subject*, 1752. Extract (b) comprises pp. 3–4, 57–9.

Unpersuaded, Wesley turns to verse, ironically adopting the stance of a Calvinist, whose thoughts he recounts in *An Essay in Answer to All which The Revd. Dr. Gill has Printed on the Final Perseverance of the Saints*, 1754. Of this ten stanzas will more than suffice, (extract (c)).

(a)

2.   By *the saints*, I understand, those who are holy or righteous in the judgment of God himself; those who are endued with the faith that purifies the heart, that produces a good conscience; those who are grafted into the good olive-tree, the spiritual, invisible Church; those who are branches of the true vine, of whom Christ ways, 'I am the vine, ye are the branches;' those who so effectually know Christ, as by that knowledge to have escaped the pollutions of the world; those who see the light of the glory of God in the face of Jesus Christ, and who have been made partakers of the Holy Ghost, of the witness and the fruits of the Spirit; those who live by faith in

the Son of God; those who are sanctified by the blood of the covenant; those to whom all or any of these characters belong, I mean by the term *saints*.

3. Can any of these fall away? By *falling away*, we mean, not barely falling into sin. This, it is granted, they may. But can they fall totally? Can any of these so fall from God as to perish everlastingly?

4. I am sensible either side of this question is attended with great difficulties; such as reason alone could never remove. Therefore, 'to the law and to the testimony,' Let the living oracles decide: And if these speak for us, we neither seek nor want farther witness.

5. On this authority, I believe a saint may fall away; that one who is holy or righteous in the judgment of God himself may nevertheless so fall from God as to perish everlastingly. ...

29. 'Can a child of God then go to hell? Or can a man be a child of God to-day, and a child of the devil to-morrow? If God is our Father once, is he not our Father always?'

I answer, (1.) A child of God, that is, a true believer, (for he that believeth is born of God,) while he continues a true believer, cannot go to hell. But, (2.) If a believer make shipwreck of the faith, he is no longer a child of God. And then he may go to hell, yea, and certainly will, if he continues in unbelief. (3.) If a believer may make shipwreck of the faith, then a man that believes now may be an unbeliever some time hence; yea, very possibly to-morrow; but, if so, he who is a child of God to-day, may be a child of the devil to-morrow. For, (4.) God is the Father of them that believe, so long as they believe. But the devil is the father of them that believe not, whether they did once believe or no.

30. The sum of all is this: If the Scriptures are true, those who are holy or righteous in the judgment of God himself; those who are endued with the faith that purifies the heart, that produces a good conscience; those who are grafted into the good olive tree, the spiritual, invisible Church; those who are branches of the true vine, of whom Christ says, 'I am the vine, ye are the branches;' those who so effectually know Christ, as by that knowledge to have escaped the pollutions of the world; those who see the light of the glory of God in the face of Jesus Christ, and who have been made partakers of the Holy Ghost, of the witness and of the fruits of the Spirit; those who live by faith in the Son of God; those who are sanctified by the blood of the covenant, may nevertheless so fall from God as to perish everlastingly.

Therefore, let him that standeth take heed lest he fall.

(b)

The doctrine of the saints final perseverance in grace to glory, being a doctrine so fully expressed in the sacred scriptures, so clearly wrote there as with a sun-beam, having so large a compass of proof, as scarce any other doctrine has; a doctrine so agreeable to the perfections of God; and the contrary so manifestly reflecting dishonour upon them, particularly the immutability of God, his wisdom, power, goodness, justice, truth, and faithfulness; a doctrine so well established upon his purposes and decrees, his counsel and covenant, and which so well accords with all his acts of grace towards, and upon his people; a doctrine so well calculated for their spiritual peace and comfort, and to promote holiness of life and conversation; a doctrine one would think, that every good man must *wish*, at least, to be true; it may seem strange, that any man believing divine revelation, and professing godliness should set himself to oppose it, and call such an opposition *Serious Thoughts* upon it, as a late writer has done; who has published a pamphlet under such a title, and which now lies before me, and which I have undertook to answer, and shall attempt to do it in the following manner. And it is to be hoped, he will think again, and more seriously, and that his latter thoughts will be better than his former. ...

Ninthly, From all that has been said it clearly appears, that the glory of all three persons in the Godhead, Father, Son and Spirit, is concerned in this affair, and they must lose it if this doctrine is not true; or if the saints should everlastingly perish, where would be the Father's glory in election, in the covenant of grace, and in the mission of his Son? Where would be the glory of the Son of God in the redemption of his people, in his sacrifice and satisfaction, and his intercession for them? And where would be the glory of the divine Spirit in the sanctification and sealing of them, if after all this they perish everlastingly? For all depends upon their final perseverance and compleat salvation. And therefore we may be assured, that since the saints are held with this threefold cord, which can never be broken, their final perseverance is certain, and their everlasting salvation sure.

Tenthly, The contrary doctrine takes away the foundation of a believer's joy and comfort; it makes the love of God changeable; the covenant of grace failable; the redemption and satisfaction of Christ insufficient; and the work and graces of the Spirit loseable; and so, must consequently fill the minds of the children of God with great doubts, fears, and distresses, if not despair, since their state and condition is so very precarious; what comfort can a believer take in his present circumstances, if they are such, as by a single act of sin, to which he is liable every moment, he may be removed from a state of grace into a state of condemnation; and notwithstanding all the favours bestowed on him, and promises made unto him, and grace given him, he may perish everlastingly? but this writer I have been considering tells[1] us, that his comfort is not affected hereby; it does not stand upon this, but upon his present knowledge, sight, faith, frames, and a good conversation; and bids men go and find a more solid joy, a more blissful comfort on this side heaven. But blessed be God, we have a better foundation for joy and comfort than all this; the true believer, tho' he lives *by faith*, he don't live *upon* it; he lives by it as *Esau* did *by* his *sword*;[2] he did not live upon it, that would have been hard living indeed, but he lived upon what it brought him; so a believer lives not on his faith, but upon Christ, and the grace of Christ, faith brings nigh unto him. He has better things than uncertain precarious frames to live upon, and receive his comforts from; even the unchangeable love of God; the unalterable covenant of grace; the faithfulness of God, who tho' *we believe not, yet he abides faithful*;[3] absolute and unconditional promises; Jesus Christ, the same to day, yesterday, and for ever; his precious blood, perfect righteousness, atoning sacrifice, and that fullness of grace which is in him.

132

To conclude: If a man may be confident of any one thing in this world, he may be *confident of this very thing*, that in whomsoever, whether in himself, or in any other, God *hath begun a good work*, he *will perform it until the day of Jesus Christ*;[4] and that *all* the true *Israel* of God *shall be saved in the Lord with an everlasting salvation*;[5] and that not one of them shall eternally perish.

Notes

1. Serious Thoughts, p. 19, 20.
2. Gen. xxxvii. 40.
3. 2 Tim. ii. 13
4. Phil. i. 6.
5. Is. xlv. 17.

(c)

29   What if I sinn'd *sometimes*
          In this *imperfect* State,
It was not like the damning Crimes
          Of a lost Reprobate;
          Sin was not Sin in *me*,
          God doth not blame his own,
Doth not behold Iniquity
          In any Chosen One.

30   What if I *foully* fell,
          I *finally* could not;
His Grace is irresistible,
          And back I *must* be brought:
          What if in Sin I liv'd,
          The firm Decree is past,
I *must* be at my Death receiv'd
          I *must* be sav'd at last.

31   How could my Folly dare
          Satan and Sin to flight?
The Judgements of my God were far
          Above out of my Sight:
          His Wrath was not for me,
          And therefore I defied
Mine enemies, from Danger free,
          In self-electing Pride.

32   Not all his threaten'd Woes
          My stubborn Heart cou'd move;

His threatenings only were for those
    Who never knew his Love:
    He cannot take away
    His covenanted Grace,
Tho' I rebel, and disobey,
    And mock Him to his Face.

33   He cannot me pass by,
    Or utterly reject,
Or judge his People, or deny
    To save his own Elect;
    He swore to bring me in
    To Heaven; 'twere Perjury
For God to punish me for Sin,
    For God to pass by me.

34   'Twas thus my wretched Heart
    Abus'd his patient Grace,
Provok'd his Mercy to depart,
    His Justice to take Place:
    Unconscious of it State,
    In Death my Soul abode,
Nor groan'd beneath its guilty Weight,
    Nor knew its Fall from God.

35   I could not be restor'd
    By pard'ning Grace renew'd,
While trampling on his Written Word,
    Self-confident I stood:
    He only saves the Lost,
    Which I cou'd never be,
I never *cou'd* be damn'd, but *must*
    Be sav'd by his Decree.

36   O my offended God
    If now at last I see,
That I have trampled on thy Blood,
    And done Despite to Thee;
    If I begin to wak
    Out of my deadly Sleep,
Into thine Arms of Mercy take,
    And there for ever keep.

37   I can no longer trust
    In my Abuse of Grace,

I own Thee Merciful and Just,
  If banish'd from thy Face:
  Tho' once I surely knew,
  And felt my Sins forgiven,
Faithful I own Thee, Lord, and true,
  If now shut out from Heaven.

38 But O! forbid it, Lord,
  Nor drive me from thy Face,
While self-condemned, and self abhor'd,
  I humbly sue for Grace:
  For thine own Mercy's Sake
  My guilty Soul release,
And now, my Pardon give me back,
  And bid me lie in Peace.

Document II.28

Notes of a General Baptist Sermon

The following are notes of a sermon by William Evershed (1717–99), a prominent General Baptist Minister in Kent and Sussex. We may note the moralistic tone and the repeated reference to the rational. The source is *William Evershed's Sermon Notes, 1791 to 1793 and 1797 to 1799*, transcribed by Peter B. Evershed (The General Baptist Assembly Occasional Paper, no. 20), London: Leonard J. Maguire, 1993, p. 6.

Account Mr John Billinghurst, Ditchling, 24 Decem 1791.

Ecclesiastes 11.8. But if a Man live many years, and rejoice in them all; yet let him remember the days of darkness, for they shall be many &c.

1 It does not appear that Solomon's words are confined to a bad sense, but rather cautionary. If the man live many years, & enjoys a comfortable and happy prosperous life, he may rejoice in it, but let his joy be rational, modest and thoughtful. Remember the day will have an end, & light & darkness will follow, which shuts the scene of human life, & closes our accounts.
2 Here is a lesson to the young, the thoughtless gay, whose blood is warm, passions strong, & surrounding temptations many; consider the nature of your rejoicing, – the days of your youth may be shortened, & the day of darkness soon come upon you.
3 Let such consider this that forget God, & rejoice in affronting the God of their life. Rejoicing in scenes of wickedness and vice, hateful to God & shameful to man, how will such endure the days of darkness.
4 Let the sons of Bacchus now consider the nature & issue of their rejoicing, is it

rational, or in the lowest degree debasing human nature, hurtful to our selves, & a preparative for every vice.

5   What then is the rejoicing of the good man & sincere Christian? It is this. He partakes of the blessing of Heaven with cheerfulness & gratitude, he enjoys with that moderation, by which he enjoys the senses of it, & is heartily thankful to God for all his good.

6   But this is not all, the good Christian has an inward rejoicing the world cannot give nor take away, the answer of a good conscience towards God, as a faithful disciple of Jesus Christ, he expects the approbation of his coming, & the days of darkness are as light to him.

Document II.29

The Articles of Religion of the New Connexion General Baptists

As we have seen, the New Connexion, founded by Dan Taylor in 1770, embraced more orthodox General Baptists and many converted during the Evangelical Revival. For the first five years of its life ministers of the New Connexion had to subscribe to the following articles, reprinted from W.L. Lumpkin, *Baptist Confessions of Faith*, Valley Forge, PA: Judson Press, rev. edn, 1969, pp. 342–4. Still Arminian, they are evangelically, not rationalistically, so (contrast Document II.28 above).

For Dan Taylor (1738–1816) see DEB, DNB.

ARTICLE 1.   *On the Fall of Man.* We believe, that man was made upright in the image of God, free from all disorder natural and moral; capable of obeying perfectly the will and command of God his Maker; yet capable also of sinning: which he unhappily did, and thereby laid himself under the divine curse; which, we think, could include nothing less than the mortality of the body and the eternal punishment of the soul. His nature also became depraved; his mind was defiled; and the powers of his soul weakened – that both he was, and his posterity are, captives of Satan till set at liberty by Christ.

ARTICLE 2.   *On the Nature and Perpetual Obligation of the Moral Law.* We believe, that the moral law not only extends to the outward actions of the life, but to all the powers and faculties of the mind, to every desire, temper and thought; that it demands the entire devotion of all the powers and faculties of both body and soul to God: or, in our Lord's words, to love the Lord with all our heart, mind, soul and strength:- that this law is of perpetual duration and obligation, to all men, at all times, and in all places or parts of the world. And, we suppose that this law was obligatory to Adam in his perfect state – was more clearly revealed in the ten commandments – and more fully explained in many other parts of the bible.

ARTICLE 3.   *On the Person and Work of Christ.* We believe, that our Lord Jesus Christ is God and man, united in one person: or possessed of divine perfection united to human nature, in a way which we pretend not to explain, but think ourselves bound by the word of God firmly to believe:- that he suffered to make a full atonement for all the sins of all men – and that hereby he has wrought out for us a compleat salvation; which is received by, and as a free gift communicated to, all that believe in him; without the consideration of any works done by us, in order to entitle us to his salvation.- Though we firmly believe, that no faith is the means of justification, but that which produces good works.

ARTICLE 4.   *On Salvation by Faith.* We believe, that as this salvation is held forth to all to whom the gospel revelation comes without exception, we ought in the course of our ministry, to propose or offer this salvation to all those who attend our ministry: and, having opened to them their ruined wretched state by nature and practice, to invite all without exception, to look to Christ by faith, without any regard to any thing in, or done by, themselves; that they may, in this way alone, that is, by faith be possessed of this salvation.

ARTICLE 5.   *On Regeneration by the Holy Spirit.* We believe, that as the scriptures assure us, we are justified, made the children of God, purified and sanctified by faith:- that when a person comes to believe in Jesus (and not before) he is regenerated or renewed in his soul, by the spirit of God, through the instrumentality of the word, now believed and embraced; which renewal of his soul naturally produces holiness in heart and life:- that this holiness is the means of preparing us for the enjoyments and employments of the heavenly world; and of preserving in our souls a comfortable sense of our interest in the Lord, and of our title to glory; as well as to set a good example before men, and to recommend our blessed Redeemer's cause to the world.

ARTICLE 6.   *On Baptism.* We believe, that it is the indispensable duty of all who repent and believe the gospel, to be baptized, by immersion in water, in order to be initiated into a church state; and that no person ought to be received into the church without submission to that ordinance.

PART III

CHURCH, MINISTRY AND SACRAMENTS

Introduction

That the Church comprises the gathered saints was not questioned by Baptists and Independents during the eighteenth century: indeed, it was the foundation of their polity. The Friends likewise distinguished themselves from what they called the world's people (amongst whom they frequently included other Nonconformists). The Presbyterians, deprived of the wider organs of their polity (though some were able to share in the deliberations of continuing regional Associations of a voluntary nature) do not appear to have pressed theoretical presbyterial points in any widespread way during the eighteenth century. Indeed, apart from affirmations of belief in the Church to be found in catechisms and sermons, Nonconformists published few major, straightforward, treatments of the nature of the Church. The issue was more frequently raised in three polemical contexts. First, as we shall see in Part Five, a number of Dissenters were keen to demonstrate that whatever else it is, the true Church is not the Anglican Establishment. Secondly, some took up cudgels against the Roman 'harlot', among them some like Samuel Bourn the Younger and Micaijah Towgood[1] who on other topics were to the orthodox disconcertingly liberal. This underlines the fear of Roman Catholic resurgence which continued to grip the hearts of many Nonconformists throughout the century. Thirdly, there were inner-Dissenting skirmishes between paedobaptists and believer Baptists over the propriety of their respective stances; and further tensions among the Baptists over the question of strict (that is, restricted to immersed believers) *versus* open communion.[2] In such disputes the new evangelicals were from time to time embroiled – notably Howel Harris in Pembrokeshire. The Lord's Supper does not seem to have been a neuralgic issue among the 'three denominations' during the eighteenth century.[3]

The Quakers, believing as they did that the whole of life was sacramental, were distinguished from the others by their attitude towards the dominical sacraments, but they no less than the Baptists, Independents and Presbyterians were concerned for adequate ministry, though we know more about the shape and role of Quaker vocal ministry than about its eighteenth-century content. Under Barclay's influence, a high view of the direct divine inspiration of the individual minister led many to shrink from speaking in meeting. A period of quietism – of meetings for worship that could be silent for weeks or months on end – set in as the century wore on, to be challenged in the next century by evangelicalism. Not indeed that devotional quietism entailed the complete cessation of male and female itinerancy, or withdrawal from the world of affairs. As we shall see in Parts Five and Six, the situation was complex. On the one hand Quakers were much involved in business, pioneering the anti-slavery movement and supporting a number of humane causes; on the other hand they maintained strict rules concerning dress, 'marrying out' and the like, which made them a people apart.

We learn much concerning the nature and functions of the ministry within the 'three denominations' from their ordination services, the major addresses of which were frequently published. In some cases, as in Exeter, Cumberland and Westmorland and Devon and Cornwall, the Associations gathered for ordinations, but in Baxter's Worcestershire Association they did not.

The reference to these wider fellowships prompts the observation that *within* eighteenth-century Congregationalism there was a certain ecclesiological tension. This is seen in the contrast between Robert Bragge's *Church Discipline according to its Ancient Standard, As it was Practis'd in Primitive Times* (1739) and Matthias Maurice's allegorical work, *Social Religion Exemplify'd in an Account of the First Settlement of Christianity in the City of Caerludd* (1750). While Bragge extols fellowship, but construes it only in terms of the association of the individual believer with a particular Church, Maurice contends for the value of synods – albeit synods with advisory status and moral authority only.[4]

Notes

1. See Samuel Bourn below: Micaijah Towgood, *A Sermon preached at Exeter, February 6 1745–6*, p. 18. For Towgood see III: 30 below.
2. See further Michael Walker, *Baptists at the Table*, Didcot: Baptist Historical Society, 1992; Peter Naylor, *Calvinism, Communion and the Baptists. A Study of English Calvinistic Baptists from the Late 1600s to the Early 1800s*, Carlisle: Paternoster, 2003.
3. See further on the Lord's Supper Bryan D. Spinks, *Freedom or Order? The Eucharistic Liturgy in English Congregationalism 1645–1980*, Allison Park, PA: Pickwick Publications, 1984, and the review of same by Alan P.F. Sell in *The Journal of Ecclesiastical History*, no. 1, January 1986, pp. 176–7; Horton Davies, *Worship and Theology in England: From Watts and Wesley to Maurice, 1690–1850*, Princeton, NJ: Princeton University Press, 1961.
4. See further Alan P.F. Sell, *Saints: Visible, Orderly and Catholic. The Congregational Idea of the Church*, Geneva: World Alliance of Reformed Churches and Allison Park, PA: Pickwick Publications, 1986, pp. 59–63. Robert Bragge (1665–1737/8) was a Congregational minister in London. For Maurice see Document IV.6 below.

Document III.1

Samuel Bourn on the Church

Samuel Bourn here speaks of the relation between the Church catholic and the particular church, and his high view of the ministry emerges clearly in his remarks upon the relationship between pastor and people.

For Bourn see Document II.12 above. The extract is from *A Sermon Occasion'd by the Death Of the Reverend Mr. Samuel Bourn, of Bolton. Who Died the 4th of March 1719, in the 72d. Year of his Age*, London, 1721, pp. 9–10. For Bourn's father (1648–1719) see DNB.

As our Union with the *Catholick* Church consists in an *Adhesion* to *Jesus Christ* as universal Head; and to all true Christians as Fellow-Members; which Union is form'd by the Communication of the Spirit on Christ's Part, and by Faith exercis'd on all proper Objects, Love and Obedience on the Part of Christians: So the Union of a *Particular* Church consists in an *Adhesion* to their *Pastor*, and to the several Members of the Society taught and ruled by him in full Subordination to Christ.

Document III.2

Samuel Bourn on the Roman Catholic Church

Samuel Bourn was typical of many Protestants in using a varied armoury to assail the Church of Rome, perceived by many as a real threat to the stability of the nation. Sometimes he reasons; sometimes he plays upon the suspicions of his readers; but he is no less opposed to bigotry whencesoever it comes – not least the Protestant 'popery' of hard-line confessionalism. His 5 November sermon was preached in 1735 on the text 1 Kings 13: 26.27. In a preface we are advised that the preacher 'very much imitated Bishop *Latimer*, had a truly Satyrical Vein, as appears from this Discourse'. In the *Dialogue* Bourn forcefully states a characteristically rational-Arminian way of understanding the Reformation as opening the way for the individual's right (over against a monopoly of the Bible by priests) to enquire into the sense of Scripture, whereas Luther thought the primary point was rather to free the Bible so that God's word might be heard. Of course, Luther could not have foreseen that during the two centuries between himself and Bourn what the latter regarded as a new Protestant confessional 'popery' was to arise. Extract (a) is from *A Vindication of the Protestant Reformation*, 1747, preface; (b) from *Popery a Craft, A Sermon delivered on the 5th of November*, 1746, p.12; (c) from *A Dialogue between a Baptist and a Churchman. By a Consistent Christian*, 1737, *passim*.

(a)
The Antichristian Kingdom of popery, which has stood so long, spread so wide and enslaved so many Nations of the World, will fall, and great will be the fall of it. This being predicated in the Scriptures of Truth, with great Clearness, ought not to be a Bar to any honest and upright Endeavours to hasten its Fall; but a powerful Spur to employ them: In regard we cannot expect that God will overturn this Spiritual Monarchy by Miracles, but by ordinary Means ... Had all nominal *Protestants been real ones, and acted up to their Protestant Principles, namely*, The Liberty of God's Scriptures and of men's Understandings and Consciences, *Popery had received a more deadly Wound than has yet been given to it* ... Christian Protestant Parents are more concerned about building Houses, furnishing Rooms, raising Trees and Flowers, improving Trade and cultivating Land, than about building up Souls for Immortality ...

(b)
Why is celibacy and a monastic Life so strictly required, and so much exalted? ... [T]his keeps all our Wealth amongst the Clergy: whereas by the Priests' Marriage it

143

would be scattered amongst the unhallowed laity. To make us amends, we are indulged all Liberties with the fair sex, and yet freed from the Expence of Mistress and Offspring ... Why are the laity denied one half of the Sacrament? To keep all the rich Wines for the Priests.

(c)
Calling a Man *Arian* or *Arminian* has sometimes produced the same Effects amongst the Dissenters, as calling him *Presbyterian* has amongst our Church Bigots; or as calling him *Heretick* has done amongst the Papists. He becomes the Object of vulgar hatred, and every Zealot has a Stone to throw at him, as if he was a mad dog.

But a little Reflection will inable you to see, that as in the Mouth of a Papist, *Heretick* is usually the Mark or Denomination of an upright, conscientious Christian; and as in the Mouth of a Church Bigot, *Presbyterian* means an honest Protestant; so, in the Mouth of a Dissenting Zealot, *Arian* and *Arminian* are almost certain Marks of a sincere, inquisitive, learned Man ...

Is not the Reformaion from *Popery* built upon every Man's *Right* to inquire into the Sense of the Bible, and his *Obligation* to profess according to his sentiments? ... [T]he *true Orthodox Way* of curing Mistakes and Errors, is by Evidence and Reason; the *Heretical Way* is by Force and Violence, Inhumanity and Ill Manners ...

May the Period hasten for a *new Reformation*, wherein our Holy Lord will, (as it is likely he will), in some degree, reject all *Parties* of Christians at this Day in the World; and form a *new People* of the good Men of the several Parties, who shall unite in the Articles of their Goodness, and sweetly bear with one another in their lesser Differences, leaving each other to the Divine Illumination.

Document III.3

Discerning the Gift of Ministry: The Northamptonshire Association

The messengers of the churches discussed the discernment of the gift of ministry at Kimbolton on 7 November1708, and at Northampton on 23 March 1709–10.

The extracts are from John Waddington, *Congregational History 1700–1800*, London: Longmans, 1876, pp.163–4.

It was propounded among the messengers *what may be judged to be the best method for the encouraging and accomplishment of young men for the work of the ministry, who are gracious, and in some measure gifted and inclined that way.* Resolved – That such young men give themselves to reading and study at spare hours – not laying aside their worldly employ – that such books as may be useful for the understanding the signification and acceptation of the word, etc., be allowed them at the charge of their parents, if able, otherwise at the common charge of the Churches; and that *a teacher be set apart in every distinct Church* if it can be; or for want thereof, one or two (related to any of the Churches in communion) to be concerned to *make it their business a day or two every month* (at such places as may be appointed for that purpose) to *examine and instruct such men in the principles of the Christian religion, both as to doctrine and discipline.*

March the 23rd, 1709–10, the brethren appointed as messengers to attend the messengers' meeting at Northampton, May 24th last past, now acquainted with the Church (not having time before to consider it), with the messengers' advice upon the queries proposed by our Church, and that they advised them upon as follows: – As to the *First*, – viz., *What methods may be most requisite to be took by a Church of Christ for finding out gifts among themselves?* Resolved, that it behoves the brethren, I. To pray and open the Scriptures in their families. II. To stir up one another in more public meetings, to speak to a word. III. That the Church call the brethren to pray in public. Forasmuch as the exercise of gifts in the Church, 1. Is the will of Christ our Lord; 2. It was the practice of the primate Churches, as appears from 1 Cor. xiv. 2, resolved that gifts consist in judgment and utterance; and therefore, 3. It was resolved – that a Church may judge that a brother hath a gift if they do discern and find upon his exercising, etc. (i.) That he be *sound in the analogy of faith*; (ii.) That he have *a chain of truth in his heart and head*, Heb. v. 12; (iii.) That he be *consistent with himself in what he delivers*; (iv.) That he be savoury in his discourse, apt to teach and have love to souls. …

As to the *Third*, – viz., *What methods to be took by the Church for the encouraging such gifts when found out* – Resolved as to this, as the messengers of Churches at Kimbolton judged, November 3, 1708. Then as to the *Fourth*, but little was said upon it. Particular Churches must act therein as they judge fit. Another query was upon these proposed – viz., *What a Church ought to do in case a person exercising be judged not to have a gift, and yet some be taken with it, and approve of it.* Resolved 1. That such an one be meekly restrained; 2. That his admirers be treated with to forbear so doing. This advice and judgment of the messengers (as to these matters) was approved by our Church, who now declared themselves to be in each particular of the same faith and judgment.

Document III.4

The Inspiration and Content of Ministry: The Quaker View of Samuel Bownas

Quaker meetings had members performing designated functions – often before the rules defining their roles were promulgated. The clerks eventually appointed by meetings acted as their secretaries and chairmen. Clerkship and the undertaking of pastoral and spiritual care in the meeting were forms of ministry just as much as the service undertaken in the vocal ministry in meetings by those designated ministers, though it is convenient here to use 'ministry' as shorthand for the last of these. Any Friend might offer vocal ministry in meeting for worship (and we should remember that business meetings were special meetings for worship during which business was transacted);

145

but from the early eighteenth century onwards monthly meetings formally recorded or acknowledged those who had an acceptable gift of vocal ministry. Elders were appointed by monthly meetings to be responsible for the meetings for worship and the ministers. Overseers had a more general pastoral responsibility for all those in the meeting. Monthly and quarterly meetings of ministers and elders were introduced in 1754. Women normally met separately for business in a parallel structure of meetings, at a local level undertaking the brunt of the pastoral care. A women's yearly meeting was not, however, established until 1784 after several decades of requests supported by American women Friends who had moved earlier in that direction. Many women were effective and influential ministers and a number travelled extensively in the ministry.

See further Lucia K. Beamish, *Quaker Ministry 1691–1834*, privately published, Oxford, 1967; David J. Hall, 'A Description of the Qualifications Necessary to a Gospel Minister: Quaker Ministry in the Eighteenth Century', *Studies in Church History*, XXVI, 1989, pp. 329–41. Gil Skidmore, 'Old Matter Opened in New Life: An Historical Introduction to Ministry in Meeting for Worship', *The Friends Quarterly*, April 1992, pp. 49–63. For Quaker women ministers see Jean E. Mortimer, 'Quaker Women in the Eighteenth Century: Opportunities and Constraints', *Journal of the Friends' Historical Society*, LVII, no. 3, 1996, pp. 228–59; Sheila Wright, *Friends in York: The Dynamics of Quaker Revival 1780–1860*, Keele: Keele University Press, 1995, ch. 3.

The two following extracts on inspiration, the content of ministry and travelling in ministry are from *A Description of the Qualifications Necessary to A Gospel Minister, containing Advice to Ministers and Elders, how to conduct themselves in their Conversation, and various Services, according to their Gifts in the Church of Christ,* 1767, pp. 25–7, 32–5, by Samuel Bownas (1676–1753), for whom see DNB.

(a)

I say then, Inspiration or Revelation from God by his Spirit, is of absolute Necessity to guide a Minister in his Ministry; and a Minister so conducted by a Gospel Power and Light, inspiring his Mind with the *How* and the *What* he shall say, will speak with the Spirit, and Understanding also; that is, he will understand by his own Experience the Work of the Spirit, and Word of Faith in his own Mind, and that what he says is true: and altho' he hath this Experience, as above, yet it is not meet for any one, in his own Time and Will, to speak thereof in an Assembly; but we are to wait for both Authority and Power, that in the Lord's Time we may speak (of what our Eyes have seen, our Hands handled, and what we have felt of the good Word of Life, and Powers of the World to come) to the People, with the same View as they, the Primitives did, *i.e.* to bring their Hearers into a right Fellowship with the Father, and his Son our dear Lord and Saviour Jesus Christ; and so shall they be one with all that truly believe in him.

But some may object, *That we may be deceived, by supposing ourselves inspired, when we are not; and that we have a Revelation, when it is nothing but an Imagination and Delusion. In such a State a Man may be deceived himself, and all who think of him as he does of himself, will in like manner be deceived, and how shall this be avoided?*

Answ. It is granted, some have been deceived themselves, and have also deceived others, but the Cause of this Deception is in themselves, for want of a humble waiting

146

to know what they are about; for a true Inspiration from God is as plainly to be distinguished from the pretended false one, as Light is from Darkness; for divine Inspiration quiets the Mind under all Opposition and Contradiction, and gives Power over the World, and the Lusts of the Flesh, and worketh the Redemption of such as are endued therewith, and are subject to it; these are very humble and low of heart, and the more their Minds are enlightened by divine Inspiration, the more they see a Necessity to watch over themselves, so that the Innocency, Meekness, and Humility suiting a true and right Minister, will appear in all their Conduct; such are slow to speak, and ready to hear and receive Instruction, and are known by them that are spiritual to be such.

But they who conceive themselves to be inspired when they are not, supposing they have a Revelation when it is nothing but an Imagination of their own Brain, are exalted in their Minds, being very heady and stubborn, slighting Instruction; more apt to teach than learn, being swift to speak, but slow to hear, judging every Body that will not receive them as true Ministers, by foretelling the Ruin and Downfall of all their Opposers; working themselves up to a strange degree of Imagination, endeavouring to drive all before them; and such as will neither hear nor heed what they say, they will be apt to call for Vengeance from Heaven upon such who offer to oppose them. This, and much more that might be mention'd, is the Conduct of these deceived and deluded Souls.

Now this Error, by the Part thus deluded, might be easily discerned, if they wou'd but give themselves Time to think and consider aright in coolness, and desire that the Lord wou'd shew them the right Way. Here is therefore great need to be cautious, and try the Spirit; that is not to receive any Thing for Inspiration or Revelation, without being well satisfied in thyself that it is such; and this cautious Fear will not be displeasing to God, but thou wilt find thy Doubts removed, and thou wilt be confirmed, what thou hast is of God, and will stand.

(b)

Then as to the State of *Infancy* in the Ministry, let it be considered, that the Ministry is a *Birth*; and when any one at first comes under the Exercise thereof, he will find a great Perturbation in himself; the Cause of which he may be as great a Stranger to, as *Samuel* was to the Voice of God in the Temple, who being called the third Time, was at length informed by *Eli* how to answer: So have some, both young Men and Women, done of later Date, *(that is)* applied themselves to such as they have apprehended had more Experience of the Work of the Lord than themselves, and after all have found it very hard to give up to the heavenly Vision; and when they have given up, it has been in so much Weakness and Fear, yea, sometimes Confusion, that they have hardly known themselves what they have said: And if in such a State any one shou'd over-run, miss in Expression, or appear in a Behaviour not so agreeable to the Minds of their Brethren, let such Brethren exercise Charity; and see to thy own Gift thou that are a Hearer, and try by virtue thereof, whether thou find'st not something of God in this Infant Minister to answer his Gift in thy own Mind; and if on such a Search thou find'st not that Satisfaction thou could'st desire, yet as it is not proper to lay sudden Hands on any one to set them up, so neither be thou rash to pull them down, but give Time for Proof, and consider the Patience of the Husband man, how he waits for a Crop after the Seed is sown. Have said so much to the Hearer, let me now advise this *Infant Minister*.

I know thou wilt find very hard Work in thyself; thy Heart will be often very heavy and sorrowful, and in great Fear and Weakness thou wilt appear as a Minister, and it may be much against thy Will to appear as such; yea, thou mayst perhaps dearly repent that ever thou gavest up to this Service, and more especially, if thou answerest not thy Expectation, which I may venture to say, none at all Times do; but as thou keepest humble and low, being honestly given up to be, and do just what the Lord by his Spirit would have thee, Resignation to the Will of God being absolutely necessary for a Minister to come to; and as thou gettest here, patiently waiting the Lord's Time, thou wilt find a greater degree of Excellency by the Spirit to enlarge thy Understanding in divine Openings; and when this grows upon thee, beware of Pride, and Self-conceit, for that has ruined many: But give the Honour hereof where due; and the more thou art enlarged, labour to be the more humble, and in so doing thou wilt find Safety.

But under these various Trials in thyself, I advise to an inward Waiting upon thy Gift, to feel the moving thereof in thy own Mind, which will by a gentle Illumination clear thy Understanding and Judgment, whereby thou wilt see thy Place and Service in the Church; and if thou find'st it thy Place to minister to others, be willing to do thy Master's Will, and stand up in the Meekness of the Spirit which moveth on thy Mind, and speak the Word thereof according to the present Opening that is before thee, regarding strictly on the one Hand, by speaking too fast and too loud, thou don't over-run thy natural Strength, Gift and Opening, which if thou happens to fall into, it will bring thee into Confusion, and thou wilt not know when to conclude, and so mayst shut up thy own Way in the Minds of thy Brethren, and bring thyself under a just Censure; therefore whenever it happens so with thee, *sit down*; for by endeavouring to mend it, thou mayst make it worse: So on the other Hand, be not too low, nor too slow in thy Speech, so as to lose the Matter that Way; but carefully keep to thy Opening, avoiding both the Extreams: Stand up in a calm and quiet Frame of Mind, as free as possible from either a Fear or Care how thou shalt come off; but follow thy Guide in all Circumspection and Humility, beginning, going on, and concluding in thy Gift: Thus wilt thou experience, what the wise Man said, to be true, *A Man's Gift maketh Room for him, and bringeth him before great Men.*[1]

Now the State I have considered this Infant Minister in, is such as requires Help by tender Advice from faithful Friends of Experience, so that I may compare him to a Babe that wants both the Breast and nursing, which shou'd be tenderly and with great Care administred, so that if he be corrected, let it be in *Love*; if encouraged, let it be with *Prudence*; both may hurt him, if not well timed, and given discreetly.

Note

1. Prov. xviii. 16.

Document III.5

Discerning the Gift of Ministry: Thomas Clarkson on the Quakers

The following extract is from Clarkson's *A Portraiture of Quakerism*, 1806, see Document II.4 above.

Way in which Quakers are admitted into the ministry – When acknowledged, they preach, like other pastors, to their different congregations or meetings – they visit occasionally the different families in their own counties or quarterly meetings – Manner of these family visits – sometimes travel as ministers through particular counties, or the kingdom at large – sometimes into foreign parts – Women share in these labours – Expense of voyages on such occasions defrayed out of the national stock.

The way in which Quakers, whether men or women, who conceive themselves to be called into the office of the ministry, are admitted into it, so as to be acknowledged by the Society to be ministers of the Quaker-church, is simply as follows:

Any member has a right to rise up in the meetings for worship, and to speak publicly. If any one therefore should rise up and preach, who has never done so before, he is heard. The congregation are all witnesses of his doctrine. The Elders, however, who may be present, and to whose province it more immediately belongs to judge the fitness of ministers, observe the tenour of his discourse. They watch over it for its authority; that is, they judge by its spiritual influence on the mind, whether it be such as corresponds with that which may be presumed to come from the Spirit of God. If the new preacher deliver any thing that appears exceptionable, and continue to do so, it is the duty of the Elders to speak to him in private, and to desire him to discontinue his services to the church. But if nothing exceptionable occur, nothing is said to him, and he is allowed to deliver himself publicly at future meetings. In process of time, if after repeated attempts in the office of the ministry the new preacher should have given satisfactory proof of his gift, he is reported to the monthly meeting to which he belongs. And this meeting, if satisfied with his ministry, acknowledges him as a minister, and then recommends him to a meeting of ministers and elders belonging to the same. No other act than this is requisite. He receives no verbal or written appointment, or power, for the execution of the sacerdotal office. It may be observed also, that he neither gains any authority, nor loses any privilege, by thus becoming a minister of the Gospel. Except while in the immediate exercise of his calling, he is only a common member. He receives no elevation by the assumption of any nominal title to distinguish him from the rest. Nor is he elevated by the prospect of any increase to his worldly goods in consequence of his new office, for no minister in this Society receives any pecuniary emolument for his spiritual labours.

When ministers are thus approved and acknowledged, they exercise the sacred office in public assemblies, as they immediately feel themselves influenced to that work.

They may engage also, with the approbation of their own monthly meetings, in the work of visiting such Quaker-families as reside in the county or quarterly meeting to which they belong. In this case they are sometimes accompanied by one of the elders of the church. These visits have the name of family-visits, and are conducted in the following manner:

When a Quaker-minister, after having commenced his journey, has entered the house of the first family, the individual members are collected to receive him. They then sit in silence for a time. As he believes himself concerned to speak, he delivers that which arises in his mind, with religious freedom. The master, the wife, and the other branches of the family are sometimes severally addressed. Does the minister feel that there is a departure in any of the persons present from the principles or practice of the Society, he speaks, if he believe it required of him, to these points. Is there any well-disposed person under inward discouragement, this person may be addressed in the language of consolation. All, in fact, are exhorted and advised as their several circumstances may seem to require. When the religious visit is over, the minister, if there be occasion, takes some little refreshment with the family, and converses with them; but no light or trifling subject is ever entered upon on these occasions. From one family he passes on to another, till he has visited all the families in the district for which he had felt a concern.

Though Quaker-ministers frequently confine their spiritual labours to the county or quarterly meeting in which they reside, yet some of them feel an engagement to go beyond these boundaries, and to visit the Society in particular counties, or in the kingdom at large. Those who feel a concern of this kind must lay it before their own monthly meetings. These meetings, if they feel it right to countenance it, grant them certificates for the purpose. These certificates are necessary; first, because ministers might not be personally known as ministers out of their own district; and secondly, because Quakers who were not ministers, and other persons who might counterfeit the dress of Quakers, might otherwise impose upon the Society as they travelled along.

Such as thus travel in the work of the ministry, or Public Friends as they are called, seldom or never go to an inn at any town or village where Quakers live. They go to the houses of the latter. While at these, they attend the weekly, monthly, and quarterly meetings of the district as they happen on their route. They call also extraordinary meetings of worship. At these houses they are visited by many of the members of the place and neighbourhood, who call upon and converse with them. During these times, they appear to have their minds bent on the object of their mission, so that it would be difficult to divert their attention from the work in hand. When they have staid a sufficient time at a town or village, they depart. One or more guides are appointed by the particular meeting, belonging to it, to show them the way to the next place where they propose to labour, and to convey them free of expense, and to conduct them to the house of some member there. From this house, when their work is finished, they are conveyed and conducted by new guides to another, and so on , till they return to their respective homes.

But the religious views of the Quaker-ministers are not always confined even within boundaries of the kingdom. Many of them believe it to be their duty to travel in foreign parts. These, as their journey is now extensive, must lay their concern not only before their own monthly meeting, but before their own quarterly meeting, and before the meeting of ministers and elders in London also. On receiving their certificates they depart. Some of them visit the continent of Europe, but most of them the churches in America, where they diligently labour in the vineyard, probably for a year a two, at a distance from their families and friends. And here it may be observed that, while Quaker-ministers from England are thus visiting America on a religious errand, ministers from America, impelled by the same influence, are engaging in apostolical missions to England. These foreign visits, on both sides, are not undertaken by such ministers only as are men; women engage in them also. They cross the Atlantic, and labour in the vineyard in the same manner. It may be mentioned here, that though it be a principle in the Quaker-society, that no minister of the Gospel ought to be paid for his religious labours, yet the expense of the voyages, on such occasions, is allowed to be defrayed out of the fund which is denominated by the Quakers their 'National Stock'.

Document III.6

An Eighteenth-Century Ordination Certificate

The text of this self-explanatory certificate is translated in *Congregational Historical Society Transactions*, IX, no. 6, September 1926, p.285. The original Latin is printed on pp. 284–5.

Certificate of the Ordination of the Revd. George Smyth,
Pastor at the Old Gravel Pit Chapel – translated from
the original document by Mr. Charles E.B. Reed.

We the undersigned Pastors of Churches and Ministers of the Most Holy Gospel do certify all who shall read this letter: – that Mr. George Smyth, Master of Arts in the University of Glasgow, after completing the curriculum of academical studies, first at London, next at Glasgow, lastly at Leyden in Holland, and after the usual call to the pastoral office (in the hamlet commonly called Hackney) – a call supported moreover by many proofs of scholarship, piety and a life conformed to the rule of the Gospel, no less than of aptness for teaching, and a highly acceptable style of preaching; – has been this day with prayers, fasting and laying on of hands, set apart by us to the aforesaid pastoral office, and duly ordained presbyter; whose authority therefore for teaching the Holy Scriptures in the public assemblies of Christians, of administering the Sacraments of the Gospel and of exercising ecclesiastical discipline (in accordance with the order of the early Church and the model of the Church Reformed) we have unanimously approved and further have given him the right hand of brotherhood. Wherefore we heartily recommend the above to all pastors of Churches and the whole of the faithful, especially to our brethren in the said hamlet, as a legitimate minister of the Divine Word, and upon him and his pious labours in the vineyard of the Lord Jesus Christ, we invoke with fervent prayers, the fruitful blessing of Jehovah.

(*Signed*)

GULIELMUS LORIMER	JERE[AH]. SMITH
EDM: CALAMY, S.T.P.	S. BROWNE
JOSH: OLDFIELD, S.T.P.	W. TONG
B. ROBINSON	THO: REYNOLDS
JOH. EVANS	W. HARRIS
	DANIEL MAYO

London 14*th January*
in the year of the Christian Era
   1716

Document III.7

Thomas Hadfield's Ordination Confession of Faith and His Changing Views

Thomas Hadfield was baptised at Chesterfield on 9 October 1701 and died 21 February 1741. He proceeded from Chesterfield Grammar School to Findern academy under Ebenezer Latham, and following some experience in medical practice he was ordained to the Presbyterian ministry in 1726 at Peckham, where he succeeded Samuel Chandler, who had removed to Old Jewry. The charge at Hadfield's ordination service was given by Thomas Reynolds (1667?–1727). Hadfield's ordination statement exemplifies a number of such affirmations during the period which set out in cosmological vein, with an emphasis upon natural theology being followed by reference to the truths of revelation. Reynolds was strongly in favour of subscription at Salter's Hall, but it would seem that with the passage of time Hadfield modified his views, as the funeral oration delivered by Chander suggests.

For Hadfield see *Evangelical Magazine*, 1824, p. 611. For Latham (matriculated University of Glasgow 1704, died 1754) see H. McLachlan, *Essays and Addresses*, Manchester: Manchester University Press, 1950, ch. 9. For Chandler (1693–1766), who trained first under J. Moore at Bridgewater academy and then, like Butler and Secker, under Samuel Jones at Gloucester/Tewkesbury, see DNB. For Reynolds see DECBP, DNB. For a full account of Presbyterian ordination services at Nottingham on 6 and 7 April 1703 see Benjamin Carpenter, *Presbyterianism in Nottingham and the Neighbourhood*, [1862], pp. 122–4.

Extract (a) is from *Ordination to the Ministry, an entrusting Men with the Gospel. A Sermon Preach'd at the Ordination of Thomas Hadfield, M.D. At Peckham in the County of Surrey, October XIX, MDCCXXVI. By Joseph Hill. With Dr. Hadfield's Confession of Faith, and his Answers to the Questions then propos'd to him by the Reverend Mr. John Beaumont. To which is Added, The Charge given by the Reverend Mr. Thomas Reynolds*, London, 1727, pp.41–8. Extract (b) is from *Death the Wages of Sin, and eternal life the Gift of God by Christ Represented in a Sermon Preached at Peckham in Surrey, March 8, 1741. On Occasion of the Death of the late Reverend*

Thomas Hadfield, M.D., Who died February 21, 1741, in the 46th Year of his Age. By Samuel Chandler, London, 1741, pp. 60–1.

(a)

Quest. 1.

It being necessary, before Persons are solemnly vested in the Office of the Ministry, that they believe all the 'Doctrines of God's Word, and be able and willing to give a reason of the Hope that is in them, with meekness and fear; you are therefore now required to confess those Truths which you believe and desire to preach unto others.

Answ. As the Being and Existence of God is the Foundation of all Religion, I am abundantly persuaded, *That there is a* God. When I seriously consider the visible Constitution of Nature; for Instance, the Number, Magnitude, Distances, Motion and Uses of the Heavenly Bodies: When I survey this Earth, and reflect upon its Figure, Gravity, and marvellous Situation, with regard to the Fountain of Light, and Heat; and the Properties of the Air, that Fuel of Life which encompasses it: When I behold the Furniture of the Earth in Plants of divers Kinds, all of them most admirable for their exquisite Structure and Beauty in Leaves, Flowers, Fruits and Seeds: When from these I descend to the Ocean, and consider its wonderful Aspect, its amazing Flux and Reflux, and the numberless astonishing Variety of Great and Small Beasts inhabiting this watery Region: Farther, when I contemplate the Fabrick of Animal Bodies, particularly the Body of Man, the exquisite Perfection, Beauty, Order and Aptness of its Parts to their proper and respective Ends; Contemplating these Things with the Subordination of one Creature to another, and the joint Concurrence of all to one common End, the Glory of God in serving his Vicegerent Man; Nay, and when to the foresaid Considerations, I yet add the common Consent and Tradition of all Ages, and the many indisputable Proofs we have from History, of Supernatural Events; weighing all these Articles in my Thoughts, I am hereupon fully convinced, that from all Eternity there must have existed a Being of absolute Perfection, whose Existence is necessary and uncased, and which it must be a Contradiction to suppose not to exist. For if ever there was a Time when there was Nothing, there never could have been any Thing; unless we can reconcile this Contradiction that Nothing could of it self arise into Being that is, that it might both be, and not be at the same Time. Nor is it less absurd to affirm, that there has been an infinite Series of changeable dependant Beings, produc'd one from another in an Eternal Progression, as natural Causes and Effects, without any One prime independent Cause of their Existence: For this Assertion supposes such Beings to exist without any Ground or Reason of their Existence. They are not supposed necessarily existent; and that they derived their Beings from the free Agency of One Necessary, Self-Existent Cause is denied, because no such Cause is supposed by the Patrons of this Scheme to exist. To be short, it is therefore so magnificently absurd to advance these, or indeed any other Arguments against the Existence of One Supreme, Independent First Cause of all Things, that even the most studied Atheism it self must be asham'd to insist upon them, and leave its Abettors secure in no other Refuge than an Obstinacy of Will to disown, rather than a Want of

Understanding to conceive, or of superior Strength of Reasons to refute what is urg'd upon them.

This Supreme Cause, of whose Necessary Eternal Existence there is such cogent and irrefragable Proof, I therefore believe must essentially and immutably be the infinite Power, Wisdom, Goodness, Truth, Righteousness, Excellence and Perfection; the prime Author, continual Sustainer, and Ultimate End of Being, Life, and Blessedness to the universal Creation, according to the several Kinds, Natures and Capacities of his Creatures; A Truth, that is demonstrable not only from Effects and constant Experience, but from *prior* Evidence, such as arises from the Perfection of One absolutely Necessary and Self-Existent Being.

The same Natural Light which thus evinces the Being and Perfections of ONE GOD, does I believe moreover and with equal Clearness evince, that universal Obedience and Conformity to his Holy Nature and Will is a Debt which the whole rational, intelligent Creation owe to this GOD, so long as their Existence and necessary Relation to Him is suppos'd; that is, so long as there are two such infinitely different Beings as God and ourselves. For from the Nature of Man, a reasonable Creature, compar'd with GOD, the Infinite, Eternal, Unchangeable Rectitude, our Maker, Owner, Supreme Lord, and consummate All-comprehending Good, it necessarily follows, that Mankind stand oblig'd by Eternal immutable Laws to obey this GOD in all the notifications of his Will to them, as ever they will act up to the Dictates of their own impartial Reason, and obtain Everlasting Perfection and Blessedness to themselves in Him.

The Knowledge of the Divine Will to Man being in many Things above the highest Improvements of unassisted Reason to attain; 'tis evident, Mankind stands in need of a Supernatural Revelation: And whereas it implies no Contradiction to suppose GOD to make such a Discovery as this to his Moral Subjects, concerning what He would have us to understand, believe and do, in order to our real Perfection and Happiness, necessarily and invincibly desir'd by us; But whereas, on the contrary, the Wisdom, Goodness, Mercy, nay, and even the Governing Justice of GOD, added to the consideration of the Necessities of Men, do afford many very probable Arguments that this GOD would some time or other, for the mention'd Ends, make Himself known to such Subjects of his Power and Providence: Consonant to this Scheme of Reasoning, I do believe, that the Everblessed GOD has evidently revealed Himself to us in all Things, necessary to our grand Spiritual and Everlasting Welfare, in those Writings known amongst us by the Names of the *Old* and *New Testament*.

And that these Writings, and the Religion therein exhibited, are from GOD, I firmly believe; When I consider their intrinsic Excellence, that they contain *Doctrines* great and glorious, many of which surpass the most elevated Heights of natural Reason to descry, but yet when revealed from a GOD of infallible Veracity, are very consistent with unprejudic'd Reason, and contain in them nothing of Contradiction thereunto: And when I consider moreover, that the *Practical Duties* injoined us in these Writings of the Old and New Testament are all of them exactly agreeable to our natural Notions of GOD, and in every View most effectually conducive to the Moral Perfection and Happiness of Man; as they forbid all, even the least Sin, as they acquaint us with the best Method of Living, the Noblest Principles of Suffering, and the most comfortable Way of dying: Beyond this, finding that these said Duties are urg'd upon Men with such *powerful Motives*, and in such an awful Manner, as it becomes the supremely wise and righteous Governour of the World to make Use of, and as reasonable Creatures in their State of Trial might expect from Him: Connecting with these Considerations the Prophecies of Christ's Birth, Life, Sufferings, Death and Resurrection, foretold many Ages before they came to pass, not in a doubtful Phrase, as the *Heathen* Oracles spake, but expressly and with particular specifying Circumstances, all which afterward were punctually fulfilled; as were also those wonderful Events which were foretold would succeed to the Cutting off the *Messiah*, such, for instance, as the total and irreparable Destruction of *Jerusalem* and the *Jewish* State for rejecting the *Messiah*; the Bringing in of the *Gentiles* to the Knowledge and Worship of the true and only God, now reconciling all Nations of the World unto Himself thro' the Blood of His dear Son: Adding to these Evidences the Multitudes of uncontroll'd Miracles wrought by Jesus Christ and his Followers, the quick and extensive Propagation of the Gospel, its having in a few Years advanced to the Ends of the then known World, not with the Advantages which a rising Opinion, such as *Mahometanism* and *Popery*, ordinarily chuses to set up withal: That Christianity, void of these Advantages, did even by the most unlikely Instruments, and amidst all possible Hindrances to it from the Lusts and Violence of Men, make so vast a Progress in so short a Space of Time, is a Miracle equal to others wrought for its Comfirmation: More than this, pondering the marvellous Preservation of the sacred Writings in the very worst of Times, and amidst the most inveterate Enemies to GOD and the Souls of Men: And once more, the very great Blessings accruing to those who conscientiously learn and practice what is therein notified and recommended: Going upon these Foundations, I am firmly persuaded that the Scriptures and the Religion taught in them are from God.

I believe then, according to the Account given of this Matter in the Scriptures of Truth, that *there are Three that bear Record in Heaven, the Father, the Word, and the Holy Ghost; and these Three*, I believe, *are One*, one GOD, as they bear the same Names, and have the same Divine Attributes and Operations ascribed to them in Scripture. I believe that in the Godhead there are three Persons, and yet but one GOD, who is over All blessed for evermore.

(b)

In the latter part of his life he altered his sentiments in some of the obstruser points of religion ... I am well assured this alteration did not proceed from fickleness and levity of temper, or a love of novelty, but from the full persuasion and maturest conviction of his judgment and conscience ... An alteration of sentiments in such circumstances, must I think created a real esteem for his memory, even amongst such of you, should there be any such, to whom such alteration might not be altogether so agreeable.

Document III.8

Thomas Craig's Ordination Confession of Faith

Thomas Craig, an evangelical Congregationalist in the wake of the Revival, was born at South Leith, Edinburgh, in 1780, and died in 1865. He was trained at Homerton College under John Pye Smith, and ministered at Bocking, Essex, from 1801 to 1863. Comparing Craig's ordination statement, which sets out from the Bible, with which our best reasoning is said to be in accord, and then proceeds conventionally enough through the major Christian doctrines with that of Thomas Hadfield, which begins as if it were an exercise in apologetics, we see something of the distance in spirit beween a Presbyterian whose rationalism was to take him gradually away from complete orthodoxy, and a later Congregationalist whose heart had been set on fire.

For Craig see *Congregational Year Book*, 1866, p. 243. For Pye Smith (1774–1851), who studied under Edward Williams of Rotherham academy, see DEB, DNB. The extract is from *An Introductory Discourse, By Samuel Newton, an Address to the Minister, by Robert Stevenson, and a Sermon to the people, By William Parry: Delivered on the Solemn Separation of The Rev. Thomas Craig to the Pastoral Office. In the Congregational Church at Bocking, in Essex, October 12, 1802, To which is prefixed, A Discourse, delivered on the preceding evening, by John Pye Smith*, London, 1802, pp. 39–40.

I consider your request, Rev. Sir, as reasonable and proper, and am persuaded that what you expect from me on the present occasion is merely a brief statement of the theological sentiments which I hold, and not an enumeration of the reasons why I first embraced them, or of the arguments by which I would now defend them against the objections of opponents.

I believe that the scriptures of the Old and New Testament were written under the inspiration of the Spirit of God. Though I suppose this inspiration to have varied both in manner and degree, according to the circumstances of the writers and the subjects they treated; yet I firmly believe that through Divine agency they were all preserved from every error, and that in religion these writings are the only rule of conduct and standard of opinion. They teach me the existence of one infinite, eternal Jehovah 'of whom, and through whom, and to whom are all things' At the same conclusion, I apprehend, every unprejudiced observer of the works of nature must arrive. For the combination of endless variety with perfect harmony in these works, as evidently demonstrates the necessity of supposing an intelligent first Cause, as an extensive, complicated and useful machine, the exertion of some *rational* agent. When I thus find that the declarations of the scriptures on this subject so perfectly accord with the dictates of sound reason, my faith in them is confirmed; and endeavouring to regulate by them my sentiments concerning the Great Eternal, I find them teaching me that, in the mysterious plan of redemption, God is to be considered as subsisting in three distinct Persons, the Father, the Son, and the Holy Spirit.

Document III.9

A Holy Calling and a Practical Business

Extract (a) is from the *Diary* of James Clegg, 11 August 1731. It briefly describes a Presbyterian ordination service in which the ministers are clearly the key persons. Extract (b), also from Clegg's *Diary*, are entries for 2–4 March 1750 and 2–16 October 1750. They reveal a mixture of ministerial hazards, pastoral duties and the need, experienced by many ministers, to supplement the stipend by earning additional income – in Clegg's case, by farming.

For James Clegg (1679–1755), who was educated under Richard Frankland at Rathmell and John Chorlton in Manchester, see DNB. For Frankland (1630–98) see DNB.

Extract (a) is from *The Diary of James Clegg of Chapel en le Frith, 1708–1755*, ed. Vanessa S. Doe, 3 vols, Chesterfield: Derbyshire Record Society, 1978, part I, p. 126; extract (b) is from 1981, part III, pp. 738–9.

(a)

Spent some time, and breakfasted with Mr. J. Mills. Then the ministers met at Mr Smalleys and heard Mr Hollands confession in private, thence we went to the meeting house, Mr Smalley begun with prayer, reading the scriptures and a Psalm Mr Waddsworth of Sheffield prayd before Sermon, I preachd from Matt 16:18: and Gave out a Psalm Mr Platts took the confession and proposd the Questions Mr. Pigot prayd at the imposition of hands and Mr Ash gave the charge and concluded with prayer. The whole work was carried on with Seriousness and decency and to the Satisfaction I hope of all present. The ministers dined together and the evning was spent at Mr William Mills's with many Friends.

(b)

2.   We met again at the Red Lyon in Bakewel dispatchd some business and dind there, after dinner Releases were signed by all parties and we parted in peace Blessed by God. I had a very narrow escape at dinner in taking part of a big Trout, I had a fish hook in my mouth and was just about to swallow it, but then discoverd what it was, and as I was entring Monsal dale a strong gust of wind blew me and my mare down on one side, had she fallen on the other side I had certainly perishd, But thro mercy I got safe home in good time but was much hurried by the strong wind full in my face.

3.   I was at home all day preparing sermons, found I had got some cold in my journey.

4.   I preachd in the forenoon from 1 Cor. 2:1, and then administred the Lords Supper to a great number but after that was so hoarse, and sore, and stuffd in my lungs, that I sent to let the people know that I could not preach in the afternoon, after dinner some Friends came to see me and staid some time. ...

13.   at home til afternoon then visited at Martinside. Spent some time there with Mr Bagshaw and Mr and Mrs Steele and returnd by chapel to order some medicines for Ms Eyre who is very ill of pain in the stomach.

14.   I was at home all day busy gardening. I sold an heifer to G. Goodwin. We hear the distemper amongst the cattle is Broke out in Rushop very near us but hope its not true. This day we had 7 teams to plow for us out of Chinley and no disaster, blessed be God.

15.   I was at home til afternoon then walkd up to chapel on business and soon returnd.

16.   I was at home til afternoon and then walkd out to visit old widow Ridgway and widow Jakson of Milton and Peter Woods Family.

Document III.10

Thomas Amory's Charge to William Richards

Here the Presbyterian divine Thomas Amory (for whom see Document I.8 above) delivers an ordination charge to William Richards. This sermon is selected for quotation here because, to qualify the slander that more liberal Presbyterian divines of the period were 'high and dry' in the pulpit (as if high Calvinists could not be equally so!), Amory speaks of joy. His text is II Corinthians 1: 24, 'Not for that we have Dominion over your Faith, but are Helpers of your Joy.'

The extract is from *Ministers not Lords over the Faith of Christians, but Helpers of their Joy: A Sermon Preached at Lewin's-Mead, Bristol, at the Ordination Of the Reverend Mr. William Richards, May the 22d. 1751*, London, [1751], pp.19–32.

II.   To represent briefly one principal Part of the *ministerial Character*, comprised under these Words of the Apostle, *being Helpers of your Joy*. The following are some of the chief Instances of this benevolent Disposition and Office.

1.   We are to *help* our Hearers to possess themselves of the *Joys of Faith*. There are few satisfactions equal to those which an honest Mind receives from a clear, rational, and strong persuasion, of the great Truths of Religion. Upon good grounds to know, and be assured, that Mankind and the World they behold and inhabit are the productions of an *infinitely perfect* Cause, who upholds all things by his unceasing Energy, supplies and governs all his Creatures by an infinitely wise and good Providence, is the ever present Father and Almighty Friend of the righteous, the grateful, the pious, and benevolent, whom by the best methods he is training up for the perfection of Goodness and of Happiness – who notwithstanding the Follies and Transgressions of the human Race sent from Heaven *his only Son, the brightness of his Glory, and the express Image of his Perfections*, to save them from Sin and Death, and to conduct them to Virtue, Piety, and Life Eternal – And who will, through Christ, forgive fully all the penitent, assist and accept the sincere, and notwithstanding their many imperfections, receive them, after death, to a state of complete, divine, and never-ending Blessedness – These are Truths so great, so noble, and so interesting, to frail and dying creatures, open to numerous Evils, conscious to many Transgressions; conscious also to large and noble Capacities for Happiness, and apprehensive of Eternity; that clearly to discern the evidences of these great Truths,

and to be fully assured of their Reality, inspires a Joy which exalts the human Heart, animates to all Virtue, and raises the Believer above all the Temptations of Vice, the Afflictions of Life, and the Terrors of Death.

The evidences of these Truths are as abundant, as the Truths themselves are important, and offer themselves to the serious and inquisitive in a striking Light. *Ministers* therefore are to be *Helpers* of their People's *Joy*, by rendering these evidences familiar to their thoughts; and by leading them to observe the demonstrations of the Perfections and Providence of the Deity in the frame and preservation of the world, and in the continually producing and supplying innumerable Creatures; the wise adjustment of the present state as a state of Trial for reasonable and immortal Beings; and the abundant Proofs which we have, that *Jesus Christ*, who confirmed all the *Truths* and *Duties* of natural Religion, and added to them such noble Encouragements and such glorious Hopes, was indeed authorised by that God, whom he resembled in the perfect purity and goodness of his Life, and who owned his Mission while living by numberless Miracles, and *declared him to be his Son with power by raising him from the dead*. By assisting even weaker Capacities to comprehend the Proofs of Truths so lovely and so important to all, by clearing the difficulties and objections which are raised against them, and by often recalling their attention to the reasons which support them, Ministers are to render their hearers *strong in the Faith*, and to be *Helpers of their Joy*.

2. They are to *assist* their People's *Joy*, by ministering to them from the Scriptures such a *Light* for the right conduct of Life, as shall make their whole path of duty plain and strait before them. It is an inestimable satisfaction to moral Agents, who consider themselves as on their Trial for everlasting Felicity, to have a distinct and comprehensive view of their Duty, and to be rationally assured what way of acting in every part of life will render them fully approved of God, and prepare them to be happy for ever. For this purpose the *grace of God appeared, bringing Salvation to all Men, teaching us, that denying ungodliness and worldly lusts, we should live soberly, righteously, and godly in the present World; looking for that blessed hope, and the glorious appearing of the great God, and our Saviour Jesus Christ.* And the principal instances of Duty are easily discerned by every honest Mind. But to trace these *general* Precepts into all their particular branches, and certainly to discover what method of thinking and acting in every relation, and in all the varying circumstances of human Life, is most worthy our Character as Men and Christians, is of the most beneficial Tendency to others, and will most immediately dispose our own minds to injoy the blessedness of Heaven – This is a work which requires frequent, close, and impartial reflection, and a judicious consideration of human Life, and of the different consequences from different Actions – and especially where our duty is plain, to discern it so clearly to be also our wisdom and happiness; and the pretences of Vice to present Satisfaction and Advantage to be fallacious, and her crooked and flowery paths certainly ending in disappointment and wretchedness; as may make our adherence to our Duty chearful and stedfast. This is not an easy attainment to persons ingaged in the necessary Cares and Business of Life, though scarce any thing be more important and desirable.

Ministers therefore are to help their People to the Joys of such a clear practical Knowledge, by first improving the Advantages which a retired and studious Life gives for acquiring this Knowledge from the Scriptures, from other judicious Writings, and from Reflections upon themselves, and upon human Life; and then communicating to others, what they have discovered of the *Extent* and *Obligations* of our Lord's Precepts of Piety and Goodness; which reach to the regulation of every Passion, the improvement of every Faculty, the answering every obligation of social Life, and using well every advantage for doing good: and by making them sensible at the same time, that their *Duty* is their *Interest, that Wisdom's ways are ways of pleasantness, and her paths peace;* that *in keeping God's Commandments there is a great reward*; and that an *imitation* of the best of Beings in Righteousness, Goodness, Purity and Truth, will assure them of his favour here, and prepare them for a divine Happiness hereafter. And what an improvement would this give to the Joy of every well disposed Person, willing to please God, to answer in some manner his Obligations to him, to do good in Life, and prepare himself for complete Blessedness in an approaching state.

3.　　The Joys of a good Conscience are of the noblest kind, and *Ministers* must be *Helpers* of their People in attaining these Joys. The satisfactions mentioned under the two preceding heads are preparatory to these, and completed in them, and nothing further is necessary to Christians becoming happy in these, but their pursuing steddily the dictates of their Faith, and their enlightened Consciences. And, *my Friends*, what Joys can equal those of a *good Conscience*? After a thorough acquaintance to stand approved to our own hearts, and upon good grounds to conclude that we are approved by God – To feel Gratitude, Love, Resignation, and Devotedness to the greatest and best of Beings prevailing in our bosoms; to be full of Faith, Love and Subjection to the Son of God, the Saviour of the World; to be animated by the most generous Concern for the good of others; and to be conscious not only to an uncorrupted Integrity, but to a divine Benevolence, a tender Compassion, and an abounding Charity – to feel our Passions beat as temperately in regard to sensible and dying Interests and Enjoyments, as becomes immortal Beings; and our Souls with that high relish pursuing the satisfactions of Knowledge, Truth, Friendship, Goodness and Devotion, which suits those who hope soon to be happy in the perfection of these with *Angels* and *Spirits made perfect* – and to be thus qualified to look up to God with a full assurance of his Complacency, forward in Life with this pleasing certainty, that all our valuable Interests are safe under his care, and onward still to Death and the everlasting State with the noble confidence, that Death will prove our great Friend, and Eternity alone be the measure of our Blessedness. These are Joys, to assist our Hearers in acquiring which is our great Business as Christian Ministers, and for this purpose to excite them to the faithful practice of their whole duty, and to a continual progress in Virtue and Piety, by all the motives of the Gospel, by the Fear and Love of God, by love to the Redeemer, and by a regard to his Virtues, Death and Resurrection; by the beauty and excellence of genuine Piety and Goodness; by the assurance of assistance from above in the noble attempt, and of divine acceptance; and of obtaining universal Honour and immortal Blessedness at the general Judgment – and by representing farther the amiableness and worth of these dispositions in our own Temper and Conduct; thus inviting and leading them to those pure streams of religious Joy, which run into an ocean of perfect and everlasting Blessedness. And not to multiply particulars.

4.   There is the *Joy of Hope*, and we should help those who attend our Ministry, to *rejoice in hope of the glory of God*. The more distinct our apprehensions are of the nature and value of the heavenly Blessedness, and the clearer our conviction is of its certainty, the higher will the Joy of Hope rise in the breast of everyone, who has *exercised himself to keep a Conscience void of Offence towards God and Man*. Frequent and spirited representations derived from the *Scriptures*, of the nature, worth, and everlasting duration of the promised Felicity, and as distinct as our present state will allow; (wherein *we walk by Faith not by Sight*) particularly as arising from an immortal health and beauty, and vigor of Body, and perfection of Mind, from the brightest and largest Views of the Perfections and Works of the Infinite Eternal, still opening upon us for ever; from the glorious presence of God and of Jesus, from the most transporting sentiments of Veneration, Gratitude, and Love to them, and from their full approbation; from an intimacy with Angels, and all the redeemed, and seeing Millions of Millions as perfect and happy, as the most generous heart can with them, exulting in their Joy and contributing to their improvement in Blessedness; from our own continued proficiency in every great and good quality, and from an unclouded certainty of our still rising higher in perfection and bliss to Eternity – such animated representations of the heavenly Blessedness, proved to be as true as delightful, from the Nature and immense Benignity of the great Father of Spirits, from the capacities of the human Soul, from the Promises, Death and Resurrection of the Son of God, and from the meetness of a Soul formed on the Precepts of the Gospel to injoy it's promised Felicity – such representations will mightily inspirit our Hearers to the practice of all Goodness, and their improvements in Goodness will naturally give them a more abundant Enjoyment of the satisfactions of a good Conscience, and thus qualify them for the Triumphs of Hope, of a clear and rational Assurance that they are *Heirs of God, and joint Heirs with Jesus Christ*. These are Joys, which mingled with the common pleasures of life, will greatly inrich them, will render the afflictions of life scarce sensible; and at the important season, when person destitute of this Hope sink into a dreadful Gloom and Despair, and when the whole World for Comfort will be found as nothing, will inable a Man to triumph over Death like St. *Paul. O Death, where is thy Sting? O Grave, where is thy Victory? I have fought a good fight, I have finished my course, I have kept the faith, henceforth there is laid up for me a crown of Righteousness, even Glory, Honour, and Immortality;* the reward assured to a *patient continuance in well doing*. Come then ye kind *ministering Spirits* and conduct me to *Paradise,* where *absent from the body I shall be present with the Lord; where is fullness of Joy and Pleasures for evermore!*

Happy they who by a life worthy of the Gospel are qualified for such divine Joys, and for such glorious Hopes, which will never make them ashamed. Thrice happy the *Ministers* who have been *helpers to many* in acquiring these, who have cheerfully devoted all their abilities and influence to this generous design; who can regard remaining Life as greatly improveable for such noble purposes, and who can every day look forward with increasing pleasure to an approaching Eternity, the Joys of which will infinitely surpass all their hopes and wishes.

This Subject would afford us a variety of important *Reflections*, particularly on the notorious Corruptions of the Church of *Rome*; and of others *like* them, who exercise a cruel *Dominion* over the *Faith* of Christians, and destroy instead of helping their Joy; and on the *contrariety* of such principles and conduct to the *nature* and *design* of *Christianity* – On our happiness as *Dissenters*, in being free from all unsurpation over Conscience; and on the *goodness* of our Cause, which is the Cause of religious Liberty and genuine Christianity, and founded on the *sole* Authority of Christ to be King and Lawgiver in his own Kingdom – On the benevolent and generous Design of the *Christian Ministry*; and the Esteem and Affection due to Christian Ministers, who faithfully pursue the design of their office; and the like – But I omit inlarging on these, that I may ask your patient attention to the two following Reflections.

1.   What has been offered should determine the *Laity*, to assert at all times their Christian *Liberty*, and to see that their Ministers keep within the bounds of their Office; and then *generously* to encourage them in doing their duty. *Stand fast in the Liberty wherewith Christ hath made you free.* It is your glory to be dutiful Subjects to the Son of God, as your Lord in matters of Faith and Conscience, and to him *only*. Should any *Ministers* then demand your implicit belief of their Doctrines, without making it appear to you that they are the Doctrines of Christ; or should they, under pretence that Scripture expressions are obscure or defective, impose their *own explications* of these, as *Articles of Faith*; should they make *new terms of Communion*, which Christ has not made, or pretending to a power of *opening* or *shutting Heaven*; attempt to persuade you, that it is not sufficient to confess your sins unto God, and by a hearty repentance, through Christ, to reconcile yourselves unto him, but that you must also confess yourselves unto them, and have their hands to your pardon – let them know, that they are not *Lords*, but *Ministers*, not your *Masters*, but your *Brethren*, which *one is your Master even Christ*; are appointed to instruct you in the Laws of Christ, not to make Laws of their own; and that you will believe and regard them no further, than they approve themselves faithful subjects of Christ our common Lord, and endeavour to promote his genuine Truths, and the practice of his Commands.

On the other hand, when you justly refuse to Ministers the Authority of *Popes*, let none of you assume this Authority to *themselves*, and expect that a Minister should take his religious sentiments from their dictates, and preach only what they believe, not what after his best Inquiry he is convinced Christ hath revealed. If a Minister appear seriously and conscientiously to study the Scriptures, as his rule of Faith, of preaching and of living, and it be the great design of his Ministry to assist you in heartily believing and practising the great and uncontroverted Truths and Duties of Christianity, hear candidly what he has to offer in favour of sentiments wherein he may differ from you; and if he cannot convince you, nor you convince him, agree to think differently as to these points, while you unite, and direct your main Zeal to cherish the Love of God, and the Faith and Love of the Redeemer, and to the practice of true Goodness in every Relation of Life, and your own best preparation for a blessed Immortality. And should his honest study of the Scriptures, and affectionate concern for your eternal Salvation, lead him to declare against dispositions and practices to which you may be indulgent, but which he apprehends may prove fatal to your best Interest, instead of regarding him as your *Enemy, for telling you the Truth*, consider impartially what he offers, and if he convinces you, imbrace the conviction, and incourage him as the best of Friends; who with the manifest hazard of your displeasure endeavours to save you from the greatest evils, and to promote your greatest good, your eternal Salvation. And while he devotes his Life and Labours to the discovering and promoting religious Truth, to the recommending and advancing real Goodness, to that which tends to make you most happy here, and divinely blessed for ever, *generously* incourage and support him, that he may pursue his good designs free from anxious Cares and distracting Wants; and let him rejoice in your Friendship who is a helper of your Joy. I speak this with the more Freedom, because it is so agreeable to the known sentiments and practice of this Christian Society.

To conclude.

2.   Is it, *my Brethren*, our great Concern as Ministers, to be *Helpers* of our People's *Joy*, to assist them in possessing themselves of the noblest satisfactions here, and in preparing their Minds for *everlasting Joys*? Let the thought of this animate our Zeal, and chear our Labours, inspirit our private Studies, and our publick Ministrations. There is a noble satisfaction attending every Instance of Kindness and Beneficence. To wish well to Mankind therefore in their best Interests, to contribute to their injoying the most valuable Satisfactions, and to their most complete Preparation for divine and immortal Joys, must yield us to exalted pleasures at present, and qualify us to be eminently blessed in that world, where Goodness will be infinitely rewarded by the best of Beings, and where to see any triumphing in eternal Felicity, to whose attainment of it we have contributed, will add infinitely to our own Blessedness.

Let the excellency therefore of our Design, and the glorious Hope that is set before us, warm our hearts, and chear us amidst difficulties, ill treatment, worldly discouragements, and slow success. Let our *Preaching*, our *Conversation*, our *Examples*, all conspire in assisting those who are committed to our Charge, to injoy abundantly the Pleasures of a good Conscience, and of heavenly Hopes. And God grant we may each of us rejoice with them now in their continual improvement, and with them triumph in the world of Bliss, finding them *our Crown of rejoicing at the coming of our Lord Jesus*, Amen.

Document III.11

Philip Doddridge on Ordination

For Doddridge see Document I.1 above. Doddridge's account of ordination and his ordination hymn comprise an appendix (pp. 69–79) to the following: *The Importance of the Ministerial Office, and the Difficulty of rightly discharging it: Considered in a*

Discourse Delivered in Norwich June 20, 1745. At the Ordination Of the Reverend Mr. Abraham Tozer. By Richard Frost. To which is added The Charge, By P. Doddridge, D.D., London, 1745.

As in the Beginning of the Charge I have touched upon the *decent Solemnities* attending the *Methods of* ORDINATION generally used among *the Protestant Dissenters*, it may not be improper to give a Brief Account of them; especially as I have been earnestly desired to do it, by a pious and learned *Clergyman* of the Established Church; who apprehends, it may obviate some Mistakes, and promote that mutual Candor among *Christians of different Denominations*, which both of us concur to wish, and labour to promote. There is indeed *a little Variety* in the Usages of different Places; but that which I have generally seen, does, I believe, prevail in most of our Churches, with the Exception, and sometimes no more than the Transposition, of a few Circumstances.

It very rarely happens, that a Minister among us is admitted to the Pastoral Office, till he has spent *some Years* as a kind of *Candidate* for it; and, so far as I can recollect, more undertake it *after*, than *before* their *Twenty-sixth Year* is completed. But as our *Theological Students* generally employ either *Four* or *Five Years* in Preparatory Studies after they have quitted the Grammar Schools, so they are *examined* by three or four Elder Ministers before they begin to preach. A strict Enquiry is made into *their Character*, and into *their Furniture*; both with respect to the *Learned Languages*, especially *the Sacred*, and also as to the various Parts of *Natural* and *Moral Philosophy*; but above all, into their Acquaintance with *Divinity*; and some Specimen of *their Abilities*, for Prayer and Preaching, is generally expected.

An unordained Minister is seldom *chosen* to the Pastoral Office in any of our Churches, (for in the *Members* of each of these Societies the whole *Right of Election* lies,) till he has resided among them *some Months*, or perhaps *some Years*; preaching stately to them, and performing most other Ministerial Offices, excepting the Administration of the Sacraments.

When *the Society*, which generally proceeds with entire Unanimity in this great Affair, has received what it judges *competent Satisfaction*, the several *Members of it* join in giving a solemn and express *Call* to take upon him the Pastoral Inspection over them: And if he be disposed to *accept it*, he generally signifies that Intention to *neighbouring Pastors*; whose Concurrence he desires in solemnly *setting him apart* to that Office.

Previous to the Assembly for this Sacred Purpose, *his Credentials* and *Testimonials* are produced, if it be required by any who are to be concerned; and Satisfaction as to *his Priniciples* is also given to those who are to carry on the Publick Work, generally by his communicating to them *the Confession of his Faith* which he has drawn up; in which it is expected, that *the great Doctrines of Christianity* should be touched upon in a proper Order, and *his Persuasion of them* plainly and seriously expressed, *in such Words* as he judges most convenient. And we generally think this is a proper and happy *Medium*, between the Indolence of acquiescing in a general Declaration of *believing the Christian Religion*, without declaring what it is apprehended to be, and the Severity of demanding *a Subscription to any Set of Articles*, where if an honest Man, who believes all the rest, scruples any one Article, Phrase, or Word, he is as effectually excluded, as if he rejected the whole.

The *Pastors* who are to bear their Part in the Publick Work, having been thus in their Consciences *satisfied*, that the Person offering himself to Ordination is *duly qualified* for the Christian Ministry, and *regularly called* to the full Exercise of it; they proceed, at the appointed Time and Place, to *consecrate him to it*, and to recommend him to the Grace and Blessing of GOD, and of our Lord *Jesus Christ*, the great Head of the Church, by *Fasting* and *Prayer*, generally accompanied with the *Imposition of Hands*; and the Publick Work of the Day is usually, so far as I have been Witness, carried on *in the following Order*, or something very near it.

It commonly opens with *a short Prayer*; and the *Reading some select Portions of Scripture* which seem most proper to the Occasion: Then *a Prayer* is offered *of greater Length and Compass* than the former, in which most of our common Concerns as *Christians* are included; which is sometime, tho' less frequently, succeeded by *another* of the same Kind. Then follows *a Sermon* on some suitable Subject, such as the Institution, Importance, Difficulty, and Excellency of the Ministerial Work, the Character and Conduct of the first Ministers of the Gospel , or the like.

After this Introduction of a more general Nature, *another Minister* (usually one of *the Eldest* present, who is a Kind of *Moderator for the Day*,) gives the Assembly a more particular Account of *the Occasion* of its being convened. *The Call of the Church* to the Candidate is then *recognized*, either in Word, or Writing, or by lifting up the Hand; and *his Acceptance* is also *declared*. He is then desired, for the Satisfaction and Edification of the Assembly, to pronounce *the Confession of Faith*, (which his Brethren have already heard and approved;) and pertinent *Questions* are put to him, relating to the *Views* and *Purposes* with which he undertakes the solemn Charge, that he may be brought under the most awful Engagements to a suitable Behaviour in it; and an express *Renunciation* of the Errors and Superstitions of the *Romish Church* generally makes a Part of *these Answers*, as well as a Declaration of *his Resolution*, by Divine Grace, *never to forsake the Ministry*, whatever Inconveniences and Sufferings it may draw after it.

This being dispatched, *the presiding Minister* comes down from the Pulpit, and *prays over the Person* to be set apart. There is no particular *Form of Prayer* on this Occasion, or on any other among us; but I have observed, that the Person who officiates is generally led in such a Circumstance, to adore the Divine Wisdom and Grace, in the Constitution and Revelation of *the Gospel*, in the Appointment of *an Evangelical Ministry*, and in supporting *the Succession of it* throughout all Ages of the Christian Church, as well as in vindicating it from *Popish* Corruption and Bondage. Some Notice is often taken of what may have seemed most remarkable in Providence, with Regard to the particular Circumstances of *the Society* then to be settled, and *the Person to be set apart* to the Ministerial Office in it; who is then solemnly *offered up* to the Service of GOD, and *recommended* to his Blessing, in all the several *Parts of his Work*, which are distinctly enumerated. And this Prayer seldom concludes without *fervent Intercession* with God, for the *Christian Church* in general, and *all its faithful Ministers* of every Denomination: And as those *rising up to succeed in the Work* are often mentioned here, so I have had the Pleasure frequently to hear *the Universities of our Island*, as well as *more private Seminaries* of learned and pious Education, affectionately recommended to the Divine Protection and Favour on such Occasions, with all the genuine Appearances of a truly Christian and Catholick Spirit. When *that Part of this Prayer* begins, which immediately relates to *the Person then to be consecrated to the Service of the Sanctuary*, it is usual for *the Speaker* to *lay his Hand on his Head*; and the *other Pastors* conveniently within Reach, (frequently to the Number of Six, Eight, or Ten,) *lay on their Hands* also, at the same Time: By which we do not pretend to convey any Spiritual Gifts, but only use it as a solemn, and expedience, tho' not absolutely necessary, *Designation of the Person* then to be set apart.

When this Prayer is over, (which often engages a very profound Attention, and seems to make a very deep Impression both on Ministers and People,) *the Charge* is given *to the newly ordained Pastor*, who generally receives it *standing* (as much as may be) in the Sight of the whole Assembly: And *an Exhortation to the People* is sometimes joined with *the Charge*, or sometimes follows it as a distinct Service, unless (which is frequently the Case,) it is superseded by *the Sermon*, or some other previous Address. *Another Prayer* follows: and *Singing* having been *intermingled*, so as properly to diversify a Service necessarily so long, the whole is concluded with *a Solemn Benediction*.

I know no Method of proceeding on such Occasions, more rational, edifying, and scriptural, than this: And I hope, few, who believe any Thing of *Christianity*, can be so ignorant or abandoned, as to *make light of such Solemnities*. But however any of *our Fellow-Servants* may judge, I have a calm, steady, and joyful Assurance, that *Transactions like these* are registered in Heaven with Approbation, and receive the Sanction and Blessing of *the great Shepherd and Bishop of Souls*.

Northampton,
Sept. 10, 1745.

Postscript

As the Want of *Psalms* or *Hymns*, peculiarly suitable to these Occasions, has often been regretted on our *Ordination-Days*, when we have generally been confined to the 132d or 133d *Psalms*, I was desired by several of my Brethren to publish *that which followed this Charge*; and I accordingly do it without any farther Apology. The Reader will easily perceive, it is a Kind of *Devout Paraphrase* on *Eph.* iv.8, & seq. And it is One of some Hundreds lying by me, on a Variety of *Scripture-Subjects*.

An Hymn.

I.

Father of Mercies, in thine House,
Shine on our Homage and our Vows!

While with a grateful Heart we share
These Pledges of our Saviour's Care.

II.

Blest Saviour! When to Heaven he rose
In splendid Triumph o'er his Foes,
What Royal Gifts he scatter'd down!
How large, how permanent the Boon!

III.

Hence sprung th'*Apostles* honour'd Name,
Sacred, beyone Heroick Fame:
Hence dictates the *Prophetick* Sage;
And hence the *Evangelick* Page.

IV.

In lowlier Forms, to bless our Eyes,
Pastors from hence and *Teachers* rise;
Who, tho' with feebler Rays they shine,
Still gild a long extended Line.

V.

From Christ their varied Gifts dervive,
And fed by Christ their Graces give:
While guarded by his potent Hand,
Midst all the Rage of Hell they stand.

VI.

So shall the bright Succession run
Thro' the last Courses of the Sun;
While unborn Churches by their Care
Shall rise and flourish, fresh and fair.

VII.

Jesus our Lord their Hearts shall know,
The Spring whence all these Blessings flow:
Pastors and *People* shout his Praise
Thro' the long Round of endless Days!

Document III.12

Samuel Bourn on Ordination

For Bourn see Document II.12 above. For Orton (1717–83) see DH, DNB. He was educated under Doddridge at Northampton, and was highly regarded by his tutor, whose biographer he became. Though a Presbyterian, he described himself as 'quite an independent', and managed to earn the respect of orthodox and radical divines alike. Extract (a) is from *A Charge Delivered at the Ordination of the Reverend Mr. Job Orton; At Shrewsbury, September 18, 1745. By Samuel Bourn*, Birmingham, 1745, p. 29; extract (b) is from Bourn's *The Protestant Dissenters Catechism*, 1747, pp. 21–2.

(a)

YOUR *Investiture* into this sacred Office has been performed (as far as Men can do it) by the laying on of the Hands of the Presbytery, or Senior Pastors (signifying their Approbation and Consent) and by the Prayers of this Assembly to the God of the Spirits of all Flesh, for a Blessing on your future Labours.

(b)

Q.   What is the Form and Manner of Ordination amongst Dissenters?

A.   Senior Pastors require sufficient Testimonials of the good Behaviour of those who offer themselves as Candidates for the Ministry; they examine them in the Languages, Philosophy, and Divinity; then, after some Time of Trial, at their own and the People's Request, they appoint a Time for their Ordination; when, the people being assembled, one Minister begins with begging a Blessing on the Work of the Day, and reading a suitable Portion of Scripture; after which a Psalm is sung; then another Minister prays at large; a third describes the Ministerial Character and Duty in a Sermon; a fourth addresseth himself to the Candidate, desires an Account of his Faith, and his Views in entering upon the sacred Office, and requires his solemn Engagement to Diligence in the Discharge of it; then one of the senior Ministers recommends him to God in Prayer, with the Imposition of his own and his Brethren's Hands; after which an Exhortation is given to the ordained Minister; and the whole Service is concluded with singing of Psalms and a Thanksgiving Prayer.

Document III.13

Joseph Priestley on Ordination

For Priestley see Document II.11. The following extract is the preface to *A View of Revealed Religion; A Sermon, Preached at the Ordination of the The Rev. William Field of Warwick, July 12, 1790. By Joseph Priestley, LL.D. F.R.S. With a Charge Delivered at the same Time by the Rev. Thomas Belsham*, London, 1790, pp. iii–viii. For Field (1768–1851) see DNB. He left Homerton College on doctrinal grounds and completed his training under Belsham at Daventry academy. For Belsham see Document II.20 above.

Though publications of the nature of *this* have seldom any extensive circulation, yet as some persons into whose hands it may fall, may want information concerning the idea of *ordination* that prevails among Dissenters, I shall observe that we (at least many of us) do not now mean by it the *giving of orders*, without which a person could not be considered as properly qualified to exercise the office of minister in a christian society. As all our societies are independent of each other, the members of each of them are, of course, the sole judges of the qualifications of the person whom they chuse to be their minister. Consequently their appointment is his proper *orders*, or *title to officiate* among them; and all that is done by the minsters who bear any part in what is usually called *the ordination service* (besides thereby virtually expressing their approbation of the choice of the congregation, and giving their minister the right hand of fellowship) is to recommend him and his labours to the divine blessing by prayer, and to give him and the people proper advice.

On this idea it is now customary with many Dissenters, especially those who are called Presbyterians, for the minister to discharge all the functions of his office, baptizing and administering the Lord's supper, as well as preaching and praying, before ordination, in order more effectually to remove the prejudices which still remain with many, founded on the idea that some powers are conferred on this occasion, powers which qualify him to do *after* this ceremony what he could not do *before*.

The proper *ordination service* therefore, consists in the *prayer over the candidate*, and the *charge*. But the congregation, and also many strangers, being usually assembled on the occasion, and especially a number of ministers being present, it has been usual for one of them to deliver a discourse, or *sermon*, on some subject relating to Christianity in general, or the ministry of it in particular; and instead of the particular *confession of faith*, which was formerly required of all candidates for the ministry (his soundness in which was then deemed essential) certain *questions* are put to him, which lead him to give as much as he thinks proper of his views of Christianity and the ministry of it, and the motives and maxims of his own conduct, for the instruction of the audience.

The ceremony of *imposition of hands*, which in primitive times accompanied the action of praying for a particular person, by which the apostles communicated spiritual gifts, and which was afterwards supposed to be necessary to the conferring of proper qualifications for the gospel ministry, is now generally laid aside by us, since we are conscious that we have nothing to impart, and wish not to encourage superstition.

Ordination being now no longer considered in the light of *conferring orders*, as in Episcopal, and the proper Presbyterian churches, many of the more liberal Dissenters neglect it altogether; thinking it to encourage superstition, and to keep up a mere *form* when the *substance* is wanting. But when the design of ordination, as above explained, is well understood, when the person ordained shall have performed every part of the ministerial duty before, as well as after, his ordination, though the name given to the service no longer suggests the idea that was formerly annexed to it, no superstition is encouraged. And since the connexion between a minister and his congregation, and especially the fist that he forms, is a very serious

169

concern, there cannot, surely, be any impropriety, but on the contrary the greatest propriety, in making it an occasion of solemn prayer; and then exhortation or admonition, from a minister of greater age and experience, to one who has but lately entered upon the office, is particularly seasonable. I cannot help, therefore, expressing my wish, that some service, to which the name of *ordination* may well enough be given, may be kept up among us, at the same time that every precaution is taken to prevent superstition with respect to it.

J. PRIESTLEY

Birmingham,
Nov. 1, 1790.

Document III.14

A Baptist Ordination in 1794

The following is an account of the service held at Worstead, Norfolk, in 1794 at which James Freeman Beard was ordained to the ministry. Lay participation in the service is clearly indicated. The account is reprinted from Charles Boardman Jewson, *The Baptists in Norfolk*, London: Carey Kingsgate Press, 1957, p. 52.

The worship of God began at 10 o'clock in the morning with singing the 2nd part of the 84th Psalm of Dr. Watts's after which Bro. Farmery of Diss engaged in prayer earnestly imploring a blessing upon the important and solemn work of the day. Brother Ridley of Ipswich introduced the work of the day and interrogated the parties particularly interested therein, agreeable to which Brother Shalders, the Senior Deacon, stood up and gave a brief account of the steps the church had taken in her widowhood state, of the particular providences occurring in bringing J. F. Beard among them and their unanimous approbation of him. Then J. F. Beard arose and gave a brief account relative to his call by grace, his call to the ministry and the leading of Providence in his removal from Woodbridge to Worstead &c which being done he gave in a confession of faith relative to the glorious doctrines of the everlasting gospel. The Senior Deacon in the name of the church recognized their call and J. F. Beard his acceptation of the pastoral office amongst them, at the conclusion of which sung 132 Psalm Dr. Watts Long Measure. After which brother Hitchcock of Wattisham gave the charge from 1 Timothy 4 ch.16 v. Sung 103 Hymn first book Dr. Watts and brother Brown of Yarmouth addressed the church from Eph. 2 ch. 19 v. Sung 132 Psalm from pause, Dr. Watts's Book and brother Kinghorn of Norwich concluded in prayer.

Document III.15

Caleb Evans on Private Judgement and Corporate Call

Caleb Evans (1737–91) was a prominent Particular Baptist minister who, following a year as assistant at Unicorn Yard, London, ministered at Broadmead, Bristol, as assistant from 1759 and as co-pastor from 1767. He served concurrently as tutor at the Baptist College, Bristol, and was principal from 1779 to 1791. The extract from his ordination statement reveals the mingling of a number of intellectual currents of his day. In addition to his evangelical Calvinism, there emerges both his concern for the right of private judgement, and his recognition that in such matters as the call to a pastorate there must be a degree of accord on doctrine and ethics.

For Evans see DEB, DNB, DWB; Norman S. Moon, 'Caleb Evans, Founder of the British Education Society', *Baptist Quarterly*, XXIX, 1971, pp. 171–90; *idem, Education for Ministry: Bristol Baptist College 1697–1979*, Bristol: Bristol Baptist College, 1979. The following extract is from *A Charge and Sermon, Together with an Introductory Discourse, and Confession of Faith, Delivered at the Ordination of the Rev. Mr. Caleb Evans, August 18, 1767, in Broad-Mead, Bristol*, 1767, pp. 13, 16.

The right of private judgment, especially in matters of religion, I apprehend is the undoubted and unalienable privilege of every rational intelligent creature. It is a privilege I claim myself, and for the use of which I am accountable only to God; and it is a privilege which I think every one *ought* to exercise, and has a right *fully* and *freely* to enjoy …

[A]s it is not possible for a conscientious people to make a choice of a minister, without being satisfied in what they apprehend to be the soundness of his faith, as well as the purity of his morals, so it does not seem consistent for any conscientious ministers to join in the ordination of another minister without having the like satisfaction.

Document III.16

Samuel Bourn on Elderly Ministers

The following text is from p. 5 of Samuel Bourn's funeral oration on II Kings 2: 3, delivered following the death of his father; see Document III.1 above.

[F]aithful old Ministers have a tender Affection for young Ministers and Students. They look upon them as their Successors in a glorious Ministry, who must stand up in their Room. As the Priesthood under the *first Covenant* was successive, the Priests not being suffer'd to continue by Reason of death; so the Gospel-Ministry passes thro' many Hands. Dying Ministers earnestly desire their Successors may be furnished with Knowledge, and Zeal, and Prudence, that they may *shine* and *burn*, and execute their great Office with Faithfulness to *Christ* and Souls. They are desirous to leave with 'em their *dying Counsels, and dying Charges.*

Document III.17

Christmas Evans on his Ministry

For Evans see Document II.22 above. The quotation is reprinted from B. A. Ramsbottom, *Christmas Evans*, Luton: Bunyan Press, 1985, p. 148.

I have been thinking of the great goodness of the Lord unto me throughout my unworthy ministry; and now, in my old age, I see the work prospering wonderfully in my hand, so that there is a reason to think that I am, in some degree, a blessing to the church when I might have been a burden to it, or rather a curse, by which one might have been induced to wish me laid in the earth that I might no longer prevent the progress of the work. Thanks be to God that it is not so! Though I deserve no better, yet I am in the land of mercy. This is unto me according to the manner of God unto His people. My path in the valley, the dangers, and the precipices of destruction upon which I have stood, rush into my thoughts, and also the sinking of many in death, and the downfall of others by immorality and their burial in Kibroth-Hattaavah, the graves of inordinate desire, together with the withering, the feebleness and the unfruitfulness of some who through the influence of a secret departure from God, and of walking in the hidden paths that lead to apostasy.

Document III.18

Benjamin Keach on Baptism

The Particular Baptist Minister Benjamin Keach (1640–1704) took up his pen against James Owen, a Welsh Independent with Presbyterian leanings, who was educated under Samuel Jones (1628–97) at Brynllywarch and Stephen Hughes (1622–88) at Swansea. A settled pastor and an itinerant preacher, he conducted an academy first at Oswestry and then at Shrewsbury. In 1693 he published *Bedydd Plant o'r Nefoedd*, to which Keach replied in 1696.

For Keach see DNB. For Owen see DNB, DWB. The following extracts comprise the title to Keach's book and the two dedications. They are reprinted from Thomas Rees, *History of Protestant Nonconformity in Wales*, London: John Snow, 1883, pp. 252–4.

Mr. Keach has given to his volume the following long and assuming title: – 'Light broke forth in Wales expelling darkness, of the English man's love to the Antient Britains; being an answer to a book intituled, "Children's Baptism from Heaven," published in the Welsh tongue by Mr. James Owen. Wherein his twelve arguments for the baptizing of the children of the faithful are examined and confuted and Infant baptism overthrown. Also proving that Baptizing is dipping the whole body in water, in the Name of the Father, the Son, and the Holy Ghost, and that believers are the only subjects of baptism. In which the Antipaedobaptists are cleared from all those unjust reproaches and calumnies cast upon them by the said Mr. Owen.'

There are prefixed to the book two dedications. The first 'To all godly Antipædobaptists, especially to them in South and North Wales;' and the second, 'To all godly Christians who are Pædobaptists, in South and North Wales.' The Antipædobaptists are thus addressed: – 'Beloved in our dear Redeemer, at your desire I have, as the Lord hath helped me, answered Mr. James Owen's book, in which he hath cast many false and slanderous reflections on you, and all other Antipædobaptists; but I have forborne returning railing for railing, though perhaps some of my words may seem a little too sharp, but his way of writing called for it. I hope the translation of his book, first out of Welsh into English, and again, the translation of my answer, out of English into Welsh, are done faithfully. If it be according to the true sense and purport of his words and meaning, the different placing of words he can have no ground to cavil at, but of that I am not capable to judge, because I understand not the Welsh tongue. He seems to reflect very severely upon some of your conversations, as if you wanted that true piety that becomes your holy profession, and also as if you wanted charity; but I hope it is his own uncharitable spirit that led him out thus to write, and that you are a people who rest not on the form of godliness without the power, and that you also love all in whom you see the image of Christ; the truth is, he of all men might have forborne such a charge, considering how short he himself appears in that respect, having laboured to cast you and all Antipædobaptists out of the universal church, and chargeth us, who dip believing men and women in the name of the Father, &c., with adultery and murder. O that the Lord would open his eye, and give him true repentance.

'Brethren, this answer hath swelled much bigger than you expected, which I am myself troubled at; but pray pardon me in this case, because this controversy was never before printed in the Welsh tongue, as I am informed, as it is here. I was therefore willing the godly in Wales, or any of the antient Britains that desired information herein, might see the main arguments that other Pædobaptists have brought for infant baptism fully answered. The substance therefore of Mr. Burkitt's late book is in this also answered, and divers others; nay, there is scarcely an argument that hath been brought for infant baptism, formerly, or of late, but it is here answered. And now to conclude, let me desire you to labour to adorn the holy gospel you profess, with a suitable and becoming conversation. It is not an external ordinance that signifies anything, without true faith and a holy life. You have lamps, but O, see that you have oil in your vessels. Not that I blame you for your great zeal for this precious, though despised, truth of Christ, considering what a glorious and illustrious institution or blessed ordinance it is,' &c.

The dedication, 'to all godly Christians who are Pædobaptists in South and North Wales,' runs in the following strain: – 'You worthy brethren and Antient Britains, I kindly salute you in the bowels of Christian love and sincere affections; I cannot but love all who have the image of my heavenly Father stamped upon their souls. It is not your opinion of Pædobaptism, though an error, that shall alienate my heart from you, nor restrain that catholic love that should run in all the veins of every one that is born of God; though I am an enemy to your opinion and practice, in that case, yet a dear lover of your persons and precious souls. *And I have so much charity to believe that it is through ignorance you err in that matter, and that God hath for some wise ends hid the truth of His holy ordinance of Gospel baptism at present from you; and do hope, did you see otherwise, you would practise otherwise; charity thinketh no evil,*' &c.

Document III.19

The Lichfield-Longdon Church Book

The Church Book was begun by the first minister, Robert Travers (whose dates are unknown) in 1695. Travers, a Presbyterian, was born at Llanboidy, Carmarthenshire, and was trained possibly under James Owen at Oswestry, and certainly under John Woodhouse at Sheriffhales. The following extract implies that Travers expected that normally both parents would be present at a child's baptism, and suggests that he took care to acquire a written promise from an absent father.

For Travers see Alan P.F. Sell, 'Robert Travers and the Lichfield-Longdon Church Book', in *idem*, *Dissenting Thought and the Life of the Churches*, Lewiston, NY: Edwin Mellen Press, 1990, ch. 9.

August 21.1731. Baptized John the Son of John Martin, exciseman, att his Mother in Laws Mrs. Motts att her house – baptized ye Son privately ye Mother present, but the Father in ye Kings business abroad, but by Letter engaged to Educate his for God [sic] Redeemer according to the claim of ye New Covenant.

Document III.20

Quaker Thoughts on Baptism

The following extract is from Benjamin Holme's *A Serious Call*, see Document II.1 above.

Concerning Baptism

Because of our Disuse of Water Baptism, and Bread and Wine, we have been very hardly spoke of, as though we denied the Ordinances of Jesus Christ; whenas there is no People that I know of, that do more truly own the Necessity of believing and being baptized than we do; but we do not understand it to be only an historical Belief of the Conception and Birth, and Life and Miracles, and also of the Death and Sufferings, and Resurrection and Ascension of Christ, or a being outwardly baptized with Water, that will entitle Men to Salvation; for we read, *that* Simon *the Sorcerer believed, and was baptized*, and yet he was so far from being in a State of Salvation, that *Peter* saith to him, *I perceive thou art in the Gall of Bitterness and in the Bond of Iniquity.*[1] But lest any should be under a Mistake, and take the Baptism of Water to be the one essential and saving Baptism, hear the Apostle *Peter*; *Whence once the Long suffering of God waited in the Days of* Noah, *while the Ark was preparing, wherein few,* that is, *eight Souls were saved by Water.* The Antitype *whereof, even Baptism, doth also now save us*; *not the putting away of the Filth of the Flesh,* [mark that] *but the Answer of a good Conscience towards God, by the Resurrection of Jesus Christ.*[2] Now it is the Baptism of Christ, by his Spirit, that brings Men to that; for it is plain, from the Instance of *Simon* before noted, that a Man may believe, and be baptized with Water, and be so far from having the Answer of a good Conscience, that he may be in the *Gall of Bitterness, and in the Bond of Iniquity*, which is the very Reverse of *Christianity*. A great many take the Commission in the 28th of *Matthew*, to be a Commission for Water-Baptism; *Go ye therefore and teach all Nations, baptizing them in the Name of the Father, and of the Son, and of the Holy Ghost.*[3] Now here is no mention of Water. Is it not reasonable to suppose, that if our dear Lord had intended that they should baptize with Water, that he would have expressly mentioned it. Although the Apostle *Paul* was not interior to the chief of the Apostles, he saith, *I thank God that I baptized none of you, but* Crispus *and* Gaius, *lest any should say, that I had baptized in mine own Name; and I baptized also the Household of* Stephanas; *besides, I know not whether I baptized any other; for Christ sent me* NOT *to baptize, but to preach the Gospel.*[4] So that what he did in that Case was by way of Condescension, as in the Case of circumcising *Timothy*, and going into the Temple and purifying himself.[5] It would be a weak Thing to plead for these Things now, because the Apostle practised them. Doth it therefore follow, that Water-Baptism should be practised now, because the Apostle *Paul*, by way of Condescension, practised it? For if he had took that Commission, *Mat. xxviii. 19.* to be a Commission for him to baptize with outward Water, we may safely conclude, that he would not have thanked God that he had done him so little Service. We do not deny, but that some other of the Apostles did also, by way of Condescension, practise Water-Baptism; but that they were commanded to baptize with Water in that Commission, I think will be too hard for any body to prove.[6] It is possible some may be ready to say, it must needs be meant of Water; because, say they, no Man can baptize with the Spirit, or into the Power and Spirit of Christ: We freely own, that no Man, as he is a Man, by his own Power can do this; neither can any Man by his own Power, as he is Man, *heal the Sick, cleanse the Lepers, raise the Dead, cast out Devils,*[7] and yet we find the Disciples were commanded to do these Things. And by the same Power, by which they did cast out many Devils, and healed the Sick, &c. they were instrumental to baptize Men into the Name and Power of Christ. *And as I began to speak*, saith Peter, *the Holy Ghost fell on them as on us at the Beginning. Then remembred I the Word of the Lord, how that he said,* John *truly baptized with Water, but ye shall be baptized with the Holy Ghost.*[8] At the great Meeting we read of in the second of *Acts*, Verse the 4th, it is said, *They were all filled with the Holy Ghost, and began to speak with other Tongues as the Spirit gave them Utterance*; yet some of the Multitude mocked, and were so ignorant of the Operation of the Holy Ghost, that they said, Verse 13, *These Men are full of New Wine: But* Peter *standing up with the Eleven, lift up his Voice and said unto them, Ye Men of*

Judah, *and all ye that dwell at* Jerusalem, *be this known unto you, and hearken to my Words, for these are not drunken as ye suppose, seeing it is but the third Hour of the Day; but this is that which was spoken by the Prophet* Joel, &c. It is hard to make Men sensible of the Operation of the Holy Ghost, and of the spiritual Baptism, while they are Strangers to the Spirit in themselves; but if it could be proved, that the Disciples in that Commission were commanded to baptize with or in Water,[9] which I believe cannot be done; how will they that are for the Sprinkling of Infants, prove their Practice from that Commission, *Go teach all Nations,* &c. for they are not capable of being taught. As to what is urged of the Jaylor,[10] and all his, and of whole Families being baptized; there is no Account that there were any Infants baptized in any of them. There is abundance of Families now, as (we may reasonably suppose) there were then, in which there are no little Children. As to that of our Saviour, where he saith, *Suffer little Children to come unto me, and forbid them not, for of such is the Kingdom,* it cannot be proved from Scripture, that he baptized any of them in, or with Water. But as to this Practice of Sprinkling Infants, it is so much without Foundation in the Scripture, that a great many People, who are not of our Society, do not hold it or own it. The Way rightly to understand this Commission, is to come to that Spirit by which it was given forth. Many urge, that our Saviour was baptized of *John*;[11] he was also circumcised, doth it therefore follow that we must be circumcised because he was circumcised? For as he was born under the Law, he fulfilled the Law, *and he is the End of the Law for Righteousness sake, to all them that believe.* When Christ came to *John* to be baptized of him, *John* forbad him, saying, *I have need to be baptized of thee.*[12] Here *John* the Baptist, who was the Administrator of Water Baptism, was sensible that he had Need to be baptized of Christ, with the Baptism of the Holy Ghost: [13]*'Suffer it to be so now,* said Christ, *for thus it becometh us to fulfil all Righteousness*: So that he fulfilled the Righteousness of *John*'s Dispensation. *John* has very clearly and excellently distinguished his Baptism with Water, from the Baptism of Christ , with the Holy Ghost, *I indeed baptize you with Water unto Repentance; but he that cometh after me, is mightier than I, whose Shoes I am not worthy to bear; he shall baptize you with the Holy Ghost and with Fire, whose Fan is in his Hand, and he will thoroughly purge his Floor, and gather his Wheat into the Garner, but he will burn up the Chaff with unquenchable Fire.*[14] This is the Messenger of the Covenant, the Prophet speaks of, *The Lord whom ye seek, shall suddenly come to his Temple, even the Messenger of the Covenant, whom ye delight in; behold he shall come.*[15]

Notes

1. Acts viii. 13, 23.
2. I Pet. iii. 20, 21.
3. Mat. xxviii. 19.
4. I Cor. 1. 14, 15, 16, 17.
5. Acts xvi. and xxi. 26.
6. Mat. xxviii. 19.

7. Mat. x. 8.
8. Acts. xi. 15, 16.
9. Mat. xxviii. 19, 20.
10. Acts. xvi. 33.
11. Luke ii. 21.
12. Mat. iii. 13, 14.
13. Verse 15–.
14. Mat. iii. 11, 12.
15. Mal. iii. 1, 2.

Document III.21

Howel Harris and the Baptists

On a number of occasions Harris found himself at odds with the Baptists. For Harris see Document II.25. The following is from Tom Beynon, *Howell Harris's Visits to Pembrokeshire*, Aberystwyth: Cambrian News Press, 1966, p. 30.

19 *March*, 1740. *Trehowell, Llanwnda*. Feed what is good in the Baptists, and weed as much as is bad in them and us all. 11 Toward Abergwaun, 2 miles (ship) by the seaside. Discoursed there in Welsh and English near 3 hours to some thousands, there being a great many of the gentry of this county here today. Had never more authority, did not speak with my own spirit on Paul's conversion. Most thundering on the words – 'Why persecutest thou me?' That religion is not in name, but in Christ. (Here was 3 parsons, I hope they had it home, that they that send the people to wander and to leave a pure Church.) When I had done I had a letter from a minister, Mr. Thomas, complaining of the Baptists. I had a letter again from John Powell charging me with many things. Discoursed with one turned over lately to the Baptists. I had love and meekness to her. Having incited them to love and calmness of spirit, went past 3 toward Tredrath [Trefdraeth- Newport]. Came to Trelert near 5. Discoursed to near 7 to many thousands. I find that John Powell last Monday seven night preached against infant baptism, so that there was nothing of the awe becoming God's worship among the people, but as if in an alehouse, one punched the other all about the house, he saying that the doctrine of infant baptism is cyfeiliornus, uffernol, melldigedig, cythreulig, etc., and that God calls none but the elect to hear the word. Here people are by the ears. Persons shan't go along the way but the first thing that is asked is 'How can you prove infant baptism?' 'Tis quite a war about this. They go 9–6 at a time to them. Men's minds are turned by these disputes from the heart to the head. I dread this war lest I should lose my love.

Document III.22

Grantham Killingworth contra John Taylor on Baptism

In 1740 the Baptist Grantham Killingworth published *The Necessity of Baptism, in order to Church membership and Christian Communion, Shewn from Christ's own words John 3: 3, 5, in Two Letters to A Learned Divine.* The Two Letters are appended to his *Remarks On the Several Answers To a Pamphlet, intitled Christianity not founded on Argument,* London, 1744, from which the following extract is taken (pp. 91–2). The learned divine was John Taylor of Norwich, for whom see Document II.13 above. For Killingworth (1699–1778) see DNB.

1.   What they call the *Abrahamic* covenant does not appear to have any thing in it like *a covenant.* It was only *a promise,* by way of prediction, of blessings that would be derived to the faithful, from *Abraham's* seed, in future, and far, far distant ages. It was not a stipulation of blessings, as this strange and perplexed notion of a covenant implies; It was not, I say, a stipulation of blessings which *Abraham* himself would ever live to see or enjoy; but of a privilege, not designed to be communicated till the times of the *Messiah.* And tho' this is declared, by St. *Paul,* to be *a preaching the gospel to Abraham,* it is only in a more improper and figurative sense: just as many prophecies and promises of the Old Testament might be said to be *preaching the gospel,* long before that holy and most spiritual institution commenced, to the whole *Jewish* nation.

2.   Circumcision is never stiled the seal of any covenant, but if it belonged to the covenant of grace, it was a seal not at all necessary with respect even to such, as are allowed to have been really interested in that covenant. For all females were utterly excluded from it, without any the least prejudice, I would hope, to their spiritual and eternal concerns. If infants therefore are excluded from baptism, they also may sustain no damage. So that the whole of this plea for infants is a heap of confusion and inconsistency; and all the warm and pathetic exclamations, that are so often mixed with it, are mere dismal sounds, that have no energy in them, can never convince the truly considerate and divested of all prejudice, nor answer any valuable purpose. Infants are as safe, their privileges as entire, and their state as good, upon this principle, without baptism, as with it' as that of one half of the *Jewish* nation was without circumcision. Why then should they be forced, without their consent, to undergo what is called the ordinance of baptism, without any encouragement from, and against the plain rules and examples of, the New Testament? But,

3.   What has been offered under the foregoing head affords, I think, a strong probability that circumcision had, and could have, no relation at all to the covenant of grace, but only to the peculiar immunities of the race and descendants of *Abraham.* For did the great God, whose tender mercies are over all his works, enter into a covenant relation with the males only? Of if an instituted seal of the covenant be such an extraordinary privilege, as our brethren profess it to be, could not one have been instituted, that would have discovered universal and more impartial goodness; that

might have been equally a seal to all that were included within the terms of the imagined covenant? But,

Finally, and to dismiss this topic, that circumcision could not belong to the covenant of grace, or to the gospel preached to *Abraham*, is manifest, even to a demonstration, from what St. *Paul* has so strenuously asserted, and copiously argued, in his epistle to the *Galatians*; where he refers it entirely to what, in the language of school-divinity, is stiled the covenant of works, according to the strict tenor of which, no man could reasonably hope for salvation.

Document III.23

John Taylor on Baptism

In 1757 Taylor (for whom see Document II.13 above) published *The Covenant of Grace, and Baptism The Token of it, Explained upon Scripture Principles*. In the following year Killingworth replied with *A Forerunner to a Farther Answer, if need be, To the Rev. Dr. John Taylor of Norwich, His Covenant of Grace and Baptism the Token of it*. Thus over some two decades the pair managed to speak past one another on this issue.

The extract is from *The Covenant of Grace*, pp. 48–50. He argues,

1.   That Baptism is a Token or Sign of the Covenant, or Grant of Blessings in Christ; and nothing but a Token or Sign. When we are baptized *into the Name of the Father, Son and Holy Ghost*, that Action doth not give us an Interest or Right in Covenant-Blessings, but only signifies and declares the Interest and Right we already have in *the Love of God, the Grace of Christ, and the Fellowship of the Holy Ghost*; or in all Covenant-Blessings. Even as Circumcision was a Seal of that Righteousness, or Grant of Favours, which *Abraham* had before he was circumcised. It is the *Promise*, which giveth the Right: and the Seal, or Token, confirms it. Therefore, those Expressions, *Be baptized for*, or into, *the Remission of Sins*; *be baptized and wash away thy Sins*, cannot be understood as if the mere Act of washing, or baptizing, removed the Guilt, or procured the Pardon of Sin: but only that it signified, that Sin was washed away, or pardoned, by the Mercy of God, to such as did sincerely repent; yet so, that if any Person had refuse to have been baptized, it could not have been supposed that their Profession, or Repentence, was sincere; nor, consequently, that their Sins were forgiven. Consequently, I remark,

2.   That Baptism doth not bring the Person baptized under new Obligations to Duty, but only signifies the Obligations which the Love and Goodness of God have already brought him under. In short, Baptism doth not make any Alteration in the religious State of the Person baptized; but only signifies and declares that State of Favour, in which he is already place by the free Gift of God in *Christ*.

3.   Baptism is now the initiating Ordinance, as Circumcision had been before: that is to say, it is the Ordinance that is administred to a Person at his first Entrance into the Church and Kingdom of God; the first visible Pledge and Token of God's

Love, assuring him of his Interest in all Covenant-Blessings, and of his Share in all Church Honours and Privileges. And this it declares and signifies once for all; and therefore it is but once administered, and not to be repeated afterwards. This is allowed by all Christians.

4. Observe; Baptism declares and signifies an Interest in Covenant-Blessings, not as they are *immediately* connected with *eternal* Salvation, but as they are *present* Privileges and Advantages: or as they are *Principles, Encouragements, Means* and *Motives* freely given on the Part of God to all Christians, *antecedently* to a Life or Course of Obedience; and, on our Part, to be understood, considered and improved, so as to excite and induce us to a Life of Obedience. Or; Baptism signifies our having passed out of the State of *Heathenism* into the *Christian* State; or into the Church and Family of God; and our being obliged to live accordingly. Which if we do, we are happy for ever: if not; neither Baptism, nor any other Christian Privilege, will be of any Avail.

These Things premised, I reckon we have now laid a very just and solid, rational and intelligible Foundation of *Infant-Baptism*. For if the Infants of believing Parents, or professed Christians, have a Right to Covenant-Blessings, they must have a Right to the Sign or Token of the Covenant, whereby their Interest in those Blessings is solemnly recognized and declared. They who have a Right to the Promise, have a Right to Baptism.

Document III.24

John Taylor contra Infant Dedication

Whilst minister at Crook, near Kendal, Samuel Bourn obliged some anti-paedobaptist members of his congregation by dedicating their child without the use of water. (See Joshua Toulmin, *Memoirs of The Revd. Samuel Bourn*, 1808, p. 23). Whether John Taylor had heard of this instance, or how widespread the practice was amongst Presbyterians, it is impossible to say; but he certainly did not approve of it, as is seen in the following extract from his *The Scripture Account of Prayer, in an Address to Dissenters in Lancashire: Occasioned By a new Liturgy some Ministers, of that County, are composing for the Use of a Congregation at Liverpool*, 1761, p. 78.

Baptism, by a strange liberty, has ... been changed into the *dedication* of children, in one instance, at least, where an Infant was only dedicated to God, but not baptized in the name of the Father, Son and Holy Ghost. This practice has a direct tendency, to dissolve, in the thought of christians, the essential connection between Baptism and the Covenant of Grace, of which Covenant, Baptism is the memorial, sign, token or seal, most properly confirming and assuring to the Infant baptised, and the rest of the Family, all the unspeakably great blessing of the Gospel, as they are freely given to us of God in Christ: and so all the comfort and encouragement to a pious life, which the Ordinance in succeeding generations is intended to inspire, will be lost to you and yours, and sunk into utter oblivion.

Document III.25

Thomas Smith's Baptismal Hymn

Thomas Smith was the Baptist minister at Shelfanger, Norfolk, for forty-seven years. He died, aged seventy-seven, in 1813. The hymn is reprinted from C. B. Jewson, *The Baptists in Norfolk*, London: Carey Kingsgate Press, 1957, p. 48.

Let young disciples feel thy grace,
Let older Christians hail the day;
And all behold the sign of peace,
And blood which washes sins away.
O shew thy power, holy Dove,
Increase our courage, strength and joy;
Revive our hope and warm our love;
Let Christ and grace our thoughts employ.

Document III.26

The Lord's Supper at Rothwell

An anonymous Anglican wrote the following account of the Lord's Supper in his *Account of the Doctrine and Discipline of Mr. Richard Davis, of Rothwell in the County of Northampton, and those of his Separation*, London, 1700, p.20. Davis (1658–1714), a somewhat angular Independent, was accused of preaching Antinomian doctrine, and caused distress to settled pastors by his evangelistic itinerating and encouragement of lay preachers. See further DWB; Alan P. F. Sell, *The Great Debate: Calvinism, Arminianism and Salvation*, Worthing: H. E. Walter, 1982 and Grand Rapids: Baker Book House, 1983; repr. Eugene, OR: Wipf and Stock, 1998, pp. 51–3 and references, p. 116 n. 93.

Every member is required to receive the Sacrament as often as it is administered. The Table stands in the midst of the Congregation, near the Pulpit. The Pastor sits in his Chair near the Table, and the Receivers on forms around about it; the People, as Spectators, at some small distance behind them.

The Pastor prays (all standing) and craves a Blessing on the Bread; then sets it apart in almost the same Words which the Church of *England* uses; then breaks it into small pieces, and puts them on divers Plates, saying, whilst he is breaking, *Thus was our Lord's body torn, mangled, broken,* &c. The Bread thus broken is carried in the Plates, by the Deacons, to the several Receivers. The Pastor sits in his Chair Eating with the rest.

As soon as the Bread is Eaten, the Pastor Prays; then pours out the Wine, saying, *Behold the Blood of Christ poured out for thee, and for me, and for all of us,* &c. *Drink ye all of this, drink large draughts of the Love of Christ,* &c. as he thinks most proper to express himself. Then he drinks and gives to the Deacons. When all have drunk the Pastor Prays, an Hymn is Sung, and the Assembly is dismissed.

They forbid all private Prayer at this Ordinance, saying, the Pastors Prayers are sufficient. They esteem it a Memorial only: Examine none before they come, saying There is no need of any more Preparation at that time than any other. In the absence or sickness of the Pastor, there must be no Sacrament.

Document III.27

The Lord's Supper at Bury Street

This extract is taken from 'From the Bury Street Records', *Congregational Historical Society Transactions*, VI, 1915, pp. 334–5.

The Lord's Supper is administered alternately by the two pastors (Dr. Watts and Rev. S. Price) (v 13) in the plainest manner, just according to the institution, first the history of the institution of this ordinance is read, either out of Matthew's gospel or the first ep. Corinthians, that it may ever be kept in mind to regulate every part of the practice; and the sermons of that day being equally suited to the design of the Lord's Supper, or a commemoration of the sufferings of Christ 'tis but seldom that any other speech or exhortation is made before the celebration.

The minister, taking hold of the plate in which the bread lies, calls upon the people to join with him in seeking for a blessing on it, which is done in a short prayer of eight or ten minutes. Then the minister says 'Having blessed this bread, we break it in remembrance of our Saviour's body, &c.' Then the loaves, which are before cut into squares, almost through, are broken by the minister into small pieces, as big as walnuts, or thereabouts, and taking the plate of bread in his hand, he says, 'This is the body of Christ, or the emblem or figure of the body of Christ, which was broken for you: take it and eat ye all of it, in remembrance of our Saviour who died for us', or such like words, which are a plain declaration that the bread represents the body of Christ, according to his own appointment: it is then distributed by the pastor to the deacons, and to one or more of the members who are appointed to it, and it is carried by them to the various members of the church. Then, after a short space, an inquiry being made if all have received the bread, and that those who have not received it are desired to stand up and signify it, the pastor proceeds, in like manner, to pour out the wine, at least into one of the cups, then he asks a blessing on the cup; and then distributes it, as before, to the members or the deacons, and they to some other members of the church, by whom it is carried round to all the seats. In many churches, the pastor is frequently speaking proper sentences or texts or scripture, to awaken the faith, hope and joy of Christians, and I cannot but approve of it in the main. But our former pastor, Dr. Chauncey, was so much against it, that it was not practiced among us. But when most of the members, on some particular occasion, met together, the two pastors proposed it to be them, whether we should keep up this practice or leave them to their own silent meditations. They seemed generally to approve our silence, and this is the reason we omit it.

After this there is a psalm or hymn sung, suited to the ordinance. Then the plate is sent round to collect for the necessities of the poor. After this, particular cases of the members are represented who desire the public prayers of the church; and then, with a prayer offered on this occasion, together with thanksgiving and the final benediction, this service is concluded.

Document III.28

Communion Discipline at Lichfield

The following is a further extract from the Lichfield-Longdon Church Book; Document III.19 above.

John Slot the Brewer now of Rath formerly had his Habitation in Rochdale in Lancashire & hath been for many years a stated member of the congregation of Protestants called Presbyterians, & had there continued, but that he finds himself necessitated to travel abroad for an honest Livelyhood, and therefore: – can seldom have an opportunity of Joyning with that Society, but expressing to me his desire to communicate *in the Lord's Super* [sic] *occasionally* with *Xn Churches* of that Denomination in those places where his business should cast him, I think it may be serviceable to the attaining that his Desire to certify thus much to those whom it may concern, as also that I have good hopes that his wil [sic] every where, behave himself as becomes the Gospel of Jesus Xt. our comon [sic] Lord: witness my hand.

Jos. Dawson M. Pastor
to the Presbyterian Congregation at Rochdale

Document III.29

Quaker Thoughts on the Lord's Supper

The following extract is from Benjamin Holme's *A Serious Call*; see Document II.1 above.

Altho' we disuse the outward Bread and Wine, we do very truly own the spiritual Supper of the Lord, which is spoken of in the *Revelations*; *Behold, I stand at the Door and knock; if any Man hear my Voice, and open the Door, I will come in to him, and will sup with him, and he with me.*[1] It is what we desire, that all religious well-minded People, who conscientiously receive the outward Bread and Wine, may open the Door of their Hearts, and receive the Lord Jesus Christ by his Spirit, that so they may know an inward Supping with him in his Kingdom; for we read, *The Kingdom of God cometh not with Observations, neither shall they say, lo here, or lo there, for behold the Kingdom of God is within you.*[2] *I will not leave you comfortless,* (said Christ our Lord) *I will come to you.*[3] *But I say unto you, I will not drink henceforth of this Fruit of the Vine, until that Day, when I drink it new with you in my Father's Kingdom.*[4]

He dwelleth with you, and shall be in you. And in that excellent Prayer, he saith to his Father, *I in them, and thou in me, that they may be made perfect in one, and that the World may know that thou hast sent me, and hast loved them, as thou has loved me.*[5] We bear Testimony to the Coming of Christ by his Spirit into Mens Hearts; and they that have known him to wash them thoroughly by the Water of Regeneration, will know inward Communion with the Lord, as the good *Christians* of old knew; *That which we have seen, and hear, declare we unto you, that ye also may have Fellowship with us; and truly our Fellowship is with the Father, and with his Son Jesus Christ.*[6] They were People of blessed Experience, and it is what we desire, that the Children of Men might come to witness this in themselves; for they that are come to have Fellowship with the Father, and with the Son, are come to the End of the outward Bread and Wine, even to the glory of the Gospel Dispensation, which is a Dispensation of Enjoyment; for as Men are inwardly reconciled, and brought into Favour with God, they come to know a Feeding of that divine and living Bread which comes down from Heaven; *I am* (said Christ) *the living Bread which came down from Heaven; if any Man eat of this Bread, he shall live for ever; and the Bread that I will give, is my Flesh, which I will give for the Life of the World. He that eateth my Flesh, and drinketh my Blood, dwelleth in me, and I in him.*[7] It is as Men witness this, that they can speak from their own Experience, what a blessed Thing it is to have inward Communion with Christ. It is the great Blessing of Wisdom's Children, that she brings them to the Substance; *I Wisdom lead in the Way of Righteousness, in the Midst of the Paths of Judgment, that I may cause those that love me to inherit Substance; and I will fill their Treasures.*[8] Reader, this is what is desired for thee, that thou mayst come to the Substance, that so thou mayst know a Feeding of that divine and spiritual Bread which can only satisfy the Soul, and a drinking of the Wine of the Kingdom; but it is hard to make the natural Man sensible of these Things; they are beyond his Reach and Comprehension. ... It doth not avail in the Sight of God, whether a Man be baptized with Water, or not baptized with Water; or whether he receives the Bread and Wine, or doth not receive it, if he be not a new Creature: We read, *If any Man be in Christ, he is a new Creature:* and as is before observed, *except a Man be born again, he cannot see the Kingdom of God.* We greatly desire that all People might have this in their own Experience, that so they might walk as becomes the Children of God, and manifest themselves to be the Followers and Disciples of Christ, by their living agreeably to his Doctrine; for I count that is the greatest outward visible Sign, that any Man can give, that he is truly a *Christian*, and a Member of Christ's Church, for him to live agreeably to the Doctrine of Christ; *By this,* said our Saviour, *shall all Men know that ye are my Disciples, if ye love one another.* Now, to love one another, to love our Enemies, to do Good for Evil, to forgive Injuries, to be just and merciful, and walk humbly, as *Christians* ought to do, are good outward visible Signs; but we believe no outward Observations will make Men *Christians*, and Members of that pure Church which Christ came to present to God, without Spot or Wrinkle, or any such Thing,[9] (but that it should be holy and without Blemish) if they do not know the Lord to work a Change in their Hearts, and redeem them out of those things which unfit them for his holy Kingdom; the Apostle saith, *He is not a Jew that is one outwardly, neither is that Circumcision which is outward in the Flesh; But he is a Jew which is one inwardly; and Circumcision is that of the Heart in the Spirit, and not of the Letter, whose Praise is not of Men, but of God.*[10] As a Man's being outwardly circumcised, and observing a great many *Jewish* Rites and Ceremonies, did not make him a true and real *Jew*, if he was not one in his Heart; so it may be truly said, he is not a *Christian*, that is only one outwardly, altho' he has been outwardly baptized, and received the Bread and Wine, and observed a great many outward Observations: If he is not one in his Heart, all his outward observations will not render him acceptable in the Sight of God.

Notes

1. Rev. iii. 20
2. Luke xvii. 20, 21
3. John xiv. 18
4. Mat. xxvi. 29
5. John xvii. 23
6. I John i. 3
7. John vi. 51
8. Prov. viii. 20,21
9. Eph. v. 27
10. Rom. ii. 28, 29

Document III.30

Micaijah Towgood on the Lord's Supper

Micaijah Towgood had a particular interest in the sacraments. He wrote his ordination thesis of 1722 on the validity of infant baptism, and in *Catholic Christianity; or, the Communion of Saints, earnestly recommended to all professing Christians, particularly to the Brethren of the Antipaedobaptist Persuasion*, he opposes all who would fence the Lord's table. Towgood (1700–92) was a contemporary of Thomas Amory at Taunton academy under Henry Grove. He subsequently ministered in a number of places in Devonshire, and served as tutor at the academy founded in Exeter (1760–71).

For Towgood see DNB; James Manning, *A Sketch of the Life and Writings of Micaijah Towgood*, 1792; Alan P. F. Sell, 'A Little Friendly Light: the Candour of Bourn, Taylor and Towgood', in *idem, Dissenting Thought and the Life of the Churches*, Lewiston, NY: Edwin Mellen Press, 1990, ch. 8. Extract (a), against Baptists who advocate closed communion, is from *Catholic Christianity*, which is appended to

Manning's *Sketch*, p. 190. Extract (b) is from *The Grounds of Faith in Jesus Christ briefly stated, and Shewn to be a solid Foundation for Peace and Joy unspeakable. With an earnest Recommendation of Catholic Christianity, and the Communion of Saints. Addressed to A candid Society of Christians at the Close of his Ministrations amongst them*, 1784, pp. 82–3, 87.

(a)

The Table they thus erect is not the Lord's Table, but a Table of their own; and as far as they thus eat in criminal separation from, and uncharitable seclusion of other ac-knowledged Christians, they eat not the Lord's Supper.

(b)

All sincere Christians are considered, however distant in Place, as eating at the SAME TABLE ... Hence ... no Christian has a right to reject any other his Fellow-Christian from partaking with him at the Lord's Table, in Account of any Difference of Sentiment in Things not fundamental, his moral Character being such as the Gospel requires ... [When Established Churchmen and Dissenters] fence around their SACRAMENTAL TABLE with Terms and Conditions and Forms and Rites which CHRIST never prescribed., and reject us from HIS TABLE, unless besides what HE enjoins, we submit also to some Injunctions and Requirements of their own ... [the Church's] CATHOLICISM [is] destroyed, and an unhappy Breach made in the COMMUNION OF SAINTS.

Document III.31

Edward Trivett's Communion Hymn

Edward Trivett ministered for fifty years from 1741 at the Baptist Church at Worstead Meeting Hill, Norfolk. Many went forward into the ministry from the Church during this time.

The following extract is from C. B. Jewson, *The Baptists in Norfolk*, London: Carey Kingsgate Press, 1957, p. 47.

The sweetest, richest best of cheer
For fainting, longing souls is here.
Heaven no choicer thing can give,
Such souls as eat forever live.
There's flesh in bread and blood in wine
The banquet in the whole divine.
No feast prepared by earthly kings
Affords such rare and dainty things.

PART IV

EVANGELISM, REVIVAL AND MISSION

Introduction

It is by now clear that at their best the eighteenth-century Nonconformists were concerned for right doctrine, and equally clear that by 'right' doctrine they could mean anything from 'that which accords with high Calvinism', to 'that which commends itself to my sincerely exercised reason and conscience'. Their practice, too (occasional hypocrisies apart), was intimately interwoven with their beliefs and, according to the positions they took upon certain theological questions, they were ardent devotees of evangelistic and missionary enterprise, lukewarm supporters of it, or firm – sometimes extremely caustic – opponents of it.

In the wake of a short selection of texts to demonstrate the existence of outcrops of evangelistic zeal prior to the Revival proper, we shall turn to these underlying issues. Should the overtures of the Gospel be taken as for all, indiscriminately, or for the elect alone? This question was laid forcefully on the table by Joseph Hussey. On the other hand, Matthias Maurice, a convert from high Calvinism, contended that hearers of the Word have a duty to believe in Christ. In this he was supported by Philip Doddridge, who himself raised the issues of evangelism at home and mission abroad. Eventually the Congregationalists began to organise for home mission. Meanwhile the Baptists were debating among themselves the propriety or otherwise of mission, with 'the three Johns' – Skepp, Gill and Brine – adopting the position of Hussey, and Andrew Fuller and William Carey advancing the opposite side of the argument.[1] In face of staunch doctrinal opposition from high Calvinists, the Baptist Missionary Society was founded in 1792, Carey sailed for India in the following year.[2] The Congregationalists, who had already initiated county unions, were not far behind in organising for world mission. They became the major sponsors of the Missionary Society (1795), to whose name the term 'London' was added as the number of similar societies grew, David Bogue being a powerful advocate of the cause.

In the meantime Methodism in its Calvinist and Arminian forms was making hay, despite opposition from the Anglicans who resented the breaches of parochial discipline involved in Wesleyan field preaching, disputed Wesley's right to ordain preachers, and on occasion orchestrated mob activity against the evangelists; from Dissenters of the more rational sort to whom 'enthusiasm' (defined by Samuel Johnson as 'a vain confidence of divine favour or illumination') was an abomination; and from high Calvinist Anglicans and Dissenters alike. The diaries of Howel Harris make it abundantly clear that the Calvinist itinerants encountered similar opposition in Wales. In both England and Wales high Calvinists and rational Dissenters, who generally had little in common with one another, found in evangelicalism, and especially in its more excitable manifestations, much matter for polemics. Certainly a formidable blend of faith and dogged determination was required by those itinerant evangelists who stayed the course.

As if to point up the contrast between expanding evangelical Dissent and both varieties of Methodism, Joseph Priestley wrote an account of the less than robust condition of the rational Dissenters.

As remarked earlier, some Baptist and Congregational ministers responded warmly to the Revival, and their traditions benefited greatly, numerically and spiritually. But the churchly destinations of converts were more varied still. Some followed Dan Taylor into his New Connexions General Baptist Churches (1770); others, like John Cennick, joined the Moravians; the Countess of Huntingdon's Connexion claimed some, and still others constituted the societies of those for whom Benjamin Ingham was the spiritual father.[3]

Notes

1. For Skepp (c. 1675–1721) see J. A. Jones, ed., *Bunhill Memorials Sacred Reminiscences of Three Hundred Ministers and other Persons of Note, who are Buried in Bunhill Fields, of every Denomination, etc.*, 1849, pp. 256–8.
2. For John Ryland (1723–92), whose singing voice was compared to the roaring of the sea, see DNB.
3. For the itinerants of the later eighteenth century see Deryck W. Lovegrove, *Established Church, Sectarian People Itinerancy and the Transformation of English Dissent, 1780–1830*, Cambridge : CUP, 1988. For John Cennick (1718–55) see DEB, DH, DNB; F. Baker, *John Cennick: A Handlist of his writings*, Leicester, 1958; J. E. Hutton, *John Cennick: A Sketch*, London, 1906. For Ingham (1712–72) see DEB, DH, DNB; R. P. Heitzenrater, ed., *Diary of an Oxford Methodist*, Durham, NC: Duke University Press, 1985; R. W. Thompson, *Benjamin Ingham and the Inghamites*, Kendal 1958.

Lights in Relative Darkness

78. An Early Eighteenth-Century Evangelical: Richard Davis

For Davis see Document III.26 above. The following passages show the kind of opposition Davis aroused (it was through the 'Kettering Inquisition' into his activities that
the Presbyterian/Congregational 'Happy Union' of 1691 had foundered); the way in
which daughter churches were formed; and the ambivalent position of John Gill who,
though he called Davis the preacher a Boanaerges (a son of thunder) and a Barnabas
(a son of consolation to depressed sinners and drooping saints), nevertheless, in 1748,
wrote the preface to the seventh edition of Davis's hymns, whilst at the same time
warning that his Calvinism was not as sound as it might have been.

Extract (a) is from Matthias Maurice, *Monuments of Mercy*, 1729, p. 74, while (b)
is from the *Second Rothwell Church Book*, entry for 17 June 1714; (c) John Gill's
preface to the seventh edition of Davis's Hymns, 1748.

(a)
A certain Gentleman in a virulent and impertinent manner ask'd him what Business
he had to go up and down to such places Babbling? for so he called the preaching
of the Gospel; Mr Davis in the presence of all, turn'd to him, and with a Countenance
which testified a good Cause and good Conscience, said, 'sir, I was upon the work
of my Lord and Master Jesus Christ, do you know him?' whereupon the Gentleman
was stuck with silence, and many more with Amazement.

(b)
At a Church Assembly on the Lord's Day 27 June 1714 – It was reported to the
Church by the messengers who were appointed to carry the dismission to the
Brethren and Sisters in and about Ringstead that on the 17th day of Inst. They were
present at Ringstead the Brethren and Sisters being assembled. After Prayer they
read the dismission in the presence of the messengers of sister church viz. Kimbolton,
Floore and Thorpe Waterfield, after which our beloved Brethren and Sisters, [then
follows the list of names of sixteen men and twenty women] in all 36 persons did
enter into covenant with one another each person individually giving themselves to
the Lord, to one another, to walk with the Lord and one another as a Church of Christ
the Lord enabling them, whereupon they, the messengers declared their membership
to cease from then and that they were a particular Congregational Church apart by
themselves and gave the right hand of fellowship in order to commune with them as
a sister church. So likewise did the messengers of other churches.

(c)

I have only one thing more to observe, that whereas the phrase of offering Christ and grace is sometimes used in hymns, which may be offensive to some persons, and which the worthy Author was led to the use of, partly through custom, it not having been, at the writing of them, objected to, and partly through his affectionate concern an zeal for gaining upon souls, and encouraging them to come to Christ; I can affirm, upon good and sufficient testimony, that Mr Davis, before his death, changed his mind in this matter, and disused the phrase, as being improper, and being too bold and free for a minister of Christ to make use of. And though I have not thought fit to alter any words and phrases in the revise of these hymns, yet in the use of them in public service, those who think proper may substitute another phrase in its room more eligible. I earnestly desire, that the Divine Spirit would make the reading and singing of these hymns of use to the magnifying of the free grace of God, to exaltation of Christ, to the debasing of the creature, and to comfort and refreshment of the Lord's people, as they have often been.

Document IV.2

Church Growth at Penmain

This account of early eighteenth-century church growth at Penmain, Monmouthshire, is quoted by Thomas Rees, *History of Protestant Nonconformity in Wales*, London: John Snow, 1883, p. 275. James Davies of Merthyr Tydfil (d. 1760), for whom see DWB, was trained at Carmarthen academy, evangelised in Glamorgan and Monmouthshire, welcomed the Revival, and later fell from favour as Arminian-inspired secessions depleted his congregation.

After some years' vacancy, they chose Mr. David Williams a Caermarthenshire man, for their pastor ; who, though a good man, yet not being a popular preacher, the church dwindled in their number continually, until about the twentieth year of this century, when the Lord returned, and visited this church, as He did others in the country about. In consequence of this the church began to increase – divers joined in communion with them ; amongst others, some young men, who became gifted men and preachers of the gospel, helped much to increase the church, as did also some particular preachers from other places ; particularly Mr. James Davis, of Merthyr Tydfil, who at that time was very popular. It was a glorious time with the church at Penmain again ; and between the year 1720 and 1739 above a hundred persons joined the congregation. This increase was not so much in the congregation at Abertilery, the Baptists prevailing in that neighbourhood, by means of the popular preaching of Mr. Enoch Francis and Mr. Morgan Griffith.

Document IV.3

Encouragement at Bourton-on-the-Water

Benjamin Beddome (1717–95), who was trained under Bernard Foskett at Bristol Baptist College and at the Independent academy at Mile End, London, ministered at Bourton-on-the-Water for fifty-five years. A number of revivals occurred during his ministry, and the cause flourished. In 1750 the church at Little Prescott Street, London, which he had attended as a student, and where he had been baptised, invited him to succeed their minister, Samuel Wilson (1720–50). It is noteworthy that the invitation was addressed both to Beddome himself and to the church. The following are their replies, as quoted by Kenneth Dix in *The Strict Baptist Historical Society Annual Report and Bulletin*, IX, 1972, unpaginated. For Beddome see DEB, DH, DNB; Norman S. Moon, *Education for Ministry*, Bristol: Bristol Baptist College, 1979 *passim*; J. Rippon, *The Baptist Annual Register*, 1795, II, 314–28. For Foskett (1685–1758) see DEB; N. Moon, *Education for Ministry*, 1979; Roger Hayden 'The contribution of Bernard Foskett,' in William H. Brackney and Paul S. Fiddes, eds, *Pilgrim Pathways. Essays in Baptist History in Honour of B. R. White*, Macon, GA: Mercer University Press, 1999, ch. 8; A. P. F. Sell, *Philosophy, Dissent and Nonconformity*, 2004.

Dearly Beloved in the Lord,

The death of your late excellent pastor has filled me with the deepest distress and concern … I cannot but rejoice in his personal gain … yet I look upon the mournful church … with that sympathy and concern which are due upon such an occasion … I have my share in your loss. You have been bereft of a pastor, I of a faithful instructor and affectionate friend …

The result of this loss is an unanimous call to me to supply his place. A call of the utmost importance to you, as your spiritual welfare is concerned in it, and of the greatest importance to me, as the reproaches of a guilty conscience, either in refusing or complying, are the worst companions I can have both in life and death.

As for your plea of absolute necessity – that it is necessary that you should have a minister, I readily own, and heartily pray that God will direct you in your choice. But that it is equally so that I should be the man, I shall never see till I have a greater opinion of my own abilities, or a much meaner of those my brethren. Other motives there are for my removal which are considerably weighty and strong. You call me from a church comparatively mean and laden with debt, to one popular, flourishing, and wealthy. You call me from a country, where I seldom enjoy the advantages of hearing and conversing with my brethren in the ministry, to a city where there are the best of preachers, and those united together by the bonds both of interest and affection. You call me from a Church to which you gave me, to a Church that first received me and called me into the ministry, and for which I still retain the sincerest regard. You call me from a place of little influence, to one of much greater, where you imagine my labours may be more profitably bestowed, and my usefulness much enlarged, and I confess that these are things mostly of consideration.

Your great love to your former minister ought not to be forgotten. Your perfect unanimity in your present case ought not to be slighted, and however it please God to dispose of me, you have given me such a testimony of your esteem and regard, as I trust I shall ever … remember. But then, … I am forced to consider that I am solemnly ordained over a people who have in general treated me with the greatest affection … many of who have been seals since I came … above a hundred having been added since my first coming amongst them, and four having proposed this month … that their hearts seem as much engaged to me as ever … To which I may add, that I very much ascribe my recovery from a late dangerous illness to their affectionate care and unwearied supplications. I say, when I consider these things, I am in a great strait. I cry to God for direction but what way I shall take, I know not.

My present determination seems to be entirely to refer myself to the church's disposal. I have therefore laid your letter before them. I opened your pressing importunities with the utmost sincerity … I have also pressed them to avoid all prejudice and passion, and after a month's time taken to consult God and one another, to return you such an answer as shall appear most equitable and consistent with their duty.

When I reflect upon my past services, and how I have been amongst them, in weakness and fear, and much trembling, I not only wonder at that degree of acceptance I have met, but think that a change in their ministry might probably cause a happy alteration in their circumstances. But then, for the same reason, I tremble at the thought of accepting a call to succeed such a man, and in such a place, where I am conscious much prudence, great courage, and superior abilities of every kind, are required. However, I would in this affair have no will of my own. I would throw myself wholly upon providence, and begging an interest in your warmest addresses at the throne of grace, refer you to the church's answer, which you may expect to receive at the before-mentioned time.

> I remain, your affectionate
> Though unworthy brother in Gospel bonds,
> B. Beddome.

The Church of Christ at Bourton, to the Church lately under the pastoral care of the Rev. Mr. Samuel Wilson deceased.

Beloved in the Lord.

We, having received your letter, cannot but sympathise with you on account of your great loss … we join with you in earnest prayers to the great Shepherd of Israel, that he would in his own due time supply the loss of so valuable a minister and pastor, though unknown to most of us. As to the representation you gave of the too general state of religion in London, we must condole with you; and, indeed, we find a like remissness in the country, which certainly affords a very gloom and dismal prospect to every considerate mind.

It is much, indeed, to be desired that there were more learned and popular ministers in London, and the more so by reason of what the Churches in the country receive from thence. … And, although you are in your letter pressing for Mr. Beddome's removal hence to London, yet we apprehend the very arguments you make use of to enforce this (such as the Church's necessity, the fear of its dispersing, or perhaps its total dissolution), would if impartially and duly considered, more strongly plead for his still abiding with us. And the more so from the considerations following. Our great love and esteem for this our learned and faithful pastor would make the parting stroke very severe and unsupportable, so that, if there were no other reason than this-this would restrain us from giving our assent to his removal. ... When we also consider ... that we were destitute for many years, notwithstanding our many cries to Almighty God, he was pleased to withhold direct answers to prayers till at length he graciously raised up, eminently qualified, and unexpectedly sent, our dearly beloved and Rev. pastor, Mr Beddome, to become our pastor. When we add to this ... his endeavours have been wonderfully blest for restoring for restoring decayed religion, the increasing of our Church ... and the raising up gifts for the help of other Churches, some of which are fixed as pastors. Nor can we help adding that God lately visited our pastor, and brought him down to the gates of the grave ... when we, following our ancient course, cried unto God, and he graciously restored his to health, and we hope to former usefulness, insomuch that several persons have lately proposed to the Church for communion, who were wrought upon under his ministry.

On these accounts, we say, and others too tedious to mention, we cannot but look upon him as an answer to our prayers, both when first given and when again restored again after hi illness. And answers of prayer are sweet and valuable mercies: and shall we act a part so ungrateful to a gracious and bountiful God, so injurious to ourselves, our families, and to others round about us, as to give up this valuable mercy? Has God answered our prayers, and shall we let go the answer? This, we apprehend, would be very provoking to God. On these accounts we cannot consent to his removal, but must, till we see occasion to alter our minds, absolutely refuse it. Yet, though we cannot comply with your request, ... we shall continue to meet you at the throne of grace, to beg that God ... would qualify and send your minister and pastor after his own heart, to you abundant joy and satisfaction.

We remain, your brethren in the faith and fellowship of the Gospel.

Document IV.4

A Church Bewidowed

The following entry for 1 July 1733 in the Wattisfield Church Book was occasioned by the death of the minister Thomas Wickes (d. 1733, aged sixty-six), for whom see John Browne, *History of Congregationalism and Memorials of the Churches in Norfolk and Suffolk*, London: Jarrold, 1877, pp. 470–1. The following extract is printed on p. 186

This church has sustained a very great and unspeakable loss, being now left in a destitute, bewidowed state, exposed to many difficulties and dangers, and the more melancholy and afflictive such a dispensation at a time when there is such a general departure from this faith as at this day; when error, infidelity, and it is in Jesus waxes cold. A day wherein the faithful labourers in Christ's vineyards are so few, and the deceitful and sophistical corrupters of the word and doctrine so many, that it appears exceedingly difficult for a church really adhering to the good old Protestant doctrines (the glory of our Reformation) to be again settled with a suitable and agreeable Pastor.

Evangelism in Dissenting Theory and Practice

Document IV.5

Joseph Hussey against the Universal Offer of the Gospel

Joseph Hussey (1659–1726) was ordained a Presbyterian and had opposed Richard Davis's Calvinism at the 'Kettering Inquisition'. From 1694, however, his Church at Cambridge underwent a change of polity, becoming Congregational, and of doctrine, becoming more high Calvinist than Davis. Hussey became especially concerned that freely to offer the Gospel in preaching carried with it the implication that fallen human beings *could* respond to it unaided. He expressed his concerns at length in *God's Operations of Grace but no Offers of Grace* (1707). Skepp, Brine and Gill stood in his line, and increasingly some came to feel that evangelism and missionary endeavour were seriously inhibited by it – hence the opposition of Andrew Fuller and others.

For Hussey see Geoffrey F. Nuttall, 'Northamptonshire and *The Modern Question*: a turning point-point I eighteenth-century Dissent', *Journal of Theological Studies*, NS XVI, 1965, pp. 101–23; Alan P. F. Sell, *The Great Debate: Calvinism, Arminianism and Salvation*, Worthing: H. E. Walter, 1982 and Grand Rapids: Baker Book House, 1983; repr. Eugene, OR: Wipf and Stock, 1998, *passim*, and references on p. 117. The following extract is from the abbreviated version of the book referred to, published at Elon College, NC: Primitive Publications, [1973].

Universal offers vs. special salvation

You do no more than preach a universal grace, while you offer Christ to all sinners. Proffers are made up of free will and human power. For Christ has been already professionally revealed in a common way to all, while the common salvation has been openly shown in the sight of the Heathen. The grace of God that brings salvation has appeared to all men: It is not said, has been offered to all men. And please to observe, that an offer, or proffer of special grace, is another special absurdity. Ministers of Christ are to preach special salvation to the elect, that they may not be wronged in having less than God's free gift declared under our labours; mere professors, or outward-court worshippers, have their share still, as to matters of form concerning Christ: that is they have the common doctrine of Christ, testified in due time, which is their share, and so they cannot be abused while they have the lot they are best pleased with: While, on the other hand, the Gospel is preached through Christ, the elect in all ages receive pardon and peace through Him, In the special salvation which He bestows.

Special grace cannot be offered; the nature of it is to be conveyed. It is not merely what is received concerning Christ, but what is to be received through Him, by the operation of JEHOVAH the Spirit. There may be a moral persuasion wrought in men by words, or by arguments and reasons proposed to them, so as to gain an orthodox persuasion of truth, opposed to any heterodox persuasion of error in the mind.

Yet such persuasion, such empty dead corrupt faith, cometh not of Him that calleth you. (Gad. 5:8) Thy Holy Spirit in effectual calling sanctifies the judgment, and works up the thoughts of the heart into principles of truth, forming a sound mind. A mere moral persuasion of the truth falls very far short of the faith of God's elect, which by preaching the Gospel forms Christ, in the heart the hope of glory.

In a word, the Lord never offers saving grace to those whom He never intends to save, because He cannot act deceitfully. But yet the Lord will send the report faithfully to them, and that to answer ends of another sort, even where He has never appointed nor intended men to believe unto salvation. To the one the Gospel is a savour of death unto death, and to the other the savour of life unto life; and who is sufficient for these things? (2 Cor. 2:16)

Document IV.6

Matthias Maurice and *A Modern Question*

Matthias Maurice (1684–1738) was the earnestly evangelical preacher who came from Wales to Rothwell in succession to Richard Davis (for whom see Document IV.1 above), where he served for twenty-four years. Turning from the high Calvinism in which he had been reared, he published *A Modern Question Modestly Answered*, London, 1737, in which he proclaimed the duty of hearers of the Word to believe it.

For Maurice see Geoffrey F. Nuttall, 'Northamptonshire and *The Modern Question*', *Journal of Theological Studies*, NS XVI, 1965, pp. 101–23; Alan P. F.Sell, *The Great Debate: Calvinism, Arminiamism and Salvation*, Worthing: H. E. Walter, 1982 and Grand Rapids: Baker Book House, 1983; repr. Eugene, OR: Wipf and Stock, 1998, *passim*, and references on pp. 118–19. The following extract is from *A Modern Question*, pp. 31–2

You dear children of God, be sober and vigilant: your Adversary is diligent, resist him steadfastly in the Faith once delivered to the Saints. That it is no part of a poor unconverted Sinner's Duty, who hears the Gospel preach'd, to believe in Christ, is what was never delivered to any by the Spirit of God. Though some have thoughtlessly and too suddenly took up that Notion, yet let them now in the Presence of God impartially compare it with the Scriptures, some Texts whereof I briefly produced (in the forgoing pages), as Persons willing to submit their souls to the revealed will of God and they will see that it is a pernicious and dangerous Error. I don't question but God can and will keep his dear converted Children from being carried away with all the bad consequences of it; but in itself it is a doctrine of darkness. Search the Scriptures, search the Scriptures earnestly, cry to the God of all Grace for Guidance into all Truth, precious acquaintance therewith, and Establishment therein, and don't readily and suddenly reject what the Churches of Christ through all Ages have embraced as their Glory. Your business lies in fervent prayer, mature Consideration of the Scriptures and humble Consultation with the godly, faithful and able servants of Christ, and all this continued in, and often repeated; and through the whole and to the last, act as dear Children of God, Followers of the Lamb, earnestly in all Things desiring Jerusalem's Peace.

Document IV.7

Philip Doddridge to His Wife

Philip Doddridge (for whom see Document I.1 above) was among the most highly respected early proponents of evangelism and mission. He writes to his wife Mercy from Yarmouth on 2 July 1741 concerning a meeting held at Denton on 30 June at which the cause of mission was advocated, and following which he wrote the tract given in Document IV.8 below.

See further, *Congregational Magazine*, NS X, 1834, p. 718; and E. A. Payne, 'Doddridge and the Missionary Enterprise', in Geoffrey F. Nuttall, ed., *Philip Doddridge*, London: Independent Press, 1951, pp. 87–90. The quotation from Doddridge's letter is given in Geoffrey F. Nuttall, ed., *Calendar of the Correspondence of Philip Doddridge, D. D. (1702–1751)*, London: HMSO, 1979 p. 137.

We spent Tuesday at Denton & it was one of the most delightful Days of my whole Life. Seventeen ministers were there of whom 8 officiated indeed excellently well. We held Kind of Council afterwards concerning the Methods to be taken for the Revival of Religion & I hope I have set them to Work to some good purpose ...

Document IV.8

Philip Doddridge to the Ministers of Norfolk and Suffolk

In 1742 Doddridge published *The Evil and Danger of Neglecting the Souls of Men, plainly and seriously represented in a Sermon Preach'd at A Meeting of Ministers At Kettering in Northamptonshire, October 15, 1741*. The Dedication is 'To the Associated Protestant Dissenting Ministers, in the Counties of Norfolk and Suffolk, Particularly Those with whom the Author had an Interview at Denton, June 30th, 1741', and the points extracted below are from this. In the sermon, from which the conclusion, pp. 36–8, is extracted, Doddridge counters objections to outreach.

It seemed most agreeable to the Deference due to the Revered Assembly, *to propose the* Scheme *in the Form of* Queries; *and which the following* Resolutions *were formed,* Nemine contradicente.

I. That it may tend to the Advancement of Religion, *that the* Ministers *of this* Association, *if they have not very lately done it, should agree to preach one Lord's-Day on* Family Religion, *and another on* Secret Prayer; *and that the Time should be fixed, in humble Hope that concurrent Labours, connected with concurrent Petitions to the Throne of Grace, might produce some happy effect.*

II.   *That it is proper, that* Pastoral Visiting *should be more solemnly attended to; and that greater Care should be taken in* Personal Inspection, *than has generally been used. And that it may conduce to this good End, that each* Minister *should take an* Exact Survey *of his Flock, and note down the* Names *of Heads of Families, the Children, the Servants, and other single Persons in his Auditory, in order to keep proper* Memorandums *concerning each; that he may judge the better of the Particulars of his Duty with Regard to every one, and may observe how his Visits, Exhortations, and Admonitions, correspond to their respective Characters and Circumstances.*

III.   *That consequent on this* Survey, *it will be proper, as soon as possible, and henceforward at least* once a Year *to visit, if it be practicable,* every Head of a Family *under our Ministerial Care, with a solemn* Charge *to attend to the Business of Religion, in their Hearts, and houses, watching over their* Domesticks *in the Fear of the Lord, We, at the same Time, professing our Readiness to give them all proper Assistances for this Purpose.*

IV.   *That it will be highly expedient, immediately, or as soon as may be, to set up the Work of* Catechising *in one Form or another, and to keep to it statedly for* one half of the Year *at least: And that it is probable, future Counsels may ripen some* Scheme *for carrying on this work, in a Manner which may tend greatly to the Propagation of real, vital,* Catholick *Christianity, in the rising Generation.*

V.   *That there is Reason to apprehend, there are, in all our* Congregations, *some pious and valuable Performs, who live in a culpable* Neglect of the Lord's-Supper; *and that it is our Duty, particularly to inform ourselves who they are, and to endeavour, by our Prayers to* GOD, *and our serious Addresses to them, to introduce them into* Communion; *(to which, I question not, we shall all willingly add,) cautiously guarding against anything in the* Methods of Admission, *which may justify discourage sincere* Christians *of a tender and timorous Temper.*

VI.   *That it is to be feared, there are* some, *in several of our* Communions *at least, who behave in such a Manner as to give* just offence; *and that we may be in great Danger of making ourselves* Partakers of other Mens Sins, *if we do not* animadvert upon them: *And that if they will not reform, or if the Crime be notorious, we ought, in Duty to* GOD, *and to them, and to all around us, solemnly to* cut them off from our Sacramental Communion, *as a Reproach to the* Church of Christ.

VII.   *That it may, on many Accounts, be proper to advise our People, to enter into little* Bands, *or* Societies, *for* Religious Discourse *and* Prayer; *each consisting of six or* Eight, *to meet for these good Purposes once in a Week, or* a Fortnight, *as may best suit with their other Engagements and Affairs.*

VIII.   *That it might be advisable, if it can be done, to* select *out of each* Congregation *under our care, a* small *Number of Persons, remarkable for experienced Prudence, Seriousness, Humility, and Zeal, to act as a* Stated Council *for promoting Religion in the said* Society: *And that it would be proper, they should have some certain* Times of meeting, *with each other, and with the* Minister, *to join their* Counsels, *and their* Prayers *for the Public Good.*

IX. That so far as we can judge, it might, by the Divine Blessing, conduce to the Advancement of these valuable Ends, that neighbouring Ministers, *in one Part of our Land and another, (especially this Country,) should enter into* Associations, *to strengthen the Hands of each other by united Consultations and Prayer: And that* Meeting of Ministers *might, by some obvious Regulations, be made more extensively useful than they often are: In which View it was farther proposed, (which unanimous Approbation,)That these* Meetings *should be held at certain* Periodical Times: – *That* each Member *of the* Association *should endeavour (if possible) to be present, studying to order his Affairs so, as to guard against unnecessary Hindrances: – That* Public Worship *should* begin *and* end sooner, *than it commonly has done on these Occasions: – That* each Pastor preach *at these* Assemblies *in his Turn: – That the* Minister of the Place *determined who shall be employed in* Prayer: – *That after a moderate Repast, to be managed with as little Trouble and Expence as may be,* an Hour *or* Two *in the afternoon be spent in* Religious Conference *and* Prayer, *and in taking into Consideration (merely as a friendly council, and without the least Pretence to any Right of authoritative Decision,) the Concerns of any* Brother, *or any* Society, *which may be brought before us for our Advice: – And finally, that every* Member *of this* Association *shall consider it as an additional Obligation upon him, to endeavour to be, so far as he justly and honourably can,* a Friend *and* Guardian *to the Reputation, Comfort, and Usefulness of* all his Brethren *in the* Christian Ministry, *near or remote, of whatever Party and Denomination.*

X. That it may be proper to enter into some father Measures, *to regulate the* Admission of Young Persons into the Ministry. – *The* Particulars *here were referred to father Consideration: but, so far as I can judge, the* Plan *proposed will be pretty nearly* this: – *That if any* Student, *within the Compass of this* Association, *desires to be* admitted as a preacher, *he apply to the* Ministers *at One of their* Periodical Meetings; *when, if they be in the general satisfied, that he is a Person of a* fair Character, *in* Sacramental Communion *with a* Christian Society, *and one who has* gone thro' a regular course *of* Preparatory Studies, *they will appoint* Three of their Number, *to examine more particularly into his* Acquaintance *with, and* Sense *of the* great Doctrines of Christianity *as delivered in the* Scripture, *and into the* Progress he has made *in* Literature, *and in general,* his Aptness to teach: *In order to judging of which, it may be proper, that a* Theological Thesis *be exhibited* in Latin, *and a* popular Sermon, *composed by the* Candidate, *be submitted to the Perusal of the* Examiners: *That if they, In their Consciences believe, he is* fit *to be employed in the* Christian Ministry, *they give him* a Certificate *of that Approbation, which he may be desired to produce at the next* General Meeting, *that his* Testimonials *may be* signed *by all the* associated Ministers *present, and He solemnly recommended to GOD by* Prayer.

Thus, Gentlemen, you have a View of the Scheme, *as it now lies before us, and as* every Article, *except* the last, *(not yet considered among us,) was* approved *at* Kettering, *at the Time above-mentioned. I will take Leave to add* One Particular more, *which has since occurred to my Thoughts, and which I here submit to* your Consideration, *and to that of my* other Reverend Brethren, *into whose Hands this may fall, especially those of* our own Association.

XI. Qu. *Whether something might not be done, in most of our* Congregations, *towards assisting* in the Propagation of Christianity Abroad, *and spreading it in some of the darker Parts of* our own Land*? In Pursuance of which it is further proposed, that we endeavour to engage as many pious People of our respective* Congregations *as we can, to enter themselves into a* Society, *in which the* Members *may engage themselves to some peculiar* Cares, Assemblies, *and* Contributions, *with a Regard to this great End. I will not swell this* Dedication *with the Particulars of that* Scheme, *which has been formed to this* Purpose; but rather chuse to insert at the Bottom of the *Page* a Copy of such an Association, *which I am endeavouring to introduce among* my own People, *and which* several *have already* signed. *'Tis a feeble* Essay; *and the Effects of it in* one Congregation *can be but very small: But if it were* generally *to be followed, who can tell what* a Harvest *such* a little Grain *might at length produce? May GOD multiply it a thousand-fold!* ...

You have all, I doubt not, prevented me, in reflecting on the Reason we have to *humble ourselves deeply* in the presence of the blessed God, while we *remember our Faults this Day.* I do not, indeed, at all question, but many of us have *set before* our People *Life and Death*; and have, in our *Publick Addresses*, urged their Return to God, by the various Considerations of *Terror*, and of *Love*, which the *Thunders of Mount Sinai*, and the *Grace of Mount Zion*, have taught us. We have, on great Occasions, *visited them*, and entered into some *ferocious Discourse* with them; and have *often*, and I would hope, more or less *daily*, *borne them on our Hearts* before God, in our Seasons of devout *Retirement*. Blessed be God, that in these Instances, we have, in any Degree, *approved ourselves faithful!* It must give us Pleasure in the Review. But, Oh, why have not *our Prayers* been more frequently presented, and more importantly enforced? Why have we not been more serious, and more pressing, in our *Private Addresses* to them, and more attentive in our *Contrivances*, if I may express it, to *catch them* in the *Net* of the *Gospel?* Let us ask our own Consciences, this Day, as in the Presence of God, If there be not Reason to apprehend, that some, who were once *our Hearers*, and it may be *our dear Friends* too, have *perished through our Neglect*; and are gone to Eternal Destruction, *for Want of our* more prudent, more affectionate, and more zealous *Care for their Deliverance?* In these Instances, *my Brethren*, though it is dreadful to say it, and to think it, yet it is most certain, that *We have been, in part, accessory to their Ruin*; and have Reason to say, with trembling Hearts, and with weeping Eyes, *Deliver us from Blood-guiltiness*, from the Blood of these unhappy souls, *oh GOD, thou GOD of our salvation!* And we have Need, with all possible Earnestness, to renew our Application to the *Blood* and *Righteousness* of a *Redeemer*; not daring to mention *any services of our own*, as Matter of Confidence in his Presence; how highly soever *others* may have esteemed them, who candidly look on the *little we do*, and perhaps make more charitable *Excuses* for *our Neglect*, than *we ourselves* can dare to urge before God. Let the Remembrance of these Things *be for a Lamentation*: And while they are so,

Let us seriously consider, *what Methods* are to be
taken, *to prevent such Things* for the Time to
come.

They that have *perished*, have *perished for ever*, and are far beyond the Reach of *our Labours*, and *our Prayers*. But Multitudes to this Day surround us, who stand exposed to the same Danger, and on the very brink of the same Ruin. And besides these *dying sinners*, who are the most compassionable Objects, which the Eye of *Man*, or of *GOD*, beholds on this Earth of ours; how many *languishing Christians* demand our Assistance? Or, if they do not expressly *demand it*, appear so much the more to *need it*? Let us look round, *my Brethren*, I will not say, upon the *Nation* in general, but on the *Churches* under our immediate Care; and say, whether *the Face of them is such*, as becomes the Societies of *those* whom *the son of GOD has redeemed with his own Blood*; and of *those*, that call themselves the *Disciples*, and *Members*, of a once *crucified*, and now *glorified Jesus*? Is their *whole temper* and *Conduct* formed upon the Model of his *Gospel*? Are they *such*, as we would desire to *present them before to Presence of his Glory*? *What is wanting, cannot be numbered*; and, perhaps, we may be ready, too rashly, to conclude, that *what is crooked, cannot be made straight.* Nevertheless, let us remember, 'tis *our Duty* to attempt it, as prudently, as immediately, and as resolutely as we can. Many admirable *Advices* for that Purpose *our Fathers* and *Brethren* have given us; particularly Dr. *Watts*, in the *First Part* of his *Humble Attempt for the Revival of Religion*, and Mr. *Some*, in his *Sermon on the same Subject*: Excellent Treaties, which reduced into Practice would soon produce the noblest Effects.

That those important *Instructions* may be *revived*, and accommodated to *present Circumstances*, with such *Additions* as those Circumstances require, we are, this Day, having united *our Prayers*, to unite *our Counsels*. I will not anticipate what I have to offer to your Consideration in the more *private Conference*, on which we are quickly to enter. To *form proper Measures*, will be comparatively easy: To *carry them* strenuously *into Execution*, will be the great Exercise of our Wisdom and Piety: May proportionable Grace be given to *animate us*, and to dispose *them that are committed to our Care*, to *fall in with us* in all our Attempts, for the Honour of God, and for their Edification and Comfort!

We shall esteem it, *my friends*, a very happy *Omen*, if *your Hearts* be *with ours* on this Occasion; and if *you* help forward so good, and so necessary a Design, by *your Prayers* to God *for us*. If *you* are sincere and affectionate in them, we may humbly hope, that He, *of whom we ask Wisdom*, will graciously *impart it to us*; and may assure ourselves, that you will not only *bear with us* in the plainest *Addresses to you*, which Fidelity may oblige us to make; but will *add all the Weight* of your Countenance and Interest, to support us in *our Applications to others*, whether *publick* or *private*. And I have cheerful Confidence, that all *will not be in vain*; but that He, who thus powerfully awakens our Minds, will so *succeed our Labours*, that many, whom we find under a Sentence of *Condemnation*, and *ready to perish* by it, will receive *the Forgiveness of their Sins*; will be recovered to a *Spiritual* and *Divine Life*; and, as the happy Consequence of all, will at length be fixed *with us*, and *with you*, in the Regions of Everlasting Security and Glory. *Amen!*

Document IV.9

John Gill on the Gospel to be Preached, and John Wesley's Rejoinder

For Gill see Document II.26 above. For Wesley see Document II.21 above. Gill's 'no free offer of the Gospel' case is answered in Wesley's dismissive verdict upon 'Anabaptists' at large, which reiterates his concern lest high Calvinism lead to practical Antinomianism. It must, however, be remembered that not all Particular Baptists took Gill's high road as, for example, the doctrinal stance of a number of the alumni of Bristol Baptist College and the deliberations of the Northamptonshire Association make plain. Extracts (a)–(g) are from works by John Gill: (a) is from his *A Complete Body of Doctrinal and Practical Divinity*, new edn, 1839, II, p. 123; (b) from *The Doctrine of Justification*, 1756, p. 118; (c) and (d) from *The Cause of God and Truth*, 1814, II, p. 47, and I, p. 106 and II, p. 54 respectively; (e) is from *A Defence of the Doctrine of Eternal Justification in Some Important Doctrines*, 1780; (f) from *A Complete Body*, I, p. 294; (g) from *Sermons and Tracts*, new edn, 1814–15, pp. 491, 459. The extract by John Wesley (h) is from his *A Farther Appeal to Men of Reason and Religion*, in *Works*, 1872, VIII, pp. 183–4.

(a)

It is a part of the ministry of the word to lay before men their fallen, miserable, lost, and undone state by nature; to open to them the nature of sin, its pollution and guilt, and the sad consequences of it; to inform them of their incapacity to make atonement for it; and of their impotence and inability to do what is spiritually good; and of the insufficiency of their own righteousness to justify them in the sight of God: and they are to be made acquainted, that salvation is alone by Christ, and not otherwise; and the fullness, freeness, and suitableness of this salvation, are to be preached before them; and the whole to be left to the Spirit of God, to make application of it as he shall see fit.

(b)

And that there are universal offers of grace and salvation made to all men I utterly deny; nay, I deny that they are made to any; no, not to God's elect; grace and salvation are provided for them in the everlasting covenant … published and revealed in the gospel, and applied by the Spirit. … Till it is proved that there are such universal offers, then Dr. Watts's reasoning on that head, will require some attention, but not till then.

(c)

The ministers of the gospel, though they ought not to offer and tender salvation to any, for which they have no commission, yet they may preach the gospel of salvation to all men, and declare that *whosoever believes shall be saved*; for this they are commissioned to do.

(d)

Evangelical repentance is not in the power of a natural man, but is the gift of God's free grace. Legal repentance may be performed by particular persons, who are destitute of the grace of God, and by all the inhabitants of a place, as the *Ninevites*, who repented externally at the preaching of *Jonah*; though it does not appear that they had received the grace of God, since destruction afterwards came upon that city for its iniquities.

God never calls persons to evangelical repentance, or requires them to believe in Christ to the saving of their souls, but he gives them that special grace, and puts forth that divine energy which enables them to believe and repent.

(e)

As God put the elect into Christ, or united them to him in eternal election, he views and considers them in him, and so justifies them, and takes infinite pleasure in their persons as members of the Mediator, in whom he always had the fullest satisfaction and delight; tho' they are under a sentence of condemnation by the law, as violaters of it, while in unbelief.

(f)

Justification is not only before faith, but it is from eternity, being an immanent act in the divine mind and so an internal and eternal one: as may be concluded ... if they bore this character of elect from eternity, or were chosen in Christ before the world began; then they must be acquitted, discharged, and justified so early ... *for there is no condemnation to them which are in Christ*, Rom.VIII.1; and therefore must be considered as righteous, and so justified.

(g)

God does not justify any because they believe in Christ. ... A man is not more justified after faith, than he is before faith, in God's account.

Nor is it *causa sine qua non*, or that without which a man cannot be justified in the sight of God ... all God's elect are justified in his sight, and in his account, before faith; and if before then without it.

Active justification is God's act, it is God that justifies; passive justification is the same act, terminating on the conscience of the believer; active justification is strictly and properly justification, passive justification is improperly so; active justification precedes faith, passive justification is by faith.

(h)

3.   One step farther from us, are you who are called (though not by your own choice) Anabaptists. The smallness of your number, compared to that of either the Presbyterians, or those of the Church, makes it easier for you to have an exact knowledge of the behaviour of all your members, and to put away from among you every one that 'walketh not according to the doctrine you have received.'

But is this done? Do all your members adorn the gospel? Are they all 'holy as He which hath called us is holy?' I fear not. I have known some instances to the contrary; and doubtless you know many more. There are unholy, outwardly unholy men in your congregation also; men that profane either the name or the day of the Lord; that do not honour their natural or civil parents; that know not how to possess their bodies in sanctification and honour; that are intemperate, either in meat or drink, gluttonous, sensual, luxurious; that variously offend against justice, mercy, or truth, in their intercourse with their neighbour, and do not walk by that royal law, 'Thou shalt love thy neighbour as thyself.'

But how is this consistent with your leading principle, – 'That no man ought to be admitted to baptism, till he has that repentance whereby we forsake sin, and living faith in God through Christ?'

For if no man ought to be admitted into church or congregation, who has not actual faith and repentance; then neither ought any who has them not, to continue in any congregation: And, consequently, an open sinner cannot remain among you, unless you practically renounce your main principle.

4.   I refer it to your own serious consideration, whether one reason why unholy men are still suffered to remain among you may not be this, – That many of you have unawares put opinion in the room of faith and repentance? But how fatal a mistake is this! Supposing your opinion to be true, yet a true opinion concerning repentance is wholly different from the thing itself; and you may have a true opinion concerning faith all your life, and yet die an unbeliever.

Supposing therefore the opinion of particular redemption true, yet how little does it avail toward salvation! Nay, were we to suppose that none can be saved who do not hold it, it does not follow that all will be saved who do: So that if the one proved a man to be in ever so bad a state, the other would not prove him to be in a good one; and, consequently, whosoever leans on this opinion, leans on the staff of a broken read.

Would to God that ye would mind this one thing, to 'make your own calling and election sure!' that every one of you (leaving the rest of the world to Him that made it) would himself 'repent and believe the gospel!' Not repent alone, (for then you know only the baptism of John,) but believe, and be 'baptized with the Holy Ghost and with fire.' Are you still a stranger to that inward baptism wherewith all true believers are baptized? May the Lord constrain you to cry out, 'How am I straitened till it be accomplished!' even till the love of God inflame your heart, and consume all your vile affections! Be not content with anything less than this! It is this loving faith alone with opens our way into 'the general Church of the first-born, whose names are written in heaven!' which giveth us to 'enter within the veil, where Jesus our fore-runner is gone before us!'

Document IV.10

Baptist Evangelism

The authors of the following extracts are Andrew Fuller (1754–1815), who became the first secretary of the Baptist Missionary Society; Robert Hall (1728–91), who ministered at Arnesby, Leicestershire; John Ryland (1753–1825), pastor at Northampton; Joseph Ivimey (1773–1834), Baptist pastor and historian; Benjamin Wallin (1711–82), Baptist minister in succession to his father at Maze Pond, Southwark, from 1740 until his death; and John Sutcliff (1752–1814), Baptist minister at Olney from 1775 until his death, and a founder of the Baptist Missionary Society.

For Fuller see DEB, DNB, ODCC, Peter J. Morden, *Offering Christ to the World. Andrew Fuller (1754–1815) and the Revival of Eighteenth Century Particular Baptist Life*, Carlisle: Paternoster, 2003, for Hall see DEB, DNB, ODCC; for Ryland see DEB, DH, DNB; for Ivimey see DEB, DNB; for Hall Sr. see DEB; for Wallin see DH; for Sutcliff see DEB, DNB. In extract (a) Andrew Fuller is quoted in C. G. Somers, ed., *The Baptist Library*, 1843, III, p. 280, while extract (b) is from his own work, *The Gospel Worthy of all Acceptation*, 1785, p. 32. Extract (c) comes from R. Hall, *Circular Letter of the Northamptonshire Association*, 1781, p. 11, and (d) from J. Ryland's *The Work of Faith … The Life and Death of the Rev. Andrew Fuller*, 2nd edn, 1818, pp. 355–6. Extract (e) is a further selection from A. Fuller, *The Gospel Worthy of all Acceptation*, p. 33, and (f) is from J. Ivimey, *A History of the English Baptists*, 1830, IV, p. 88. Extract (g) is taken from Robert Hall's Sr. *Help to Zion's Travellers*, 1781, p. 103 f., while (h) is from J. Ivimey's *A History of the English Baptists*, 1830, IV, p. 41. Benjamin Wallin's *The Folly of Neglecting Divine Institutions*, 1758, pp. IV–V is the source of (i), while (j) is from Andrew Fuller's *The Promise of the Spirit*, 1810, reprinted in his *Works*, 1824, III, p. 359. The authors of (k) are J. Sutcliff, J. Ryland and A. Fuller, *The Difficulties of the Christian Ministry, and the Means of Surmounting Them*, 1802, pp. 2–3, while (l) is from J. Sutcliff's *Jealously for the Lord of Hosts*, 1791, pp. 14–15.

(a)

For a minister to withhold the invitations of the gospel till he perceives the sinner, sufficiently as he thinks, convinced of sin, and then to bring them forward as something to which he is entitled, holding up his convictions and distress of mind as signs of grace, and persuading him, on this ground, to think of himself one of God's elect and warranted to believe in Christ, is doing worse than nothing.

(b)

The same law that obliged Adam in innocence to love God in all his perfections, as displayed in the works of creation, obliged Moses and Israel to love him in all the glorious displays of himself in his wonderful works of providence, of which they were witnesses. And the same law that obliged them to love him in those discoveries of himself obliges us to love him in other discoveries, by which he has since more gloriously appeared, as saving sinners through the death of his Son. To suppose that we are obliged to love God as manifesting himself in the works on creation and providence, but not in the work of redemption, is to suppose that in the highest and most glorious display of himself he deserves no regard.

(c)

It is somewhat singular that this notion of faith, as consisting in an assurance of a personal interest in Christ, which was in the last age reckoned a distinguishing tenet of those that were then called Antinomians, should be principally maintained by the most zealous Arminians of the present day.

(d)

We have some who have been giving out of late that, 'If Sutcliff and some others had preached more of Christ, and less Jonathan Edwards, they would have been more useful'. If those who talk thus preached Christ half as much as Jonathan Edwards did, and were half as useful as he was, their usefulness would be double what it is. It is very singular that the Mission to the East should have originated with men of these principles; and, without pretending to be a prophet, I may say, If ever it falls into the hands of men who talk in this strain, it will soon come to nothing.

(e)

The sufferings of Christ, in themselves considered, are of infinite value, sufficient to have saved all the world, and a thousand worlds, if it had pleased God to have constituted them the price of their redemption.

(f)

Mr Fuller too, by some of his explanations respecting the sufficiency of the atonement as a sacrifice equal in value to have effected the salvation of all mankind, was supposed to have pleaded for universal redemption; nothing, I am persuaded, was farther from his intention, as he considered the Holy Spirit's application of the atonement confined to the objects of the Father's election, and of the Son's redemption. … The writer has long been of opinion that if instead of proving by the above representations the general invitations of the gospel to the unconverted to be scriptural, it would be much more easily supported, and be better understood, by a reference to the manner in which the Lord Jesus and his inspired apostles preached the gospel. Who can deny but that those infallible specimens support the practice of calling on the unconverted to 'repent and believe the gospel'.

(g)

If anyone should ask, have I a right to apply to Jesus the Saviour, simply as a poor, undone, perishing sinner, in whom there appears no good thing? I answer, Yes; the gospel proclamation is, whosoever will, let him come. … the way to Jesus is graciously laid open for every one who chooses to come to him. His arms of mercy are expanded to receive the coming soul. Fear not, poor sinner, to approach him. He will not, on any account, cast thee out. John VI.37. … There is no preventative bar in the sinner's way to the Saviour, but what ariseth from a carnal heart, such as impenitency for sin, an attachment to self-righteousness, and an avowed aversion to the holy perfection of God in his sovereign methods of grace.

(h)
The principles of this admirable little work were those of modern Calvinism in opposition to the system of high or hyper-calvinism, which had so generally prevailed in our churches, chiefly in consequences on the preachings and writings of Mssers Brine and Gill.

(i)
They who neglect ... divine institutions on a pretence that inward and spiritual devotion is all God requires, are under a plain delusion ... More is required in Gospel-worship than a barely to hear the Word in the assemblies of the faithful ... We learn from the New Testament that they who received the Word were soon baptized and joined the disciples, who in every place were with one consent united in a church-state and communed together under their several officers in the ordinances of the Lord.

(j)
The *true* churches of Jesus Christ travail in birth for the salvation of men. They are the armies of the Lamb, the grand object of whose existence is to extend the Redeemer's Kingdom.

(k)
We suppose a Christian church to be a society of professing Christians, voluntarily united for spiritual purposes ... Men are not born Christians. They are made such by the Holy Spirit. They are not members of a Christian church by natural birth; but become such by their own act and deed. Possessing one common principle, the principle of love, having drank into one spirit, the spirit of Christ, they naturally associate.

(l)
Are they [i.e. God's people] not the *Salt* of the earth? It is not proper that the *Salt* should lie all in one heap. It should be scattered abroad. Are they not the *Light* of the world? These taken collectively should, like the Sun, endeavour to enlighten the whole earth. As all the rays, however, that each can emit, are limited in their extent, let them be dispersed, that thus the whole globe may be illuminated. Are they not *Witnesses* for God? It is necessary they be distributed upon every hill, and every mountain, in order that their sound may go into all the earth, and their words unto the end of the world.

Document IV.11

William Carey on the Lord's Missionary Commission

William Carey (1761–1834), an ardent advocate of overseas mission, became the first missionary of the Baptist Missionary Society (1792), sailing for Calcutta with his wife and children and John Thomas on 13 June 1793.

For Carey see DEB, DH, DNB, ODCC. The following is a section of his promotional sermon, *An Enquiry into the Obligations of Christians To use Means for the Conversions of the Heathens. In which the Religious State of the Different Nations of the World, The success of Former Undertakings, And the Practicality of Further Undertakings, are Considered*, 1792.

An Enquiry Whether The Commission Given By Our Lord To His Disciples Be
Not Still Binding On Us.

Our Lord Jesus Christ, a little before his departure, commissioned his apostles to Go, and teach all nations; or, as another evangelist expresses it, Go into all the world, and preach the gospel *to every creature*. This commission was as extensive as possible, and laid them under obligation to disperse themselves into every country of the habitable globe, and preach to all the inhabitants, without exception or limitation. They accordingly went forth in obedience to the command, and the power of God evidently wrought with them. Many attempts of the same kind have been made since their day, and which have been attended with various success; but the work has not been taken up, or prosecuted of late years (except by a few individuals) with that zeal and perseverance with which the primitive Christians went about it. It seems as if many thought the commission was sufficiently put in execution by what the apostles and others have done; that we have enough to do to attend to the salvation of our own countrymen; and that, if God intends the salvation of the heathen, he will some way or other bring them to the gospel, or the gospel to them. It is thus that multitudes sit at ease, and give themselves no concern about the far greater part of their fellow-sinners, who to this day, are lost in ignorance and idolatry. There seems also to be an opinion existing in the minds of some, that because the apostles were extraordinary officers and have no proper successors, and because many things which were right for them to do would be utterly unwarrantable for us, therefore it may not be immediately binding on us to execute the commission, though it was so upon them. To the consideration of such persons I would offer the following observations.

First, If the command of Christ to teach all nations be restricted to the apostles, or those under the immediate inspiration of the Holy Ghost, then that of baptizing should be so too; and every denomination of Christians, except the Quakers, do wrong in baptizing with water at all.

Secondly, If the command of Christ to teach all nations be confined to the apostles, then all such ordinary ministers who have endeavoured to carry the gospel to the heavens, have acted without a warrant, and run before they were sent. Yea, and though God has promised the most glorious things to the heathen world by sending his gospel to them, yet whoever goes first, or indeed at all, with that message, unless he have a new and special commission from heaven, must go without any authority for so doing.

Thirdly, If the command of Christ to teach all nations be confined to the apostles, then, doubtless, the promise of the divine presence in this work must be so limited; but this is worded in such a manner as expressly precludes such an idea. *Lo, I am with you always, to the end of the world.*

That there are cases in which even a divine command may cease to be binding is admitted – As for instance, if it be *replaced*, as ceremonial commandments of the jewish law; or if there be *no subjects* in the world for the commanded act to be exercised upon, as in the law of septennial release, which might be dispensed with when there should be no poor in the land to have their debts forgiven, Deut.XV:4. or if, in any particular instance, we can produce a *counter-revelation*, of equal authority with the original command, as when Paul and Silas were forbidden of the Holy Ghost to preach the word in Bythinia, Acts XVI:6,7. Or if, in any case, there be a *natural impossibility* of putting it into execution. It was not the duty of Paul to preach Christ to the inhabitants of Otaheite, because no such place was then discovered, nor had he any means of coming at them. But none of these things can be alleged by us in behalf of neglect of the commission given by Christ. We cannot say that it is repealed, like the commands of the ceremonial law; nor can we plead that there are no objects for the command to be exercised upon. Alas! the far greater part of the world, as we shall see presently, are still covered with heathen darkness! Nor can we produce a counter-revelation, concerning any particular nation, like that of Paul and Silas, concerning Bythinia; and, if we could, it would not warrant our sitting still and neglecting all the other parts of the world; for Paul and Silas, when forbidden to preach to those heathens, went elsewhere, and preached to others. Neither can we alledge a natural impossibility in the case. It has been said that we ought not to force our way, but to wait for the openings, and leadings of Providence; but it might with equal propriety be answered in this case, neither ought we to neglect embracing those openings in providence which daily present themselves to us. What openings of providence do we wait for? We can neither expect to be transported into the heathen world without ordinary means, nor to be endowed with the gift of tongues, &c. when we arrive there. These would not be providential interpositions, but miraculous ones. Where a command exists nothing can be necessary to render it binding but a removal of those obstacles which render obedience impossible, and these are removed already. Natural impossibility can never be pleaded so long as facts exist to prove the contrary. Have not the popish missionaries surmounted all those difficulties which we have generally thought to be insuperable? Have not the missionaries of the *Unitas Fratrum*, or Moravian Brethren, encountered the scorching heat of Abyssinia, and the frozen climes of Greenland, and Labrador, their difficult languages, and savage manners? Or have not English traders, for the sake of gain, surmounted all those things which have generally been counted insurmountable obstacles in the way of preaching the gospel? Witness the trade to Persia, the East-Indies, China, and Greenland, yea even the accursed Slave-Trade on the coasts of

Africa. Men can insinuate themselves into the favour of the most barbarous clans, and uncultivated tribes, for the sake of gain; and how different soever the circumstances of trading and preaching are, yet this will prove the possibility of ministers being introduced there; and if this is but thought a sufficient reason to make the experiment, my point is gained.

It has been said that some learned divines have proved from Scripture that the time is not yet come that the heathen should be converted; and that first *the witnesses must be slain*, and many other prophecies fulfilled. But admitting this to be the case (which I much doubt)[1] yet if any objections is made from this against preaching to them immediately, it must be founded on one of these things; either that the secret purpose of God is the rule of our duty, and then it must be as bad to pray for them, as to preach to them; or else that none shall be converted in the heathen world till the universal down-pouring of the Spirit in the last days. But this objection comes too late; for the success of the gospel has been very considerable in many places already.

It has been objected that there are multitudes in our own nation, and within our immediate spheres of action, who are as ignorant as the South-Sea savages, and that therefore we have work enough at home, without going into other countries. That there are thousands in our own land as far from God as possible, I readily grant, and that this ought to excite us to ten-fold diligence in our work, and in attempts to spread divine knowledge amongst them is a certain fact; but that it ought to supersede all attempts to spread the gospel in foreign parts seems to want proof. Our own countrymen have means of grace, and may attend on the word preached if they choose it. They have the means of knowing the truth, and faithful ministers are placed in almost every part of the land, whose spheres of action might be much extended if their congregations were but more hearty and active in the cause: but with them the case is widely different, who have no Bible, no written language, (which many of them have not,) no ministers, no good civil government, nor any of those advantages which we have. Pity therefore, humanity, and much more Christianity, call loudly for every possible exertion to introduce the gospel amongst them.

Note

1. See Edwards on Prayer, on this subject, lately re-printed by Mr Sutcliffe.

Document IV.12

David Bogue on Right Sentiments in Religion

David Bogue (1750–1825), the Congregational minister at Gosport, where he opened an academy, was a founder of the London Missionary Society (1795), and also of the Religious Tract Society (1799) and the British and Foreign Bible Society (1804).

For Bogue see DEB, DNB. The following extract is from *The Great Importance of having Right Sentiments in Religion: A Sermon Preached at an Association of Ministers, at Ringwood, Hants, On Tuesday, the 29th of July*, 1788, pp. 34–41, in which he contrasts the prevailing spirit of warm-hearted evangelicals with that of the Rational Dissenters.

Another mark of right sentiments is, that the persons, who feel their influence, take pleasure in reading the word, in meditation, in prayer, and in the worship of God both in public and in private. Let us try the two systems by this test. Evangelical principles produce this temper and conduct. He is considered as inattentive and culpable who does not make conscience of morning and evening devotions in his closet. The friends of this system think lightly of that profession of religion which does not influence a man to prayer in his family from day to day. They account the sabbath a delight, they love the house of God, and take pleasure in a constant attendance on public worship, as the great business of the day; and not satisfied with social worship on the sabbath only, like the primitive Christians, they have meetings on the week-days for this purpose, and endeavour to redeem from business some time in order to receive spiritual edification and comfort. There are few societies of evangelical dissenters, where exercises of this nature are not to be found. Here then is an evident resemblance to the temper and practice recommended and exemplified in sacred Scripture.

Can we discover the same feature in those that take the name of Rational Believers? Do they delight as much in the worship of God? Whether some time at the beginning and close of the day be consecrated to secret devotions, I leave it to the consciences of such to determine. But, while I do not pry into their retirements, I would ask, is family religion a common thing among them? and is the morning and evening sacrifice of prayer and praise presented by the assembled family to the great Jehovah? Is public worship as much esteemed, and are as frequent opportunities embraced of attending upon it, by them as by those of an evangelical form? And do we as frequently find persons in their societies meeting together for pious conversation and for prayer? From the observations that I have made, I am afraid there will be found a great defect here in that system. Should we not consider this as a strong objection to its truth and excellence? Perhaps I may be told that worship is but a means of religion. If, in one point of view, it be considered as the means, in another it is one of the most important parts of religion. In the description given us of heaven, worship is represented as the most important, and as the noblest part of the employment of the blessed inhabitants: and can we imagine that, which is spoken of as the highest part of religion in heaven, not to be a grand part of the religion of saints on earth?

It was given as a mark of right sentiments, that they inspire the soul with peace and hope at the approach of death. This is evident from the nature of the Christian doctrine, and from the words of holy men in Scripture, in the views of death. The question is, which of the two systems tends most to produce the same disposition; and amongst whom is there the greatest measure of joy and peace in believing, during the conflict with the king of terrors? I can say, without fear or contradiction, that evangelical Christians discover exactly the same disposition with the saints in holy writ. At the approach of death, when faith is in lively exercise, they rejoice in Christ Jesus; they bless that grace which called them, and has kept them; and they express their hope of eternal blessedness through the righteousness of God their Saviour. They adopt the language of Paul in 2 Tim. I. 12, and say 'For, I know whom I have believed, and I am persuaded that he is able to keep that which I have committed unto him against that day.' And they exult in the words of the same inspired writer, I Cor. XV. 55, 56, 57. 'O death, where is thy sting? O grave where is thy victory? The sting of death is sin, and the strength of sin is the law; but thanks be to God, who giveth us the victory through our Lord Jesus Christ.' Numerous instances of this temper occur in the memoirs of the great reformers from popery, of eminent divines in the last and in the present century, and of thousands of holy men and women in private stations. Here is a cloud of witnesses to bear testimony to the supporting and comforting power of the Gospel in the hour of death. Those of us that minister in holy things, have seen many examples of a good hope through grace in dying Christians of our flocks. We have heard them express their trust in the promises of God, their expectation of eternal life as the gift of God through Jesus Christ, and the hope of a speedy entrance into the joy of their Lord; and we have sometimes heard them declare the great peace and sweet consolation that their souls enjoyed, while nature was suffering a rapid decay, and their bodies were sinking by weakness and pain into the arms of death. This, I think, is a proof that evangelical principles are powerful and good.

But is the same lively hope and joy as frequently found among those that deny the divinity and atonement of Jesus Christ? Do we commonly read, in the accounts of their death, of such consolation and peace? Is it found in religious societies, who adhere to this system, that at the last hour they enjoy the same comforts as evangelical believers? It is a common thing for them to rejoice in the hope of the glory of God? They have not the same ground of hope; and the sentiments of many of them, who expect a state of insensibility between death and the resurrection, afford but a poor prospect for many hundred years to come. If, when I die, I am to have no more feeling than the clods of valley that cover the mouldering clay, till the archangel's trumpet call the body from the grave, I have but little reason to rejoice at the hour of death. If it be but seldom that a lively hope and sacred joy in death are produced by these sentiments, there must be something in them defective and wrong; feeling that they are not productive of the same effects that were produced in the primitive believers by their sentiments, and that evangelical Christians now feel from theirs.

A servant zeal, for the salvation of precious souls, I mentioned as another mark, by which right sentiments may be known. They, that have felt the influence of good principles upon themselves, will be deeply concerned for the eternal happiness of others. Now, the enquiry is, whether shall we find the largest portion of this spirit, among those of evangelical principles, or the advocates for a different system? Which of the two are the most anxiously thirsting after the salvation of their fellow-creatures? Which heads of families are most diligent in teaching their children the principles of religion; in praying with them and for them; in sanctifying the sabbath day, and in keeping themselves and their household at the greatest distance from undue conformity to the world? In which congregations is there the most lively and fervent preaching to convert perishing sinners, and the most frequent meetings for the purposes of religion? Which ministers are most diligent in preaching the word; in catechising the children and youth; in visiting the sick; in praying with the afflicted; and in exhorting sinners to cry to God for mercy and grace? Let this comparison be stretched through every part of the country, and I judge it will be found that evangelical dissenters are most zealous for converting souls to Christ, and their congregations are in a more flourishing state; whereas languor and indifference, in a very considerable degree, seem to have diffused their soporific influence over those of a different system; and the greater part of their congregations, though under the ministry of men of talents and learning, are gradually dwindling away. Is there nothing amiss in principles that do not produce more powerful and beneficial effects? Allow me to mention another circumstance. In the course of the last forty years, a great number of itinerant preachers has appeared through every part of the land, exhorting men to turn unto the Lord. If ye commend not the regularity of their zeal, ye must at least applaud its fervour, and their well-meant endeavours to do good. If the MAN, who travels from country to country to visit the abodes of the miserable and to procure some alleviation of distress to the guilty in their dungeons, receives the approbation of every heart for the zeal of his philanthrophy and benevolence, and his fellow-citizens wish to erect a statue in his honour; is not a considerable portion of praise due to those, who, pitying the wretched cafe of perishing sinners go from place to place, in order to save them from endless misery, and to free them into glorious liberty of the children of God? Of what sentiments are these men? All agree in the grand evangelical principles. Perhaps not an Arian or Socinian is to be found amongst them. I have heard of several of these preachers, who turned from evangelical sentiments to the other system: but, no sooner had they done so, than their zeal immediately forsook them; and, quitting their itinerant labours, they became on a sudden stationary and cold. That you may not think this mark applicable to one or two particular sects only, examine what ministers in the established church are labouring most zealously for the salvation of souls. You will find those of evangelical sentiments justly entitled to the pre-eminence. If then the common effect of those sentiments, which they call rational, be great coldness and indifference about the salvation of immortal souls, surely there is something in them wrong; and they give different views of the natural state of man from the Scriptures of truth. I make no account of warm treaties that the press is daily pouring forth in favour of Socinianism. If men be zealous in their study for the propagation of their favourite opinions, and cold in the Pulpit, and in their prayers, and among their flock, this is not the zeal recommended in the word of God. Even the diligence of a few, who hold these sentiments, will not overthrow the general rule, more than the zeal of the emperor Antonius and the slave Epictetus will prove Paganism to be the true religion, and Christianity to be false.

Once more: I mentioned that right sentiments may be known by this mark, that they are rejected and accounted foolishness by the self-righteous, and the children of human wisdom. Such is the reception that Christianity met with at its first appearance in the world; and such is the reception that it always will meet with from persons of a similar temper. Who will say, that there are not now men as much conceited of their knowledge and learning as the Greek philosophers were? Is it not possible to find many who have as high an opinion of their own righteousness as the Pharisees among the Jews? To such persons true Christianity will be a stumbling block and foolishness. What are the doctrines that these men cannot brook and bear? Are they not those which evangelical Christians hold? Namely, that God was manifest in the flesh in the person of Christ; that, by the atonement and righteousness of Christ alone, we obtain pardon and justification; that our natures, which are wholly depraved, must be renewed by the Holy Ghost; and that as we are all condemned by God's righteous law, we must all be saved by an act of grace. They cannot bear to be told, that the most learned, who can read all the languages that were written upon the cross, must fall down at the foot of the cross, and acknowledge that his salvation flows intirely entirely from free grace, in the same door of mercy with the most profligate and vile; and that the decent matron and the man of benevolence and compassion must, along with the drunkard, the harlot, and the publican, equally acknowledge eternal life to be the gift of God through Jesus Christ. These are the doctrines that the spirit of worldly pride and of worldly wisdom cannot endure; and the rejection of them is an evidence of their truth. We meet with nothing of this kind in the other system. …

Document IV.13

David Bogue's Call to Mission

The Baptists having launched their missionary society in 1792, Bogue was concerned that paedobaptists should do likewise. Hence the following open letter, which appeared in the *Evangelical Magazine*, September 1794.

Christian Brethren,

God has favoured us with knowledge of the way of salvation, through a crucified Redeemer. Our obligations to him on this account are inexpressible; and I trust, we are often prompted, from the fullness of our hearts, to ask, 'What shall we render unto the Lord for all his benefits?' If in many things we are anxious to make a suitable return, there is one thing with respect to which, if weighed in the balance of the sanctuary, we shall be found wanting. A survey of the state of the world presents to us more than one half of the human race destitute of the knowledge of the gospel, and sitting in darkness and in the shadow of death. Their deplorable condition, it is utterly impossible for words to describe! And what have we done for their salvation? There are hundreds of millions of poor Pagans ignorant of the true God, and falling down before stocks and stones. There are hundreds of millions more, blinded by the delusions of Mahomet, and unacquainted with Jesus, as the only mediator between God and man, whom to know is eternal life. If we have never thought of these things, there is much reason to lament our criminal unconcern for the honour of God, and for the salvation of the perishing souls of men. If they have been the subject of our serious consideration; with such a scene before our eyes, what methods have we employed, that all these myriads of Pagans and Mahometans might be delivered from the power of darkness, and translated into the kingdom of God's dear Son!

While we are forced to acknowledge that we have as a body done nothing, we may justly reflect that we are under the strongest obligations to do everything in our power. We all know that it is the supreme end of our existence to glorify God. But can we suppose that though we endeavour personally to live to his honour, our obligations are fulfilled, while we have employed no methods, as a Christian body, to lead our brethren in Pagan lands to glorify him also, by making them acquainted with his nature, government, and grace? We profess 'to love the Lord Jesus Christ in sincerity;' but are we not bound thereby 'to shed abroad the sweet odour of his name in every place,' till it be diffused throughout all the dark parts of the earth, the habitations of ignorance and cruelty? We are commanded to 'love our neighbour as ourselves;' and Christ has taught us that every man is our neighbour. But do we display this love, while we allow gross darkness to cover the Pagan and Mahometan nations, and are at no pains to send them the glad tidings of salvation through the sufferings and death of the son of God? Perhaps we have not considered our duty, resulting from that command, which was directed from the supreme authority to every follower of the Lamb, 'Go ye into all the world, and preach the gospel to every creature.' That has not yet been done. It ought to be done without delay; and every Christian is called upon to act his part, and cannot without criminality withhold his exertions towards procuring obedience to the command of his Redeemer and his Lord. Gratitude calls loudly to us to be active instruments in the hands of Christ, in proclaiming to the most distant parts of the earth that grace of which we hope we have ourselves been made partakers. Justice, too, unites her strong and imperious voice, and cries, 'Ye were once Pagans, living in cruel and abominable idolatry. The servants of Jesus came from other lands, and preached his gospel among you. Hence your knowledge of salvation. And ought not ye as an equitable compensation for their kindness, to send messengers to the nations which are in like condition with yourselves of old, to entreat them that they turn from their dumb idols to serve the living God, and to wait for his Son from heaven? Verily, their debtors ye are.'

But it may be asked, 'Why are we in particular called on to exert ourselves in this work?' Will it satisfy you if I answer, that I am one of you, and think myself on this account obliged to speak more immediately to you? A connection with a society or denomination of Christians should certainly influence us to seek the welfare of that society, and authorises us to invite its members to discharge the duties incumbent on them. Besides, all other bodies of professing Christians have done, and are doing, something for the conversion of the heathen. The labours of the church of Rome have been far more abundant than those of all other sects whatever. O that they had conveyed Christianity pure to the blinded Pagans! The Church of England has a society of considerable standing, for the propagation of the gospel. The Kirk of Scotland supports a similar institution. The Moravian brethren have, if we consider their numbers and their substance, excelled in this respect the whole Christian world. Of late the Methodists have exerted themselves with a most commendable zeal. An association is just formed by the Baptists for this benevolent purpose, and their first missionaries have already entered on the work. We alone are idle. There is not a body of Christians in the country, except ourselves, but have put their hand to the plough. We alone (and it must be spoken to our shame) have not sent messengers to the heathen, to proclaim the riches of redeeming love. It is surely full time that we had begun. We are able. Our number is great. The wealth of many thousands of individuals is considerable. I am confident that very many among us are willing, nay desirous, to see such a work set on foot, and will contribute liberally of their substance for its support. Nothing is wanting but for some persons to stand forward, and to begin.

We have the greatest encouragement, Brethren, to engage in this work of love. The sacred Scripture is full of promises, that the knowledge of Christ shall cover the earth, as the water covers the channel of the sea; and every promise is a call and a motive to enter on the service without delay. It is the cause of God, and will prevail. Should we even fail in the attempt, we shall not lose our labour; for though the heathen should not be gathered by our means, 'yet we shall be glorious in the eyes of out God.' But we have no reason to expect such an issue. For all who are engaged have met with such success, as to animate others to unite their vigorous endeavours. In no one place have pious and persevering missionaries laboured in vain.

Some, perhaps, may ask, 'What can we do? We are willing to assist; but how can our assistance avail?' Need I say, Brethren, that our duty is to use the means of Divine appointment? In every age of the church, the propagation of the gospel has been by the preaching of the ministers of Jesus Christ. By the same method are we to propagate the gospel now. It is highly probable that some zealous men would present themselves, who are well qualified to go immediately on a mission among the heathen. But in general they will require some previous instruction; and therefore it will be necessary to found a seminary for training up persons for the work. An able and eminently pious minister, in a central situation, must be sought for, to superintend it; and as the education of a missionary must be, in many respects, widely different from that of those who preach in Christian countries, it may be expected that every man of talents will unite his endeavours to render the plan of instruction as well adapted to answer the end in view, and in every respect as complete as possible. For the support of the seminary and of the missionaries, funds must be provided; and I do not think I am too sanguine in my expectations when I say I am fully persuaded, that in every congregation among us, annual subscribers will be found, and an annual collection granted. And that the produce of these, aided by occasional donations, and by legacies from lovers of our Lord Jesus Christ, will be sufficient for maintaining at least twenty or thirty missionaries among the heathen. What pleasing and glorious effects may result from their labours, it is impossible for the human mind to calculate!

With objects before us so grand, and prospects so delightful, I conjure you, Brethren, to exert yourselves in the cause of your Redeemer and of perishing souls. An insulated individual, and not having an opportunity of consulting with others, I take this method of recommending the subject to your serious attention. Think of it in your most pious moments. Let it be matter of prayer before God; and make it the topic of your conversation one with another. As it is the duty of pastors of the church 'to be forward in every good work,' I call upon the ministers of the metropolis to consult together on this important subject, and without loss of time propose some plan for the accomplishment of this most desirable end; that our Lord Jesus Christ may have 'the heathen for his inheritance, and the uttermost parts of the earth for his possession.'

August 26, 1794.

Document IV.14

The Fundamental Principle of the [London] Missionary Society

The following declaration was included in the Plan and Constitution of the [London] Missionary Society in 1796.

As the union of Christians of various denominations in carrying on this great work is a most desirable object, so, to prevent, if possible, and cause of future dissension, it is declared to be a *fundamental principle of The Missionary Society* that its design is not to send Presbyterianism, Independency, Episcopacy, or any other form of Church Order and Government (about which there may be difference of opinion among serious persons), but the glorious Gospel of the blessed God, to the heathen; and that it shall be left (as it ought to be left) to the minds of the persons whom God may call into the fellowship of His Son from among them to assume for themselves such form of Church Government as to them shall appear most agreeable to the Word of God.

Document IV.15

Mission at Home

While the Hampshire Association of Independent churches had been founded as early as 1781, David Bogue being a leading light in this project, most counties turned their attention to mission at home in the wake of the formation of the London Missionary Society. Among these was Surrey, where the Surrey Mission Society was constituted in 1797, James Bowden (1745–1812) of Tooting being its first secretary.

For Bowden see John Waddington, *Surrey Congregational History*, London: Jackson, Walford and Hodder, 1866, pp. 124–5, 315–17 (from which the following extracts are drawn); Edward E. Cleal, *The Story of Congregationalism in Surrey*, London: James Clarke, 1908, pp. 212–13. Extract (a) is taken from an address which Bowden delivered in Tooting on 14 December 1797; (b) and (c) are from Bowden's memoranda.

(a)
Dear Brethren, – We are happy in being able to state that our former address on the subject of a County Mission was not circulated in vain. The generous contributions

of many who perused it, have already empowered us to enter the field of service. Ministers connected with the society have explored various places, within the reach of their personal exertions, where religious advantages were greatly needed, are stately engaged in preaching the gospel with very encouraging prospects of success. Two missionaries, engaged at the last quarterly meeting, are prepared to commence their labours in the more distant parts.

(b)

December 14, 1810. – Another year opens before me, and the year that is past I must review with various emotions. It was certainly a year of great and special mercy in many respects. My bodily health has been very little interrupted, and no breach by death has been made in my family. Outward comforts have abounded; the blessing of the Lord hath attended my ministry; and I have enjoyed much delightful enlargement at times in the service of my Lord and Saviour. Never, I believe, has there been a period wherein the power and glory of the Lord were beheld in so many works of grace in the sanctuary. Prayer was remarkably answered in the case of my friend Mr. L——; but lest I should be exalted above measure, there has been given me a thorn in the flesh, a messenger of Satan sent to buffet me. One severe trial after another has followed in quick succession. Repeated words and acts of unkindness from those I love wound my spirit, and even pierce my heart. My dear partner, through trouble of mind, is suffering in a great degree the gradual loss of sight, attended with great debility in the whole nervous system. Yet, blessed be God, He still enables me to possess my soul in patience, and yet the promise, My grace is sufficient for thee, has not failed.

(c)

March 6, 1812 – I have now nearly completed thirty-six years of my ministry, which commenced the first sabbath in May, 1776. During these many years I have seen many and great mercies: personal mercies, family mercies, and mercies attending my ministry. At the close, however, a distressful storm has been permitted to arise, during which singular supports and consolations have been granted. Painful circumstances have constrained my retiring. This is indeed to me a distressing necessity; but shall I receive good at the hand of the Lord, and shall I not receive evil? Sometimes I fear lest there should be found marks of displeasure in this dispensation. Yet my soul has been brought truly near to God by these trials; and had God been determined to put me away in anger, He surely would not have shown me such things as these. I trust that in all this is the will of God concerning me, even my sanctification. Lord, not my will, but thine, be done. Now, behold, here I am, with respect of bodily strength and a devoted heart as well prepared as for several years past for ministerial labours. Lord, what wilt Thou have me to do? If it be his pleasure, He will show me an open door to the service of the sanctuary. But if He thus say, I have no pleasure in thee; here am I, let Him do with me as seemeth good unto Him.

'Behold thy servant, Lord,
   Devoted to thy fear;

Remember and confirm thy Word,
   For all my hopes are there.'

(Signed)   James Bowden.

Document IV.16

Joseph Priestley on the State of the Rational Dissenters

While things evangelical moved on apace, the Rational Dissenters, in many parts, fell into the doldrums. However Joseph Priestley (for whom see Document I.11 above) found a way of looking on the bright side, as is shown in the following extract from his *A Free Address to Protestant Dissenters, As such* (1769; 2nd enlarged edn, 1771) in his *Works*, London, 1817–31, XXII, pp. 289, 292–3.

It is possible that some of those who are called *Rational Dissenters* may be discouraged by the *smallness of the party*, and the seemingly declining state of the interest. But this is an objection that will hardly bear to be avowed, and can only have weight with weak minds. The cause of *truth and liberty* can never cease to be respectable, whether its advocates be few or many. Rather, if the cause be just and honourable, the smaller is the party that support it, the fewer there are to share that honour with us. It can never be matter of praise to any man to join a multitude, but to be singular in a good thing is the greatest praise. It shews a power of discernment, and fortitude of mind, not to be overborne by those unworthy motives, which are always on the side of the majority, whether their cause be good or bad. ...

So long as the Dissenting interest is a nursery for men of liberal and enlarged minds, who make it their study to restore Christianity to its primitive simplicity, and many such it can boast of at present; so long as it is the cause of civil and religious liberty, which it can never cease to be; and so long as it is a check upon the disorders into which the established clergy would otherwise sink, which also it can never cease to be, it must appear a truly *respectable* interest, in the eyes of all men who are capable of entertaining just and generous views of things, though it be ever so inconsiderable with respect to numbers.

As to the number of *Dissenters* in England, it must be considered, that, notwithstanding the seeming declension of what we call the rational part of Dissenters, there is perhaps rather an increase than a decrease upon the whole. Those who are called *Independents*, retain all the zeal of the old Puritans; and though several of their societies are become daily what we call more *free* in their sentiments, they receive daily recruits from the *Methodists*; and many very numerous societies of Independents have been formed entirely out of that body. Even these new-made Dissenters will by degrees necessarily come to think freely, and supply the places of those rational, but lukewarm Dissenters, who are daily absorbed either in the *church* or in *irreligion*; and thus may the *circulation*, at least, be kept up.

I cannot help considering the *Methodists* as raised up by Divine Providence, at a most seasonable juncture, as a barrier against the encroachments of ecclesiastical tyranny, in the declension of the old Dissenting interest. For, whatever be the real views of their leaders, one great point in favour of the Dissenting interest is gained with all the Methodists; which is, that though they communicate with the Church of England, they are no longer attached to the hierarchy, as such. That blind and bigotted attachment, which is the great hold that the clergy have on the minds of the common people, is broken, the moment they can choose to worship God without the walls of the parish church, and without the use of the Common Prayer-Book. Their minds are, from that time, at liberty to consider the expediency of different forms of worship, and to adopt that to which their judgment shall give the preference; and as public worship is universally conducted among them in the same manner as among Dissenters, they are already *in the way* to us, from the Established Church. When such a spirit of reformation is raised, it will not be in the power of those who have the most influence among them to say, *Hitherto shall it go and no farther.* It is not improbable, that a great revolution may take place in their affairs, when the heads of two or three of their present leaders shall be laid in the grave.

Itinerancy and Evangelism

Document IV.17

Some Experiences of Howel Harris and Others

For Howel Harris see Document II.25 above; for James Clegg, Document III.9; for George Whitefield, Document II.25; for Selina, Countess of Huntingdon (1707–91), founder of her connexion and doughty promoter of Calvinistic evangelicalism, see DEB, DNB, ODCC; Edwin Welch, *Spiritual Pilgrim: A Reassessment of the Life of the Countess of Huntingdon*, Cardiff: University of Wales Press, 1995, and Boyd Stanley Schlenther, *Queen of the Methodists: The Countess of Huntingdon and the Eighteenth-Century Crisis of Faith and Society*, Durham: Durham Academic Press, 1997; for John Wesley see Document II.21 above; for Jonathan Scott (1735–1807), a Countess of Huntingdon preacher who was prominent in the planting of twenty-two evangelical Congregational churches in Staffordshire, and influenced the formation of others in Shropshire, Cheshire, Derbyshire and Lancashire, see DEB; for John Johnson (c. 1760–1804), a Countess of Huntingdon preacher, trained at Trevecka, see DEB, DNB; the identity of John Wesley's adverse but serious critic 'John Smith' is unknown; for Peter Jaco (1728–81), the Wesleyan itinerant from Cornwall, see DEB; for John Furze, Methodist itinerant, see DEB; for William Roby (1766–1830), Countess of Huntingdon preacher turned Congregational minister, see DEB, DNB and W. Gordon Robinson, *William Roby (1766–1830) and the Revival of Independency in the North*, London: Independent Press, 1954.

The first extract is from *Howel Harris's Visits to Pembrokeshire* (transcribed by Tom Beynon, Aberystwyth: Cambrian News Press, 1966, pp. 42, 44–5, 48, 60, 144–5; the second from James Clegg's *Diary*, ed. V. S. Doe, Chesterfield: Derbyshire Record Society, 1979, part II, pp. 446–7, January 1742; and the third from George Whitefield to the Countess of Huntingdon, in his *Letters*, 1771, letter DCCCXXV. Extract (d) is from John Wesley's Sermon CXXXI in *Works*, London: Wesleyan Conference Office, 1872, VII, pp. 410–11; while (e) is part of the obituary notice for Jonathan Scott, *Congregational Magazine*, III, 1820, p. 401. A portion of the memoir of the Rev. John Johnson follows (f): *Evangelical Magazine*, April 1805; and in (g) John Wesley writes to Miss Bishop on 18 October 1778 (*Letters*, ed. J. Telford, London: Epworth Press, 1931, VI, pp. 326–27), while in (h) 'John Smith' writes to John Wesley on 11 August 1746 (*Works* (bicentennial edn), Oxford: Clarendon Press, 1982, XXVI, p. 213 f). Extract (i) is from Wesley's Sermon CXV (*Works* VII, pp. 279–80), while portions of his Journal are reproduced at (j) (*The Journal of the Rev. John Wesley*, London: Epworth Press, 1938). Part of a letter from Peter Jaco to Wesley is reproduced at (k) (J. Telford, ed., *Wesley's Veterans*, 7 vols, 1909–14, II, pp. 12–13), and (l) is from *The Life of Mr. John Furze*, 1770, pp. 345, 342–3. An extract from *The Newcastle Chronicle* (XI, no. 1250, 14 June 1788; transcribed from the original newspapers held at the Central Library, Newcastle-upon-Tyne) follows at (m), and at (n) we find William Roby's words in a letter of 4 July 1789 (John

Waddington, *Congregational History, Continuation to 1850*, London: Longmans, Green, 1878, p. 49.)

(a)

5 Dec., 1740. *Newgwll.* Toward St. David's, 5 miles. There discoursed from 11 to 1 on 'This is life eternal.' Was made a most dreadful Boanerges, and many cried bitterly though it rained wetting us to the skin. All stayed. Postea toward Trefin, 5 miles. Many came to me to say what God had done to their souls through me. Discoursed there to past 5, though wet to the skin. Exposed the Dissenting carnal ministers. To the society to 9, there discoursed a very long time on assurance, then to Longhouse; there the Lord surrounded me with His mercies. Tol. Discoursed to near 2.

10 Dec., 1740. *Maenclochog.* Discoursed with the woman of the house that had been born again, I hope, in hearing me about 9 months ago, when I was so sorely set upon by the Baptists. She never has that savour with John Powell as she had with me (though he has the light of all the scriptures). He has done great mischief in these parts, incensed poor people vastly, and brought poor children over to them that were very raw. He said of 6 errors I held. I find the Baptists had rather I should not come this way. I hope I come in the fear of God, and am owned and helped by him. So many things meet in John Powell – pride in clothes, resentment, self in boasting himself, passions dreadful, disturbing spirit, censuring, party zeal, stirring up animosities, drinking to excess, lightness and rashness, and seeming want of awe and sight of God in His works; that I am staggered about him whether God send him. Am almost persuaded to expose him. 'Tis a pity so glorious a harvest should be so mauled. I heard of Thomas Matthias at Fishgate when some hot headed bigots came to him to tell him we are set upon here, you must stand for us today. He said, what am I come so often among you, and this is the effect of all my preaching among you, he never mentions anything but to edification, I find my soul bids him God speed. But I dread John Powell, he comes after me to draw down what good work I have been endeavouring to build. I feel no bitterness, or envy, or rancour, but have an even spirit, and am stirred by a sense of my duty and concern for God's work to expose him, the flesh is against it as I know he is a bitter enemy far more knowing than me, and has vast many followers. …

26 Feb., 1741. *Cardigan Town ......* Came to Trehaidd past 3, where I was received with much welcome and love, and no opposition to about 7 or 8,000. Discoursed on the broken heart, most thundering and dreadful to the whole heart to near 6. I hear of a minister near the seaside that when the servants were gone out to sing Psalms, he brought the hounds to drown their voices. O! horrid. Some Baptists this way said that dogs were more proper objects of baptism than infants, and made game at a schoolmaster that catechised the children.

5 May, 1741. *Llandilow.* [Landeloy]. Now all are against me preaching and exhorting. – Presbyterians, Baptists and Churchmen. 1. For assurance as I do. 2. For talking about experience and opening the heart. All this country is in darkness. Discoursed. …

29 *April*, 1748, *Carmarthen.*   After settling some jars among them, I went in a humble spirit to discourse where all the students and Dissenting ministers came to hear that are so enraged and bitter. The Lord was near me indeed. I was led meekly and yet boldly clearly with much demonstration, and in much love and gentleness on 'I am black yet comely', in Welsh and English. Kept a private society. Settled here about the school, and went thence to Merthyr. The Lord again gives me the honour of setting up schools about the country, and chatechizing in the societies. Arianism is strong everywhere, they can't bear to hear of a dying God. There I discoursed. Felt true love to the young students and the Dissenters, longing that God should come down among them though even all the people thereby leave us. Had a commission against Arianism and Pharisaism in our own people, all 3 being very strong. Most home in the oneness. Declared through grace I myself would stand out against 500 of you, even old ministers, not respecting old age nor anything in this, took from them to my side Dr. Owen, Dr. Watts, Matthew Henry, the Old Vicar, etc. No wonder they inveigh against our Church, she is too orthodox in her Articles and Creed and Prayers for you to bear her. If you had said anything against me, I could bear it, but since you have gone to rob my God of His glory, I can't be easy. How can I receive benefit and good from a carnal man? Why, I have but one Mediator, and I don't deal with the man. 'Tis plain they had laid a scheme to have us all over, and now this stopped by this.

(b)
4.   David Taylor the Methodist came amongst us again and many flock to hear him, if any good be done I shall rejoyce. I ought to do so by whatever person it is done.

5.   I was at home all day preparing Sermons, at night we had more of our neighbours to supper, had some discourse with them about David Taylors doctrine which I find leads to antinomianism, which they are not sufficiently apprehensive of in its tendency.

6.   was at Spire Hollin where some time was spent in prayer and praise.

12.   I was calld to a Daughter of Lewis Bagshaw at Down Lee, walkd thither in snow or rain. calld on Thos Mellor, returnd wet on my feet and all over. at night was invited by two messenger to see and talk with the methodist who preachd today at Milton, and was invited to Job. Bennets at night. I enquird after his authority to preach, he could not pretend to any but an inward motion of the spirit. I then enquird what doctrines he preachd and found them Antinomian to the highest degree. he tells his hearers they are all lost in Adams sin. that they can do nothing at all towards their own recovery, nor need to do any thing, Christ having done all, he makes no manner of account of repentance, or holiness or righteousness of his own as long as he livd, I shewd him from Scripture and reason the necessity of holiness and virtue, of obedience and good, til he was silenced but he would not be convincd so I left him. I bless God that I was enabled to deal so plainly and faithfully with him in the presence of so many of his friends. some were satisfied and returned thanks, but some others flock after him stil, and I fear to their hurt.

15.   Son John set out early for Manchester, and some time after I set out for Chinley house, some time was spent there in prayer and praise, I preachd form 1 Thes 5:18 and gave an account after of my conference with the Methodist, I find he

has created very great uneasiness and disturbance in the minds of many. He goes to houses where he is never invited and tells the more serious and pious women, they are whores, fornicators, Adulterers and murderers etc.

(c)

Honoured Madam   Exeter, March 21, 1750

I think it is now almost an age since I wrote to your Ladyship, but travelling and preaching have prevented me. Immediately after writing my last, I preached to many thousands, at a place called Gwinnop [sic]. The rain dropped gently upon our bodies, and the grace of God seemed to fall like a gentle dew and sprinkling rain upon our souls. It was indeed a fine spring shower.

In the evening I rode sixteen miles to St. Ives, and preached to many that gladly attended to hear the words; a great power seemed to accompany it. On the morrow, being the LORD'S day, I preached twice to large auditories, and then rode back again rejoicing to Gwinnop. In the way, I had the pleasure of hearing that good was done, and had fresh calls to preach elsewhere. In the morning I was to church, and heard a virulent sermon from these words, 'Beware of false prophets'. On Saturday the preacher was heard to say, Now Whitefield was coming, he must put on his old armour! It did but little execution, because not scripture proof, and consequently not taken out of God's armory. On Monday I preached again at Redruth, at ten in the morning, to near (as they were computed) ten thousand souls. Arrows of conviction seemed to fly fast. In the evening I preached to above five hundred, at twelve miles distant and then rode about sixteen miles to one Mr. B ——'s, a wealthy man, convinced about two years ago. In riding, my horse threw me violently on the ground, but by God's providence, I got up without receiving much hurt. The next day we had a most delightful season at St. Mewens, and the day following a like time, at a place called Port Isaac. In the evening, I met my dear Mr. Thompson again at Mr. Bennet's, a friendly minister aged fourscore, and on Thursday preached in both his churches. Blessed seasons both! On Friday we went to Biddeford, where there is perhaps one of the best little flocks in all England. The power of GOD so came down while I was expounding to them, that Mr. Thompson could scarce stand under it. I preached twice; a commanding, convincing influence went forth a second time, and one came to me the next morning under awakenings. The LORD JESUS has here brought home a lawyer; and one of the youngest and closest reasoners that I ever met with is now under deep convictions. On Monday evening I came to Exeter, and with great regret shall stay till Friday. For I think every day lost, that is not spent in field preaching. An unthought of and unexpectedly wide door is opened in Cornwall, so that I have sometimes almost determined to go back again ...

(d)

In the same year there broke out a wonderful work of God in several parts of New-England. It began in Northampton, and in a little time appeared in the adjoining towns. A particular and beautiful account of this was published by Mr. Edwards,

Minister of Northampton. Many sinners were deeply convinced of sin, and many truly converted to God. I suppose there has been no instance in America of so swift and deep a work of grace, for an hundred years before; nay, nor perhaps since the English settled there.

3.   The following year, the work of God spread by degrees from New-England towards the south. At the same time it advanced, by slow degrees, for Georgia towards the north. In a few souls it deepened likewise; and some of them witnessed a good confession, both in life and in death.

4.   In the year 1738 Mr. Whitefield came over to Georgia, with a design to assist me in preaching, either to the English or the Indians. But as I was embarked for England before he arrived, he preached to the English altogether, first in Georgia, to which his chief service was due, then in south and north Carolina, and afterwards in the intermediate provinces, till he came to New-England. And all men owned that God was with him, wheresoever he went; giving a general call to high and low, rich and poor, to 'repent, and believe the gospel.' Many were not disobedient to the heavenly calling: They did repent and believe the gospel. And by his ministry a line of communication was formed, quite from Georgia to New-England.

5.   Within a few years he made several more voyages to America, and took several more journeys through the provinces. And in every journey he found fresh reason to bless God, who still prospered the work of his hands: there being more and more, in all the provinces, who found his word to be 'the power of God unto salvation.'

6.   But the last journey he made, he acknowledged to some of his friends, that he had much sorrow and heaviness in his heart, on account of multitudes who for a time ran well, but afterwards 'drew back unto perdition.' Indeed, in a few years, the far greater part of those who had once 'received the word with joy,' yea, had 'escaped the corruption that is the world,' were 'entangled again and overcome.' Some were like those who received the seed on stony ground, which 'in time of temptation withered away.' Others were like those who received it among thorns: 'the thorns' soon 'sprang up, and chocked it.' Insomuch that he found exceeding few who 'brought forth fruit to perfection.' A vast majority had entirely 'turned back from the holy commandment delivered to them.'

7.   And what wonder? for it was a true saying, which was common in the ancient Church, 'The soul and the body make a man; and the spirit and discipline make a Christian.' But those who were more or less affected by Mr. Whitefield's preaching had no discipline at all. They had no shadow of discipline; nothing of the kind. They were formed into no societies: They had no Christians connexion with each other, nor were ever taught to watch over each other's souls. So that if any fell into lukewarmness, or even into sin, he had none to life him up: He might fall lower and lower, yea, into hell, if he would; for who regarded it?

(e)

His condition in life, his youth, the sprightliness of his imagination, the earnestness of his address, produced an amazing and happy effect. He preached in the streets, on the quays (of Bristol), and at Kingswood, among the colliers. He spread the gospel through the several neighbouring counties of Wiltshire, Somersetshire, and especially

Gloucestershire. In the latter county many were awakened and truly converted to God, where, by his labours also, several congregations, now large and flourishing, were founded. One of these was established at Wotton-under-Edge. This drew much of his regard. He there built a tabernacle, and attached to it a dwelling-house, which he always afterwards continued to occupy as the centre of his retreat and excursions in the country.

About the year 1780, two or three persons went over from this place to Hanley, in Staffordshire, to hear the celebrated Captain Scott, whose itinerant labours as a minister of the Gospel were very useful in this part of the country, and waited upon him at the conclusion of the service to request that he would preach at Congleton. Although no room was provided, he came, and preached either in the street or the yard of the inn at which he lodged. Rowland Hill, who happened to be in the neigh-bourhood, preached the next week in the open air. In 1781, or the beginning of 1782, Mr. Scott fitted up a room at his own expense, supplied by himself, or by some neighbouring minister, or one of the students, under the care of John Whitridge, of Newcastle. In 1790 Captain Scott erected, at his own expense the chapel in Mill Street.

(f)

Having experienced the power of divine truth on his own heart he became strongly inclined to the ministry of the gospel. Several of his friends advised him to seek or-dination in the established church; but conscientious scruples respecting some parts of its liturgy, and a warm attachment to the people, among whom he had been brought to a knowledge or the truth, determined him to offer his services to the late Countess of Huntingdon's connection. He was admitted into her college at Trevecka, in Wales, where he pursued his preparatory studies; and was one of the first of the six students who were ordained on the plan of secession: after which he laboured in numerous places as an itinerant, amidst diversified circumstances, and with consider-able success.

At length, he became more stationary at Wigan, where he was the instrument of gathering a respectable congregation, of erecting a commodious chapel, and was eminently useful. Many now living, and others already gone to glory, will have cause, to all eternity, to bless God for his ministry.

His preaching excursions in the neighbourhood of Wigan were frequent, and in every direction. In some of them, the wrath of man, and the interposing providence of God, were remarkably exemplified. At Chorley his life was endangered. The first time he preached there in the public street, a man threw a bone at him, with great violence, weighing upwards of two pounds, which very narrowly missed his head. – Having announced his intention of preaching there again, this same person pre-pared for more violent disturbance. In the former part of the day he paraded the streets, mocking the preacher, and promising the rabble fine sport in the evening. At the appointed time Mr. Johnson appeared, and entered upon the service. Just as the riot was commencing, a number of colliers came up. It was apprehended that they would join in the tumult; but having heard a few sentences, they, contrary to all ex-pectation, apprehended this turbulent fellow, – dragged him into a stable, – confined him there, and then returned and heard the remainder of the sermon in a peaceable manner. The unhappy man was so irritated by his disappointment, that he contemplated more effectual measures. Some days afterwards, coming out of the country, he overtook a person driving an empty cart. He got into it, and began to boast of what he would do to the preacher, if he should come again. After talking with much indignation and profaneness on this subject, he laid himself down in the cart, and apparently fell asleep. Having driven into the town, the carter called and shook him, to awake him; but behold, the persecutor was dead!

At Bretherton, likewise, Mr. Johnson preached amidst great opposition. One evening the tumult was so great, that he was obliged to stop, and dismiss the congregation. In returning to his lodgings, being pelted with stones, he caught hold of a man by the collar of his coat, and demanded the names of the persons who threw them; but he could not obtain information. The next morning he applied to the rector of the parish, a justice of peace, for a warrant to apprehend the persons who had disturbed the congregation; but the magistrate, irritated against those whom he termed *schismatics*, refused to grant one. Application was then made to another justice, the rector of a neighbouring parish, who ordered the warrant desired. After much difficulty it was served upon the man, and he was bound to appear at the quarter-sessions at Wigan. In the mean time a warrant was executed on Mr. Johnson; in which he was charged with having assaulted the man before mentioned. This warrant was issued by the very magistrate who refused to grant one for apprehending the disturber of public worship.

Early on the day of the trial, the man against whom the prosecution was directed, and his associates, came tumultuously into the town with ribbands in their hats, anticipating their triumph.

When the jurymen were called, one of them not answering to his name, an indifferent person was called out of the court in his stead. Mr. Johnson's license, and license of the house were produced. The counsel disputed the signature of the latter; and asked for evidence that it was the hand-writing of the deputy-register. To produce this immediately, appeared to be impracticable: enquiry, however, being made, a gentleman came forward, and declared the signature to be genuine.

The witnesses on the part of Mr. Johnson were then examined: two were also called on behalf of the defendant. The former, pressing through the crowd, said, 'make way, I'll swear through them all:' – and accordingly he swore that the person accused did not make any disturbance. – The second witness came forward with apparently the same impious intention; but the oath being administered' a solemn awe seized his mind, and he was heard to say, 'I'll not forswear myself for anybody.' Impelled by this sentiment, he acknowledged, to the confusion of his companions, that the man had behaved in a riotous manner.

The jury, with all this evidence before them, hesitated. Some alleged most shameful motives of party-spirit, personal obligations, and private interest, as arguments for not giving in their verdict against the defendant; and other were ready to yield to their representations. He only who was called out of the court to supply the place of the absent jurymen, protested against them; declaring, that he would sooner starve to death than, contrary to his conscience, bring in the criminal not guilty. They earnestly urged his compliance, but, indignant at their solicitations, the honest man rose up, saying, 'Gentlemen, if these are the reasons on which you intend to proceed, I must discharge my duty by mentioning them to the court:' – and was turning about for this purpose, when they caught him by the coat, and requested him to forbear, promising that they would accede to his views. The foreman of the jury then came forward, and said, 'Gentlemen, we are very sorry, but we are obliged to bring in the man Guilty.' – He was accordingly sentenced to imprisonment till he should pay the fine which the law directs. – His party being defeated in this case, had not courage to bring on the other; though the man who had obtained the warrant against Mr. Johnson, had actually brought a torn waistcoat to exhibit in court against him.

From Wigan, Mr. Johnson removed to Tildesley, where he erected another chapel, the expence of which, though vested in trustees for the use of the congregation, had laid very considerably on himself.

After residing there a little while, he was prevailed upon, by the urgent request of the Countess of Huntingdon, to cross the Atlantic, to superintend the concerns of the Orphan-house, which the Will of Mr. Whitfield had entrusted to her care. Here he experienced considerable inconveniences, on account of his determining to instruct the negro-slaves belonging to the house, contrary to the then existing laws. But his principle sufferings were occasioned by the death of his honourable Patroness.

With the account of her death, he received power to assert the trust of the Orphan-house according to her will. About a month after this, he received a letter from the Speaker of the House of Representatives, informing him that a bill had passed that house, declaring the property vested in the Countess of Huntingdon to be life-estate; and vesting the same in certain trustees nominated by the said act: thereby annulling her Ladyship's Will, and alienating the Orphan-house, &c. from the trust which she had appointed. Soon after this, Mr. Johnson received further intelligence that, on a certain day, the trustees appointed by the General Assembly would come to take possession of the estate. They came accordingly. But he like a faithful steward, resisted the claim; resolving not to give up possession till he was compelled to do so by the highest legal authority. The commissioners retired; and, in the evening, two constables were sent, from whom Mr. Johnson experienced the most abusive treatment. Still he remained in the house; but the next day he was forced out of possession. Both he and Mrs. Johnson were dragged violently off the premises; and he was placed in a state of imprisonment. During his confinement he received some flattering proposals of being constituted the President of the Orphan-house, with a liberal stipend, on condition that he would submit to the new regulations; but these he disdained to accept. At length he was officially liberated. Still he persisted to maintain his right of possession; but being left without support, he was unable to prosecute any further appeal.

Driven by these circumstances from the western continent, he returned to England, and fixed his residence again at Tildesley. Here his sufferings were renewed. The immediate payment of a considerable sum of money, which he had borrowed for the erection of the chapel, was demanded; which being unable to pay, he was thrown into prison. This, though an afflictive dispensation to himself, was a merciful one to others. It changed the scene of his labours, but it did not interrupt the exercise of his ministry. He preached the glad tidings of the gospel to the prisoners. Three or four of them were brought to an earnest concern for their souls, and became experimentally acquainted with the method of salvation by Christ. The kindness of his friends did not suffer him to continue in this painful situation; they soon obtained his liberation, and restored him to his stated charge.

Some time after, knowing that St. George's Church had been long unoccupied, and feeling for the populous neighbourhood, he entered into an agreement with a respectable gentleman, for the privilege of preaching in it, hoping to raise a congregation from the vast number of inhabitants who, having no place of worship very near them, were tempted to spend the Sabbath in idleness. His expectations were not disappointed. He had the pleasure to see a considerable body of people collected here by his various labours; and, it is hoped, his usefulness among them has been great.

Considering Mr. Johnson as a man, his talents were diversified: they would have qualified him to shine in other departments of life. His mechanical genius was very considerable: his musical and poetical talents were far above mediocrity: his inventive powers would very eminently appear, if his scheme of an universal language, the prospects of which he offered to the public, should ever be called for: his discursive mind inclined him to cultivate general knowledge. In his literary pursuits, the Hebrew language was the object of his favourite study. In his Master's service he was especially distinguished by ardent zeal, by undaunted fidelity, and by a fervent and steady attachment to the distinguishing doctrines of the gospel. His stern integrity, and his earnest desire to be useful, sometime placed objects before him in too prominent a view, and involved him in difficulties which he might otherwise have escaped; but even in the midst of these, though he suffered in his person and his circumstances, his character remained unimpeachable.

(g)
The original Methodists were all of the Church of England; and the more awakened they were, the more zealously they adhered to it in every point, both of doctrine and discipline. Hence we inserted in the first Rules of our society. 'They that leave the Church leave *us*.' And this we did, not as a point of prudence, but a point of conscience. We believe it utterly unlawful to separate from the church unless sinful terms of communion were imposed; just as did Mr. Philip Henry, and most of those holy men that were contemporary with them.

'But the ministers of it do not preach the gospel.' Neither do the Independent or Anabaptist ministers. Calvinism is not the gospel; nay, it is farther from it than most of the sermons I hear at church. These are very frequently un-evangelical; but those are anti-evangelical. They are (to say no more) equally wrong; and they are far more dangerously wrong. Few of the Methodists are now in danger from imbibing the grand error – Calvinism – from the Dissenting ministers. Perhaps thousands have done it already, most of whom have drawn back to perdition. I see more instances of this than any one else can do; and on this ground also exhort all who would keep to the Methodists, and *from* Calvinism, 'Go to the church, and not to the meeting.'

But, to speak freely, I myself find more life in the Church prayers than in the formal extemporary prayers of Dissenters. Nay, I find more profit in sermons on either good temper or good works than in what are vulgarly called gospel sermons. That term is now become a mere *cant* word. I wish none of our society would use it. It has no determinate meaning. Let but a pert, self-sufficient animal, that has neither sense nor grace, bawl out something about Christ and His blood or justification by faith, and his bearers cry out, 'what a fine gospel sermon!' Surely the Methodists have not so learnt Christ. We know no gospel without salvation from sin.

(h)

Well, then, how shall we account for the considerable success of your itinerant ministry? It must be owned that you have a natural knack of persuasion, and that you speak with much awakening warmth and earnestness, that God has blessed you with a strength of constitution equal to the indefatigable industry of your mind. These natural abilities, then, without having recourse to anything supernatural or miraculous, might alone account for the measure of your success. Yet there is another thing which gives you more advantage, and occasions you to make more impression than all these put together, and that is the very irregularity and novelty of your manner. 'The *tinners, keelmen, colliers* and *harlots*', say you, 'never came near the church, nor had any desire or design to do so.' But when it was told them, There is a man preaching upon yonder mountain, they came in as great flocks to such a dispenser of divinity as they do to a *dispenser of physic who dances on a slack rope*. Such a doctor may by a stratagem have more patients, and consequently if he has equal skill may do more good than Dr. Mead, who confines himself to the unalarming and customary carriage of a chariot; yet since it is next to certain that the rules of the college once broken in upon, many unskilful persons will take upon them to get patients by the novelty of the slack rope, it is likewise next to certain that if we cast up the physic account at the end of any one century we shall find that surprise and novelty have done much more harm than good, and that it was upon the whole much better to go on in the slower but safer way of the college ...

I fear you do not know every evil seed that may still lurk in your own breast. Are you sure there is no spark of vanity there? No love of singularity? No desire of distinction, *digito monstrari et dicier, hic est?* [to be pointed at, and to have it said of you, 'That's the one']. At least turn your emulation into a right channel, God can make you as conspicuous in a regular as you are endeavouring to make yourself in this irregular way.

(i)

I wish all of you who are vulgarly termed Methodists would seriously consider what has been said. And particularly you whom God hath commissioned to call sinners to repentance. It does by no means follow from hence, that ye are commissioned to baptize, or to administer the Lord's Supper. Ye never dreamed of this, for ten or twenty years after ye began to preach. Ye did not then like Korath, Dathan and Abiram, 'seek the priesthood also'. Ye knew, 'no man taketh this honour unto himself, but he that is called of God, as was Aaron,' O contain yourselves within your own bounds; be content with preaching the gospel; 'do the work of Evangelists; proclaim to all the world the loving kindness of God our Saviour; declare to all, "The kingdom of heaven is at hand: Repent ye, and believe the gospel!" I earnestly advise you, abide in your place; keep your own station. Ye were, fifty years ago, those of you that were then Methodist Preachers, *extraordinary messengers* of God, not going in your own will, but *thrust out*, not to supersede, but to 'provoke to jealousy' the ordinary messengers. In God's name, stop there! Both by your preaching and example provoke them to love and to good works. Ye are a new phenomenon in the earth, – a body of people who, being of no sect or party, are friends to all parties, and endeavour to forward all in heart-religion, in the knowledge and love of God and man. Ye yourselves were at first called in the Church of England; and though ye have and will have a thousand temptations to leave it, and set up for yourselves, regard them not; be Church-of-England men still; do not cast away the peculiar glory which God hath put upon you, and frustrate the design of Providence, the very end for which God raised you up.

(j)
[2 May 1759] May 2, *Mon.* – I preached at Warrington about noon to a wild, staring people (very few excepted), who seemed just ripe for mischief. But the bridle was in their jaws. In the evening I preached at Manchester.

[20 March 1760] *Mon.* 24 – About noon I preached at Warrington. Many of 'the beasts of the people' were present; but the bridle from above was in their teeth, so that they made not the least disturbance.

[17 July 1764] *Tues.* 17. – I preached at Warrington. But what a change! No opposer, nor any trifler now. Every one heard as for life, while I explained and applied 'Why will ye die, O house of Israel?'

[7 April 1766] *Mon.* 7. – I preached at Warrington, about noon, to a large congregation, rich and poor, learned and unlearned. I never spoke more plain; nor have I ever seen a congregation listen with more attention. Thence I rode to Liverpool, and thoroughly regulated the society, which had great need of it.

[5 April 1768] *Tues.* 5. – About noon I preached at Warrington; I am afraid, not to the taste of some of my hearers, as my subject led me to speak strongly and explicitly on the Godhead of Christ. But that I cannot help, for on this I *must* insist as the foundation of all our hope.

[30 March 1772] *Mon.* 30. – At one I preached at Warrington. I believe all the young gentlemen of the academy were there, to whom I stated and proved the use of reason, from those words of St. Paul, 'In wickedness be ye children, but in understanding be ye men.'

[3 April 1779] After preaching at Alphraham and Chester, on *Wednesday* I went on to Warrington, the proprietor of the new chapel had sent me word that I was welcome to preach in it; but he had now altered his mind, so I preached in our own; and I saw not one inattentive hearer.

[26 March 1780] On *Easter Day* I set out for Warrington Mr. Harmer read prayers both morning and afternoon. We had a large congregation in the morning, as many as the church could contain well contain in the afternoon, and more than it could contain in the evening. At last there is reason to hope that God will have a steady people even in this wilderness.

[21 May 1781] *Mon.* 21. – I went over to Warrington and preached in the evening. Fearing many of the congregation rested in a false peace, I endeavoured to undeceive them by closing applying those words, 'Ye shall know them by their fruits.'

[7 April 1781] *Sat.* 7. – At noon I preached at Preston-on-the-Hill, and in the evening at Warrington.

[8 April 1781] *Sun.* 8. – The service was at usual hours. I came just in time to put a stop to a bad custom, which was creeping in here; a few men, who had fine voices, sang a psalm which no one knew, in a tune fit for opera, wherein three, four, or five persons sung different words at the same time! What a burlesque upon public worship! No custom can excuse such a mixture of profaneness and absurdity.

(k)

In the year 1753 you proposed my going to Kingswood School, and accordingly, having settled the terms, I set out for Bristol in April, 1754; but, to my great disappointment, I found the school full, and a letter from you desiring me to come immediately to London. This, together with your brother's telling me that if I returned back to my business he should not wonder if I turned back into the world, determined me to comply with your desire. At the conference in London, May 4, 1754, I was appointed for the Manchester Circuit, which then took in Cheshire, Lancashire, Derbyshire, Staffordshire, and part of Yorkshire. Here God so blessed my mean labours that I was fully convinced He had called me to preach His gospel. Meantime my hardships were great. I had many difficulties to struggle with. In some places the work was to begin; and in most places being in its infancy, we had hardly the necessaries of life; so that after preaching three or four times a day, and riding thirty or forty miles, I have often been thankful for a little clean straw, with a canvas sheet, to lie on. Very frequently we had also violent oppositions. At Warrington I was struck so violently with a brick on the breast that the blood gushed out through my mouth, nose, and ears. At Grampound I was pressed for a soldier; kept under a strong guard for several days without meat or drink but what I obliged to procure at a large expense; and threatened to have my feet tied under the horse's belly, while I was carried eight miles before the commissioners: and though I was honourably acquitted by them, yet it cost me a pretty large sum of money as well as much trouble.

(l)

I was invited to preach in Salisbury Plain, near the New Inn. ... A very great company was gathered together, from the neighbouring villages. ... as soon as I began to preach, a man came straightforward, and presented a gun at my face; swearing he would blow my brains out, if I spake another word. However, I continued speaking, and he continued swearing; sometimes putting the muzzle of the gun to my mouth, sometimes against my ear. While we were singing the last hymn, he got behind me, fired the gun and burned off part of my hair. But he did lose his labour, for he was so soundly beaten that he kept his bed for several weeks.

[The Rev. Joseph Horler preaches before the Earl of Shaftesbury]
'Take heed brethren, lest there be in any of you an evil heart of unbelief, in departing from the living God – that is the Church. ... There is sprung up among us a new religion, called "Methodism": it is like the plague. They that have it infect whole families. Now in such a case, if one were to come and warn you, to shut the door, and keep out the man and his distemper, would you not be thankful? I am now come to do you this kind office. I will describe the persons in three particulars. In the first place, they look just like toads that are crept out from under a faggot pile. In the second place, they pretend to be led by the spirit; and when they are "under his guidance", as they call it, they look like toads that are crept out from under a dung heap, and croak just like them. In the third place, they look just like toads that are dragged from land's end to land's end under a harrow.'

I was curious to observe, what notice his Lordship took of the preacher who stood bowing at his side, as he went out of church. He passed by him without making the least motion, or taking any notice of him at all.

After he was got home, he sent a footman to tell the Preacher, 'If you please you may come and dine with his Lordship.' When he came, and was sat down, the Earl asked his name. He answered, 'My name is Joseph Horler.' His Lordship then asked, 'Mr. Horler, what have you been doing?' He answered, 'Preaching, my Lord.' 'What have you been preaching?' 'The Gospel, my Lord.' 'I deny that Mr. Horler; you have been preaching against the Government.' He said, 'I ask your Lordship's pardon: I do not know that I have.' 'Nay,' said his Lordship, 'have not the King, Lords and Commons all agreed that every Englishman shall worship God according to his own conscience? And are there not licenses granted for this very purpose? But pray, who are those toads who creep out of the dung-heap? I hope they are not your neighbours! Let me hear of it, Sir, no more. I will hear no more of it. I will send a note to the Vicar, to let me know, when I am in the country, any day that you are to preach; and I will be sure not to be in the church that day.'

(m)

On Sunday last the Rev. Mr Wesley preached in this town to a numerous concourse of people; his prayers and sermon were admirably adapted to the capacities of his hearers. This venerable itinerant patriarch, now eighty-four years of age, has nearly completed half a century, unwearied, in his vocation: And however we may have reprobated his apostasy in politics during the American War; been disgusted with the injudicious farrago of prescriptions in his system of quackery; surprised at the numerous contradictions and inadvertances in his multifarious writings; laughed at his credulity in giving place to the most ridiculous of stories about hobgoblins and spirits, in his Arminian Magazine; or stared at him in the capacity of a flying stationer, selling his own sermons and pamphlets; yet, when we view this reverend veteran in the rostrum, pouring forth the warmest effusions of human benevolence, and, with uplifted hands, soliciting this Father of Mercies, with the most vigorous efforts of prayer, to bless all his hearers, on recollecting this old adage *humanum est errare*,[1] we forget all human foibles, and are impressed with the highest veneration for the character of this indefatigable, though almost exhausted labourer in the vineyard, and charitably hope that his labour has not been in vain.

Note

1.   To err is human.

(n)

Wigan, *July*, 4, 1789.

Mr. Wesley's people are our greatest enemies, who envy our prosperity, and go to the greatest lengths is blaspheming our doctrine. They have repeatedly given themselves the trouble of going over the neighbourhood where I preach, in the barn, to warn the people against hearing me, and to say their horrid things of Calvinism – assuring the people that I repeat whatever they are pleased to put into my mouth, and then leave them with 'and he is a very bad man.' The last time I preached, one of their preachers – an occasional one – and another or two who *think themselves something*, came to hear, or rather to carp; but I disappointed them by saying nothing about doctrines, but preached an alarming discourse from 'Prepare to meet thy God;' but, however, they were determined to find fault, for I said man had not by nature a free will to do good. This served them to begin with, and then they lugged in the doctrines, and stayed with the poor ignorant people who had been hearing till twelve o'clock at night, spoiling their mouths, which are apt to speak lavishly of 'love' with the blackest aspersions on the poor preacher and his doctrines.

Document IV.18

Howel Harris Queried by His Vicar

The following is a letter from the Rev. P. Davies of Talgarth, to Howel Harris. It is reprinted from Thomas Rees, *History of Protestant Nonconformity in Wales*, London: John Snow, 1883, pp. 334–5.

Talgarth, Feb., 1735–6.

Sir, – When first I was informed that you took upon you to instruct your neighbours at Trefecca on a particular occasion – I mean, of the nature of the Sacrament – and inforce their duty, by reading a chapter out of that excellent book, 'The Whole Duty of Man,' I thought it proceeded from a pious and charitable disposition. But since you are advanced as far as to have your public lectures from house to house, and even within the limits of the church, it is full time to let you know the sin and penalty you incur by so doing. The office you have freely undertaken belongs not to the laity and farther than privately in their own families: and if you will be pleased to take your Bible in hand, you will there find the heavy judgments which God inflicted upon the sacrilege and impiety of those who presumed to invade the office ministerial. If you will consult the histories of this as well as other nations, you will see the dismal and lamentable effects of a factious zeal, and a puritanical sanctity: for it is an easy matter to seduce ignorant and illiterate people, and by cunning insinuations from house to house, induce them to embrace what tenets you please. I have yet one heavy crime to lay to your charge, which is this: – that after you have expatiated, upon a Sunday, upon the 'Whole Duty of Man' to your auditors, which, in my opinion, is wrote in so plain and intelligible a manner that it is incapable of paraphrase, unless it be to obscure and confound the author's meaning, you concluded with a long extemporary prayer, with repetitions, tautologies, &c. Pray consider how odiously this savours of fanaticism and hypocrisy. What I have already said will, I hope, dissuade you for the future from such practices. But if the admonition of your minister will *not* prevail, I will acquaint your brother of it; and if you will persist in your way, I must acquaint my diocesan of it, which will prove an immoveable obstruction to your ever getting into Holy Orders; for your continuance in it will give me, as well as others, just reason to conclude that your intellectuals are not sound.

I am your well-wisher, and assured humble servant,

P. Davies.

Document IV.19

An Independent's Support for Howel Harris

Edmund Jones (1702–93) was an Independent minister of evangelical Calvinistic persuasion. In 1738 he encouraged Harris to make his first visit to Monmouthshire and, because he disapproved of Harris's loyalty to the Established Church, he supported some Methodist societies in becoming Independent churches. He itinerated in Wales and England, and was a welcome visitor at Trevecka.

For Jones see DWB. His letter is reprinted from Thomas Rees. *History of Protestant Nonconformity in Wales*, London: John Snow, 1883, pp. 339–42.

August 7, 1741

Dear Brother, – I received your kind and very welcome letter, and see your great self-denial in it, a matter of conviction to most, and worthy of imitation to all that see it. But going to Longtown, where I am at the writing of this, I parted with it to my friend Mrs James the very day I had it. Blessed be God, who blesses Mr. Whitfield's and your labours after him so much in and about London. I am very desirous of his great success in Scotland, where religion was at first planted, and afterwards defended by some most glorious providences that I have read of. Oh! how wonderful are you both honoured, while I am of so little use that I cannot but mourn over it, and be ashamed of myself, though I do, from time to time, offer my service to God's cause, and ask Him what will He have me to do for Him. Many are they that hate me; and my friends are but few; yea, the labourers in my Lord's harvest would not allow me even to glean after them; and while the men of this world give a sheaf or two, especially the more generous among them, to poor workmen, nobody would do me that kindness; but when I offered to take up any ear of corn that lay before me, another enviously would take it, yea, and run to take it. Thus Dissenters and those who were not for discipline dealt with me; thus the bigoted Churchmen, the Baptists, and even the Methodists have dealt with me in many new stations: but if this be the Lord's will, I am content, and adore and bless it; and only desire that I would not be of no use before the Lord. Let me die now rather than devour His mercies and be of no service to His cause. However, my dear spouse, who hath had the presence of the Lord last Thursday, from about ten o'clock till about sunset, in such a manner as made her cry out wonderfully, so that I never in my life saw the like before, tells me positively that the Lord will yet raise my head, and will yet own me to cast a light about me; and which I cannot but believe, because God was immediately with my dear spouse, yea, and she tells me God will help building up the meeting-house, and, when it is finished, give His presence in it. But do not think from this that I am deserted, though I thus write, for thus I think, and have been carried to write without any previous intention.

I am fully of your mind, dear brother, that there are but few that wholly come out from the world to follow Christ. But there is a cursed conformity to it, and the fear of being counted fools makes men conform to some of the world's principles, and self-love and self-seeking make them conform to its practices; not considering that according top men's conformity or nonconformity to the world, they are conformable to, or dissenters from Christ, and consequently good or bad.

I now begin to collect some help for the building of the meeting-house, and will go about both the meetings and societies, where I am anything acquainted and shall be received. If you are acquainted with some desirable Dissenting ministers and people, I desire you would ask them some small assistance towards the building of our meeting-house; somewhat which they can easily spare. Propose it only to those in whom you may perceive faith to believe they shall be rewarded; and not to any others. If you will do me some service this way, it will be a great kindness indeed, and perhaps in time I shall reward you; but if I do not, God will. There are more of our Dissenting ministers, who are friends to the Methodists, than you mention this side of the country, beside Mr. Henry Davies, Mr. Philip Pugh, and myself, viz. – Mr. Lewis Jones, Mr. Joseph Simmons, Mr. Owen Rees, Mr. William Williams, Mr. Cole, &c.; but perhaps they will not act much; but you know our Lord's saying – 'He that is not against us is on our side;' and I cannot but observe that they are our best men who are favourable to you, and that they are for the most part dry and inexperienced, or Arminians, that are against you – at least, who are bitter. Though indeed, while all of us allow you to exhort, though unordained, and not called in the usual way, but are called extraordinarily, yet we cannot still allow of others going on without a rule, much more that there should be a succession of them still rising up; for this may be a means of bringing an unnecessary persecution upon the church of God, and of shutting the door of liberty in this nation; for though we have seen enough already to excite persecution, yet on men's part nothing but pure duty should be the eternal cause of it.

I desire you would prevail with Mr. Whitfield to procure journals of the labours of the Tennents whom you mention in your letter, and give so good an account of. I am glad the followers of Wesleys came over to you, and wish the truth may crush all their errors. Carry it tenderly to their persons; but to their errors give not a place, no, not for an hour, as the apostle phrases it; but pray and preach it down. I am glad Mr. Whitfield hath borne his honest and bold testimony against lukewarmness and worldliness of Dissenters, and against the loose walking and levity of some of their ministers. There was the greatest need in the world of it; but Mr. Whitfield doth it in a prudent, though yet home manner; and had you, dear brother, done this with less passion and intemperance of spirit, and with more prudence and distinction, observing a regard to their persons, you might have done much good; but as it was, I fear it did but little good. It is my presumption upon your honesty and self-denial makes me venture to tell you this much; but I see our own much greater fault. We should have borne our just reproof, and be humble, and confess our great degeneracy before God and man, and strive to reform: some were humble, and took it so; but most were proud, and rose upon it, to our greater shame and guilt; especially since it came from the man whom God owned so much to do good. We should have borne with you as with younger, if not as weaker brethren; and where, through Satan's temptation, some of you carried things somewhat intemperately and too far, yet we should have either held our peace, or have used entreaties and mild argumentations; but Satan puffed us on the other side to undue resentments, as it did some of you to undue provocation on the other hand.

I wish some of the sound Dissenting ministers separated from the erroneous and loose Dissenters; but perhaps it will come to that. Both the ministers of Penmain deny that there is any need of discipline among them, and call my attempts of discipline by the opprobrious names of rigid, punctilious, and novel customs; upbraid my friendship with the Methodists, whom they call my new friends, but tell me that I had as well or better, or to that purpose, have accorded with my old friends, &c. Thus these men refuse to be reformed – the more is the pity. I forgot in its proper place to desire you not to seek anything for my meeting-house, which we intend to build, of Mr. Samuel Price, because he doth me kindness yearly, but of Mr. Goodwin, Mr. Hall, and Mr. Hill, &c., if his congregation is not small, and can only support their minister, which is the case with some congregations; and where that is the case it is not proper to mention it.

I am concerned to hear how Accord and Rogers, and some other person, whose name I have not heard, should turn Anabaptists. Were they Antinomians, or no? Let me know in yours. And, dear brother, I here take occasion to desire you to guard your people from Antinomian errors, when you lead them into the doctrine of free grace, for that is a rock where many have split; and when they become Antinomians, they will readily turn Anabaptists: and while you exclaim so much against the luke-warmness of our Dissenters, do not neglect warning of the spiritual pride and intemperate spirit of the Baptist Dissenters, which are yet worse, though accompa-nied with zeal which other lukewarm Dissenters want; otherwise you may occasion the turning of your friends to the Anabaptists. So subtle is the enemy, that under pretences of advancing free grace, he hath pushed on thousands to the Antinomian whirlpool; for which reason I humbly give this caution.

Let me have an account of these men, and of what Mr. Stennet hath done in the matter. Your answer to mine, which I desire may be soon, in expectation of which, I remain your unworthy brother and servant in the Lord Christ,

Edmund Jones.

P.S. – If you can get Dr. Goodwin's works at second-hand, very cheap, in London, as perhaps you may (else do not buy them), bring them down with you, or a second-hand Flavel, and I will pay you for them, to dispose of them to young preachers.

For Mr. Howel Harris, to be left at Mr. James Hutton, bookseller, at the Bible and Sun, near Temple Bar, London.

Document IV.20

John Evans on the Jumpers of Wales

For John Evans see Document II.22 above. The extract, concerning the more ecstatic expressions of Revival fervour, is from his *A Sketch of the Denominations of the Christian World*, pp. 184–6.

About the year 1785, I myself happened very accidentally to be present at a meeting, which terminated in *jumping*. It was held in the open air, on a Sunday evening, near Newport, in Monmouthshire. The preacher was one of Lady Huntingdon's students, who concluded his sermon with the recommendation of *jumping*; and to allow him the praise of consistency, he got down from the chair on which he stood, and jumped along with them. The arguments he adduced for this purpose were, that David danced before the ark, that the babe leaped in the womb of Elizabeth, and that the man whose lameness was removed, *leaped* and praised God for the mercy which he had received! He expatiated on these topics with uncommon fervency, and then drew the inference, that *they* ought to shew *similar expressions* of joy, for the blessings which Jesus Christ had put into their possession. He then gave an empassioned sketch of the sufferings of the Saviour, and hereby roused the passions of a few around him into a state of vio-lent agitation. About nine men and seven women, for some little time, rocked to and fro, groaned aloud, and then *jumped* with a kind of frantic fury. Some of the audience flew in all directions; others gazed on in silent amazement! They all gradually dis-persed, except the *jumpers*, who continued their exertions from eight in the evening to near eleven at night. I saw the conclusion of it; they at last kneeled down in a circle, holding each other by the hand, while one of them prayed with great fervour, and then *all* rising up from off their knees, departed. But previous to their dispersion, they wildly pointed up towards the sky, and reminded one another that they should soon meet *there*, and be *never* again separated! I quitted the spot with astonishment. Such disorderly scenes cannot be of any service to the deluded individuals, nor can they prove beneficial to society. Whatever credit we may and ought to allow this class of Christians for good intentions, it is impossible not to speak of the practice itself, without adopting terms of unqualified disapprobation. The reader is referred to *Bingley's* and *Evans Tour through Wales*, (the latter author is a clergyman at Bristol), where as many particulars are detailed respecting the *Jumpers* his curiosity will receive a still farther gratification. It pains the author of the present work, that he has it not in his power to give a more favourable account of them. The decline of so unbecoming a practice will, it is to be hoped, be soon followed by its utter extinction.

Document IV.21

Enthusiasm Scorned by Horace Walpole and Rebuked by a Resident of Norfolk

In extract (a), Horace Walpole (1717–97), man of letters and sophisticated luminary of the aristocratic class, describes in scornful tones a service at which John Wesley preached. The chapel was presumably that of the Countess of Huntingdon's Connexion in Bath, where marble eagles, similar to Walpole's own at Strawberry Hill, are in evidence as pulpit supports.

For Walpole see DNB. The letter is from P. Tonybee, ed., *Letters of Horace Walpole*, Oxford: Clarendon Press, 1903–25, VII, pp. 49–50.

Extract (b) is the work of a man at once crafty and almost, with his intense feeling of shock pain, self-mocking. The anonymous letter appeared in the *Norwich Mercury*, 22 February 1752, under the heading, 'The fruits of enthusiasm'. It is quoted in E. J. Bellamy, *James Wheatley and Norwich Methodism in the 1750s*, Peterborough: Methodist Publishing House for the World Methodist Historical Society, revised edn, 1994, pp. 71–3.

(a)

To John Chute, Bath, October 10, 1766

My health advances faster than my amusement. However, I have been at one opera, Mr. Wesley's. They have boys and girls with charming voices, that sing hymns, in parts, to Scotch ballad tunes; but indeed so long, that one would think they were already in eternity, and knew how much time they had before them. The chapel is very neat, with true Gothic windows (yet I am not converted); but I was glad to see that luxury is creeping upon them before persecution: they have neat mahogany stands for branches, and brackets of the same in taste. At the upper end is a broad *haut-pas* of four steps, advancing in the middle: at each end of the broadest part are two of *my* eagles, with red cushions for the parson and clerk. Behind them rise three more steps, in the midst of which is a third eagle for pulpit. Scarlet armed-chairs to all three. On either hand, a balcony for elect ladies. The rest of the congregation sit on forms. Behind the pit, in a dark niche, is a plain table within rails; so you see the throne is for the apostle. Wesley is a lean elderly man, fresh-coloured, his hair smoothly combed, but with a *soupçon* of curl at the ends. Wondrous clean, but as evidently an actor as Garrick. He spoke his sermon, but so fast, and with so little accent, that I am sure he has often uttered it, for it was like a lesson. There were parts and eloquence in it; but towards the end he exalted his voice, and acted very ugly enthusiasm; decried learning, and told stories, like Latimer, of the fool of his college, who said, 'I *thanks* God for everything.' Except a few from curiosity, and *some honourable women*, the congregation was very mean.

(b)

Sir,

... I must ... by your means declare the fatal Consequences of Enthusiastic Rage, and if I profit or not by it myself, yet I hope many good Families may by my unhappy Misfortunes endeavour to avoid, hinder, or more cheerfully acquiesce in them ... I observed about last Michaelmas to my great sorrow, that Margery my cook did not behave at our Morning and Evening Devotions with that Decency and religious Awe, as I had taught her was becoming one, who was in the immediate Presence of the Supreme Being, instead of attending the Prayers as usual, she mutter'd to herself incoherent Stuff, so that those who kneeled by her, could hear nothing but 'Sweetest Jesus! Loveliest Lord! Dearest Spouse!' with Grace and Spirit and inward light and Heart's Blood and Wounds, and several other Words and Phrases jumbled together without any Sense or Signification so delivered; to the great Disturbance of me and my Family in our religious Worship.

Soon after John the Butler would not say Amen at the Conclusion of each Prayer; which caused great Schism and Division amongst us, and made it impossible to perform our Duty with Decency and Order. I argued with them on the unreasonable-ness and irreverence of such Behaviour, but to no Purpose; so they, as was absolutely necessary, (unless they would comply with our old Rules) separated, and performed their Devotions by themselves in their own Method.

This passed sometime without any material Disturbance, only I saw with Concern that the Love and Respect usual in my Family began sensibly to decline, and Neglect of social Duties, as well as secular to encrease. Several Dinners were spoiled by the Negligence of my cook, the Poor complained that the small beer was not so good as it used to be, and Margery who used to appear as neat as a Cook, began now to be ragged and dirty, for she lost her own Time by wandering abroad in the Evening to hear a gifted Man ... a 'reddifying' Teacher, as she called him.

But how the edifying is manifest by what follows. –

Her poor aged Mother whom she lately assisted, was now, by withdrawing her Assistance, reduced top the utmost Extremity, and forced to the Workhouse, where she soon died with Sorrow and Grief; whilst the pious Preacher, this gifted Man, enriched himself with the Presents of this poor infatuated Wretch, and of many other dear Sisters enslaved by the like Infatuation.

This I own grieved me to the Heart; was a cutting Sorrow, and could heardly [hardly] bear it with Christian Patience. I told her her behaviour was inhuman, cruel, and such as our Blessed Saviour sharply reprehend in the Jews, who neglected to provide for their Parents because of Corban, Mark 7.11. I explained the Meaning of it, and shew'd that any such voluntary Dedication of their Monies and Goods to any Person, was barbarous Cruelty, and an unnatural Act, when their Relations must perish for want of what is thus squandered on one, who if a good Man would refuse it with Horror and Detestation; and concluded by shewing that the Poor have the Gospel preached unto them. Her Excuse was in her own Words, 'She was a Jacobite … and had not the Spirit.' I replied whatever she was, or whatever Spirit she had, she could not have a worse than hers, a spirit of Inhumanity; and so she went from me little better for my Instructions, as will appear hereafter.

Be it known the (tho' 'tis no great News) that at the End of my Garden I have a small House for certain necessary Occasions, which I name not lest I should offend delicate Ears, or more delicate Noses, by this Time you may know it by the smell. One Day as I was walking in my Garden, thinking of the melancholy Broils and unhappy Divisions of my Family, I was suddenly alarmed with the Voice of my Cook from that same House; a voice so melancholy, of such dismal Tone, as if she was then in the utmost Extremity, and at the Point of Death; crying out, 'Come quickly, O come quickly, Come quickly.' I had immediately complied with her Request, and attended to relieve her, had not the immodesty of such Behaviour occur'd to me; so I ran in, and sent Sarah my Chamber-Maid to her Assistance, but she presently returned as pale as Ashes, and told me the Margery made such a dreadful Moan, that she fear'd meeting her Ghost as it should come from her Body, so she durst not go unless some one bore her company; I order'd the butler (as no one else was at hand) to attend her, he complied, but I believe made no great haste, so that, when they approached the House, Margery was just coming out; which so terrified the foolish Chamber-Maid, who expecting to find her dying, that she fainted at the sight of her Apparition as she supposed it to be, and the Butler ran back as swift as possible, with a faultering Tongue told me she was dead, that he met her Apparition with a Pair of Eyes as big and of just such a colour as our warming-pan Lid, and that in running away he looked back behind him, and saw her ascend into Heaven, for Sir, her says, she was a pious dear Soul and had the Spirit.

I had not time top reply to such Enthusiastick Nonsense before Margery appeared, haling in the Poor Chamber-Maid as a dead Corpse; after Care was taken of the affrightened Servants by letting them blood, I summoned Margery or Margery's Ghost before me, I examined her strictly of the Cause which produced those dreadful Consequences, and the whole of it was, that whilst she in that House was easing the Necessities of Nature, the Spirit she said commanded her to sing to sweet Jesus in one of Mr. W——y's Hymns.

I am now looking in Dyche's Dictionary to spell a hard Word which I should write next, but a violent Noise in my Kitchen calls for my Attendance, but I am forced to lay it aside and abruptly subscribe myself,

Yours etc.

P.S. The Troubles in the Kitchen afford me many more wonderful and melancholy Frays, which as this is received shall be communicated for the good of my native City, as Time and Materials occur.

PART V

CHURCH, STATE AND SOCIETY

Introduction

The toleration afforded by the Act of 1689 was valued greatly by the Dissenters, but they knew it could be wrested from them at any time, such was the resentment against it on the part of many Anglicans. Quakers continued to suffer for the non-payment of tithes, and also for refusing to make affirmations in court – a substitution for oath-swearing sanctioned by an Act of 1696 – because to some an affirmation seemed to be simply an oath by another name. Rural Friends also suffered more than other Dissenters when the prohibitive price of bread led many to suspect Quaker mill owners of sharp practice.

Among the most implacable opponents of Whigs and Dissenters in the early years of the eighteenth century was the High Church Tory Henry Sacheverell.[1] On 20 October 1714, the day of George III's coronation, Sacheverell preached a rabble-rousing sermon in the Parish Church of Sutton Coldfield, its congregation swollen by the presence of about two hundred Jacobites from Birmingham. Trade was depressed, and many feared an invasion by the Pretender. Riots ensued in 1715, and Dissenting meeting houses were attacked – nowhere more than in Staffordshire, as can be seen from the estimates of damages subsequently produced by the King's commissioners:

Total for Staffordshire: £1,722 17 8
Total for Shropshire : £1,063 16 2
All other counties : less than £1,000.00 each
Total for the country : £5,580 4 7½[2]

Contemporaneously, there was considerable Dissenting anxiety over the Schism Bill of 1714.[3] The Bill was occasioned by fear of the dangers to the state which might ensue from the fact that Dissenters from the Church of England were running schools and seminaries. Licensed schoolmasters only would be permitted to teach and licences would be granted by the archbishop, bishop or ordinary only to those who could provide a certificate signed by their parish minister and one churchwarden testifying that they had received the sacrament according to the rite of the Church of England at least once during the previous year. Applicants would also be required to take the oath against transubstantiation as provided in the Test Act of 1693. The penalty for failure in these matters was to be three months' imprisonment. Further, licences would be invalidated if, once teaching, a schoolmaster used any catechism other than that of the Book of Common Prayer. All of which was perceived by Dissenters as a great threat to their academies and schools. In the event, the death of Queen Anne on 1 August, the very day on which the Bill was to have become law, kept it from the statute books – a fact hailed as a mighty providence by many Dissenters, not least by the Independent Thomas Bradbury, who is said to have preached on the text relating to Jezebel, 'Go, see now this cursed woman, and bury

her: for she is a king's daughter' (II Kings 9: 34).[4] Providence notwithstanding, as
late as 1733 no lesser person than Philip Doddridge was (unsuccessfully) prosecuted
by the chancellor of the diocese of Peterborough for teaching without a licence.[5]
Eventually, by the Nonconformist Relief Act of 1779,[6] schoolmasters were permitted
to teach provided that they declared their Protestant Christian status and their adherence to Scripture before a magistrate.

In the meantime some Dissenters, particularly Presbyterians, by meeting the
conditions of the Occasional Conformity Act of 1711, had been elected to corporations, sometimes, as at Nottingham, forming the majority group. In 1732 the
Protestant Dissenting Deputies organised themselves to represent the Dissenting
interest to the monarch and the government.

Additional legal impediments included Lord Hardwicke's Marriage Act of 1753.[7]
By this Act all marriages (except where both parties were either Quaker or Jews)
had to be solemnised by a clergyman of the Church of England using that Church's
rite. As provided under an Act of Henry VIII the Archbishop of Canterbury could
still grant special licences to marry at any convenient time or place.[8] Hardwicke's
Act remained in force until 1836.

In addition to legal difficulties there were social ones. Nonconformity having been
legalised, the development of the 'Church and chapel' – even the 'Church *versus*
chapel' – divide proceeded apace, and lingers to this day. In the eighteenth century,
with its socio-ethical concern for the orders of society, many Anglicans knew precisely where to position Nonconformists, and some of them went out of their way
to obstruct and intimidate them.

Towards the end of our period the Birmingham riots of 1791 and the subsequent
self-exile of Priestley typify the mood of the more vociferous elements of the Church
and King party, and also suggest that in a period of revolutionary fervour abroad,
the rational Dissenters, both because of the revolutionary sympathies of some of
them, and because of their denial of orthodox-doctrine-deemed-societally-cohesive,
were now more of a constitutional threat than the Roman Catholics.

In a somewhat lower key, the Establishment principle was challenged by a number
of Dissenting divines on theological and other grounds during the eighteenth century.[9] The writings of the Presbyterian Micaijah Towgood on this question were greatly
valued and frequently quoted until well into the following century.

To the end of the century subscription as required by the Test Acts was deeply resented by Andrew Kippis and others as an intolerable imposition for which no good
arguments could be adduced. The requirement was, however, something of a money-
spinner, as when, knowing that loyal Nonconformists would not subscribe, the City
of London repeatedly offered the position of Sheriff to Nonconformists and imposed
a fine of £600.00 upon those who declined the honour – thereby raising some
£15,000 towards the cost of building the Mansion House!

Turning to broader political affairs, we find a considerable diversity of opinion
among the Nonconformists, with the Old Dissent tending towards the Whigs, and
the Wesleyans to the Tories. But this generalisation must be qualified by the realisation that within Dissent there were contrasting views on such specific matters as
American Independence and the French Revolution; and that on some matters,

notably the anti-slavery cause, for the original promotion of which the Quakers take the credit, rational and evangelical Dissenters and Wesleyans increasingly spoke with one voice. Similarly, poverty, prisons and Sunday Schools (which gave basic education to those otherwise deprived of it) were common causes among many Nonconformists as the century progressed. Nor should we overlook the enlightened attitude of such Quaker medical men as J. C. Lettsom and John Fothergill, who were harbingers of the pioneering work in the care of the mentally ill at the Retreat in York, founded by Friends at the end of the century.[10]

Social advocacy took many forms, as did social prophecy, as witness Rowland Hill's poster against the theatre, which certainly reveals contempt for an amusement deemed degrading, and possibly suggests a desire to undermine the competition.

Notes

1. For Sacheverell (1674?–1724) see DNB, ODCC; G. Holmes, *The Trial of Dr. Sacheverell*, London: Eyre Metheun, 1973. For a study of Saceverell and other eighteenth-century riots in one locality see, for example, Alan P. F. Sell, 'The Walsall Riots, the Rooker Family and Eighteenth-Century Dissent', in *idem, Dissenting Thought and the Life of the Churches: Studies in an English Tradition*, Lewiston, NY: Edwin Mellen Press, 1990, ch. 11. See also *idem*, 'Through Suffering to Liberty: 1689 in the English and Vaudois Experience', in *idem, Commemorations: Studies in Christian Thought and History*, Calgary: University of Calgary Press and Cardiff: University of Wales Press, 1993, ch. 5.

2. Figures reproduced by A. G. Matthews, *The Congregational Churches of Staffordshire*, London: Congregational Union of England and Wales, [1924], p. 128.

3. 12 Anne. Stat. 2, c. 7.

4. Walter Wilson, *History and Antiquities of Dissenting Churches and Meeting-houses in London, Westminster and Southwark*, 1808, III, p. 514. For Bradbury (1677–1759) see DNB, and for full references, Alan P. F. Sell, *Dissenting Thought and the Life of the Churches*, p. 401 n. Bradbury's meeting house in Stepney was burned by a mob on 1 March 1709–10; he declined the Queen's attempt to buy his silence with a bishopric; and when a would-be assassin attended his church in order to acquaint himself with his intended victim he was converted – a matter concerning which Wilson claims to have 'indubitable proof', *History and Antiquities*, III, p. 512.

5. For relevant letters see Geoffrey F. Nuttall, ed., *Calendar of the Correspondence of PhilipDoddridge, D.D. (1702–1751)*, London: HMSO, 1979, pp. 69–70.

6. 19 George III, c. 44.

7. 26 George II, c. 33.

8. For the legal details thus far noted see T. Bennett, *Laws against Nonconformity*, Grimsby: Roberts & Jackson, 1913.

9. See further Alan P. F. Sell, 'Dubious Establishment? A Neglected Ecclesiological testimony', in *idem, Dissenting Thought and the Life of the Churches*, ch. 22; *idem, Testimony and Tradition: Studies in Reformed and Dissenting Thought*, Aldershot: Ashgate, 2004, ch. 11.

10. For Fothergill (1712–80) and Lettsom (1744–1815) see DNB. James J. Abraham, *Lettsom his Life, Times, Friends and Descendants*, London: Heineman, 1933, includes a chapter on Lettsom and prison reform. Lettsom wrote, *Memoirs of John Fothergill*

M.D., 1786; and see R. Hingston Fox, *Dr John Fothergill and His Friends*, London: Macmillan, 1919. For Fothergill's correspondence see C. G. Booth and B. C. Corner, *Chain of Friendship*, Cambridge, MA, 1971. For the Retreat see Mary R. Glover, *The Retreat at York*, York: Sessions, 1984; K. A. Stewart, *The York Retreat in the Light of the Quaker Way*, York: Sessions, 1992: Samuel Tuke, *Description of the Retreat, an institution near York, For Insane Persons of the Society of Friends*, York: Sessions, 1813.

Post-Toleration Trials and Tribulations

Document V.1

A Disturbance at Ludlow

For James Owen see Document III.18 above. The following is quoted by Thomas Rees, *History of Protestant Nonconformity in Wales*, London: John Snow, 1883, p. 249.

On the Sabbath day, Nov. 12, 1693, a meeting for religious worship was held at Ludlow, in a house legally licensed; during which time an alarm was sounded from the parish church, by ringing the bells backward, whereby great numbers of people gathered together, and in a riotous manner exceedingly disturbed the said meeting by clamorous noise and throwing in vast numbers of stones, bats, &c., many of them of several pounds weight, to the defacing of the house, breaking the windows, to the great terror and apparent hazard of the lives of the persons within, and the abrupt breaking up of the religious worship. The people who met, peaceably departing, were many of them set upon in the streets, abused, stoned, beaten, and pursued through the town. The bailiffs and constables of the town were that day absent, withdrawn to a small alehouse out of town to pass the Sabbath in, whereby no relief could be had against the said rioters.

Document V.2

Some Quaker Experiences

Eighteenth-century Friends are usually seen as withdrawn from the world and intro-spective, channelling their energy, integrity and application into building successful commercial enterprises. John Bellers (1654–1725) stood out from this pattern, as we shall see. The Society corporately was anxious to enjoy good relations with the state and to stay remote from politics. The limitations imposed on Dissenters reduced op-portunities for formal political involvement. Nevertheless when appropriate, Friends petitioned parliament or the Crown, and were not averse to sending relevant literature to members of both houses. Tithe remained an issue throughout the century, as the pamphlet *Reasons why the People called Quakers do not pay Tithes*, 1777, and Joseph Phipps's *Animadversions on the Practice of Tithing under the Gospel*, 1796, make plain. In addition, Thomas Ellwood's *The Foundation of Tithes Shaken*, 1678, was re-printed in 1720, and Anthony Pearson's *Great Case of Tithes*, 1657, was reprinted on a number of occasions during the eighteenth century. Tithe was seen both as an unjust and unjustly implemented imposition on behalf of the state church, and as an area where weaker brethren could be tempted to compromise their principles for a quieter life or an unthreatened livelihood. Provision for affirmation instead of oath-swearing removed one of the other forms of persecution (though not all Quakers were happy to affirm). Friends resolutely refused to join in occasions of public celebration or illuminations, and suffered accordingly.

The three following quotations on tithe are drawn from the printed epistles of the Yearly Meeting for (a) 1701, (b) 1725 and (c) 1751.

(a)

And we have an account, from divers parts, of Friends' great sufferings in England and Wales, to the value of above £5,000, since the last year's account; and there are still continued thirty-seven Friends prisoners, although there have been thirteen discharged since the last Yearly Meeting: and the sundry sufferings do appear to be mostly on the claim of tithes; and divers of them by the old destructive course of proceeding to excommunication, imprisonments, and sequestrations, notwithstanding the sundry late acts (declared to be) 'For the more easy recovery, &c.', which severe proceedings Friends may tenderly acquaint the bishops and civil magistrates of.

Our testimony against tithes and forced maintenance in this gospel day, being received from Christ, our head and high priest, is not of our own making or imposing, nor from the tradition of men, but what we have from him, by whose divine power we were raised up to be a people, and by which we have been preserved to this day: knowing that his ministry and gospel are free, according to his own express command, 'Freely ye have received, freely give'.

(b)

It is also advised, and earnestly recommended, that inasmuch as it doth appear there is in some places a shortness and deficiency in bearing a faithful testimony against tithes, that, in any Monthly Meetings which have such members, after a deliberate dealing with them in the wisdom of truth and the meek spirit of the gospel, for their help and information, Friends have recourse, for their further proceedings, to the Yearly Meeting minute, anno 1706.

The accounts of the sufferings of Friends, which this year we have received from the counties of England and Wales, do amount unto four thousand seven hundred and twenty pounds and upwards, and are chiefly for tithes and church-rates so called. Two Friends, prisoners, have been discharged since last year; and there doth at present remain but one Friend prisoner on truth's account. Whereupon we have repeated occasion to observe to you the goodness and mercy of God in this, as in many other particulars.

(c)

The accounts of Friends' sufferings brought in this year, being chiefly for tithes and church-rates so called, amount in England and Wales to the sum of three thousand and twenty-five pounds and upwards; and those from Ireland, to the sum of one thousand seven hundred and sixty pounds and upwards. There are four Friends now remaining prisoners; two of them in consequence of processes in the Ecclesiastical Courts.

Document V.3

Wesleyan Excitements in the West Midlands

The following extract is from an anonymous source, *Some Papers Giving An account of the Rise and Progress of Methodism at Wednesbury ... As Likewise of the late Riot in those parts*, 1744.

In the beginning of November 1742, or near to that Time, Mr. Charles Westley and a young Clergyman, whose Name is Greaves, first made their Appearance in Wednesbury. When Notice of their coming was first given to the Inhabitants, it was said Mr. Westley was to be sent among them, in order to reform the Colliers, and other illiterate and ignorant Persons; and Intimations were given that a Charity School was designed to be built and endow'd at Wednesbury, wherein poor Children should be instructed and train'd up in the Principles and Practice of the Christian Religion.

Mr. Charles Westley is said to have made the strongest Asservations to the then Vicar, that nothing should be done by him or his Followers to alienate the Affections of the People from him, (the Vicar) or to withdraw them from the Church of England, but that it should be their constant Endeavour to unite them more strongly to both. By these, and such like specious Pretences, the People became prejudiced in their Favour, and received them gladly. Mr. Westley preached publickly in the Streets and Fields, and drew great Numbers of People after him. He told them he did not come to collect Money among them, or to draw anything from them: but only to instruct them in the Purity of the Christian Doctrine: and to confirm this, a Person who ac-companied him, gave a Guinea to be distributed in Bread among the Poor, and did some other Acts of Charity.

Mr. John Westley came next, about six Weeks afterwards. He preached publickly, as his Brother had done; and before he left them he proposed the establishing of a Society; (which Society at present, in Wednesbury and in the neighbouring Parishes, consists of near Two hundred People) into which each Person that enter'd was to pay a certain Sum, and to subscribe weekly, according to his Ability: He likewise proposed a Subscription amongst them towards the building a Place of Worship or a Tabernacle, as they rather chose to call it. These Propositions differing very widely from what had been declared at the first setting out, began to open the Eyes of the serious and thinking sort of People. After Mr. John Westley, came one Williams, a Man not in Orders, but said to be sent by Westley, and to come from Wales, who in his publick Harangues vilified the Orders of the Church of England, and the whole Body of the Clergy, calling them dumb Dogs, that would not bark; and that they pretended, when they offer'd themselves for Holy Orders, to be moved by the Holy Ghost, but that it was all a mere Farce, and that they knew nothing of the Influence of the Holy Spirit. After him came a Bricklayer, and then a Plumber and Glazier, both said to come from London, who Both publickly prayed and usurp'd the Office of a Preacher. Every three weeks or Month, one of the Mr. Westleys, or of the other Persons now mentioned, came amongst them. Some of the Doctrines they propagated, were, That every Person must have an absolute Assurance of his Salvation, or he would certainly be damn'd; That all who did not adhere to, and follow them, were not in a State of Salvation; and that this had been the Case of our Forefathers for several Generations past; That every true Christian did arrive at such a Degree of Perfection, as to live entirely free from all Sin, and that those who had not made this Progress, were no Christians at all; that every Person must receive the Holy Ghost in a sensible Manner, so as to feel and distinguish all its several Motions, which sometimes would be quite violent.

In consequence of which Doctrine, several People, either through the Force of Imagination, Enthusiasm, or Hypocrisy, would fall down in Fits, under violent Agitations of Body, and make strange hideous Noises. This their Preachers called Conviction, which when they had been under for some time, they then received the Holy Ghost and were assur'd of their Salvation. The Ill Effects of these Doctrines soon appeared: Instead of that Peace, Charity, and Good-will, which their Preachers boasted to be the Fruits thereof; Malice, Spleen, and endless Feuds, sprang up in their room. The Methodists became prejudiced against their lawful Minister, and spoke ill-natur'd and unjustifiable things of him. They likewise, upon every Dispute they had with their Neighbours of the Church of England, would tell them they were eternally damn'd, and even Children would tell their Parents the same. These things exasperated illiterate and unthinking People, and have been the Principal Cause of all the Disturbance that has since happen'd.

The first Insult was given to a small Party of Wednesbury Methodists, as they re-turned form Darlaston singing their Hymns, where they had been at an appointed and stated Place of Meeting: The Persons who assaulted them were Darlaston people, who beat and abused the Methodists, by flinging Stones and Dirt at them. The Methodists applied to a Justice of the Peace, and he granted them a Warrant on this Occasion; but upon hearing the Matter, he told them that they themselves had been the first Beginners and the chief Cause of the Tumult, and might thank themselves for what had happen'd.

Some Time after this, about the middle of Summer, there arose a Mob, consisting of Darlaston and Walsal People and some from Bilston, who broke the Windows of most of the Methodists Houses in Wednesbury, Darlaston, and West-Bromwick. After this their Teachers did not come near them for some Time. The first that came were Greaves and Williams, who preached only in private Houses. In a little Space after that Mr. John Westley ventured again; and the Mob, hearing of it, beset the House where he was, took him Prisoner, and carried him to the House of a Justice of the Peace; but the Justice not caring to act in the Affair, did not think fit to be seen: so the Mob returned with their Prisoner, and after some Insults offered him they set him at Liberty again. After that Greaves and Williams ventur'd to preach publickly as usual; and in Christmas 1743, Mr. Whitfield coming to Birmingham, where there is likewise a Society, was invited over to Wednesbury, where he pub-lickly preached in the Streets for several Days. At last, on Saturday, the 4th of February 1743, Mr. Charles Westley and Williams came to Wednesbury, which was soon spread abroad; and it was rumour'd that a Mob would rise on that Occasion on the Tuesday following, being Shrove-Tuesday. Upon which Mr. Westley and

Williams went off on the Monday; and on the Day following, the Mob, about half of which were said to be Colliers, consisting chiefly of Darlaston people, and some from Bilston, came to Wednesbury, forcibly enter'd the Houses of several Methodists, ransack'd, tore to Pieces, and carried off their Goods, and what they could not carry off they spoil'd notwithstanding their utmost Endeavour to disperse them.

The next Day the Mob rose again, went as far as Aldridge about five Miles off, and committed the same Outrages there; and intended to have proceeded in the same Manner through all the neighbouring Places, where there were any Mehodists; but Wednesbury and Walsall raised a Mob against them, which being superior in Number, overaw'd and dispersed them, and all has remained quiet ever since.

The Damage done by this Mob, according to the best Information amounts to Five Hundred Pounds or upwards.

P.S.   The Mob threatened to pull down the Houses of two of the Gentlemen who endeavour'd to persuade them to disperse, and go to their own Homes.

Document V.4

The Trials of a Caernarvon Schoolmaster

William Edwards, a member of the Independent Church at Pwllheli, was employed by Dr Daniel Williams's trustees at a charity school in Caernarvon. Here he writes to the secretary of the Trustees, giving details of the opposition he faces.

The letter is reprinted from Thomas Rees, London: John Snow, 1883, *History of Protestant Nonconformity in Wales*, pp. 377–9.

Caernarvon, January 3, 1744.
Sir, – I am this day to appear at the Bishop's Court, in Bangor. Mr. William Williams, vicar of Llanbeblig and Caernarvon, has put me in, on the account of my school. He, the said vicar, came the 13th day of August last, about eleven o'clock at night, heading a mob, in a most insulting and riotous manner, to the door of my house, knocked and commanded me to open the door quickly, or else that he would break it. I was just going to bed, and had stripped all to my shirt. I opened the door, and asked him, 'In the name of God, what is the matter?' He answered, 'You shall know, you rascal!' 'Well' said I, 'what is it you want to know?' He gave me foul names, and told me an untruth to my face; namely, that I raised a mob in town. 'How can you tell such a falsehood,' said I. He replied, 'You brought strangers to town, which was the cause of it.' 'That is another falsehood,' said I, 'whoever told it you. Here is fine doings, Mr. Williams! Heading a mob to frighten, abuse, and disturb homes and old people, one seventy years, and the other a blind woman of seventy-four, without the least cause given! What had I ever done against you? What ill have I spoken of you, or wherein have I ever affronted you, that you should thus abuse me?' I argued with him as smoothly as I could, but nothing would do but foul names and foul language, and threatening to do me all the diskindness he could. He said that

he would see me in gaol, if he lived a year longer. He went away at last with the mob when he was weary. As he was going, I said, 'Here is a fine preparation to a Sabbath day's work!' for it was Saturday night he gathered the mob. I argued with him, 'How could I bring strangers to town, that I never knew – never seen their faces in my life before: If there was harm in their coming, they only passed through the town, stayed a quarter of an hour, or less, on horseback at the door; and had they stayed all night, and longer, what harm was in their coming, more than other people? They were honest men!' &c. Now these strangers were two Dissenting ministers from Montgomeryshire, namely, Mr. Lewis Rees, of Llanbyrnmair, and Mr. Jenkin Jenkins, of Llanfyllin,[1] going to Anglesea, to preach at a house recorded there by one William Prichard, of Penmynydd. I met with these gentlemen, and showed them the sign of the 'Boot.' Some enemies took notice of this, and suspected that they were Presbyterians, and that they would be preaching that night somewhere. They went and told the vicar the story, and he raised the said mob to go and search for this preaching; and they have done mischief enough in several places, such as breaking houses, and beating people. Indeed, none of them did me any harm, because he was with them; they left it between him and me, otherwise they would have done mischief enough here, for he was with them nowhere but with me; and so he being with them, God was pleased, by that means, to keep me from further mischief in that foul and stormy night. And now to vent his malice, he has put me in the Bishop's Court, as I said above. This man designs my ruin, and will effect it, if he can. He and the new Chancellor have a mind to extirpate religion out of the country. The Chancellor has now excommunicated a very godly and devout young man, a member of our congregation, for teaching people to read Welsh, and perhaps it will be so with me at last; I do not know what to do, and in this case I am not able to contest with him. I have no money to spend; my salary is too small to maintain me and my old blind wife, and a girl to attend us: food, drink, and clothing, house rent, and firing, being very dear here. It is too small to provide all this; but I must live as well as I can upon it, having nothing in the world besides to live upon. A very poor living it affords; but God be praised for it, as it is, it is better, far better, than I deserve. I have not a penny to spare to contest with him, and defend myself from his tyranny; that he knows very well, and my ruin would be his rejoicing. Therefore, good gentlemen, I humbly crave your assistance, with your advice, how and what I shall do in the case; but I am resolved not to leave the school till they confine me in gaol, as he has threatened. Your speedy answer to this is humbly desired by your afflicted, and most obedient and humble servant,

To Mr. Francis Barkstead,   WILLIAM EDWARDS.

at Hoxton, near London.

Note

1. Afterwards Dr. Jenkins, tutor of the Academy at Caermarthen.

Document V.5

Local Opposition in Lichfield, and George Burder's Response

The Church Book of Lichfield's Congregational Church, begun in the handwriting of the second minister, William Salt, opens with the paragraphs reproduced in extract (a). Extract (b), by George Burder, was presumably occasioned by the 'considerable opposition' his co-religionists of Lichfield endured.

William Salt (1784?–1857) twice held the Lichfield pastorate: Lichfield (1807–31), Erdington (1831–7), Hinckley (1737–49) and Lichfield (1849–57). For Burder (1752–1832), Congregational minister, secretary of the London Missionary Society, and keen supporter of the Religious Tract Society and the British and Foreign Bible Society, see DEB, DNB. For the full context and references see Alan P. F. Sell, 'George Burder and the Lichfield Dissenters', in *idem, Dissenting Thought and the Life of the Churches*, Lewiston, NY: Edwin Mellen Press, 1990, ch. 10.

(a)

The city of Lichfield has been proverbial for ages past in the opposition of its inhabitants to the introduction of the Gospel: so that while the light of Divine Truth was spreading in most other towns in the neighbourhood, the ministers and friends of religion were discouraged in their wishes to come to this place by the cloud of thick darkness which appeared to envelope and surround this city: and even so late as about the year 1780 we cannot hear of more than one poor woman who was in the habit of going out of town several miles to hear the Gospel.

But God who had mercy in store was pleased to hear the prayers of His people on behalf of this place – several persons previous to the year 1790 were brought to a knowledge of the truth, and soon became earnestly desirous to promote the spiritual welfare of their friends and neighbours; they therefore with the advice and encouragement of ministers and Christian friends, engaged a building in Tunstalls yard in Sandford Street; this was repaired and fitted up for public worship. In July 1790 this place was opened by the Rev. G. Burder of Coventry and the Rev. J. Moody of Warwick, and continued to be supplied by neighbouring ministers or by a minister stationary for a time in Lichfield until 1796. During this period very little success appeared to attend the endeavours, the congregation was reduced to so small a number, that it was determined to desist from regular preaching, and soon after the attempt was given up, and the place shut up for several years.

Now the enemy triumphed, and those few who had favoured the meeting were at times shamefully treated on the account. About the year 1802 several persons were by the providence of God brought to reside in the town and neighbourhood, who were much concerned to have the preaching of the Gospel resumed, and tho' not without considerable opposition, they had the above-mentioned place reopened, and occasional services were again established.

(b)

In the month of January, I composed and printed an answer to a virulent little pamphlet published at Lichfield by the opposers of the Gospel. The controversy, provoked by a clergyman of High-church pretensions, produced results very different from those which he both desired and anticipated. The impression on the public mind was such as to favour the 'furtherance of the Gospel.'

Document V.6

An Early Morning Baptist Service in Norfolk

The Baptist Church at Aylsham, Norfolk, was founded in April 1791, when Joseph Kinghorn baptised two men and three women there. Local opposition prompted the Church to gather secretly for early morning worship, as Kinghorn describes in the following extract.

For Kinghorn (1766–1832), who trained for the ministry at Bristol Baptist College and regarded himself as a Calvinist, but not one of the 'over-high people', see DEB, DNB. The following extract is reprinted from C. B. Jewson, *The Baptists in Norfolk*, London: Carey Kingsgate Press, 1957, p. 63.

At four o'clock I rose, walked down to the river, met a few friends at a place appointed under a willow tree, in proper readiness: we joined together in prayer, begging God's blessing on his own commands, and then went down into the water. ... Besides the silence of the morning, there was a thick fog which hid us from observation ... nor was the voice of anything to be heard to interrupt us or excite any tremor, the birds only were heard who, indeed, filled the air with their music.

Document V.7

The Priestley Riots

On 17 July 1791 John Gwinnell wrote the following letter from Worcester to Robert Preston of Frederick Place, London. The letter is reprinted from John Waddington, *Congregational History 1700–1800*, London: Longmans, Green, 1876, pp. 652–4.

For Priestley see Document I.II above. For the context see David L. Wykes, '"A Finished Monster of the True Birmingham Breed": Birmingham, Unitarians and the 1791 Priestley Riots', in Alan P. F. Sell, ed., *Protestant Nonconformists and the West Midlands of England*, Keele: Keele University Press, 1996, ch. 3.

A few days previous to the meeting of the Revolutionists at Birmingham to celebrate the downfall of French despotism, some very inflammatory handbills were distributed, tending to poison the minds of the lower class against the Established Church and State; and on the evening preceeding the meeting of the 14th July, some people (supposed to be in the interest of Dr. Priestley) had printed in large characters on every church door throughout Birmingham, 'This useless Barn to be let or sold.' This so enraged the friends of the Established Church, that during the time that the

Revolutionists were at dinner at the hotel, a mob surrounded the house, assailed the windows of it with bricks and stones, and obliged the company for a time to retire in great confusion. About six o' clock the rioters had increased to five thousand, and advanced in a body to the house of Dr. Priestley, which they very soon levelled to the ground, and totally destroyed his valuable mathematical instruments, pictures, etc.; and he himself narrowly escaped with his life to Kidderminster. The mob then proceeded to his Meeting-house, which, with two others, were soon in ruins. They continued parading the streets the whole of Thursday night, calling loudly for the head of Priestley, and offering a *handsome reward* for it. On Friday morning their numbers were increased to above twelve thousand. The inhabitants, fearing the dreadful consequences of such a force, did not open their shops or windows all that day or the next, but sent an express to Coventry for the assistance of the military. The Mayor of that city, dreading an insurrection there, remonstrated with the commanding officer of the regiment, and they were restrained from leaving Coventry. This refusal animated with redoubled vigour the enthusiasm of the mob, who immediately attacked the house of Mr. Taylor, an eminent banker, a friend and companion of Dr. P., which they very deliberately unroofed and set on fire, and, with five others, were soon consumed to ashes. The next object of their revenge was a Mr. Russell, a magistrate, who had shown much activity by endeavouring to suppress the riot. His house, with three others, were totally destroyed. Mr. Thomson's house and several others suffered on Friday evening before I left the town. All these depredations were committed without the smallest opposition, and the houses of all suspected persons were searched to find Dr. Priestley, who arrived at Worster from Kidderminster this day, and immediately set off for London. The report since I left Birmingham is, that on Saturday night the town was on fire in seven different places, that part of a regiment of cavalry arrived from the north, and that others were hourly expected; so that we may hope in a short time to hear of a stop being put to these horrid subversions of laws and liberties.

Document V.8

John Harrison's Plan for a Mollifying Liturgy

In 1793 John Harrison published, *Specimens of the Manner in which Public Worship is Conducted in Dissenting Congregations: With a Service for Baptism; the Celebration of the Lord's Supper; and the Burial of the Dead.* His objective was to show that while the doctrines of some Dissenters might not accord with those held by the majority of Christians, their principles and worship posed no threat to civic stability.

John Harrison served at Market Place church, Kendal (by now decidedly Unitarian), from 1796 until his death, aged seventy-two, in 1833. For Harrison see Francis Nicholson and Ernest Axon, *The Older Nonconformity in Kendal*, Kendal: Titus Wilson, 1915, pp. 366–94. The following extract is from pp. 368–70.

That a general odium has been raised against Dissenters, in every part of the Kingdom, can be matter of information to none; for the effects of it have been manifested in a way, disgraceful to a Country that has any pretensions to civilization, or any right to boast of her freedom. The most absurd calumnies, when levelled against *them*, have met with ready credit; and men of truly constitutional principles, whose attachment to their country is firm, and (to say the least of it) equally enlightened with that of their calumniators, have been reproached as inveterate Republicans and enemies to the Constitution both in Church and State.

In many cases it may be the wisdom and duty of the injured, to support the misrepresentations of their enemies with that calm temper, which bespeaks true dignity – but must they, when conscious of the purity of their intentions, hear themselves stigmatised as vipers who carry a sting ready to be plunged into the bosom of the country which nourishes them, and remain silent under the odious imputation? Must they be continually marked out as objects of distrust and suspicion, and rest satisfied without attempting their own justification? Is it not on the contrary, an act of injustice to themselves, and of charity to those, who misrepresent their principles through ignorance, to shew from incontrovertible evidence, that there is nothing in their tenets which can lead them to become enemies to the civil constitution of this Kingdom? Religion and Politics are indeed so distinct from on another, that it seems difficult to conceive how any particular system of religious faith, can be naturally and peculiarly allied to any particular political system. It would be impossible, for instance, to prove that the doctrines of the Established Church are more suitable to the nature of our Government, than those of any other Church whatever. The only inference meant to be drawn from this observation, is, that it is the greatest injustice to charge, indiscriminately, all with disaffection to the *civil*, who from pure motives of Conscience, dissent from *ecclesisastical* establishment of their country.

To prove the injustice of this charge is the Author's principal object. He would long since have attempted it, had not the most effectual mode of attaining it required some deliberation. Appeals have been made to History, by many writers, to prove the invariable attachment of Dissenters to the constitution which was established in the last century; but the prejudices against them have proved too inveterate to give way to these attacks – their fancied disaffection is supposed to arise from their religion; and till the absurdity of this supposition be unmasked, they must still hear the reproaches of all others the most grievous to ingenuous minds.

Under these mortifying circumstances, the following plan was at length suggested and immediately adopted; to lay before the public a set of Prayers agreeing in sentiment, as nearly as possible, with those in general use amongst the rational Dissenters, in their public worship, together with offices for Baptism, administration of the Lord's Supper, &c. These, as they would exhibit a general and accurate view of their religious principles, it was thought, might convince the candid, however they may vary from the creed of others, that they contain nothing that can biass the political opinions of those who use them. Not a single trace will be found of disaffection to that form of Government, under which this nation has so long flourished. On the contrary, upon proper occasions, Dissenters have always been in the habit of petitioning for the continuance of this blessing, in language as earnest and sincere as that of the Established Church.

Document V.9

Samuel Horsley's Invective

Samuel Horsley (1733–1806), bishop of St Asaph, who took up the cudgels on behalf of the Trinity against Priestley, had little patience with Dissenters, whom he regarded as fellow-travellers with those of seditious intent.

For Horsley see DECBP, DNB, ODCC. The following extract (which drew replies from Robert Hall, for whom see Document IV.10 above; and from John Townshend (1757–1826), the Congregational minister at Bermondsey who was beset by Arians on the one side and Antinomians on the other, for whom see DEB, DNB) is reprinted from John Waddington, *Congregational History, Continuation to 1850*, London: Longmans, Green, 1878, pp. 132–3.

In this country, I believe, they know very well that bold undisguised Atheism, proceeding directly and openly to its horrid purpose, will never be successful. They must have recourse, therefore, to cautious stratagem. They must pretend that their object is not to demolish, but reform. And it was with a view of giving colour to this pretence, that the impudent lie, for such I have proved it to be, has been propagated in this country of their reverence for pure Christianity, and for the reformation. In their first attempts in this way, we trust they have been foiled. The Patriarch of the sect is fled, and the orators and oracles of Birmingham and Essex Street are dumb; or if they speak, speak only to be disregarded.

Still the operations of the evening are going on – still going on by stratagem. The stratagem still a pretence of reformation; but the reformation, the very reverse of what was before attempted. Instead of divesting religion of its mysteries, and reducing it to a mere philosophy in speculation, and to a mere morality in practice, the plan is now *to affect a great zeal for orthodoxy;* to make great pretensions to an extraordinary measure of the Holy Spirit's influence; to alienate the minds of the people from the Established clergy, by representing them as sordid worldings; without any concern about the souls of men; indifferent to the religion which they ought to teach, and to which the laity are attached; and destitute of the Spirit of God. *In many parts of the kingdom new conventicles have been opened in great number; and congregations formed of one knows not what denomination.* The pastor is often, in appearance at least, an illiterate peasant, or mechanic. The congregation is visited occasionally by preachers from a distance. Sunday Schools are opened in connection with these conventicles. There is much reason to suspect that the expenses of these schools and conventicles are defrayed by *associations*, formed in different places for the preachers, and schoolmasters are observed to engage in expenses for the support and advancement of their institutions, to which, if we may judge form appearance, their own means must be altogether inadequate. The poor are even bribed by small pecuniary gifts from time to time, to send their children to these schools of, they know not what, rather than to those connected with the Established Church, in which they would be bred in the principles of true religion and loyalty. It is very remarkable that these new congregations of nondescripts have been mostly formed since the Jacobins have been laid under the restraint of those two most salutary statutes, commonly known by the names of the Sedition and the Treason Bill – *a circumstance which gives much ground for suspicion that sedition and Atheism are the real objects of these institutions, rather than religion.* Indeed, in some places, this is known to be the case. In one topic the teachers of all these congregations agree: abuse of the Established clergy, as negligent of their flocks, cold in their preaching, and destitute of the Spirit. In this they are joined by persons of a very different cast; whom a candour, of which they, on their part, set but a poor example, is unwilling to suspect of any ill design; though it is difficult to acquit them of the imputation of an indiscretion in their zeal, which, in its consequences may be productive of mischief very remote, I believe, from their intentions. It is a dreadful aggravation of the dangers of the present crisis in this country, that persons of real piety should, without knowing it, be lending their aid to the common enemy, and making themselves accomplices in a conspiracy against the Lord and against His Christ. The Jacobins of this country, I very much fear, are, at this moment, making a tool of Methodism, just as the illuminées of Bavaria made a tool of freemasonry; while the real Methodist, like the real freemason, is kept in utter ignorance of the wicked enterprise the counterfeit has in hand.

What measures it may become the wisdom of the legislature to adopt to stop the growing evil, is a point on which I shall not touch in this assembly.

Document V.10

William Kingsbury's *An Apology for Village Preachers*

Where the church/chapel divide existed, it was nowhere closer to hand than in the villages of England and Wales. In the following extract from his pamphlet of 1798 Kingsbury, Congregational minister at Above Bar chapel, Southampton, gently advises hostile Anglican clergy that the best way to deal with village preachers is to perform so productive a ministry as to make them redundant.

Kingsbury (1744–1818) studied at Mile End academy under John Conder (1714–81) and Thomas Gibbons (1720–85), for all whom see DNB. The following extract is from John Waddington, *Congregational History, Continuation to 1850*, London: Longmans, Green, 1878, p. 131.

With regard to the clergy of the Establishment, … I hope I have said nothing throughout these sheets disrespectful of those who fulfil their ministry. It has been my happiness, in common with others of my brethren, to be acquainted with some of the order whom we have loved and honoured. We have read the writings of the clergy on various subjects with delight and improvement. We cordially pray for and rejoice in their success in promoting the knowledge of the pure gospel. Glad should we be to see incumbents and their curates going forth on the afternoons and evenings of Sundays, and on the week days, in those villages and hamlets within their own precincts, *where there are no parish churches*; to preach faithfully, and to teach from house to house, the soul-reviving and soul-sanctifying truths of their Articles, Homilies, and Liturgy. *Let them be the leading labourers in this abundant harvest, and gather in as many sheaves as they can; we will follow them as gleaners, to pick up what they leave. Nay, we will go into another part of the wide field where the husbandmen are few, or negligent.* It is not our aim to make proselytes to a party, by preaching about ecclesiastical, any more than civil politics. It is not our wish to bring one man from the Church of England to become a mere notional rigid Dissenter. We are not such bigots as to confine salvation within the pale of a church; but we long for the disobedient to be turned from the error of his way. And, might I be permitted to offer a hint to the clergy of the Establishment, as to the means most likely to be effectual to suppress village preaching by Dissenters, and to revive real religion in the Church of England, and throughout the land, I would say, it is not to misrepresent, malign, and persecute men; but to exceed or equal them in labour, and to render their assistance unnecessary.

The Establishment Question

Daniel Williams on Occasional Conformity

Under the Toleration Act of 1689 Dissenters could, by occasional conformity – that is, by receiving communion in their parish church – qualify for government and civic office. The Toleration Act of 1711, known as the Occasional Conformity Act. (10 Anne, c. 1), was introduced to prevent this practice, and to ensure that those Dissenters who took communion in their parish churches did not thereafter return to their former Dissenting churches. The Presbyterian divine Daniel Williams (1643?–1716), in most things a moderate, took a firm stand against the Act and strongly opposed the principle and practice of occasional conformity.

For Williams see DECBP, DNB, DWB. The following extracts are from a sermon Williams preached at the Merchants' Lecture at Salters' Hall on 22 January 1711–12, reprinted by John Waddington, *Congregational History 1700–1800*, London: Longmans, Green, 1876, pp. 109–10, 112.

For near two hundred years these human impositions have divided the nation, and caused warm and public contests. The consequences are to be lamented; for many thousands of faithful ministers have been silenced from time to time; love among Christians destroyed by mutual censure; many violent persecutions against multitudes, for no pretended crime except Nonconformity; foundations shaken; civil rights hazarded; much time and pains employed about the defence of these inventions, which had otherwise been laid out to the real benefit of souls. From these our Popish enemies have been oft (and still are) encouraged to attempt and hope the restoration of Popery. It is too notorious that very many place the most of their religion and hopes of eternal life in their observance of these, though they remain ignorant and regardless of the essentials of Christianity. By these the most wicked and profane come to be necessitated to receive the Sacrament, and gain a handle to asperse and abuse men who appear to be truly godly. How many persons fit to serve the Government are rendered useless and incapable? These are some of the fruits of our impositions; and yet the *imposers* acknowledge that they are but small things, indifferent matters, no part of worship, not necessary to salvation, and what the Church may alter. Whereas *we*, on the other side, can't, without sinning against the dictates of our consciences, comply with or declare for them; and are persuaded we cannot be faithful to the interest of Christ Jesus, unless we in our stations endeavour a reformation of such *terms* of the Gospel ministry and communion of saints as He never appointed, and both are and will be attended with such pernicious consequences. ...

We find it expressly charged (2 Tim. I. 8) – *Be not ashamed of the testimony of Christ, nor of me, His prisoner*; which informs us that when some are eminently exposed for the testimony of Christ, it is a fault in others to carry towards them, as if ashamed to own them (Heb. x. 33; 2 Tim.iv. 10, 16). To apply this to our case. Such of you as shall now forsake our public Assemblies, do refuse to share in the reproach of our incapacity for public offices, for you desert them to continue your public employment in a time when those who are present in them are not allowed to be in any office. If all we Dissenters were in office, then all these public Assemblies must cease, and be reduced to the number of nine persons at most (besides the family). For why may not all such do the same as you? Moreover, by absenting from our Assemblies, you withhold from them whatever reputation, safety, strength, and assistance your presence would afford.

Document V.12

Isaac Watts's Reception of Locke on Toleration

John Locke's *A Letter Concerning Toleration* (1689) was cordially welcomed by numerous Dissenters – not least by Isaac Watts (for whom see Document I.2 above), who declared (*Works*, Leeds: Edward Baines, 1800, V, p. 503) that it

led me as it were into a new region of thought, wherein I found myself surprised and charmed with truth. There was no room to doubt in the midst of sun-beams. These leaves triumphed over all the remnant of my prejudices on the side of bigotry, and taught me to allow all men the same freedom to choose their religion, as I claim to choose my own.

Document V.13

Isaac Watts on the Blessing of Religious Liberty

The following self-explanatory extract is from Watt's *Works*, Leeds: Edward Baines, 1800, III, p. 167.

Let us again give thanks to our God, who has so formed our civil constitution and government, at this day, that we have liberty to worship God, through Jesus Christ the Mediator, in his own appointed ways; that we are not persecuted from corner to corner, but in every place, we are permitted to erect synagogues for divine service, and to attend on our God in those ordinances, on which he has stamped his own name. How many scattered Christians are there up and down in the popish nations, where they are forbid to meet in any place for the solemnizing of true Christian worship? How many nations are there where the places of protestant worship are utterly demolished, and Christians are not suffered to unite their prayers and praises to the God whom they adore, in spirit and in truth? Let us yet again give thanks to God, that, in the course of his providence, we have convenient places to assemble for his pure religion; that we are provided with so many advantages, that we are not exposed to the inconveniences of wind, or rain, or sultry seasons, and are secured from the disturbances of a sinful world. Let us bless God, that he has so plentifully stored the provinces of this land, with such buildings, that we are not exposed to the labour and the hardships of long travel, which was a burdensome ceremony imposed on the Jews, who were required to wait upon their God *three times a year*, where he recorded his name, at Shiloh, or at Jerusalem; but we may meet him nearer at hand, and receive his public blessings, in so many of the streets of this great city, and in so many of the towns and villages of the British isles.

And you, my friends of this congregation, have abundant occasion and reason for thankfulness, that God by his providence has based your assembly in so convenient a place, wherein you begin this day to pay him your worship. May you long enjoy it in undisturbed peace! O blessed be his name, that many of you have found God with you in former places of assembling, and that you are daily training up under his divine instructions and blessings, for the worship and happiness of the heavenly state, and for his more joyful and immediate presence.

Document V.14

Thomas Reynolds on the Schism Bill

With the Schism Bill nearing the statute books, many Dissenting preachers turned to pertinent texts and ardent prayer. Among these was the Presbyterian minister Thomas Reynolds's (1667?–1727), who preached on Ecclesiastes 7: 14 at St Helens. Reynolds was educated under Charles Morton at Newington Green academy, and then at Geneva under Turretine and Utrecht under Witsius.

For Reynolds and Morton (1627–98) see DNB. The following extracts from Reynolds's sermon are reprinted from John Waddington, *Congregational History 1700–1800*, London: Longmans, Green, 1876, pp. 155–7, 159.

My brethren, this being the first opportunity we have had, both ministers and our several congregations, to unite our prayers, since a law so much to our disadvantage has obtained the royal assent; and it falling to my turn, according to our usual quarterly course, to preach to you, I confess it has given me much thought what I should say in the present juncture, and upon the most melancholy occasion that has happened since my entrance upon the ministry. I hope I can truly say, I am desirous to know my duty, and faithfully to practise it, as I am also to direct and assist you to my power in what I think to be yours. I am sensible there are two things which we that are employed in the ministry do greatly need, and for which I am satisfied my brethren do concur with me in begging your prayer. These are *wisdom and courage:* the one, that we may not in anything baulk or flinch from our duty; the other, that we may not transgress or go beyond it. I would not offend in either extreme. I shall now do what I think to be my part, and leave it with God.

I cannot, therefore, forbear saying, that whoso shall consider the present face of things with respect to us *Protestant Dissenters;* the steps that have been lately taken with success against us; in how tender a part we are now affected, over and above what we were before by the Bill to prevent Occasional Conformity; how far we are abridged of those privileges we had for many years enjoyed with very little inter- ruption; how many are in danger of immediate ruin, or of making shipwreck of a good conscience to preserve themselves form it , to the great scandal of religion and the grief of good people: again, whoso shall reflect how we are joined with the Papists, and put upon the same foot with them, as if equally threatening danger to the Established Church, and that the design of the present law is to take care that whatever liberty be granted for the present to us, our posterity shall be effectually debarred of it; how God also is removing from us those that have been most eminent and useful , whilst men are doing what they can to deprive us of a succession in their room; whoso shall add to this, how we are all of us now exposed to the censures and insults of the ignorant multitude, being set forth as wicked schismatics, and this, too, with such aggravations as I know not whether it be advisable for me to mention, and therefore shall leave it to your own recollection. Finally, whoso shall further consider the improvements bad men may make of this law, by straining it to the great vexation and disturbance of innocent people; whoso, I say, will allow himself time sedately and seriously to think of these things, will, I believe, unless he be very stupid, admit it to be a *day of affliction* and adversity with us.

Our duty at such a time is to '*consider*,' not barely to pore upon our affliction, but in order that we may know what we are to do, and how we are to behave ourselves at such a time.

Consider the nature of our affliction. What is now come upon us is a further ad- dition to what has been done by a former law, by means of which many have already fallen under great hardships. Some have been exposed to great temptations for the sake of a livelihood; others have been debarred from joining in public worship with their brethren; and many families have been actually reduced to great difficulties and straits. How much this *new law* is like farther to affect us, a little time will begin to discover. This does not only renew our sorrow, but our troubles are enlarged and rendered much heavier, as this new law does, in my opinion, strike deeper than any- thing that hath yet been framed against us.

What can go nearer our hearts than to be debarred the opportunity (as many will now be) of giving our children a free and liberal education, and of fitting them for that service in their generation which they are capable of ? What can more sensibly affect us than the not being allowed to breed them up in our own way, which we and others must think we are bound to do so long as *in our consciences we judge* to be most agreeable to the mind and will of God? How can we but be deeply concerned whilst we are obliged either to deliver our children to be instructed and educated in a way that is dissonant from us, or to keep them in ignorance of the *learned sciences*, so as at the best they shall be only capable of living by mechanical arts and labour, and in time, through decay of knowledge, become fit to be made, as the poor

Gibeonites, 'hewers of wood and drawers of water'? What an affliction this is, everyone that has children can sensibly judge. What grief and difficulties this must expose many thousands to, who does not apprehend? Consider, *whence all this evil is come upon us.*

It is natural and but too common with us to stop at second causes, and to carry our reflections no farther than the instruments of our troubles, upon whom *we are apt to bestow too plentifully our invectives, and sometimes to launch forth into those indecencies which the Christian religion (an institution of meekness and patience) does by no means encourage.* I own we ought to maintain very feeling apprehensions of the afflictions and hardships that are upon us, that we may the more reverence the Providence of God, and at the same time testify to men that we are not insensible of their displeasure; but, then, in expressing our resentment, we are to take care we do not exceed those bounds religion has set us, and should make our *principal business to observe the Hand of God in our adversity*, by whose permission these evils are come upon us, and without which it were not in the power of any creature to do us the least hurt or damage. ...

Why, after so many years' peaceable enjoyment that has been granted us, should our brethren be so very angry with us? What have we done to deserve these hardships we are laid under? Will any say we are enemies to the Civil Constitution and Government? We solemnly profess we are not; and for proof of this, we appeal to all the world about us, to all that know our principals and behaviour. If, after this, we may not be believed, we have no more to say, but refer ourselves to the *great Searcher of Hearts.*

Is it for our Dissent from the Established Church? How can we help dissenting, whilst those things are required and imposed which we cannot conform to without sin? Will they, by an instituted and unnecessary imposition, *force us to Dissent*, and then *punish* us for dissenting? We pray them to think of our affliction.

Document V.15

The Title Deeds of Selandine Nook Baptist Church

The following document, couched in terms designed to meet prevailing legal requirements, is typical of many in that the reference is frequently to 'Protestant Dissenters' rather than to 'Baptists'. It is reprinted from Anon., *Foundations*, Halifax: Edward Mortimer, 1933, pp. 62–4.

This indenture made the Seventh day of February in the year of our Lord one thousand seven hundred and forty two in the sixteenth year of the reign of our Sovereign Lord George the Second by the Grace of God of Great Britain France and Ireland. King Defend' of the Faith etc *Between* Joseph Morton of Saladine Nook in the parish of Huddersfield and County of York, Yeoman, and John Morton of the same place, Clothier, Edmund Morton of Intakehead in the parish aforesaid Clothier. Stephen

Brook of Elland in the parish of Halifax aforesaid, Chapman John Greenwood the elder of Sowerby in the parish of Halifax aforesaid Yeoman, and James Hargreaves of Hepton Bridge, Shallooner on the other part *Witnesseth* that for and in consideration of the sum of five shillings of lawful money of Great Britain to the said Joseph Morton in hand paid by the said John Morton, Edmund Morton, Stephen Brook, John Greenwood, James Hargreaves or some or one of them before the sealing and delivery of these presents the receipt whereof is hereby acknowledged and for other good and valuable causes him thereunto moving he the said Joseph Morton Hath granted assigned and conformed and by these presents doth grant, assign and conform unto the said John Morton, Edmund Morton, Stephen Brook, John Greenwood and James Hargreaves and their survivors during the term of nine hundred years now ensuing the date hereof that new erected chapel or meeting house with seventwo square yards of ground hereunto adjoining and being at IntakeHead in the said parish of Huddersfield which said chapel or meeting house is for the use of the Protestant dissenters usually called by the name of Baptists. To have and to hold the new erected chapel or meeting house together with the said parcel of land thereunto adjoining to the said John Morton, Edmund Morton, Stephen Brook, John Greenwood and James Hargreaves and their survivors during the said term of nine hundred years to be fully compleated and ended yielding and paying yearly and every year during the said term unto the said Joseph Morton his heirs and assigns the yearly rent of one peppercorn if demanded. And the said John Morton, Edmund Morton, Stephen Brook, John Greenwood, James Hargreaves the survivor and survivors of them shall hereafter during the said term of nine hundred years when and so often as needs shall require by and with such collection or other contributions, as shall from time to time be made by and amongst the said protestant dissenters take a special care that the said new erected chapel or meeting house be kept in good and sufficient repair that the same be kept fit and commodious for a chapel or meeting house for the said Protestant Dissenters in a religious worship and upheld and continued for the said use and to and for no other intent and purpose whatsoever during the said term and to the intent that there may be a due constant and perpetual execution (during the said term) of the trusts aforesaid. It is declared and agreed by and between the parties aforesaid to these presents that the said Joseph Morton for himself and his heirs Exors and admins, and every of them doth covenant grant and agree to and with the said John Morton, Edmund Morton, Stephen Brook, John Greenwood and James Hargreaves and the survivor and survivors of them by these presents in manner following. That is to say that at such time or times and all times during the said term when and so often as the number of the Trustees aforesaid shall by death or otherwise come or happen to be but only two or fewer it shall and may be lawful to and for the then surviving trustee or trustees by and with the assistance and approbation of the Minister Pastour or Teacher of the said Protestant Dissenters for the time being to be assembled in the said new chapel to elect and nominate so many other persons as shall make up the then surviving trustee or trustees five or more in number which new elected trustees and the survivors of them shall from time to time and at all times during the said term be employed and concerned in the execution and performance of all and every the Trusts aforesaid and from time to time during the said term have the like full power privilege and authority of nominating and electing other persons to succeed in power and trust aforesaid. In witness whereof the said Joseph Morton hath hereunto set his hand and seal the day and year above expressed.

S. S. & D. in the presence of

John Denton.

David Crosley.

Jos. Miller. Joseph Morton

[The following endorsement is appended to the Deed]

Memorandum. Before the sealing and delivery of these presents we the within mentioned Trustees do agree that we will on our part perform the covenants and agreements relating to us as witness to our hands.

John Morton.

Edmund Morton.

Stephen Brook.

John Greenwood.

James Hargreaves.

Document V.16

Samuel Chandler Declines the Blandishments of the Establishment

Samuel Chandler (1693–1766), a Presbyterian divine with Arian leanings, was a contemporary of Butler and Secker at Samuel Jones's academy at Tewkesbury, completing his studies at Leiden. He proceeded from bookselling to book writing, and ministered at Old Jewry, London.

For Chandler see DECBP, DNB. The following extract is from Thomas Amory's preface to *Sermons … by the late Reverend Samuel Chandler*, I, 1768, p. xii.

[T]he high reputation which [Chandler] had gained, by his defences of the Christian religion, procured him from some of the governors of the established church, the offers of considerable preferments, which he nobly declined. He valued more than these the liberty and integrity of his conscience, and scorned for any worldly considerations to profess as divine truths, doctrines which he did not really believe, and to practice in religion, what he did not inwardly approve. An honourable sacrifice to truth and honesty, and well compensated by the affection and generosity of his people; as far as such sacrifices are recompensed on this side of the grave.

Document V.17

Micaijah Towgood contra the Establishment

Micaijah Towgood (for whom see Document III.30 above) was a noted opponent of the theory of Church Establishments. He had published *The Dissenter's Apology* in 1739, but returned to the theme following the appearance of three letters *To a Gentleman Dissenting from the Church of England* (1743, 1745, 1745). These were by John White (1685–1755), vicar of Ospringe, Kent (for whom see *Alumni Cantabrigienses*, compiled by John and J. A. Venn, Cambridge: CUP, 1922, I, iv). Towgood's response is *The Dissenting Gentleman's Answer to the Reverend Mr. White's three letters; in which a separation from the Establishment is fully justified; the Charge of Schism is refuted and retorted; and the Church of England and the Church of Jesus Christ, are impartially compared, and set in Contrast, and found to be Constitutions of a quite Different Nature*, 1746. A *Second Letter* followed in 1747, and a *Third and Last Letter* in 1748. Extract (a) is from the *Answer*, pp. 30–32; extract (b) is from the *Third and Last Letter*, p. 21.

(a)

Now here, Sir, I am pressed with an *insuperable Difficulty* how to reconcile this Constitution of the *Church of England* with the Constitution of the *Church of Christ*. Are they not most indisputably *two different* Societies, subject to *two different*, sometimes *opposite*, Authorities, animated and governed by *two different* Heads? In CHRIST's *Church*, HIMSELF is the *only* Sovereign and Head; HE only hath Power to decree Ceremonies and Rites, to fix Terms of Communion and Authority in Points of Faith: Nor hath any *earthly Prince* Power to make Laws in *his* Kingdom, which shall bind the Consciences of *his* Subjects; or sovereignly to dictate to *his* Servants and Ministers what they shall believe, and what they shall preach. Yea, *his Subjects* are expressly commanded and charged to receive nothing as *Doctrine of Parts of Religion*, which are only *Commandments of Men*.

But in the *Church of England* there is ANOTHER *Sovereign, Law-giver*, SUPREME HEAD besides JESUS CHRIST, an *Authority* which commands Things which CHRIST never commanded, which teaches Doctrines HE never taught, which enjoins Terms of Communion, and Rites of religious Worship, which CHRIST never enjoined. What now can I judge, Sir! What do you yourself judge! but that the *two Churches* are two distinct and *quite different* Societies (for in *one* and *the same* Society, surely there cannot be TWO *Supreme Heads*), that they are framed after different Models, consist of different Members, are governed by different Officers, Statutes, and Laws. Consequently, my SEPARATION or DISSENT from *the one*, does, by no Means infer my SEPARATION from *the other*. Yea, what am I to judge but that by the Allegiance I owe to CHRIST my ONLY *supreme Head* and *King* in spiritual Matters, I am *obliged* to enter my Protest against the Pretensions and Claims of any OTHER *supreme Head*. For, can a Man *serve two Masters?* Can he be subject at the same Time to TWO *supreme Heads?* Can he be faithful to CHRIST, the *only* KING in the Church, and yet acknowledge ANOTHER *King*, as a Fountain of all Magistracy and Power therein? Surely he cannot.

Permit me, good Sir, to exercise your Patience a Moment or two more upon this remarkable *Contrast*, and I will dismiss the ungrateful Subject.

By the Constitution of the *Church of Christ*, tis expressly ordered and declared – That *the* WOMAN *shall not be suffered publickly to teach, nor to usurp Authority over the Man*. But the WOMAN is permitted *publickly to teach*, yea, to limit and controul in *spiritual* and *religious* Matters, and authoritatively to INSTRUCT all the *Bishops*, and *Clergy*, and *Men* in the Land. Thus did Queen *Eliz.* thus did Queen *Anne*, and thus hath *every Queen* Authority to do that sits upon our Throne; Authority to *prescribe* and *dictate* to all, both Ministers and People, what the one are to preach, and the other to receive. And was it not, Sir, a very comely and edifying Sight, to behold the two Houses of Convocation waiting upon the good *Queen (Anne)* in the Case of *Whiston's* Books upon the Trinity, to be *instructed* by her Majesty, whether they were to be condemned as *heretical*, or not. That venerable and learned Body had solemnly decreed them to be *dangerous* and *heretical;* but this their *Censure* was of no Force, till they had laid it before *the Queen*, to have *her* Judgement upon the Point. Upon her Majesty's Determination it entirely depended, whether *Whiston's* Tenets were to be *rejected* by the *Church of England* as erroneous, or not. Her Majesty, in the Case, was of a different Opinion from her two Houses of Convocation; she thought not fit to censure the Books: So her single Opinion, strange to relate! her single Opinion carries it against that of *her Bishops* and *Clergy*. She over-rules and sets aside all their Proceedings, *restrains* and *counteracts* them in one of the very chief of their *Pastoral* Functions, the guarding against Errors and Heresies in the Church.

Behold here, Sir, a WOMAN exercising spiritual ecclesiastical Authority over *the Man!* Yea, behold *the Representative* of the Clergy of the whole Land, a most learned, grave and venerable Body, waiting upon A WOMAN, to learn from her Mouth, what *the Church* is to believe, and what to reject, as to this great *Mystery of Faith:* Upon A WOMAN who could be supposed to know as little of this Matter as of the Motion of the Stars; yet, by her sole Determination, (I repeat it with Astonishment, and you hear it, no doubt, with Perplexity and Grief) *your Church* was uncontroulably and authoritatively directed in this deep and mysterious Point.

I ask you, Sir, in the *Name of* GOD, Is *this* the Constitution and Frame of the *Church of* CHRIST? Is it not *a Constitution* of a quite different Nature; a Society not DIVINELY, but *humanly* instituted; and, therefore, by your own Definition, NOT the *Church of Christ?* And may not, think you, a Person separate from it, without any the least Danger of thereby separating himself from the one scriptural, apostolic, and catholic Church? ...

(b)

What you call then the *ecclesiastical* is really, you see, no other than a Branch or Limb of the *civil* Constitution; and what you call the *Church* is in truth no more an *essential*, much less *an half* Part of our CONSTITUTION, than the *Treasury*, the *Army* ,or either of the *Courts* of *Westminster-hall*. Should, now, the Wisdom of the *Legislature* think proper to new form any of these *Constitutions;* for instance, the Method of dispensing Justice in any of our *Law-Courts* (which *Courts*, by the way, are all of much longer standing than the Constitution of our present *Church*) by which a Saving would arise of vast Sums to the Public, and *Justice* be dispensed in a more *rational* and *easy* way: Would you not smile to hear some zealous Gentlemen of the Robe stand forth and insist, – *That these* COURTS *were an essential and an half Part of the* CONSTITUTION; *and that therefore whoever mov'd for, or so much as wish'd, an* ALTERATION *in either of them, could not be safely trusted with any Share of the public Power, and was really in Truth an Enemy to the* STATE – ? The learned Gentlemen of that Robe, Sir, no doubt, alike smile to hear you thus reasoning as to the *Church.*

Document V.18

Joseph Priestley contra Religious Establishments

For Priestley see Document I.11 above. On a number of occasions Priestley inveighed against religious establishments. In his *Lettres physiques et morales sur les montagnes et sur l'histoire de la terre de l'homme* (1778), the Swiss geologist and meterologist Jean André De Luc (1727–1817) lodged a number of objections against Priestley's *Disquisitions relating to Matter and Spirit*, 1777. The following is Priestley's reply to one such objection. It is in the preface to the second edition of his *Disquisitions*, (1782), in his *Works*, London: 1817–31, III, pp. 214–15.

M. De Luc seems willing to allow that I might be justified in publishing my opinions, provided I were *persecuted* for them, which he says I am not, except so far as I am excluded by them from all preferment in the church. And he takes this occasion of intimating, that I may not have sufficiently considered the necessity of some *establishment of religion*, in order to prevent controversy in the public exercises of it. I answer, that I wish to have nothing to do with any establishment of religion by civil power. Our Saviour and the apostles certainly never looked to any such thing. They made no provision for it, and Christianity did much better when, for three hundred years it had no such support, than it has since done with it; notwithstanding there were sects enow among Christians in those ages, and therefore the inconvenience which M. De Luc so much dreads, must have affected them, as well as it does us.

But, in fact, establishments have not removed this inconvenience, if it be any. Few sectaries differ more form one another than members of the church of England do contrive to differ among themselves. The same is the case in the church of Rome. The doctrines publicly preached in the pulpits of the church of England are just as different from one another as those in Dissenting congregations. M. De Luc is a foreigner, and therefore may not be acquainted with the fact, but it is notorious. I think, therefore, he would be at some loss to shew what *good end* the establishment of religion in this country answers. I will undertake to point out to him many *bad* ones. On the other hand, let him look to America, and say what evils have arisen from a want of establishments. ...

Document V.19

Richard Price on Toleration and Religious Liberty

For Price see Document I.9 above. The following extracts are from *The Evidence for a future Period of Improvement in the State of Mankind, With the Means and Duty of promoting it, Represented in a Discourse, Delivered of Wednesday the 25th of April, 1787, At the Meeting-House in the Old Jewry, London, To the Supporters of a new Academical Institution among Protestant Dissenters*, 1787. The academy was that at Hackney (1786–96), where Price himself served briefly as tutor.

In philosophical knowledge, great advances have been lately made. New fields of philosophy have been opened since the time of Sir ISSAC NEWTON. Our ideas of the extent and grandeur of the universe have been carried much farther than he carried them, and facts in the system of nature discovered, which could they have been intimated to him, would have been pronounced by him impossible. Standing on his shoulders and assisted by his discoveries we see farther than he did. How daring then would be the man who should say, that our successors will not see farther than we do?

This increase of natural knowledge must be accompanied with more enlarged views and liberal sentiments in religion; and we find that this has been its effect. There is, indeed, no circumstance in the present state of the world which promises more than the liberality in religion which is now prevailing. God be thanked, the burning times are gone; and a conviction of the reasonableness of universal toleration is spreading fast. Juster notions also of the origin and end of civil government are making way; and an experiment is now making by our brethren on the other side of the Atlantic of the last consequence, and to which every friend of the human race must wish success. There a total separation of religion from civil policy has taken place, which will probably read a lesson to the world that will do it infinite service. Alliances between church and state and slavish hierarchies are losing credit, long experience having taught their mischief. The nature of religious liberty is better understood than ever. In the last century, those who cried out the loudest for it meant only liberty for themselves because the advocates of truth. But there is now a conviction prevailing that all encroachments on the rights of conscience are pernicious and impious; that the proper office of the civil magistrate is to *maintain peace*; not to support *truth*. – To defend the *properties* of men, not to take care of their *souls*. – And to protect *equally* all honest citizens of all persuasions, not to set up one religious sect above another.

Sentiments so reasonable must continue to spread. They promise an open and free stage for discussion, and general harmony among the professors of Christianity. O happy time! when bigotry shall no more persecute the sincere enquirer, and every one shall tolerate as he would wish to be himself tolerated …

I have been shewing you how much the state of the world encourages you. A spirit of enquiry is gone forth. A disdain of the restraints imposed by tyrants on human reason prevails. A tide is set in. A favourable gale has sprung up. Let us seize the auspicious moment, obey the call of Providence, and join our helping hands to those of the friends of science and virtue, – Think not, however, that you have no difficulties to encounter. It will not be strange if an alarm should be taken about the danger of the church. There is a jealousy natural to church establishments (especially when undermined by time and the spread of knowledge) which may produce such an alarm. In this case it would be a most unreasonable alarm, for if our religious establishment can bear discussion, and stands on good ground as its friends must believe, what harm can be done to it by an institution, the design of which is, not to inculcate the peculiarities of any sect, but to communicate such general instruction, and to promote such a spirit of enquiry and candour, as shall form worthy citizens for the state, and useful ministers for the church? – This, however, is a consideration that will not prevent opposition. The enemies of reformation may be alarmed. Ignorance and intolerance may clamour. But their opposition cannot be successful. The liberal temper of the times must overpower them. Bigotry and superstition must vanish before increasing light. We see the clouds scattering. We live in happier times than our fore-fathers. The shades of night are departing. The day dawns; and the Sun of righteousness will soon rise with healing in his wings. Let us keep our attention fixed on this reviving prospect. Animated by it, let us persevere in our exertions, knowing that, as far as we are on the side of liberty and virtue, we are on the side which must at last prevail.

Let us, however, at the same time take care not to forget a caution which I have before given, and cannot too often repeat. While we proceed in our exertions with perseverance and zeal, let them be accompanied with peaceableness, and dispositions perfectly charitable.- Some of our fellow-christians are eagerly maintaining a pre-eminence in the Christian church, which Christ has prohibited; and struggling to preserve the power they claim as interpreters of Christ's laws, and kings in his kingdom. They either do not see the great change that is going forward; or, if they *do* see it, they have not the wisdom to suit their conduct to it, and to prepare for its effects. – Others of our brethren continue to hold as sacred some of the doctrines of the dark ages. The mist, which opening day is dispersing, still lurks round them. Imagining the acceptance of the Deity to be confined within the circle of their own faith, they cannot view mankind with the same satisfaction that we do. They have not yet felt the chearing power of a religion which makes nothing essential but an honest heart; and they look, perhaps with pain on your attempts to serve the cause of truth and piety. But though, in this respect less happy than ourselves and as we think not so well informed, they may be truly worthy; and we should learn not to condemn them, whatever sentiments, with respect to us, a mistaken Judgement may lead them to entertain.

My own experience has induced me to speak thus to you. I have been an object of censure for actions which I consider as some of the best in my life. But being conscious that I have meant well, and believing that I have not laboured quite in vain, the censure I have met with has made no impression on me. I look back with complacency; and I look forward with joy, in hope of a time when those good men who now dislike me on account of the difference of our religious opinions and views, will be as ready to embrace me as I am to embrace them.

Document V.20

Andrew Kippis contra Subscription

Andrew Kippis (1725–95), Presbyterian minister, was trained under Philip Doddridge at Northampton academy, and eventually served the congregation at Princes Street, Westminster, where he remained for forty-three years. He taught at the Hoxton and Hackney academies.

For Kippis see BCE, DECBP, DNB. For Doddridge see Document I.1 above. The following extract is from his *A Vindication of the Protestant Dissenting Ministers, With Regard to their late Application to Parliament*, London, 1773, pp. 29–30.

We dissent, because we deny the right of any body of men, whether civil or ecclesiastical, to impose human tests, creeds, or articles; and because we think it our duty, not to submit to any such imposition, but to protect against it, as a violation of our essential liberty to judge and act for ourselves in matters of religion. We dissent because we apprehend that the church of England, in requiring a subscription to her doctrines and ceremonies, claims and exercises a power derogatory to the honour of our great Master, the sole legislator in this own kingdom; and because we believe ourselves bound, as his professed disciples and subjects, to stand up for his honour, in opposition to all encroachments upon his undivided, incommunicable authority.

Independently, therefore, of the truth of the Thirty-nine Articles, the generality of Dissenting Ministers object to the imposition of these Articles. Persuaded as they are of the sufficiency of Scripture, and of the liberty which every one ought to have of following the guidance of his own conscience in religious concerns, they will not susbscribe to human formularies, which they themselves believe, when such formularies are pressed upon them by an incompetent and usurped authority.

Document V.21

The Protestant Dissenter's Catechism

The *Catechism* was the work of Samuel Palmer (1741–1813), biographer of Nonconformity, who studied under Caleb Ashworth at Daventry. The order of the clauses in the answer to the first question is interesting: an older Arian might have placed the sufficiency of Scripture in first place; an evangelical might have placed the second clause first; but many rational divines would have approved of Palmer's order.

For Palmer see DNB. For Ashworth see Document II.11 above. The following extract is from *The Protestant Dissenter's Catechism, Containing I. A Brief History of the Nonconformists: II. The Reasons of the Dissent from the National Church. Designed To instruct and establish Young persons among the Dissenters in the Principles of Nonconformists*, London, 1773, pp. 23–4.

Q.1 *What are the* grand principles *on which the Protestant Dissenters* ground their separation *from the church by law established?*

A. The right of private judgement and liberty of conscience, in opposition to all human authority in matters of religion; the acknowledgement of Christ alone as head of his church, and the sufficiency of the holy scriptures as the rule of faith and practice.

Q.2 *Doth not the scripture require us to be* subject to the civil magistrate as the minister of God, for conscience sake?

A. Not in matters of religion, much less in things contrary to the law of God, for God cannot deny himself; so that all human laws, which are inconsistent with the divine, ought to be disobeyed.

Q.3 *But is every private man* to judge for himself, *whether the laws of his country are agreeable to the laws of God?*

A. Certainly in the affairs of religion, every man ought to judge for himself, since every man must give an account of himself to God, who has given us an infallible rule in his word to guide us, and reasonable faculties to understand it; which private persons are as capable of using, to discover the way of truth and duty, as magistrates and large bodies of men. Besides, religion is a personal thing, and no further deserves the name than as it is the effect of conviction and choice.

Document V.22

Theophilus Lindsey on the Outcome of the Feathers Tavern Petition

Theophilus Lindsey (1723–1808), vicar of Catterick and friend of Priestley, was a sponsor of the Feathers Tavern Petition which was presented to Parliament on 6 February 1772, the object of which was to abolish subscription to the Thirty-nine Articles of Religion in favour of an affirmation of belief in the Bible. The petition failed, Edmund Burke being its principal opponent. Embracing Unitarian views, Lindsey left the Church of England in 1773, and removed to London where from April 1774 he preached in a room in Essex Street which had been acquired with the help of Price, Priestley and others.

For Lindsey see BCE, DECBP, DNB, ODCC. The following extract from a letter to W. Turner records Lindsey's eyewitness account of the second hearing of the Petition, on 5 May 1774. It is reprinted from H. McLachlan, *Letters of Theophilus Lindsey*, Manchester: University of Manchester Press, 1920, pp. 49–51.

My business is to tell you that we have had a debate in the Commons this day of betwixt three and four hours, serious and important in many respects, thought not so successful as we could have wished. For the clerical Petitioners, Sir William Meredith opened the cause well, upon the increasing hardships of the petitioning clergy, the contradiction of the doctrines they were to subscribe, the contradiction of their adversaries to each other and their inconsistency – instancing in the

Calvinism of our Reformers and the Arminianism of our present Church – its Doctors, Tucker, Warburton, and Tottie, were particularly named. Happily for the debate, though plainly against the will of the Ministry, Sir Roger Newdigate got up with his usual zeal, and played off his ammunition of Feby. 1772 – the martyr Charles, etc., with some little additional matter against the proto-martyr of Essex Street. This little fling, which was less angry than could have been expected, was over and above compensated for by the kinder construction of others. Lord North spoke out – his old argument – the disturbing things that were well – the few that were dissatisfied, only one had quitted the Church, and another, Evanson of Tewkesbury, under prosecution – the clergy of the present Church the most learned and harmonious that ever were – no Petitioners now, only a motion of Sir W. M. for they knew not who. Sir Geo. Saville replied in a most serious manner, and like a Christian, that it was not a matter of political expediency, but of high moral importance; but his voice was so feeble, and I at a distance, that I heard imperfectly. Mr. Edmund Burke go up, made some reply to Sir George, pleaded for a strict establishment narrowly watched, but with the most unbounded toleration to the Dissenters. Dwelt much on the present prosecution of Evanson, spoke highly of his moral character, but severely against him or any one else making alterations in the Liturgy, or, in the pulpit, contradicting the reading-desk. I was sorry to see this pass as the sense of the House, because it may distress some of my friends and encourage Mr. Evanson's prosecutors. Lord Geo. Cavendish got up – answered him well on the point of the necessity of a review of our Establishment, and relaxing our subscription – manly, and like a serious Christian throughout, but recurred at last to his plan on Feb. 6, 1772, of that House recommending it to the King to put the bishops on meeting the reformation that was so much wanted. Lord Caermarthen, the D. of Leeds' son, next spoke, and did very well on the court side for so young a man, pleading for an adherence to both our civil and religious establishments, with an allowance of toleration to Dissenters. Mr. Fred Montagu replied very well to him, and to some things dropped from Sir Roger Newdigate; spoke warmly and handsomely in behalf of the motion referring the matter to a Committee of Religion, which was Sir William Meredith's proposal, but declaring himself at the same time for some Articles, and speaking with high veneration of the national church. Mr. Chas. Fox adopted Burke's idea, but insisted vehemently on the Dissenters being relieved – said they had a connivance but no toleration. Sir Richd. Sutton came next, declared himself for some Articles, but an utter dislike for the present set, and gave his full vote for the motion. Sir George Germayne and others were rising, but the question was called for so loud that an end was put to the debate, and the motion rejected without a division.

Document V.23

The State of the Parties

Extract (a) is from a letter of 28 June 1782 from Theophilus Lindsey to William Tayleur. It is reprinted from H. McLachalan, *Letters of Theophilus Lindsey*, Manchester: University of Manchester Press, 1920, p. 124. Extract (b) is from Edward Williams in reply to a question from Dr Green of America (John Waddington, *Congregational History 1700–1800*, London: Longmans, Green, 1876, pp. 678–80). Edward Williams (1750–1813), Independent minister and academy tutor, was educated under Benjamin Davies at Abergavenny academy. Following pastorates at Ross-on-Wye and Oswestry – where he had charge of the academy which removed there from Abergavenny on Davies's departure to Homerton College – and Carr's Lane, Birmingham, he served as principal of Rotherham Independent academy from 1795 until his death. He was a supporter of the London Missionary Society, and his principal theological work was *An Essay on the Equity of Divine Government*, 1813, which was concerned with the relations of divine sovereignty and human freedom. He influenced many in Wales to return to evangelical Calvinism in preference to both the Arianism of the Carmarthen academy and the high Calvinist reaction to it.

For Williams see DEB, DB, DWB; W. T. Owen, *Edward Williams, D.D. His Life, Thought and Influence*, Cardiff: University of Wales Press, 1963. For Davies (1739?–1817) see DWB.

(a)

Good Dr. Price, though an Arian, is one of the strictest Unitarians I know. On this account, he holds the worship of the Church of England to be wholly idolatrous, and scruples not to speak of it as such. What makes me thus abruptly mention him is my having been with him a few days ago, when he was very low-spirited on account of the poor state in which the Rational Dissenters were, both in the country as well as in the Town. Their congregations are crumbling away to nothing – the lower part joining the Methodists, those more at ease, the Church; all which, he said, would not have happened if Unitarians had informed their people properly, and spoken of the established worship as became them.

(b)

Birmingham, *August* 20 1794.

Dear Sir, – As to Dr. Green's first inquiry, 'What proportion do the Dissenters bear to the Established Church?' the answer is, as near as I can calculate, about one to eight, including the Friends, Baptists, and those who prefer associating with Dissenting Churches on the Lord's-day. Perhaps about two out of eight are perfect Gallios, who care nothing at all about religion, and frequent no place of worship except at a marriage, a baptism, or a burial. It then follows that about five out of eight are of the Established Church, taking town and country on an average through England and Wales. Of these Churchmen, about one in sixteen may be termed Evangelical or Calvinistic, including such Methodists as have not declared for the right of private judgement by actual dissent.

The second inquiry is, 'In number and influence, do they appear to be on the gaining or on the losing hand?' In numbers, I think the Dissenters are on the increase; but we must distinguish upon the sources of that increase. Some congregations appear stationary for a number of years; some, especially *among the less orthodox, on the decrease;* and others on the advance, both as to the size of the congregations and the rising and supporting of new ones.

As to influence, it is necessary to discriminate the objects of it. The Arian and Socinian have but little influence with either the Government of the populace; the orthodox Dissenters have much with the latter, and by the former they are considered as more innocent and well meaning, because *they confine themselves more to religion.* Their principles are more conformable to the articles of faith established, and they meddle less with the *turbulent politics* of the day; whereas the Socinians, or, as they prefer to be called, Unitarian Dissenters, have influence principally with the speculative class of readers, who, destitute of the fear of God and respect for vital godliness, pursue with avidity every bold attempt to pull down superstitions, or novel ideas and criticism, calculated to gratify unhallowed curiosity. But in the eye of Government, they are a party greatly suspected, not because of their number so much as their political investigations, their confessed learning and parts, their opulence, and especially their declared, open opposition to all hierarchies.

'Are Arianism and Socinianism still making progress among them, or are they declining?' Arianism is hardly to be met with. Those who were wont to be denominated Arians are generally sinking into Socinianism, and almost universally associated with the latter. Religious associations of ministers are seldom heard of among either of them; and congregational discipline, as to what relates to the religious welfare of the societies, is generally neglected. To which we may add, family worship, and personal examination as to principles, temper, and Christian deportment, however extolled, are, there is reason to fear, but little attended to practically.

'What proportion of the Dissenters is probably made up of the denominations of persons just mentioned?' Probably, one in six of the Dissenters, or one in forty-eight of the community, But as their struggles for greater enlargement of liberty, by the repeal of penal statutes in force against the Dissenters, and especially those whereby they are rendered incapable of civil offices under the Crown, have rendered them an obnoxious party in the view of the clergy, the Government, and their adherents; and as they almost universally are understood to disapprove of the coalition against France, they resemble a plant that lately made vigorous shoots, but now, through defect of moisture, begins to wither. It is remarkable that amongst all their complaints of hard treatment noticed in their sermons and publications (which, by the way, are fondly nursed by the reviews in general), we hear of no extra meetings for prayer among them, nor humiliations before God, seeking relief from Him – no, not during nor after those riots in which they were the principal sufferers. Indeed, prayer meetings are with them strange things.

'Has vital religion a general or remarkable prevalence in any part of South Britain at present?' I believe it is generally allowed, by those who are best acquainted with the subject, that in Wales there has been for many years a greater prevalence of vital religion, are more frequent and glorious revivals, than in any other part of this king-dom. The spirit of hearing these, even at this time of general languor, is astonishing. It is not an uncommon thing to see, at an association of ministers, five or six thousand hearers deeply affected.

I remain, your affectionate friend and brother,

E. W.

To Rev. Mr. Saltem, of Bridport, Dorset.

Politics

Document V.24

John Bellers and a European Union of States

In his writings the Quaker philanthropist John Bellers (1654–1725) touched themes that would be taken up later not only by Friends, and he was esteemed by both Robert Owen and Karl Marx. He was involved in Quaker business meetings, and in promoting the wider circulation of Barclay's *Apology*. Following revocation of the Edict of Nantes (1685) he was concerned for Huguenots emigrating to North America, and bought five thousand acres of land for them in Pennsylvania. His writings concern education, the welfare and gainful employment of the poor, the improvement of medical care, and the establishment of a European union of states. He appears to have been the first person in Europe publicly to advocate the abolition of capital punishment.

For Bellers see DNB. The following extract is from *Some reasons for an European State*, 1723, reprinted from George Clarke, *John Bellers: His Life, Times and Writings*, London: Routledge & Kegan Paul, 1987, pp. 150–2.

An Abstract of a Model, for the good, and perpetual respose of Christendom; by that Great Prince, King Henry *the 4th of* France; *as in the* Memoirs *of the Duke of* Sully, *and published by the Bishop of* Rodez, *(once Tutor to the present King,* Lewis *the 14) in his Life of* Henry *the 4th.*

I.   He believed, that he ought to establish in his own Kingdom, an unshaken Peace, by Reconciling all Spirits, both to him, and among themselves, by taking away all causes of bitterness.

And that moreover, it was necessary for him to chuse People Capable and Faithful, who might see, in what his Revenue, or Estate might be better'd, and instruct him so well in all his Affairs, that he might discern himself the more Feasible, from Impossible Enterprizes.

He granted an Edict to the *Protestants*, that the two Religions might live in Peace.

He made an Order to pay his Debts, and those of his Kingdom, contracted by the disorder of the Times, and the profuseness of his Predecessors.

II.   That done, he continually laboured, to joyn all Christian Princes, by seeking all occasions to Extinguish disorders, and pacify differences among them.

He began to make his Friends and Associates, the Princes and States, which seemed best disposed towards *France;* as the States of *Holland,* the *Venetians, Swisse,* and *Grisons.*

And also, he endeavour'd to Negotiate with the three puisant Kingdoms of the *North, England, Denmark, and Sweedland,* to discuss and decide their differences.

And to do the same thing among the Electors and Estates, and Cities Imperial.

And he sounded the Lords of *Bohemia, Hungary, Transilvania*, and *Poland*, to know if they would concur with him.

These were the dispositions of his great design, of which, the Platform, or Model follows.

He desir'd perfectly to Unite all Christendom into one Body to be called,

The Christian Commonwealth

For which effect, he Proposed to part it into 15 Dominions, or Estates, as the most he could do, to make them of equal Power and Strength, and whose limits should be so well specified, by the Universal consent of the whole 15, that none could pass beyond them.

The 15 Dominions were,

1. The *Pontificate*, or *Papacy*.
2. *Empire* of *Germany*.
3. *France*.
4. *Spain*.
5. *Great Britain*.
6. *Hungary*.
7. *Bohemiah*.
8. *Poland*.
9. *Denmark*.
10. *Sweedland*.
11. *Savoy*, or Kingdom of *Lumbardy*.
12. The *Signory* of *Venice*.
13. The *Italian* Commonwealth, or little Princes, and Cities of *Italy*.
14. The *Belgians*, or Low Countries.
15. The *Swisses*.

Now to regulate the differences, which might arise between these Confederates, and to decide them: There should have been established, an Order, and Form of procedure, by a general Councel, composed of 60 persons, 4 on the part of every Dominion, which should have been placed in some City, in the midst of Europe, as *Mets, Nancy, Collen*, or others.

There should likewise have been established 3 others, in 3 several Places, every one of 20 Men, which should all three, make report to the grand Councel.

And by consent of the General Councel, which should be called THE SENATE OF THE CHRISTIAN COMMONWEALTH: There should be established an Order and Regulation, between Sovereigns and Subjects, to hinder on one side, the Oppression and Tyranny of Princes; and on the otherside, the Tumults and Rebellion of Subjects.

There should likewise by raised a Stock of Money, and Men, to which every Dominion should contribute, according to the Assessment of the great Councel: For the Assistance of the Dominions bordering upon Infidels, from their Asualts, to wit, *Hungary* and *Poland*, against among themselves, without destroying one another? O unhappy Men! an Enemy hath surely sow'd these Tares in *Christendom*, not so much because of different Principles, as of an uncharitable Unchristian Temper.

Having said thus much of the Mischiefs that attend Religious Feuds and Wars, to prevent which for the future, I would Propose a New sort of General Council of all the several Christian Perswasions in *Europe*.

The Vertuous and Sincere of all Nations being of one Religion, for we finds them in General Councel and Convocation Assembled together in Heaven, to Adore and Praise God and the Lamb. Rev. 7. v. 9.

God being no Respecter of Persons, but in every Nation he that feareth him, and worketh Righteousness, is accepted of him. Acts 10.

It's the Hypocrite and Prophane that are Excluded, it being the Integrity of the Heart that God accepts, which he, and not Man, is Judge of.

All the Powers on Earth cannot make one Man sincere by force; tho' they may make Millions conformable.

Document V.25

The Protestant Dissenting Deputies

The Deputies, constituted in London in 1732, saw themselves as the spokesmen for the whole of Dissent, and the link between Dissent and the monarch and government, See Bernard Lord Manning, *The Protestant Dissenting Deputies*, Cambridge: CUP, 1952.

Extract (a), concerning the origin of the Deputies is from Anon., *A Sketch of the History and Proceedings of the Deputies*, 1813, pp. 1–3.

Extract (b) is the Deputies' Statement of 1739 (Manning, *Protestant Dissenting Deputies*, pp. 30–1), circulated among MP's, which details their objections to the Test Acts. Their tone is that of humble supplication, prompted partly by minority-consciousness, partly by commercial considerations. As the century proceeded, and with the rise of the radicalism associated with John Wilkes (who, though a roué, was a Dissenter of some sort, who enjoyed widespread Nonconformist support), a more confident note was struck, as in the Feathers Tavern Petition.

(a)

On the 9th November, 1732, a general meeting of Protestant Dissenters was held, at the meeting-house in Silver-street, London, to consider of an application to the legislature for the repeal of the Corporation and Test Acts. At this meeting a Committee of twenty-one persons was appointed, to consider, and report to a subsequent meeting, when, and in what manner, it would be proper to make the application. Another general meeting being held on the 29th of the same month, the Committee reported that they had consulted many persons of consequence in the state; that they found every reason to believe such an application would not then be successful; and therefore could not think it advisable to make the attempt. This report was not very cordially received. The Committee was enlarged by the addition of four other gentlemen, and instructed to reconsider the subject. It was at the same time resolved, that every congregation of the three denominations of Protestant Dissenters, Presbyterians, Independents, and Baptists, in and within ten miles of London, should be recommended to appoint two Deputies; and to a general assembly of these Deputies, the Committee were instructed to make their report. ...

It soon became evident that whatever might be the fate of their attempts to procure a repeal of the Corporation and Test Acts, the Dissenters would derive considerable advantage, in other respects, from establishing a permanent body to superintend their civil concerns. It was accordingly resolved, at a general meeting of the Deputies, held at Salter's Hall meeting-house, on the 14th of January, 1735–6, 'That there should be an annual choice of Deputies to take care of the Civil Affairs of the Dissenters'. In order to carry this resolution into effect, it was further resolved, 'That the chairman do write to the ministers of the several congregations, some convenient time before the second Wednesday in January next, to return the names of their Deputies to him fourteen days before'.

The first meeting of the Deputies, elected in pursuance of these resolutions, was held at Salter's Hall meeting-house, January 12, 1736–7, when Dr Benjamin Avery was called to the chair. The meeting, after some preliminary business, adjourned for a fortnight, to give each member time to determine upon the most proper persons to form a Committee of twenty-one, on whom the principal business of the year was to be devolved. Accordingly, on the 26th of the month, the Deputies met, and elected their Committee by ballot. These several elections – of the Deputies by the congregations, and of the Committee by the Deputies – have been continued annually from that time to the present.

(b)

The Protestant Dissenters can and do readily take the oaths of allegiance and supremacy required by these Acts; but some of them scruple receiving the sacrament after the manner of the church of England; and many of them refuse to take the sacrament, after the manner of any church, as a qualification for an office.

It is humbly hoped, therefore, that so much of these acts as relates to the taking the sacrament as a qualification for offices, may be repealed, for the following reasons:

1.   Every man has an undoubted right to judge for himself in matters of religion. No one therefore ought to be punished, by being deprived of any of the common rights of subjects, and branded with a mark of infamy, merely for exercising this right in things that no way affect the public welfare and prosperity of the kingdom.

2.   The sacrament of the Lord's supper was appointed only for religious purposes; and the using it as a qualification for civil offices, seems, in a great measure, to have occasioned that disregard and contempt of this institution in particular, and of religion in general, of which all good men have so long and justly complained.

3.   As the Dissenters are universally acknowledged to be well affected to His Majesty and the established government, they think it hard, that by the Corporation

Act they are rendered incapable of holding offices in the corporations where they live, though in many places their property is at least equal to that of their neighbours; especially since many of them have been fined for not taking upon them such offices; and in particular, as a very large fine is now insisted on, by the city of London, from a known Dissenter, for not serving the office of sheriff, and a prosecution for the same is actually commenced.

4.   Many persons of substance and capacity being excluded by this act, the government of several corporations has fallen into the hands of the meaner sort of people, to the great prejudice of such corporations, the discouragement of industry, and the decay of trade. ... [N]othing seems more likely to heal our divisions, put an end to party names and distinctions, and unite the friends of liberty, than removing those incapacities from a body of men, whose dissent is founded on the right of private judgement, and who are confessedly a great support and security to the religion and liberties of this kingdom.

Document V.26

Quaker Political Attitudes

The two following extracts from the Yearly Meeting epistles of the Society of Friends for 1730 and 1746 show Friends being urged to be loyal to the state. In 1746 there was also a loyal address from the Yearly Meeting to King George II following the defeat of the '45 which might be seen as too partisan. Later Friends were urged not to become involved in election campaigns, but to make wise use of their votes when they possessed them. The Written epistle of 1774 (extract (c)) deals specifically with this point. The Written epistles were occasional letters circulated by the Yearly Meetings in manuscript only. Their texts can be found in the archives of many meetings, as well as in the Library of Friends' House, London.

(a)
And, in regard we have been favoured by the government with the enjoyment of our religious liberties, in common with other Protestant dissenters, and, in an especial manner, relieved by the legislature in several cases, which peculiarly concern us as a people; we, therefore, think ourselves obliged earnestly to advise all Friends, that they be particularly careful to behave with all dutifulness and gratitude, and especially to discountenance every the least appearance of indecent freedom, or mark of dissatisfaction, in word or writing, relating to the government.

(b)
And, dear friends, from what we have lately beheld of the calamities of the sword, we have cause to bow in thankfulness to the Lord; who, by his overruling providence, hath checked its progress in this nation. Let us pray, that the Lord would hasten the promised time , when he shall judge among the nations, and shall rebuke many people, and they shall beat their swords into ploughshares, and their spears into

pruning-hooks; nation shall not lift up sword against nation, neither shall they learn war any more. (Isa. ii.4.) And let us also, as the Lord shall open our hearts, and influence our minds, make our supplications and prayers for kings, and for all that are in authority; that we may lead a quiet and peaceable life, in all godliness and honesty: for this is good and acceptable in the sight of God our Saviour. (1 Tim. ii. 2, 3.)

And, as it hath pleased the Lord, in his abundant mercy, to appear for the deliverance of us and the nation in general, in time of outward distress, and to preserve the king and his government from the wicked attempts of those who rose up against them, and to continue unto us the enjoyment of our civil and religious liberties, it is our duty to express our thankfulness to the Lord, and to acknowledge his might, manifested in the day of danger; not only in words and expressions, but in an awful and reverent walking in all holy conversation and godliness, to the praise and honour of his holy name, who is blessed for ever.

(c)

Dear Friends

Our Minds being at this time exercised in a deep Concern that Friends *every where* may walk so circumspectly in every part of their Conversation as to shew forth the Peaceableness and Purity of the truly Christian Principles we profess, and that no Inconsistency therewith, may at any Time appear but that the whole of their Conduct may tend to the Exaltation of the Cause of Truth, and as we apprehend the time for a General Election is approaching, we are engaged affectionately to advise that all in Membership with us, whether Electors, or not, would guard against inconsiderately engaging themselves in these Matters, or being drawn in by Party, but preserving their Judgments calm and free, that those who are qualified, may be as unanimous as they will care, in quickly voting for such Candidates whose Characters and Conduct are the most virtuous, and whose Abilities seem to promise Service to the Public.

And, Dear Friends, as Occasions of this Nature, are generally attended with Intemperance and Dissipation, we earnestly beseech that your Deportment may be strictly guarded in those Respects, and that none under our Name, may be allured into any active, or leading part in these Cases. The corrupt immoral Practices which have frequently attended, are a Scandal to the Christian Name, and would be very reproachful on any of our Profession, Wherefore if any amongst us should be prevailed upon to become Managers, or Agents in Elections, let such be visited, and laboured with to convince them of the hurtful Consequences that may ensue.

We remind you of the Declaration concerning Israel formerly, that they should dwell alone, and not be numbered amongst the Nations, by which we would be understood that Friends ought to refrain from touching the defiling Practices which so much abound in public Elections, and by a circumspect Conduct, may adorn the Profession we make, and be Examples to our Neighbours, giving no just Occasion of Offence to any.

Document V.27

Richard Price and John Wesley on the American War of Independence

For Price see Document I.9 above; for Wesley see Document II.21 above. In connection with this war Price is at his most radical, as extract (a) makes plain. The divergent responses to this war clearly demonstrate the extent of the political gulf between the fervently patriotic Wesleyans and the rest of Nonconformity, as extracts (b) and (c) show.

Extract (a) is from R. Price, *Observations on the Nature of Civil Liberty*, 1776, pp. 44–7; extract (b) is from J. Wesley, *Letters*, ed. John Telford, London: Epworth Press, 1931, VI, p. 161; extract (c), in which the page references are to Price's *Observations*, is from J. Wesley, *Observations of Liberty*, 1776, pp. 104–5.

(a)

Though clearly decided in my own judgment on this subject, I am inclined to make great allowances for the different judgments of others. We have been so used to speak of the Colonies as *our* Colonies, and to think of them as in a state of subordination to us, and as holding their existence in *America* only for our use, that it is no wonder the prejudices of many are alarmed, when they find a different doctrine maintained. The meanest person among us is disposed to look upon himself as having a body of subjects in *America;* and to be offended at the denial of his right to make laws for them, though perhaps he does not know what colour they are of, or what language they talk. – Such are the natural prejudices of this country. – But the time is coming, I hope, when the unreasonableness of them will be seen; and more just sentiments prevail.

Before I proceed, I beg it may be attended to, that I have chosen to try this question by the general principles of Civil Liberty; and not by the practice of former times; or by the *Charters* granted the colonies, – The arguments *for* them, drawn from these last topics, appear to me greatly to outweigh the arguments *against* them. But I wish to have this question brought to a higher test, and surer issue. The question with all liberal enquirers ought to be, not what jurisdiction over them *Precedents, Statutes,* and *Charters* give , but what reason and equity, and the rights of humanity give. – This is, in truth, a question which no kingdom has ever before had occasion to agitate. The case of a free country branching itself out in the manner *Britain* has done, and sending to a distant world colonies which have there, from small beginnings, and under free legislatures of their own, increased, and formed a body of powerful states, likely soon to become superior to the parent state. – This is a case which is new in the history of mankind; and it is extremely improper to judge if it by the rules of any narrow and partial policy; or to consider it on any other ground than the general one of reason and justice. – Those who will be candid enough to judge on this ground, and who can divest themselves of national prejudices, will not, I fancy, remain long unsatisfied. – But alas! Matters are gone too far. The dispute probably must be settled another way; and the sword alone, I am afraid, is now to determine what the rights of *Britain* and *America* are. – Shocking situation! – Detested be the measures which have brought us into it: And, if we are endeavouring to enforce injustice, cursed will be the war. – A retreat, however, is not yet impracticable. The duty we owe our gracious sovereign obliges us to rely on his disposition to stay the sword, and to promote the happiness of all the different parts of the Empire at the head of which he is placed. With some hopes, therefore, that it may not be too late to reason on the subject, I will, in the following Sections, enquire what the war with *America* is in the following respects.

1. In respect of Justice.
2. The Principles of the Constitution.
3. In respect of Policy and Humanity.
4. The Honour of the Kingdom.
  And lastly, The Probability of succeeding in it.

(b)

I do not intend to enter upon the question whether the Americans are in the right or in the wrong. Here all my prejudices are against the Americans; for I am an High Churchman, the son of an High Churchman, bred up from my childhood in the highest notions of passive obedience and non-resistance. And yet, in spite of all my long-rooted prejudices, I cannot avoid thinking, if I think at all, these, an oppressed people, asked for nothing more than their legal rights, and that in the most modest and inoffensive manner that the nature of the thing would allow.

(c)

31. The supposition, then, that the people are the origin of power, or that 'all government is the creature of the people', though Mr. Locke himself should attempt to defend it, is utterly indefensible. It is absolutely overturned by the very principle on which it is supposed to stand, namely, that 'a right of choosing his Governors belongs to every partaker of human nature.' If this be so, then it belongs to every individual of the human species; consequently, not to freeholders alone, but to all men; not to men only, but to women also; not only to adult men and women, to those who have lived one-and-twenty years, but to those that have lived eighteen or twenty, as well as those who have lived threescore, But none did ever maintain this, nor probably ever will; therefore, this boasted principle falls to the ground, and the whole superstructure with it. So common sense brings us back to the grand truth, 'There is no power but of God.'

32. I may now venture to 'pronounce, that the principles on which you have argued, are incompatible with practice,' even the universal practice of mankind, as well as with sound reason; and it is no wonder 'that they are not approved by our Governors, 'considering their natural tendency, which is, to unhinge all Government, and to plunge every nation into total anarchy

This, in truth, is the tendency of the whole book; a few passages of which I shall now recite, begging leave to make a few remarks upon them, But I must ask the reader's pardon, if I frequently say the same thing more than once; for, otherwise, I could not follow the author.

33.   'All the members of a state' (which necessarily include all the men, women, and children) 'may intrust the powers of legislation with any number of delegates, subject to such restrictions as they think necessary.' (Page 8.) This is 'incompatible with practice:' It never was done from the beginning of the world; it never can; it is flatly impossible in the nature of the thing. 'And thus, all the individuals that compose a great state partake of the powers of legislation and government.' *All the individuals!* Mere Quixotism! Where does that state exist? Not under the canopy of heaven. 'In this case, a state is still free,' (but this case has no being,) 'if the representatives are chosen by the unbiased voices of the majority.' Hold! this is quite another case; you now shuffle in a new term: The *majority* we were not talking of, but *all the members* of a state. The majority are not *all the individuals* that compose it; and pray, how came the minority to be deprived of those rights which you say are 'unalienable from human nature?' – 'But we disguise slavery, keeping up the form of liberty, when the reality is lost.' It is not lost; I now enjoy all the real liberty I can desire, civil as well as religious. The liberty you talk of was never found; it never existed yet. But what does all this lead to, but to stir up all the inhabitants of Great Britain against the Government?

34.   To inflame them still more, you go on: 'Liberty is more or less complete, according as the people have more or less share in the Government.' This is altogether contrary to matter of fact: The greater share the people have in the Government, the less liberty, either civil or religious, does the nation in general enjoy. Accordingly, there is most liberty of all, civil and religious, under a limited monarchy; there is usually less under an aristocracy, and least of all under a democracy. What sentences then are these: 'To be guided by one's own will, is freedom; to be guided by the will of another, is slavery?' (Page 11.) This is the very quintessence of republicanism; but it is a little too barefaced; for, if this is true, how free are all the devils in hell, seeing they are all guided by their own will! And what slaves are all the angels in heaven, since they are all guided by the will of another! See another stroke: 'The people have power to model Government as they please.' (Page 12.) What an admirable lesson, to confirm the people in their loyalty to the Government! Yet again: 'Government is a trust, and all its powers a delegation.' (Page 15.) It is a trust, but not from the people: 'There is no power but of God.' It is a delegation, namely, from God; for 'rulers are God's ministers,' or delegates.

35.   How irreconcilable with this are your principles! Concerning our Governors in England, you teach, 'A Parliament forfeits its authority by accepting bribes.' If it does, only the Governor of the world has, even the wiser Heathens being judges; but which no man upon the face of the earth either has or can have. No man, therefore, can give the power of the sword, any such power as gives a right to take away life: Wherever it is, it must descend from God alone, the sole disposer of life and death.

Document V.28

Richard Price's Fast Sermon

In his Fast Sermon of 1781, Richard Price sums up the attitudes underlying his political writings, and firmly sets his consideration of the evils which befall individuals and nations in the context of the over-arching governance of God and the prospect of 'a future better state'.

The extracts are from *A Discourse addressed to a Congregation at Hackney, on February 21, 1781 Being the day appointed for a Public Fast*, 1781. Price's texts are II Peter 1: 2 and II Peter 3: 13.

Numberless are the calamities to which we are liable in this world. There are few of us who have not some share of trouble allotted us, either in our persons, or families, or fortunes. But, if happily exempted from troubles of this kind, there are troubles of a public nature which are very shocking and which at present throw a dark cloud over all our views and hopes. In such circumstances we are necessarily led to look out for consolation. It would be dreadful to suffer under present evils and to be under a necessity perhaps of looking forward to future greater evils, without any considerations that have a tendency to abate anxiety and mitigate pain. But this is not our condition. There are many springs of comfort to which in the worst circumstances we may have recourse, and which will help to reconcile us to our lot, and to give us patience and fortitude. Most of them, however, are of little moment compared with the two following; I mean, 'the consideration of the perfect government of the deity', and 'the prospect of a future better state'. These are the grand springs of consolation amidst the evils of life and wretched is the person who, either from scepticism, or inattention, or viciousness of character, loses the hope and satisfaction which they are fitted to afford. Were the course of events under no wise and good direction, or were the present scene of trial and tumult the whole we are to enjoy of existence, were the universe forlorn and fatherless, did joy and grief, defeat and success, prosperity and adversity, arise fortuitously, without any superintendency from a righteous and benevolent power; or, were we, after being witnesses to the scramble among the children of men, and making our way through this distracted world, to close our eyes for ever, and to sink to rise no more; were, I say, this our state, we might as well lose all spirit and give up ourselves to bitter sorrow and despondence. But, on the contrary, if there is a perfect order established in nature, and infinite wisdom and goodness govern all things, and if also the scene will mend hereafter, and we are to sink in death only to rise to new heavens and a *new earth wherein dwelleth righteousness*, and to have *an entrance* ministered to us into an everlasting kingdom of peace and virtue; if I say, this is our true situation we have abundant reason for comfort. The lot appointed us is glorious. We may contemplate the course of events with pleasure. We may look forward with triumph, and make ourselves easy and happy at all times. ...

But it is time to proceed to the main point I have had all along in view, or the use we ought to make of this subject for our comfort under the evils which prevail among the kingdoms of this world. Let me press you to make this use of what I have been saying. Withdraw your minds from temporal objects and amidst the devastations, the slaughters and cruelties around you, look forward to a better state. I pity from my heart those whose principles will not allow them to do this, who, believing they are made only to struggle and fret for a short time on this earth, can look no higher. Men who think thus meanly of themselves must be proportionately mean in their dispositions and pursuits. They must think meanly of the divine administration. They must want the strongest motives to noble exertions, and can have nothing to preserve them from despondence when they reflect on the present state of civil society and government. No reflection can be more painful to a reasonable person. The occasion for civil government is derived from the wickedness of mankind, and the end of it is to provide securities for our person, property and liberty. But it is a very insufficient security and often proves the cause of intolerable distressed, by arming the ambitious with power and enabling them to trample on their fellow-creatures. General experience has proved this and the history of the world is but little more than a recital of the oppressions and rapines of men entrusted with powers of government, and the calamities occasioned by the endeavours of mankind to defend themselves against them. This is particularly exemplified in the history of our own country, the annals of which are full of accounts of hard struggles between liberty and tyranny.

Free governments are the only equitable governments, but how few of them are there in the world and what seats of contention do we often find in them? This contention is even necessary to their existence, for all governments tend to despotism and will end in it if no opposition checks them. Nothing corrupts more than power. Nothing is more encroaching and, therefore, nothing requires more to be watched and restrained. The safety of a free people depends entirely on their maintaining a constant and suspicious vigilance, and as soon as they cease to be quick at taking alarms, they are undone. But the vigilance and jealousy necessary to the security of free governments have been the occasion of dreadful convulsions. They are apt to degenerate into faction and licentiousness, and an impatience of all controul; and very often exertions apparently the most ardent in favour of public liberty, have proved to be nothing but the turbulence of ambitious men and a vile struggle for places and the emoluments of power.

I make these observations to render you more sensible of the imperfection of all earthly governments. If they are free they are subject to intestine broils which keep them in a constant ferment and sometimes end in insurrections and civil wars. If they are slavish they may be indeed more quiet, but that quiet is founded on a depression of the human mind, which is the greatest of all calamities. ...

But lastly, let us on this subject take care not to forget that the happiness I have described will be the happiness only of virtuous men. All I have said has supposed this and my text plainly expresses it. For so (that is, by adding to faith, fortitude, prudence, temperance, patience, godliness, brotherly kindness and charity) *an entrance shall be ministered to you abundantly into the everlasting kingdom of our Lord and Saviour Jesus Christ, for if ye do these things ye shall never fall.* The wicked are nuisances and pests and there can be no happiness where they are. *Know ye not*, says St. Paul, *that the unrighteous cannot inherit the kingdom of God. Be not deceived. Neither fornicators, nor adulterers, nor thieves, nor covetous, nor drunkards, nor revilers, nor extortioners, shall inherit the kingdom of God.* Christ, by taking upon him our natures, acquired power to raise us from death and to gather together all the virtuous into a state of future existence where, with him at their head, they are to be formed into one joyful society, and to be exalted to the highest honours under a government of peace and righteousness which shall never be destroyed. This is the doctrine which the Scriptures teach us, but the same Scriptures teach us, with respect to the vicious part of mankind, that after being raised up from death they are to be consigned to a state of punishment, where they will suffer a *second death*, from which there will be no redemption.

What remains then but that we now resolve to avoid every evil way and devote all that is to come ouf our lives to the practice of righteousness. This must be your resolution if you wish to get to the kingdom of heaven. And let me, on the present occasion, desire you particularly to consider that in the practice of righteousness is included the faithful discharge of all your duties as member of civil society. The conversation of a Christian is not so in heaven as to render him indifferent to what passes on earth. He that expects to be a citizen of the heavenly Jerusalem ought to be the best citizen of this world. He who hopes for a place under a government of eternal peace and virtue will make the best subject to any earthly government under which his lot is cast. He will be the warmest friend to liberty and the most ready to spend his substance, or to pour out his blood in defence of the rights of his country. Act, fellow-christians under the influence of these sentiments and, while others think of nothing but making their way in the world, do you strive to make your way through the world, exhibiting always in your tempers and conduct, a zeal for virtue, and a conscious dignity becoming those who expect honour and glory, greater than this world can bestow, *in the everlasting kingdom of Jesus Christ. ...*

Will you on this occasion bear with me if I say that it has been my study to form my own conduct agreeably to this exhortation. My life has been hitherto spent in such endeavours as I am capable of to promote all the best interests of my country and of mankind. I can, in particular, reflect with pleasure on the part I have taken in that dispute with the colonies which has for some years made us the derision of Europe and to which we owe all our present difficulties. Convinced that our claim of a right to dispose of their property and to alter their governments without their consent, was an unjust claim, and, in general, that provincial governments are the most rapacious and oppressive of all governments, and that the subjection of countries to one another has always been and must always be the worst sort of slavery. Convinced, I say, of this and believing also that a war with our colonies, supposing it just, was in the highest degree impolitic, I could not avoid publishing my sentiments in a pamphlet to which few of you can be strangers. This pamphlet was published five years ago at the commencement of our present troubles. I endeavoured to explain in it the nature of civil liberty and legitimate government, and to set forth particularly the danger to which the war with America would expose us. I argued in it freely against the war. But I only argued. I did not enter into personal invectives or speak disrespectfully of any particular men, and a kingdom ceases to be free as soon as the members of it cease to enjoy the liberty of canvassing in this manner public measures.

It was not possible that I should have any indirect view in this publication. I was led to it by no kind of advice or solicitation. It was extorted from me entirely by my judgment and feelings in opposition to my inclinations. So true is this and so conscious am I of having acted, in this instance, from pure motives that it has ever since laid the foundation of a comfort in my own mind which has made me perfectly insensible to all censures. Nor would I now for any emoluments part with the satisfaction I feel when I recollect my attempts, by that publication and the publications that followed it, to serve my country, and to propagate just notions of government and a zeal for that liberty on which the happiness of man essentially depends and without which he is a creature scarcely superior to a beast. I was far from having reason to expect that any thing I could write would influence the managers of our affairs. I must say, however, that had they been influenced by it this kingdom, instead of being on the brink of ruin, would now have been enjoying its former prosperity.

I cannot help reminding you here that I insisted strongly, in the publications I have mentioned, on a peculiarity in the state of this kingdom which made any war, but more especially such a war as that with America, dreadfully hazardous, and that I represented particularly the danger there was that the colonies would be driven to form an alliance with France, that this jealous rival would seize the opportunity to ruin us, that a general war would be kindled, and that a catastrophe might follow in this country never before known among nations. These representations when written were apprehensions only. A great part of them may be now read as history. When I say this I do not mean to boast of any sagacity. It was easy to foresee these consequences and there are many distinguished and excellent persons, in every respect my superiors, who entertained the same apprehensions and who have given the same warnings. But though I am only one and one of the least of many who have stood forth on this occasion, yet it has happened that no one has fallen under a greater load of abuse. You will be sensible how improper an object of abuse I have been if you will consider,

First, that detesting all abuse in political as well as religious discussions I have myself always avoided it.

Secondly, that I have done no more than what it is in a particular manner the duty of a Minister of the Gospel of peace to do; I mean, endeavoured to prevent the carnage of war and to promote peace and righteousness.

Thirdly, what most of all justifies me is that events have proved that I was right in my opinion of the pernicious tendency of the measures against which I wrote.

Upon the whole, I must repeat to you that there is nothing in the course of my life that I can think of with more satisfaction than the testimony I have borne and the attempts I have made to serve the cause of general liberty and justice, and the particular interest of this country at the present period. A period big with events of unspeakable consequences and perhaps one of the most momentous in the annals of mankind.

But I have detained you too long and talked too much of myself. You are my friends and know me, I hope, too well to question the uprightness of my views. May you be blest with every comfort this world can give and with eternal happiness in that country beyond the grave which is now the hope and will soon be the refuge of the virtuous. In that country alone I wish for honour and there God of his infinite mercy grant that we may all at last meet!

Document V.29

Dissenting Attitudes towards the French Revolution

The French Revolution, which coincided with the Dissenters' renewed campaign for relief at home from the Test and Corporation Acts, occasioned much Nonconformist comment. The authors of the following extracts are Joseph Priestley, for whom see Document I.11 above; Joseph Kinghorn, for whom see Document V.6 above; and Samuel Kenrick and James Wodrow. Kenrick (1728–1811), for whom see *The Monthly Repository*, VII, 1812, pp. 9–11, and Wodrow (1730–1810), for whom see *The Monthly Repository*, VI, 1811, p. 122 – an extract from *The Glasgow Courier* of 20 December 1810 – were fellow students at Glasgow University. Wodrow was minister at Stevenston from 1759 until his death; Kenrick, a rational Dissenter, was a founder of the Bewdley Bank. They studied under William Leechman, whose *Life* Wodrow wrote, and who was said to have emancipated Kenrick from Calvinism, so that he became ' a decided Unitarian'.

In extract (a) Samuel Kenrick writes to James Wodrow in December 1789 (Doctor Williams's Library (DWL) MS 24.157.152). In J. Priestley's *Familiar Letters to the Inhabitants of Birmingham*, 1791, pp. 53–6, 171–2, extract (b), we have an example of religio-political radicalism taken to an extreme, and a profoundly utilitarian piece of reasoning. Here is a conflict model of society, an anticipation of the Whig reforms of the 1830's, which provoked the Oxford Movement. Extract (c) is quoted from a letter of Joseph Kinghorn, the Norwich Baptist, to his father. Written in November 1792, the letter is quoted in *Baptist Quarterly*, XXIV, no. 5, 1972, pp. 209–10. Here a Dissenter begins to have reservations – and tends in the direction of biblical chiliasm.

With revolutionary violence increasing and the war intensifying, the *Protestant Dissenter's Magazine*, March 1794, comes round strongly to a pro-government stance (extract (d)). In extracts (e)–(i) we have further letters from S. Kenrick to J. Wodrow: 20 April 1791 (DWL MS 24.257.160); 28 October 1792 (DWL MS 24.157.177); 14 August 1793 (DWL MS 24.157.181); 10 January 1794 (DWL MS 24.157.186); 22 January 1794 (DWL MS 24.157.187). In 1791 Kenrick approves of Tom Paine's radicalism; by 1792 he is having doubts; by 1793 the 'atrocious act' of the execution of the King and Queen has made him despair. All he now sees in France is tyranny which, by 1794, is literally unspeakable. Kenrick was not alone among Dissenters in passing through such changes of attitude towards the French Revolution.

(a)

On the 4th. of last Mo. Dr. Priestley preached a sermon at both the presbyterian meeting Houses in Birmingham, wch, is since published, exhorting the dissenters to persist in their application to parliament. Dr. Price you see preached a revolution sermon on the same day before Lds. Stanhope & Effingham &c & after dinner offered the copy of an address to the National assembly at Paris, on their steadiness and success.

(b)

If men are not to interpose their authority in matters of religion, they ought to refrain, not only from making *articles of faith*, and rules of *moral conduct*, to bind the consciences of men (which they allow to be within the province of God only) but they ought not to enforce any decrees of men respecting religion by *civil penalties*. For this is evidently setting up *a kingdom of this world*, and applying human authority to matters of religion, things with respect to which Dissenters hesitate not to say that every man should be left to himself, to be guided by the dictates of his own conscience, of which God is the only sovereign.

If I break the peace of society, if I injure my neighbour, in his person, property, or good name (things which human laws were intended to guard) I ought to be punished by those who administer such laws. But if I do any thing by which I offend *God* only, and not man, I should be left to the judgment of God, in this world or the next. These are very plain rules, and yet they are evidently violated whenever any body of men, clergy or laity, lay down rules respecting religion, and enforce them by civil penalties.

It follows from these plain principles, that whether I chuse to profess any particular mode of religion at all, my neighbours and fellow citizens have no right to compel me. I do not molest them, and therefore they ought not to disturb me. If, therefore, I do not chuse to give any part of my property to the maintenance of religion, it does not concern *them;* and to compel me to pay money on a religious account, is real *injustice;* though sanctioned by law. The civil magistrate has the power of the stronger, and I, as the weaker, must submit; but it is on the same principle that I submit to an highwayman, or a robber, at whose mercy I necessarily am. He may say that he has a right to take my money, but he makes himself the judge, and to me his decision may appear unjust.

If we interpret the scriptures by the conduct of the apostles and that of the early christians for three centuries, you will be satisfied that I do not carry this principle too far. In the New Testament you will find that, whatever any man gave to the support of religion, it was perfectly *voluntary*. The primitive church had bishops, deacons, and other officers, who, giving their whole time to the instruction, &c. of others, were maintained from the common flock; and the christians of those times must have been at great expence in building places of public worship, maintaining their poor, &c. But all these expences, great as they were, were defrayed by voluntary contribution.

It will be said that, in that age, there was no civil power that *could* be applied in favour of christianity. But neither our Saviour nor the apostles gave any direction about such a thing as *a civil establishment of christianity*, when christians *should* have the power of making one. And yet, as our Saviour distinctly foresaw, and frequently referred to, the universal prevalence of his religion, he must have known that it would be wanted, if that change in the external circumstances of his religion would authorize such a measure.

But what apprehension could the apostles have of the *use* of a civil establishment of christianity, when they found no want of it in their own times? Read all their epistles, and you will find no wish expressed by the writers of them, of any civil power to inforce the laws of Christ. Nay, without the aid of any civil power, christianity gained ground in the world, to the over-turning of the long-established system of heathenism, which was supported by that power. With what face, then, can any christian at this day say that civil power is *necessary* to christianity, when it never flourished so much as when it was entirely destitute of it, and opposed by it?

Christians should consider their religion as *disgraced* by any alliance with civil power. The voluntary zeal of the sincere professors of christianity would at this day, as well as in former times, supply all the funds which are really wanted for the support of religion; and if men offend against the laws of religion, they should, as our Saviour prescribed, and the apostles practiced, be cut off from christian societies, and be considered as persons with whom they have no religious connection; but not punished by fines, imprisonments, or any civil inconveniences whatever, such as are the consequence of your excommunications. In this manner christianity is actually supported by all Dissenters, compelled as they are to bear their share in the support of a much more expensive system, by which they are oppressed.

It will hardly be said that the authority of the civil magistrate was necessary for the *appointment*, as well as the *payment*, of bishops, and other ministers in christian churches. For not only in the time of the apostles, but long after the undue interference of the civil power in matters of religion, it would have been thought an intolerable grievance; if all christian societies had not had the free choice of their own ministers of every kind. But men who have been used to servitude of any kind, get in time the habit of acquiescence, and sometimes fancy that there is a real advantage in what is most disgraceful to them. Thus you are very well content to have no vote at all in the nomination of your own *servants*. For *ministers* of the gospel are no other than their title imports, being persons who are employed by christian societies for a certain stipend, to do a certain duty.

These are the pure and rational principles of christian churches; such as we find in the scriptures, and in all the primitive times. But how have we deviated from them; and in consequence of it, how has the church of Christ adopted the maxims of the kingdoms of this world? Men have assumed authority, such as your church expressly avows, to *determine controversies of faith*. They have made numberless regulations about religion, and they have enforced the observance of them by fines, imprisonments, and dreadful punishments of various kinds, so that what is now called *the church* is as much a *kingdom of this world*, as *the state*.

The great argument for these civil establishments of christianity is that religion promotes good morals, and that good morals are necessary to the well being of civil society. Now I am far from denying the usefulness of religion, and especially of christianity, in this respect; and on this account I have written so much (more, I believe, than any other person in this country) to prove its divine authority, and to explain its principles. But the friends of church establishments have made a great deal too much of this argument. Civil society has subsisted very well under all forms of religion, even the heathen ones. For the Roman empire was well regulated before

297

the knowledge of christianity, yea better than several christian countries since. And christianity will operate in favour of good morals without being *established*, and even more so than when it is. The man who truly fears God, and believes a future state, will be a good moral man, and an useful member of society, though the prince and the state should not concern themselves about it. Nay he will be virtuous, when they are wicked.

Besides, though religion, or the belief of a God, a providence, and a future state, have its *use* with respect to society, it is not absolutely *necessary* for that purpose. Good laws, and a proper administration of civil government, will be sufficient to keep men from injuring one another. It is a common interest to restrain those vices which are injurious to the community, and the force of the community may easily applied for this purpose. Only let there be a good legislature, good judges, and good civil officers (which temporal interest of all states will provide) and you need not fear but that the internal peace of any country, which is the only proper object of civil government, will be sufficiently secured.

Great numbers of persons in this country, and many more abroad, are actually without religion. They believe in no God, or future state; they frequent no place of public worship, and they know no more of the Bible than they do of the Koran; and yet, with respect of *the peace of society*, they behave like other people, and are no more disposed to disturb others than others are disposed to disturb them.

Besides there is no danger of mankind in general being without religion. Nay, I am well persuaded there would be much more of it without any establishment than with one; and that religion which we will voluntarily adopt and support will have more influence on their morals and be more favourable to the good of society than any which any state will adopt and enforce. ...

These, my friends, are only a part of the complex system of your church establishment. On which ever side you view it, you will see similar weaknesses, such as, without gunpowder, or any high wind, threaten an approaching fall. The universities, in particular, from which, perhaps with the best intentions with respect to us, you exclude our youth, call most loudly for reformation. But this must be the result of your own thinking and exertions. You must not expect that the clergy will promote any reformation of a system in the continuance of which they are so much *interested.* You must do it *yourselves*, by petitions to the legislature; and if you be in earnest, and any thing like unanimous, you will be heard. Is it not a disgrace to a protestant country, that there should, in so many important respects, be greater abuses in its church government than in that of the Catholics; that our *civil* constitution should be so excellent, and yet its *ally*, as it is called, the *ecclesiastical* part, of the same system, be so imperfect?

The *use* of this expensive system is to provide for the instruction of the country in the principles of christianity; but it by no means answers its end. For it is not one half of the inhabitants that are taught any religion at all. They attend no public worship, and it is not the interest of the clergy to promote their attendance; because their incomes are altogether independent of it. In popish countries the case is far otherwise. In all of *them* care is taken, by one means or other, that every person is instructed in his religion, and every open neglect of the known duties of it is regularly animadverted upon. The state, in my opinion, has no business to meddle with it; but if it pretend to do it at all, and if an order of men be amply provided for on this account, care should be taken that the end of the institution be answered. At present, the whole kingdom is taxed, and in the most inconvenient manner possible, for the maintenance of religion; when, after all, the religion of a very great proportion of those who have any is provided for out of their own private purses, and they who do not chuse to have any, which is the case of the greatest part of both the highest and the lowest classes of people, are not so much as admonished on the subject.

Whenever the *wants of the state* shall make it necessary to examine strictly into its *resources* and *expenditure*, the great sum that is now given for the maintenance of religion, will either be wholly withdrawn, or care will be taken that it be better applied. Would it not be better, for instance, if the government made some provision for having all the poor taught to read and write; that when, by this means, they had acquired the *civilization*, and capacity for judging, which they now want, they might chuse a religion for themselves, than impose upon them, one which they are not capable of examining. This scheme for communicating *knowledge* in general, would not cost the country one tenth part so much that it now does to have them taught *religion*, which, after all, is not taught to any purpose.

(c)

The troubles on the Continent I strongly hope are the fore-runners of peace & that their national ferment will tend to their purification. ... I had some conversation a few weeks ago with a Roman Catholic Clergyman who very frankly answered every question I put to him respecting the state of the Church and Clergy of France from which I thought I could clearly see that Babylon is falling with vengeance. He represented almost the whole nation as in rebellion against the Pope that there was no legal Church authority in the Kingdom – the decrees of the National Assembly infringing on the Pope's Prerogative so much as to set his authority aside. The successes of the French are truly astonishing by last week's papers tho the scenes occasioned by intestine wars are really dreadfull beyond imagination. What is in futurity God only knows. The signs of the destruction of Jerusalem by Babylon too much apply to us Ezek. 22, 23 &c &c there is scarcely a circumstance which we do not see in England as far as ancient language can be considered as analogous to modern times.

(d)

A material charge against the Dissenters has lately been drawn from their supposed partiality for FRENCH PRINCIPLES. Where is the evidence for this fact? It is certain that the majority of the Dissenters are abhorrent of these principles. Among no descriptions of men in this country, or even in Russia or Turkey, are there any more inveterate in their opposition to the present government of France. It is notorious that many Dissenters sacrifice some speculative opinions, not peculiar to themselves, in declaiming against the usurped power in that country, as they represent it, through a dread of similar innovations in this. Has a single pamphlet been produced by any

Dissenter, in vindication of the late proceedings of the convention? And at the grand burst of the revolution, when the British government openly signified no disapprobation of so extraordinary an event, were the Dissenters more enthusiastic in their admiration, more serious in developing the minutiae of the transaction, than others who can be selected, from the church, from the bar, and from the senate itself?

(e)

The great merit of Paine's immortal work, is, the clear narrative he has given of what passed before his own discerning eyes, from the beginning to the end of this astonishing Revolution – this will be a precious morsel to the philosopher, the historian as well as politician to the latest generation. Tho' the great stroke was instantaneous – it was decisive & effectual & the destruction of the Bastille was the ever memorable signal of the downfall of despotism, wch. Vanished like the baseless fabric of a vision, leaving not a wreck behind.

(f)

For my own part I cannot approve of the French extending even liberty so rapidly. It wd. please me better to see things firmly established first at home – & that they would erect there the Temple of Liberty for surrounding nations to admire and imitate. If from what they have already done – amidst so many furious storms and tempests – we may venture to foretel what they may farther do wth. the influence and stability wch. they now possess – it is impossible to fix a limit to their carreer.

(g)

They seem resolved to destroy & have in part accomplished their purpose, all sense or order & subordination in the minds of men, the only sure basis on which the fabric of civil & political liberty can stand. … I should think it probable by the atrocious act Instead of the silken cords of Liberty, the faction will be obliged to rule them with a rod of Iron. And as to the forreign nations it was very natural for their rulers to interpret the Quixote effects of that faction to extend the fanaticism of Democracy among their neighbours, into a design or attempt to spread anarchy & confusion.

(h)

France exhibits an awful spectacle to rash hot-headed tyrants – & Liberty, however disfigured by rage & violence & besmeared wth. The mingled blood of slaves & patriots, still rears her triumphant head, & proclaims aloud to the astonished world, that her Cause is invincible.

(i)

I cannot enter on the subject of the state of things in France as I am quite exhausted. I cannot join with you in considering the success they have had as the triumph of Liberty however modified by your alter expressions. Their present Govt. is a most ferocious Despotism marked with more outrages of injustice & cruelty than any other at present in Europe, and as the professed friends of Liberty they have dishonoured & hurt its sacred its glorious cause more than its worst enemies.

Social Questions

Document V.30

Quakers on Poverty

Extract (a) is from the Yearly Meeting epistle of 1720, extract (b) is by John Bellers, for whom see Document V.23 above, extract (c) is from the Yearly Meeting epistle for 1757 (all at Friends House, London).

(a)

As mercy, compassion and charity are eminently required in this New Covenant dispensation we are under; so, care of the poor and indigent among us, to see there be no beggar in our Israel, is the concurrent advice of this meeting, that all poor Friends among us may be taken due care of, and none of them sent to the parish to be relieved; that nothing be wanting for their necessary supply; which has been according to our ancient practice and testimony. And it has long been of good report, that we have not only maintained our own poor, but also contributed our share to the poor of the respective parishes wherein we dwell.

Whereupon it is agreed by this meeting, that to the questions already put in our Yearly Meeting, this be added; viz.

How are the poor Friends among you taken care of? ...

(b)

TO THE YEARLY, QUARTERLY, AND MONTHLY MEETINGS OF
GREAT BRITAIN, AND ELSEWHERE.

As the foregoing Proposal in Behalf of the POOR,
was dedicated and delivered to both Houses
of PARLIAMENT *this last Sessions, I now send*
it to you, with the Addition of the following
Considerations.

Whereas it hath been observed, that our *Week-Day Meetings* are thinner now then they were Thirty or Forty Years ago, which some are wondering at, they not discerning the *Signs of the Times.*

When our *Friends* first appeared with a Testimony in this Nation, the People generally seemed to be Religious, and many were then ready to say, *Men and Brethren, what shall we do to be saved? a*nd consequently flocked to our Meetings, as the *Doves to the Windows;* and being as the *Good Ground*, received the Word and Doctrine joyfully.

But the present Age produceth another Sort of Men, who have little Regard to Religion, but are persuing the Pleasures and Vanities of this World, being too much as the *Stony, Thorny, or Highway Ground.*

Of such there will come but a few to our Meetings, by which the Seed of the Kingdom may be sowed among them, and therefore other Hearers should be sought after, which require other Management, besides the Ministry to induce them to it.

Which shews that we are come to another Hour of the Day, wherein another Sort of Work doth offer itself; which when the invited Guests did not come in, the Command was,

> *To go to the Streets and Lanes of the City,*
> *And into the Highways and Hedges,*

And compel them to come in, (not by Penal Laws, but) by offering such a Method of Living (to those who had no Land nor Oxen) as will supply all their Wants, Natural, as well as Spiritual.

A good Education of Youth, hath a great influence towards reducing them to the *Nature of good Ground,* and then our present Ministry may have the same Influence upon them, as the Ministry of our first Friends had upon the People of their Time.

It may be observed that our *Peel-Meeting* is fuller now than it was 30 or 40 Years ago, (and the late inlarging of that Meeting-House implies it) which in some Measure is owing to *Friends Workhouse at Clarkenwel;* besides there are Two Meetings in a Week at that House, which was not 20 Years ago.

And if we can raise as many Workhouses as there are Meetings, every Meeting would find some Benefit by them.

But as that will seem to some, to be an intollerable Burden to Friends, which therefore I shall endeavour to explain to be Practical. It may be observed that some of the Boys in *Friends Workhouse* at *Clarkenwel,* by their present Employment of Spinning, are capable to earn their own Living.

Therefore I propose, that Offers shall be made to others that are not *Friends, That their Boys* (only at first) *shall be kept there for* 18d. *a Week, a Head,* (which will put it out of Doubt that *Friends* will not lose by that Proposal) *their Parents admitting them to be under the Rules of the House.* On which Terms it may be supposed, that sufficient may be had to fill many Workhouses.

But to make the Undertaking the more effectual, and beyond all Contradiction, I recommend, *The Scheme of a College of Industry, of all Useful Trades and Husbandry,* as is mentioned in the First Part.

By which Scheme it doth appear, that a Hundred Labourers so imploy'd, can raise Food and Clothing, and other Necessaries for Two Hundred Persons, which Two Hundred next Year, may raise all Necessaries for Four Hundred; and then Four Hundred next Year, will raise all Necessaries for Eight Hundred: Which by that Geometrical Proportion, in a few Years, may come to many Thousands, and be a Means to introduce the Poor into the Love of Vertue and Industry.

And as every Lover of Vertue and Piety, will gladly incourage an Expedient that will answer those great Ends, so I hope every one will be cautious of contradicting the Proposition I make; before they have well considered it, and can demonstrate it to be either useless or impracticable, least they be found *Fighters against God.*

For he that shall obstruct an Undertaking of so great a Consequence, will be answerable for all the Evils that his Opposition shall be the Occasion of.

And this Proposal is the more valuable, considering that tho' our Saviour said, *How hard is it for a Rich Man to enter the Kingdom of Heaven:* Yet,

That it was the POOR *which received the Gospel.*

By which it plainly appears the Duty of all good Christians, to use their utmost Endeavours for the gathering and instructing of the Poor, of which their Children are the most easily procured by such Colleges, and then will be the more ready to receive a good Education, of which the Consequence may be very great.

First, Considering that the Children of this Age, will be the Men and Women of the next.

Secondly, That the Poor are much more numerous then the Rich, and their Souls are of as much value.

Thirdly, That the Vertuous and Industrious, will be capable of purchasing the Estates of the Vitious and Extravagant, when they have spent them.

Fourthly, That its frequent for some Parents, who by Industry and Temperance, have raised Estates, to have extravagant Children, or Heirs, that spend them.

Therefore its the Interest, as well as Duty, of every prudent and good Man, to endeavour that the Poor may be provided for the future, as well as at the present Time.

That when their Heirs may be reduced to Poverty they may be put in a Station capable to have the Gospel preached unto them, and all their Wants supply in a Way of Temperance and Industry.

Wherefore if every single Person have a Duty (as well as Interest) incumbent upon them of doing such a Good, much more are all *Religious Bodies* bound, who so much excel Single Persons, in Council, Interest, and Ability, as they are in Number.

Therefore I in a more particular Manner, now address my self to *Friends,* of the Yearly, *Quarterly, and Monthly Meetings, in* Great Britain, *&c.* in Behalf of the Poor, and the spreading of Truth, and the Gospel of Peace.

Which *Good Works* will shew the Truth of our Faith, (that worketh by Love) and will convince many People, *That God is among us of a Truth;* our Blessed Saviour having said, *In this shall all Men know that you are my Disciples, if that you love one another.*

But it is one Symptom *That Iniquity abounds, where Love grows cold.*

Yet if such Charity, with Vertue and Industry continues, and increaseth with us, *We shall be as a Light set upon a Hill.*

Joseph was such a Light in *Egypt,* by a timely and effectual Provision of Sustenance for the Wants of that Nation, that gave him so great an Interest with *Pharaoh,* and Influence among the People.

In no Action of our Lives can we shine more, than in a prudent Education and Management of the Poor, by which it will appear, *That We have been with Jesus;* and it may be a Means for us, *To become as the Stone cut out of the Mountain without Hands, which came to fill the whole Earth.*

The Method I propose by Colleges of Industry, will not only provide Food, but Clothing, and all other Necessaries of Life for many Thousands that now want them, not only for Seven Years, but for many Sevens, producing a continual Fountain of Supply.

And will be to all other Workhouses and Charity Schools, As Moses's *Rod was to the* Egyptians, except they shall use the same Method, with as much Integrity, Vertue, and Industry.

I hope none will be as the Evil Spies, of whom it is writ,

Numb.xiii. ver. 32. *They brought up an evil Report of the Land, and caused the People to murmur, for which they were not admitted to enter it.*

But to the Rich more particularly, I would remember them of the Messages which *Mordecai* sent to Queen *Esther,*

Esther iv. ver. 14. *Who knoweth whether thou art come to the Kingdom* (thy Estate) *for such a time as this.*

Matth..x. ver 16. *Be ye Wise as Serpents, and Harmless as Doves.*

Luke vii. ver. 35. *Wisdom is justified of all her Children.*

Prov. viii. vers. 16. *I Wisdom dwell with Prudence.*

Isa. xxxiii. vers. 16. *Wisdom shall be the Stability of thy Times.*

If my Advice, and Proposal of a *College of Industry*, had been put into Practice, which I writ, and dedicated to *Friends*, Twenty Eight Years ago, or Two Years after, when it was recommended by Forty Five *Friends*, in the following Words (of whom Thirty Two of them are since fallen asleep) I believe we should have been double the Number we are now; and also have stirr'd up, and provoked others by our Example, to that Great and Good Work of effectually providing for the poor, by imploying and reforming of them, whose great and many Vices and Miseries, cry aloud for it.

London, the 1st of the
4th Month, 1723.   *John Bellers.*

(c)

We think it incumbent upon us, in this Time of *Scarcity*, particularly to impress it upon our Brethren, to open their Hearts and Hands freely for the Relief of the Poor and Needy of all Denominations: Those in Affluence especially ought ever to bear in Mind, that none are intrusted with Riches, that they may indulge themselves in Pleasures, or for the Gratification of Luxury, Ambition or Vain-glory; but to do Good, and to communicate thereof; by which the Afflictions of the Distressed will be mitigated, and even outward Substance render'd a Means of laying up a good Foundation against the Time to come: *For he that hath Pity upon the Poor, lendeth to the* Lord, *and that which he hath given, will He pay him again.*[1]

Note

1.   Prov. xix. 17.

Document V.31

Quakers on the Slave Trade

Well before the anti-slave trade campaign gathered momentum the Society advised members against involvement, and opposition to the trade became evident earlier than might have been expected. The first passage quoted here is from 1758. American Friends collectively and individually (notably Anthony Benezet and John Woolman) attempted to persuade British Quakers of the importance of the cause. From the 1780's onwards the anti-slave trade campaign was a regular theme in the Yearly Meeting epistles. Benezet's works included *A Caution and Warning to Great Britain and her Colonies in a Short Representation of the Calamitous state of the enslaved Negroes in the British Dominions* ... , Philadelphia, 1776, reprinted in London with the abridged title, 1777, and 1784; and *Some Historical Account of the Slave Trade, its Nature and Lamentable Effects* ... , Philadelphia, 1771, reprinted in London in 1772 and 1778. John Woolman's *Journal* was printed three times in London in 1775, and in Dublin in 1776, 1778 and 1794. It was included in his *Works*, Philadelphia, 1774. See Phillips P. Moulton, *The Journal and Major Essays of John Woolman*, New York: OUP, 1971. As the anti-slave trade campaign gathered momentum the Meeting for Sufferings in 1783 issued for the wider public *The case of our fellow-creatures, the oppressed Africans*, by John Lloyd and William Dillwyn. The following year copies were sent to all Members of Parliament, and in all 12,000 copies of the first two printings were circulated.

Extracts (a), (b) and (c) are from the Yearly Meeting epistles of 1758, 1784 and 1796 respectively.

(a)

We also fervently warn all in profession with us, that they be careful to avoid being in any way concerned in reaping the unrighteous profits arising from that iniquitous practice of dealing in negroes and other slaves; whereby, in the original purchase, one man selleth another, as he doth the beast that perishes, without any better pretension to a property in him than that of superior force; in direct violation of the gospel rule, which teacheth every one to do as they would be done by, and to 'do good' unto all; being the reverse of that covetous disposition, which furnishes encouragement to those poor ignorant people to perpetuate their savage wars, in order to supply the demands of this most unnatural traffic, whereby great numbers of mankind, free by nature, are subjected to inextricable bondage; and which hath often been observed to fill their possessors with haughtiness, tyranny, luxury, and barbarity, corrupting the minds, and debasing the morals of their children, to the unspeakable prejudice of religion and virtue, and the exclusion of that Holy Spirit of universal love, meekness, and charity, which is the unchangeable nature, and the glory of true Chrisitanity. We therefore can do no less than, with the greatest earnestness, impress it upon Friends everywhere, that they endeavour to keep their hands clear of this unrighteous gain of oppression.

(b)

The Christian religion being designed to regulate and refine the natural affections of man, and to exalt benevolence into that charity which promotes peace on earth, and good-will towards all ranks and classes of mankind the world over; under the influence thereof, our minds have been renewedly affected in sympathy with the poor enslaved Africans; whom avarice hath taught some men, laying claim to the character of Christians, to consider as the refuse of the human race, and not entitled to the common privileges of mankind. The contempt in which they are held, and the remoteness of their sufferings from the notice of disinterested observers, have occasioned few advocates to plead their cause. The consideration of their case being brought weightily before the last yearly-meeting, friends were engaged to recommend endeavours for putting a stop to a traffick so disgraceful to humanity, and so repugnant to the precepts of the gospel. The report of the measures adopted in execution thereof, hath afforded comfort and satisfaction to this meeting; and it hath been our concern to recommend to our friends, to whose care this business is committed, to persevere in all prudent exertions for attaining the desirable end. And it is our earnest desire, that none under our name may weaken or counteract our endeavours by contributing, in any way, to the support of this iniquitous commerce.

(c)

Respecting the Slave Trade, though we have no good tidings to proclaim, we feel unwilling to pass it over in silence. As a body, we have been among the foremost to expose its turpitude; and, although it doth not appear at present to be our duty to take any publick step as the advocates of this degraded class of our fellow creatures, we still continue to view the commerce with unremitting abhorrence: and we much desire that no one, once touched with a sense of their complicated woe, may suffer its being thus dreadfully protracted, to efface the impression from his memory, or sympathy from his heart.

Document V.32

John Howard and Prison Reform

John Howard (c.1726–90) was an Independent of the evangelical Calvinist kind, who became a pioneer of prison reform, and whose work lives on in the Howard League for Penal Reform (1866). His reports on British and European prisons did much to bring public notice the shameful conditions of gaols and the inhumane treatment of prisoners in many parts. He published *The State of Prisons in England and Wales, with Preliminary Observations and an Account of some Foreign Prisons*, 1777, and *An Account of the Principal Lazarettos in Europe*, 1789. In his later work hospitals also came within Howard's investigative purview. He died whilst on a field trip to Russia.

For Howard see BCE, DEB, DNB, ODCC. The following is an example of one of his reports from his 1777 work.

County Gaol At Chelmsford.

Gaoler: Selina Taylor.
  Salary, none.
  Fees, Debtors ⎫
    ,,   Felons ⎬ £0 15 4
  Transports, to London or Gravesend, £1 5 0 for each, if not more than seven; for
    each above seven, £1 1 0.

Prisoners.
  Allowance, Debtors ⎫ A pound and a half of bread a day, and a
    ,,   Felons ⎬ quart of small beer. (see Remarks.)
  Garnish, Debtors,   £0 4 6
    ,,   Felons,   0 3 0

Number of	Debtors.	Felons.
1774, Feb. 4	30	30
,, Dec. 6	13	31
1775, Oct. 19	19	14
1776, Nov. 20	22	7

Chaplain.
  Duty – Sunday, Monday, Wednesday.
  Salary, £40.

Surgeon. Mr Griffenhooft.
  Salary, £25, for felons and the bridewell prisoners.

Remarks.
  A close prison, frequently infected with gaol distemper. Inquiring in October,
    1775, for the head turnkey, I was told he died of it.
  In the tap room there hung a paper on which, among other things, was written:
    'Prisoners to pay Garnish, or run the Gauntlet.'
  Debtors have a bushel of coals a day from about the 12th November to Lady Day,
    and £5 a year by a legacy from Elizabeth Herris from lands in Brentwood, paid
    by the rector or minister of the parish of Chelmsford on the 24th December. By
    a memorial hung up in the tap room it appears the bequest was acknowledged
    by the testatrix 14th June, 1746. It was generous in the Justices to grant debtors
    the same allowance as felons, and very judicious to fix that allowance to a *cer-
    tain weight.*
  It gave me pain to be informed that there had been no divine service for above a
    year past, except to condemned criminals.
  There is a new gaol, which exceeds the old one in strength, &c., almost as much
    as in splendour. The County, to their honour, have spared no cost. The
    Magistrates cannot but know the plan. The prison is nearly finished. It can
    therefore be of no service to offer any remarks upon this *stately* fabrick.

Table of Fees.

Essex. At General Quarter Sessions, &c., a Table of Fees settled, to be taken by the Keeper of His Majesty's Gaol, pursuant to an Act made in the second year of King George II., viz.;

For the chamber rent, bed and bedding of each debtor, provided that no more than two be put into one bed, nor more than two beds in one room	0	0	4
For the chamber rent, bed and bedding of each prisoner upon criminal process *per week*, provided that no more than two be put into one bed nor more than two beds in one room	0	3	6
For the Turnkey's Fee into gaol	0	1	0
For the Turnkey's Fee out of gaol	0	1	0
For the Gaoler's Fee upon each prisoner's discharge ...	0	13	4

Recommended and confirmed by us the Justices of Assize this 19th day of July, 1729.

R. Eyre.	Tho. Bramston.
Law: Carter.	Tho. Walford.
	John Cheveley.

Signed by us Justices of Peace in and for the said County this 19th day of July, Anno Dom., 1729.

Rodt. Abdy.
Henry Maynard.
Benj. Moyer.

Document V.33

Sunday Schools

From the 1760's onwards some gave thought to the education of the young in particular, and especially those of underprivileged backgrounds. Among these was the Anglican-turned-Unitarian Theophilus Lindsey (for whom see Document V.22 above), whose Sunday school was opened in 1765 whilst he was vicar of Catterick. The movement received great impetus from Robert Raikes of Gloucester (1736–1811), who used the *Gloucester Journal*, of which he was the proprietor, to publicise the work. Early concerned with general as well as with Christian education, and in some cases employing paid teachers, the church-based Sunday schools increasingly confined themselves to things religious as the campaign for popular education succeeded during the nineteenth century, while there also arose secular Sunday schools for those of that persuasion.

For Raikes see DEB, DNB, DC, P. B. Cliff, *The Rise and Development of the Sunday School Movement in England 1780–1980*, Redhill: Lutterworth Press, 1986; J. P. Ferguson, ed., *Christianity, Society and Education: Robert Raikes, Past, Present and Future*, London: SPCK, 1981. Extract (a) is from Robert Halley, *Lancashire: Its Puritanism and Nonconformity*, Manchester: Tubbs and Brook, 1869, II, p. 472 n., where the quotation is from *History of Blackley Chapel*, p. 105. Extract (b) is by John Sutcliff, for whom see Document IV.10 above, writing in the *Circular Letter of the Northants Association*, 1786, p. 10.

(a)

Sunday schools were established in Manchester in 1784, in accordance with certain resolutions passed at a public meeting of the inhabitants convened by the borough-reeve and constables. The following advertisement, which appeared in the *Manchester Mercury* of January 2, 1792, illustrates the manner in which they were managed: 'The Committee of the Sunday Schools request the visitors in Manchester will deliver to the Overseers of the poor a list of the names of all the children who are instructed in each respective school, also the names of their parents or friends with whom they reside. It is presumed that every school is provided with a book, in which are entered the names of all the children who attend, and marked every Sunday whether *present* or *absent*. The book being produced to the Overseers once or twice every month will answer the full intent. All parents receiving pay from the town and neglecting to send their children regularly to a Sunday School will by this means be strictly noted.'

(b)

It may be hoped that the prevailing practice of establishing schools upon the Lords's-day may be attended with the most beneficial effects. The proper education of youth is a matter of the highest importance. ... According to the present laudable plan, many are in great measure preserved from what would be hurtful; and, by being taught to read and regularly brought to the public worship of God, are in the way to learn that which ... may be profitable to themselves, and render them more useful members of society at large.

Document V.34

A Moral Tale for Children

Anna Letitia Barbauld (1743–1825) was the only daughter of John Aikin, Presbyterian academy tutor at Warrington (for the oration at whose funeral see Document V.69 below). Learned in French, Italian, Latin and Greek, she was acquainted with many of the divines, philosophers, writers and social reformers of her day, and was herself a widely respected essayist and poetess. Following her husband's death she undertook the editorship of a series of the fifty best English novels.

For A. L. Barbauld see DNB. The following extract is Hymn X from her *Hymns In Prose For Children*, 1781.

Look at that spreading oak, the pride of the village green: its trunk is massy, its branches are strong. Its roots, like crooked fangs, strike deep into the soil, and support its huge bulk. The birds build among the boughs: cattle repose beneath its shade: the neighbours form groups beneath the shelter of its green canopy. The old men point it out to their children, but they themselves remember not its growth: generations of men one after another have been born and died, and this son of the forest has remained the same, defying the storms of two hundred winters.

Yet this large tree was once a little acorn; small in size, insignificant in appearance; such as you are now picking up upon the grass beneath it. Such an acorn, whose cup can only contain a drop or two of dew, contained the whole oak. All its massy trunk, all its knotted branches, all its multitude of leaves, were in that acorn; it grew, it spread, it unfolded itself by degrees, it received nourishment from the rain, and the dews, and the well-adapted soil, but it was all there. Rain and dews, and soil, could not raise an oak without the acorn; nor could they make the acorn anything but an oak.

The mind of a child is like the acorn; its powers are folded up, they do not yet appear, but they are all there. The memory, the judgment, the invention, the feeling of right and wrong, are all in the mind of a child; of a little infant just born; but they are not expanded, you cannot perceive them.

Think of the wisest man you ever knew or heard of; think of the greatest man; think of the most learned man, who speaks a number of languages and can find out hidden things; think of a man who stands like that tree, sheltering and protecting a number of his fellow men, and then say to yourself, the mind of that man was once like mine, his thoughts were childish like my thoughts, nay, he was like a babe just born, which knows nothing, remembers nothing, which cannot distinguish good from evil, nor truth from falsehood.

If you had only seen an acorn, you could never guess at the form and size of an oak; if you had never conversed with a wise man, you could form no idea of him from the mute and helpless infant.

Instruction is the food of the mind; it is like the dew and the rain and the rich soil.

As the soil and the rain and the dew cause the tree to swell and put forth its tender shoots, so do books and study and discourse feed the mind, and make it unfold its hidden powers.

Reverence therefore your own mind; receive the nurture of instruction, and the man within you may grow and flourish. You cannot guess how excellent he may become.

It was long before this oak showed its greatness; year after year passed away, and it had only shot a little way above the ground, a child might have plucked it up with his little hands; it was long before any one called it a tree; it is long before a child become a man.

The acorn might have perished in the ground, the young tree might have been shorn of its graceful boughs, the twig might have been bent, and the tree would have been crooked; but if it grew at all, it could have been nothing but an oak, it would not have been grass or flowers, which live their season and then perish from the earth.

The child may be a foolish man, he may be a wicked man, but he must be a man; his nature is not that of any inferior creature, his soul is not akin to the beasts that perish.

O cherish then this precious mind, feed it with truth, nourish it with knowledge; it comes from God, it is made in his image: the oak will last for centuries, but the mind of man is made for immortality.

Respect in the infant the future man. Destroy not in man the rudiments of an angel.

Document V.35

Rowland Hill against the Theatre

Although David Garrick, one of the eighteenth century's most distinguished actors, once said, 'I'd give a hundred guineas to be able to say "Oh!" like Whitefield', and although according to his intonation Whitefield could move an audience to tears or rejoicing when he uttered the word 'Mesopotamia', many Nonconformists were by no means as complimentary to the theatre. The following is a broadsheet posted at Richmond on Saturday, 4 June 1774, close to the playbill for that day. Rowland Hill (1744–1833), though he denied the name 'Dissenter' and was in fact an Anglican deacon (denied priests' orders owing to his irregular preaching), itinerated widely and was connected for most of his ministry with undenominational chapels (which were built for him) where his evangelical and practical Calvinism received a ready hearing. His most important ministry was at the 3,000-seat Surrey Chapel, from 1783 until his death. An enthusiast for evangelical unity, he supported the London Missionary Society, the Religious Tract Society and the British and Foreign Bible Society.

For Hill see DEB, DH, DNB. The broadsheet is reprinted from *Congregational Historical Society Transactions*, XII, no. 5, April 1935, pp. 218–21.

BY COMMAND OF THE KING OF KINGS, *(a)*
AND AT THE DESIRE OF ALL WHO LOVE HIS APPEARING. *(b)*
AT THE THEATRE OF THE UNIVERSE, *(c)*
ON THE EVE OF TIME *(d)* WILL BE PERFORMED,
THE GREAT ASSIZE': OR, DAY OF JUDGMENT. *(e)*

THE SCENERY

Which is now actually preparing, will not only surpass every thing that has a yet been seen, but will infinitely exceed the utmost stretch of human conception, *(f)*. There will be a just representation of all the Inhabitants of the World, in their various and proper colours; and their customs and manners will be so exact, and so minutely delineated, that the most secret thought will be discovered, *(g)*

'For God shall bring every Work into Judgment, with every secret thing whether it be Good or whether it be Evil.'
– *Eccl. xii.* 14.

This THEATRE will be laid out after a new Plan, and will consist of PIT and GALLERY only; and contrary to all others, the GALLERY is fitted up for the reception of Persons of High (or Heavenly) Birth. (*h*) And Pit for those of Low (or earthly) Rank. (*i*) N.B. – The Gallery is very spacious. (*k*) and the Pit without bottom. (*l*)

To prevent inconvenience, there are separate Doors for admitting the Company; and they are so different, that none can mistake that are not wilfully blind. The Door which opens into the Gallery is very narrow, and the steps to it somewhat difficult; for which reason there are seldom many people about it. (*m*) But the Door which gives entrance into the Pit is very wide and commodious, which causes such numbers to flock into it, that it is generally crowded. (*n*) N.B. – The straight Door leads towards the right hand, and the broad one to the left. (*o*) It will be vain for one in a tinselled coat and borrowed language, to personate one of High birth, in order to get admittance into the upper places, (*p*) for there is One of wonderful and deep penetration, who will search and examine every individual; (*q*) and all who cannot pronounce Shibbolith (*r*) in the language of *Canaan*, (*s*) or who has not received a white stone and a new Name; (*t*) or cannot prove a clear title to a certain portion of the Land of Promise, (*u*) must be turned in at the left hand Door. (*w*)

The PRINCIPAL PERFORMERS are described in *I. Thess. iv.* 10, 2 *Thess. i.* 7,8,9, *Matth.xxiv.* 30,31; and *xxv.* 31,32, *Daniel vii.* 9,10, *Jude* 14 to 19, *Rev. xx.* 12 to 15, &c. But as there are some People much better acquainted with the contents of a Play Bill, than the Word of God, it may not be amiss to transcribe a verse or two for their perusal: –

'*The Lord Jesus shall be revealed from Heaven with his mighty Angels, in flaming fire, taking vengeance on them that obey not the Gospel*', but, '*to be glorified in his Saints. (x) A fiery stream issued, and came forth from before him; thousand thousands ministered unto him, and ten thousand times ten thousand stood before him; the Judgment was set, and the Books were opened. (y) And whomsoever was not found written in the Book of Life, was cast into the Lake of Fire*'. (*z*)

ACT FIRST
OF THIS GRAND AND SOLEMN PIECE WILL BE OPENED BY
AN ARCHANGEL WITH THE TRUMP OF GOD!!!
'FOR THE TRUMPET SHALL SOUND AND THE DEAD
SHALL BE RAISED.'

ACT SECOND
PROCESSION OF SAINTS,
In white, with Golden Harps, accompanied with Shouts of Joy and Songs of Praise. (*a*)

ACT THIRD,
WILL BE
AN ASSEMBLAGE OF ALL THE UNREGENERATE. (*b*)
The MUSIC will chiefly consist of Cries, (*c*) accompanied
with WEEPING, WAILING, MOURNING,

LAMENTATION, And WOE. (*d*)
TO CONCLUDE WITH AN ORATION BY
THE SON OF GOD

It is written in the 5th of *Matthew*, from the 31ˢᵗ verse to the end of the chapter; but for the sake of those who seldom read the scriptures, I shall here transcribe two verses: – 'Then shall the King say to them on his Right Hand, "Come ye blessed of My Father, inherit the Kingdom prepared for you from the foundation of the World." Then shall he say also unto them on his left hand, "Depart from me, ye cursed into everlasting Fire, prepared (not, indeed, for you, but) for the Devil and his Angels."'

AFTER WHICH THE CURTAIN WILL DROP.

– Then! O to tell!

John v. 28, 29 .... Some rais'd on high, and others doo'd to hell!
Rev. v. 9.–*xiv.* 3,4 .... These praise the Lamb, and sing redeeming Love,
Luke xvi. 22, 23 .... Lodg'd in his bosom, all his goodness prove;
—— *xix.* 14, 27 .... While those who trampled under foot his grace,
Matth. xxv. 30. 2 *Thess. i.* 9. Are banished now, for ever from his Face.
*Luke xvi.*26 .... Divided thus, a Gulf is fixed between,
Matth. xxv. 46 .... And everlasting, closes up the scene.

'Thus I will do unto thee, O Israel; and because I will do this unto thee, prepare to meet they God, O Israel'. *Amos iv.* 12. TICKETS for the PIT; at the easy purchase of following the vain pomps and vanities of the Fashionable World, and the desires and Amusements of the Flesh; (*e*) to be had at every Flesh-pleasing Assembly. 'If ye live after the flesh, ye shall die'. *Rom.viii.* 13.

TICKETS for the GALLERY, at no less rate than being converted, (*f*) forsaking all (*g*) denying self, taking up the Cross, (*h*) and following Christ in the Regeneration. (*i*) To be had nowhere but in the Word of God, and where that word appoints.

> 'He that hath ears to hear, let him hear. And be not deceived; God is not mocked. For whatsoever a man soweth, that shall he also reap'. *Matth. xi.* 15. *Gal. vi.* 7.

N.B. No money will be taken at the door, (*k*) nor will any Tickets give Admittance into the Gallery, but those sealed by the Lamb.

'Watch, therefore, be ye also ready; for in such an hour as ye think NOT, the Son of Man cometh'. *Matth. xxiv.* 44.

(*a*) Rev. xix. 16. I Tim. vi. 15. (*b*) 2 Tim. iv. 8. Titus ii. 13. (*c*) Rev. xx. 11. Matth. xxiv. 27. (*d*) Rev. x. 6, 7. I Cor. xv. 51, 52. (*e*) Heb. ix. 27. Jude xv. Psalm ix. 7, 8. Rev. vi. 17. 2 Cor. v. 10. (*f*) I Cor. ii. 9. (*g*) Matth. xii. 36–xxv. 32. I Cor. iv. 5. Rom. ii. 12, 16. (*h*) John iii. 3, 5. I Peter i. 23. Rom. viii.14. (*i*) James iii. 14, 15. Rom. iii. 8. (*k*) Luke xiv. 22. John xiv. 2. (*l*) Rev. ix. 1, 2; xix. 20. (*m*) Matth. vii. 11. (*n*) Matth. vii. 15, etc. (*o*) Matth. xxv. 31. (*p*) Matth. vii. 21–2–3; xxii. 11. (*q*) Psalm liv. 20–1. Jerem. xvi. 10. 2 Tim. ii. 19. John x. 14. (*r*) Judges xii. 6. (*s*) Isaiah xix. 18. Zeph. iii. 9. (*t*) Rev. ii. 17. (*u*) 2 Cor. xiii. 5. Gal. iii. 29. Heb. ix. 1–8–9. (*w*) Heb. iii. 17,

18, 19. Rom. xiii. 9. Psalm ix. 17. (*x*) 2 Thess. i. 7, 10. Matth. xxiv. 31. (*y*) Dan. vii. 10. (*z*) Rev. xx. 12, 15. (*a*) Rev. xiv. 2, 3; xv. 2, 3, 4. (*b*) Matth. xiii. 49, 50.; xxv. 32, 41. I Cor. vi. 9, 10. (*c*) Luke xxiii. 30; Psalm cxii. 10. Rev. vi. 16, 17. (*d*) Luke xiii. 28; Matth. xiii. 49,50; Rev. i. 7; Ezek. ii. 10. (*e*) James iv. 4; I John ii. 15, 16, 17. I Tim. v. 6. Eph. ii. 2, 3. (*f*) Matth. xvii. 3. Acts iii. 19; viii. 18 to 24. (*g*) Luke xiv. 33; xviii. 28 to 30. (*h*) Luke ix. 23 to 26; xiv. 27. (*i*) Matth. xix. 28, 29. (*k*) Acts viii. 18 to 24. (*l*) 2 Cor. i. 22. Eph. i. 13, 14; iv. 30. (*m*) Rev. vii. 3. Eph. iv. 30.

LEWIS & Co., Printers, 95, Bunhill Row.

PART VI

NURTURE, PIETY AND CHURCH LIFE

Introduction

Of all the parts in this collection, this, as is appropriate, is the most miscellaneous, for it reflects religious life as it was for most Nonconformists. Few were philosophers, theologians, evangelists, politicians or social reformers, but many were concerned with the nurture of the young, with the life of devotion – a sphere in which women writers made a particular contribution, with the affairs of their church, with worship, and with honouring (though not praying for) the faithful departed and preparing for the life to come. The extracts which follow are intended to afford a glimpse into the academies the Nonconformists founded, the souls they nurtured, the churches and ministers they knew, the discipline they practised and the worship they offered.

Formal Education

Document VI.1

School for Poor Friends

This 1718 epistle by John Bellers is reprinted from George Clarke, *John Bellers: His Life, Times and Writings*, London: Routledge & Kegan Paul, 1987, pp. 223–5. For Bellers see Document V. 24 above.

An epistle to the quarterly meeting of *London* and *Middlesex*

Dear Friends,
As Christ laid it down for a standing and Effectual *Foundation*, for his *Church* to build on, when he said;

That *Loving God with all the Heart, and with all the Soul, and with all the Mind, and our Neighbour as our self* were the two *great Commandments*, on which *Hang all the Law and the Prophets:*

So it's also recommended by that great Apostle *James*, when he wrote. That *pure Religion and undefil'd before God and the Father, is to visit* (or Relieve) *the Fatherless and the Widows in their Affliction and to keep unspotted from the World.*

Therefore a *Virtuous Education* that may keep the YOUTH *unspotted from the World*, and a sufficient Provision for the Imployment of the *Able* POOR, with a charitable Subsistence from the *Disabled*, is one of the most Essential visible Parts of the true Apostolick Christian Religion.

Which I have often consider'd for many Years: and having now a fresh Occasion given me, from the late Advice of the *Yearly Meeting* to the *Quarterly Meetings* for their *Providing a good Education for Friends Children*, I offer the following Proposals, our present Education being defective, for want of a full Provision for Friends Children under all Circumstances.

For tho' there are good *Schools* near *London*, for such whose Parents are able and willing to be at the Charge of *Eighteen* or *Twenty Pound* a Year, for their *Board*, etc. and in the *North* for such as will give *eight* or *ten* pounds.

Yet there are many of our *Friends*, in and about *London*, who are not able to pay 18 or 20 1. a Year, nor willing to send their Children so far from them as the *North*.

Therefore it is highly necessary to find some *Method* for the *Education* of the *Children* of such Parents.

For keeping their Children at Home, and sending them daily to what School is nearest them, it may be of very pernicious Consequence, by the Company and Conversation they may meet with either at School or out of it.

And for *Londoners* sending their Children into the *North*, it's so far from their Parents, that they may be dead before they can see or hear from them. And it would many times be an extream Difficulty for either of the Parents, much more for both of them, to go to see a Sick Child, however great their Desire may be for it.

And farther, none of these *Schools* are any Provision for many that can give but 5 1. a Year, and yet are above wanting the *Charity* of others, whose *Children* ought also to be consider'd for an *Education*; and possibly one Half of *our Friends* may be under those Circumstances.

The PROPOSALS.

For all which good Purposes, I propose our Hospital, *at* Clerkenwell, *as capable to be a sufficient Provision at present, for such of our Friends Children as may desire it in the City of* London *and* Middlesex. *And as it farther prospers, it will be a good Pattern for every County in the Kingdom.*

First, A *Child* may be *Boarded* there, with the present Diet and Rules, at *four Shillings* a Week without Working.

Secondly, Children, whose Parents will allow them to *work*, if they can earn 12d. 18d. or 2 s. a Week, they may be abated weekly, out of the 4 s. a Week, that their Work comes to, which will be a great Ease to many Parents in their Charge.

Thirdly, Many Children that do some Work will Learn much the better for it, Children loving change of Imployments; whilst an Idle Education is an Education to Idleness: Some Imployment being an Advantage to all Children.

Fourthly, Considering, that all the House-Room that is there may be us'd to Entertain Children: There may be many more Provided for, than there are at present.

Fifthly, As there shall be sufficient Number of Children, there may be all Sorts of *Learning* and *Languages* Taught there, where maybe also a Library.

And in Time all Sorts of *Handicraft Trades*, which in *Germany* and *Turkey* is reckoned so Essential a Part of *Education*, that the *German Princes* and the *Grand Signior* are all Taught some *Mechanick* Trade.

And in *Holland* it is a Proverb, *That their Children make Toys for the* English *Children to Play with.*

But to remove one Obstacle to these *Proposals*, it is necessary to change it's Name from a *Work-house*, to be either an *Hospital* or a *College*, but rather the latter; because some Parents will not put their *Children* to so contemptible a Place of Education, as a *Work-house* or an *Hospital*.

The *first* sounding too much like a Bridewell, and the *second* like an *Almshouse*. Whereas a *College* bespeaks a more *Liberal Education*.

And this House, when *Sr. Thomas Row* had it, was call'd *The College* of INFANTS, and so Inscrib'd upon the *Gate*.

And such Colleges, under good Management, may be so enlarg'd as to be made a Means to leaven may of the Poor of the Kingdom with a Love to Vertue and Piety. In the first coming out of our Ministers, their Ministry was the only Means then to convince the People; but since we are become a considerable Body in the Nation, there is a Duty incumbent on this Body, to exert it self in all Christian Offices to propagate Vertue, Charity and Piety among Men; Good Examples being more convincing than Precepts.

Note, What I have proposed for the using Part of our *Hospital* at *Clerkenwell*, for a *Boarding-School*, is not to put the House to any Charge, because those Friends that put their Children there, are either to pay what will keep them, or their Children's Work is to make up what their Parents pay short.

And therefore it will be needful for you, to extend your Acts of *Charity*, to such other Objects as may most want them: And in particular an *Infirmary* or *Hospital* for the Sick would be very useful; and you might take in the *Poor Children of Friends* in the neighbouring Counties, upon the usual Terms, rather than let the House want filling.

And it is *Advantage* sufficient to the *Monthly-Meetings*, that they can have their *Poor* kept there (on them Terms) cheaper and better than any where else.

But for any to think, that the *Monthly-Meeting* should be eased of their *whole Charges*, which they pay for their Poor there, if there were a *Fund* sufficient, would be to *rob* the *Poor* (that might otherwise be there provided for) to give to the *Rich* in easing them, and prevent the *rich* Men whilst living the Opportunity of shewing their *Charity* (which is their *Duty*) to the *Poor*, and consequently of receiving the *Blessing* that doth attend it; which will also leave the Living Poor to expect from the *Dead* their Support: But on the contrary, as the Fund shall Increase, I offer the following *Considerations*, for the Enlargeing of your *Charities* in time to come; and further recommend to your Perusals my former *Proposals for a College of Industry*.

Document VI.2

Thomas Secker and James Clegg on Their Student Days

Excluded from the universities, the Dissenters established academies for the education of their young men. Prior to the Toleration Act academies and tutors were seriously at risk of having legal proceedings taken against them: Richard Frankland's academy migrated no fewer than five times. Post-Toleration a more settled existence was possibly, though academies would still remove on the acceptance by their principal tutor of a new pastorate, and not all of them enjoyed a long life. Academy students were supported by the Presbyterian Fund (1689), the Congregational Fund Board (1695) and the King's Head Society (1730). The education given was by no means exclusively theological, neither was every student destined for the ministry. On the contrary, some academies – supremely that at Warrington, the 'Athens of the North' – pioneered education in the sciences, and the best of the academies could hold their own with the universities in terms of curriculum and teachers. In the second half of the eighteenth century, under the impact of the Revival, new evangelical academies were founded – as at Trevecka and Newport Pagnell. In these the emphasis was not so strongly on general academic education: indeed, as we have seen, philosophy, for example, received short shrift in some of them.

For the academies see H. McLachlan, *English Education under the Test Acts*, Manchester: Manchester University Press, 1931, Irene Parker, *Dissenting Academies in England*, Cambridge: CUP, 1914; Alan P. F. Sell, *Philosophy, Dissent and Nonconformity 1689–1920*, Cambridge: James Clarke, 2004; J. W. Ashley Smith, *The Birth of Modern Education: The Contribution of the Dissenting Academies 1660–1880*, London: Independent Press, 1954; David L. Wykes, 'The Contribution of the Dissenting Academy to the Emergence of Rational Dissent', in Knud Haakonssen, ed., *Enlightenment and Religion: Rational Dissent in Eighteenth-Century Britain*, Cambridge: CUP, 1996, ch. 5. See also the series on 'Early Nonconformist Academies', *Congregational Historical Society Transactions*, VI, 1915.

In extract (a), from T. Gibbons, *Memoirs of Dr. Isaac Watts*, 1780, pp. 346–53, Thomas Secker, the future Archbishop of Canterbury, aged eighteen, writes to his sponsor, Isaac Watts, concerning life in Samuel Jones's academy which had in 1712 removed from Gloucester to Tewkesbury. For Secker (1693–1768) see DNB, ODCC. For Jones see Document I.9 above. For Watts see Document I.2 above. In extract (b), from his *Diary*, ed. V. Doe, Chesterfield: Derbyshire Record Society, 1981, part III, p. 913, the Presbyterian minister James Clegg recalls his student days, making clear his early distaste for 'Rigid Calvinism'. The work of Richard Franklan's Rathmell academy was continued in Manchester by John Chorlton, for whom see Document II.12 above. For Frankland (1630–98) and Clegg see Document III.9 above.

(a)

Before I give you an account of the state of our academy, and the other things you desired me, please to accept my hearty thanks for that service you have done me, both in advising me to prosecute my studies in such an extraordinary place of education, and in procuring me admittance to it. I wish my improvements may be answerable to the advantages I enjoy: but however that may happen, your kindness has fixed me in a place where I am very happy, and spend my time to good purpose; and where, if I do not, the fault will all be my own.

I am sensible how difficult it is to give a character of any person or thing, and because the most probable guesses we make very often prove false ones. But, since you are pleased to desire it, I think myself obliged to give you the best and most impartial account of matters I can.

Mr Jones then I take to be a man of real piety, great learning, and agreeable temper; one who is very diligent in instructing all under his care, very well qualified to give instructions, and whose well-managed familiarity will always make him respected. He is very strict in keeping good orders and will effectually preserve his pupils from negligence and immorality. And accordingly I believe there are not many academies freer in general from those vices than we are. In particular my bedfellow, Mr Scott is one of unfeigned religion, and a diligent searcher after truth. His general carriage and agreeable disposition give him the esteem of everyone. Mr Griffith is more than ordinary serious and grave, and improves more in everything than one could expect from a man who seems to be not much under forty; particularly in Greek and Hebrew he has made a great progress. Mr Francis and Mr Watkins are diligent in study and truly religious. The elder Mr Jones, having had a better education than they, will in all probability make a greater scholar; and his brother is one of quick parts.

Our *Logic*, which we have read once over, is so contrived as to comprehend all *Heereboord*, and the far greater part of *Mr Locke's* Essay, and the *Art of Thinking*. What Mr Jones dictated to us was but short, containing a clear and brief account of the matter, references to the places where it was more fully treated of, and remarks on, or explications of, the authors cited, when need required.

At our next lecture we gave an account both of what the author quoted and our tutor said, who commonly then gave us a larger explication of it, and so proceeded to the next thing in order. He took care, as far as possible, that we understood the sense, as well as remembered the words of what we had read, and that we should not suffer ourselves to be cheated with obscure terms which had no meaning. Though he be no admirer of the old Logic, yet he has taken a great deal of pains both in explaining and correcting taken a great deal of pains both in explaining and correcting *Heereboord*, and had for the most part made him intelligible, or shown that he is not so.

The two Mr Jones's, Mr Francis, Mr Watkins and Mr Sheldon, and two more gentlemen are to begin Jewish Antiquities in a short time. I was designed for one of their number, but rather chose *Logic* once more: both because I was utterly unacquainted with it when I came to this place, and because the others having all, except Mr Francis, been at other academies will be obliged to make more haste than those in a lower class, and consequently cannot have so good or large accounts of anything, nor so much time to study every head. We shall have gone through our course in about four years time, which I believe nobody that once knows Mr Jones will think too long.

I began to learn *Hebrew* as soon as I came hither, and find myself now able to construe, and give some grammatical account of about twenty verses in the *easier* parts of the *Bible* after less than an hour's preparation. We read every day two verses apiece in the *Hebrew Bible* which we turn into *Greek* (no one knowing what his verses shall be, though at first it was otherwise). And this with *Logic* is our morning's work.

Mr Jones also began about three months ago some critical lectures in order to the exposition you advised him to. The principal things contained in them are about the *Antiquity of the Hebrew Language, Letters, Vowels, the Incorruption of the Scriptures*, ancient *Divisions of the Bible*, an account of the *Talmud, Masora* and *Cabala*. We are at present up on the Seqtuagint, and shall proceed after that to the *Targumim*, and other versions etc. Every part is managed with abundance of perspicuity, and seldom any material thing is omitted that other authors have said upon the point, though very frequently we have useful additions of things which are not to be found in them. We have scarce been upon anything yet but Mr Jones has had those writers which are most valued on that head, to which he always refers us. This is what we first set about in the afternoon; which being finished, we read a chapter in the *Greek Testament*, and after that *Mathematics*. We have gone through all that is commonly taught of *Algebra* and *Proportion*, with the six first books of *Euclid*, which is all Mr Jones designs for the gentlemen I mentioned above, but he intends to read something more to the class that comes after them.

This is our daily employment, which in the morning takes up about two hours, and something more in the afternoon. Only on Wednesdays in the morning we read *Dionysius's Periegesis*, on which we have notes mostly geographical, but with some criticisms intermixed; and in the afternoon we have no lecture at all. So on Saturday in the afternoon we have only a thesis, which none but they who have done *Logic* have any concern in. We are also just beginning to read *Isocrates* and *Terence* each twice a week. On the latter our tutor will give us some notes which he received in a college from *Perizonius*.

We are obliged to rise at five o'clock every morning and to speak *Latin* always, except when below stairs among the family. The people where were we live are very civil, and the greatest inconvenience we suffer is, that we fill the house rather too much, being sixteen in number besides Mr Jones. But I suppose the increase of his academy will oblige him to remove next spring. We pass our time very agreeably betwixt study and conversation with our tutor, who is always ready to discourse freely of anything that is useful, and allows us either then or at our lecture all imaginable liberty of making objections against his opinions and prosecuting them as far as we can. I almost forgot to mention our tutor's library which is composed for the most part of foreign books, which seem to be very well chosen, and are every day of great advantage to us.

Thus I have endeavoured, Sir, to give you an account of all that I thought material or observable amongst us. As for my own part, I apply myself with what diligence I can to every thing which is the subject of one of our lectures, without preferring one subject before another; because I see nothing we are engaged in, but what is either necessary, or extremely useful for one who would thoroughly understand those things which most concern him, or be able to explain them well to others. I hope I have not spent my time, since I came to this place, without some small improvement both in human knowledge, and that which is far better, and I earnestly desire the benefit of your prayers that God would be pleased to fit me better for his service both in this world and the next. This, if you please to afford me, and your advice with relation to study, or whatever else you think convenient, must needs be extremely useful, as well as agreeable, and shall be thankfully received by your most obliged, humble servant.

T. Secker

(b)

1699

When I left Rathmel I placed myselfe in Manchester for the benefit of the Library and the Conversation of other young Scholars that lived there and I boarded with Dr. Wild in Fennel Street where Mr. Richard Miln of Millrow near Roachdale also boarded, I had been very intimately acquainted with him at Rathmel and his conversation was of use to me at Manchester, but in a little time he was calld to be minister at Stockport and I removd from Dr. Wild's to Mr Chorlton. Several young men who had been under Mr Franklands tuition at Rathmel also came about that time and placd themselves under Mr. Chorlton who was admirably qualified for a Tutor, as well as a preacher. He Read Lectures to us in the forenoon in Philosophy and Divinity and in the afternoon some of us read in the Public Library, twas there I first met with the works of Episcopius, Socinus Crellius etc. The writings of Socinus and his followers made little impression on me, only I could never after be entirely reconcild to the common doctrine of the Trinity but then begun to incline to that Scheme which long after Dr. Clark espousd and publishd but I admird the clear and strong reasoning of Episcopius and after that could never well relish the doctrines of Rigid Calvinism. But all this time I continued too much addicted to levity and keeping company and made not that good improvement of the advantages I had that I ought to have done. Some acquaintance I fell into in that Town that led me into evils that I have great reason to lament, but after I had spent little more than a year there I left the town and boarded with Jos. Dawson the pious serious Dissenting Minister in Roachdale and his good advice and pious conversation was of great use to me.

Document VI.3

Samuel Clark's Advice to Philip Doddridge

On 3 October 1721 Clark wrote as follows to his protégé, Doddridge, for both of whom see Document I.1 above. The extract is included a second time because of Doddridge's importance in theological education.

I am sensible of the difficulties pneumatology has attending it. The only method of extricating oneself out of them is to see that we have clear ideas of all the terms we use, whether single, or connected with propositions, and that we take nothing for granted without sufficient evidence; and, which flows from the other two, that we do not pretend to reason upon things about which we have no ideas: that is, that we do not pretend to impossibilities. Mr. Locke's Essay is so useful to direct the mind in its researches, that methinks it should have been read before you entered upon pneumatics. ... As to your contemplations upon the being and attributes of God, take heed of suffering your mind to rest in barren speculations. Whatever clear and enlarged ideas you attain to of the divine excellencies, see that they have proportionable effect upon the soul, in producing reverence, affection, and submission.

Document VI.4

'Of Academical Exercises': Northampton Academy

The following extract is from the *Constitutions Orders & Rules relating to the Academy at Northampton agreed upon by the Tutors & the several Members of it in December 1743 & then Established as the future Conditions of Admission into the Academy or Continuance in it.* The document contains further sections: 'Of Attendance on Family Prayer & Lecture at appointed Times'; 'Of the Hours Place & Order of meals'; 'Of Shutting the Gate & Retiring to Bed'; 'Rules relating to the Chambers & Closets'; 'Rules relating to the Library'; 'Rules relating to the Office of the Monitor'; 'Rules relating to Conduct abroad'; 'Miscellaneous Rules'. The *Constitution*, transcribed and slightly edited by Malcolm Deacon from DWL MS (New College, London MS 2/4), is reprinted from his *Philip Doddridge of Northampton*, Northampton: Northamptonshire Libraries, 1980, pp. 191–2.

Constitutions Orders & Rules relating to the Academy at Northampton agreed upon by the Tutors & the several Members of it in December 1743 & then Established as the future Conditions of Admission into the Academy or Continuance in it.

Sect I.   Of Academical Exercises

1.   In the first year Translations are to be made from Latin into English & vice versa as appointed by the Tutors to be shewed them at the Day & Hour appointed, & in the last three months of this year Orations are to be exhibited in Latin & English alternately every Thursday which is also to be the Time of the following Exercises.
2.   In the first half of the Second Year these Orations are to be continued & in the latter Part of the Year each is in his Turn to exhibit a Philosophical Thesis or Dissertation.
3.   In the third year Ethical Theses or Dissertations are to be exhibited weekly as above, & toward the End of this Year & during the Fourth Theological.
4.   The Revolution of these is to be so adjusted that every Student may compose at least six Orations, Theses or Dissertations before the Conclusion of his fourth year, & if the numbers of Students should be such that more Theses be exhibited than can be disputed on weekly with the Allowance of one vacant Thursday in the Month Disputations are to be held on the Remainder at any Time in the Morning in the presence of the Assistant Tutor on Days when the Principal Tutor is obliged to be absent.
5.   All the Subjects to be disputed upon are to be given out with the Names of the Respondent & Opponent affixed to the particular Questions at least as soon as the Academy meets after the long Vacation & that at Christmas, & where it can be done with certainty before it breaks up at those Vacations.
6.   The Absence of the Tutor is not to occasion the Omission of any of these Exercises & if the person to exhibit them be disabled by Illness or otherwise unavoidably prevented the next in Order is to take his Place & the Turns to be exchanged; in order to provide for which each Exercise is to be delivered into the Tutor's Hand on the Day he shall appoint at what he judges a proper Distance of Time between that of its Assignment & Exhibition.
7.   Exercises are to be first written in a paper Book, then reviewed & corrected by one of the Tutor's after that fairly transcribed & after they have been exhibited in the Manner which shall be appointed a fair Copy of them with the Authors' Names annexed shall be delivered to the Tutor.
8.   Two sermons on given Subjects are to be composed by every Theological

Student in his eighth half year to be read over by him in the Class & having been there corrected to be preached in the Family if the student does not propose preaching in publick before he leave the Academy & besides these at least six schemes of other Sermons on given Texts are to be exhibited in the Class during the fourth year by each Student.

9. If any Student continue a fifth year he is to compose at least one Sermon & exhibit two Schemes every Quarter whether he do or do not preach in Publick. Besides which he is this fifth year to exhibit & defend two large Theological Theses; or if he stay but a part of the 5th year a proportionable Part of these Exercises is to be performed.

10. Four Classics viz One Greek & one Latin poet, One Greek & one Latin prose writer as appointed by the Tutor are to be read by each Student in his Study & Observations are to be written upon them to be kept in a distinct Book & communicated to Tutor whenever he shall think fit.

11. Each Student of the upper Class may be allowed to propose a difficult Scripture to the principal Tutor every Thursday Morning to be discussed & examined by him the next Thursday Morning. But it will be expected that the person proposing them write some Memorandums of the Solution to be afterwards subjected to Review.

12. From the Entrance on the 2[n]d to the end of the 8th half year each Theological Pupil will be expected to write either at Meeting or afterward in a proper Book notes of all the Sermons he hears to be examined by the Tutor when he shall require & the neglect of this shall be deemed the Omission of a Stated Exercise & as such shall expose to yt[it] a proper Fine.

13. On the four Thursdays immediately preceding the Long Vacation (or in Case of an unavoidable Hinderance then on the next Lecture Day following that on which there has been an Omission) the whole Academy is to meet at Ten in the Morning & all the Forenoon is to be spent in the Examination of Students in the several Studies of the preceding year. And on the two first of these Days Disputations shall be held by the two upper Classes in the presence of the Juniors that they may learn by Example the Method of Disputation & this is the only Exercise of this Kind at which the Junior Classes may be present.

14. In case of a Total Neglect of preparing an appointed Exercise sixpence is to be forfeited to the Box & two pence if a rough Dra[ft of] it be not ready for the first Examination a Fortnight after it is assigned, at which Time it is to be brought to the Tutor without being particularly called for; not is Forgetfulness to be allowed as any Excuse when the Order has been registered in the Library Book.

Document VI.5

Job Orton on the Daventry Academy

On the death of Philip Doddridge in 1751 the academy removed to Daventry, and Caleb Ashworth was appointed tutor. The following was written to him by Job Orton.

For Ashworth see Document I.11 above; for Orton see Document III.12 above. The extract is reprinted from John Waddington, *Congregational History 1700–1800*, London: Longmans, Green, 1876, pp. 495–6.

I really think the students lived too well at Northampton ... I hope I need not caution you against that error in the good Doctor in saying true things to and of almost any-body ... When Dr. Doddridge expounded in the morning, it was seldom less than an hour, which is quite too much ... I hope you will never be the slave of any persons, either Independents or Presbyterians, orthodox or otherwise. Set out upon a generous plan the be steady. ... Pecuniary penalties are very proper, but of late years they an-swered no end, because the students never paid them, but they were put down to their account, which was no punishment to them. Insist upon their paying every week. Especially warn the students against metaphysical and philosophical prayers, but *let not your animadversions be severe, as the good Doctor's often were, when he thought they were not evangelical, which intimidated and discouraged many of his pupils. Errors that will naturally mend by years and experience should be gently treated.*

Document VI.6

Joseph Priestley's Recollections of Daventry Academy

For Priestley see Document I.11 above; and see Tony Rail and Beryl Thomas, 'Joseph Priestley's Journal while at Daventry Academy, 1754', *Enlightenment and Dissent*, XII, 1994, pp. 49–113. The following is from Priestley's *Works*, London, 1817–31, I, part I, pp. 21–5.

(25.) My aunt, and all my relations, being strict Calvinists, it was their intention to send me to the academy at Mile-end, then under the care of Dr. Conder. But, being at that time an Arminian, I resolutely opposed it, especially upon finding that if I went thither, besides giving an *experience*, I must subscribe my assent to ten printed articles of the strictest Calvinistic faith, and repeat it every six months. My opposi-tion, however, would probably have been to no purpose; and I must have adopted some other mode of life, if Mr. Kirkby (above-mentioned) had not interposed, and strongly recommended the academy of Dr. Doddridge, on the idea that I should have a better chance of being made a scholar. He had received a good education himself, was a good classical scholar, and had no opinion of the mode of education among the very orthodox Dissenters, and being fond of me, he was desirous of my having every advantage that could be procured for me. My good aunt, not being a bigoted Calvinist, entered into his views, and Dr. Doddridge being dead, I was sent to Daventry, and was the first pupil that entered there. My step-mother also, who was a woman of good sense, as well as of religion, had a high opinion of Dr. Doddridge, having been some time house-keeper in his family. She had always recommended his academy, but died before I went thither.

(26.) Three years, viz. from September 1752, to 1755, I spent at Daventry, with that peculiar satisfaction with which young persons of generous minds usually go through a course of liberal study, in the society of others engaged in the same pursuits, and free from the cares and anxieties which seldom fail to lay hold on them when they come out into the world.

(27.) In my time, the academy was in a state peculiarly favourable to the serious pursuit of truth, as the students were about equally divided upon every question of much importance, such as liberty and necessity, the sleep of the soul, and all the articles of theological orthodoxy and heresy; in consequence of which, all these topics were the subject of continual discussion. Our tutors also were of different opinions; Dr. Ashworth taking the orthodox side of every question, and Mr. Clark, the sub-tutor, that of heresy, though always with the greatest modesty.

(28.) Both of our tutors being young, at least as tutors, and some of the senior students excelling more than they could pretend to do in several branches of study, they indulged us in the greatest freedoms, so that our lectures had often the air of friendly conversations on the subjects to which they related. We were permitted to ask whatever questions, and to make whatever remarks we pleased; and we did it with the greatest, but without any offensive, freedom. The general plan of our studies, which may be seen in Dr. Doddridge's published lectures, was exceedingly favourable to free inquiry, as we were referred to authors on both sides of every question, and were even required to give an account of them. It was also expected that we should abridge the most important of them for our future use. The public library contained all the books to which we were referred.

(29.) It was a reference to 'Dr Hartley's Observations on Man,' in the course of our Lectures, that first brought me acquainted with that performance, which immediately engaged my closest attention, and produced the greatest, and in my opinion the most favourable effect on my general turn of thinking through life. It established me in the belief of the doctrine of Necessity, which I first learned from Collins; it greatly improved that disposition to piety which I brought to the academy, and freed it from the rigour with which it had been tinctured. Indeed, I do not know whether the consideration of Dr. Hartley's theory contributes more to enlighten the mind, or improve the heart; it affects both in so super-eminent a degree.

(30.) In this situation, I saw reason to embrace what is generally called the heterodox side of almost every question. But notwithstanding this, and though Dr. Ashworth was earnestly desirous to make me as orthodox as possible, yet, as my behaviour was unexceptionable, and as I generally took his part in some little things by which he often drew upon himself the ill-will of many of the students, I was upon the whole a favourite with him. I kept up more or less of a correspondence with Dr. Ashworth till the time of his death, though much more so with Mr. Clark. This continued till the very week of his melancholy death, by a fall from his horse, at Birmingham, where he was minister.

(31.) Notwithstanding the great freedom of our speculations and debates, the extreme of heresy among us was Arianism; and all of us, I believe, left the academy with a belief, more or less qualified, of the doctrine of *atonement*.

Document VI.7

Creeping Unitarianism at Carmarthen Academy

Robert Gentleman (1746–95) was a popular preacher, whose theology tended towards Arianism, but whose spirit was evangelical. He was reared under the ministry of Job Orton at Shrewsbury, trained under Caleb Ashworth at Daventry, and, following a pastorate at Shrewsbury, he became tutor at Carmarthen academy in 1779. As early as 1755 the Congregational Fund Board had withdrawn support from that academy owing to the Arianising theology promoted there. Gentleman resigned in 1784 on acceptance of the pastorate at Kidderminster, whereupon the academy removed to Swansea under Solomon Harris (1726–85), who died within a year.

For Gentleman see DNB; for Harris see DWB. For the academy see D. Elwyn Davies, 'Education and Radical Dissent in Wales in the Eighteenth and Nineteenth Centuries', *Transactions of the Unitarian Historical Society*, XIX, no. 2, April 1988. pp 92–101. The following reminiscence of John Williams, the biographer of Thomas Belsham, is reprinted from John Waddington, *Congregational History 1700–1800*, London: Longmans, Green, 1876, p. 637.

The writer well remembers as early as the year 1783, when he first entered as a student at Carmarthen (or rather at Rhyd Gors, in the neighbourhood), under the superintendence of Rev. Robert Gentleman, the senior class, and indeed almost all the students who had paid any attention to the subject, were avowedly Unitarian, in the strictest sense of the term; and when in the succeeding year he removed to Hoxton, he found the same sentiments generally prevailing in that institution. The class which completed their course at the conclusion of the session, Midsummer, 1785, were all declared Unitarians, excepting one; and the other classes, with few exceptions, were generally disposed to receive, and ultimately embraced and avowed, the same sentiments; and at the time of his leaving Daventry, where the writer finished his academical course in the year 1789, these were the opinions of the majority of his fellow-students who were then entering upon the Christian ministry, yet they were invited by some of the leading Dissenting congregations to the pastorship.

Document VI.8

The Bristol Case for an Educated Ministry

The following is the work of the Bristol Education Society, 1770. The document is re-printed from Norman S. Moon, *Education for Ministry*, Bristol: Bristol Baptist College, 1979, pp. 129–31.

'The importance of a liberal education, more especially to candidates for the Christian ministry, is so exceedingly obvious, that one might almost think it impossible that any considerate, intelligent person should not be convinced of it. Yet there are, it is well known, some very worthy people who, from a mistaken view of things, not only call in question the importance of such an education, but even seem to imagine it is rather prejudicial than useful. Now, if these prejudices are well founded, every scheme formed for the education of pious youths designed for the ministry ought to be discountenanced. But if, on the other hand, it should appear that these prejudices are unreasonable, and that a learned education is highly useful, then every institution calculated for that purpose must be deserving of the warmest and most effectual encouragement. It is proposed, therefore, as introductory to an account of the BRISTOL EDUCATION SOCIETY, to offer a few thoughts on the usefulness and importance of learning to a Gospel minister; and, likewise, to lay down the plan of instruction at present pursued in that particular seminary, which it is the more immediate design of this Society to countenance and support.

That all the learning in the world is, of itself, by no means sufficient to complete the ministerial character is readily acknowledged; and it is, therefore, a very great absurdity to think of training up young persons to the Christian ministry in the same indiscriminate manner as to any other profession. If a man be not truly religious, and furnished with talents adapted to the work of the ministry, let him have as much learning as may be, it cannot be expected that he should be an acceptable and useful minister. And it is much to be apprehended that an abuse of learning, in this repect, hath contributed more than anything to bring it into disrepute. Let it, therefore, be remembered, all that is pleaded for in this introduction, is the usefulness and importance of learning in *subordination* to what is more essentially requisite to the ministerial character. Many persons without any of the advantages of learning, we freely confess, have been very able, laborious, and successful ministers of the Gospel. But not a few of these ministers themselves, so far from decrying learning a useless, have sensibly felt their own want of it, and with an amiable candor acknowledged the disadvantages they lay under on that account. And, indeed, it is highly unreasonable, as well as ungrateful, for those who are destitute of learning, to exclaim against it, since they are not to be supposed very competent judges of the matter, and are themselves under peculiar obligations to the WORKS of the learned. The expressions of an eminent divine upon this subject, in a late important publication, are remarkably strong: 'Here I cannot but observe the amazing ignorance and stupidity of some persons who take it into their heads to decry learning and learned men. For what would they have done for a Bible if it had not been for them as instruments? And if they had it, so as to have been capable of reading it, God must have wrought a miracle for them, and continued that miracle in every nation, in every age, and to every individual; I mean the gift of tongues in a supernatural way, as was bestowed upon the Apostles on the Day of Pentecost; which there is no reason in the world ever to have expected. Bless God, therefore, and be thankful that God has, in His Providence, raised up such men to translate the Bible into the mother tongue of every nation, and particularly into ours; and that He still continues to raise up such, who are able to defend the translation made against erroneours persons and enemies of the truth; and to correct and amend it in lesser matters in which it may have failed, and clear and illustrate it by their learned notes upon it.'

It has been suggested by some that LEARNING is designed to perfect the work of the Spirit of God. But this is a mere slander. The only question is, Are we to expect miracles, as in the Apostolic age, to qualify us for the work of the ministry; or, are we to use ordinary means? That we are not to expect miracles all will allow, and, if not, then surely we are to use ordinary means. And so far is this from interfering with the work of the Spirit, that it appears to be the only way in which we may reasonably expect His continued influences; and it seems rather to be tempting the Spirit of God to expect that in an *extraordinary*, which we are authorised to expect only in an *ordinary* way. We have already observed that no man can be an acceptable minister of the Gospel if he be not a converted man, and furnished with those ministerial gifts or talents which God alone can communicate; but, then, is he not to endeavour, in the use of proper means, to improve these talents? Suppose a man who is not able to read should yet appear to be an eminently good man, and to have such a peculiar readiness in expressing his sentiments, both in prayer and religious conference, as should lead a Christian society to judge he might be useful in the work of the ministry; must not this man be taught to read lest it should be supposed to interfere with the work of the ministry; must not this man be taught to read lest it should be supposed to interfere with the work of the Spirit of God? Or, if he is taught to read the Scriptures in the languages in which they were written, that he may be able the better to enter into the genuine spirit and meaning of the sacred writers and judge for himself the propriety and force of any Scripture criticism; if he is taught the rules of just reasoning, and how to arrange his ideas in the most clear and orderly manner; if he is led into the knowledge of ancient customs, and the history of past ages, by which he may be enabled to elucidate many passages of Scripture; if he be made acquainted with the rudiments of natural philosophy, by which his ideas of the Divine perfections and the work of God may be enlarged and elevated; in short, if he be led through such a course of instruction as hath a natural tendency, with the blessing of God, to enable him to exercise his ministerial talents with more general acceptance and usefulness, what injury is done to him? Or, what reflection, can it be pretended, is hereby cast upon the work of the Spirit of God? Is it lawful for a person who may be called to the ministry, to learn to read, if he was not before capable of it? Is it lawful for him to avail himself of a learned exposition or commentary? Is it lawful for him to premeditate what he intends to say upon any subject, and seek out acceptable words? And is it *unlawful*, then, to proceed one step further? Must we stop *precisely* here? Or, may we not learn the languages in which the Scriptures were written, with other things of a similar nature? The opposers of learning, to be consistent with themselves, should neither read not study at all, since, upon their principles, they are hereby attempting to help or mend the work of the Spirit of God.

The truth is, whatever prejudices may be formed in the minds of some men against learning, it is certain that since the times of the Apostles, who had those miraculous helps which superseded every kind of learning. Divine Providence hath, in every age, put the greatest honour upon it. Consult the history of the Church, and you will uniformly find trough every period of it, with *very few* exceptions, that those ministers who have been the most laborious and successful in their work, have been as eminent for sound learning as for substantial piety. Nor is it to be doubted but that, whenever there is a revival of religion amongst us, men will be raised up, not only eminent for spiritual gifts, but who will endeavour zealously to improve those gifts, for the attainment of all that knowledge which, with the blessing of God, may render them able ministers of the New Testament. For though we have no sort of doubt but that the great Head of the Church could, if He pleased, carry on His work, not only without *learned* ministers but without *any* ministers at all; yet, as He sees fit, for the most part, to fulfil His designs in the use of means, it is in this way we are to expect His presence and blessing. There is, moreover, this further advantage arising from learning, it will enable a minister to become an instructor of youth, by which his sphere of usefulness may be enlarged, and he may be enabled to procure, with reputation, a subsistence for himself and family, in many situations, where otherwise he could not.

The Seminary countenanced by the Society, which now solicits the assistance of the friends of religion and learning, is at present under the direction of the Rev. *Hugh Evans*, assisted by the Rev. Messrs. *Caleb Evans*, and *James Newton*, who are ready cheerfully to exert their united endeavours to accomplish, as humble instruments in the hands of Divine Providence, the pious intentions of the generous subscribers to this institution.

Document VI.9

John Taylor's Advice to His Students

John Taylor, for whom see Document II.13 above, became the first divinity tutor at Warrington academy in 1757. The following advice to his students is reprinted from his *A Scheme of Scripture Divinity*, 1762, pp. vi–vii.

I. I do solemnly charge you. In the Name of the God of Truth, and of our Lord Jesus Christ, ... that in all your Studies and Inquiries of a religious Nature. Present or future, you do constantly, carefully, impartially and conscientiously, attend to Evidence, as it lies in the holy Scriptures, or in the Nature of things, and the Dictates of Reason: cautiously guarding against the Sallies of Imagination, and the Fallacy of ill-grounded Conjecture. II, That you admit, embrace, or assent to, no Principle or Sentiment, by me taught or advanced, but so far as it shall appear to you to be supported and justified by proper Evidence from Revelation, or the Reason of things. III, That, if at any time hereafter, any Principle or Sentiment by me taught or advanced, or by you admitted and embraced, shall, upon impartial and faithfull Examination, appear to you to be dubious or false, you either suspect or totally reject such Principle or Sentiment. IV. That you keep your Mind always open to Evidence. That you labour to banish from your Breast all Prejudice, Prepossession, and Party-zeal; ... and that you steddily [sic] assert for yourself, and freely allow to others, the unalienable Rights of Judgment and Conscience.

Document VI.10

The Curriculum at Warrington Academy

It was not the introduction of 'useful' or 'commercial' subjects which made the Dissenting academies singular in their age – recent research has shown that dozens of 'commercial schools' sprang up in the eighteenth century; it was the depth to which the studies were taken in such mini-universities as Warrington which was of prime significance.

For the academy see P. O'Brien, *Warrington Academy 1756–86: Its Predecessors and Successors*, Wigan: Owl Books, 1989; William Turner, *The Warrington Academy*, reprinted from the *Monthly Repository*, 1813–15, Warrington: Library and Museum Committee, 1957. The following extract is from the Report of the Warrington academy, 25 June 1761, with introduction and comments by H. McLachlan, from the latter's *English Education under the Test Acts*, Manchester; Manchester University Press, 1931, pp. 210–12.

In 1760 the 'Plan' of education for the full course and for the special three years' course was published. A student taking the full course was to spend his first year learning languages and elementary mathematics. In his second year, the study of languages was continued, and Logic, more advanced Mathematics, 'Natural History' and an 'Introduction to Natural Philosophy' were taken. The third year was chiefly occupied with Natural and Moral Philosophy, and occasional classes in Belles Lettres and Mathematics. In the fourth year, Moral Philosophy and Theology, and in the last 'those studies that peculiarly relate to his Profession and those Exercises which are to prepare him for a proper Discharge of the Public Office he has in view' were to occupy his time and thought. Throughout the course, translation, composition, and exercises in speaking supplemented the lectures and classes.

Senior students were expected to give assistance to juniors 'in the preparation of their lectures.'

The course for lay students is here given in greater detail, since the provision for these in the academics is not generally set forth, nor did any other academy have so large a proportion of them amongst the total number of students.

First Year:
  (1)   Elementary Mathematics (Arithmetic, Algebra and Geometry).
  (2)   French.
  (3)   Universal Grammar and Rhetoric.
Weekly exercises:
  (1)   Translations out of French into English.
  (2)   The composition of an essay on some easy subject in English.
  (3)   Specimens of letters in the epistolary style to imitate.
Second Year:
  (1)   Mathematics (Trigonometry; Navigation if desired).
  (2)   Natural Philosophy, and 'the easier Parts of Astronomy applied to the use of the Globes, and the general system of the Universe.'
  (3)   French.
Exercises:
  (1)   Translating out of English into French.
  (2)   Specimens of French Letters to imitate.
  (3)   'Some English Composition.'
Third Year:
  (1)   Natural Philosophy and 'some of the principal Experiments in the Elements of Chemistry.'
  (2)   'A short system of Morality ... concluding with the Evidences of the Christian Religion.'
Exercises:
  (1)   Dissertations in some moral, political, or commercial Subjects.
  (2)   French–English, English–French translations.

Further, lay students were to give attention to pronouncing the English language well, and in this connection attend lectures on Oratory and Grammar, and during 'the whole of their course' they were to learn 'the best methods of Book-Keeping,' 'to improve their Writing,' and 'to make some Progress in the Art of Drawing and Designing.' To this end a special tutor was appointed from time to time to give instruction in Writing, Drawing and Book-keeping. Shorthand would be taught if desired. Finally, 'one or two lectures' were to be given every week on Geography during the whole course in which 'the principal problems upon the Globes will be resolved; the Use of Maps represented; and the Natural History, Manufactures, Traffick, Coins, Religion, Government, etc., of the several Countries will be enlarged upon.'

Such was the curriculum of laymen in the Academy. That from first to last the staff of the Academy was an exceptionally strong team may be seen from the list of tutors with subjects and dates.

Divinity: John Taylor, D.D., 1757–61.
          John Aikin, D.D., 1761–80.
          Nicholas Clayton, D.D., 1780–3.
Classics: John Aikin, D.D., 1758–61.

Languages and Belles Lettres: J. Priestley, LL.D., 1761–7.
Languages and Natural History: J. Reinhold Forster, LL.D.,1767–70.
                           La Tour, 1770–?.
Belles Lettres: John Seddon, 1767–70.
                Gilbert Wakefield, A.B., 1779–83.
                Pendlebury Houghton, 1778–9.
Natural Philosophy and Mathematics: John Holt, 1757–72.
                           George Walker, F.R.S. 1772–4.
                           W. Enfield, LL.D., 1774–83.
Rector Academicus: John Seddon, 1767–70.
                W. Enfield, 1770–83.

Document VI.11

Howel Harris Addresses Young Academicians

The distance in objectives and atmosphere separating the older academies from the newer evangelical ones is clearly indicated in the following diary entry by Howel Harris, for whom see Document II.25 above. His remarks delivered in 'Arianising' Carmarthen are significantly different in temper from those of John Taylor at Document VI.9 above. The extract is from T. Beynon, *Howell Harris's Visits to Pembrokeshire*, Aberystwyth: Cambrian News Press, 1966, p. 126.

29 Dec., 1746.   *Glancothi*,   When I did read some things written by Mr. Gr. Jones against us I was easy, and all my cry was that God's mind alone should be known by us all. Went hence to Llandyfaelog, there the people being gone away, I discoursed very affecting, and many seemed affected. To Carmarthen, where in hearing Bro. John Richard opening the mystery of the believer, being dead and alive, weak and strong etc. I had light. Thankful in seeing the light, wisdom, gifts and authority given him in such a place, then I discoursed. I had vast freedom of wisdom all through, and to reason with the young academians, and to shew the danger of philosophy. How Paul seemed a babbler to the wise unenlightened Athenians, and if so, I don't wonder if I do to you. Was cutting to the young students that go forth to preach without knowing their own misery, or Christ. Without this all their learning is nothing. I justified lay preaching – of Apollos, and yet shewed we did not despise ordination, etc. Supped with a gentleman.

Document VI.12

Thomas Barnes at the Opening of Manchester Academy

Himself trained at Warrington, the Unitarian minister Thomas Barnes (1747–1810) delivered the address at the opening of the new Manchester academy in 1786. Barnes was the resident tutor, and the academy survived until 1803, when it removed to York. Barnes himself, in failing health and quite unable to maintain discipline among the students, had resigned in 1798.

For Barnes see DECBP, DNB. For the academy see V. D. Davis, *A History of Manchester College from its Foundation in Manchester to Its Establishment in Oxford*, London: Allen & Unwin, 1932; Barbara Smith, ed., *Truth, Liberty and Religion: Essays Celebrating Two Hundred Years of Manchester College*, Oxford: Manchester College, 1986. The following extract is from Thomas Barnes, *A Discourse delivered at the Commencement of the Manchester Academy, September Fourteenth, One Thousand Seven Hundred and Eighty Six*, Warrington, [1786], p. 14.

Of all subjects. DIVINITY seems most to demand the aid of kindred, and even of apparently remoter sciences. Its objects are, GOD and MAN: and nothing, which can either illustrate the perfections of the one, or the nature, capacities, and history of the other, can be entirely unimportant. But how extensive a field do these subjects open? Natural Philosophy, in its widest sense, comprehending whatever relates to the history or properties of the works of Nature, in the Earth, the Air, the Ocean, and including Natural History, Chemistry, &c. has an immediate reference to the one – and to the other belong, all that Anatomy and Physiology can discover relating to the body, and all that Metaphysics, Moral Philosophy, History, or Revelation declare concerning the mind. But here again the field still opens upon us. For History, as well as Revelation, demands the knowledge of Languages: and these again, of Customs and of Arts, of Chronology and Manners – the stream of science still branching out into more and wider channels. And to the highest finishing of the mind are necessary, those subject which belong to cultivated Taste, which regulate the Imagination and refine the Feelings, and which give correctness to vigour, and elegance to strength.

Document VI.13

The New Independent Academy at Rotherham

For the Rotherham academy see Kenneth W. Wadsworth, *Yorkshire United Independent College*, London: Independent Press, 1954. For Edward Williams see Document V.23 above.

The following letter from 'Excited' was published in the *Evengelical Magazine*, III, 1795, pp. 465–7.

Whatever tends to the glory of God, in the salvation of man, may be considered as a subject worthy the view of the religious public. Confident of your inclination to insert in the Magazine what may be both pleasing and profitable, I beg leave to give some short account of the new Independent Academy at Rotherham, in Yorkshire, under the care of the Rev. Dr. Williams. I do this the more cheerfully, as the institution was unanimously voted to appear in your periodical work, at a special meeting holden at Huddersfield, June 18.

To raise up ministers is the special work of our Lord Jesus Christ, and belongs to him as the Head of his church. He called men from the common employments in life, in the days of his flesh, and gave them a commission to go and preach his Gospel. With this commission was connected the necessary qualifications for the due discharge of their sacred functions, in an extraordinary way. Were it his pleasure, he could raise up men without the aid of human literature now, and make them eminently subservient to the advancement of his cause. But perhaps we have no good reason to expect it; and though it has been sometimes the case, it has by no means been common in any age of the church. The knowledge of the Gospel is obtained by the special teaching of God; but the knowledge of languages, by which we make that Gospel known; the decent attire in which it appears before the world; and especially if it is decorated with any ornaments, or strengthened with arguments taken from philosophy, must be the work of the schools of the prophets. It is therefore matter of joy that so many institutions for raising up youth, and sending them into the world with credit and reputation, are established; that so much good has been done by them, and that there is the pleasing prospect of still further us fullness.

By the blessing of God, we have had reason for thankfulness for an institution similar to this, in which many of the Independent ministers in this county, and some in others, received their education. Perhaps no institution of the kind, has been on the whole, and for the extent to which it went, more singularly blessed. The men who have come from thence have been, for the most part, both orthodox and experimental. They have preached what they have known of the word of life, and promoted the spirit and power of true religion. By their instrumentality, decayed congregations have been revived, and many new ones raised up. Of late years, indeed, the Almighty has frowned upon us, and we have found it necessary to ask his direction in the choice of a tutor, whose heart was set on the prosperity of Zion, and whose life was an ornament to his profession. We humbly hope that our proceedings in this business, have met with the approbation of the friends of the former institution; and, while we gratefully acknowledge their former favours, we beg leave to ask their continuance, and especially as the enlarged plan upon which we now go will require a much greater support.

The directions of Providence have been wonderfully seen in the several stages of this business hitherto. Where to turn our thought, or upon whom to fix as tutor, was difficult; nor was a suitable situation much less the object of our concern. After several special meetings, and much prayer to God, a committee was appointed; to whom we are under great obligation for their diligence and attention. Being much pleased with the correspondence of Dr. Williams, with his general character, and the great reputation with which he had discharged the office before; our friends mentioned him as a person eminently qualified, if he could be obtained. This proposal was universally approved. The Doctor has since seen it his duty to accede to the invitation as tutor to the academy; and also to comply with the request of the church at Rotherham, as their pastor. For the performance of both these important offices, we pray that he may be filled with all wisdom and spiritual understanding.

The constitution of the academy, in respect to religion, will perhaps be best understood by the sixth and thirteenth resolutions of the meeting holden at Halifax, September 11, 1794. Resolved, – That no person be chosen tutor, or sub-tutor, but such as are of most approved piety, learning, diligence, fidelity, and Calvinistic Independent dissenters; and if they who are chosen should afterwards depart from their once professed Calvinistic principles, the subscribers shall be at liberty to dismiss them. – That none but truly serious men be educated for the sacred ministry: Such as wish to enter the academy, shall bring a recommendation from the minister and church to which they belong, as persons who know the power of divine grace upon their hearts; that, along with this recommendation they shall produce, in writing, reasons of the hope that is in them: And the committee shall then examine them, as to their religious and moral conduct, and qualifications for entering upon an education for the important work they have in view.

It is pleasing to see the appearances there are in the world for the advancement of the kingdom of Christ. With these we wish to join our humble efforts, and earnest prayers; hoping that God will make them subservient to the advancement of the general cause. To make our design the more effectual, it is earnestly desired that the several churches would pay a particular attention to the seriousness and character of the young men they recommend. Literature, however useful in other respects, can never inspire the heart with love to God, and a sincere concern for the salvation of men. Learning is no substitute for grace. It is not the honour and respectability of that particular party of Christians to which we belong, we have in view, but the conversion and edification of mankind in general: and we are fully convinced that these desirable ends will never be accomplished by an unconverted ministry. Unhallowed victims on the altar of God, are worse than none at all. It is hoped therefore that the public will strengthen our hands, and encourage our hearts, not only by their prayers and contributions, but also, and especially, by their diligent care, to bring forward such young men, as shall, by the blessing of God, be burning and shining lights in the Christian church. Thus shall we have the abundant pleasure to see our infant cause flourish; new resources will be opened in different places for its support; Zion will extend its boundaries; other churches will be raised, and old ones fed with the bread of Life; yea it will grow and increase with the increase of God.

Above all, let us in this affair still continue to acknowledge God, and pray for his blessing, without which our attempts will be vain. 'Unless the Lord build the house, they labour in vain who build it.' Have we not seen very splendid and promising beginnings, in this way, come to nothing? The united strength of literature, property, and exertion, have been found too feeble to support a cause not founded on the *Rock*. 'He that honoureth not me,' saith Christ, 'honoureth not the Father.' Brethren, what is it for which we come forward? Is it not that which is dearer to us than our lives? That which unites the happiness of man with the glory of God? Not the mere form of Christianity, but as containing its life and spirit. Christianity clothed with all its evangelical doctrines, fed and nourished with the constant supplies of experimental power, and exemplified in the ornaments of meek and quiet spirit, and the practice of every moral virtue, – nothing less than this is our object. Attached to a cause so glorious in its nature, and so happy in its consequences, surely we may have the confidence to ask, and the encouragement to expect, the blessing of God, and the support of good men.

EUMENES.
EXCITED

Document VI.14

The Promise and Rules of William Roby's Independent Academy, Manchester

For Roby see Document IV.17 above. The following is the Solemn Promise to be made and Rules to be Observed by students entering William Roby's Independent Academy, Manchester, c. 1804. It is reprinted from R. Slate, *History of the Lancashire Congregational Union*, 1840, p. 18.

To Robert Spear, Esq.

We, the undersigned, who shall be educated for the Christian ministry at your expense, do declare that we devote the remainder of our lives to the service of God in the Gospel of His Son; resolving, through Grace, not to abandon the work of preaching the Gospel as we shall be enabled, on any account, except compelled by absolute necessity.

Having thus put our hands to the plough, we consider it our duty not to draw back; but to be ready to preach the Gospel wherever openings in Providence may occur; while, if need be, we minister to our necessities with our own hands, and thus prove, to our brethren and to the world, that when we entered as labourers into our Lord's vineyard, it was not with an intention to improve our worldly circumstances or to raise ourselves to stations in Society superior to those we formerly held.

We understand that we are admitted into the Seminary on trial; and that we are to be continued only while we give satisfaction as to character, abilities and behaviour.

During our continuance, we will readily submit to the general rules of the Institution, and to any other regulations which the further experience of the Patron and the Tutor may recommend to our attention.

With our allowance for support we declare ourselves satisfied; and, in order to prosecute our studies without interruption, we engage to follow no occupation for further subsistence till our present connexion with this seminary is dissolved. ...

1. That each candidate for admission be required to send a written account of his doctrinal sentiments, his religious experience, and the circumstances which inclined him to the Christian Ministry.
2. That each candidate produce satisfactory testimonies respecting his religious character, and his natural abilities; and if he has not been previously accustomed to preach or to exhort, that he be required to do so before his admission,

in the presence of competent judges, in order to determine his natural aptitude to teach.

3. That each student, on his admission, sign the inscribed address to Mr. Spear, with professed approbation.

4. That the Hours of Study – except in particular cases – be from six to eight in the morning; from nine to twelve in the forenoon; from two to five in the afternoon; and from six to eight in the evening; and that these be employed according to direction.

5. That the general term of Education be two years; but that this be occasionally abridged or extended if the Patron and Tutor conceive that circumstances require it.

6. That the Students, during their continuance at the Seminary, consider themselves under obligation to preach when and where the Patron and Tutor may appoint.

7. That no Student, during the term of his studies, form any kind of connection, especially with a Female, which might retard his improvement, without giving immediate information thereof to the Patron or the Tutor.

8. That no Student be out of his Lodging after 10 o'clock at night; without assigning some very satisfactory reason.

9. That the Students watch over one another in Love, and after private admonition, if it fail, inform the Patron or Tutor of any inconsistency of conduct, or change of sentiment, discovered in any of their Brethren, and that neglect in this case be considered as subjecting the party to a proportional degree of guilt.

10. That the Students pledge themselves to give an ingenuous answer to all such questions as the Patron or Tutor may at any time propose to them respecting their sentiments, their conduct, or their studies.

11. That every Month, each Student renew his professed approbation both of the original address, and of the general rules of the institution.

Encouragement and Aids to Devotion

Document VI.15

Isaac Watts on Prayer

For Watts see Document II.2 above. The following extracts are from his A Guide to Prayer; or, a Free and Rational Account of the Gift, Grace and Spirit of prayer; with plain Directions how every Christian may attain them, 1715.

The gift of prayer is one of the noblest and most useful in the Christian life, and therefore to be sought with earnest desire and diligence; and in order to attain it, we must avoid these two extremes:

I.   A confining ourselves entirely to precomposed forms of prayer. II. An entire dependence on sudden motions and suggestions of thought.

I.   The first extreme to be avoided is, a confining ourselves to set precomposed forms of prayer. I grant it lawful and convenient for weaker Christians to use a form a prayer rather than not perform that duty at all. Christ Himself seems to have indulged it to His disciples in their infant state of Christianity (Luke 11: 1, 2). I grant also that sometimes the most improved saints may find their own wants and desires, and the frames of their own hearts so happily expressed in the words of other men, that they cannot find better; and may therefore in a very pious manner use the same, especially when they labour under a present deadness of spirit, and great indisposition for the duty. It is also evident, that many assistances may be borrowed by younger and older Christians from forms of prayer well composed, without the use of the whole form as a prayer. And if I may have leave to speak the language of a judicious author that wrote more than forty years ago, I would say with him, that forms may be useful, and in some cases necessary: for,

1.   'Some, even among Christians and professors, are so rude and ignorant, though it may be spoken to their shame, that they cannot tolerably express their desires in prayer; and must such utterly neglect the duty? Is it not better during their gross ignorance, to use the help of others gifts and composures than not to pray at all? or to utter that which is senseless and impious? I speak it not to excuse their ignorance, or that they should be encouraged to rest satisfied herein, but for the present necessity.

2.   'Some again, though they can do it privately, and so far as may suffice in their secret address to God; yet when they are to pray before others want either dexterity and fitness of expression, readiness of utterance, or confidence to use those abilities they have, whom yet I will not excuse from sinful bashfulness.

3.   'It is possible that some bodily distemper, or sudden distraction, may befall such as are otherwise able, which may becloud their minds, weaken their memories,

and dull their parts, that they may be unfit to express themselves in extemporary conceptions. This may happen in case of melancholy, cold palsies, or the like distempers. I conclude then, that in the cases aforesaid, or the like, a form may be profitable and helpful. Nor is it a tying up of the Spirit, but if conscionably used, may be both attended with the Spirit's assistance, and find acceptance with God. Yet it will not hence follow that any should satisfy themselves in such stated and stinted forms: much less, that those who have praying abilities, should be enforced by others to rest in them. If ignorance, bashfulness, defect of memory, or other distemper, may render it excusable and necessary to some, is it fit all should rest in their measure? Where then will be that coveting earnestly the best gifts? Or why should those that are excellently gifted that way be hindered from the use and exercise of that gift, because others want it.' Thus far this worthy writer.

Now though the use of forms in such cases be not unlawful, yet a perpetual confinement to them will be attended with such inconveniences as these:

1.   It much hinders the free exercise of our thoughts and desires, which is the chief work and business of prayer, viz to express our desires to God: and whereas our thoughts and affections should direct our words, a set form of words directs our thoughts and affections; and while we bind ourselves to those words only, we damp our inward devotion, and prevent the holy fire kindling within us; we discourage our active powers and passions from running out on divine subjects, and check the breathings of our souls heaven-ward. The wise man tells us (Proverbs 14: 10): 'The heart knoweth his own bitterness; and a stranger doth not intermeddle with his joy.' There are secret joys, and unknown bitternesses, which the holy soul longs to spread before God, and for which it cannot find any exact and correspondent expressions in the best of prayer-books: now must such a Christian suppress all those thoughts, and forbid himself all that sweet conversation with his God, because it is not written down in the appointed form?

2.   The thoughts and affections of the heart that are truly pious and sincere are wrought in us by the Spirit of God, and if we deny them utterance because they are not found in prayer-books, we run the danger of resisting the Holy Ghost, quenching the Holy Spirit, and fighting against the kind designs of God toward us, which we are so expressly cautioned against (1 Thessalonians 5: 19), and which a humble Christian trembles to think of.

3.   A confinement to forms cramps and imprisons those powers that God hath given us for improvement and use; it silences our natural abilities, and forbids them to act; and it puts a bar upon our spiritual faculties, and prevents their growth. To satisfy ourselves with mere forms, to confine ourselves wholly to them, and neglect to stir up and improve our own gifts, is one kind of spiritual sloth, and highly to be disapproved. It is hiding a talent in the earth, which God has given us on purpose to carry on a trade with heaven. It is an abuse of our knowledge of divine things to neglect the use of it in our converse with God. It is as if a man that had once used crutches to support him when he was feeble would always use them. Or because he has sometimes found his own thoughts happily expressed in conversation by another person, therefore he will assent to what that other person shall always speak, and never speak his own thoughts himself.

4.   It leads us into the danger of hypocrisy and mere lip-service. Sometimes we shall be tempted to express those things which are not the very thoughts of our own souls, and so use words that are not suited to our present wants, or sorrows, or request, because those words are put together, and made ready beforehand.

5.   The confinement of ourselves to a form, though it is not always attended with formality and indifference, yet it is very apt to make our spirits cold and flat, formal and indifferent in our devotion. The frequent repetition of the same words doth not always awaken the same affections in our hearts, which perhaps they were well suited to do when we first heard or made use of them. When we continually tread one constant road of sentences, or track of expressions, they become like an old beaten path in which we daily travel, and we are ready to walk on without particular notice of the several parts of the way; so in our daily repetition of a form we neglect due attention to the full sense of the words. But there is something more suited to awaken the attention of the mind in a conceived prayer, when a Christian is making his own way toward God, according to the present inclination of his soul, and urgency of his present wants: and to use the words of a writer lately cited, 'While we are clothing the sense of our hearts in fit expressions, and as it were digging the matter of our prayers out of our own feelings and experience, it must needs keep the heart closer at work'.

6.   The duty of prayer is very useful to discover to us the frame of our own spirits, but a constant use of forms will much hinder our knowledge of ourselves, and prevent our acquaintance with our own hearts, which is one great spring of maintaining inward religion in the power of it. Daily observation of our own spirits would teach us what our wants are, and how to frame our prayers before God; but if we tie ourselves down to the same words always, our own observation of our hearts will be of little use, since we must speak the same expressions, let our hearts be how they will. As therefore an inward search of our souls, and intimate acquaintance with ourselves, is a means to obtain the gift of prayer, so the exercise of the gift of prayer will promote this self-acquaintance, which is discouraged and hindered by the restraint of forms.

In the last place, I mention the most usual, most evident and convincing argument against perpetual confinement of ourselves to a form; and that is, because it renders our converse with God very imperfect: for it is not possible that forms of prayer should be composed that are perfectly suited to all our frames of spirit, and fitted to all our occasions in the things of this life, and the life to come. Our circumstances are always altering in this frail and mutable state. We have new sins to be confessed, new temptations and sorrows to be represented, new wants to be supplied. Every change of providence in the affairs of a nation, a family, or a person requires suitable petitions and acknowledgements. And all these can never be well provided for in any prescribed composition. I confess all our concerns of soul and body may be included in some large and general words of a form, which is no more suited to one time, or place, or condition, that to another: but generals are cold and do not affect us, nor affect persons that join with us, and whose case he that speaks in prayer should represent before God. It is much sweeter to our own souls, and to our fellow worshippers, to have our fears, and doubts, and complaints, and temptations, and sorrows represented in most exact and particular expressions, in such language as the soul itself feels when the words are spoken. Now, though we should often meet with prayers precomposed that are fitted to express our present case, yet the gift of prayer is as much better than any form, as a general skill in the work of preaching is to be preferred to any precomposed sermons; as a perfect knowledge in the art of physic is better than any number of receipts; or as a receipt to make a medicine is preferable to one single medicine already made. But he that binds himself always to read printed sermons will not arrive at the art of preaching; and that man that deals only in receipts shall never become a skilful physician; nor can the gift of prayer be attained by everlasting confinement to forms. …

Let the nature of this duty of prayer, as divided into its several parts, be impressed upon your hearts, and dwell in your memories.

Let us always remember that it contains in it these several parts of worship, namely, invocation, adoration, confession, petition, pleading, profession or self-resignation, thanksgiving, and blessing; which that we may retain the better in our minds, may be summed up in these four lines:

> Call upon God, adore, confess,
> Petition, plead, and then declare
> You are the Lord's, give thanks and bless,
> And let Amen confirm the prayer.

And by a recollection of these several parts of prayer, we may be assisted to go on step by step, and to improve in the gift of performance of this part of worship.

Document VI.16

The too Great Neglect of Family Worship

The following extracts are from *A Letter to the Protestant Dissenters, Relating to the too great Neglect of Family-Worship, And Decay of practical Religion Amongst us,* London, 1720, pp. 3–5, 6, 7, 8, 9, 15. It was published 'By the Direction of some London Ministers'.

The Protestant Dissenting Ministers in *London,* conferring together some Years ago, about the State of those Flocks of which the Holy Ghost had made them Overseers; found cause to lament the too general Neglect of Family, and Practical Religion among them. Such a Neglect, those Fathers, could not but lay near to their Heart, and forthwith considered what it was proper for them to do, in order to excite the Negligent to their Duty, and to quicken those who were cold, or careless in it: This Consideration ended in a Resolution to write and preach upon the important Occasion; and we hope the Effects were answerable. – We who now watch for your Souls are apprehensive, Sirs, of the same Evil in our Day; and in Faithfulness to

God, to you, and our selves, think it our Duty to give you this publick Warning of your Sin and Danger. We are sorry and ashamed there should be cause to exhibit such a Charge as this, against the Professors of a pure Religion: We hoped you had better learned Christ than to have deserved such a Reproof; and had so well understood your Duty to God and your Families, as not to have needed such an exhortation. We know there are some who make great Conscience of Family-Religion amongst us; but, that there is too general a Neglect of it, is too evident in Fact; and were this only among *the Men of the World, who have their Portion in this Life*, it would not surprise us; but to observe it among Men professing Godliness, fills our Hearts with Grief, and forces us to speak what we wish there were no need for you to hear. We are too nearly concern'd in this matter to be any longer silent; your Ministers would be chargeable with Unfaithfulness, should they overlook such a Neglect. To intermeddle in the Civil Affairs of your Families would be criminal in us, but should you take amiss our Concern for the Religion of them, it would be a Crime in you. Ye are our Witnesses how much we sympathize with you in Cases afflictive; and can you think we shall not lament what we apprehend offensive to God among you?

It is not easy for us to tell you, Sirs, how deeply we are concern'd at this great and threatening Evil; God has built you a Tabernacle, but you have not erected an Altar for him; nay some have pulled down his Altar, after spiritual Sacrifices had been offer'd upon it for a long time. You appear on solemn Days at God's House, but in your own you acknowledge Him not; your Children, and Servants, may for all you, live without God in the World: We hear of no Family Instruction, no singing the Praises of God, and the Redeemer among you; nay not so much as reading the Scriptures, and Prayer. – This Neglect we have reason to fear is a growing Evil, reaching from Parents to Children, and spreading among both Rich, and Poor, which makes our Grief and Confusion so much the greater; and puts those Words of the disconsolate Prophet into our Mouths, *O that our Heads were Water, and our Eyes a Fountain of Tears!*

We would gladly be instrumental in reviving real Religion among you, and to that end are desirous to use our Interest with you wisely and seriously to consider the Causes and Consequences of that Neglect we are now lamenting.

The Causes of the Neglect of Family-Religion we apprehend to be such as these.

1.   The ill Constitution of Families at the first by unsuitable Marriages and Relations. …

2.   Omitting it at first setting out in the World. …

3.   Excess of Modesty, and Bashfulness of Mind. …

4.   Is not the Decay of serious Religion, and Abatement of Zeal in the Heads of Families, another Cause of this Neglect? …

5.   Multiplicity of worldly Affairs, and inordinate Regards to worldly Good. …

To conclude. The *Morning* and *Evening Sacrifice* being a standing Institution under the Law, and *praying always with all Prayer* being an express Precept of the Gospel, we hope, professed Christians will be persuaded to look upon Family-Worship as their Duty, and not satisfy themselves in any longer Neglect of it.

But you will hear more of this Matter from the Pulpit. The Ministers of *London* intend in some convenient time to preach upon this Subject by common Consent. This was formerly done by the Brethren of both Denominations, and is now design'd as an Expression of hearty Zeal and Concern for the Interests of serious Religion, under such visible Decays amongst us.

Document VI.17

Quaker Exhortations to Parents and Others Concerning Personal Devotion

Beyond the encouragement they received in meeting for worship and in family prayer and worship at home, there is plenty of material in the abundant printed literature of Quakerism to sustain the devotional lives of individuals. Much inspiration was drawn from the journals and lives of the early Friends, but the literature was steadily added to. Obituaries, for example, were collected in *Piety Promoted*, a nine-part work of which the first appeared in 1701 and the last in 1796; and in *A Collection of Testimonies* (1760). Friends also made use of material from other traditions – perhaps most notably the writings of such continental quietists as Fénelon, Madame Guyon and Thomas à Kempis, all of whom were translated or published by Quakers. Exchanges with North American Quakers were frequent, and among the best-known and most challenging of personal testimonies from that quarter was that of John Woolman (1720–72), for whom see DNB, ODCC. Nor were the Scriptures to be ignored. The Yearly Meeting's epistles contained regular exhortations to their use, particularly in the family.

Extract (a) from the epistle of 1732 is one of many that was used in the Society's Book of Discipline. Extract (b) is advice from the Yearly Meeting of 1752 on self-examination and attending meeting. It was also used in the printed book of *Extracts from the minutes and advices of the yearly Meeting of Friends held in London from its first institution*, 1783.

(a)

And, dear friends, we tenderly and earnestly advise and exhort all parents, and masters of families, that they exert themselves in the wisdom of God, and in the strength of his love, to instruct their children and families in the doctrines and precepts of the Christian religion, contained in the Holy Scriptures; and, that they excite them to the diligent reading of those sacred writings, which plainly set forth the miraculous conception, birth, holy life, wonderful works, blessed example, meritorious death, and glorious resurrection, ascension, and mediation of our Lord and Saviour Jesus Christ; and to educate their children in the belief of those important truths, as well as in the belief of the inward manifestation and operation of the Spirit of God on their own minds, that they may reap the benefit and advantage thereof, for their own peace and ever-lasting happiness, which is infinitely preferable to all other considerations. We therefore exhort, in the most earnest manner, that all be very careful in this respect; a neglect herein being, in our judgment, very blameworthy; and further, where any deficiency of this sort appears, we recommend to Monthly and Quarterly Meetings, that they stir up those whom it may concern to their duty therein.

(b)

Dear Friends! When we call to Remembrance the fervent Zeal, Faith, and Constancy of our worthy Elders and Predecessors in the Truth, who through manifold Sufferings were enabled to bear a faithful Testimony to the Purity and Spirituality of the Gospel Dispensation, an earnest Desire is raised in us, that we who succeed them in the same Profession may be excited to follow their Example. In order whereunto, we recommend to every particular Member of our Society, a strict and serious Self-Examination, Whether we are really concerned for the Glory of God, and the Honour of his Name? Are our Hearts united unto him, and one unto another? Do we live answerable to the Principles of our Profession? Do we walk as becometh the Followers of Christ? Do we not depart from the Testimonies of Truth, or the known Doctrines of his Gospel, through Fear of Penalties enacted by human Laws? Do we in our Conversation among Men live in the Practice of *Christian* Humility and Self-Denial? *Doth our Light so shine before Men, that others seeing our good Works, may glorify our Father which is in Heaven?* [Matt. 5: 16]. Upon such an impartial Enquiry into our selves, let every Particular of us hearken and *hear what God the Lord will speak, for he will speak Peace unto his People, and to his Saints, but let them not turn again to Folly* [Ps. 85: 8]. But if upon such a solemn Search, any of us shall find, that we have declined from the Testimonies borne by our faithful Predecessors: That we have gone astray, and been too remiss in our Conduct and Conversation: That we have been too conformable to the Customs and Manners of the World, and have not walked according to the Plainness and Purity of our Profession: Let us humble our selves before the Lord, and turn unto him with all our Hearts, who is *long-suffering and gracious, and delighteth in Mercy, who reconcileth the Penitent, healeth their backslidings, is the Repairer of Breaches, and the Restorer of Paths to* walk *in* [Isa. 58: 12]. Such an holy Care and Watchfulness in every Particular over himself, will be greatly conducive to a general Love and Unity, to the confirming and strengthening our Church-Fellowship and Communion, and to the making us one another's Joy in the Lord.

And, as in our Epistle of the last Year, we were concerned to recommend to the Monthly Meetings the Appointment of solid and judicious Friends to visit the Families of their Brethren in *Christian* Love, and therein to inform, admonish, and advise as Occasion may be: We again beseech you, Let the tender Advice of such as shall undertake so Brotherly an Office, meet with a kind and Friendly Reception, that in the mutual giving and receiving of wholsome Counsel and Advice, you may co-operate to the Help and Furtherance of each other's Faith, the reviving of our ancient Testimonies, and establishing the Church on its first and fixed Foundation.

And, *Dearly beloved Friends*, As we become thus united to God, and one unto another, we shall experience the attracting Power and Force of Divine Love, drawing and strongly inclining our Hearts to a constant Attendance at the appointed

Times and Places for the publick Worship of God, who is *Love*, and he that *dwelleth in Love, dwelleth in him* [Jn. 4: 16]. This Divine Love induced our worthy Elders to Maintain their Religious Assemblies with an invincible Constancy: For they following the Call of Christ their Heavenly Shepherd, resorted earnestly to those Places of Feeding, where he ministred Food to the Hungry, and Waters of Life to those that were a-thirst, and filled with the Consolations of his Spirit the Souls of those who waited upon him in Sincerity and Truth. The same Spiritual Comforts and Advantages are to this Day measurably enjoyed by those, who with the like ardent Desires, and earnest Breathings of Soul, are humbly waiting to receive them. Let us therefore, *Brethren*, as many of us as have been remiss in this great and necessary Duty of religiously assembling together, be excited to double our Diligence for the Time to come, and with an holy Awe and Reverence bow before the Lord, and draw near *unto the Throne* of his *Grace, that we may obtain Mercy, and find Grace to help in Time of Need* [Heb. 4: 16].

Document VI.18

Samuel Bourn's Prayers for Young Christians

For Bourn see Document II.12 above. The following items are selected from *The Young Christian's Prayer Book. Dedicated To the Young People in Birmingham and at Coseley*, Birmingham, 1733, p. x (preface), 69–72, 81–3.

I would have you make a wide difference between saying your Prayers, *or* reading Prayers, *and* Praying; *the* former *is the service of* meer Children, *or of* Men in Pay, *and has no Religion* at all in it; *the* latter *is the Service of a rational and religious Creature, who sees and feels its dependance on God.*

To pray with Understanding and Judgment includes FAITH; *Faith in God's Ability to help, in his Readiness to do it, in Christ's Mediation for you, and in God's appointment of Prayer as a Condition of his Favour, and as a Preparative of the Soul for Mercy.*

By this short Account you see how many great Characters must concur to make up an Intelligent Prayer.

2.   *Always pray, with a* serious *Mind, a* Heart called off *from the World, and offered up to God. Fear lest this excellent Service degenerate into a* customary, *dead* Task, *wherein neither your selves, nor God, take any Pleasure. The Tempers and Dispositions of the Heart in Prayer is the* chief Thing *in God's account; let me exhort and perswade you then to aim at this great Point, 'That your Prayers be always accompanied with an inward desire to please God in all your Actions; with a just, friendly, forgiving, reconcilable Inclination towards all about you; and with a real Intention to depart from all Iniquity; which if practis'd, will prove the Insincerity, and hinder the Efficacy of your Prayers.*

In this judicious *and serious* Manner, *enter* young Christians, *into your Closets, Morning and Evening, and pray to your Father, who seeth in Secret, and doubt not you will find your Account in it, by a present Acceptance with God, and a future Reward from him. …*

XXX.   A Young *Man in the* Country, *at* Prayer.

Great God! Heaven is thy Throne, and Earth thy Foot-Stool, and thou dost whatever pleaseth thee in Heaven, and amongst the Inhabitants of the Earth; Yet thy work is perfect, and all thy ways are Judgment, nor is there *any Respect of Persons* with thee, but in every *Nation*, and in every *Dwelling*, he who feareth thee, and worketh Righteousness is accepted with thee.

Though thy wise Providence has placed me in a *Country Station*, where I want *many Advantages*, arising from nearness to the House of God, from the Company of Ministers, and other wise and good men, and from a Variety of Books, which the Young Men *in Town* enjoy; Yet I desire Chearfully to accept, and Faithfully to improve my Lot; I bless God the *Way to Heaven* lies open from every Place, and God is ready to hear every Creature wherever it lives and prays.

I am sensible, in many a Youth Wisdom and Virtue have grown under *fewer Advantages* than I possess; I beg the Sacred Influence of thy Spirit, that I may also grow in every Quality of mind, which will render me acceptable to God and Man. If I want many *Helps*, I am free from many *Hindrances*, and many *Temptations*, which surround Young People in populous Places, and in a croud of Company and Business; Assist me, in a serious Judment, to set the one over against the other, and to acquiesce in the Wisdom of thy Disposals: I wou'd be so far from a murmuring and complaining Temper, that I desire to admire the Felicity of my Situation, which gives me so much *Happy Leasure* for Contemplation, Reading and Prayer.

Assist me, O gracious God, to view *Thee*, in all thy surrounding Works, which declare thy Astonishing *Greatness*, thy Almighty *Power*, thy Unsearchable *Wisdom*, and thy neverfailing *Goodness;* Thy Works of Creation and Providence are visible where ever I go, for the Earth is thine, and all its Fulness.

Every Day that I walk out to my Business in the Field, or to take my Evening Walk, may I *lift up my Thoughts* to thee, ascribing all Perfections, all Praise, Honour and Glory to thee, *Who hast* created the Sun, Moon and Stars' even all the Host of Heaven; *Who* makest the Day dark with Night, and changest the Shadow of Death into the Morning; *Who* Thunderest Marvelously with thy Voice, and whose Lightenings enlighten the World; *Who* bringest the Wind out of thy Treasuries, and causest the Vapours to ascend; *Who* saith to the Snow, 'Be thou upon the Earth,' and callest for the Waters of the Sea, and pourest them out upon the Face of the Earth; *Who* causest Grass to grow for Cattle, and Herb for the service of Man; *Who* renewest the Face of the Earth crownest the Year with thy Goodness, so that the Pastures are cloathed with Flocks, and the Vallies covered with Corn.

My Station, my Business, my Diversions do all lead me to contemplate thee, O blessed God! *Who* providest Food for all Creatures, and Feedest the Fowls of the Air, Who hast created Sheep and Oxen for the service of Man, yea every Beast of the Field; *Who* openest thine Hand, and satisfiest the desires of all Living; and whose

Delights are with the Sons of Men, for whose sake thou hast Ordained all these Things.

By such Meditations as these, and by other Holy Exercises may I be obtaining and improving an Acquaintance with thee; And what other Helps I have from my Parents, my Ministers, from Books and Company, teach me to value them, and to use them in the best Manner.

Preserve me from falling in with any *sinful Customs* of the Place I live in, May all my Recreations be innocent and blameless, promote the Health of my Body, and Chearfulness of my Mind.

May my Bible be my chief Companion, and by reading that Blessed Book may I be led to know more of thy Unspeakable Love to me, and to all the World, in and through Jesus Christ, who came in so surprising and unexpected a Manner to visit such vile Creatures as me, who dwell in House of Clay, to prepare for us Habitations in Heaven.

From the Bottom of my Soul wou'd I praise thy Fatherly Goodness for his Manifestation in Flesh, for the numerous Testimonies of his Love, throughout his whole Life, and for that Astonishing Grace in humbling himself to Death for us, for his Resurrection from the Dead, and his Ascension to Heaven; for his great Authority over all Things, his Compassionate Intercession; for the Assistance of his Spirit, and the Assurances given us of his Coming again to the Salvation of all his Saints; of which number may I be one, through his Mediation, To whom be the Glory of his whole Mediatorial Office, now and for ever. *Amen*

XXXIV.   The Prayer of a Young *Woman in* Courtship.

O most High and Holy Majesty, who art before all Things, independently blessed in thy self, and art disposed to make all thy Creatures blessed and happy suitably to their Nature and Capacities; I bow down my self before thee, under a sense of my own Insufficiencies, and that nothing can make me truly happy *without thy Love and Favour.*

Possess'd of this Belief, I desire in the first Place to *choose thee*, O God, as the Strength of my Heart, and the Portion of my Soul; for whom have I in Heaven but thee, and what is there in all the Earth desirable compared with thee; Having avouched thee, the Lord, to be *my God*, I hope thou wilt be my Guide through Life, and at Death my Exceeding great Reward,

I am a poor young thoughtless Creature, subject to many *false Judgments* and *foolish Passions*, and dare not trust my self in the *lesser Affairs* of Life; I need Wisdom from above in the Conduct of Every Day, and much' more in the *great Article* of choosing a *Companion for Life*; And since thy Providence seems putting this Matter now to my Choice, I pray thou wouldst assist all *my own Deliberations* on a matter so Momentous; and over-rule for my good the *Consultations* of my Parents and Friends, that the Issue may be well.

Keep up in my Soul a continual and an aweful Apprehension of thy Presence and All-seeing Eye over me, that this may dispose me to the strictest Watch over my Thoughts, Words and Actions; that no *Appearance of Evil* may attend my Behaviour;

God forbid I shou'd ever admit a Thought of those Sins which War against the Soul, and kill the Seeds of Religion.

Let the Purity of my Mind, the Innocency of my Intention, the Unspotted Chastity of my Whole Conduct keep off all undue Advances, and banish all indecent Talk from my Ears.

Indue me with a distinguishing Judgment, and dispose and enable me to weigh and Measure a Man rather by the *Qualities of his Mind* than by the Mein of his Person, the Air of his Address, or the Bulk of his Fortune.

As I hope thou hast already in thy great Goodness, given me a Love to Wisdom and Piety, I beg thy gracious Hand will prevent my being ever Yoak'd with a Fool, a Sot, or a Knave; May no Worldly Inducements whatever draw me into an irreligious Match, or an absurd Choice.

But teach and incline me to fix upon one who will always consider me as his *dearest Possession* in Life, who will every Day contribute to my Comfort and Happiness, and whose wife, sober, religious Behaviour will be my growing Satisfaction.

In order to which desirable State of Life, bestow on me, O God all those inward Excellencies, and real Virtues which will render me ever more and more acceptable to a Man of the truest Judgment and Penetration; that if a Married State be my Lot it may be an Addition to the Happiness of each of us in the *present Life*, and no Bar to our Preparation for Happiness *hereafter.*

Fit me for all the Duties and Offices of every Station of Life; And if ever I stand at the Head of a Family, May I fill up that great Place with all Wisdom and Prudence.

But however these Affairs issue, keep my Heart immutably fix'd on thee and thy Ways; Raise me up to great Degrees of Sacred Goodness, translate my best Affections from all these lower Objects, in every undue Measure, and place them upon *him* who is fairer than the Children of Men, and cause unseen Things to exceed in mine Eye, and to out-shine all the fading Splendor of Earthly Objects: Possess me with so strong a sense of thy Love to me in Christ Jesus as shall cure me of a *Worldly Spirit*, of all *Sloth of Mind*, and sinful *Solicitude* about the Events of time.

In whatever State and Relation of Life I am, I pray that my *Love* to any thing here below may not degenerate into Fondness, nor my *Joy* and Chearfulness into Lightness and Vanity, nor my *Seriousness* and Sorrow turn into Melancholly and Discontent, nor my Just *Anger* proceed to Hatred and Contention, nor my *Industry* in Business sink into Earthliness of Mind, or grow into Carelesness and Distrust, nor my *Discretion* and Prudence ever put on the Form of Craft, Dissimulation and Deceit.

But in all Things may I behave with Christian Innocency, and true Wisdom, that I may adorn the Doctrine of my Lord and Saviour Jesus Christ in all my Actions. To him be Praises and Thanksgivings for ever and ever *Amen.*

Document VI.19

Philip Doddridge's *The Family Expositor*

As an aid to home Bible study, Doddridge's *The Family Expositor, or a Paraphrase and Version of the New Testament With Critical Notes, and A Practical Improvement of each Section*, was published in six volumes between 1739 and 1756.

The following is from the preface to volume I of the first edition. For Doddridge see Document I.1 above.

I should think any impartial reader must immediately see, and every judicious critic be daily more confirmed in it, that the New Testament teaches us to conceive of Christ, not as a generous Benefactor only, who, having performed some actions of heroic virtue and benevolence, is now retired from all intercourse with our world, so that we have no more to do with him than to preserve a grateful remembrance of his character and favours; but that he is to be considered as an ever-living and ever-present Friend, with whom we are to maintain a daily commerce by faith and prayer, and from whom we are to derive those supplies of Divine grace, whereby we may be strengthened for the duties of life, and ripened for a state of perfect holiness and felicity. This is evident, not only from particular passages of scripture, in which he is described as always with his church, (Mat. xxviii. 20,) as present where ever two or three are assembled in his name, (Mat. xviii. 20,) as upholding all things by the word of his power, (Heb. i. 3,) and as Head over all to his church, (Eph. i. 22,) but indeed from the whole scope and tenor of the New Testament. These views are therefore continually to be kept up; and for any to pretend that this is a round-about method, (as some have presumed to call it,) and that men may be led to virtue, the great end of all, by a much plainer and more direct way, seems to me only a vain and arrogant attempt to be wiser than God himself, which therefore must in the end appear to be folly, with whatever subtlety of argument it may be defended, or with whatever pomp of rhetoric it be adorned.

The New Testament is a book written with the most consummate knowledge of human nature; and though there are a thousand latent beauties in it, which it is the business the glory of true criticism to place in a strong point of light, the general sense and design of it is plain to every honest reader, even at the very first perusal. It is evidently intended to bring us to God, through Christ, in an humble dependence on the commuuications [sic] of his sanctifying and quickening Spirit; and to engage us to a course of faithful and universal obedience, chiefly from a grateful sense of the riches of Divine grace manifested to us in the gospel. And though this scheme is indeed liable to abuse, as every thing else is, it appears to me plain in fact, that it has been, and still is, the grand instrument of reforming a very degenerate world; and according to the best observations I have been able to make on what has passed about me, or within my own breast, I have found that, in proportion to the degree in which this evangelical scheme is received and relished, the interest of true virtue and holiness flourishes, and the mind is formed to manly devotion, diffusive benevolence, steady fortitude, and, in short, made ready to every good word and work. To this therefore I am determined at all adventures to adhere; nor am I at all ashamed or afraid of any scorn which I may encounter in such a cause; and I would earnestly exhort, and entreat, all my brethren in the Christian ministry to join with me, as well knowing to whom we have committed our souls; and cheerfully hoping, that he, by whom we have hitherto, if faithful in our calling, been supported and animated; will at length confess us before the presence of his Father, and the holy angels, in that day, when it will be found no dishonour to the greatest and wisest of the children of men to have listed themselves under the banner of the cross, and constantly and affectionately to have kept their Divine Leader in view.

I cannot flatter myself so far as to imagine that I have fallen into no mistakes in a work of so great compass and difficulty; but my own conscience acquits me of having designedly misrepresented any single passage of scripture, or of having written one line with a purpose of inflaming the hearts of Christians against each other. I should esteem it one of the most aggravated crimes to make the Life of the gentle and benevolent Jesus a vehicle to convey such poison. Would to God, that all the party names, and unscriptural phrases and forms, which have divided the Christian world, were forgot; and that we might agree to sit down together, as humble loving disciples, at the feet of our common Master, to hear his word, to imbibe his Spirit, and to transcribe his life in our own!

Spirituality

Document VI.20

Three Prayers of Anne Gwin

These prayers were written in the early eighteenth century by the Quaker Anne Gwin (1692–1715), for whom see *A Memorial of Anne Gwin, A Prudent and Virtuous Maiden*, 1715, pp. 30–1, 34–5.

(a)

Lord, Let me be made a Partaker of thy Wisdom, which is pure and peaceable, gentle and easie to be entreated, full of Mercy and good Fruits, without Partiality and without Hypocrisie. And Lord, give me, if it be thy Will, a true generous Heart, that I may slight and look over Injuries; But, Lord, I beseech thee let me not be lifted up with any vain Conceit whatsoever, but let me walk truly humble before thee, that I may come to have Self of no Reputation, that I may carry my self humbly and meekly to my Neighbours. But, O Lord, when I examine my Heart, I find it too much given to resent Injuries and Affronts. I fear, O God, it comes from a Spirit of Pride. My God, lay open my Heart, let me not flatter my self, knowing well, Lord, that *thou resistest the Proud, but givest Grace unto the Humble*. Lord, thou hast been pleased, though but young, to try me with great Afflictions, and what hath come very near to me, as the Sickness of my dear Father, whom I tender as my Life, and the Loss of my Relations, which has been I hope for the making of us better. Lord, sanctifie those Afflictions. And, Lord God, if it stands with thy ever blessed Will, I now humbly beg thee to continue to us the greatest of all temporal Mercies, the Life of my dear Parents. Thou hast given us good and tender Parents, and somewhat of this World's Goods, which are Blessings we deserve not more that Thousands who are deprived of them: But, Lord, it was thy great Loving-kindness, for which O Lord, I return Praise and Thanksgiving.

(b)

O great God, thou that art the most able Physician of my Soul, I beseech thee, look down and heal me: take notice of me, I pray thee: take away my Sins, Lord, with the Blood of thine immaculate Lamb, who died to take away the Sins of the World. Lord, let not *his Blood* be spilt in vain for me and many more: but, Lord, teach me *how to pray aright*, for I cannot speak a *good Word*, nor think a *good Thought of myself*, without my God and my Helper, to whom all Praise is due that *my poor weak Soul* can render unto thee, who art blessed now henceforth for ever, and for evermore, saith my Soul.

(c)

O Lord God of Heaven and of Earth, and of all things therein; Lord, I am now come to put my self in Remembrance of the many signal Favours I have received of late of thine Hands. Lord Jesus, instruct me in what I shall say or do to thy Praise: my Heart is full of the Cares of this Life, and the Desire of the deceitful Enjoyments of this World does, I am afraid, take my Mind from a due, and ever-minding of thy great and unspeakable Mercies; which is, Lord, when I cried unto thee in great Sorrow of Heart that thou hast been pleased to hear my Prayer. There is never a Day or Moment but that we ought to live in the Remembrance of thy great Mercy, for every Breath we draw, for the Health and Ease we enjoy; so that we can take some Delight in those Enjoyments thou hast made me, unworthy, a Partaker of; a Stomach to my Meat, and Meat to satisfie my Stomach; Cloths for my Body, which a great great many who are beter than myself want.

Document VI.21

Elizabeth Singer Rowe on God's Inexpressible Love

The author Elizabeth Singer Rowe (1674–1737), for whom see DNB, was a member of Isaac Watts's congregation. The following example of her intense, searching piety is from the posthumous *Devout Exercises of the Heart*, 1737, ch. 9.

IX. *Inexpressible Love toward God*

Thou radiant sun, thou moon, and all ye sparkling starts, how gladly would I leave your pleasant light to see the face of God! Ye crystal streams, ye groves and flowery lawns, my innocent delights. How joyfully could I leave you to meet that blissful prospect! And you delightful faces of my friends, I would this moment quit you all to see Him whom my soul loves – so loves that I can find no words to express the unutterable ardour. Not as the muser loves his wealth, nor the ambitious his grandeur, not as the libertine loves his pleasure, or the generous man his friend: these are flat similitudes to describe such an intense passion as mine. Not as a man scorched in a fever longs for a cooling draught, not as a weary traveller wishes for soft repose: my restless desires admit of no equal comparison with these.

I love my friend: my vital breath and the light of heaven are dear to me. But should I say I love my God as I love these, I should belie the sacred flame which aspires to infinity. 'Tis thee, abstractly thee, O uncreated beauty, that I love. In thee my wishes are all terminated, in thee, as in their blissful center, all my desires meet, and there they must be eternally fixed. It is thou alone that must constitute my everlasting happiness. Were the harps of angels silent, there would be harmony for me in the whispers of thy love. Were the fields of light darkened, thy smiles would bless me with everlasting day. ... All their beams of grace, joy and glory are derived from

355

thee, the eternal Sun, and will merit my attention no further than they reflect thy image, or discover thy excellencies.

Even at this distance – encompassed with the shades of death and the mists of darkness – in these cold melancholy regions, when a ray of the love breaks in on my soul, when through the clouds I can trace but one feeble beam, even that obscures all human glory, and gives me a contempt for whatever mortality can boast. What wonder then will the open vision of thy face effect. when I shall enjoy it in so sublime a degree that the magnificence of the skies will not draw my regard, nor the conversation of angels divert my thoughts from thee? … Mend thy pace, old lazy Time, and shake thy heavy sands; make shorter circles, ye rolling planets. When will your destined courses be fulfilled? Thou restless sun, how long wilt thou travail the celestial road? When will thy starry walk be finished? When will the commissioned angel arrest thee in thy progress and, lifting up his hand, swear by the unutterable name 'that time shall be no more'? O happy ending, my impatient soul springs forward to salute thee, and leaves the lagging days, and months, and years far behind. …

If I were only to reason upon this subject, I might say, What motive could earth, could hell, could heaven itself propose to tempt my soul to change its love? What could they lay in the balance against an infinite good? What could be thrown in as a stake against the favour of God? Ask the happy souls who know what the light of his countenance imports, who drink in joy and immortality from his smiles – ask them what value they set on their enjoyment. Ask them what in heaven or earth should purchase a moment's interval of their bliss. Ask some radiant seraph, midst the fervency of his rapture, at what price he values his happiness. And when these have named the purchase, earth and hell may try to balance mine. Let them spread the baits that tempt deluded men to ruin; let riches, honor, beauty, and bewitching pleasure appear in all their charms, the sensuality of the present and past ages, the Persian delicacy and the Roman pride. Let them uncover the golden mines and disclose the ruby sparkling in its bed; let them open the veins of sapphires and show the diamond glittering in its rock; let them all be thrown into the balance. Alas, their weight is too little, and too light! Let all pageantries of state be added, imperial titles and the ensigns of majesty; put in all that boundless vanity imagines, or wild ambition craves, crowns and sceptres, regal vestments and golden thrones. The scale still mounts. Throw in the world entire: 'tis insubstantial, and light as airy vanity.

Are these thy highest boasts, O deluding world? Ye ministers of darkness, have you nothing else to offer? Are these your utmost proposals? Are these a compensation for the favor of God? Alas, that boundless word has a meaning which outweighs them all: infinite delight, inconceivable joy, are expressed in it. The sight of his countenance signifies more than angels can describe or mortality imagine. And shall I quite all that an everlasting heaven means for empty shadows?

Go, ye baffled tempters, go offer your toys to madmen and fools! They all vanish under my scorn and cannot yield so much as an amusement to my aspiring thoughts. The sun, in all its spacious circuit, beholds nothing to tempt my wishes. These winding skies, in all their ample round, contain nothing equal to my desires. My ambition has far different ends, and other prospects in view. Nothing below the joys of angels can satisfy me.

Let me explore the words of life and beauty, and find a path to the dazzling recesses of the Most High. Let me drink at the fountain-head of pleasure, and derive all that I want from original and uncreated fulness and felicity.

O divine love, let me launch out into thy pleasurable depths, and be swallowed up in thee. Let me plunge at once into immortal joy, and lose myself in the infinite ocean of happiness.

Till then I pine for my celestial country, till then I murmur to the winds and streams, and tell the solitary shadows my grief. The groves are conscious of my complaints, and the moon and starts listen to my sighs. By their silent lights I talk over my heavenly concerns and give a vent to my divine affections in mortal language. Then, looking upward, I grow impatient to reach that milky way, the seat of joy and immortality.

> Come love, come life, and that bless'd day
> For which I languish, come away,
> When this dry soul these eyes shall see,
> And drink the unseal'd source of Thee.

O come, I cry, thou whom my soul loveth! I would go on, but lack expression, and vainly struggle with the unutterable thought.

Tell me, ye sons of light, who feel the force of the celestial fires, in what language do you paint their violence? Or, do the tongues of seraphs falter? Does the language of paradise lack equivalents here, and immortal eloquence fail? Surely your happiness is more perfect than all your descriptions of it. Heaven echoes to your charming notes as far as they reach. while divine love, which is your song, is infinite, and knows no limits of degree or duration.

Yet I would say, some gentle spirit come and instruct me in your art: lend me a golden harp and guide the sacred flight. Let me imitate your devout strains, let me copy out your harmony. And then

> Some of the fairest choir above
> Shall flock around my song,
> With joy, to hear the name they love
> Sound from a mortal tongue.

Blessed and immortal creatures, I long to join with you in your celestial style of adoration and love. I long to learn your ecstacies of worship and joy, in a language which mortals cannot pronounce. and to speak the divine passion of my soul in words which are now unspeakable.

Document VI.22

Philip Doddridge on Honouring God as Death Approaches

For Doddridge see Document I.1 above. His *The Rise and Progress of Religion in the Soul*, 1745, is one of the spiritual classics of the eighteenth century. Here Doddridge's pastoral sensitivity is to the fore, and his indebtedness to the experimental style of the Puritans is clear.

Thus, my dear reader, I have endeavoured to lead you through a variety of circumstances that occur in the Christian life. And I can truly say, that I have marked out to you the path which I myself have trod, and in which it is my desire still to go on. I have ventured my own everlasting interests on that foundation, on which I have directed you to adventure yours; and the most considerable enjoyment, which I expect or desire in the remaining days of my pilgrimage on earth, are such as I have directed you to seek, and endeavoured to assist you in attaining. Such love to God, such constant activity in his service, such pleasurable views of what lies beyond the grave, appear to me (God is my witness) a felicity incomparable beyond any thing else which can offer itself to our affection and pursuit: and I would not for ten thousand worlds resign my share in them, or consent even to the suspension of the delights which they afford, during the remainder of my abode here.

I would humbly hope, through the divine blessing, that the hours you have spent in the review of these plain things may have turned to profitable account, and that you have either been brought into the way of life and peace, or been induced to quicken your pace in it. Most heartily should I rejoice in being further useful to you, and that even to the last. Now there is one scene remaining; a scene, through which you must infallibly pass; which has something in it so awful, that I cannot but attempt doing a little to assist you in it; I mean the dark valley of the shadow of death. I could earnestly wish that for the credit of your profession, the comfort of your own soul, and the joy and edification of your surviving friends, you might die, not only safely but honourably too; and therefore, I would offer you a few parting advices. I am sensible, indeed, that Providence may determine the circumstances of your death in such a manner, as that you may have no opportunity of acting upon the hints I now give you. Some unexpected accident may, as it were, whirl you to heaven before you are aware; and you may find yourself so suddenly there, that it may seem a translation rather than a death. Or it is possible the force of a distemper may affect your understanding in such a manner, that you may be quite insensible of the circumstances in which you are; and so your dissolution (though others may see it visibly and certainly approaching) may be as great a surprise to you, as if you had died in full health.

But as it is on the whole probable, you may have a more sensible passage out of time into eternity; and as much may, in various respects, depend on your dying behaviour, give me leave to propose some plain directions with relation to it, to be practised, if God give you opportunity, and remind you of them.

That you may be the more at leisure, and the better prepared for this, 'enter into some serious review of your own state, and endeavour to put your soul into as fit a posture as possible, for your solemn appearance before God.' For a solemn thing indeed it is, to go into his immediate presence. Renew your humiliation before God for the imperfections of your life, though it has in the main been devoted to his service. Renew your application to the mercies of God as promised in the covenant of grace, and to the blood of Christ as the blessed channel in which they flow. Resign yourself entirely to the divine disposal, as willing to serve God, either in this world or the other, as he shall see fit. And sensible of your sinfulness, on the one hand, and of the divine wisdom and goodness on the other, summon up all the fortitude of your soul to bear as well as you can, whatever his afflicting hand may further lay upon you, as one who would maintain the most entire subjection to the great and good Father of spirits.

Whatever you suffer, 'endeavour to shew yourself an example of patience.' Let there not be a murmuring word; and when you feel any thing of that kind arising, look by faith upon a dying Saviour, and ask your own heart, 'was not his cross much more painful than the bed on which I lie? Was not his situation among blood-thirsty enemies infinitely more terrible than mine? Did not the heavy load of my sins press him in a much more overwhelming manner than I am pressed by the load of these afflictions? and yet he bore all as a lamb that is brought to the slaughter.' Let the remembrance of his sufferings sweeten yours: yea, let it cause you to re-joice. Count it all joy, that you have an opportunity yet once more of honouring God by your patience, which is now acting its last part, and will, perhaps, in a few hours, be superseded by everlasting blessedness. And I am not willing to hope, that in these views, you will not only suppress all passionate complaints, but that your mouth will be filled by the praises of God. So that you will be enabled to commu-nicate your inward joys in such a manner, as may be a lively and edifying comment upon these words of the Apostle, 'tribulation worketh patience, and patience ex-perience: and experience hope; even a hope which maketh not ashamed, while the love of God is shed abroad in our hearts, by the Holy Ghost which is given unto us.'

Now is the time when it is especially expected from you, that you bear an honour-able testimony to religion. Tell those that are about you, as well as you can (for you will never be able fully to express it) what comfort and support you have found in it. Tell them, how it has brightened the darkest circumstances of your life; tell them, how it now reconciles you to the near views of death. – Your words will carry with them a peculiar weight at such a season: there will be a kind of eloquence, even in the infirmities with which you are struggling, while you give them utterance; and you will be heard with attention and with credit. Tell others what you feel of the vanity of the world, and they may learn to regard it less. Tell them what you feel of the substantial supports of the gospel: and they may learn to value it more.

'Give a solemn charge to those that are about you, that they may spend their lives in the service of God, and govern themselves by the principles of real religion.' You may remember that Joshua and David, and other good men did so, when the days drew near in which they should die. And you know not how the admonitions of a dying friend, or of a dying parent, may impress those who may have disregarded what has been said to them before.

And in this last address to your fellow-mortals, 'be sure that you tell them how entirely and how cheerfully your hopes and dependence in this season of the last extremity are fixed on what the great Redeemer has done and has suffered for sinners.' Let them see, that you die, as it were, at the foot of the cross; nothing will be so comfortable to yourselves, nothing so edifying to them. Endeavour that the last act of your soul, while it continues in the body, may be an act of humble faith in Christ. 'Come unto God by him; enter into that which is within the vail, as with the blood of sprinkling fresh upon you.'

Once more, 'to give you comfort in a dying hour, and to support your feeble steps, take the word of God as a staff in your hand.' Let books and mortal friends now do their last office for you. Call, if you can, 'some experienced Christian, who has felt the power of the word of God upon his own heart, and let him bring the scripture, and turn you to some of those precious promises, which have been the food and rejoicing of his own soul I shall here give you a collection of a few such admirable scriptures. And to convince you of the degree in which I esteem them, I will take the freedom to add, that I desire they may (if God give an opportunity) be read over me, as I lie on my dying-bed, with short intervals between them, that I may pause upon each, and renew something of that delightful relish, which, bless God, I have often found in them.

Can any more encouragement be wanting, when he says, 'Fear not, for I am with thee; be not dismayed, for I am thy God: I will strengthen thee, yea, I will help thee; yea I will uphold the with the right-hand of my righteousness.' And God is not a man that he should lie, or the son of man, that he should repent: Hath he said, and shall he not do it? Or hath he spoken, and shall he not make it good? The Lord is my light and my salvation, whom shall I fear? The Lord is the strength of my life, of whom shall I be afraid? This God is our God for ever and ever : he will be our guide even unto death. Therefore, though I walk through the valley of the shadow of death, I will fear no evil; for thou art with me, thy rod and thy staff they comfort me. O continue thy loving kindness unto them that know thee, and thy righteousness to the upright in heart! For with thee is the fountain of life; in thy light shall we see light. – Thou wilt shew me the path of life; in thy presence is fullness of joy, at thy right-hand there are pleasures for evermore. As for me, I shall behold thy face in righteousness; I shall be satisfied when I awake with thy likeness; for I know in whom I have believed, and am persuaded that he is able to keep what I have committed to him until that day. Therefore my heart is glad, and my glory rejoiceth; my flesh also shall rest in hope. For if we believe that Jesus died, and rose again; those also that sleep in Jesus, will God bring with him. – I give unto my sheep eternal life (said Jesus the good shepherd,) and they shall never perish, neither shall any pluck them out of my hand. This is the will of him that sent me, that every one that believeth on me should have everlasting life; and I will raise him up at the last day. Let not your heart be troubled; ye believe in God, believe also in me. In my Father's house are many mansions; if it were not so, I would have told you; I go to prepare a place for you, I will come again, and receive you to myself; that where I am, there ye may be also. Go tell my brethren, I ascend unto my Father and your Father, and to my God and your God. Father, I will that those whom thou has given me be with me where I am, that they may behold my glory which thou hast given me; that the love wherewith thou hast loved me, may be in them, and I in them. – He that testifies these things, saith, Surely, I come quickly. Amen, even so, come Lord Jesus! O death, where is thy sting? O grave, where is thy victory? Thanks be to God, who giveth us the victory through our Lord Jesus Christ. Thus may that God, in whose sight the death of his saints is precious, cheer and support you and me in those last extremities of nature! May he add us to the happy number of those who have been more than conquerors in death! And may he give us those supplies of his Spirit which may enable us to pour out our departing souls in such sentiments, as those I would now suggest: though we should be no longer able to utter words, or to understand them if they were to be read to us! Let us at least review them with all proper affections now, and lay up one prayer more for that awful moment! O that this, and all we have offered with regard to it, may then come in remembrance before God.

Document VI.23

John Wesley's Spirituality

For John Wesley see Document II.21 above. For Wesley's conversion see Henry D. Rack, *Reasonable Enthusiast*, London: Epworth Press, 1989, ch. 4. The following account of his quest of pardon is found in Wesley's *Journal*, 24 May 1738, *Works*, 1872, I, p. 103.

I continued thus to seek it (though with strange indifference, dulness and coldness, and unusually frequent relapses into sin), till Wednesday, May 24. I think it was about five this morning, that I opened my Testament on those words, ... 'There are given unto exceeding great and precious promises, even that you should be partakers of the divine nature' (2 Peter i. 4). Just as I went out I opened it again on those words, 'Thou are not far from the kingdom of God'. In the afternoon I was asked to go to St Paul's. The anthem was, 'Out of the deep have I called unto Thee, O Lord: Lord, hear my voice. O let thine ears consider well the voice of my complaint. If Thou, Lord, wilt be extreme to mark what is done amiss, O Lord, who may abide it? For there is mercy with Thee; therefore shalt Thou be feared. O Israel, trust in the Lord: for with the Lord there is mercy, and with Him is plenteous redemption. And he shall redeem Israel from all his sins'.

In the evening I went very unwilling to a society in Aldersgate Street, where one was reading Luther's preface to the Epistle to the Romans. About a quarter before nine, while he was describing the change which God works in the heart through faith in Christ, I felt my heart strangely warmed. I felt I did trust in Christ, Christ alone, for my salvation: and an assurance was given me, that He had taken away my sins, even mine, and saved me from the law of sin and death.

Document VI.24

John Butterworth's Craving for Assurance

The Baptist John Butterworth (1727–1803) of Goodshaw, Rossendale, Lancashire, was Baptist minister at Cow Lane, Coventry, for fifty years. He published an oft-reprinted concordance and dictionary, and a refutation of Priestley's Unitarianism. Butterworth exemplifies the truth that for some Dissenters doctrine could be as much an occasion for spiritual wrestling as was temptation.

For Butterworth see DEB, DNB. The following is reprinted from Clyde Binfield, *Pastors and People: The Biography of a Baptist Church, Queen's Road, Coventry*, Coventry: Queen's Road Baptist Church, 1984, pp. 25–6, who in turn draws from M. Irene Morris, *Three Hundred Years*, [1926].

The doctrine of assurance of faith and of knowing our own sins pardoned, was much insisted upon by the Methodist preachers. This I wanted to know, for I was not certain that I was a subject of grace ... I sometimes thought I would cease praying, nor hold my peace till the Lord should speak peace and pardon to my soul ...

... One night I resolved to continue all night till God appeared, but about 2 o'clock sleep overtook me ... One morning I was deep in thought on this subject, reasoning with myself why I was still in unbelief, when these words dropped upon my mind:– 'By grace ye are saved through faith, and that, not of yourselves, it is the gift of God.' This word '*gift*' revolved in my mind. A gift, thought I, is not merited, if it were, it would be a debt, and not a gift ... This led me to think that there was some truth in the doctrine of election, and that it was not upon foresight of faith and obedience but of pure sovereignty, and that faith and obedience were the fruits and effects of election, and not causes thereof. My sentiments began to change from Arminianism to Calvinism ... This was about my nineteenth year, in the bloom of youth and health.
...

One day I was reading in a book called 'The Marrow of Modern Divinity', a sentence from Luther ... 'I would run into the arms of Christ if he stood with a drawn sword in His Hand'. This thought came bolting into my mind – so will I too – and those words of Job occurred: 'Though he slay me yet will I trust in him'. My burden dropped off. My soul was filled with joy and peace through believing in Christ, a venturesome believing, as Mr. Belcher calls it ...

About this time I had strong desires of preaching Christ to my fellow sinners.

Document VI.25

The Experience of Theophilus Lobb

Theophilus Lobb (1678–1763) was trained both for ministry, at Thomas Goodwin's Pinner academy, and for medicine, which professions he sometimes combined and between which he sometimes oscillated.

For Lobb see DNB. For Goodwin (1650?–1716?) see DNB. Lobb's account of his experience is reprinted from John Greene, *The Power of Faith and Godliness exemplified, In some Memoirs of Theophilus Lobb, M.D. F.R.S.*, London, 1767, pp. 11–14.

O most dreadful and yet most gracious God! I beseech thee, for the passion of thy son, accept of thy poor prodigal, prostrating himself at thy door. I am, by my wicked practice a son of death, a child of hell: but, of thine infinite grace, thou hast promised mercy to me, if I will but turn to thee. Therefore upon the call of thy gospel, I am come in; and throwing down my arms, I submit myself to thy mercy.

I acknowledge that I have wickedly sided with thine enemies: but I here renounce them all, firmly covenanting with thee, not to allow myself in any known sin; but conscientiously to use all the means, I know thou hast prescribed, for the destruction of all my corruptions; and it is my resolution, through thine assistance, to forsake all that is dear to me in this world, rather than to turn into the ways of sin, and to watch against all its temptations, lest they should withdraw my heart from thee:

And since thou hast graciously offered to be my God through Jesus Christ, I do here call heaven and earth to record this day, that I do solemnly vouch thee for the Lord my God, and give up myself, soul and body, for thy servant, promising and vowing to serve thee in holiness and righteousness, all the days of my life.

And I do here accept of Christ, as the only way by which sinners may have access to thee; and renouncing my own righteousness, depend on him alone for justification. And subscribing to all his laws as holy, just, and good, I solemnly take them as the rule of my thoughts, affections, words, and actions; promising, that tho' my flesh may contradict and rebel, yet, I will endeavour to order my whole life according to his direction, and will not allow myself in the neglect of any thing I know to be my duty.

I am indeed, subject to many failings; but the gracious declarations of thy word encourage me to hope, that unallowed miscarriages shall not make void this covenant.

O almighty God, the searcher of all hearts, thou knowest that I make this covenant with thee, this day, without any known guile of reservation. I beseech thee, discover to me whatever flaw or falsehood there may be therein; and help me to make and execute it aright.

And now, glory be to thee, O God the Father (whom I shall be bold, from this day, to call my Father, and look upon as my God, in Christ) that thou hast found out such a way for the recovery of sinners. Glory be to thee, O God the Son! Who hast loved me, and washed me from my sins, in thine own blood, and art become my Saviour. And glory be to thee, O God the Holy Ghost! who, by thine almighty power, hast turned my heart from sin to God.

O merciful Jehovah, the Lord God omnipotent! thou art become my covenant friend, and I, through thine infinite grace, am become thy covenant servant; Amen, so be it. And the covenant which I have made on earth, let it be ratified in heaven.

Theophilus Lobb.

Document VI.26

Thomas Gibbons's Diary

Thomas Gibbons (1720–85), who trained under Abraham Taylor at Deptford and John Eames at Moorfields, exemplifies those Dissenting ministers who served now with the Presbyterians – in his case as assistant at Silver Street, London – now with the Independents, for in 1743 he undertook the pastorate of the Independent Church at Haberdashers' Hall. From 1754 he served concurrently as a tutor at the Homerton academy established by the Calvinistic King's Head Society in 1730, with Abraham Taylor as theological tutor. The academy removed to Mile End in 1754.

For Gibbons see DNB. For Taylor see Document I.4 above. For Eames (d. 1744) see DNB. The extracts from Gibbons's *Diary* for 1754 are reprinted from *Congregational Historical Society Transactions*, I, 1901–4, pp. 328–9.

Lord's Day. 14. Preached in the Morning from Hos. 14.2. In the Afternoon from 1 Pet. 4.18, on the Account of the Death of Mrs. Ann Clarke, Daughter of the Revd. Saml. Clarke, an ejected Minister, & Author of Annotations on the Bible.

Thursd. 25. Set apart the Morning of this Day for Prayer & Exhortation on Account of our Removal to a new Habitation.

Frid. 26. Gave up great Part of this Day to Mr. Davies in soliciting Charity for his Errand into Great-Britain, to wit, that of founding a College in the New-Jerseys. Collected this Day 7 Guineas & Half. Collected for him in all about 40 Guineas from our Church and Congregation.

May. Tuesd. 21. Attended Pinners'-Hall. Met the Deputation from *the Fund*, viz: Dr. Guyse, Mr. Bradbury, Mr. King, & Mr. Hall, who were in Commission to notify the Choice of the 13th Instant of the Revd. Mr. Conder for the Province of Divinity, & Mr. Walker & my self, to have a share, according to what we should agree upon, in the Work of Academical Tuition.

Wed. 22. Met the Deputation from the Society, viz:, Dr, Guyse, *Mr. Hall*, Mr. Brewer, Mr. Will Fuller, Mr. Wealthdale, Mr. Eade, who were appointed to notify to the same Purpose as above the Choice of the King's Head Society of the same persons, on Tuesday the 14th Inst. Each of us delivered in, according to what we had settled among ourselves, a List of the Branches of Tuition we intended to undertake in Case we complied with the Request of the two Bodies.
My List stood as follows:–

Logick	Ethics	Stile in gener:
Metaphysics	Rhetorick	Pulpit Stile.

N.B. The choice of my Self was in both Bodies very unanimous; the like was Mr. Walker's Case. The Society quite so as to Mr. Conder & the Fund generally …

August. Frid. 2. Met some Gentlemen of the King's Head Society in the Evening. Every Thing is settled as to the Tuition. Now for Strength of Body and Soul comfortably and usefully to perform the Work devolved upon me! May thy Grace, O God, be sufficient for me, and thy Strength perfected in my Weakness!

Tuesd. 20. At Ipswich. Visited two Malefactors under Sentence of Death. [He visited them again the two following days.]

September. Mond. 16. Introduced my work of Tuition among the Students at Plaisterers' Hall by delivering an Address to them relating to the Part of Education I had undertaken, and their Duty as Candidates for the Ministry.

October. Wed. 9. [at Ipswich]. Engaged in the Ordination of Mr. Gordon as Copastor with Mr. Notcutt, by preaching to the people from 1 Cor. 15.58. Mr. King gave the Charge.

November. Frid. 1. Mr. Hart & Mr. Fuller were chosen Deacons.

Thursd. 7. Prepared a Discourse as a Charge to the new Deacons.

December. Wed. 11. Spent the Day at Mr. Conder's at Mile End, where was Time spent in Prayer by Dr. Guyse, Mr. Hall, & Mr. Brewer on occasion of the Removal of the Academy there, & c.

Frid. 13. No Lectures to-Day, as the Students are busy in Removal from Plaisterers' Hall to Mile End.

Wed. 25. Went with my Child to the Chappel at St. James's, & saw the King & Royal Family.

Document VI.27

The Last Days of Anne Crowley

Some Expressions of Anne Crowley, the Quaker (1757–74), was published in 1774, and reprinted in that year and in 1784. The following quotation is from the second edition.

On First-day, the 6th of the Second Month, she sent for her three Brothers separately to her Bed-side, and in a most affectionate and tender Manner cautioned them against *The Gaiety, Riches and Grandeur of the World*, and exhorted them *To walk in the Path of Virtue, to keep close to divine Instructions, and likewise to watch and pray continually*; adding, *I find it needful even on my Death Bed*. To one of them, she said, *Give up, O give up! remember that the Fear of the Lord is the Beginning of Wisdom; seek thou that Wisdom now in the Days of thy Youth – step gently along, and keep thy Mind low and humble before him*. After laying still a little Time, she said, *Though painful my Days and wearisom my Nights, as* Samuel Fothergill *said, yet I am preserved in Resignation and Patience*. Her Sisters being in the Room, she intreated them *To live together in Love, and be affectionate to each other*. One of them observing, 'What Pleasure it would 'give them if she was to get well,' her Reply was, *No, I shall not add much to your Pleasure, my Home will soon be in Heaven*.

She wished, *That every one that frequents publick places of Diversions, and follows the deceitful Pleasures of this World, would be persuaded, after giving themselves up to those Scenes of Folly, to dedicate the Remainder of their Time to the Service of the Lord their God*; and added, *that in so doing they would find the greatest and most lasting Happiness*.

Document VI.28

John Fry's Poem

A volume of *Select Poems, containing religious epistles, &c.* was published by the Quaker John Fry (1701–75) in 1774 (the edition used here), and reprinted in 1781, 1783 and 1793 – the last two editions containing additional material.

On inward Poverty, and a rambling Mind, in religious Meetings.

I.

O That my Mind could still refrain
From ev'ry foolish Thought!
And all my mental Rovings be
To true Subjection brought!

II.

That when my Heart is bent to seek
The Lord for Help and Peace,
All Thoughts that would my Mind divert
Might then entirely cease.

III.

Tho', when retir'd, I've often felt
Some inward Consolations,
Yet when I would again retire,
I've met with sore Probations.

IV.

Perhaps about Indiff'rent Things
My Thoughts have been employ'd,
Which for a while were not supprest,
Nor any Good enjoy'd.

V.

But O that I, with Diligence,
May labour more and more,
That so the Lord may condescend
His Favours to restore.

VI.

That I may feel my Strength renew'd,
Temptations to resist,
Which if I humbly wait to find,
He surely will assist.

VII.

Because his Arm is cloth'd with Strength,
   And full of heav'nly Might,
His Ear is open to the Poor,
   Whose Aid is his Delight.

VIII.

To him, in Streights, may I apply,
   Whilst I remain on Earth,
As he alone can give me Life,
   And break the Pow'r of Death.

IX.

Tho' frail I am, and frail we are,
   And on this Side the Grave
A State of Frailty ev'ry one
   Must still expect to have;

X.

But to the Lord we all should look
   In Times of deep Distress;
And in Prosperity as much,
   Tho' then we seek him less.

XI.

'Tis his reviving heav'nly Love
   Can only dissipate
The idle Ramblings of the Mind,
   Altho' exceeding great:

XII.

'Tis this alone can chase away
   Our vain Imaginations,
And change the Rovings of our Minds
   To proper Contemplations:

XIII.

Wean all our Thoughts from earthly Things,
   Save only for our Use;
And those receive as with a Mind
   Averse to Things profuse.

XIV.

This sov'reign Help, this gracious Aid,
   This awful humbling Pow'r,

Is that for which we ought to wait,
    And seek for ev'ry Hour.

Document VI.29

Ann Moore's Desire

Ann Moore was a courageous Quaker itinerant in Spain. The following extract is from *The Journal of Anne Moore 1710–1783*, printed in M. H. Bacon, ed., *Wilt Thou Go On My Errand? Three Eighteenth-Century Journals of Quaker Women Ministers*, Wallingford, PA: Pendle Hill, 1994, pp. 357–9.

I have also a desire to mention another trial I afterwards met with: it being our lots to be cast in Spain in the time of lent, where we continued until it was over, and towards the conclusion, came on their procession of the host, the images of our Saviour, their saints the apostles and the Virgin Mary through the streets and on the parade by the seaside, before the window of the room where I lodged, they erected an altar on which they placed the coffin that contained the image of our Saviour, and stood round it with the rest of the images fixed on great square tables borne up on men's shoulders. While they were erecting the altar, the power of the Lord was upon me in such a manner that I trembled as one in a strong ague and a cry ran through my heart, O Lord, let them see as thou has let my poor soul see, that Christ within is the hope of the saints' glory, which became so close and heavy, I began greatly to fear that if I did not proclaim this which so powerfully ran through my heart, I should lose favour with the Lord; and great indeed was my distress, yea more than pen or tongue can declare, and my cries to the Lord were, O Lord! What can I do, I fear that I shall not stand, nor be strong enough to go through this great work, and so bring dishonour to thy cause and confusion of face on my dear friends; and then it would be better I had never been born; besides they cannot understand me. In this awful state I remained upwards of two hours until all fear of what man could do was taken away. Then beholding my hands which looked like one prepared for the grave, I went to the fire, and sat down alone, my companions being gone to another town there was no soul for me to speak to or ask counsel of. Thus I sat resigned to the will of the Lord, my God, waiting for him to point out to me, where He would have me go, whether to the church, or to the place where they had erected the altar. I had not sat long before I sensibly felt the will was accepted for the deed, as was the ram instead of Isaac [Gen. 22: 13]. Glory, honour, and praise to the Lord God and the Lamb forever and ever. Thus did my soul sing His praise in secret, and being bowed low before him, my joy as far exceeded the declaration of pen or tongue as my baptism and sorrow before had done. A day of days not easily to be forgot. Yea, I have thought like letters engraven in a rock not easily to be erased. O! praises, thanksgiving and glory to the Lord God and the Lamb, forever and ever, Amen, Saith my soul and more.

    I have wrote the above that my dear children may see what the high and holy one who inhabits eternity, has done for their mother that they may be engaged to be inward with him, who is and ever was a present help to all his depending children: for O sweet Lord and Saviour, he gave me power at that time to resign my life, and also my dear children, expecting my life would be taken for the testimony I should have to bear. May my dear children remember this, and believe the word of the Lord who said, Whoever will lose his life for my sake shall find it [Matt. 10: 39]. And all he requires of his creation man is to resign the whole heart, then he lets us see that he is a God of order and requires no more of us than He will give us ability to perform. But a tried people will the Lord our God have under which trials we are sometimes laid so low, that we feel according to our measure, as our dear Saviour did, when He said, I have a baptism to be baptized with [Matt. 20: 22]. O how am I straitened until it be accomplished, but glory to his worthy name he went through faithfully and now sits in glory and honour, which will be the end of all His faithful servants who sell all and follow him.

Document VI.30

Diary of a Deacon

It appears that the anonymous author of the following diary extracts became an Independent deacon in 1778. He seems to have belonged to the White Row church, London, and to have had relatives whom he visited in Yorkshire. For the following extracts, together with Albert Peel's speculations as to who the deacon might have been, see *Congregational Historical Society Transactions*, XV, no. 4, April 1948, pp. 180–81.

5th July, 1772. Mr. Hitchen after the Ordinance took a Sollem Farewell of the Church for a Littel time as he and Mrs. Hitchen setts out for Yorkshire.
Friday, 7th Aug., 1772. Church meeting before the Breaking bread Day. Mr. Hitchen arived so tired that he could not Preach so Mr. Chater Praid and Mr. Crozer and then sung and Mr. Hitchen concluded with Praier. ...
    21st Sep., 1773. ... Mr. Hitchen desired the Church to stay when he related a very Affecting Case of a Bad Member being in the Poultry Counter for Sodommy and was cut off from being a Member with us.
1774. 9th Jan. [Hitchen still very ill. Mr. Ryland from Northampton.]
11th Jan. [Hitchen dies].
14th Jan., Friday. At our Church Meeting we sung then Mr. Wheatly and Mr. Eming and another Brother Praied and wee sung and another Brother Praied and concluded the Exercise and a Precious Opportunity it was to me – and then Mr. Flowers tould us about the Church Buring our once dear Pastare Mr. Hitchin for we shall see him no more.
20th. 20 mourning coaches.

Document VI.31

Christmas Evans Recalls His Youth

For Evans see Document II.21 above. The quotations are reprinted from B. A. Ramsbottom, *Christmas Evans*, Luton: The Bunyan Press, 1985, pp. 14–15.

The fear of dying in an ungodly state especially affected me (even from childhood), and this apprehension clung to me till I was induced to rest upon Christ. All this was accompanied by some little knowledge of the Redeemer; and now, in my seventieth year, I cannot deny that this concern was the dawn of the day of grace on my spirit, although mingled with much darkness and ignorance. …

The spirit of energetic supplication was given to me early. A sense of danger prompts the soul to seek deliverance. Earnestness in prayer grew with me, though I frequently feared it would become extinct. Still, it was not entirely extinguished, even in those days of darkness when I but barely perceived that the merits of Christ were the only plea, without reference to anything of our own. After I came to know and feel that the righteousness of Christ formed the only ground to be depended upon before God, I was able with every sense of unworthiness to approach Him with a stronger expectation. The Christian must have a rock in the merits of the Redeemer to rest upon; and here he finds 'a place of refuge, and a covert from the storm and the rain.'

Document VI.32

The Serious Thoughts of the Young John Elias

John Elias (1774–1841), a Calvinistic Methodist minister, was one of Wales's most popular preachers. With his oratorical devices he combined an evangelical yet determined Calvinism. He was active in promoting the Presbyterian Church of Wales, and was a leading drafter of its Confession of Faith (1823) and its constitutional deed (1826).

For Elias see DEB, DNB, DWB. The following is extracted from Edward Morgan's *Memoir* of Elias, reprinted under the title *John Elias: Life, Letters and Essays*, Edinburgh: The Banner of Truth Trust, 1973, pp. 6–7.

I was deeply impressed, from my childhood, with serious thoughts respecting God, judgment, and the world to come. I used to be terrified in my dreams with apprehensions about the day of judgment, and fears of going into hell, though I was very ignorant.

When I was seven years old, I had the small-pox. I was greatly afflicted with the disease: it was very heavy. Indeed there was a doubt for weeks about my recovery. I lost my memory for some days: my eyes were closed, and I was blind for a fortnight. But the Lord was pleased to restore me. I remember when I began to recover, and to open my eyes, that my grandfather came to my bedside, weeping, and addressing me thus: 'My dear boy, do you remember what your lesson is?' I answered, 'Yes', and mentioned some chapter in the book of Jeremiah. The old man rejoiced greatly when he saw that I could remember in spite of my affliction the portion of Scripture I was reading when I was taken ill, and that there were hopes that I should have the use of my eyes again to read the Bible. I was long in a low state, and often afflicted for three or four years.

When I began to walk after my affliction, I went as usual with my grandfather to the parish church every Sabbath. He used to lift me up to some elevated place to read the responses after the minister, according to the accustomed order. The old man in every way would teach me to avoid immoral practices, such as lying, swearing, dishonesty and Sabbath-breaking. The Lord blessed his counsels to keep me from those things.

Sometimes I was enticed by children of my own age, and some older, to follow them on Sabbath evenings as we came out of church, and to engage in what they called innocent play, that is, without making any noise. Sometimes, on such occasions, I was unable to say the Lord's Prayer, and could not sleep by reason of guilt and terror. Once I heard a lad swearing (I was not allowed to keep company with such boys). I thought it was splendid of the boy to say such words. I went far from all people to the middle of a field to attempt uttering the swear-word. Alas, I said it! Upon which such fear and terror seized me that I thought the earth would open and swallow me to Hell on the spot. ...

There used to be great strivings within me respecting the Sabbath; my conscience would insist upon keeping it holy, but my sinful bias would crave for a little amusement with my companions. But I could not silence conscience; I had no liberty to follow the multitude. My parents were not at that time careful about the Sabbath. Sometimes neighbours likeminded with themselves would come to them on the Sabbath, and would converse with them on improper subjects for God's day. I wept much on this account. Sometimes I would remonstrate with them, but they would not hear me! One Sabbath my parents sent me on an errand to the house of my mother's father, about four miles away. I was seized with great trouble of mind; on my way I saw one of the mountains before me black and smoky, after the heath had been set ablaze on it on Saturday night. I thought the day of judgment had come, that the earth was beginning to burn, and that I was going to judgment by breaking the Sabbath. Such was my distress and great terror that I was obliged to cry out; I endeavoured to pray that I might be spared from going to judgment in my sins. Notwithstanding this I was ignorant of God, and the way of salvation.

Document VI.33

The Experience of Ann West

Ann West (1783–1871) was a Methodist who lived at St Breake, Cornwall. Her private papers are quoted in the *Journal of the Cornish Methodist Historical Association*, VII, no. 4, 1988, from which the following early entries are drawn. Extract (a) is from 1799; extract (b) is from 1801.

(a)

From what I have read, heard and remarked, in Christian experience, I learn that almighty God hath many and varied ways in bringing His creatures acquainted with Himself. Some are drawn to seek an acquaintance with God by the terror of His law, as thundered forth fro the Mount; whilst others are drawn to seek Him by the cords of love, having their hearts gently opened; and many again are allured to seek an acquaintance with Him through a discovery of His excellent perfections. God is not only pleased to reveal Himself as the Mighty God, doing wonders, but also as 'The Lord God, gracious and merciful etc.' Now the latter discovery seemed to operate most powerfully on my mind. At a very early age I had many discoveries of the excellencies of the Divine Being, such as His Holiness and Love; but in the years of 1796, and 1797, when at the age of thirteen and fourteen I was at a boarding-school, in Plymouth, I had further discoveries made to my mind, whilst attending the ministry of Dr. Hawker. Then it was that I saw something excellent in religion – that the people of God were a happy people, and that religion had in it something amiable, something calculated to make one wise and happy. How to possess this 'one thing needful' I knew not. I desired to walk in the ways of God, and I loved His people, but how to become one myself was the grand concern. I had no acquaintance with any religious character, and was now about to leave school, so should have no further opportunity of hearing the Dr. again. I learnt from his preaching that prayer was necessary, so in my poor way I began to pray secretly, for I feared the jeers of those among whom I lived.

I returned home fully determined to be very good, but alas! I soon experienced that my resolutions were like 'the morning cloud, and early dew' that passeth quickly away.

I will forbear saying anything about the minister I now had to sit under, but oh! What will these pretended Guides do when they meet their starved flocks at the Bar of God?

After leaving school, and returning home, having no one to take me by the hand, I soon drank into the spirit of those with who I associated, and joined in all the country amusements, such as cards, dancing, etc., etc., but after a while I could find no delight in these fleeting enjoyments. The anticipated pleasure at the dance or the card-table would disappoint, and I should return home with an aching void. I recollect whilst at the last dance I ever attended at a very respectable person's house, I felt so dissatisfied, that on my return home I determined never to attend such places of amusement again, I seemed to be created for superior enjoyments. And now the period drew near when the Day Star from on high was to dawn on my heart.

In 1799 (I know not by what inducement) I strolled into the Methodist Meeting-house at Trevanson. [Trevanson was then the post-town, but is now reduced to a small hamlet.]

Here I was as a beast before God, full of ignorance and prejudice; for I had been taught to believe that the Methodist Preachers were 'False Prophets', 'Wolves in sheep's clothing'. Indeed so ignorant was I, that I knew not even if any reverence were due to the place of Meeting. I could not tell what to do, till some one pointed me to a seat, which I took most gladly, and watched the motions of others to be the rule for my own conduct.

But oh! the goodness and mercy of God? How unsearchable are His ways? Here it was I was to learn the things concerning Himself, and be brought acquainted with His people.

The Preacher [Mr. Gellard] soon entered and went into the Pulpit. I was much struck with his appearance and manner. After singing and prayer, he took for his text, – Mal. III, 16–17, 'Then they that feared the Lord spake often one to another,' etc. In the course of his sermon he described the character of those 'that feared the Lord', with their happy privileges; and then showed how all might become 'His jewels', and sweetly he persuaded his hearers thereto. And blessed be God, before the close of the meeting my prejudices were removed, and I was led to say in my heart, 'This is the people – unknown till now – that I have so long desired to be acquainted with;' 'this people shall be my people, and their God my God'. And strange to say, I that very night joined hand and heart with the Methodists [this was in 1799] and I hope with them to live and die.

The Society remained after the congregation was dismissed. I remained with them, and received my first Ticket. The passage on it was, 'Escape for thy life etc.'

I had not as yet been to a class meeting, but I thought on receiving my Ticket, 'what a privilege is this, how great a mercy to be united with the people of God'. My cry was for grace to walk circumspectly, lest any misconduct of mine should bring disgrace on the cause I had espoused, or reproach on the people who had thus kindly given me the right hand of fellowship. This feeling operates to the present time; I would sooner die this moment than by any irregular conduct bring reproach on the cause of God.

From this period I went comfortably on my way to Zion; each day brought fresh light, life and love, without any terrors of mind, (I had always a hope) till I could say in confidence, – 'Oh God, Thou art my God'. Just as in the morning we discover the dawn, one ray of light succeeds another, till our room is filled, without our knowing the precise moment when darkness passed away and the full light of day began. We should not say the room was in darkness because we could not ascertain the exact time when the Sun shone forth, and dispersed the shades of night – so the Sun of Righteousness beamed forth upon my soul, gradually enlightening my mind, and bringing me acquainted with Himself.

I went on thus for more than two years rejoicing in the God of my salvation – notwithstanding some severe outward opposition.

(b)

Despair would sometimes take hold of me, and the old Giant would often thrust me into his darkest dungeon, and make me roar out for help. [but] 'Neither secret prayer, nor class meetings were ever wilfully neglected, although we had no regular leader for more than that time. To the latter cause I attribute my remaining so long in that painful state, which no pen is adequate to describe' …

The Lord again remembered His people at Wadebridge, and sent them a faithful class-leader, who was well acquainted with the human heart, the devices of Satan, and the great plan of Redemption. He was very careful to make himself acquainted with the state of his charge, before he would apply the remedy, hence he took great pains to understand my case. This he did by seeking opportunities when alone, as well as in the class of conversing with me. He found it difficult at first, as I was got into a silent, sullen way. So completely had Satan shut my mouth that I have gone to class meeting many a time during this period without speaking a word. Here we see the propriety of dealing tenderly with the feeble of the flock. Had I perhaps not received all this love and tenderness from my elders, I might have gone back, and walked no more with them.

Not long after this I was walking in the Church Park, Trevorder, just under the sycamore trees, and the Lord visited my soul, and made me very happy. The words of my leader were brought to my recollection, – 'Surely,' thought I, 'this is pardon; my God is reconciled.' My soul was at that moment filled with peace and joy. So strong was the evidence, that I have not once doubted of its reality even in the darkest moments, although at that time there was not any passage of scripture applied. But, there were many in the following days; indeed the whole Bible seemed full of promises to ME.

Soon after this restitution of Divine favour and love, the Lord discovered to me that His work must be carried on and matured, so that I might bring forth all the fruits of the Spirit, and, that this must be effected by the sanctifying influences of His Blessed Spirit. My prayer now was that He would renew my soul in righteousness, and true holiness, that I might experience the Blood of Christ to cleanse from all sin, that all unholy tempers and dispositions, especially levity and selfwill might be destroyed; and so intense were my desires for this blessing that I frequently awoke praying to be sanctified wholly.

Document VI.34

Joseph Hussey on Marriage

Joseph Hussey, whose decided doctrinal views we have already encountered (see Document IV.5 above), would seem to have been no shirk when it came to church discipline. The following is the transcript of a letter he wrote to a member who had married outside of the church. On the back is found the transcript of Susan Orlebar's response.

The letter and reply are reprinted from *Congregational History Society Transactions*, 1904–5, pp. 137–8.

Susan Orlebar

For I will salute your person by your old name. You having committed heinous offences and sins against the Ld. Xt. And us of this Congregational Church of saints, & in open slander against the gospel before the world, declared your sin as Sodom and hid it not, we have voted to meet the 2d Thursday of Jany 1700 in order to humble ourselves before the Ld., and by giving you up in the name of the Lord C. to Satan cut you off by the terrible sentence from any relation to the Church; that you may find it utter destruction to the flesh, & that your spirit, if you belong to Xt. may be saved in the Day of the L. Jesus. – These are therefore to give you notice in as-much as the Church is bound by the indispensable laws of Xts Government to proceed in the sharpest way against you for your manifold scandals. We shall if the Lord will effect it the Day and Month above written.

Given at our Church meeting, Thursday Novr 7th 1700.

Jos. Hussey Pastor

Robt. Willson
Saml. Aungier
Philip Saunders

Colchester Novr 28 1700

I Susan Handley do solemnly declare and am ready to make oath, that I know of no other Reason for this severe sentence to be pronounced against me by the Within named Joseph Hussey & others, but that I set my hand to a paper wherein I obliged myself not to marry any one but who should be believed to be of the same society and thereby leaving the congregation.

Subscribed by Susan Handley in the presence of me,

JOS. POTTER, Mayor.

Document VI.35

The Yearly Meeting's Concern for Marriage

Marriage in Quakerism requires special mention. The legality of Quaker marriage was not accepted by the Established Church in the earlier years, though it was upheld by the civil courts after 1661. The procedure was open and carefully supervised by the appropriate meeting. Lord Hardwicke's Marriage Act of 1753 excluded Quakers and Jews from the requirement that all marriage ceremonies take place in the parish church, provided that Quaker married Quaker and Jew, Jew. As time went by the rules on marriage as much as those on dress and speech emphasised the setting apart of Friends as a peculiar people, while the disownment of those who married outside the Society was a major factor in the decline of numbers of members – a decline which reached crisis point in the middle of the nineteenth century. In his essay of 1859, *Quakerism Past and Present; being an Inquiry into the Causes of its Decline in Great Britain and Ireland*, John Stephenson Rowntree showed that during the eighteenth century marriages in the Society of Friends were one-fifth less frequent than in the population at large, with adverse consequences for birthright membership of the Society.

See further Edward H. Milligan, *Quaker Marriage*, Kendal: Quaker Tapestry Scheme, 1994. The following extracts emphasise the need for proper behaviour and the undesirability of mixed marriages. Extract (a) is from the Yearly Meeting epistle of 1707; extract (b) from that of 1719.

(a)

And, we being sensible of the hurt that may happen by persons under the profession of truth, in drawing out the affections of one another, without the knowledge and consent of parents or guardians; do, for preventing such mischief, deliver it as our sense and judgment, that in case any person reputed a Quaker, shall endeavour to entangle the affection of any young woman professing truth, or shall make suit unto her in order to marriage, without the privity and consent of her parents or guardians, first had and obtained (whether such parents or guardians be Friends or not), that such persons ought not to be allowed or permitted to proceed in any meeting of Friends, in order to the accomplishing of such intended marriage, until they shall have removed the offence, and given satisfaction both to such parents or guardians, and to the meeting of Friends to which they do belong, by an open and due acknowledgement of the offence, and condemnation of themselves therefore, and shall have obtained the consent of such parents or guardians.

And, it is further advised, that after parents and guardians have suffered their children to engage one another in affections, they do not break off upon any worldly account; but [that they] wait upon and seek the Lord for their children, in proposals of marriage, before they give any encouragement thereunto.

(b)

At this our meeting, we are being given to understand, that, in divers places, there are some who profess the truth with us, who deviate from the way thereof, by contracting marriages with such as are not of our society, contrary to the repeated advice of this meeting, to the dishonour of our holy profession, and the hindrance of truth's prosperity; in order therefore, that a stop may be put to an undue liberty in such marriages, and the evil consequences thereof, we do hereby tenderly advise and desire, that all parents and guardians of children do take especial care, as much as in them lieth, to prevent their children from running into such marriages; and that Friends of each particular meeting, as also of the Monthly Meetings to which such persons belong, do, in the wisdom and power of truth, use their endeavours to put a stop to the said evil, by admonishing such as may attempt to marry as aforesaid, to desist before they accomplish the same; but if they refuse to take counsel, or privately go on to marry as aforesaid, that then such persons be dealt withal according to the good order of truth, and judgment fixed upon all such as take such an undue liberty.

It is a matter of sorrow and grief to us, that notwithstanding the good advice and counsel formerly given from this meeting against pride, yet, it appears in many places, there is not that due regard had to the counsel given as ought to be: wherefore it is again advised, that such parents and guardians, who have the care and oversight of children, be first concerned to be good examples to them. Secondly, be careful to train them up in the nurture and admonition of the Lord; and be concerned to have the sense of truth on your own spirits; otherwise you cannot bring them to a sense of truth on their spirits: and without that, your work will be but of small advantage: but if you find truth hath hold of their minds, then have you a help in them, to work with you against those youthful inclinations to vanity.

Document VI.36

Moses West on Marriage

The following extract is by the Quaker Moses West, from his *A Treatise concerning Marriage, wherein The Unlawfulness of Mixt-Marriages is laid open from the Scriptures of Truth*, 1707, pp. 24–7. This work was reprinted nine times during the eighteenth century.

When the Apostle exhorted the *Believers* of old *not to be unequally yoked together with Unbelievers*, 2. Cor. 6. 14. may we supposed he intended to restrain the *Prohibition*, only to those *absolute and notorious Unbelievers who were* Pagans, *or* Heathens? Or did he extend to all, that did not believe the Manifestation of Christ *Outwardly* in the Flesh? The *Jews* did believe in God, and that Christ the Son of God, *should come*: But they did not believe in him as He *was then come* and manifest in the Flesh among them. Might the *Christian Believers*, notwithstanding that, have mingled in Marriages with the Unbelieving *Jews*, because of their general Belief in God, and in *Christ to come*, tho' they *rejected* him in his *then present Appearance*? Would that have been an Equal Yoking? So likewise, if one that believes, not only the *Outward* Appearance of Christ, with Respect to his having come in the Flesh but his Inward Appearance also, with Respect to his being come *in the Spirit*, by his Divine Light and Grace, to Rule in the Hearts of his People, and thereby to both direct and enable them, as they attend thereto, how to *perform* divine Worship and Service to God, should marry one that denies, and opposes that *Inward* and *Spiritual* Coming and Appearance of Christ in the *Heart*, and sticks only to his Belief of his *Outward* Coming and Appearance in the *Flesh* at *Jerusalem*: Would such a Couple be equally yoaked?

But, not to press the Comparison too close, because I would both avoid Offence, and use what Brevity I can; I say, if two Persons of *different Judgments* about Matters of Faith and Religious Exercises (as going to Meetings, Preaching, Praying, Thanksgiving &c.) should incline to marry each other, presuming in their *fond Affections*, that, notwithstanding that *Disagreement*, they may live comfortably together, they will find *too late* that they were greatly mistaken. For although, if it were only a Disagreement in their Tempers or Natural Dispositions, which concerned only their *outward Conversation* one towards the other, or the Management of their Temporal Affairs, it might be hoped they might live *tolerably* together: Yet where the Difference is of so high a Strain and Nature, as concerns the Peace of *Conscience*, and Safety of the *Soul*, on either Side; that cannot be reconciled, without the *Conversion* of one of them, which is out of Man's Power, of himself, to effect. Wherefore although such may talk of and promise to themselves *Unity* in such *Contrariety*: Yet by that Time *their Folly shall have corrected Them*, they will find Cause to be of another Mind. And if their Love to God and Religion, be not quite *consumed* by those *Passionate Flames*, which engaged them into that *unwarrantable* Undertaking; they will feel *after Marriage*, their Spirits more plainly and *warmly conflicting* one with another, and striving to bring each other into a *Conformity* unto that Way of Worship, which he or she is in, and then, which soever of them prevails, the other must lose Peace of *Conscience* (the *Greatest* of all Losses) unless such *Compliance* spring from a *True* and *Unfeign'd* Conviction that the Worship so conformed to is the *Right*. Which is more than may reasonably be expected by any, who are guilty of *Tempting* the Lord with such Mixt-Marriages.

Besides, *when Two* of Disagreeing Persuasions in Religious Exercises, do join in Marriage, no Man can reasonably think, that there *Affection* to each other is grounded on, or governed by Religion; and if not that, it must be by some *Wordly End*: And to choke such a Marriage with a Pretence of Hope, to convert each other to what each believeth is right, is in plain English, no better than *a sinning, that Grace may abound*; *a doing Evil, that Good may come of it.*

Document VI.37

Statement of the Meeting for Sufferings, 1783

The basic framework of Quaker church government inherited from the seventeenth century remained in use throughout the eighteenth, though it grew in complexity. The Yearly Meeting was at the top of a pyramidal structure whose base was the countrywide local meeting for worship, with or without their own meeting houses. The local meetings joined together for administrative purposes into monthly meetings (151 in 1694,

108 in 1800), the monthly meetings into quarterly meetings typically covering a county. Information and exhortation passed through the structure in both directions, instructions came down from superior meetings. Business at the higher level did not have to wait for the Yearly Meeting, there was an executive body, the meeting for Sufferings, which met weekly until late in the century. There were other meetings with administrative roles as well. The Yearly Meeting made the rules and offered advice that applied nationally. Meetings answered in writing formal queries sent out by their superior meetings, gathering strictly factual information as well as more subjective judgements concerning the spiritual state of the Society. The queries were amended and added to as time went by, reflecting changing needs, concerns and circumstances. Information was requested on Friends' sufferings and imprisonments, on formal conversions – that is, on the number of convicements, not the nature of personal conversion experiences, on meeting houses built, and on the answer to an additional query from the Yearly Meeting of 1703: 'How have the Several Advices of this Meeting been put into Practice?' The whole body of the advices and minutes of continuing relevance from the Yearly Meeting was codified in 1738 in a volume issued in manuscript to the meetings the *Christian and brotherly advices Given forth from time to time By the Yearly Meeting in London Alphabetically Digested under Proper Heads*. This collection was printed in 1783 and made more widely available. In 1784 a Women's Yearly Meeting was established after several decades of requests supported by American women Friends who had moved earlier in that direction.

See further David J. Hall, 'Christian and Brotherly Advices', *The Friends' Quarterly*, July 1981, pp. 506–15; Richard E. Stagg, 'Friends' Queries and General Advices: A Survey of Their Development in London Yearly Meeting 1682–1928', *Journal of the Friends' Historical Society*, XLIX, 1959–61, pp. 209–35. For the Women's Yearly meeting see *London Yearly Meeting during 250 Years*, London: Society of Friends: 1919; Margaret Hope Bacon, 'The Establishment of London Women's Yearly Meeting: a Transatlantic Concern', *Journal of the Friends' Historical Society*, LVII, no. 2, 1995, pp.151–65. The following extract comprises the bulk of the preface to *Christian and brotherly advices*, 1783.

The Yearly Meeting, having been apprehensive that, in some quarterly and monthly meetings, due care hath not been taken to preserve, and enter regularly in the books kept for that purpose, those minutes and advices, which from its first institution have occasionally been communicated to them, for establishing and conducting the discipline of the church, hath seen meet to direct that those minutes and advices should be carefully extracted and properly arranged under suitable heads, and be comprised in one volume, for the general service of the society. This important work having been committed to the care of the meeting for sufferings, it was with much labour and great attention performed, and was laid before the Yearly Meeting in 1781; when a considerable number of judicious friends then present were appointed to come up to London in the tenth month ensuing, to join the meeting for sufferings in examining the same: most of whom, in conjunction with that meeting, met accordingly, and, having given their attendance with unremitting assiduity, in much concord and to mutual satisfaction, were favoured after many sittings to go through the work, comparing every part with the original records, and the whole, as contained in the following pages, was agreed to by the Yearly Meeting in 1782, and directed to be printed: in order that,

1st.   Every quarterly and monthly meeting may be furnished with a complete and correct collection of the several minutes and advices issued by the Yearly Meeting for regulating the affairs of the society:

2dly.   That these minutes and advices, being more generally made known, may be more uniformly observed and put in practice, that order, unity, peace, and harmony, may be preserved throughout the churches:

3dly.   That, in an especial manner, the youth of the present and succeeding generations may be early and fully instructed in our religious principles, and in the nature and design of our Christian discipline, and, through divine assistance, be enabled to adorn our holy profession, by a consistent conduct and circumspect conversation, in all godliness and honesty; thereby avoiding the reproach which many, through a defection in principle, or a degeneracy in practice, have brought upon themselves and the body of which they profess to be members:

4thly.   That the unfaithful, the immoral, and the libertine professors may be seasonably reminded of their danger and of their duty, as well as of the great labour, which, in much gospel love, hath been from time to time bestowed for their help and recovery; and that such as continue to despise and reject the convictions of truth, and the counsel of their brethren, and refuse to be reclaimed, may be made sensible that they themselves are the sole cause of their separation from our religious fellowship and communion: for when any, by their inconsistent and disorderly conduct, or by imbibing and adopting principles and practices contrary to the doctrine which we have received, have first openly manifested their disunity with the society, it is but just and requisite, that, after endeavouring and waiting to restore them without effect, the body should testify its disunity with such erring and refractory members: at the same time earnestly desiring that they may be convinced of the error of their ways, and that through unfeigned repentance, and a consistent, orderly conduct in future, they may be reunited to the body. This being the utmost extent of our discipline respecting offenders, it is very evident, that, from the right exercise thereof, no degree of persecution or imposition can be justly inferred; for the imposition rests entirely on the part of those who insist on being retained as members, whilst at open variance with the body either in principle or practice.

We are not, however, without a clear sense that this publication will prove insufficient to produce the desired effect, unless we are very careful to move and act under the immediate influence of the spirit of Christ in the pure love of the gospel; a close adherence to which would render a multiplicity of rules unnecessary.

And whilst we are earnestly recommending this work to the notice and regard of friends, we cannot omit to press upon them a diligent reading of the Holy Scriptures, as superior to all other writings for instruction; and it must yield great satisfaction to observe how consonant these advices are to the doctrine and precepts of Christ and his apostles.

Although this collection is printed solely for the use of our own society, yet, should it get abroad and meet the publick eye, it is not doubted but every serious and candid reader will observe, throughout the whole, the constant and earnest endeavours of the Yearly Meeting for the promotion of virtue and religion. And notwithstanding it be too obvious to be denied, that there are amongst us many sorrowful instances of a grievous departure from the godly zeal, purity, probity, simplicity, and self-denial, so conspicuous in our worthy predecessors; yet, by comparing the later advices with those of a more ancient date, and observing the continued care and concern of the Yearly Meeting to guard and testify against every appearance of evil, and every mark of declension, it must be allowed, that as a religious body we are the same people our forefathers were, in faith, in doctrine, in worship, in ministry, and in discipline.

And although it be our lot to live in an age of great dissipation, luxury, and profaneness, when the genuine fruits of the spirit of Christianity are so rarely seen, that every thing sacred and serious seems threatened to be overwhelmed by the torrent of vice and irreligion; yet we are bowed in thankfulness to the Author of all good, in that we have abundant cause to believe there are still many, of various ranks and ages, mercifully preserved both among ourselves, and in other Christian communities, who, through faithfulness to the measure of grace which is given to every one to profit with, have been strengthened to retain their integrity, and hold fast the profession of their faith without wavering.

Document VI.38

Deliberations of the Northern Association of Particular Baptists

The following extract, transcribed by S. L. Copson, is reprinted from his *Association Life of the Particular Baptists of Northern England 1699–1732*, [Didcot:] Baptist Historical Society, 1991, pp. 108–9

The Elders and Messengers of several Associated Churches assembled together at Hamsterly in the County of Durham ye 6th and 7th days of June Ano Dom.1716 to ponder, weigh, Consider, Examine, Resolve, Determine & Conclude of & upon all such questions debates and Objections yt may arise out of the letters or be p.posed to this Association by the respective Representatives of the Sd Churches according to the light we are attended wth.yt God may have the praise through Jesus Christ our precious Lord, to whom be glory for evermore. Amen.

Imprimis. Qu 1. Whether any Remote part or wing of any Church or Churches of Jeus Christ may orderly & upon Scriptural grounds silence and stop the Mouths of any of their Gifted Brethren whom she hath formerly Approved of, without the Bodies consent, being blameless in Doctrine life and Conversation yea, or nay?

Answ 1. That such disorderly Actings & proceedings is noe less than open breaches of the plain Rule of Gods Sacred Word. Matth 18.15.16.17. Numbers 11.26,27,28,29.

2. That such groundless inconsiderate ways is wholly detrimental to the Constitution of a Church. Matth 12.25.

Qu 2. When may it be truly said that a Church hath lost its State?

Answ.   To Answer this question Directly will lead into a vast laberinth so great and wide at this time to be perfectly comprehended for it necessarily requireth a discovering what a State is and wherein it Consisteth which must at this time be omitted & because some Persons may be desirous to have the Solution of this question shall proceed in a few particulars.

1.   The State of a Church may be said to be lost when she swerveth and wandereth from the Fundamental principles of Religion. Gal 3.1,2,3.

2.   When she hath universally lost the true [ ] of her love & pursueth and practiceth unwarrantable courses. Matth 15.7,8,9. Mar 7.7.

3.   When she is universally fil'd with disorders in her Discipline.

4.   When she becomes so blind and ignorant that she utterly refuseth wholesome Councel and advice though never so seasonably given her. Matth 23.37.

That it is the hearty desire of the Messengers of the respective Churches to whom we belong that there be due consideration upon the great and wonderfull deliverance we have had from the late threatening Judgments of popery & tiranicall slavery and the mercies we still share in the enjoyment of Gospel priviledges under a favourable government and lest the appearing difficulties of these mercies continuance should at ye last be taken from us, there be deep humiliation before the Lord to this end, That the Church endeavour in setting apart by fasting and prayer the last Friday of the 3 ensuing Months to meet at the Throne of Grace & there chiefly spread before the Lord these following things.

1.   The lamentable stupidness deadness & dullness that the Churches of Jesus Christ is attended with & labours under Notwithstanding manifold circumstances of mercies daily following us.

2.   Too much satisfaction and ease under the apprehension of the melancholy sense of the declining condition of the Churches.

3.   The Jarring differences, discords & very unseemly carriages faults and falings out of Brethren, and seeming inclination rather to widen than repair the breaches in Gods House.

4.   The Churches under these Circumstances in open ways of high provocations against our Precious Lord in the extent of his mercies, And that we may be recovered and reclaimed 'ere it be too late it is earnestly desired.

1. That the Churches humbly begg that deserved future impending Judgments may be diverted & daily offertures of mercy noe longer abused.

2. That each and all of us be exceeding carefull to discharge our duty of thankfulness to the Father of mercies for his late wonderfull great and amazeing deliverance of our existances priviledges & immunities out of the hands and from the power malice and rage of the implacable enemy of our souls rageing in his adherents against the Cause and interest of our Lord and Saviour Jesus Christ.

3ly That the sinking Interest of Christ may be revived his work more regarded and encouraged in the midst of all the Churches.

4ly That the Churches may be emptied of vain Janglings and be filled with a Spirit of love & of a sound mind.

5ly That repeated experiences of favourable circumstances loaded upon us, may greatly excite us to diligence in duty.

6ly That in the pursuit of our duties God would enable us with plentifull effusions of the Holy Spirit, whereby we may worship him in Spirit and in Truth.

7ly That all our enjoyments may be sanctified to us to the praise and glory of God the Father through Jesus Christ our only Lord.

8ly That we may be enabled to foresee the evil and hide ourselves.

9ly That our lives and conversations may be as becomes Children professing godliness.

Lastly It is concluded wth submission to providence that the next general meeting be at Hamsterly on Wednesday and Thursday in the second whole week after Whitsuntide in the year 1717.

Document VI.39

The Covenant of the Baptist Association in Wales, 1790

The following is reprinted from Charles W. Deweese, *Baptist Church Covenants*, Nashville, TN: Broadman Press, 1990, pp. 130–1, whose source is John Rippon, *The Baptist Annual Register for 1790, 1791, 1792, and Part of 1793*, pp. 65–6.

It is proper that the members of a church should bind themselves to the Lord, and to each other, by covenant. We often find that the people of Israel entered into covenant, and bound themselves by vows, Deut. V. 27. and xxix. 10–12. Neh. X. 28. &c. And we have some reason to conclude, that under the New Testament, some engaged by covenant; for they are mentioned as *truce-breakers* under the form of godliness, 2 Tim. Iii. 3. 5. Reason and experience shew, that no society can be supported orderly, comfortably, and peaceably, without it. This covenant at least implies these things; (1) that the persons bind themselves to strive against sin, and for the faith; or in other words, to lay aside the service of Sin and Satan, and cleave to the Lord, his worship and service; and adhere to the people of God, the excellent of the earth, especially to those of the same fellowship, remembering the old commandment and the new is, *Love one another*; (2) that they are to watch over one another in love, to exhort each other; and if it be needful, to reprove and rebuke one another, but in the spirit of the Gospel, and according to the rule of God's word; (3) that he who is overtaken in any fault should receive reproof, rebuke, or advice, in humility, confessing his fault, and forsaking it; (4) that none should behave as busy bodies and tale-bearers, mentioning the business of the church to the people of the world; (5) that all should endeavour to keep their place in the church, not forsaking the assembling of themselves together, as the manner of some is; (6) that they should be willing and ready to contribute what may be necessary and meet for the support of the *cause of Christ*, and that according to what they have, and not to what they have not.

Document VI.40

Covenant of the Baptist Church, Bourton-on-the-Water

This is the covenant of the church of which Benjamin Beddome (see Document IV.3 above) was minister. It is reprinted from C. Deweese, *Baptist Church Covenants*, Nashville, TN: Broadman Press, 1990, pp. 122–4.

We whose Names are underwritten having been Members & much the Major Part of a Church or Separate Congregation late under the Pastoral Care of the Rev. Mr. Joshua Head decd. is still desirous to walk together in all the Ordinances of Iesus Christ, as much as may be, blameless, (seeing that Church by reason of different apprehensions of some of the Brethren about the Choice of a Pastour; hath been, in the presence, & by the Advice of some neighbouring Ministers, peaceably dissolv'd) do now freely & heartily give up our selves afresh to God and Father & his Only Son our Lord & Lawgiver; & to one another according to his Will. And so becoming a new Church or Sacred Society incorporated by the Gospel Charter, do now in the presence of God & those that are here Witnesses of our Order unanimously agree in the Name & fear of Christ.

1st   That we will, to the utmost of our Power, walk together in one Body, & as near as may be with one Mind, in all sweetness of Spirit, and saint like Love to each other, as highly becomes the Disciples of Christ

2dly   That we will jointly contend, & strive together for the Faith & Purity of the Gospel, the truths of Iesus Christ, & the Order, Ordinances, Honour, Liberty, & Priviledges of this his Church against all Opposers

3dly   That we will with all care, Diligence, & Conscience labour & study, to keep the Unity of the Spirit in the Bond of Peace, both in the Church in general, & in particular between one another

4thly   That we will carefully avoid all Causes & Causers of Divisions as much as lyes in us, & shun those that are Seducers & false Preachers of Errours & Heresies

5thly   That we will sympathize & have a fellow feeling (to our power) with one another in every Condition, & endeavour to bear each others Burthens, where we are joyfull or sorrowfull tempted or otherwise, that we may be mutual Helps to one another, & so answer the End of our near Relation

6thly   That we will forbear, & bear with one anothers weaknesses & Infirmities in much Pity, Tenderness, Meekness, & Patience not daring to rip up the weakness of any to those without the Church, nor to those that are within, unless it be according to Christ's Rule & Gospel Order, endeavouring all we can for the Glory of the Gospel, & for the Credit of this Church willing to cover, & hide one anothers Slips & common failings that are not sinfull

7thly   That we will, as our God shall enable us, cleave fast to each other to the utmost of our power; & that if perilous Times should come, & a Time of Persecution (which God for our nonproficiency may justly send) we will not dare to draw back from our holy profession, but will endeavour to strengthen one anothers hands, & encourage one another to Perseverance, let what will fall to our Lot

8thly   We do promise to keep the Secrets of our Church entire without divulging them to any that are not Members of this particular Body, tho' they may be otherwise near & dear to us; for we believe the Church ought to be as a Garden enclosed & a fountain sealed

9thly   Those of us that are or may be single persons do fully design never to enter into conjugal Bonds with any that are Unbelievers for we believe it to be a Sin to be unequally yoked, that it tis contrary to Rule of Christ, & the ready way to hinder our souls peace, growth, & eternal Wellfare

10thly   That we will communicate to one another of the good Things of this Life, as God hath or may prosper us, so far as Ability will suffer, or any of our Necessities shall be thought to require

11thly   That we will endeavour to watch over one anothers conversation for Good, not for each others halting, yet so as not by any means to suffer sin to rest in the bosom of our Brogher but to remove it by using all possible Means to bring the person to repentance & Reformation of Life; & that we will endeavour to provoke one another to Holiness, Love & good Works

12thly   We do all purpose constantly to attend the Meetings appointed by the Church, both on the Lord's days & other Days, nothing hindring except Distances, sickness, or the Works of Mercy & Necessity

13thly   That We will make Conscience of praying for one anothers Wellfare at all times, but especially in Time of Distress, as Poverty, Sickness, Pain, Temptation, Desertion, or the like; & that we will pray for the Peace & Growth of the whole Church in general & for our Ministers & the success of their Ministry in an especial manner.

Signed at Bourton on the Water the 30th day of Ianuary 1719–20.

Document VI.41

Covenant of the Dedham Independents

For Congregational covenants see Alan P. F. Sell, 'Confessing the Faith in English Congregationalism', in *idem, Dissenting Thought and the Life of the Churches*, Lewiston, NY: Edwin Mellen Press, 1990, ch. 1. The following is reprinted from *Congregational Historical Society Transactions*, IX, 1924–6, p. 261.

Done at Dedham, Sepr. 30th, 1741

We, whose Names are under written, having Solemnly given up our Selves to the Lord, and having by Prayer, with fasting implored the gracious Presence of God with us and his Blessing upon us Now also, in the Presence of God and of the Pastors of Several other Churches of Jesus Christ do give up our Selves one to another, by the Will of God as a Church of Jesus Christ; Promising by the help of God, to Subit unto all Ordinances of Christ, as administred in this Church.

Fransiss Hawkins
William Richardson
Saml. Jarrold
Willm. Rudkin
Ellen King
Elizabeth Kirk Parrick

Witnesses
Wm. Notcutt
Bezaleel Blomfield
Benjm. Vowell

Document VI.42

Covenant of the Oakenshaw Baptists

The following extracts are from the covenant of 1760 of the Baptist Church at
Oakenshaw, Lancashire. The doctrinal portions are Calvinistic, but great emphasis is
placed upon the bearing of members towards one another. The extracts are reprinted
from Robert J. V. Wylie, *The Baptist Churches of Accrington and District*, Accrington:
W. Shuttleworth, 1923, pp. 15–16.

We will conscientiously endeavour to discharge our duties in those families to which
we belong. As masters and parents we will teach, admonish, and correct those whom
God hath put under our care; nor will we tolerate any wickedness in our sight of
hearing, such as drunkenness, cursing and swearing, lying, jesting, foolish and filthy
talking, or and scoffing or ridiculing religion, without taking notice of it and showing
our dislike to it, and reproving for it sharply. We will also work with our hands, as
God has commanded, and employ our leisure moments in reading the Word, in useful
conversation, and in prayer with and for our families. We that are wives, children,
and servants, will be in subjection to our superiors in all things, wherein we may
without sin; and endeavour to render our lives as useful and religion as amiable as
we possibly can, in those families to which we appertain, so that the Name of Christ
and His doctrine be not blasphemed.

... To endeavour to discharge our duty one to another as members of Christ's
body by loving one another in deed and truth ... sympathising with one another's
sorrows, bearing one another's burdens, and seeking out one another's good, temporal and spiritual. ... To abstain from shy looks and distant carriage; all whispering,
railing, and backbiting; all contempt and scorn; all contention and strife about things
to no profit; as also coveteousness and slackhandedness; all hardheartedness and
unconcernedness about one another's distress, and all carelessness about one another's good unto edification ... avoid the sinful custom of going from house to house
as talebearers ... to deal honestly with the worldly, not cheating them and over-reach-
ing them in buying or selling, but being punctual in all our promises to them, though
it be to our loss. ...

Document VI.43

Covenant and Confession of theWalsall Independents

Distressed by the proclamation of Arian doctrine, twenty-eight orthodox members and two deacons seceded from Bank Court Presbyterian Church, Walsall, and constituted themselves as an Independent Church on 21 September 1763. As compared with the Dedham covenant, that of Walsall is much more strongly doctrinal, and behind the positive doctrinal statement there lurks, by implication, the repudiation of doctrinal formulations which these saints no longer wish to hear. The church's origin in doctrinal secession is perhaps reflected in the fact that as compared with the Oakenshaw Baptist covenant it has much less to say concerning Christian behaviour.

The following text is reprinted from Alan P. F. Sell, *Dissenting Thought and the Life of the Churches*, Lewiston, NY: Edwin Mellen Press, 1990, pp. 349–50

We whose names are hereunto subscribed, being desirous to form ourselves into a Church of Christ, do make this confession of our Faith in the great & Important Doctrines of the Gospel.

We believe in One God, who is infinite, eternal & unchangeable in all his perfections, & that there are three persons in the Godhead, Father, Son, & Holy Ghost, the same in Substance, equal in power & glory. We believe that God created Adam after his own Image, capable of yielding perfect obedience to the Diving Law, & also that God appointed him to be the federal, or covenant Head of all his posterity; so that upon his standing they would have stood; but he falling, all his posterity fell with him, & were thereby involved in sin & misery; agreeable to the Apostles declaration, By one man's obedience many were made sinners.

The Holy Scripture informs us, that God of his free & undeserved mercy appointed his Son Christ Jesus as God-man to be the Redeemer of all those that believe in him, & that he, having taken upon him our nature, obey'd and suffer'd as the surety of his people, & gave his life a Ransom for many: so that by his obedience we become Righteous. We hold it as an important Truth of the holy Scripture, that man in his unrenewed state is at enmity with God, & that without regeneration by the Holy Spirit we cannot enter into the Kingdom of Heaven.

Tho' salvation is absolutely of grace, yet, We are firmly persuaded, that it is the indispensable Duty of every one that believeth to maintain good works. For without Holiness no man shall see the Lord. We believe that all those whom God has justified by the Righteousness of Christ, & sanctified by his holy Spirit, shall be kept by his mighty power unto Salvation.

We learn both from reason & Scripture that a Church of Christ has a Right to require satisfactory Evidence of Repentance towards God and Faith in our Lord Jesus Christ, of every one who desires admission into it; & that it also has a Right, to dismiss its Members to another Church, to admonish Offenders, & to put away from amongst themselves Disorderly persons, according to the Rules prescribed by our Lord & his Apostles. And after having solemnly humbled ourselves before God, & sought Counsel from him; We, hoping thro' grace that we have given up ourselves first to the Lord, do now give up ourselves to each other in Church fellowship in his name; desiring to watch over One another with all Christian tenderness, & to walk together in all the Ordinances & commandments of the Lord.

Being desirous to study the things that make for peace We Agree that all matters among us, relating to the Church shall be determined by the Vote of the Major part of the Members of this Church.

These are the Articles of our Faith in the great Doctrines of the Gospel & this Solemn profession, We make before God, desiring mercy of the Lord to be found faithful. Done at our first Church Meeting on September the Twenty first, & in the year one Thousand Seven hundred and Sixty three.

Document VI.44

Covenant of the Independents of Blanket Row, Kingston-upon Hull

In 1769 a secession from the Presbyterian Church at Dagger Lane, Hull, occurred owing to the suspicions of some that the views of the minister, John Burnett, were less than fully orthodox. The seceders built a small chapel in Blanket Row, and a larger one in Fish Street in 1782; their heirs removed to the Fish Street Memorial Church in 1898. Their strongly orthodox Confession of Faith runs to twenty paragraphs, and is preceded by the following covenant which, like many of the period, begins in breast-beating fashion (though, unlike some, stopping short of describing the saints as 'poor worms lost in Adam'). The covenant is reprinted from *Congregational Historical Society Transactions*, IX, 1924–26, pp. 248–9.

We, who by Nature were Sinners, ready to perish, having by the good Spirit and abundant Grace of God, been led to see our dreadful State by Nature, as fallen in Adam, and far from God, and having we trust, tasted of the Grace of God in converting, promised, and communicated Mercy; we do sincerely, unfeignedly, and without Reserve, desire to give up ourselves unto the Lord and each other, to walk together in all the Commandments and Ordinances of the Lord blameless – to watch over one another in Love – to exhort with Diligence, and rebuke with Meekness and without Partiality – to pray for and seek the Edification of each other in all things pertaining to Life and Godliness. And this we do in the most solemn and serious Manner, having sought the Divine Presence amongst us, and called for the Blessings of our Covenant God to distill upon us. And as a further Testimony we do subscribe the same with our Hands, agreeable to the Prediction of Gospel Times: *One shall say, I am the Lord's; and another shall call himself by the Name of Jacob; and another shall subscribe with his Hand unto the Lord, and surname himself by the Name of Israel. – Isaiah xliv., 5.*

Document VI.45

The Stevington Church Book

Given their conviction that the Church comprises saints – the twice-born – and that evidence of this happy state is revealed by a godly walk, many Baptist and Congregational church meetings found it necessary to discuss and deal with members who erred. Accordingly, many church books devote a significant proportion of their space to disciplinary matters. The following extracts are from the church book of the Dissenting Church at Stevington, Bedfordshire, which was founded as an Independent Church in 1655, but shortly after became Baptist. The extracts are reprinted from H. G. Tibbutt, *Some Early Nonconformist Church Books*, The Publications of the Bedfordshire Historical Record Society, LI, 1972, pp. 42–3

A Church meeting on the 13 day of the 3d. month.
William Stratton and Ann Hopkins declared some experiences, and were approved. On the 17th day William Stratton, Ann Hopkins and Ellin Stoakes were baptized by brother Taylor in brother Negusis pond.

- - - - - the 18 of September, 1711.
Simon Hearcock came to Ste[fin]ton.

The 8 day of November 1711 then at a Church meeting.
Brother Hearcock and his wife did joyen as members to this Church of Christ at Stefinton, and then too things was agreed upon:
1. That after wating and due care to instruction the parcons into ther duty of baptism, and thay do continueu dark as to ther duty, yet to receive them into this Church of Christ, provided that thay walke as becometh the gospal of Christ.
2. Members of other churches that wallke as becometh the gospal of Christ to have commuening with this Church of Christ

In the yeare of our Lord 1711.
[Simon Hearcock] was called by this Church Christ … office, to which he did except of. And the 15 day of November 1711 a salom day of prayr was keep in order thereunto by this Church of Christ; and the 10 day of January 1711 the work of ordna[ti]on was finished by this Church of Christ. The elders that was then to assist in that worke was Mr Massom of Luton and Mr Dutton and others.

Hear foloweth the letter of recommendation from the church of Heail Weston to the Church of Christ at Steventon, faithfully subscribed in order:
To the Church of Christ at Stepenton the Church of Ch[rist at] Heail Weston sendeth greeting. Dearly beloved in the Lord, we wish grace and peace from above to be multiplied upon you. Whereas our beloved brother Hearcock and his wife are by divine providence cast among you, and have desird their dismission from us to joyn with you in the fellowship of the gospel, we, accoarding to their request, have granted

the same; and do hereby recommend them as persons (while here) walking in the fear of God; and wish they may be blessings to you and you to them; and on their actual joining to you we shall look upon their particula[r] relation to us to cease. So commending of you all to divien protection and blessiong, desireing a constant re-membrance of us in your prayers, we remain yours in the bonds of the blessed gospel in ----- all love to serve. Farewell. Subscribed with the church's consent: Richard Rawlin, pastor, Oliver Bigg, Thomas Asplin, John Moon, John Parrell, Thomas Mesheus. October 14th, 1711 . ...

November 22 day, 1711. Brother Scrivenor - - - - -
February 3 day, 1711/12 was the first Lord's Day we broke bred with this Church of Christ.
July 22 day, 1712, this Church of Christ keepe a day of prais to God for good wether for harves and for other things.
January 11 day, 1712/13, at the Church meeting brother Lovell was called to the offes of a deacon in this Church of Christ, and he did undertake to provied for the pooer of this Church with the mony that was collected at the Lord's Tabol, and also to provied bred and wien for the Lord's Tabol. At the same Church meeting, brother Tayelr and his wife had thear dismishion from this Church of Christ at Arnsby under Mr. Winkels.
February 5 day, 1713, this Church of Christ keep a day of prayer for brother Lovell's ordination in the offes of a deacon for this Church of Christ.

Document VI.46

Isaac Watts's Church Book

The following letter of Isaac Watts is from the records of Bury Street Independent Church, London, and is reprinted from *Congregational Historical Society Transactions*, I, 1901–4, pp. 32–4. For Watts see Document I.2 above.

To ye Church of Christ assembling in Mark Lane, Feb. ye 8th 1701–2.
Beloved in our Lord,
When You first called in to minister ye Word of God among you, I took the free-dom to acquaint you That, in Ye chief Doctrines of Christianity, I was of ye same mind with your former Revd Pastor Dr Jno. Owen; who being dead yet speaketh: and I have been glad to find by three years' experience yt you retain ye same Principals [sic] yt he preacht amongst you; now since thro' Your great affection & undeserved respect to me you have thought fit to call me to ye Great & Solemn Office of A Pastor, I cannot but take ye same freedom to hope that you are of one Mind wth him in ye chief points of Church Discipline. Tho' I call no man Master upon Earth, nor confine my belief to ye judgment of another, yet I cannot but own yt in ye study of Gospel Order, I have found much Light and Assistance from his Works, & from those of your late Revd Pastor Dr Isaac Channey. But being desir'd by You to give

some hints of my Principals [sic] in Writing, in order to future satisfaction and continuance of Peace and love (if ye Lord shall fix me with You) I have briefly written a few things whereby you may Discover something of my knowledge in ye Mind & Will of Christ concerning his Churches.

First, I believe yt Jesus Christ ye King of Saints has given command and power to his Saints to form themselves into Spiritual Societies & Corporations for his publick Glory and their own edification.

2. That every such Society of Saints, covenanting to walk wth God and one another in all ye Rules & Institutions of ye Gospel is a Church of Christ.

3. That every such Church has power to increase its own Number by ye addition of members, or to purge it self of corrupt Members, before it be organiz'd and made compleat by having fixed Officers among them.

4. That this Society of Saints ought to look on themselves [as] more nearly united & related to one another than to other Christians; and consequently to pray wth and for each other, to visit one another, to exhort, comfort and assist one another, & maintain such A love and Communion to & wth each others as yt they may look like fellow members of ye Same Body both Visible & invisible.

5. The Members of such an incompleat Church before any Pastor is settled among them may pray together, and exhort one another; yet this Church has not power in itself to administer all Ordinances amongst them. But when they have chosen a proper Officer to be over them in ye Lord, And when he is ordained by their publick Call, his public acceptance, & by solemn separation of him to yt work, by fasting & prayer, then unto yt Officer is this power committed.

6. It follows thence yt tho' ye Pastor be named & chosen to this Office by ye People, yet his Commission & power to administer all divine Ordinances is not derived from ye People, for they had not this power in themselves; but it proceeds from ye Lord Jesus Christ, who is ye only King of his Church & ye principal of all power; & he has appointed in his Word yt ye call of his Church and solemn Ordination shall be ye means whereby his Ministers are invested with this Authority.

7. That in ye ordination of A Pastor to A Particular Church our Lord Christ, as ye supream Governor & head of his Church, setts him in an office of Spiritual Rule, over a willing People who freely commit themselves to his care; even as Christ also in & by his Word & his Providence now commits them unto his care & charge, of wch he must give an Account.

8. Hence it follows that Pastoral Acts, such as teaching, feeding, guiding, & overseeing Y^e Flock, exhorting, reproving, comforting them, are not perform'd in ye Name of ye People, but in ye Name, stead, & place of Christ, by ye Pastor, as his Representative in yt Church, & as his Embassador to it; As a Shepheard in ruling, leading, & feeding his Flock acts not in ye name of ye sheep; but in ye name & place of him yt owns them, & yt has committed them unto his care; & therefore these Pastoral Acts are to be received by ye People as clothed wth ye Authority of our Lord Jesus, so far as they agree wth his Mind & Will; according to those Scriptures 2 Corn. 5. 20,' Now then we are Embassadors for Christ, as tho' God did beseech you by us, we pray you in Christ's stead, be ye reconciled to God.' 13 Jno. 20,' He yt receiveth whomsoever I send receiveth Me.' And this regard is also due to such Acts

of yᵃ Pastor from every member, because they have given themselves up to him in yᵃ Lord.

9.   Yet I believe yt even wth regard to these Pastoral Acts Christ has given to his Churches so far A Judgment of discretion, yt they are not bound to submit blindly to yᵉ government of yᵉ Pastor, unless he approve himself therein to Act according to yᵉ Mind & Will of Christ in his Word: and it is yᵉ neglect of this Consideration yt has brought in yt unbounded Authority & usurped dominion of yᵉ Priests, & yt implicit Faith & blind obedience of yᵉ People in yᵉ Antichristian Church.

10.   I believe also yt in all those other exercizes of Church Order wch are not merely Acts of yᵉ Pastor, but also Acts of the Church, such as receiving & casting out Members, Appointing places of stated or occasional worship, setting apart days of Prayer, & times for Church Meetings. A Pastor ought to do nothing without yᵉ Consent of yᵉ People; and tho' yᵉ wholeoffice of A Pastor herein lyes not merely in declaring yᵉ mind and consent of yᵉ Church, yet this is part of that business & service that he oweth to yᵉ Church.

11.   That in yᵉ admission of Members into yᵉ Church, 'Tis necessary yt yᵉ People be well satisfied wth yᵉ Person they receive into their fellowship, as well as yᵉ Pastor to receive him under his care; and yt yᵉ Church has liberty to make objections if they are dissatisfied wth his fitness for Church Communion; nor can yᵉ Pastor receive in any Member of cast out any one, contrary to yᵉ mind of yᵉ People, or without their actual free consent.

12.   I belive [sic] yt when yᵉ Pastor admits a Member upon yᵉ profession of his Faith and Hope and yᵉ satisfaction of yᵉ Church, he doth in yᵉ Name of our Lord Jesus Christ & by yᵉ consent of yᵉ Church receive him into fellowship wth Christ & wth yt Church in all Gospel Priviledges & Ordinances.

13.   The Duties of A Pastor are chiefly such as these: preaching and labouring in yᵉ Word & Doctrine, praying earnestly for his Flock in publick & in private, Administring yᵉSeals of yᵉ Covenant of Grace, Baptism & yᵉ Lord's Supper, being instant in Season & out of Season, teaching & exhorting, comforting & rebuking, wth all long suffering & doctrine, contending for & preserving yᵉ Truth, approving himself an example to yᵉ Flock, Visiting yᵉ Sick & yᵉ Poor, praying wth them & taking care of them, making enquiries into yᵉ State of his Flock especially as to spiritual affairs, endeavouring to stir up & promote Religion in their Households & Families, & labouring by all means & methods of Christ's appointment to further their Faith & Holiness, their comfort & their increase. And 'tis the Duty of yᵉ People to attend upon his ministrations, to pray for him, to encourage & support him, & wherein soever he acts according to yᵉWill of Christ to receive him wth all due regard.

14.   That it is yᵉ proper business of yᵉ Pastor also to present Persons and Cases to yᵉ Church, and to ask yᵉ Votes of Consent of YE Church as one yt is sett to go before yᵉ Flock; except when he is necessitated to be absent, or thro' any Indispositions incapable when present, or where ye Pastor himself is so far concern'd in yᵉ case to be proposed as may render it improper for him to propose it.

15.   For yᵉ better performance of all these things, & by reason of yᵉ various necessities of a Church, other Officers are also appointed by Christ, of several Names

in Scripture, especially for Churches where ye Members grow numerous; all whose business is to assist ye Pastor in those Affairs wch cannot so fully be managed by himself alone, each of them acting according to their proper place, office, and business, wch ye Lord has appointed them unto in his Word.

Lastly: That in ye management of every affair in ye Church there ought to be a Spirit of Gentleness, Meekness, Lowliness of mind, Love, Affection & tenderness, both in yE Pastor and People towards each other; for Jesus ye Great Shepherd of his Church was most humble & compassionate, most gentle & meek, & his Saints are called his Sheep, from their like Dispositions; and yt ye edification of ye Church being one great end for wch Christ has given this office to his Ministers, all lesser concerns and differences ought to be managed wth a continual regard to this great end, and for ye publick honour of Christ in his Churches. Thus I have given a short account of some of the chief Principals [sic] of Gospel Order.

If I am so unhappy in any of my expressions to be obscure, & to want explaining, I am ready at any time to declare my meaning, & also to give the reasons of my judgment in any of ye foregoing Articles, shewing yt they not only agree wth ye judgment of your Reverend Pastors aforenamed, but – wch is more considerable – that they are all in my apprehension suitable to ye Will of Christ concerning Churches & Pastors revealed in his Word.

Christian Friends dearly beloved, I cannot but tell you that while I have been writing these Articles, especially ye 7th, 8th, & 13th, I shrink at ye very thoughts of Your call of me to so weightly an office in ye Church of Christ; And I find such discouragements from ye awfulness and greatness of ye work, yt makes me cry out feelingly *Who is sufficient for these things?* And this inclines me still to suspend my Answer, & to renew my request to you (tho' often in vain renewed) of quitting all thoughts of me, & choosing one whose gifts, graces, & ablilitys may be more capable of discharging so Vast A Trust, & filling up ye Duties of so Sacred an office.

Yors in ye service of ye Gospel,

Is. WATTS.

Document VI.47

Isaac Watts's Letter to the Bury Street Church

The ailing Isaac Watts addressed the following letter to the Church of which he was pastor on 4 November 1713. It is reprinted from John Waddington, *Congregational History 1700–1800*, London: Longmans, Green, 1876, 114–17.

To the Church of Christ, meeting in Bury Street, of which the
Holy Spirit hath made me overseer.

Dearly beloved in our Lord, – Grace, mercy, and peace be multiplied to you from God our Father, and our Lord Jesus Christ.

It has been a very sore aggravation of my long sorrows that I have not been able to encourage your Christian visits, to converse with you singly, to receive your consolations, and relate my own experience. Nor have I been capable to express my constant concern for your welfare by writing to you together as a Church, as I often designed. But you are upon my heart more than ever, whilst God chastises my former want of zeal by *silencing me for a season*. I bow to his wisdom and holiness, and am learning obedience by the things that I suffer, and many lessons of righteousness and grace, which I hope hereafter to publish amongst you; as I have been long pleading with Him for pardon for my negligence, so I ask you also to forgive. Long afflictions are soul-searching providences, and discover the secret of the heart and omission of duties, that were unobserved in the day of grace. May the blessed Spirit reveal to each of us why He continues to contend with us! I cannot reckon up all my obligations to you for your kind support of me under my tedious and expensive sicknesses, and for your continued and constant prayers for my recovery, which gave me the first ground of hope that I should be restored, which hope and expectation still remain with me, and I think are supported by the Word and Spirit of God. It seems at present more needful for you that I abide in the flesh (Phil. i. 24–26), and I trust I shall yet abide for your furtherance and joy of faith, that your rejoicing may be more abundant in Christ Jesus for me, by my coming to you again. And whilst I am confined as the prisoner of God, I request the continuance of your supplications for patience and sanctification as well as health. I rejoice also to hear of your union, your love, and your attendance on the worship of the Church. This has been a great comfort to my thoughts in the time of my affliction and absence; yet I am in pain for your edification, because you have no one among you to administer the spiritual and sealing ordinances; and since it is your earnest desire to know my opinion on that affair that lies before you, I have at several seasons been enabled to write it under these heads: – 1. That there were in the primitive Churches several preaching elders, bishops, or overseers. 2. That where their gifts were different, some were called pastors, or elders for exhortation, to feed the flock, and to exhort the saints; and others were called teachers, or elders for doctrine, to instruct the hearers in the principles of Christianity, chiefly the younger Christians, and to bring in new converts. 3. The Scripture does not determine when, or how often, one or other should preach or administer holy ordinances; and yet it is necessary there should be some rule to decide it, lest ambition or controversy should arise among the elders in this matter. 4. The Scripture makes no distinction, nor subordination of power, betwixt them in the Church, but seems to give all elders an equality of power. 5. Therefore I believe the Church (to which the light of nature and Scripture hath given all power in things indifferent, that are necessary to be determined) has power to appoint the times, seasons, and places of their ministrations. 6. It is for the certain advantage of a Church to have more elders than one in it, that they may more frequently visit the Church, more fully take care of them, and regularly administer all holy ordinances; if one or other be sick or absent, may also better keep the Church together, and encourage young converts to join themselves to it. 7. That it is for the advantage of a Church to have such an elder chosen, whose gifts have been tried and approved in the Church, and been owned and blessed of God for the good of souls. Such a one may most likely please and profit.

Now with regard to our Church in particular – 1. It is my opinion that, whether I live or die, if such an elder be chosen by the universal desire and voice of Church, it will be much for their advantage, in all probability. 2. Whether I live or die, if another elder be chosen with the desire of a few persons, and the opposition of a few, and the bare, cold assent of the major part it will not be for the advantage of the Church; and I am sure my worthy brother, Mr. SAM PRICE, on whom your thoughts are set, hath too tender a sense of your spiritual interests, and too wise a sense of his own, to accept of such an imperfect call to fixed office in the Church. 3. If another elder be chosen, with pretty general desire of the Church (though not universal), it will be for the advantage of the Church if I live, and am restored to your service; and I shall rejoice to have you supplied with all ordinances in my absence by a man that I can most entirely confide in; and, on my return, shall rejoice to be assisted in all services to the Church by one whom I love and esteem highly; and I write as much with an eye to your future benefit as to your present want. 4. If God, for my sins, shall refuse to employ me again (for I have justly deserved it), and if He shall deny the long and importunate requests of his people (for He is a great Sovereign), I trust He will direct and incline your hearts to choose and establish one or more elders among you, who may give universal satisfaction, and especially to such as may now be less satisfied, and may be for your future edification and increase. 5. If my beloved brother PRICE be chosen as one elder among you, I hope your diligent and sincere attendance on his instructions will give you more abundant sense of his true worth, of the exactness of his discourses, of the seriousness of his spirit, and of the constant blessing of God with him – all which I have observed with much pleasure.

Now I have fully delivered my sentiments in this affair, and you see how sincere and hearty I am in it. Yet I will give you two reasons why *I do not think it fit to propose it to the Church* – 1. Because it is the *proper business of the Church to seek after elders and officers of itself*, from a sight and sense of their own spiritual interests, both as Christians and as a united body; especially considering the elder you propose to choose is *not to be my deputy or servant*, but *your minister and overseer* in the Lord. 2. Because I never would have anything of such importance done in the Church *by the influence of my desire, without your own due sense and prospect of your own edification and establishment as a Church of Christ*. Nor would I influence you in this affair, unless the judgment of your minds concur with mine; for *as I never had any interest divided from the interest of the Church, so I hope I never shall*.

And now, brethren, dearly beloved, I intreat you, by the love of Christ to you, and by the love you bear to Christ, our common Lord, that there may be no contentions among you. I should be glad to find every affair that belongs to the Church determined by as many voices as, I trust, I have hearts and affections among you. However, *with freedom let every one speak his sentiments as under the eye of Christ, the great Shepherd, without bias or resentment, and with zeal for the Church's interest. Let everything that is debated be with great calmness*, and so much the more in my absence, each of you believing concerning one another that you sincerely seek the honour of Christ, and the union and peace of the Church, as I believe concerning you all. Let each of you be ready to lay aside his own former opions or resolutions, as you shall see reason arise, for the common welfare. If there should be quarrels and wranglings, reflections and hard speeches, it would be a grief too heavy for me to bear, and the most effectual way to overwhelm my spirit, and delay my return to you; and as I know you have the utmost tenderness of my peace, you ought to be as tender of each other's spiritual advantage, and the union and peace of the body, and to indulge no secret whispers of backbitings that may hinder the edification of your brethren by the ministrations of the Church. But I will not give myself leave to entertain such suspicion concerning you, *who have so many years walked together in constant love*. I pray heartily that the all-wise God and Jesus Christ our Lord may preside in you consultations, direct your hearts, and determine all things for you, that you may be extablished and edified, and be a joy and blessing to each other, as you have been, and I trust will be, to your most affectionate and afflicted pastor,

Nov. 4, 1713.   Isaac Watts.

Document VI.48

Philip Doddridge's Induction at Northampton

Philip Doddrige recorded the occasion of his induction in the Northampton Church Book, and to it he appended the confession of faith he delivered on that occasion. For Doddridge see Document I.1 above. The extract is reprinted from John Waddington, *Congregational History 1700–1800*, London: Longmans, Green, 1876, pp. 279–80.

After repeated solicitations, long deliberations, and earnest prayer to God for direction, I came to a resolution to accept the invitation of my dear and most affectionate friends at Northampton, on Saturday, December 6, 1729, and certified the Church of that resolution by a letter that evening. I removed from Harborough, and came to settle here on Wednesday, December 24. On Thursday, March 19, 1729–30, was solemnly set apart to the pastoral office by prayer and fasting, and imposition of hands. Mr Goodrich began with prayer and reading Eph. iv. Mr Dawson prayed; then Mr. Watson preached from 1 Tim. iii. 1. Mr Norris then read the call to which I declared my acceptance. He took my confession of faith and ordination vows, and then proceeded to set me apart by prayer. Immediately Mr. Clark of St. Albans gave the charge to me; Mr. Saunders, of Kettering, the exhortation to the people; and Mr. Mattock concluded the whole solemnity by prayer. It was a delightful, and I hope it will prove a very profitable day. I write this memorandum of it under the remainder of a painful and threatening illness, which detained me from my public work the ensuing Sabbaths. The event is still dubious, but I leave my life and my dear flock in the hand of the Great Shepherd, hoping what passed on my ordination day will be an engagement to me to live more usefully or an encouragement to die more cheerfully than I should otherwise have done. Amen.

Document VI.49

Matthias Maurice on Congregational Polity

For Maurice see Document IV.6 above. The following extracts are from Maurice's *Social Religion Exemplified*, 1737, I, pp. 124, 142.

The formal reason for a Church, is its Covenant ... Members of Churches stand in a special visible Relation to each other, and this Relation is voluntary, and thereby by Agreement Persons are receiv'd and Persons are rejected. ...

We poor Sinners, having destroy'd ourselves by Sin, yet being brought through Grace and everlasting Love to look upon him, in whom our Help is laid, under a Sense of our exceeding Sinfulness, mourn and repent before the Lord: And do here openly, and without Reserve, resign ourselves and ours up wholly to *Christ* the compleat Saviour of Sinners, in Church Fellowship and Communion; resolving and promising in his Strength, to believe his Promises, live by Faith on him, in whom they are all yea and *Amen*, obey his Precepts, hearken to the Voice of his Providence, serve him, and each other, according to all the Laws, Statutes and Ordinances of his House ... *Christ* has promised his Presence to a Church of his, meeting in his Name: all the Members of a Congregational Church profess this. *Christ* we humbly hope, his Face being sought, guides this Church in Wisdom according to his Word: All Reason tells us, the *Majority* must be the Church: and then, all reason in the World the *Minority* should cheerfully concur.

Document VI.50

The Mynyddbach Church Book

The following extracts from the Mynyddbach, Carmarthenshire, Independent Church Book are reprinted from Thomas Rees, *History of Protestant Nonconformity in Wales*, London: John Snow, 1883, pp. 269–70.

Anne Rees, widow of Harry Evan Morgan, was received to church communion at Mynyddbach, the 5th day of December, 1736. Being very old and illiterate, she has but little knowledge; however, she is much altered in her conversation from what she was formerly.

Edward John Harry was received to church communion at Mynyddbach, Feb. 26th, 1737. His knowledge is very defective, yet he has the character of being an earnest man. Great alteration is seen in him from what he was before.

Evan David Evan was received to church communion at Mynyddbach, June 18 1738. He is very young, yet he has a good stock of knowledge, and he has the character that he lives accordingly.

Evan Thomas Evan, near Cwmysgyfarnog, was examined and received to church communion at Mynyddbach, the 17th of February, 1745. He was examined one month before, and we delayed to receive him, until we would endeavour to catechize him better, and lead him to more knowledge of the fundamental principles of religion.

Document VI.51

William Roby Defies the Church Meeting

In the New Testament the saints are sinners, and thus it has ever been. Every church polity is, accordingly, open to abuse, not least the congregational. The realisation of unanimity in Christ in every church meeting may perhaps be designated an eschatological aspiration. Meanwhile some ministers may draw a certain comfort from the fact that some of those who have gone down as pastoral exemplars have borne the brunt of saints in recalcitrant mood.

For Roby see Document IV.17 above. The following extract, by an anonymous church member, is reprinted from W. Gordon Robinson, *William Roby*, London: Independent Press, 1954, p. 36.

We had most distressing church meetings. We saw our dear Pastor stand upon his feet for four or five hours without intermission. We heard him assailed in the most uncourteous, the most unchristian manner, and what was peculiarly distressing to myself and many others, while the greater part of the members were ready to shed their blood to defend him, from a strange sort of something I cannot define, we suffered him to fight these hot battles almost alone. ... One of our Brethren informed me that he went home with him after one of these stormy meetings and though he had possessed himself in the meeting with much apparent composure, yet as soon as he got into the street he burst into tears and went weeping all the way home.

At length the church was roused to action – and this was what roused them. He said in a mild though decisive tone, we had no prospect of peace, and without peace we could not expect prosperity. He would therefore resign his charge. It is impossible to describe the sensations that we felt when these words were uttered. We all retired in silence like so many persons under sentence of death. Soon however a church meeting was called. Every member was present except the few troublers, including the aged, infirm, diseased and the lame, and with only one dissenting voice came to the conclusion of separating the troublers and gave our Minister an affectionate invitation to continue with us. Peace was again restored and prosperity followed.

Document VI.52

The Welsh Calvinistic Methodist Society Meetings

The society or experience meetings were seed-beds of Christian nurture in Welsh Calvinistic Methodism. In extract (a) George Whitefield records in his journal entry of 7 March 1739 Howel Harris's success in establishing such societies; in extract (b) William Williams, Pantycelyn, the Methodist cleric, hymn writer and preacher who did much to promote the experience meetings, outlines the ordering of such meetings.

For Whitefield see Document II.25 above; for Harris see Document II.25 above. For Williams (1717–91) see DEB, DH, DNB, DWB. Extract (a) is from *George Whitefield's Journals*, London: The Banner of Truth Trust, 1960, pp. 228–9. Extract (b), translated by Mrs Lloyd-Jones, is reprinted from William Williams, *The Experience Meeting*, London: Evangelical Press, 1973, p. 31.

(a)

Wednesday, March 7 [1739]. Arose before twelve at night, sang psalms, and prayed, and the wind being fair, we had a speedy passage over to the Welsh shore. Our business requiring haste, God having, of His good Providence, sent one to guide us, we rode all night, stopped at Newport to refresh us, where we met with two friends, and reached Cardiff about eleven in the morning.

The town, I soon found, was apprehensive of my coming, and therefore, whilst I was giving a word of exhortation to some poor people at the inn, Mr. Seward went to ask for the pulpit; being denied, we pitched on the Town Hall, which Mr. Seward got by his interest, and at four in the afternoon, I preached from the Judge's seat to about a hundred hearers. Most were very attentive; but some mocked. However, I offered Jesus Christ freely even to them, and should have rejoiced if they would have accepted Him; but their foolish hearts were hardened. Lord, make them monuments of Thy free grace!

After I came from the seat, I was much refreshed with the sight of my dear brother Howell Harris, whom, though I knew not in person, I have long since loved in the bowels of Jesus Christ, and have often felt my soul drawn out in prayer in his behalf. A burning and shining light has he been in those parts, a barrier against profaneness and immorality, and an indefatigable promoter of the true Gospel of Jesus Christ. About three or four years God has inclined him to go about doing good. He is now about twenty-five years of age. Twice he has applied (being every way qualified) for Holy Orders, but was refused, under a false pretence that he was not of age, though he was then twenty-two years and six months. About a month ago he offered himself again, but was put off. Upon this, he was, and is still resolved to go on in his work; and indefatigable zeal has he shown in his Master's service. For these three years (as he told me from his own mouth) he has discoursed almost twice every day for three or four hours together, not authoritatively, as a minister, but as a private person, exhorting his Christian brethren. He has been, I think, in seven counties, and has made it his business to go to wakes, &c., to turn people from such lying vanities.

Many alehouse people, fiddlers, harpers, &c., (Demetrius-like) sadly cry out against him for spoiling their business. He has been made the subject of numbers of sermons, has been threatened with public prosecutions, and had constables sent to apprehend him. But God has blessed him with inflexible courage – instantaneous strength has been communicated to him from above, and he still continues to go on from conquering to conquer. He is of a most catholic spirit, loves all who love our Lord Jesus Christ, and therefore he is styled by bigots, a Dissenter. He is contemned by all who are lovers of pleasure more than lovers of God; but God has greatly blessed his pious endeavours. Many call and own him as their spiritual father, and, I believe, would lay down their lives for his sake. He discourses generally in a field, but at other times in a house, from a wall, a table or any thing else. He has established nearly thirty Societies in South Wales, and still his sphere of action is enlarged daily. He is full of faith, and the Holy Ghost.

(b)

EUSEBIUS: And now, tell me how things should be ordered, when the society meets together like this. Give me some instruction, for I am anxious to know the best way to keep warmth and life in the worship of the Lord.

THEOPHILUS: First of all, let there be prayers and pleadings to God to lead you in the way which pleases Him, whether in singing praises, or continuing in prayer, catechizing some, comforting the weak-minded rebuking the heedless and careless, or in whatever else has to be done, that all should be done according to the mind and the will of the Lord. As of old ancient Israel was called upon to follow the pillar of cloud and fire, so His saints today are to follow the voice and the leading of His Spirit, so that if His Spirit does not honour one exercise, our duty is to turn to some other. If catechizing is not seen to be progressing with enlightenment, warmth and life, it is better to spend the time in singing or praying, or in some exercise that will promote conviction, instruction and comfort.

EUSEBIUS: But if we are to catechize, who is suitable for the task, pray? For I have heard some men catechizing without one glimmer of light, or any degree of warmth in their examination, so that they darken the minds, not only of those being questioned, but also of the whole gathering, and possibly spend as much time with one as would be needed to catechize six.

THEOPHILUS: Quite true; to catechize is a special gift not possessed by one in a hundred.

Document VI.53

A Vindication of the Calvinistic Methodist Associations

The Associations in question were gatherings at which a number of sermons would be preached on two successive days – in some cases to congregations exceeding ten thousand. The quarterly meetings were instituted to promulgate and defend evangelical doctrine against heresy, and to promote holiness. The following is from a tract of 1776, quoted by John Waddington, *Congregational History 1700–1800*, London Longmans, Green, 1876, pp. 594–5.

It is a fact very notorious, and which cannot admit of a doubt, that numbers of the Protestants of our days have forsaken several of the leading principles and doctrines which the venerable Reformers maintained and preached, which they found the most successful instruments, under the Divine blessing, in demolishing the fabric of Popery, and which were preached with so much success by our pious and suffering fathers, the Puritans. Now, the associating ministers openly acknowledge their apprehensions, that the rejection of those principles tends to eat up and consume the very vitals of genuine piety, to promote carnal confidence and sinful security, to undermine the very foundation of Christian consolation, to rob us of the chief and only effectual motives to evangelical obedience, and, in one word, to deprive us of the substance of the gospel, and to leave us nothing in its room but the bare religion of nature.

Now, let all men of piety, and that know anything of religion beside wearing its external garb, judge whether there is not too much ground for such apprehension. 'When the true and proper divinity of the Son and Spirit of God is openly denied and opposed; when the original guilt and native pollution of human nature is exploded; when salvation by sovereign grace is traduced as a licentious doctrine; when the doctrine of efficacious grace is rejected, and human power exalted to sit on its throne and to usurp its honours; when the great gospel truth of satisfaction to divine justice by the sacrifice of Christ is treated with contempt, the imputation of His righteousness denied, and the acceptance of men with God founded on their own fancied goodness and virtue.' Those ministers not only heard and saw that what they apprehended to be a new gospel was thus introduced, but beheld the most convincing evidences that as these new doctrines spread and prevailed, in the same proportion the power of godliness decayed. In some measure to remedy this evil it was agreed upon that quarterly meetings of ministers should be set up, to circulate by rotation in their several churches, in which there might be an opportunity freely to profess and openly to vindicate those precious gospel truths which others so openly opposed and calumniated. This is the true original and rise of the quarterly meetings.

Document VI.54

Methodist Conference Minutes and Organisation

The secret of Methodism's success was not only its evangelistic imperative and its joyful liberating message (the 'optimism of grace', as it has been called), but the remarkable discipline and control exercised by the leadership over the circuits and societies. John Wesley was certainly one of the greatest organising geniuses of all times. In extracts (a) and (b) we see control spreading over societies and bands (the latter soon grew into élite groups of the totally dedicated, cells within the ecclesiolae, so to speak). Extract (c) is from the so-called Large Minutes which leaves the reader in no doubt that the Methodist people were strictly under authority in respect of belief, conduct, reading and attire. Extract (d) records Wesley's Rules for his Preachers – men (and briefly women) whose daily living was strictly regulated. Extracts (e) and (f) show how the discipline concerning the methodical movements of preachers was worked out in Worcestershire/Gloucestershire.

The first extracts is from *Minutes of the Methodist Conference*, 1862 edn (1744–98), I, pp. 1 f.; the second is from J. Wesley, *Works*, 1872, VIII, pp. 273–4; extract (c) is from *The Large Minutes*, in Wesley's *Works*, VIII, p. 299 f., while at (d) we find J. Wesley's *The Twelve Rules of A Helper*, approved by the Conference of 1744, but re-printed in amended form in 1753. The earliest plan of the Worcester/Gloucester Circuit (e) is reprinted from J. Noakes, *Worcester Sects*, 1861, pp. 317–18, as is (f), the Same Circuit's Plan for 1797, pp. 319–20.

(a)
Monday, June 25th, 1744
The following persons being met at the Foundery: John Wesley, Charles Wesley, John Hodges, Henry Piers, Samuel Taylor, and John Meriton; after some time spent in prayer, the design of our meeting was proposed, namely, to consider:

1.   What to teach;
2.   How to teach, and
3.   What to do, i.e. how to regulate our doctrine, discipline and practice.

But first it was inquired whether any of our lay brethren should be present at this Conference. And it was agreed to invite from time to time such of 'em as we should judge proper. It was then asked, Which of 'em shall we invite today? And the answer was: Thomas Richards, Thomas Maxfield, John Bennet, and John Downes, who were accordingly brought in. Then was read as follows:

It is desired
    That all things may be considered as in the immediate presence of God;
    That we may meet with a single eye, and as little children which have everything
        to learn;
    That every point may be examined from the foundation;
    That every person may speak freely whatever is in his heart; and
    That every question proposed may be fully debated, and bolted to the bran.

(b)
Directions given to the Band-Societies, December 25, 1744

You are supposed to have the faith that 'overcometh the world'. To you therefore, it is not grievous: –
    I.   Carefully to abstain from doing evil; in particular: –
    1.   Neither to buy nor sell anything at all on the Lord's day.
    2.   To taste no spirituous liquor, no dram of any kind, unless prescribed by a
physician.

3. To be at a word both in buying and selling.

4. To pawn nothing, no, not to save life.

5. Not to mention the fault of any behind his back, and to stop those short that do.

6. To wear no needless ornaments, such as rings, ear-rings, necklaces, lace, ruffles.

7. To use no needless self-indulgence, such as taking snuff or tobacco, unless prescribed by a Physician.

II. Zealously to maintain good works; in particular: –

1. To give alms of such things as you posses, and that to the uttermost of your power.

2. To reprove all that sin in your sight, and that in love and meekness of wisdom.

3. To be patterns of diligence and frugality, of self-denial, and taking up the cross daily.

III. Constantly to attend on all the ordinances of God; in particular: –

1. To be at church and at the Lord's table every week, and at every public meeting of the Bands.

2. To attend the ministry of the word every morning, unless distance, business, or sickness prevent.

3. To use private prayer every day; and family prayer, if you are at the head of a family.

4. To read the Scriptures, and meditate therein, at every vacant hour. And, –

5. To observe, as days of fasting or abstinence, all Fridays in the year.

(c)

Minutes of several conversations between The Rev. Mr. Wesley and others; from the year 1744, to the year 1789

It is desired, that all things be considered as in the immediate presence of God; that every person speak freely whatever is in his heart.

Q. 1. How may we best improve the time of this Conference?

A. (1.) While we are conversing, let us have an especial care to set God always before us.

(2.) In the intermediate hours, let us redeem all the time we can for private exercises.

(3.) Therein let us give ourselves to prayer for one another, and for a blessing on this our labour.

Q. 2. Have our Conferences been as useful as they might have been?

A. No: We have been continually straitened for time. Hence, scarce anything has been searched to the bottom. To remedy this, let every Conference last nine days, concluding on Wednesday in the second week.

Q. 3. What may we reasonably believe to be God's design in raising up the Preachers called Methodists?

A.   Not to form any new sect; but to reform the nation, particularly the Church; and to spread scriptural holiness over the land.

Q. 4.   What was the rise of Methodism, so called?

A.   In 1729, two young men, reading the Bible, saw they could not be saved without holiness, followed after it, and incited others so to do. In 1737 they saw holiness comes by faith. They saw likewise, that men are justified before they are sanctified; but still holiness was their point. God then thrust them out, utterly against their will, to raise a holy people. When Satan could no otherwise hinder this he threw Calvinism in the way; and then Antinomianism, which strikes directly at the root of all holiness.

Q. 5.   Is it advisable for us to preach in as many places as we can, without forming any societies?

A.   By no means. We have made the trial in various places; and that for a considerable time. But all the seed has fallen as by the highway side. There is scarce and fruit remaining.

Q. 6.   Where should we endeavour to preach most?

A. (1.)   Where there is the greatest number of quiet and willing hearers. (2.) Where there is most fruit.

Q. 7.   Is field-preaching unlawful?

A.   We conceive not. We do not know that it is contrary to any law either of God or man.

Q. 8.   Have we not used it too sparingly?

A.   It seems we have; (1.) Because our call is, to save that which is lost. Now, we cannot expect them to seek *us*. Therefore we should go and seek *them*. (2.) Because we are particularly called, by 'going into the highways and hedges', which none else will do, 'to compel them to come in'. (3.) Because that reason against it is not good, 'The house will hold all that come'. The house may hold all that come to the house; but not all that would come to the field.

The greatest hinderance to this you are to expect from rich, or cowardly, or lazy Methodists. But regard them not, neither Stewards, Leaders, nor people. Whenever the weather will permit, go out in God's name into the most public places, and call all to repent and believe the gospel; every Sunday, in particular; especially were there are old societies, lest they settle upon their lees. The Stewards will frequently oppose this, lest they lose their usual collection. But this is not a sufficient reason against it. Shall we barter souls for money?

Q. 9.   Ought we not diligently to observe in what places God is pleased at any time to pour out his Spirit more abundantly?

A.   We ought; and at that time to send more labourers than usual into that part of the harvest.

But whence shall we have them? (1.) So far as we can afford it, we will keep a reserve of Preachers at Kingswood. (2.) Let an exact list be kept of those who are proposed for trial, but not accepted.

Q. 10.   How often shall we permit strangers to be present at the meeting of the society?

A.   At every other meeting of the society in every place let no stranger be admitted. At other times, they may; but the same person not above twice or thrice. In order to this, see that all in every place show their tickets before they come in. If the Stewards and Leaders are not exact herein, employ others that have more resolution.

Q. 11.   How may the Leaders of classes be made more useful?

A. (1.)   Let each of them be diligently examined concerning his method of meeting a class. Let this be done with all possible exactness at the next quarterly visitation. And in order to this, allow sufficient time for the visiting of each society.

(2.)   Let each Leader carefully inquire how every soul in his class prospers; not only how each person observes the outward Rules, but how he grows in the knowledge and love of God.

(3.)   Let the Leaders converse with the Assistant frequently and freely.

Q. 12.   Can anything farther be done, in order to make the meetings of the classes lively and profitable?

A. (1.)   Change improper Leaders.

(2.)   Let the Leaders frequently meet each other's classes.

(3.)   Let us observe which Leaders are the most useful; and let these meet the other classes as often as possible

(4.)   See that all the Leaders be not only men of sound judgment, but men truly devoted to God.

Q.13.   How can we farther assist those under our care?

A. (1.)   By meeting the married men and women together, the first Sunday after the visitation, – the single men and women apart, on the two following – in all the large societies: This has been much neglected.

(2.)   By instructing them at their own houses. What unspeakable need is there of this! The world say, 'The Methodists are no better than other people'. This is not true. But it is nearer the truth than we are willing to believe. ...

Q. 14.   How shall we prevent improper persons from insinuating into the society?

A. (1.)   Give tickets to none till they are recommended by a Leader, with whom they have met at least two months on trial.

(2.)   Give notes to none but those who are recommended by one you know, or till they have met three or four times in a class.

(3.)   Give them the Rules the first time they meet. See that this be never neglected.

Q. 15.   When shall we admit new members?

A.   In large towns, admit them into the Bands at the quarterly love-feast following the visitation: Into the society, on the Sunday following the visitation. Then also read the names of them that are excluded.

Q. 16.   Should we insist on the Band rules, particularly with regard to dress?

A.   By all means. This is not time to give any encouragement to superfluity of apparel. Therefore give no Band-tickets to any till they have left off superfluous ornaments. In order to this, (1.) Let every Assistant read the 'Thoughts upon Dress' at least once a year, in every large society. (2.) In visiting the classes, be very mild, but very strict. (3.) Allow no exempt case, not even of a married woman. Better one suffer than many. (4.) Give no ticket to any that wear calashes, high-heads, or enormous bonnets.

To encourage meeting in Band, (1.) In every large society, have a love-feast quarterly for the Bands only. (2.) Never fail to meet them once a week. (3.) Exhort every believer to embrace the advantage. (4.) Give a Band-ticket to none till they have met a quarter on trial.

Observe! You give none a Band-ticket before he meets, but after he has met.

Q. 17.   Have those in Band left off snuff and drams?

A.   No. Many are still enslaved to one or the other. In order to redress this, (1.) Let no Preacher touch either on any account. (2.) Strongly dissuade our people from them. (3.) Answer their pretences, particularly curing the colic. ...

Q. 29.   What general method of employing our time would you advise us to?

A.   We advise you, (1.) As often as possible to rise at four. (2.) From four to five in the morning, and from five to six in the evening, to meditate, pray, and read, partly the Scripture with the Notes, partly the closely practical parts of what we have published. (3.) From six in the morning till twelve, (allowing an hour for breakfast,) to read in order with much prayer, first, 'The Christian Library', and the other books which we have published in prose and verse, and then those which we recommended in our Rules of Kingswood School.

Q. 30.   Should our Helpers follow trades?

A.   The question is not, whether they may occasionally work with their hands, as St. Paul did, but whether it be proper for them to keep shop or follow merchandise. After long consideration, it was agreed by all our brethren, that no Preacher who will not relinquish his trade of buying and selling, (though it were only pills, drops, or balsams,) shall be considered as a Travelling Preacher any longer.

Q. 31.   Why is it that the people under our care are no better?

A.   Other reasons may concur; but the chief is, because we are not more knowing and more holy.

Q. 32.   But why are we not more knowing?

A.   Because we are idle. We forget our very first rule, 'Be diligent. Never be unemployed a moment. Never be triflingly employed. Never while away time; neither spend andy more time at any place than is strictly necessary.' ...

Q. 43.   Has the office of an Assistant been well executed?

A.   No, not by half the Assistants. (1.) Who has sent me word, whether the other Preachers behave well or ill? (2.) Who has visited all the classes and regulated the Bands quarterly? (3.) Love-feasts for the Bands have been neglected: Neither have persons been duly taken in and put out of the Bands. (4.) The societies are not half supplied with books; not even with those above-mentioned. O exert yourselves in this! Be not weary! Leave no stone unturned! (5.) How few accounts have I had, either of remarkable deaths, or remarkable conversions! (6.) How few exact lists of the societies! (7.) How few have met the married and single persons once a quarter!

Q. 44.   Are there any other advices which you would give the assistants?

A.   Several. (1.) Take a regular catalogue of your societies, as they live in house-row. (2.) Leave your successor a particular account of the state of the Circuit. (3.) See that every Band-Leader has the Rules of the Bands. (4.) Vigorously, but calmly, enforce the Rules concerning needless ornaments, drams, snuff, and tobacco. Give no Band-ticket to any man or woman who does not promise to leave them off. (5.)

As soon as there are four men or women believers in any place, put them into a Band. (6.) Suffer no love-feast to last above an hour and an half; and instantly stop all breaking the cake with one another. (7.) Warn all, from time to time, that none are to remove from one society to another without a certificate from the Assistant in these words: (Else he will not be received in other societies:) 'A. B., the bearer, is a member of our society in C.: I believe he has sufficient cause for removing'. I beg every Assistant to remember this. (8.) Everywhere recommend decency and cleanliness: Cleanliness is next to godliness. (9.) Exhort all that were brought up in the Church, to continue therein. Set the example yourself; and immediately change every plan that would hinder their being at church at least two Sundays in four. Carefully avoid whatever has a tendency to separate men from the Church; and let all the servants in our preaching-houses go to church once on Sunday at least.

Is there not a cause? Are we not unawares, by little and little, sliding into a separation from the Church? O use every means to prevent this! (1.) Exhort all our people to keep close to the Church and sacrament. (2.) Warn them all against niceness in hearing, – a prevailing evil. (3.) Warn them also against despising the Prayers of the Church. (4.) Against calling our society, 'the Church'. (5.) Against calling our Preachers, 'Ministers'; our Houses, 'Meeting-houses': Call them plain preaching-houses, or chapels. (6.) Do not license them as Dissenters. The proper paper to be sent in at the Assizes, Sessions, or Bishop's Court is this: 'A. B. has set apart his house in C. for public worship, of which he desires a certificate'. N.B. The Justice does not license the house, but the Act of Parliament. (7.) Do not license yourself till you are constrained; and then, not as a Dissenter, but a Methodist. It is time enough when you are prosecuted to take the oaths. And by so doing you are licensed.

Q. 45.   But are we not Dissenters?

A.   No: Although we call sinners to repentance in all places of God's dominion; and although we frequently use extemporary prayer, and unite together in a religious society; yet we are not Dissenters in the only sense which our law acknowledges, namely, those who renounce the service of the Church. We do not, we dare not, separate from it. We are not Seceders, nor do we bear any resemblance to them. We set out upon quite opposite principles. The Seceders laid the very foundation of their work in judging and condemning others: We laid the foundation of our work in judging and condemning ourselves. They begin everywhere with showing their hearers how fallen the Church and Ministers are: We begin everywhere with showing our hearers how fallen they are themselves. What they do in America, or what their Minutes say on this subject, is nothing to us. We will keep in the good old way.

(d)

1753

Q.   What are the Rules of a Helper?

1.   Be diligent, never be unemployed a moment, never be triflingly employed. Never while away time, nor spend more time at any place than is strictly necessary.

2.   Be serious. Let your motto be 'Holiness to the Lord'. Avoid all lightness, jesting, and foolish talking.

3.   Converse sparingly and cautiously with women particularly with young women.

4.   Take no step towards marriage without solemn prayer to God, and consulting with your Brethren.

5.   Believe evil of no one unless fully proved: take heed how you credit it. Put the best construction you can on everything. You know the Judge is always supposed to be on the prisoner's side.

6.   Speak evil of no one: else your word, especially, would eat as doth a canker. Keep your thoughts within your own breast till you come to the person concerned.

7.   Tell everyone what you think wrong in him, lovingly and plainly: and as soon as may be, else it will fester in your own heart. Make all haste to cast the fire out of your bosom.

8.   Do not affect the gentleman. A Preacher of the Gospel is the servant of all.

9.   Be ashamed of nothing but sin; no, not of cleaning your own shoes, when necessary.

10.   Be punctual. Do everything exactly at the time. And do not mend our Rules, but keep them: and that for conscience' sake.

11.   You have nothing to do but to save souls. Therefore spend and be spent in this work. And go always, not only to those who want you but to those who want you most.

12.   Act in all things, not according to your own will, but as a son in the Gospel, and in union with your Brethren. As such, it is your part to employ your time as our Rules direct: partly in preaching and visiting from house to house; partly in reading, meditation and prayer. Above all, if you labour with us in our Lord's vineyard, it is needful that you should do that part of the work which the Conference shall advise at those times and places which they shall judge most for His glory. Observe: It is not your business to preach so many times, and to take care merely of this or that Society, but to save as many souls as you can: to bring as many sinners as you possibly can to repentance: and, with all your power, to build them up in that holiness without which they cannot see the Lord. And remember, a Methodist Preacher is to mind every point, great and small, in Methodist Discipline. Therefore you will need all the grace and all the sense you have, and to have all your wits about you.

(e)

The brother that goes on the circuit from *Worcester* sets off immediately after breakfast on Friday Morning, dines at *Mrs Cannings*, schoolmistress, at *Bengeworth*; Saturday morning, after breakfast, to *Broad Marston*, *Mr Henry Eden's*; Sunday forenoon, preach at *Broad Marston*, and in the evening at *Weston*, *Mr Adkins*; Monday, dine at *Mrs Guy's*, *Hampton*, near *Bengeworth*, and after come to *Pershore* to preach, at *Mr Jones's*, barge owner; Tuesday morning, return to *Worcester*; Wednesday go to *Stourport*, *Mr Cowell's*; Thursday, to *Bewdley*, *Mr James Lewis*, near the church, shoemaker; Friday, to *Kidderminster*, *Mr James Bell*, shopkeeper, Mill Street; Saturday evening, preach here also, and Sunday morning, which falls to their turn in this manner once in a month, because the next preacher that comes to this part of the circuit, goes back from *Kidderminster* to *Bewdley* on the Saturday morning in order to preach there the opposite Sunday morning once in the month. From each of these places *Bewdley* and *Kidderminster*, the preacher returns after Sunday morning preaching to dine at *Stourport*, and preach at half-past two and six in the evening. Monday, after breakfast, you go to the *Clee Hills*, through *Cleobury* – a new place (society this year begun, 1791). Tuesday of late has fallen vacant, through giving up a place in that country. I hope the *Lord* will open a door for you somewhere to fill up this day. Wednesday, dine at *Stourport*, preach at night. Thursday morning, return to *Worcester*, having now completed your fortnight's round. The next preacher then takes the above circuit. You stay in Worcester a whole fortnight.

(f)
The preacher who goes to the country circuit sets off from *Worcester* on Saturday morning to *Ombersley*, where is a new society of eighteen members formed this year. On Sunday, preach at *Droitwich*, at nine o'clock in the morning, return to Mr. Groves's at Ombersley to dine, and preach again at Droitwich in the evening. N.B. *Droitwich* is a new place opened this year, and in which we have a very good prospect. Here call at Miss *Russell's*. From hence proceed on Monday to *Bromsgrove*, *John Bott's* needle maker. In this place is a society of nineteen members, steady, but not very lively, Tuesday: Mr. *Samuel Randle's*, *Netherwood*. The prospect in this place is not very good, as the congregations are very small; yet there is a society of eight members, not very lively. Wednesday: *Worcester*, a day of rest. Thurday: *Bengeworth*, Mrs. *Canning's*, schoolmistress. Here is the oldest a society in this part of the kingdom – once a large and flourishing one, but now reduced to fourteen members, and these not much in earnest. Friday: dine at Mr *Nathaniel Eden's*, *Honeyburn*, and then proceed to Mr *William Eden's* at *Broad Marston*. Preach at night at *Pebworth*. Here we have no society, as the few serious peoble who attend here belong to *Broad Marston* society. Saturday: *Weston*, Mr *Caleb Adkins*. Here is a lively society of twenty-four members. Mr. *Adkins* is one of the circuit stewards. Sunday: in the morning in some of the little villages in the neighbourhood of *Weston*, and in the afternoon or evening, *Broad Marston* as above. Monday: *Bidford*, Mr *Russell's*. Here is a new society of twenty-five members, in earnest, but ignorant and weak. Tuesday: Great *Allon*, Mr. *Hemming's*. We have preached here for some months, but have not attempted to form a society. Wednesday: *Alcester, Michael* Flaherty, carpenter. We have not preached long in this place. Thursday: *Pershore*, at *Owner Jones's* house. There was once a society in this place, but it was dissolved before I came to the circuit. We gave up preaching there for some months, but at the earnest entreaty of some poor people returned to it again. Friday: return to Worcester for the fortnight.

Document VI.55

Methodist Discontent: The Rise of the New Connexion

The Wesleyan bureaucratic and centralised regime seemed to many to accompany a heavy-handed authoritarianism, and responses to this perception were varied. Sunday school teachers built local empires of their own increasingly in separate buildings; local preachers resented their exclusion by the itinerants from major pulpits; society members objected to the appointment as trustees of their local chapels of wealthy laymen who often lived at a distance and seemed to be able to do as they pleased; those in the provinces were frequently suspicious of domination by London. In extract (a) John Pawson wonders, following the death of John Wesley, whether an Episcopal system in place of Conference control might not be the best solution. In extract (b) Pawson writes of dispute at Bristol in 1794, when a fiery young minister, Henry Moore, administered the sacrament contrary to the wishes of the trustees who promptly locked him out of the New Room. Eventually in 1795 a Plan of Pacification was adopted by Conference which, in spite of great hopes in some quarters, exemplified by extract (c), really served only to add fuel to the flames. Already Alexander Kilham, an unprepossessing man and a poor speaker, had written an anti-Conference tract – extract (d) – whose violent radicalism earned him and his followers the nickname 'Tom Paine Methodist'. He was expelled in the following year (extract (e)) – a move resented by many discontented Wesleyans, and deeply resented by Kilham's Alnwick circuit, as extract (f) (in which Mr E. is Steven Eversfield, junior minster in the Alnwick circuit, and William Hunter is Chairman of the Newcastle District) makes plain. Extracts (g) and (h) show that the situation was complex: in Liverpool the trustees seem to be siding with the rebels; in Chester to be harassing them. The Chester document also demonstrates that some societies which later threw their lot in with the Kilhamites had been in existence for a number of years. Kilham was little more than a safety valve for the expulsion of discontents. He was too hot-headed and unstable to be a leader. Fortunately, in William Thom the infant denomination, founded in 1797, found a tactful, reconciling statesman, and lay persons really shared power in the Methodist New Connexion. Extract (i) shows that the air has been cleared; even so, until the rise of a number of New Connexion grandees such as the Firths of Sheffield and the Ridgeways of the Potteries, the denomination continued to struggle, as extracts (j) and (k) make clear. The Methodist New Connexion remained an almost entirely urban denomination.

John Pawson (1737–1806), Charles Atmore (1759–1826), Joseph Benson (1748–1821), Samuel Bradburn (1751–1816) and Henry Moore (1751–1844), for all of whom see DEB, were Methodist ministers. Atmore, Benson and Moore are in DNB. For Alexander Kilham (1762–98) see DEB, DNB, ODCC. The extracts are from the following sources: (a) John Pawson to Charles Atmore, 13 December 1793, John Bowmer and John A. Vickers *Letters of John Pawson*, WMHS Publications, 1994, I, pp. 156–7; (b) John Pawson to Joseph Benson, 5 September 1794, ibid., 1995, II, p. 4; (c) Samuel Bradburn to John Reynolds, 12 April 1796, Methodist Archives, John Rylands University Library of Manchester, Manchester, PLP 1.14.9; (d) A. Kilham, *The Progress of Liberty*, 1795, pp. 18–19; (e) Henry Moore to his wife, 26 July 1796, MS letter at Drew University, USA; (f) Mrs Kilham to A. Kilham, 20 August 1796, Methodist Archives; (g) Isaac Wolfe to Alexander Kilham, 9 May 1797, Methodist Archives; (h) Anon., *An Address to the People called Methodist*, Chester, 26 December 1793; (i)

Methodist New Connexion Minutes, 1797; (j) John Pawson to Joseph Benson, 23 January 1798, *Letters of John Pawson*, 1995, II, p. 130; (k) David Morley to Alexander Kilham, February 1798, MS letter at John Rylands University Library of Manchester.

(a)

It will by no means answer our end to dispute one with another which is the most Scriptural form of Church government, but we should consider our present circumstances, and try to agree upon some method by which our people may have the Ordinances of God, and we may at the same time be preserved from divisions. I care not a rush whether it be Episcopal or Presbyterian. I believe neither of them Scriptural. But our Preachers and people in general are prejudiced against the latter, and therefore if the former will answer our end, we ought in our present circumstances to embrace it. Indeed, I believe it will suit our present plan far better than the other. My reason for thinking so is, we have a great many very little men among us, who cannot get forward except they are under proper governors.

The design of Mr Wesley will weigh very much with many, both Preachers and people, which now evidently appears to have been this. He foresaw that the Methodists would soon after his death become a distinct body of people. He was deeply prejudiced against Presbyterian, and as much prejudiced in favour of Episcopal government. In order therefore to preserve all that is valuable in the Church of England among the Methodists, he ordained Mr Mather and Dr. Coke Bishops. These he undoubtedly designed should ordain others. Mr Mather told us so at the Manchester Conference, but we did not at all understand him. We could not see how a Scotch Presbyterian Bishop could support the Church of England. The mystery was here. By the Church of England was meant the body of Methodists, who were to have the Doctrine and Discipline of the Church of England among them. I can see no way to come to any good settlement but that which I mentioned before. The District meetings do not answer the end at all. My very soul is weary of them. And in reality we have no government. I do therefore most sincerely wish that Dr. Coke and Dr. Mather may be allowed to be what they are, Bishops. That they should ordain two more chosen by the Conference. That these four should have the government put into their hands, for one year, each one in his own District. They being stationed, one suppose in London, one in Bristol, one in Leeds and one in Newcastle. We can give them what degree of power we please, but I would not cramp them. If any of them should abuse their powers, woe be to them, for they would never be intrusted with it any more. And even supposing these four had authority to station the Preachers, who would have any cause to fear? Not a man in Connection who is good for anything. It is only a parcel of poor worthless creatures that we do not know where to find a place for, that will have any occasion to shrink back from this plan. I am so weary of Districts and of the shadow of being a Chairman that I would give my vote that either Mr. Mather or Dr. Coke should be King in our Israel rather than that we should be as we are.

We must have Ordination among us at any rate. We have so many little, very little, men in the connection. Men who would quite disgrace that sacred Ordinance were they to have anything to do with it.

(b)

The following considerations weigh very much with me. Ever since the death of Mr. Wesley we all know that the trustees have been trying to lessen our influence with the people, and as far as they can prevail here they at the same time lessen our usefulness also. We all know that of late their avowed design has been to divide us and they have done all they could in order to it. Those trustees at Bristol have got possession of a most extravagant degree of power, committed to them by the owner of those premises when he did not understand what he was doing, which they would never part with, no not to the owner of the premises himself, although oft entreated so to do. They have now without any good or lawful reason exercised this unjust power in excluding a man of God, a faithful minister of Christ, a man of long approved integrity, none more so, that I know of in the whole Connection, from preaching in their Chapels, although appointed by the Conference. And will Mr. Benson sanction this? Can any Methodist preacher countenance this! Here I stand and wonder. Why so! What will be the consequence if you suffer these trustees to exercise their power? Why, they will no doubt exercise the same power in all time coming. And then please them with preachers if you can. How many then will you find in the whole Connection that you will be suffered to station in Bristol? Will J. Brittle or Frank Wrigley stand the first chance? I fear not. But bad as this is, it is not the worst. It will no sooner be known that the trustees in Bristol exercise this power in the choice of preachers, but all the large towns in the kingdom will claim the same power, and whether their Deeds give it to them or not, they will use it. Witness the trustees of Stockport in the case of poor Billy Simpson last year. You know how this is so.

(c)

The business of the Lord's Supper is settled. The leading men on each side are agreed, or nearly so. It will not be Messrs Mather, Thompson and Benson against Pawson, Hanby and Taylor etc etc. No! These will be one! And who is to stand against them? Kilham and Company!! Alas! They know not what they are about – look at their influence and connexions!

(d)

If it be matter of astonishment that the Methodist conference should submit to such decrees as this, there are several things to be observed on the subject. 1. Many of the preachers protessed against this rule, and would not on any account vote for it. 2. Others were satisfied with the explaination of the word separation, which Messrs Thompson, Benson, and others gave of it. 'They *positively declared*, that it was not one, two, five, ten, twenty, a hundred, or any number of persons leaving the society, that made a separation, unless they had a preacher at their head'. 3. Others submitted to it, under a firm persuasion, that it would only continue for one year: or at *the farthest*, for two or three years. 4. But the greatest part of those who voted for it, did it to prevent a division of the preachers and the people. Not one in twenty would have submitted to such an *arbitrary rule*, if it had not been with a view to preserve *some kind of peace* amongst us.

412

I forbear examining the 6th, 7th, 8th, 9th, and 10th, rules of pacification: as well as the 3rd, and 4th articles of the addenda: with several things, that may be found in the second part, concerning discipline. Let every impartial reader make his own reflections upon them. Most of them sufficiently prove, that we are not yet come out of Egypt. If we are freed from the house of bondage, they only declare us to be in the wilderness, on our way to the promised land.

Let us conclude this part of the pamphlet with a few reflections, which naturally arise from the subject we have been considering.

1   Liberty of conscience, is one of the most valuable blessings which a people can enjoy. It leaves every person perfectly free to examine all the doctrines and discipline of the different national churches, and dissenting congregations, that are established. Creeds, articles and confessions of faith, homilies, &c, &c, are all brought to the law and the testimony; and every thing is rejected, that does not agree with the word of God: which is the only and sufficient rule, both of our faith and practice. For a man to live where this blessing is enjoyed, and not to avail himself of its advantages, discovers such a want of respect for himself, as can never be sufficiently execrated, If bigotry, superstition, attachment to modes of worship, which have not been examined; and to creeds and articles of faith, which never have been seriously thought upon, should compose our religion in such a state, will it not be to our present condemnation, and to our eternal reproach?

2   In these nations we have a very great portion of liberty of conscience. Our excellent laws allow us to prove all things in religion, and to hold fast that which is good. If we are *forced* to support the church by tithes and offerings, we are not constrained to be members of her body. We may renounce her doctrines and discipline with impunity, and worship God according to the desire of our heart. Our fathers looked with *earnest desire* to these days, and rejoiced at the prospect of the followers of Jesus, ever being blessed with them.

3   Is it not amazingly strange, that any sect or party should refuse to give to their brethren, what the laws of our country so cheerfully allow? Is it not cruelty and persecution to restrict one another in those things, which are not essential to the salvation of the soul? Does not every man that would force his brother, to submit to any modes of worship, against his own mind, act the part of a spiritual tyrant, and lord it over God's heritage? We detest the conduct of persecuting Neros, and all the bloody actions of the great Whore of Babylon, and yet in our measure, we tread in their steps. If a man of any sect or party, should force his creed of faith upon us, and constrain us to worship in his way contrary to our will, or prevent us from worshiping according to the convictions of our own mind, he is a Nero to us – a true son of the great Whore of Babylon.

(e)

Wednesday morning, 27. After a few preliminary observations, it was ordered that the Secretary should read over the Articles again with the answers, which was accordingly done, and Mr. Kilham was called upon to add to these answers anything which he should think proper. He made a few additions, but nothing material. He was then ordered to withdraw, and the Conference, having considered the case, ordered,

That any letters which were in Mr. Kilham's favour should be read, but that no letters *against* him with respect to his plans &c. should be read, which was done accordingly. The charges were then read over again one by one, and the question put on each. They were all unanimously pronounced *Unproved* and *Slanderous*. The following Motion was then made. 'Whereas Mr. Kilham has brought several charges against Mr. Wesley and the body of preachers, of a scandalous and criminal nature which charges he declared he could prove, and yet on examination he could not prove one of them; and also considering the disunion, strife &c. which he has occasioned, we adjudge him unworthy of being a member of the Methodist connexion. This was carried unanimously, not one person against it. He was then called and the judgment read to him. Thus this business is ended, unless he repent, which would rejoice my heart; but there is no appearance of it at present. Thus, my dearest, I have given you a hasty account of this painful matter. The preachers are as the heart of one man.

(f)
Poor George Ferguson was almost raving. He told Mr E the first preacher that came to his house when he was got to bed, he would load a pistol and go to his bedside and say, were you one that lifted a hand against Mr K and then present the pistol to his head and make him beg pardon or blow his brains out. Amidst our sorrows we had may a hearty laugh at the various scenes that passed in different families. Mr E endeavoured to preach moderation to all that came to him but it was in vain to very many. The Morpeth and Placey [sic] friends have determined not to receive the preachers ... Mr Hunter read Dr Coke's letter in this chapel, which grieved the people exceedingly. Many went out, others threw open the doors to disturb. Everything at present wears ... the face of confusion.

(g)

May 9 1797

[W]e are not looking to Conference, we have no more to do with Conference than with the Inquisition in Spain. We are now going on our way peaceably ... We the Trustees have taken possession of our New Chapel in Maguire St for our preacher to preach in. ... We are now out of connexion with them ...

(h)
[W]e took the field ourselves, and determined that we would no longer maintain our union with those Trustees, neither would we pay class-money or quarterage towards the support of the preachers under their superintendence, until some sort of justice should be done to our cause ... we accordingly formed ourselves into a society at Commonhall lane ... since 30th October 1793 the local preachers have ... preached for us ...

(i)

Dear Brethren,
                                                        August 7, 1797
                                                        Leeds,

We think it our duty to inform you by the earliest opportunity, of the measures we have taken, in order to satisfy those of our Brethren, who have been made more or less uneasy by sundry publications circulated through the Societies: and we trust, that on a serious consideration of the regulations we have agreed to at this Conference, you will see, that the sacrifices in respect to authority which we have made on the part of the whole Body of Travelling Preachers, evidence our willingness to meet our Brethren in every thing which is consistent with the existence of the Methodist Discipline, and our readiness to be their servants for Jesu's sake.

(j)

They have been doing all in their power in London. They have had meetings at a man's house in Wood Street for some time. ... A few of the lowest of the Local preachers and a few of the Workhouse preachers met with them, and could they have made a party, they would no doubt have invited Kilham. But if I am rightly informed, they are nearly broken up ...

(k)

We go on poorly, but have no doubt but we should do better had we preaching. The last meeting we had (on Tuesday last) it was agreed that we were to look out for a place & count the ... costs & then you will hear more from us. There are some openings about 8 or 10 miles round London, but it is thought best to begin here first ...

Worship

Document VI.56

Quaker Thoughts on Worship

These are the thoughts of Benjamin Holme, for whom see Document II.1 above, from his *A Serious Call in Christian Love To all People To turn to the Spirit of Christ in Themselves*, 1753, pp. 107–11. He considers the place of women in worship.

3.   *Concerning* Worship

We live in a Time in which there is great Difference, even among those called *Christians*, about Religion and the Worship of God. Difference about Religion and the Worship of God is no new Thing; the *Jews* and *Samaritans* differed to such a Degree, that it seems they did not deal with one another. It is very much amiss, where Religion sours People, and makes them rigid, and bitter one against another.[1] *Christianity is Love*, and he that is a *Christian* in his Heart, is full of Pity and good Will to them that are under a Mistake in Matters of Religion; and the worst that he wishes for all such, is, that the Lord may direct them right; for they that have the Mind of Christ, would not have any Soul to err, either in Faith or Practice. Our Saviour in his Discourse with the Woman of *Samaria*, has clearly described the true and spiritual Worship; *But the Hour cometh, and now is, when the true Worshippers shall worship the Father in Spirit and in Truth; for the Father seeketh such to worship him. God is a Spirit, and they that worship him, must worship him in Spirit and in Truth.*[2] Now we believe, that as God is a Spirit, he may be truly worshipped, as we are gathered in his Spirit, though there be not a Word outwardly spoken among us, as Christ said, *Where two or three are gathered together in my Name, there am I in the Midst of them;*[3] and the holy Prophet faith, *They that wait upon the Lord, shall renew their Strength: They shall mount up with Wings as Eagles; they shall run, and not be weary; and they shall walk, and not faint.*[4] Although I believe a great many pious good *Christians* can say, as they have waited humbly upon the Lord, in true Silence of all Flesh, with their Minds truly staid upon him, they have enjoyed that divine Comfort which has been beyond what they could express in Words; yet this of *silent Waiting* is a great Mystery to many People. There is a divine Teacher near Men, even in their own Hearts, which is sufficient to teach them, as they take heed thereto. It is to be feared, that many People too much depend upon the Teachings of Men, and neglect the divine Teacher in themselves; *But the Anointing which ye have received of him, abideth in you; and ye need not that any Man teach you, but as the fame Anointing teacheth you of all Things, and is Truth, and is no Lie; and even as it hath taught you, ye shall abide in him.*[5] Now we understand the holy Man here, to speak in a large Sense; he told them, that they needed not that any

Man taught them, but as the fame Anointing taught them, &c. We do very much own outward Preaching and Praying, where it proceeds from this divine Anointing. If it please God to speak by this through any Instruments, whether Male or Female, we believe there should be Liberty amongst us, for every one to speak as he requires it of them; *For ye may all prophesy one by one, that all may learn, and all may be comforted; and the Spirit of the Prophets are subject to the Prophets.*[6] *And they were all filled with the Holy Ghost, and began to speak with other Tongues, as the Spirit gave them Utterance.*[7] We believe the true Preaching, and Praying, is that which proceeds from the Holy Spirit; *We know not what we should pray for as we ought, but the Spirit itself maketh Intercession for us, with Groanings which cannot be uttered.*[8] *I will pray with the Spirit, and I will pray with the Understanding also: I will sing with the Spirit, and I will sing with the Understanding also.*[9]

This is the Preaching, and Praying, and Singing, which we own, that is by the Direction and Assistance of the Holy Spirit. Now some being against Womens *speaking* in the Church, urge what the Apostle faith, *Let your Women keep Silence in the Churches, for it is not permitted unto them to speak; but they are commanded to be under Obedience, as also faith the Law, and if they will learn any Thing, let them ask their Husbands at Home, for it is a Shame for Women to speak in the Church.*[10] *Let the Women learn in Silence with all Subjection; but I suffer not a Woman to teach, nor to usurp Authority over the Man, but to be in Silence.*[11] We do not take this to be a prohibiting holy Women to speak, whom the Lord calls thereto; and I think it would be very much amiss to say, that the Apostle *Paul* was against holy Women speaking, whom God called to speak; but such troublesome and unruly Women as disturbed the Church by their Questions, and usurped Authority over the Man, which he was against, we are against. If the Apostle *Paul* had been against holy Women Praying and Prophesying, why should he lay down a Rule how they ought to behave themselves when they Pray or Prophesy? *But every Woman that Prayeth or Prophesieth with her Head uncovered, dishonoureth her Head.*[12] And he commends to the Believers divers good Women, *I commend unto you* Phebe *our Sister, which is a Servant of the Church.*[13] All good Ministers of Jesus Christ, are Servants to the Church. And he advised his true Yoke-fellow, *to help those Women which laboured with him in the Gospel*; so that he was an Encourager of holy Women, that laboured in the Gospel: We read, that *Anna* spoke in the Temple, *and she was a Widow of about Fourscore and Four Years, which departed not from the Temple, but served God with Fastings and Prayers, Night and Day; and she coming in that instant, gave Thanks likewise unto the Lord, and spake of him to all them that looked for Redemption in* Jerusalem.[14] And we read, that *Philip* the Evangelist had four Daughters, Virgins, and they did all Prophesy. And *Joel* also prophesied that God would pour forth of his Spirit, *&c. But this is that,* saith *Peter, which was spoken by the Prophet* Joel; *and it shall come to pass in the last Days, saith God, I will pour out of my Spirit upon all Flesh, and your Sons and your Daughters shall prophesy, and your young Men shall see Visions, and your old Men shall dream Dreams, and on my Servants, and on my Handmaidens, I will pour out in those Days of my Spirit, and they shall prophesy.*[15] Now although Prophesying is several Times taken in the Scripture for foretelling Things to come; read *Jeremiah,*[16] and several other

417

Prophesies of the Prophets; yet it is also taken for edifying the Church; *But he that prophesieth, speaketh unto Men to Edification, and Exhortation, and Comfort. He that speaketh in an unknown Tongue, edifieth himself; but he that prophesieth, edifieth the Church.*[17] *Mary* was sent by Christ to declare of his Resurrection, *Jesus saith unto her, touch me not, for I am not yet ascended to my Father; but go to my Brethren; and say unto them, I ascend unto my Father, and your Father, and to my God, and your God.*[18] And the Woman of *Samaria* was instrumental to bring many of her Neighbours to believe in Christ; she said, *Come see a Man that has told me all that ever I did, is not this the Christ? And many of the* Samaritans *of that City believed on him, for the Saying of the Woman, which testified, he told me all that ever I did.*[19] Now it is to Christ, as he inwardly appears in Men's Hearts by his Light and Spirit, that we desire all may come. It is he that shews Men when they do amiss. Christ within, *which is the Hope of the Saints Glory,*[20] is a great Mystery to many People. *When it pleased God*, saith the Apostle *Paul, to reveal his Son in me, that I might preach him among the* Heathen, *immediately I conferred not with Flesh and Blood:*[21] Here was the Son of God revealed in him. Now that all may have a right Understanding of the Things of God, we desire that they may come to him that hath the Key of *David*, that opens the Mysteries or the Kingdom of God to Men.

Notes

1. John iv. 9
2. John iv. 23, 24
3. Mat. xviii. 20
4. Isa. xl. 31
5. 1 John ii. 27
6. 1 Cor. xiv. 31, 32
7. Acts ii. 4
8. Rom. viii. 26
9. 1 Cor. xiv. 15
10. 1 Cor. xiv. 34, 35
11. 1 Tim. ii. 11, 12
12. 1 Cor. x. 5
13. Rom. xvi. 1, to 13
14. Luke ii. 37, 38
15. Acts ii. 16, 17, 18.
16. Jer. xxi.
17. 1 Cor. xiv. 3, 4.
18. John xx. 17.
19. John iv, 29, 39.
20. Col. i. 27.
21. Gal. i. 16.

Document VI.57

John Taylor on Prayer in Worship

A letter dated 16 October 1760 was sent to a number of brethren by a group of Presbyterian ministers in Liverpool, requesting assistance towards the production of 'a rational liturgy' Among the recipients of this letter was John Taylor, who took exception to the idea of a formal liturgy, however rational, but, on the other hand, while advocating free prayer, did so 'only so far as it is rational'.

For Taylor see Document II.13 above. The following extracts are from his *The Scripture Account of Prayer, In an Address to the Dissenters in Lancashire; Occasioned By a new Liturgy some Ministers, of that County, are composing for the Use of a Congregation at Liverpool*, London, 1761, pp. 7–8, 10–11, 12–13, 20, 22–3.

My dear countrymen,

It is the peculiar honor and high distinction of the human nature, that we are the only creatures in the earth capable of converse with the most high God; which, as he is the most consummate perfection, must be the noblest use of our rational powers; and, as he is the only source of all happiness, must be of infinite importance to our well-being. We have not one faculty of body or mind, nor any one injoyment of life, absolutely in our own hands; all our springs are in God, and upon him we continually depend for life, and breath, and all things. This naturally directs our defires and expectations, under all present infirmities, deficiencies and difficulties, to the goodness and tender mercies of our almighty Father.

Prayer is a duty of natural religion; but it is most clearly explained, strongly inculcated, and highly recommended in the holy Scriptures, by the most illustrious examples. ...

But, my Friends, it is become a matter of some debate amongst you, in what method Prayer, especially publick Prayer, is most properly performed; whether by reading Prayers already composed, confining our thoughts to the sense of what we read; or by free and extempore Prayer, dictated by the sense, state and disposition of our own minds, and accommodated to any occasion or event of life.

In order to form a judgment upon this point, it should be previously observed.

I.   That Prayer doth not properly consist in language, how curious and elegant soever, but in the real sense, and sincere desires of the mind. It is the heart, not the tongue that prays. It is the true and sincere devotion of the heart only, that can make our Prayers acceptable to God. ...

II.   That by *free* or *extempore* Prayer is not to be understood any crude unpremeditated effusion, in an entire dependance upon some supposed sudden extraordinary motion or suggestion of the Spirit of God. We are not incouraged, at least, in our age of the Church, to expect the assistance of the Spririt, but in conjunction with our own sincere endeavors: and *free* or *extempore* Prayer, in the just and rational sense of it, supposes a due degree of previous care to funish the mind with proper materials and language, digested into good order and connection, that a person may be enabled regularly to adapt his thoughts and expressions, not only to general topics, or such things as are common to all cafes and Christians, but also to special providences, and the particular circumstances of those, who join with us in this act of divine worship. This I call the *gift* of Prayer, which is but an imperfect attainment, if it is not attended with the *spirit* of Prayer; meaning thereby a praying frame of heart, or that pious temper whereby a person is inclined and disposed to lift up his foul to God, and to hold communion with him; not excluding such aids of the holy Spirit as are promised to the faithful discharge of all Christian duties.

These things being stated and explained, it stands very clear in my thoughts, and appears to be very reasonable concluded by the body of Dissenters, that free Prayer, dictated by the sense, state, and disposition of a mind duely prepared for it, is the most eligible. ...

Happy, beyond expression, is the man, who is thus qualified for communion with God. He worships him in spirit and truth, in the pure, spiritual, lively devotion of the foul, and stands in no need of other assistance. His heart is his Prayer-Book, vastly preferable to the most curious compositions: he hath attained to some perfection of beauty in this service; he feels the pleasure and power of it in his own breast, and shews it before men in all its loveliness and attractive force. ...

Reading of Prayers cannot give a Minister any character of esteem in a Dissenting Congregation, where it is considered as a very low manner of performing the office. If a Minister prays by heart or memory which is the least that is done among Dissenters, he must at the same time shew some previous care and application to qualify himself for the duty, and some present thought and attention in the discharge of it, and so may appear to be deserving of some respect; which must arise to a high degree of esteem when the propriety of expression and sentiment, together with the life and servor of utterance, plainly indicate that the address proceeds from the immediate conceptions and sense of a well prepared and truly pious and devout mind. Thus it is an admirable, excellent, and honorable gift. And the Apostle exhorts us *earnestly to covet the best gifts.* I Cor. xii. 31.

Document VI.58

Pulpit Dress between the Times

The following self-explanatory anecdote is recounted by Robert Halley in *Lancashire: Its Puritanism and Nonconformity*, Manchester: Tubbs and Brook, 1869, II, p. 424 n. For Halley (1796–1876), Congregational minister and principal of New College, London (1857–72), see DEB, DNB.

Letter of Rev. Mr. Blake and MS. Of Rev. Richard Bowdon, cited in Dr. Raffles's *Collections*. Dr. Raffles has preserved a curious anecdote of this good Welshman which, if not true, deserves to be. It is given on the authority of one of his successors. During the time of his ministry, the black cap of the puritan minister was going out of fashion in genteel congregations. Some of the young people of Darwen had been to Liverpool, and had seen the graceful wigs which polite ministers wore in that town. Esteeming their minister worthy of so honourable a decoration, they generously purchased one for him. The old gentleman, pleased with this mark of respect from his young friends, somewhat incautiously, without consulting the elders, appeared the next Sunday doing duty in his fashionable wig. It was a sad scandal to the elders. Was their minister conforming to the fashions of the world? Or was it a new sort of conformity to the Church? Had he appeared in a surplice, they could not have been more offended. They left the place, and in the afternoon their seats were vacant. The good minister was sorely distressed. He wished to conciliate both old and young, and succeeded by appearing the next Sunday with his black cap over his wig, the graceful curls of which hung beneath it. Endeavouring to 'please all men in all things,' he seems to have succeeded.

Document VI.59

William Hazlitt on Samuel Taylor Coleridge's Sermon

The essayist William Hazlitt (1778–1828), son of a Unitarian minister, records an occasion on which he heard Samuel Taylor Coleridge (1772–1834), then in his Unitarian phase, preach.

For Hazlitt see BCE, DNB. For Coleridge see BCE, DH, DNB, ODCC. The following extract is from P. P. Howe, ed., *The Complete Works of William Hazlitt*, London: J.M. Dent, 1933, p. 108.

It was in January, 1798, that I rose one morning before daylight, to walk ten miles in the mud, and went to hear this celebrated person preach. Never, the longest day I have to live, shall I have such another walk as this cold, raw, comfortless one, in the winter of the year 1798. *Il y a des impressions que ni le tems ni les circonstances peuvent effacer. Dusse-je vivre des siècles entiers, le doux tems de ma jeunesse ne peut renaître pour moi, ni s'effacer jamais dans ma memoire.* When I got there, the organ was playing the 100th psalm, and, when it was done, Mr. Coleridge rose and gave out his text, 'And he went up into the mountain to pray, HIMSELF, ALONE.' As he gave out his text, his voice 'rose like a steam of rich distilled perfumes,' and when he came to the two last words, which he pronounced loud deep, and distinct, it seemed to me, who was then young, as if the sounds had echoed from the bottom of the human heart, and as if that prayer might have floated in solemn silence through the universe. The idea of St. John came into mind, 'of one crying in the wilderness, who had his loins girt about, and whose food was locusts and wild honey.' The preacher then launched into his subject, like an eagle dallying with the wind.

The sermon was upon peace and war; upon church and state – not their alliance, but their separation – on the spirit of the world and the spirit of Christianity, not as the same, but as opposed to one another. He talked of those who had 'inscribed the cross of Christ on banners dripping with human gore.' He made a poetical and pastoral excursion, – and to shew the fatal effects of war, drew a striking contrast between the simple shepherd boy, driving his team afield, or sitting under the hawthorn, piping to his flock, 'as though he should never be old,' and the same poor country-lad, crimped, kidnapped, brought into town, made drunk at an alehouse, turned into a wretched drummer-boy, with his hair sticking on end with powder and pomatum, a long cue at his back, and tricked out in the loathsome finery of the profession of blood.

> 'Such were the notes our once-lov'd poet sung.'

And for myself, I could not have been more delighted if I had heard the music of the spheres. Poetry and Philosophy had met together. Truth and Genius had embraced, under the eye and with the sanction of Religion. This was even beyond my hopes. I returned home well satisfied …

Document VI.60

A Visiting Preacher's Disquiet

In 1772 John Reynolds, Independent minister at Haverhill, Suffolk, whence he proceeded to Camomile Street, London (1773–1803), preached at Bishop's Stortford. In his diary he records his disquiet at the demeanour of the congregation. For Reynolds (1739–1803) see J. A. Jones, ed., *Bunhill Memorials*, London: James Paul, 1849, pp. 227–8. The following extract is from M. G. Lewis, *The Congregational Church Water Lane, Bishop's Stortford 1662–1962*, pp. 13–14.

Lord's Day, Oct. 18, 1772. … Went to Meeting – Preached from Psalm 37, 25. The people dead (?). O how awful to sleep and die under such a ministry – found but little Liberty in speaking to them. … In the afternoon upon Phil. 3.3 – was helped to speak close to conscience, to lift up my voice like a trumpet. … This sort of preaching many of them did not relish: it was too alarming, too searching. I could not escape without censure and a sneer. …

Spent evening at Mr. Hawks's. I could not forbear informing them what I had observed today as to behaviour of many in the worship of God and after it. That their treating me with incivility was a small matter, but their contempt of the Gospel was likely to prove a damning sin; and they would find it a weighty matter at last.

My Friends could not help lamenting this from what they had see and observed.

Document VI.61

General Baptist Discord over Hymns

The singing of hymns in worship proved a cause of tension among eighteenth-century General Baptists in the 1730s and 1750s, the more orthodox Northamptonshire churches being among the most concerned. Some permitted metrical psalms only, others argued that the singing of a mixed multitude of believers and unbelievers was not tolerable. When recourse was had to the General Assembly the official reply urged tolerance and appealed to the freedom of congregations to find their own way on this matter. Particular Baptists do not seem to have been troubled by the inhibitions noted to anything like the same degree.

In the following note reprinted from *Lancashire: Its Puritanism and Nonconformity*, Manchester: Tubbs and Brook, 1869, II, p. 327, Robert Halley reflects upon Baptist hymn singing.

Taylor, in his *History of the General Baptists* [1818], tells us some of their early churches thus conducted their 'service of song' (vol. i. p. 425). 'The best,' he cites an old authority among them, 'and for aught I can find, the only certain way to be used to sing the praise of the Lord is this – That such persons as God hath gifted to sing His mighty acts, should have their liberty and convenient opportunity to celebrate the high praises of God *one by one*.' If any man 'had a psalm' he was to have liberty to sing it, and the others were to 'wait on his gifts,' that is, to be quiet until he had done. This method of singing solo does not seem to have been quite confined to the General Baptists, for, as Taylor himself says, some Particular Baptists separated from the General Baptist church in Paul's Alley, not only on account of difference in doctrine, but also on account of the introduction of singing in concert. The good people of Hill Cliffe were very particular, and would, I doubt not, carefully eschew everything associated with general redemption even singing, if so associated. – See Wilson's *History of Dissenting Churches*, [1810], vol. iii. p. 230.

Document VI.62

Caleb Ashworth's Guidance to Musicians

For Ashworth see Document I.11 above. Extract (a) is from the preface to his *A Collection of Tunes Suited to the several Metres commonly used in Publick Worship, set in Four Parts, and with an Introduction to the Art of Singing and Plain Composition*, London, n.d., pp. 22–3. Extract (b) is from *A Collection of Tunes: Part II. Containing Anthems and Other Tunes, More proper to Entertain and Improve those who have made some Proficiency in the Art of Singing, than to be introduced into public Worship*, 1762, no. 15. The tune is arranged by Ashworth, and the words are possibly his. The carol may be heard on the CD *While Shepheras Watched: Christmas Music from English Parish Churches, 1740–1830*, Hyperion CDA66924. As Sally Drage and Peter Holman explain in the CD notes, Nonconformist country psalmody was generally written in three parts with the melody in the tenor line, though with the expectation that the upper two parts would be doubled at the octave, making five parts in all.

(a)

A few Miscellaneous Advices in regard to Singing.

1.   Let not a learner covet to run on too fast; but make himself perfect in rising and falling by degrees and intervals, and each tune, both as to the air and time, before he proceeds further.

2.   Let a learner's first care be to sing true, and to give the just sound of the notes; he may afterwards learn graces and ornaments. In regard to these the best instructor is a kind of musical taste, a good imagination and ear. These may be improved by observing a master who has an agreeable air and manner; but can receive little assistance from rules. No. 10. is the direction commonly given for making a *trill*, which is usual at the last note but one in the upper part before a close, and in some other cases. It is made by alternately sounding two notes as long as the time will allow, always beginning, and resting a little, on the highest and ending somewhat distinctly on the lowest.

3.   Let every person take the part to which his voice is adapted. If one whose organs are best suited to the bass will sing tenor, he hangs as a weight on the others, is sure to sink the tune, and his voice must be rough and forced.

4.   A person should never exert all the strength of his voice, as if he aimed to sing as loud as he was able. This destroys the musick of the voice, and makes it impossible to pass on with sufficient swiftness, where the notes are short. Catching at a note, and jerking along, are likewife disagreeable. There is a kind of ease and seeming negligence, in which consists the beauty of singing.

5.   It is particularly disagreeable to conclude a line, &c. with a strong rough voice. The sound should not break off abruptly, but die away gradually. All the parts should gently cease together; but it is more especially wrong when the sound of the upper parts is heard after the bass.

6.   Some persons insensibly contract an awkward distortion of face, or attitude of body. This will scarce ever be cured, unless and observer will frequently, and in an obliging manner, acquaint them with it: and they are willing to receive the hint kindly, and make an early reformation.

7.   Many good singers have an unhappy way of pronouncing the words; some mumble so as scarce to make any articulate sound; some have an awkward, vulgar pronunciation; and others, through inattention, continually put one word for another. These faults should be early and carefully guarded against.

8.   A wrong pronounciation is most discernable when it affects the beginning of a line: yet it is more difficult to pronounce the first syllable true than any other, especially if it begins with a vowel. Care and pains at first will prevent it. For want of being aware or attending to it, some always begin such lines with the consonant with which the last ended, and others always begin them with a T, and M, a Y &c. so that if the first syllable begins with a vowel you are sure to hear the horrible sound of tau, mnau, yau, &c.

9.   It cannot be thought amiss to conclude an essay intended to assist persons in learning to sing with a view to conduct this exercise with more propriety on sacred occasions, by reminding the reader that singing is an act of religious worship. While persons are learning the art, indeed, they can scarce be considered as ingaged in a devout exercise. If therefore they choose to sing a tune in the words of a psalm, it is most proper to choose those that are not peculiarly devotional. Such are the verses printed pl. 5, &c. But when it is performed as a part of worship, the utmost care should be taken, not only to avoid all levities and indecencies of carriage, which are intolerable; but to adopt no expressions which we cannot conscientiously use, to enter thoroughly into the sentiments of the psalm, and to have the heart affected with them. Thus singing with the understanding and the affections, we make melody in our hearts unto the Lord; but if otherwise, whatever harmony our voice may make, we affront and provoke almighty God. Happy will it be if this hint is attended to, whatever else in this essay is overlooked or forgotten.

(b)

Document VI.63

From Distinction to Doggerel: Representative Eighteenth-Century Hymns

The proposition 'Hymns were the creeds of the Nonconformists' has the status of a truism in the minds of some. It cannot be denied that much doctrine was communicated to, and affirmed by, large numbers of people through hymns. Scripture passages, the cycle of the natural year, the seasons of the Christian Year, national rejoicing and disasters, the issues of life, the aspirations of the believer – these were among many inspirations to hymn writing. But hymns could also be used to make polemical doctrinal points, and on the whole these are the ones which have not found their way into modern hymnals. Many of the hymns of Isaac Watts and Charles Wesley live on and are widely used across the Christian denominations. Other hymns have remained within the traditions within which they were written. There is no need to reprint Watts's 'When I survey the wondrous Cross', Doddridge's 'O God of Bethel, by whose hand Thy people still are fed', Wesley's 'Christ the Lord is risen today', William Williams's 'Guide me, O Thou great Jehovah', or the Baptist John Fawcett's 'Blest be the tie that binds'. Instead there follow eight hymns designed to remind readers of lesser known hymns by Watts and Doddridge (a) and (b); a strongly – even technically – doctrinal hymn of Charles Wesley (c); the Baptist Benjamin Wallin's hymn on the call to the ministry (d); verse two from a hymn based on Ephesians 6; 11–13 in which Joseph Hart (1712–68), the Independent minister and hymn writer (for whom see DEB, DH, DNB), moves almost imperceptibly from biblical exposition to high Calvinist technicalities (e); another of Hart's in which he marries the injunctions of Scripture with the orders of society (f); a characteristic hymn by the Baptist Anne Steele (1717–78) – one of many women hymn writers of the period, for whom see DEB, HD, DNB (g); and finally the majestic missionary hymn (now suspect in some circles on the ground of its alleged triumphalism, and its assumption that everything which is not Christian is gloomy and dark) by William Williams, Pantycelyn (h).

(a)

> There is a land of pure delight,
> Where saints immortal reign;
> Infinite day excludes the night,
> And pleasures banish pain.

2   There everlasting spring abides,
> And never-withering flowers;
> Death, like a narrow sea, divides
> This heavenly land from ours.

3   Sweet fields beyond the swelling flood
> Stand dressed in living green;
> So to the Jews old Canaan stood,
> While Jordan rolled between.

4   But timorous mortals start and shrink
> To cross this narrow sea,
> And linger shivering on the brink,
> And fear to launch away.

5   O could we make our doubts remove,
> Those gloomy doubts that rise,
> And see the Canaan that we love
> With unbeclouded eyes:

6   Could we but climb where Moses stood,
        And view the landscape o'er,
    Not Jordan's stream, nor death's cold flood,
        Should fright us from the shore.

(b)

    My gracious Lord, I own Thy right
        To every service I can pay;
    And call it my supreme delight
    To hear Thy dictates and obey.

2   What is my being but for Thee,
        Its sure support, its noblest end,
    Thy ever-smiling face to see,
        And serve the cause of such a friend?

3   I would not breathe for worldly joy,
        Or to increase my worldly good,
    Nor future days or powers employ
        To spread a sounding name abroad:

4   'Tis to my Saviour I would live,
        To Him who for my ransom died;
    Nor could untainted Eden give
        Such bliss as blossoms at His side.

5   His work my hoary age shall bless,
        When youthful vigour is not more,
    And my last hour of life confess
        His love hath animating power.

(c)

1   Let earth and heaven combine,
        Angels and men agree,
    To praise in songs divine
        The incarnate Deity,
    Our God contracted to a span,
    Incomprehensibly made man.

2   He laid His glory by,
        He wrapped Him in our clay;
    Unmarked by human eye,
        The latent Godhead lay;
    Infant of days He here became,
    And bore the mild Immanuel's name.

3   Unsearchable the love
        That hath the Saviour brought;
    The grace is far above
        Or man or angel's thought:
    Suffice for us that God, we know,
    Our God, is manifest below.

4   He deigns in flesh to appear,
        Widest extremes to join;
    To bring our vileness near,
        And make us all divine:
    And we the life of God shall know,
    For God is manifest below.

5   Made perfect first in love,
        And sanctified by grace,
    We shall from earth remove,
        And see His glorious face:
    Then shall His love be fully showed,
    And man shall then be lost in God.

(d)
1   My soul, thy Saviour's call attend,
        With trembling His commands revere;
    Arise, saith He, for thee I send:
        To My elect My Gospel bear.

2   Unlearn'd, my lips can never speak
        As Thy great oracles become:
    Ah, Lord, wilt Thou a child so weak
        Employ to bring Thy chosen home?

3   Of all Thy servants I'm the least
        To whom Thou hast Thy grace made known,
    And most unworthy to attest
        The glorious Gospel of Thy Son.

4   Thy sov'reign will, O Lord, be done,
        I yield myself to Thy command;
    The meanest instruments are known
        To prosper in Thy glorious hand.

5   Thy promise yelds me great support,
        'My grace sufficient is for thee';
    Thou art my refuge and my fort:

Sufficient is Thy grace for me.

(e)

Bind thy golden girdle round thee,
　　Truth to keep thee firm and tight;
Never shall the foe confound thee,
　　While the truth maintains thy fight,
Righteousness within thee rooted
　　May appear to take thy part;
But let righteousness imputed
　　Be the breastplate of thy heart.

(f)

1　Christians, in your sev'ral stations,
　　Dutiful to all relations,
　　　　Give to each his proper due.
　　Let not their unkind behaviour
　　Make you disobey your Saviour:
　　　　His command's the rule for you.

2　Parents, be to children tender;
　　Children, full obedience render
　　　　To your parents in the Lord.
　　Never slight nor disrespect them;
　　Nor through pride, when old, reject them!
　　　　'Tis the precept of the Word.

3　Wives, to husbands, yield subjection;
　　Husbands, with a kind affection,
　　　　Cherish as yourselves your wives.
　　Masters, rule with moderation,
　　Sway'd by justice, not by passion;
　　　　To the Scriptures square your lives.

4　Servants, serve your masters truly,
　　Not unfaithful, nor unruly,
　　　　To the good, nor to the bad;
　　Not refusing what you're bidden,
　　Nor replying when you're chidden;
　　　　'Tis the ordinance of God.

5　This shall solve th' important question,
　　Whether thou'rt a real Christian,
　　　　Better than each golden dream.
　　Better far than lip-expression,

429

Towering notions, great profession;
    This shall shew your love to Him.

(g)

1   The Lord forgets his wonted grace,
     Afflicted Zion said;
   My God withdraws his smiling face,
     Withdraws his heavenly aid.

2   Shall the kind mother's gentle breast
     No soft emotion share;
   But, every tender thought supprest,
     Forget her infant care?

3   The helpless child, that oft her eyes,
     Have watch'd with anxious thought,
   While her fond breast appeas'd his cries-
     And can he be forgot?

4   Strange as it is, yet this may be,
     For creature-love is frail;
   But thy Creator's love to thee,
     O Zion, cannot fail.

5   No, thy dear name engraven stands,
     In characters of love,
   On thy almighty Father's hands;
     And never shall remove.

6   Before his ever-watchful eye
     Thy mournful state appears
   And every groan, and every sigh
     Divine compassion hears.

7   These anxious doubts indulge no more,
     Be every fear supprest;
   Unchanging truth and love, and power,
     Command thy cares to rest.

(h)

O'er the gloomy hills of darkness
    Look, my soul; be still, and gaze;
All the promises do travail
    With a glorious day of grace:
       Blessed jubilee!

Let thy glorious morning dawn.

2   Kingdoms wide that sit in darkness,
      Grant them, Lord, Thy glorious light;
  And from eastern coast to western
      May the morning chase the night;
        And redemption,
    Freely purchased, win the day.

3   May the glorious day approaching
      End their night of sin and shame,
  And the everlasting gospel
      Spread abroad Thy holy name
        O'er the borders
    Of the great Immanuel's land.

4   Fly abroad, thou mighty gospel!
      Win and conquer, never cease;
  May thy lasting wide dominion
      Multiply and still increase:
        Sway Thy sceptre,
    Saviour, all the world around.

'The Long Cloud of Witnesses'

Document VI.64

John Howe's Consolations

The eminent Puritan divine John Howe (1630–1705) wrote the following *Consolations to my Wife and other Relations, supposing they hear of my Death.*

For John Howe see DNB, ODCC. The *Consolations* are reprinted from Edmund Calamy's *Life* of Howe, 1724, pp. 65–6.

1.   Whom or what have you lost? A poor Creature that could never be of much use to you.

2.   You are to consider me, not as lost in my prime; but as now I am sensibly under great decays, and not likely to continue long, except some means hitherto not thought on, should have been tried. What a Summer had I of the last? seldom able to walk the Streets; and not only often disabled by Pain, but Weakness. And what great Advantage to you would it have been to see me die? I know not when I have had so much ease and health as in this Journey.

3.   God not only hath determin'd the thing, we must die, but all Circumstances, when and where, and after what manner, and all wisely and well. Why should you be grieved, that he hath done well? Not only well in itself, but well for you, if you love him?

4.   You must e'er long follow, and shall not be always in this World without me.

5.   What there is of Evil in the case, admits of Remedy. Draw so much nearer to God, and cease from Man: Mind Heaven more, and your Loss is made up.

6.   I have thro the Grace of God, preach'd immortal Truth, which will survive, and may be to your Advantage.

7.   As to you who have Dependence upon me for worldly concernments: I was never a good Projector for the World; so the Loss is not great. How many, Dear to God, make a shift in a worse Condition! Forget not the motto, *God will provide*. He that feeds Ravens, and takes care of Sparrows, will he not take care of you? Are you of his Family, and will he not take care of his own? Instead of distrust and repining, give *Thanks* O bless him with all your Soul, that he hath revealed and given himself to you for an everlasting Portion; and whole Covenant is to be your God, and the God of yours.

8.   Let it be some satisfaction to you, that I go willingly, under no dread, with no regret, but with some comfortable Knowledge of my Way and End.

Document VI.65

Samuel Johnson's Tribute to Isaac Watts

'Dictionary' Johnson (1709–84), see DNB, included this sketch of Isaac Watts in his *Lives of the Most Eminent English Poets*, London: Frederick Warne, n.d., pp. 451–2.

As his mind was capacious, his curiosity excursive, and his industry continual, his writings are very numerous, and his subjects various. With his theological works I am only enough acquainted to admire his meekness of opposition, and his mildness of censure. It was not only in his book, but in his mind, that orthodoxy was united with charity.

Of his philosophical pieces, his Logic has been received into the universities, and therefore wants no private recommendation: if he owes part of it to Le Clerc, it must be considered that no man, who undertakes merely to methodise or illustrate a system, pretends to be its author.

In his metaphysical disquisitions, it was observed by the late learned Mr Dyer, that he confounded the idea of *space* with that of *empty space*, and did not consider that though space might be without matter, yet matter being extended could not be without space.

Few books have been perused by me with greater pleasure that his 'Improvement of the Mind', of which the radical principle may indeed be found in Locke's 'Conduct of the Understanding', but they are so expanded and ramified by Watts, as to confer upon him the merit of a work in the highest degree useful and pleasing. Whoever has the care of instructing others may be charged with deficience in his duty if this book is not recommended.

I have mentioned his treatises of theology as distinct from his other productions; but the truth is, that whatever he took in hand, was, by his incessant solicitude for souls, converted to theology. As piety predominated in his mind it is diffused over his works: under his direction it may be truly said *Theologæ Philosophia ancillatur*, philosophy is subservient to evangelical instruction. It is difficult to read a page without learning, or at least wishing, to be better. The attention is caught by indirect instruction, and he that sat down only to reason, is on a sudden compelled to pray. It was therefore with great propriety that, in 1728, he received from Edinburgh and Aberdeen an unsolicited diploma, by which he became a Doctor of Divinity. Academical honours would have more value, if they were always bestowed with equal judgment. He continued many years to study and to preach, and to do good by his instruction and example; till at last the infirmities of age disabled him from the more laborious part of his ministerial functions, and, being no longer capable of public duty, he offered to remit the salary appendant to it; but his congregation would not accept the resignation. By degrees his weakness increased, and at last confined him to his chamber and his bed; where he was worn gradually away without pain, till he expired Nov. 25, 1748, in the seventy-fifth year of his age.

Few men have left behind such purity of character, or such monuments of laborious piety. He has provided instruction for all ages; from those who are lisping their first lessons, to the enlightened readers of Malebranche and Locke; he has left neither corporeal nor spiritual nature unexamined; he has taught the art of reasoning, and the science of the stars. His character therefore, must be formed from the multiplicity and diversity of his attainments, rather than from any single performance; for it would not be safe to claim for him the highest rank in any single denomination of literary dignity; yet perhaps there was nothing in which he would not have excelled, if he had not divided his powers to different pursuits.

As a poet, had he been only a poet, he would probably have stood high among the authors with whom he is now associated. For his judgment was exact, and he noted beauties and faults with very nice discernment; his imagination, as the 'Dacian Battle' proves, was vigorous and active, and the stores of knowledge were large by which his fancy was to be supplied. His ear was well tuned, and his diction was elegant and copious. But his devotional poetry is, like that of others, unsatisfactory. The paucity of its topics enforces perpetual repetition, and the sanctity of the matter rejects the ornaments of figurative diction. It is sufficient for Watts to have done better than others what no man has done well. His poems on other subjects seldom rise higher than might be expected from the amusements of a man of letters, and have different degrees of value as they are more or less laboured, or as the occasion was more or less favourable to invention. He writes too often without regular measures, and too often in blank verse; the rhymes are not always sufficiently correspondent. He is particularly unhappy in coining names expressive of characters. His lines are commonly smooth and easy, and his thoughts always religiously pure; but who is there that, to so much piety and innocence, does not wish for a greater measure of sprightliness and vigour! He is at least one of the few poets with whom youth and ignorance may be safely pleased: and happy will be that reader whose mind is disposed by his verses or his prose, to imitate him in all but his non-conformity, to copy his benevolence to man, and his reverence to God.

Document VI.66

Mercy Doddridge's Letter to Her Children

Mercy Maris was an orphan, born in Worcester but raised by an uncle at Upton-on-Severn. She married Philip Doddrige on 22 December 1730 and died 7 April 1790, aged eighty-two. She wrote as follows to her children following the death of their father in Lisbon on 26 October 1751. The letter is reprinted from John Waddington, *Congregational History 1700–1800*, London: Longmans, Green, 1876, pp. 438–41.

Lisbon, *November* 11, N.S., 1751.
My Dear Children, – How shall I address you, under this awful and melancholy providence. I would fain say something to comfort you; and I hope God will enable me to say something that may alleviate your deep distress. I went out in a firm dependence, that, if Infinite wisdom was pleased to call me out to duties and trials as yet unknown, He would grant me superior aid and strength that would support and

keep me from fainting under them; persuaded that there was no distress or sorrow into which he would lead me, under which His gracious and all-sufficient arm could not support me. He has not disappointed me, nor suffered my heart and eyes directed to Him to fail. 'God all-sufficient, and my only hope,' is my motto; let it be yours. Such indeed have I found Him: and such I verily believe you will find Him too in the time of deep distress.

Oh, my dear children, help me to praise Him! Such supports, such consolations, such comforts has He granted to th meanest of His creatures, that *my mind, at times, is held in perfect astonishment, and is ready to burst into songs of praise, under its most exquisite distress.*

As to outward comforts, God has withheld no good things from me, but has given me all the assistance, and all the supports that the tenderest friendship was capable of affording me, and which I think my dear Northampton friends could not have exceeded. Their prayers are not lost. I doubt not but I am reaping the benefit of them, and hope that you will do the same.

I am returned to good Mr. King's. Be good to poor Mrs. King. It is a debt of gratitude I owe for the great obligations I am under to that worthy family here. Such a solicitude of friendship was surely hardly ever known as I meet with here. I have the offers of friendship more than I can employ, and it gives a real concern to many here that they cannot find out a way to serve me. These are great honours conferred on the dear deceased, and great comforts to me. It is impossible to say how much these mercies are endeared to me, as coming in such an immediate manner from the Divine Hand. To His Name be the praise and glory of all!

And now, my dear children, what shall I say to you? Ours is no common loss. I mourn the best of husbands and of friends removed from this world of sin and sorrow to the regions of immortal bliss and light. What a glory, what a mercy is it that I am enabled with my thoughts to pursue him there! You have lost the dearest and the best of parents, the guide of your youth, and whose pleasure it would have been to have introduced you into life with great advantage. Our loss is great, indeed! But I really think the loss the public has sustained is still greater. But God can never want instruments to carry on His work. Yet, let us be thankful that God ever gave us such a friend; that He has continued him so long with us. Perhaps if we had been to have judged, we should have thought that we, nor the world, could never less have spared him than at the resent time. But I see the hand of Heaven, the appointment of His wise Providence in every step of this awful dispensation. It is His hand that has put the bitter cup into ours; and what does He now expect from us, but a meek, humble, entire submission to His will! We know this is our duty. Let us pray for those aids of His Spirit which can only enable us to attain it. A Father of the fatherless is God in His holy habitation; as such may your eyes be directed to Him! He will support you; and that He may, is not only my daily but hourly prayer.

We have never deserved so great a good as that we have lost; and let us remember, that the best respect we can pay to his memory is to endeavour, as far as we can, to follow his example, to cultivate those amiable qualities that rendered him so justly dear to us and so greatly esteemed by the world. Particularly I would recommend this to my dear Philip. May I have the joy to see him acting the part worthy the relation to so amiable and excellent a parent, whose memory, I hope, will ever be valuable and sacred to him and to us all! Under God, may he be a comfort to me, and a support to his family! Much depends on him. His loss I think peculiarly great. But I know an all-sufficient God can over-rule it as the means of the greatest good to him.

It is impossible for me to tell you how tenderly my heart feels for you all – how much I long to be with you, to comfort you and assist you! Indeed, you are the only inducements I now have left to wish for life, that I may do what little is in my power to form and guide your tender years. For this purpose I take all possible care of my health. I eat, sleep, and converse at times with a tolerable degree of cheerfulness. You, my dears, as the best return you can make me will do the same, that I may not have sorrow upon sorrow. The many kind friends you have around you, I am sure, will not be wanting in giving you all the assistance and comfort that is in their power. My kindest salutations attend them all.

I hope to leave this place in about fourteen or twenty days. But the soonest I can reach Northampton will not be less than six weeks' or two months' time. May God be with you, and give us, though a mournful yet a comfortable meeting! For your sakes, I trust my life will be spared; and I bless God, my mind is under no painful anxiety as to the difficulties and dangers of the voyage. The winds and waves are in His hands, to whom I resign myself, and all that is dearest to me. I know I shall have your prayers, and those of my dearest friends with you.

Farewell, my dearest children. I am your afflicted but most sincere friend and ever-affectionate mother,

M. Doddridge.

Document VI.67

A Son Recovers and a Son Dies

Extract (a), on the serious illness and subsequent recovery of his son, is from the *Diary* of James Clegg, ed. V. S. Doe, Chesterfield: Derbyshire Record Society, pt. I, p. 98 (30 October 1730), and part II, p. 475 (31 December 1742). For Clegg see Document III.9 above. Extract (b) concerns the death of Edward, son of Dr Edward Williams of Rotherham academy. For Dr Williams see Document V.23 above. The obituary notice is reprinted from *The Patriot*, V, no. 272, Thursday 10 November 1836, p. 472.

(a)
I spent some time in prayer with my wife and children and some time in secret wrestling with him from whom alone we could hope for help. Alas sleep departed from during the night, and my heart was filld with fears and trouble. I apprehended God was now entring into Judgment with me for the sins I committed whilst I livd in Manchester and that I had moreover provokd him thus to break me by too confident and presumptuous hope that my son would, being so sober and diligent and in so good a way of business would some time make a considerable figure in the world

and be a great support to his parents in our decling years; such thoughts and expectations I had cherishd too mush, my dependence had thus been drawn away from God
to the creature. How easily can he dash such confidence and presumption to pieces,
alas how frail, what broken reeds are all created props and supports. I communed
with my heart on my bed and my spirit made diligent search, and resolvd and
promisd if God would spare my son I would shew my selfe thankful and make it my
great care and business in the world henceforward to advance the honour of God
and the eternal welfare of immortal souls. May this never be forgotten, these vows
never be broken.

[The boy recovered] 31.   at home all day, some part of it spent in fasting and
prayer for pardoning mercy and healing and renewing grace, great reason I had to
lament the evils committed in the year past and great reason to acknowledge with
thankfulness the Favours of Divine providence, Hitherto the long suffering god is
pleasd to spare, to protect and mercifully to provide for a sinful creature. Bless the
Lord O my Soul and all that is within me.

(b)
On the 30th ult., at Brighton, aged 36, Mr Edward Williams, youngest son of the late
Rev. Dr. Williams, of Rotherham, Yorkshire. After for many years wandering as a
prodigal, on the 5th of nov., 1835, he reached the house of the Rev. Mr. Goulty, of
Brighton, and made himself known. Immediate care was taken of him, for his father's
sake. He was then in such a state that the kindness affected his heart, softened his
spirit, and disposed him to receive the Gospel. The instructions of early life revived;
he yielded to the power of Divine truth, and through months of affliction (the result
of former habits, with the force of which he had often to struggle) he exhibited evidences of a renewed mind, which afforded pleasing satisfaction. His death was rather
sudden, from the rupture of a blood vessel on the lungs, but 'the end was peace'.
The restoration of such a character to his valued family, together with his apparent
conversion to God, are among the events of Divine Providence and grace, which
testify that the seed of the righteous is not forsaken.

Document VI.68

Funeral Episodes

The following are self-explanatory notes from Robert Halley, *Lancashire: Its
Puritanism and Nonconformity*, Manchester: Tubbs and Brook, 1869, II. Extract (a) is
on p. 298, extract (b) on pp. 446–7.

(a)
I remember that when I was a child, after some repairs had been done to the
Independent Meeting at Deptford, the proper nail had not been restored to its place
above the pulpit. On the next Sunday was a funeral sermon, and the omission had
not been observed until it was time to carry the mourning hat of the Rev. John

Theodore Barker to its proper place. As he was an orderly sort of man, and the bereaved family of some consideration, the service was delayed a few minutes while the undertaker, in the presence of the waiting congregation, had the 'nail fastened in a sure place, 'and the hat properly hung upon it.

(b)
While resident in Lancashire he published a little book entitled *The Good Old Way*, of which, his biographer says, 'more than a hundred thousand' were sold. Of his *Village Sermons* it was computed some years before his death that 'between sixty and seventy thousand volumes has been circulated,' – Wilson's *Dissenting Churches of London* [1810], vol. iii. p. 470.

The growth of the Independent congregation during the ministry of Mr. Charrier in Lancaster, in so far as it was consequent upon the decline of the Presbyterian interest, may to some extent be attributed to the strange conduct of the Arian minister of that town, who although a very attractive preacher when he was in good humour, was almost incessantly quarrelling with his people. On occasion of the death of a lady of his congregation connected with several of the principal families of the town, he observed a large audience expecting to hear her funeral sermon. After announcing his text, he said, 'I perceive an unusually large audience. You are come no doubt to hear the character of Mrs.——; but you will all be disappointed, for be it known to all of you that I and my people are at open war. I see or know nothing of them except as they appear on Sundays in the corners of their pews. As the deceased was a constant attendant here, let us hope she is gone to a better world.'

In order to express his disapproval of the illiberality of his people in contributing inadequately to his support, he would frequently lay aside on Sunday evening the clothes in which he had preached, and walk through the principal streets of the town dressed in a ragged coat, patched breeches, old shoes, and dirty linen, taking care, as he had opportunity, to tell those who accosted him that he was dressed in a style befitting the contributions made for his support. I cite these particulars from the MSS. Of Dr. Raffles, who says of them 'communicated by Mr. Charrier.'

Document VI.69

William Enfield's Sermon at John Aikin's Funeral

John Aikin (1713–80), father of A. L. Barbauld, for whom see Document V.34 above, was Philip Doddridge's first student at Kibworth academy. He then went to Aberdeen University, where the divinity tutors weaned him from Calvinism to Arianism. After a period as Doddridge's assistant, and as pastor at Market Harborough, he removed to Warrington on the opening of the academy there in 1757. He served as classical tutor, succeeding to John Taylor's divinity chair in 1761, on the latter's death.

For Aikin see DNB. For Taylor see Document II.3 above. The following extracts are from the funeral sermon by William Enfield (1741–97, a Presbyterian divine trained under Caleb Ashworth at Daventry), *A Funeral Sermon, Occasioned by the Death of* the Late Rev. *John Aikin, D.D. Professor of Divinity in the Academy in Warrington,* Warrington, 1781. For Enfield see DNB. For Ashworth see Document I.11 above.

1 Corinthians xi. 1.

Be ye followers of me, even as I also am of Christ.

From the history of life and actions of Saint Paul recorded in the New Testament, and from his own familiar epistles, in which the genuine dictates of an honest heart are every where expressed without the smallest indication of artifice or concealment, it manifestly appears that humility was one of the most striking features in his character. Far from making that ostentatious display of his virtues, which we observe in the writings of some of the antient philosophers, in a degree which might lead one to suspect, that, in their catalogue of virtues, vanity had taken the place of modesty; this Christian Apostle, after the example of his divine Master who was 'lowly of heart', disclaimed every pretension to superior merit, and ascribed all his attainments to the favour of Heaven. 'By the grace of God I am what I am'.

Yet we find this eminent pattern of humility, proposing his own conduct as an object of imitation to his fellow Christians, and particularly exhorting them to exercise the same prudent condescension, and disinterested benevolence towards each other, which they had seen exemplified in his conduct towards them. 'As I please all men in all things, not seeking mine own profit, but the profit of many, that they may be saved; be ye followers of me, even as I am of Christ'.

Let him not, however, on this account, be charged with having deviated from his general character: let the occasion and the motive be admitted as a sufficient apology for his conduct. For, why should he who had devoted himself to the service of his brethren and the support of their common cause, at the expence of every worldly interest, scruple to call upon them to follow his example?

But, whatever opinion be formed of the consistency of the Apostle's conduct in this instance, or in general concerning the propriety of making, on any occasion, a direct display of one's own merit, no doubt can be admitted with respect to the utility of holding up to public view, pictures of eminent wisdom and virtue in the characters of others. It is universally acknowledged, that example is a more efficacious and agreeable instructor than precept; impressing the imagination, and interesting the feelings, at the same time that it informs the understanding; and firing the breast with that generous emulation, which is the most powerful incentive to great and useful actions.

I will therefore make no apology for directing your attention, on the present occasion, to the character of an Individual, whose talents, attainments, and virtues, placed him far above the common level of human nature, and shone through the veil which his modesty cast over them, with a lustre and influence which commanded universal admiration; – who had an unquestionable title to the testimony which our Saviour bare to John his fore-runner, 'He was a burning and a shining light'.

Whilst I am attempting to delineate the principal features of this eminent character, let it not be supposed that, with the numerous tribe of venal panegyrists, I am substituting a work of fancy in the room of a copy from nature. The picture shall be drawn from the life; and I trust, those who had the happiness of knowing the original, will be at no loss to discover the likeness. Nor let it be imagined, that, in undertaking this difficult task, I am influenced by the poor ambition of obtaining the applause of survivors by a studied eulogium on the deceased; or by the weak expectation of giving any additional lustre to a name, which shines with the unborrowed rays of substantial merit. On an occasion like this, let it be supposed that I am influenced by higher and better motives; – let it be believed, that I am induced by a desire, of paying the last public tribute of respect to the memory of a man I esteemed – a character I revered – a friend I loved; and of assisting my audience in learning the lessons of wisdom and virtue which such an example is adapted to teach.

The great and good man of whom I speak, was endued with natural powers, which qualified him for high attainments and extensive usefulness; and the talents which he had received from the great Lord of nature, he did not suffer to remain unemployed. Clearness of perception, strength of judgment, vigour of imagination, and warmth of feeling, were in him most happily united.

With this rare combination of natural advantages, he early devoted himself to learning, in that profession in which he apprehended his abilities and acquisitions would be most useful to the world. And by a judicious disposition, and an assiduous improvement of his time, both during the period of his elementary studies, and through all the labours of his more advanced years, he obtained an acquaintance with literature and science, more extensive and accurate than usually falls to the share of one man.

In the several branches of learning, which are more immediately connected with the profession of the Christian ministry, he was an eminent master. All the great questions concerning the nature, faculties, and operations of the human mind – concerning the foundation and extent of moral obligation – concerning the principles of civil government and law – concerning the attributes and providence of the Supreme Being – concerning the divine authority of the Mosaic and Christian revelation – and lastly, concerning the general design and spirit, and the peculiar doctrines of Christianity – with the arguments usually urged in support of the different opinions which have been entertained on these subjects, – lay before his understanding in methodical arrangement, always ready to be called forth as occasion required. Nor was his mind a mere common-place of metaphysical and theological knowledge. On every topic of this kind which engaged his attention, he deliberated calmly, reasoned clearly, and formed a judgment for himself with caution and impartiality.

The Holy Scriptures he studied with that close and minute attention, which was the result of a sincere desire to understand these sacred volumes, and to deduce from them an uncorrupted system of religion and morals. In these important studies, he not only made a judicious use of every aid which could be derived from the labours of critics and commentators, but availed himself of every light, which an extensive knowledge of ancient history both ecclesiastical and civil, a good acquaintance with the writings of the Fathers of the Christian Church, and a critical skill in the original languages of the Old and New Testament, could afford him.

Nor were his researches confined to the more immediate objects of his profession, morals and theology. He took an extensive range through the fields of ancient learning, and formed an intimate acquaintance with the philosophers, historians and poets of Greece and Rome. Regarding these invaluable remains of antiquity as the most perfect models of correct and elegant composition, and as an inexhaustible treasury of rational entertainment to a cultivated mind; he studied them, at the same time with all the accuracy of a judicious critic, and with all the discernment and feeling of a man of true taste. From the walks of literature, he often turned aside into the paths of natural science, and in these occasional excursions, he gathered up much valuable knowledge, respecting the general laws of the material world, the distinct properties of bodies, and the history of nature, animate and inanimate. In short, there is scarcely a province in the extensive and daily enlarging empire of human knowledge, which his philosophic and inquisitive mind did not visit, though his particular engagements or inclinations might lead him to fix his more stated residence in one region rather than another.

But let it not be from hence surmised, that his learning was too extensive to be deep and solid. The ignorant and the indolent are apt to take it for granted, that every man who is a general scholar, must for that reason be superficial one. But the industrious bee doth not extract her sweets from the flowers she visits, the less perfectly, because she roves from plant to plant, and from field to field: nor doth the philosopher less completely execute his purpose in any single branch of study, because he has activity of mind and patient assiduity sufficient to enable him, when one vein of the quarry is exhausted, to open another. Of this the present example is a sufficient confirmation: for notwithstanding the variety of his pursuits, he did not satisfy himself with skimming over the surface of knowledge, but penetrated its most deep and hidden recesses.

With an understanding thus richly furnished, this excellent man possessed the most rational and steady PRINCIPLES of religion and virtue.

The first object of his researches was, to discover those truths which are the foundation of moral wisdom. Subjects merely speculative he occasionally examined, either in the way of amusement, or in the ordinary course of instruction. But those questions which are intimately connected with the conduct of life, and happiness of rational beings, he studied with a degree of attention and solicitude, which discovered a deep sense of their importance.

Whilst he readily acknowledged the existence, and the powerful operation, of original principles in human nature, he was no advocate for that indolent philosophy (so well adapted to the spirit and manners of the present age) which has raised an unnatural contest between *Reason* and *Common Sense*, and instructed men to trust to their feelings rather than to their understanding. He thought it the duty of every rational being to employ his powers of reasoning and judging in the search of truth, and to endeavour to deduce the practical rules of life and manners from such theoretical propsitions as have been established by conclusive argumentation. Accordingly, he employed his most serious thoughts in framing a consistent and connected system of belief, which, though not wholly free from difficulties, might however have the support of probable evidence from reason or testimony. On these grounds – perhaps the only grounds which ought to satisfy a wise man – he built his opinions concerning the great subjects of morals, religion and Christianity. And from these opinions he deduced practical maxims of conduct, which he at all times conscientiously observed; strictly adhering to whatever he judged to be suitable to the nature and condition of man, conducive to the happiness of the species, and confirmable to the laws of God.

The laws of God, as promulged in the Gospel of Christ, he obeyed with religious exactness. Acknowledging the divine authority of this great Legislator after having examined with the most anxious attention the grounds of his claim; the precepts of Christianity, and the sanctions by which they are supported, operated with all their energy upon his mind to produce the character of a sincere and exemplary CHRISTIAN.

His ideas of the Supreme Being, and of the nature of his moral government, were worthy of the Christian Philosopher: and they were so constantly present to his mind, and so deeply impressed upon his heart, that they formed a settled habit of piety which influenced all his actions, and produced a lively sense of religion which animated all his devotions. His piety was not merely a principle; it was a sentiment, which constantly possessed his mind, and which discovered itself in the solemnity with which he always performed the duties of religious worship, and in the reverence with which he at all times spoke of the Deity. In this respect he resembled that religious philosopher, Mr. *Boyle* of whom it is related, that he never mentioned the name of God without visible expressions of profound veneration.

Conceiving it to be the great object of the Christian Revelation, to give mankind an assurance of a future state of rewards and punishments, and thus to connect the actions and events of the present life with the life to come; he regarded it as the first Christian duty, to 'seek for glory, honour, and immortality by a patient continuance in well doing', and held it as a maxim, which with a sincere Christian will admit of no exception, That wherever the interests of this world and the next interfere, the former ought to give way to the latter.

He could not persuade himself to adopt those relaxed ideas of the system of Christian morals, by which many accommodate their principles to the taste of a luxurious and licentious age, and while they indulge every favourite inclination without control, still imagine themselves good Christians. This attempt to lower the standard of Christian morals, till it is brought to some sort of agreement with fashionable opinions, and affords some indulgence to fashionable follies and vices, he considered as the most dangerous corruption of Christianity.

The principles of this good man were not of that plaint kind, which could easily adapt themselves to every occasion. Had he been placed in a situation which would have required an extensive intercourse with mankind, they would probably have subjected him to difficulties, of which the man of the world has no apprehension. They would have required him to struggle against the tide of licentious manners: but they would have supported him in the struggle; they would not have suffered him to be carried away by the torrent. They would have laid upon him the hard necessity of refusing the bribes, with which avarice and ambition would have tempted him to practice 'the deceits of unrighteouness': but they would have enabled him to view the seducing bait with honest indignation; and in the consciousness of his integrity they would have given him a prize, which mines of silver could not purchase.

Happy for him, however, it was, that his situation and profession in life excused him from these painful trials, and permitted him to practice every lesson of contentment, moderation and inflexible integrity, which Christianity teacheth, without being exposed to the ridicule of unprincipled libertines, or to the insolent disdain of those who have loaded themselves with the spoils of iniquity. His humble station, it is true, did not afford him the envied distinctions which attend the rich and mighty: but his great mind, inured to seek, and not doubting to find, sufficient stores of happiness within itself, taught him to despise them. So much did he value the treasures of wisdom and virtue above the gifts of fortune, – so tenacious was he of the precious stores he possessed, – that he has often declared, that he should be fearful of receiving a great increase of riches, lest they should rob him of that philosophic tranquility and self-possession, and those intellectual and moral pleasures, which he valued above every thing else.

The fame rational and Christian principles, which gave him such elevation and strength of mind, likewise taught him the lessons of humility and charity.

In the midst of all his great attainments, and the distinction and respect which these procured him, he always discovered the utmost diffidence of his abilities, and was himself the only person unacquainted with his merit. Far from 'thinking of himself more highly than he ought to think', he never assumed to himself the confequence which every one else perceived to belong to him. In some cases this excess of modesty was perhaps painful to himself: on some accounts, it was doubtless to be regretted by others; particularly, as it has deprived posterity of all opportunity of reaping benefit from his labours: but, let us not, for this, refuse the tribute which is due to a virtue which all good men agree to admire, and which is 'in the fight of God of great price'.

Benevolence was in this good man, something more than gentleness and sensibility of nature; it was a principle and habit, grafted on the stock of natural temper by reflection, and established by the authority of religion. Hence it was uniform and steady in its operation, disposing him to every good work. It was this spirit of Christian charity which diffused an air of courtesy and urbanity over his whole manner, free from the smallest tincture of insincerity. It was this spirit which inclined him to 'follow peace with all men', – which prevented even the sons of discord from being his enemies, and which united him to his friends and connections, by bonds which nothing but death could have dissolved. Lastly, it was this spirit which led him to the exercise of moderation and candour, in a degree which reflects distinguished honour upon his character, and merits particular notice.

Not that he was indifferent to the cause of truth, or unconcerned for the support of pure religion. No man was ever more in earnest in the search of the former, or more desirous of serving the interests of the latter. But his good sense, extensive reading, and deep thinking, enabled him to perceive the difficulties which attend every system of philosophy and religion, and the numerous avenues by which prejudice and misapprehension find their way into the human mind. He felt the full force of the reflection which was made by one who has obtained, by way of distinction, the appellation of *the wise man*, – a reflection which those who know the most, are always most inclined to adopt – 'I said, I will be wise, but it is far from me'. Hence he was always open to conviction himself, and always disposed to allow the utmost scope for freedom of inquiry to others. He knew how to encourage a liberal spirit, to indulge inquisitiveness, and even to endure contradiction; and could bear every thing but ignorant conceit, and obstinate pertinacity. There are not a few who will patiently allow you to controvert their opinions in some points, while you confine yourself within a certain latitude; but if you venture farther, their apprehensions are alarmed; their temper is discomposed; and you have little chance of obtaining a fair hearing. The good man whose character I am describing, carried his liberality and candour much farther. Perceiving that freedom of discourse, as well as of thinking, is necessary to the discovery of truth, he listened with a candid ear to every argument which was proposed with ingenuity and modesty.

Good Christians of every sect, and honest men of every persuasion, had a share in his esteem. Merit of every kind he was capable of distinguishing, and was always inclined to respect. As a philosopher, the society of wise and learned men was his delight. As a Christian, he loved every true friend of religion and virtue as his brother. As a citizen, he lamented the disorders and corruptions of the state, and prayed for the prosperity of his country. As a man, he interested himself in whatever concerned the improvement and happiness of mankind.

Such were the endowments, such the virtues, which distinguished the character of this valuable man. How faithfully, how successfully, these talents were employed in the service of mankind, now remains to be related.

The influence of his eminent attainments and excellent qualities, was long and largely experienced in his domestic relations. To the virtues of the husband and the father, those who best knew their value, and are now, with tears of affection and gratitude, lamenting their loss, will bear a willing testimony. Of the skill and success with which he performed the duties of parental education, the world is in possession of proofs, which will live to distant posterity.

In the capacity of a Christian minister, he discharged the offices of the sacred character with dignity and reputation. But infirmities of constitution soon rendering it hazardous for him to speak in public, he directed his labours into the channel of private education. Afterwards, through many of the most valuable years of his life, he was more publicly employed in communicating the rich stores of leaning and science which he had with so much judgment and industry collected, to young men destined for various stations in life, and particularly to such as were devoted to the Christian ministry.

In these important labours he discovered a degree of ability, wisdom and fidelity, which commanded universal respect from those who attended upon his instructions. Upon every subject, he laid before them a full and methodical detail of the principal arguments, advanced on each side by the best writers; subjoining his own observations, which were always the result of patient thinking and mature judgment: but at the same time leaving his pupils at full liberty to examine the merits of every question, and form an opinion for themselves. Unbiassed himself, he used neither artifice nor influence to bias others. To this may be added, that he conveyed his ideas with a clearness of method, precision of language, and energy of elocution, which commanded attention, and gave a peculiar dignity and weight to his instructions. – And whilst he was careful to furnish those who were educating for the Christian ministry with all the knowledge proper to the profession, he was equally solicitous to instil into their minds the principles, and to inspire them with the spirit, of Christianity. His lectures on Morals and Theology, and his comments upon the Holy Scriptures, were adapted to improve the heart, as well as to inform the understanding. In this manner did this judicious and faithful Preceptor approve himself a 'well-instructed scribe, able to bring out of his treasures things new and old'. And he had the happiness of seeing his labours in this important branch of education amply rewarded, in the growing reputation and usefulness of those who, having sat at the feet of this *Gamaliel*, have from time to time gone forth into the churches of Christ, 'thoroughly furnished' for their office, 'workmen who need not be ashamed'. In their faithful labours in the cause of religion and virtue, 'being dead, he yet speaketh'.

Here let me be permitted to mention with grateful respect, the essential support and reputation, which the *Seminary of learning*, in which he presided from its first institution, has derived from his numerous and important services, which have so largely contributed to accomplish the laudable designs of its generous founders, to overcome the difficulties which have from time to time risen up to obstruct its success, and to give it that degree of stability, and that prospect of increasing usefulness, which it at present enjoys. As long as this Seminary continues to be distinguished by sound learning just and liberal principles, and virtuous manners, to long let the name of AIKIN be there remembered with respect and veneration.

But it is of more general concern, and reflects higher honour on his memory, to add, that the assiduous labours of his long and valuable life were a public blessing to the world, by advancing useful knowledge, and propagating the genuine principles of religion and virtue. On these accounts he deserves to be ranked among the benefactors and friends of mankind, and to be remembered with distinction by distant prosterity. But, though posterity should neglect to give his name a place in the tablet of *fame*, it cannot be doubted, that it will be enrolled in the tablet of *merit* by the hand of the Almighty, and preserved with honour in the records of eternity.

The natural close of a life distinguished by such high attainments and useful virtues, is an old-age of tranquillity, and a peaceful death. In this manner it was that this exemplary Christian 'finished his course'. Just at the period, when an apprehension of increasing infirmities, more perceived by himself that his friends, had induced him to form the design of retiring from his public labours, whilst he was yet in possession of his excellent talents, and in the actual exercise of them, he was called to receive the eternal 'recompence of reward', and permitted, without the painful prelude of lingering sickness and decay, to 'enter into the joy of his Lord'.

'Blessed are the dead, who thus die in the Lord; for they rest from their labours and their works follow them'. 'Mark the perfect man, and behold the upright, for the end of that man is peace'.

Is there not, my brethren, in the character we have been contemplating, a voice which speaks aloud this language; 'Be ye followers of me, even as I also have been of Christ'? To such a voice, who will not be disposed to lend a willing and obedient ear?

445

Among those who have listened with admiration to the doctrine of this wise Preceptor, and gathered up the rich fruits of knowledge which have fallen from his lips, none will, I trust, be found, who will pay less regard to the silent but authoritative language of his character, than they have been accustomed to pay to his living instructions. From the disciples of such a master much is to be expected; especially from those to whom his labours were more particularly devoted, the candidates for the Sacred Profession. From these it will be expected, that they retain that high idea of the dignity and sanctity of the clerical character, and that strong perception of the religious and moral obligations connected with it, which they must, in some degree at least, have imbibed from the precepts and example of their Teacher. It will be expected that, thus instructed, they enter upon their office under a deep conviction of the reality and importance of religious and moral principles, and with a sincere desire to render some essential service to mankind, by judiciously and faithfully discharging the functions of the Christian ministry. It will be expected that, considering themselves as professional advocates in the cause of truth, virtue, and religion, and herein intrusted with an important charge, for which they are accountable to the public, and to the great Lord of all, they will support the dignity of their profession, by unspotted purity of character, by a manly gravity of deportment, by cultivating a taste for science and literature, and by assiduous endeavours, both in public and private, to propagate rational principles and virtuous manners.

If these expectations should, in any instances, be frustrated; if any who have been taught by this eminent Instructor should enter upon the sacred office with a light and trifling mind – inattentive to the nature of the character they are assuming – insensible of the weighty duties belonging to it; or should hereafter bring disgrace upon their profession by giving themselves up to indolence, dissipation, or licentiousness; – But let me be excused from pursuing into its consequences a supposition, which it is, I trust, unnecessary to make: let me presume, that no one will act so inconsistently with the veneration which he professes to entertain for the memory of this great and good man, as to trample under foot his most solemn instructions.

I must not conclude without suggesting, in a few words, an important reflection, which men of every rank and profession may deduce from the character which has been exhibited. In this character you have seen the happy fruits of intellectual and moral culture: you have seen how much it is in the power of Wisdom to do for her followers: you have seen, that an improved understanding, honest principles, and virtuous manners, can give a man the true enjoyment of himself, qualify him for extensive usefulness, procure him universal respect, and enable him to live happily and to die in peace. Go to the most successful devotees of Wealth – divinity whom all the world worshippeth – and call upon them to declare, whether it has been in her power, to do as much for them. Filling their coffers, has she at the same time enriched their understanding? Increasing their power of doing good, has she withal increased the inclination? Surrounding them with that splendor which captivates vulgar admiration, and procures the external expressions of deference and respect; has she likewise endued them with that sterling integrity, which commands the tribute of heart-felt esteem? Placing within their reach the instruments of luxurious enjoyment, has she also given them a contented mind, and provided them with a 'more enduring substance', which will abide with them when the gifts of fortune shall 'take to themselves wings and fly away'? – If these are things which Wealth has never done for her most favoured votaries – which lie wholly beyond her power; let her no longer presume to maintain the unequal contest with Wisdom: let all mankind agree in acknowledging, that 'the merchandise of wisdom is better than the merchandise of silver; and the gain thereof, than fine gold'. 'Wisdom is the principal thing, therefore get wisdom; and with all thy getting, get understanding'.

Documents VI.70

Memorials of Faithful Ministers

Many an eighteenth-century minister was commemorated by an elegy, a memorial, or both. The following three examples are drawn at random from different decades of the century.

Extract (a), the inscription for the Independent minister John Spilsbury is reprinted from George Hunsworth, *Baxter's Nonconformist Descendants; or, Memorials of the Old Meeting Congregational Church, Kidderminster*, Kidderminster: Edward Parry, 1874, p. 25. Extract (b) is the inscription on a Memorial Stone in the grounds of Market Place Chapel, Kendal, of which Caleb Rotheram (1694–1752), Presbyterian divine and tutor (for whom see DECBP, DNB), was the first minister. The words are reprinted from F. Nicholson and E. Axon, *The Older Nonconformity in Kendal*, Kendal: Titus Wilson, 1915, pp. 310–11. Extract (c) is found on the title page of John Evans's funeral sermon for Daniel Turner (1710–98), Baptist minister at Abingdon for fifty years, moderate Calvinist and advocate of open communion. For Turner see DEB. Evans assisted Turner at Abingdon for the last nineteen years of Turner's life, and his funeral sermon was on the text 'He was a good man and full of the Holy Ghost and of faith' (Acts 11:24).

(a)

HERE LIES

(For whom he will death strikes and levels low; –
Himself at length the Lord shall overthrow:)

JOHN SPILSBURY,

The Only Child of his Father, of the same Name,
Who was also a very eminent Minister at Bromsgrove.
Having voluntarily devoted Himself
To the Sacred Ministration of the Word of God,
He became the faithful and excellent Paster
Of a Church at Kidderminster,
A place formerly made famous by the name of BAXTER.
For a period of Thirty-three years
He diligently instructed and encouraged
The Flock which had freely committed itself to his charge,
By his Public Discourses and his Affectionate Prayers
By 'doing the Works of an Evangelist',

And also by the bright Example of a Life
Of Faith and primitive Piety,
Even in an age which was abandoned to sin.
He was a diligent cultivator
Of Christian Uprightness and Unity,
Of Charity to the Poor,
And of Affability towards all.
As all who knew him loved him whilst he lived,
So when he died all good men wept for him.

JAN. 13, A.D. 172$\frac{6}{7}$, AGED 60

———

Alas, the good hath fallen! One whose life
Was useful in the service of his Lord.
How happy is He now whose children dwell
With Him in Heavenly brightness! And how rich
The spot of earth which holds a Saint's Remains!

(b)

In Memory
Of
The Rev, Caleb Rotheram, D.D.
Who died June 8th 1752, Aged 59.
He was the esteemed Minister of the
Congregation worshipping at this Chapel
For 36 years.
His remains are deposited at Hexham
Where he died.

As a protestant Dissenter he was
A credit to his profession;
For he was a friend, a faithful friend,
To Liberty,
The distinguishing principle
Of that profession

(c)
Of no Distemper, of no Blast he died;
But fell like Autumn fruit that mellow'd long;
Ev'n wondered at because he dropt no sooner:
Fate seem'd to wind him up for fourscore years;
Yet freshly ran he on nine winters more,
Till, like a Clock worn out with eating Time,
The Wheels of weary Life at last stood still.

Select Bibliography

The following works cut a relatively wide swathe. More specialised books and articles are listed in the notes to the introductions and texts to which they apply.

Bassett, T. M., *The Welsh Baptists*, Swansea: Ilston House, 1977.

Bolam, C. G., Jeremy Goring, H. L. Short, and Roger Thomas, *The English Presbyterians From Elizabethan Puritanism to Modern Unitarianism*, London: Allen & Unwin, 1968.

Braithwaite, W. C., *The Second Period of Quakerism*, (1919), 2nd edn, Cambridge: CUP, 1961.

Brown, Raymond, *The English Baptists of the Eighteenth Century*, London: Baptist Historical Society, 1986.

Cragg, Gerald R., *Reason and Authority in the Eighteenth Century*, Cambridge: CUP, 1964.

Davies, Rupert and E. Gordon Rupp, (eds), *A History of the Methodist Church in Great Britain*, vol. 1, London: Epworth Press, 1965.

Dexter, Henry Martyn, *The Congregationalism of the last Three Hundred Years, As seen in its Literature*, London: Hodder & Stoughton, [1879].

Drysdale, A. H., *History of the Presbyterians in England: Their Rise, Decline, and Revival*, London: Publication Committee, Presbyterian Church of England, 1889.

Haakonssen, Knud, (ed.), *Enlightenment and Religion. Rational Dissent in Eighteenth-Century Britain*, Cambridge: CUP, 1996.

Hamilton, J. Taylor, and Kenneth G. Hamilton, *History of the Moravian Church. The Renewed Unitas Fratrum 1722–1957*, Bethlehem, PA: Interprovincial Board of Christian Education, Moravian Church in America, 2nd edn 1983.

Jones, R. Tudur, *Congregationalism in England 1662–1962*, London: Independent Press, 1962.

Jones, R. Tudur, *Hanes Annibynwyr Cymru*, Swansea: Union of Welsh Independents 1966. Eng. trans., *Congregationalism in Wales*, ed. Robert Pope, Cardiff: University of Wales Press, 2004

Jones, Rufus M., *The Later Periods of Quakerism*, vol. I, London: Macmillan, 1921.

Langton, Edward, *History of the Moravian Church. The Story of the First International Protestant Church*, London: Allen & Unwin, 1956.

Rees, Thomas, *History of Protestant Nonconformity in Wales from its Rise in 1633 to the Present Time*, London: John Snow, 1883.

Sell, Alan P. F., *Dissenting Thought and the Life of the Churches. Studies in an English Tradition*, Lewiston, NY: Edwin Mellen Press, 1990.

Smith, Joseph, *A Descriptive Catalogue of Friends' Books*, 2 vols, London, 1867, *Supplement*, 1893.

Stephen Leslie, *History of English Thought in the Eighteenth Century*, (1876), New York: Harcourt, Brace & World, 2 vols, 1962.

Taylor, Adam, *The History of the English General Baptists*, 2 vols, London, 1818.

Torbet, Robert G., *A History of the Baptists*, London: Carey Kingsgate Press, 1966.

Underwood, A. C., *A History of the English Baptists*, London: Kingsgate Press 1947.

Waddington, John, *Congregational History: 1700–1800*, London: Longmans, Green, 1876.

Waddington, John, *Congregational History: Continuation to 1850*, London: Longmans, Green, 1878.

Walsh, John, Colin Haydon, and Stephen Taylor, *The Church of England c. 1689–c. 1833. From Toleration to Tractarianism*, Cambridge: CUP, 1993.

Watts, M. R., *The Dissenters*, vol. I, Oxford: Clarendon Press, 1978.

Whitley, W. T., *Baptist Bibliography, being a register of the chief materials for Baptist history, whether in manuscript or in print, preserved in Great Britain, Ireland, and the Commonwealth. Compiled for the Baptist Union of Great Britain and Ireland*, 2 vols, London: The Kingsgate Press, 1916–1922.

Whitley, W. T., *A History of British Baptists*, London: Kingsgate Press, 1932.

Williams, William, *Welsh Calvinistic Methodism. A Historical Sketch of the Presbyterian Church of Wales*, 2nd enlarged edn, London: Presbyterian Church of England, 1884.

Index of Persons

Rees, Anne 397
Rees, Lewis 256
Rees, Owen 238
Rees, Thomas 6, 172, 192, 236, 237, 251, 256, 397
Reid, Thomas 34–6
Renty, Jean Baptiste de 113
Reynolds, John 422
Reynolds, Thomas 152, 266
Richard, John 335
Richards, Thomas 402
Richards, William 158
Richardson, William 386
Ridgeway family 410
Ridgway, Mrs. 158
Ridley, John 170
Rippon, John 193, 383
Rivers, Isabel 14
Robinson, Benjamin 152
Robinson, Elmo Arnold 50
Robinson, W. Gordon 223, 398
Roby, William 223, 236(n), 339, 398
Rodez, Bishop of 282
Rogers, Mr. 239
Romaine, William 98, 99
Rotheram, Caleb 447, 448(b)
Rowe, Elizabeth Singer 355–7
Rowe, Thomas 14, 20
Rowntree, J. S. 4, 7, 376
Rudkin, William 386
Russell, Mr., of Bideford 409
Russell, Mr., of Birmingham 259
Russell, Miss 409
Rutt, J. T. 84, 86
Ryland, John 207, 208(d), 209(k)
Ryland, John Collett 190, 369
Ryle, Gilbert 5, 7

Sacheverell, Henry 247, 249
Sadler, Thomas 91
Sallust 11
Salt, William 257(a)
Saltem (J. Saltern) 281
Sandeman, Robert 98, 99(b), 100
Saunders, Philip 375
Saunders, Thomas 396
Saville, George 278
Schlenther, Boyd S. 223
Schofield, Robert E. 32

Scott, Daniel 321
Scott, Jonathan 223, 227(e)
Scrivenor, John 390
Secker, Thomas 71, 152, 270, 320, 321(a)
Seddon, John 335
Sell, Alan P. F. 12, 20, 34, 50, 51, 66, 74, 75, 98, 128, 142, 174, 181, 185, 193, 197, 198, 249, 257, 258, 321, 385, 387
Seward, William 399
Seymour, A. C. H. 12
Shaftesbury, *see* Cooper, A. A.
Shaftesbury, Earl of 235
Shalders, Mr. 170
Sheils, W. J., 55
Sheldon, John 322
Short, H. L. 66
Sigstedt, C. O. 102
Simmonds, John 47
Simmons, Joseph 238
Simpson, Billy 412
Simpson, John 97
Skepp, John 189, 190, 197
Skidmore, Gil 146
Slate, R. 339
Sloss, James 81, 83(f)
Slot, John 183
Smalley, Christopher 157
Smith, Barbara 336
Smith, J. W. Ashley 321
Smith, Jeremiah 152
'Smith, John' 223, 228(f), 232(h)
Smith, John Pye 156
Smith, Thomas 181
Smyth, George 151
Socinus (Fausto Paolo Sozzini), 92, 324
Solly, Henry 90–91
Somers, C. G. 207
Southall, Kenneth H. 7
Spangenberg, A. G. 93
Spear, Robert 339
Spilsbury, John 447
Spinks, Bryan D. 142
Stagg, Richard E. 379
Stanhope, Charles 295
Steele, Mr. 157
Steele, Mrs. 157
Steele, Anne 426, 430(g)
Stell, Christopher 7
Stennett, Mr. 240